MARY ELLEN MARK
AMERICAN ODYSSEY

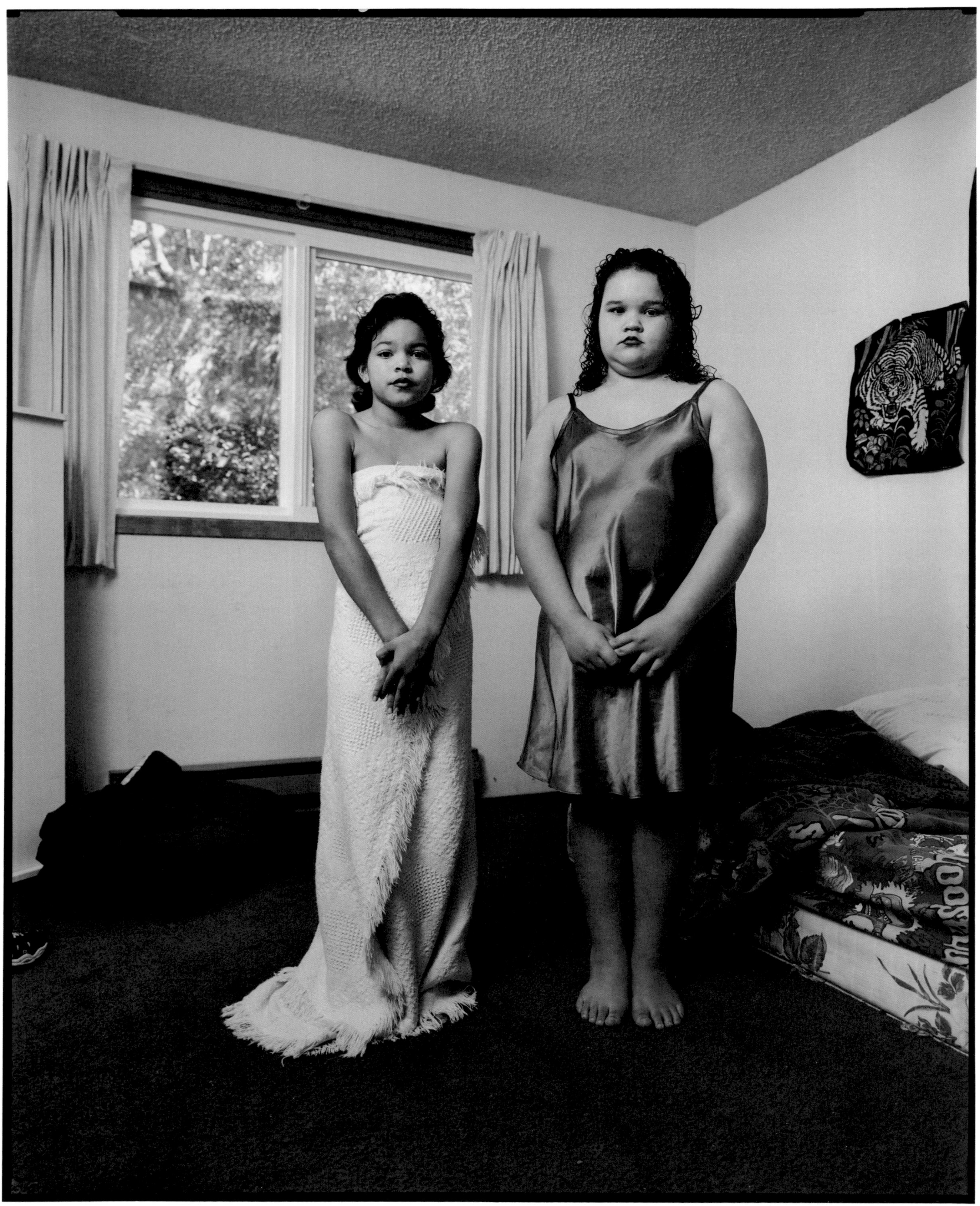

Keanna and La Shawndrea dressed up, Seattle, Washington, 1999

MARY ELLEN MARK
AMERICAN ODYSSEY
1963–1999

POEM BY
MAYA ANGELOU

APERTURE

HUMAN FAMILY

MAYA ANGELOU

I note the obvious differences
in the human family.
Some of us are serious,
some thrive on comedy.

Some declare their lives are lived
as true profundity,
and others claim they really live
the real reality.

The variety of our skin tones
can confuse, bemuse, delight,
brown and pink and beige and purple,
tan and blue and white.

I've sailed upon the seven seas
and stopped in every land,
I've seen the wonders of the world,
not yet one common man.

I know ten thousand women
called Jane and Mary Jane,
but I've not seen any two
who really were the same.

Mirror twins are different
although their features jibe,
and lovers think quite different thoughts
while lying side by side.

We love and lose in China
we weep on England's moors,
and laugh and moan in Guinea,
and thrive on Spanish shores.

We seek success in Finland,
are born and die in Maine.
In minor ways we differ,
in major we're the same.

I note the obvious differences
between each sort and type,
but we are more alike, my friends,
than we are unalike.

We are more alike, my friends,
than we are unalike.

We are more alike, my friends,
than we are unalike.

FOR MARTIN

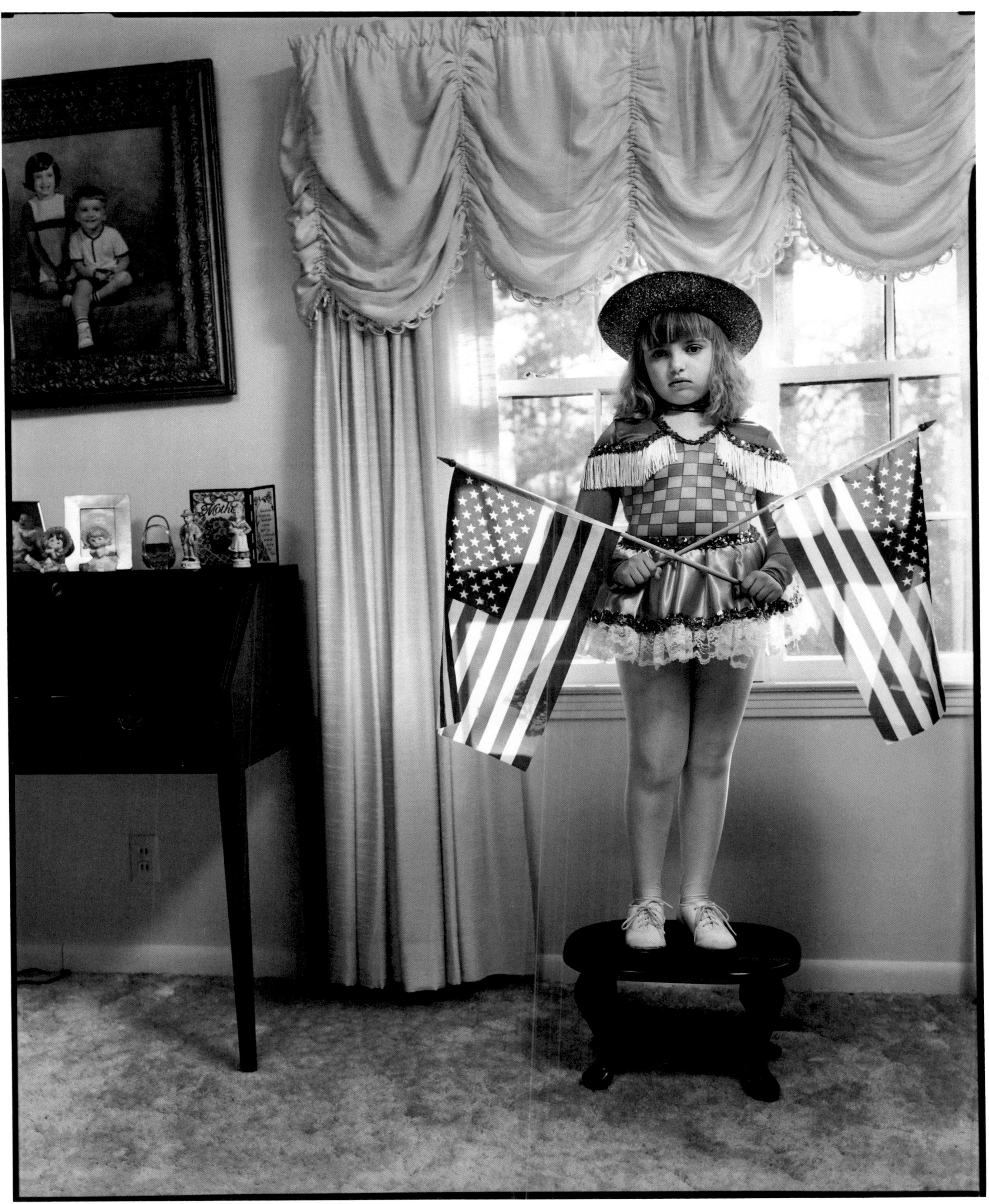

Elise Collins, Union, South Carolina, 1995

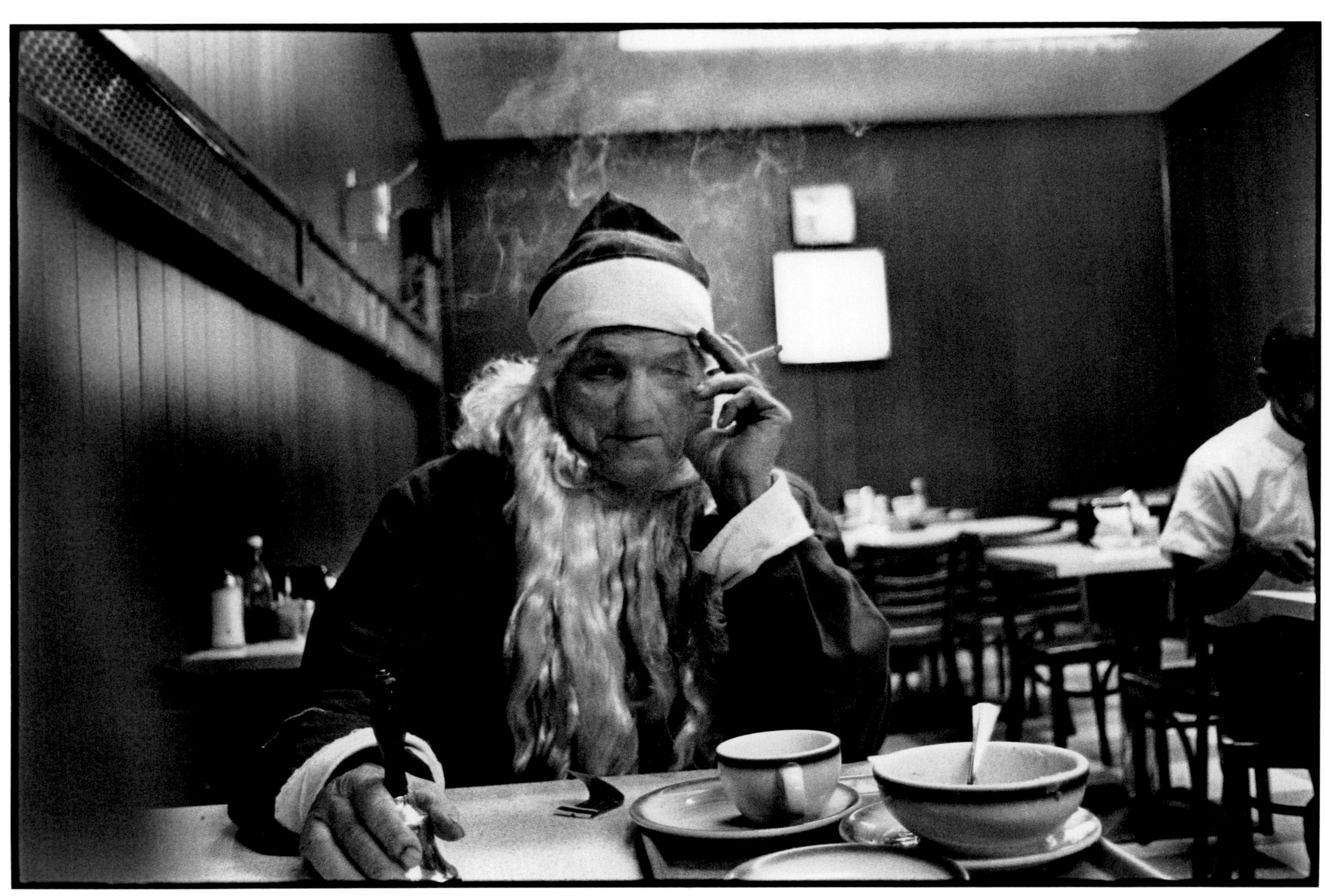

Santa Claus at lunch, New York City, 1963

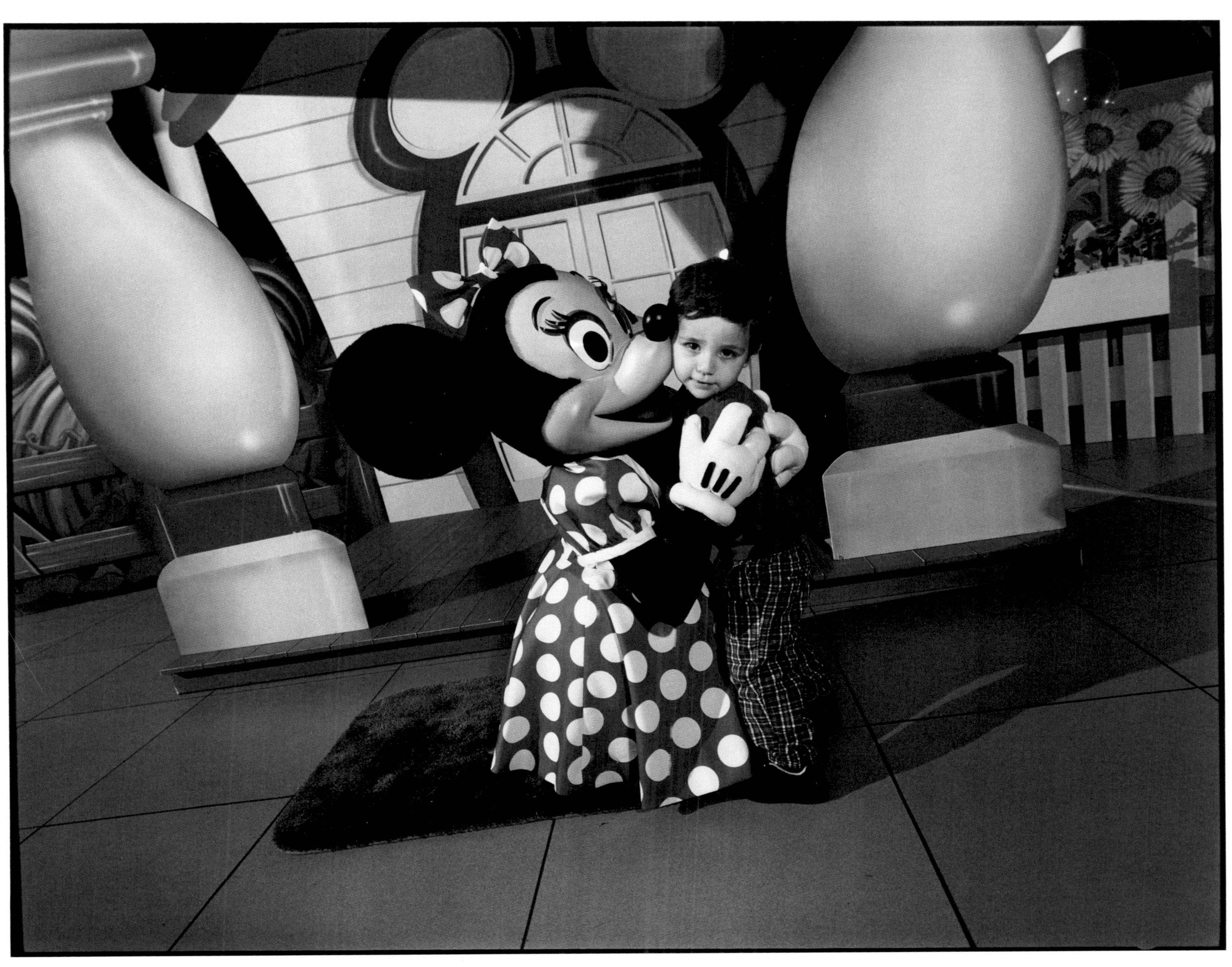

Minnie Mouse, Parma Mall, Ohio, 1997

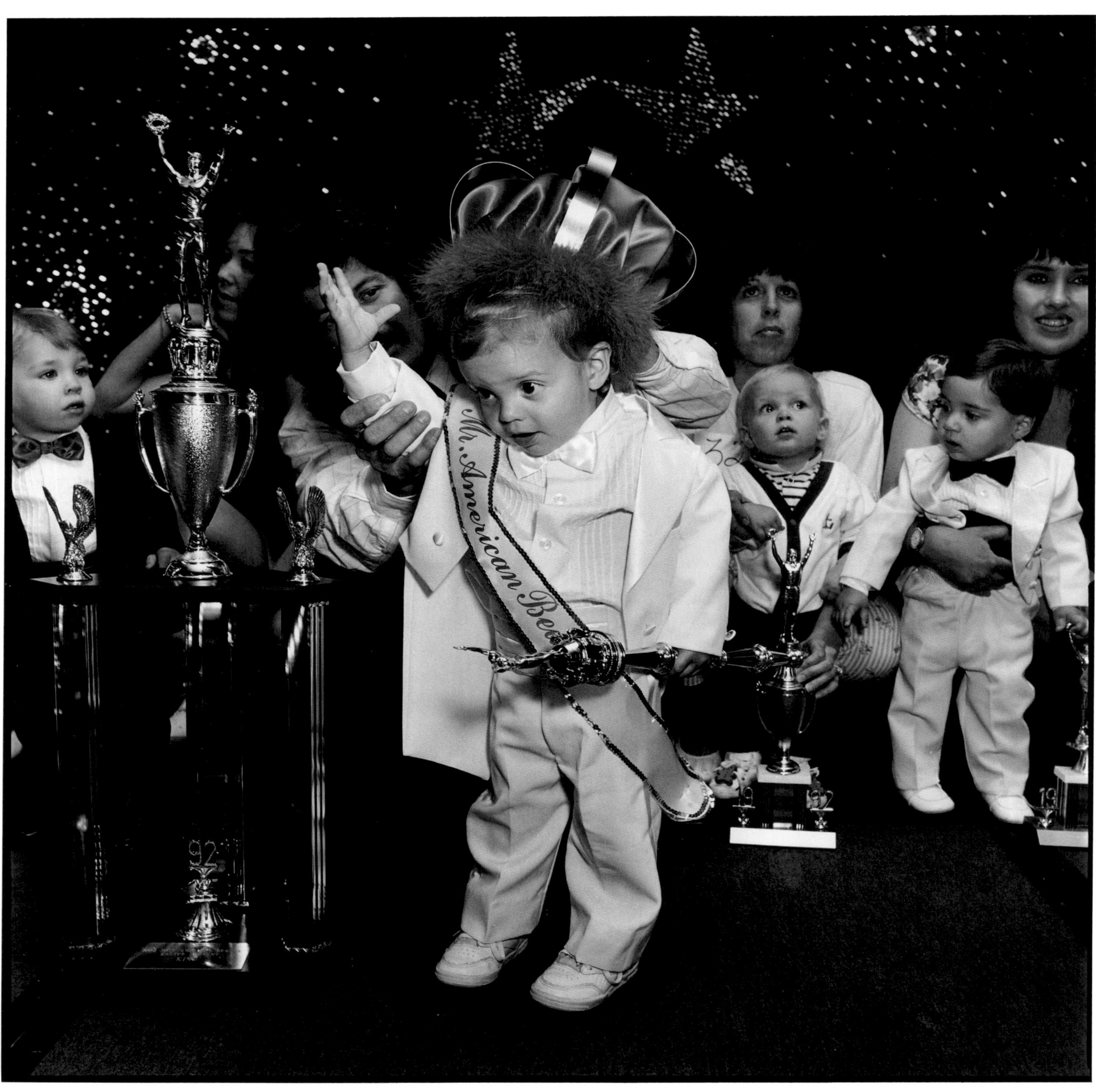

Baby beauty pageant winner, California, 1992

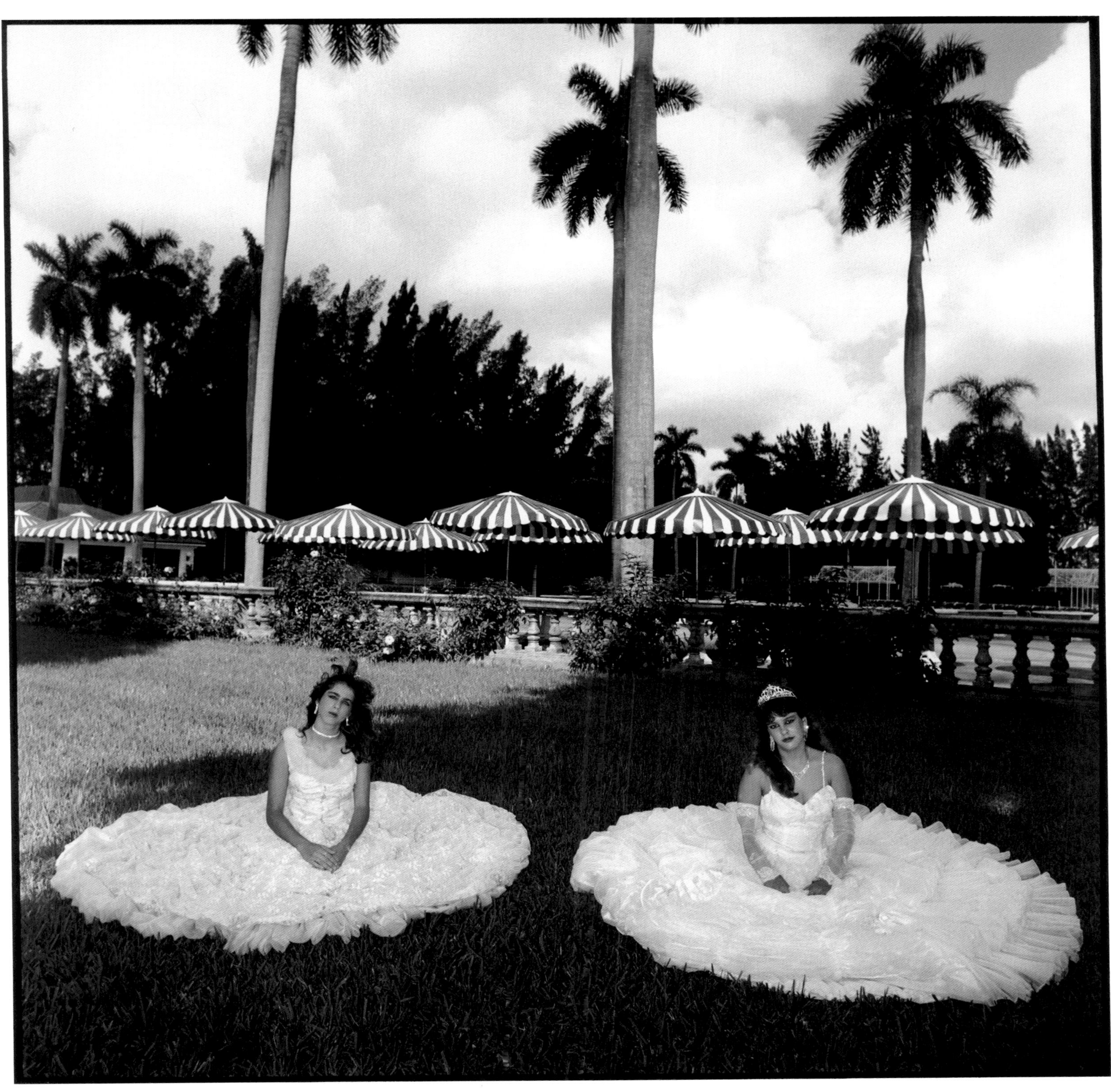

Quinciсñera, Miami, Florida, 1986

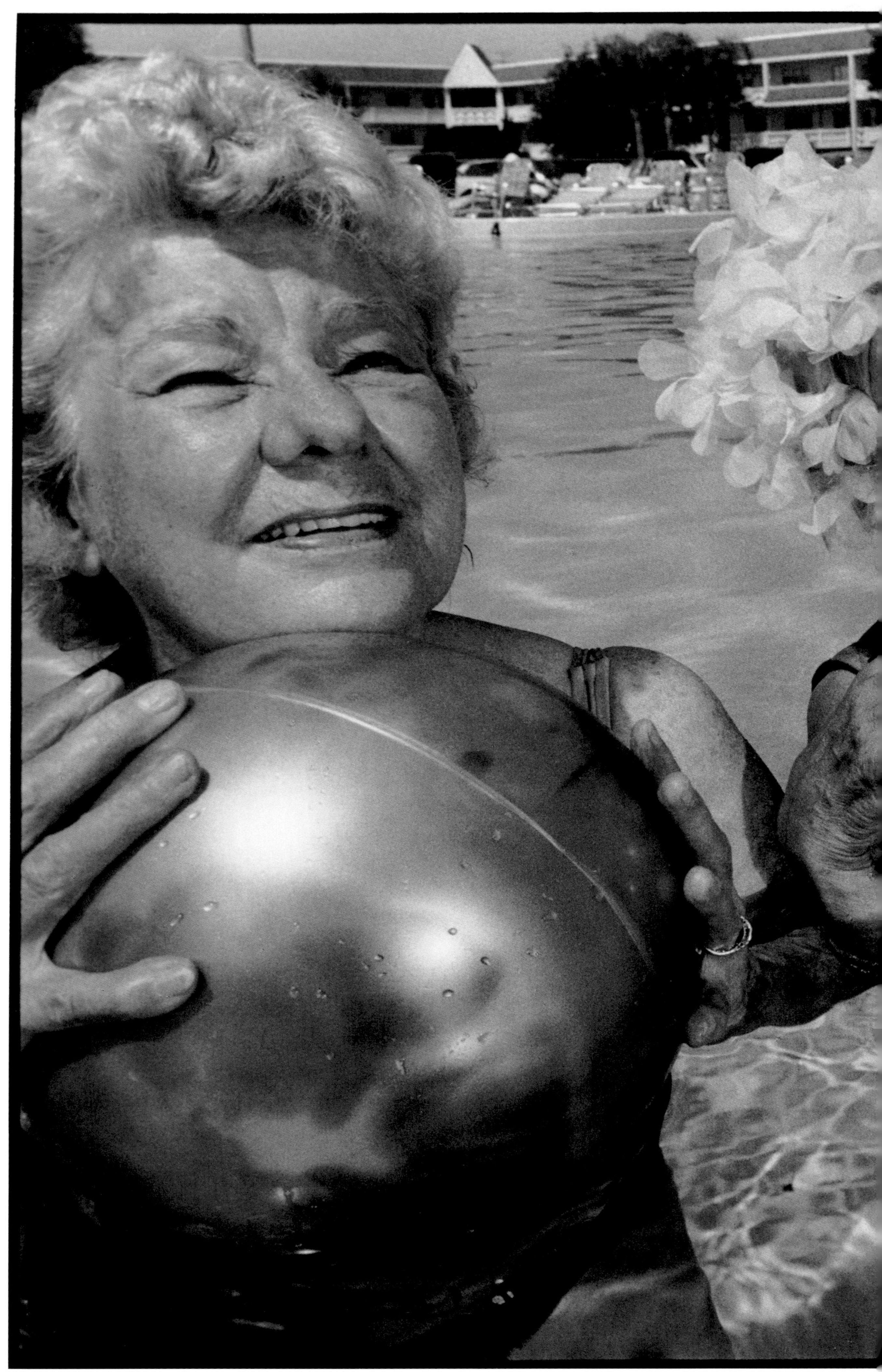

Water exercise group,
St. Petersburg, Florida, 1986

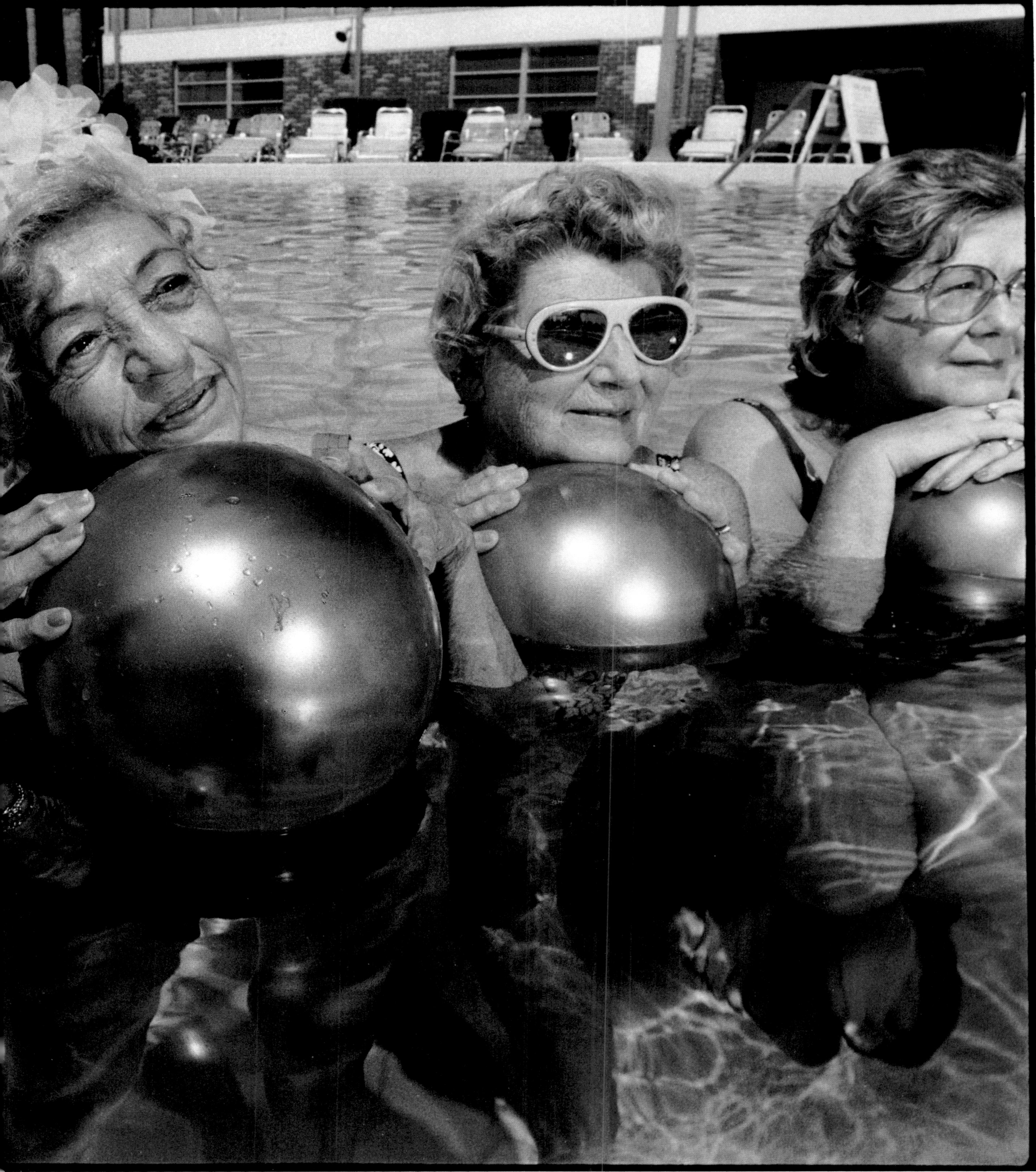

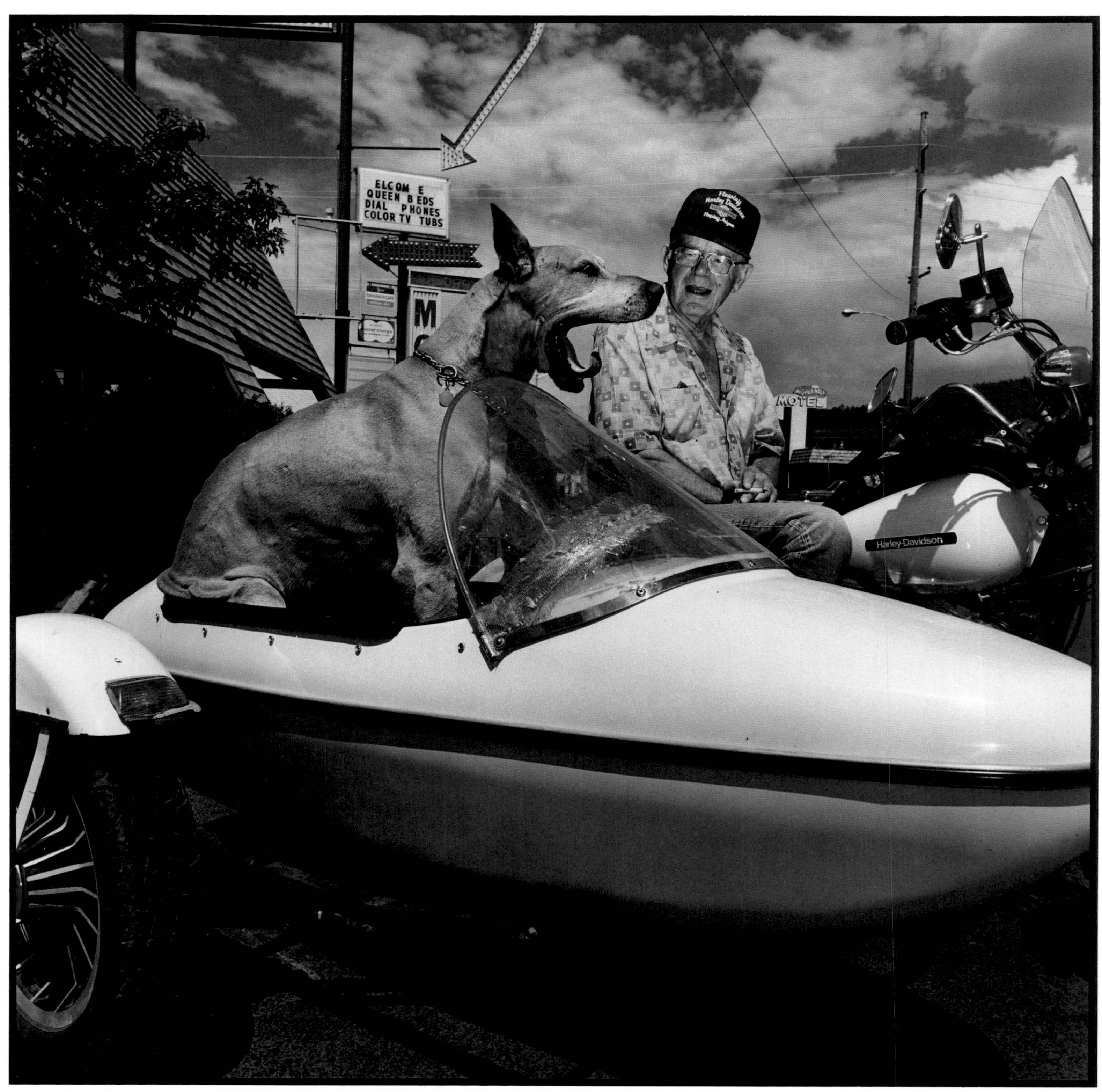

Yawning dog, Williams, Arizona, 1988

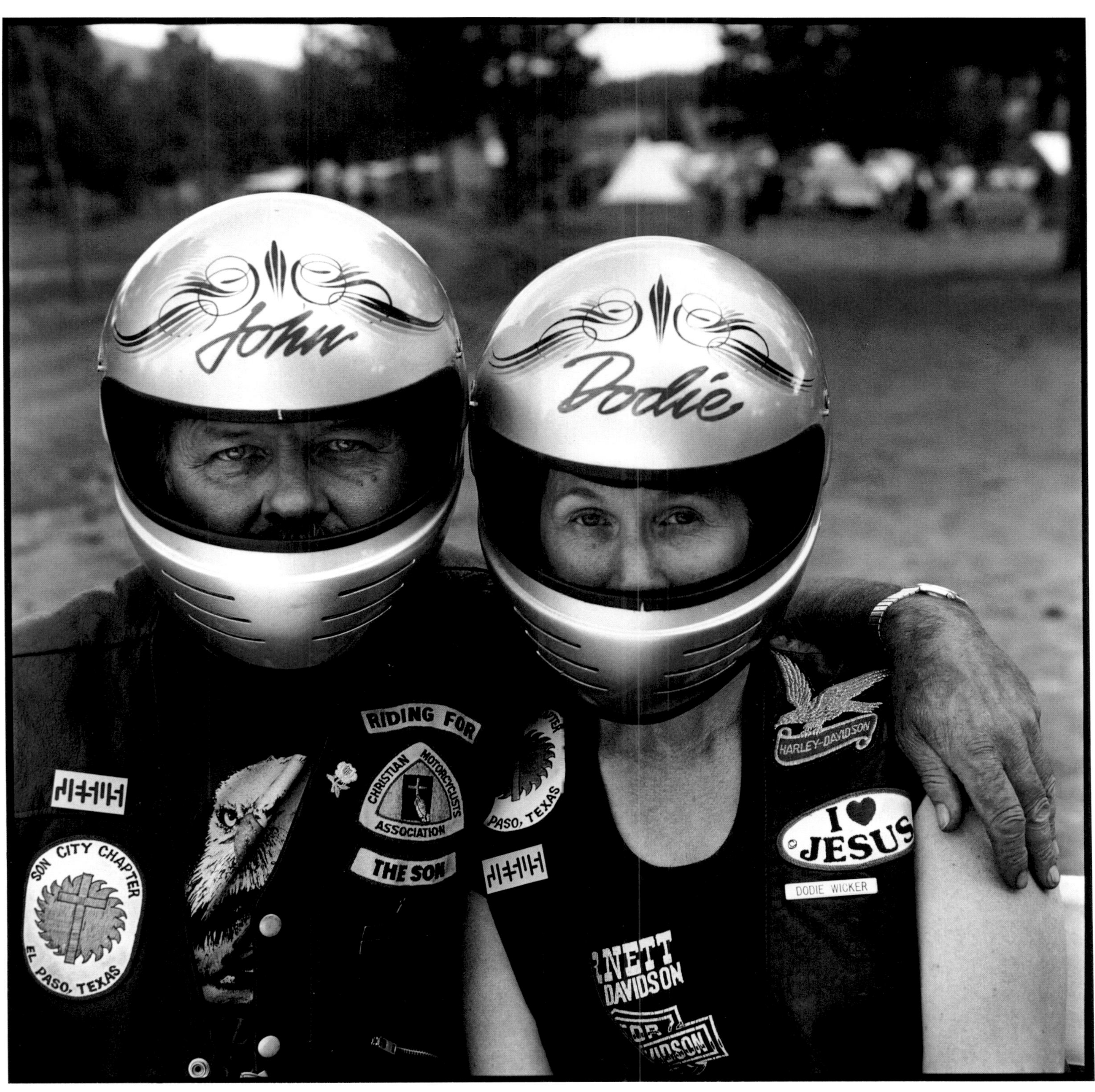

Christian bikers, Williams, Arizona, 1988

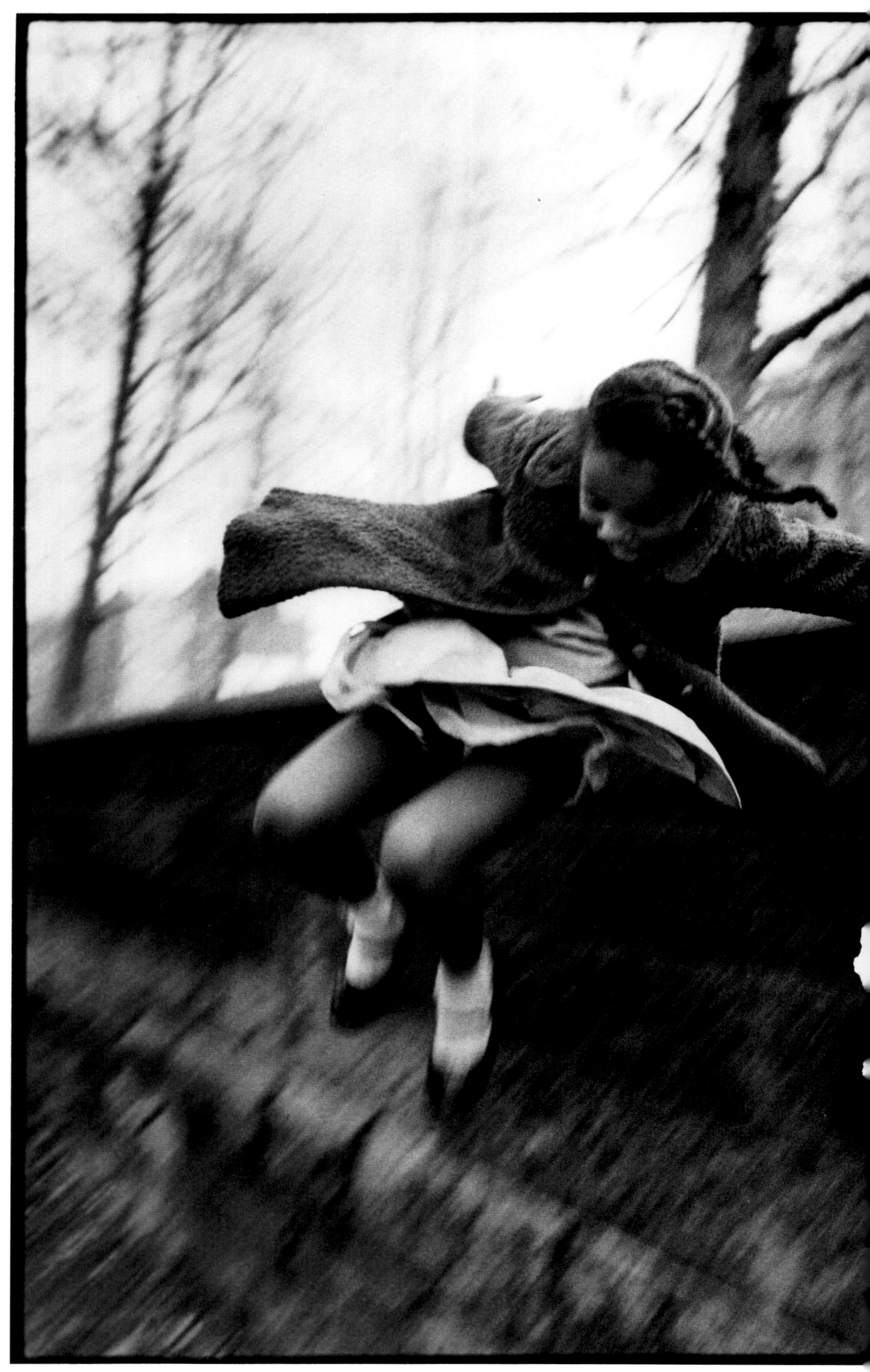

Central Park, New York City, 1967

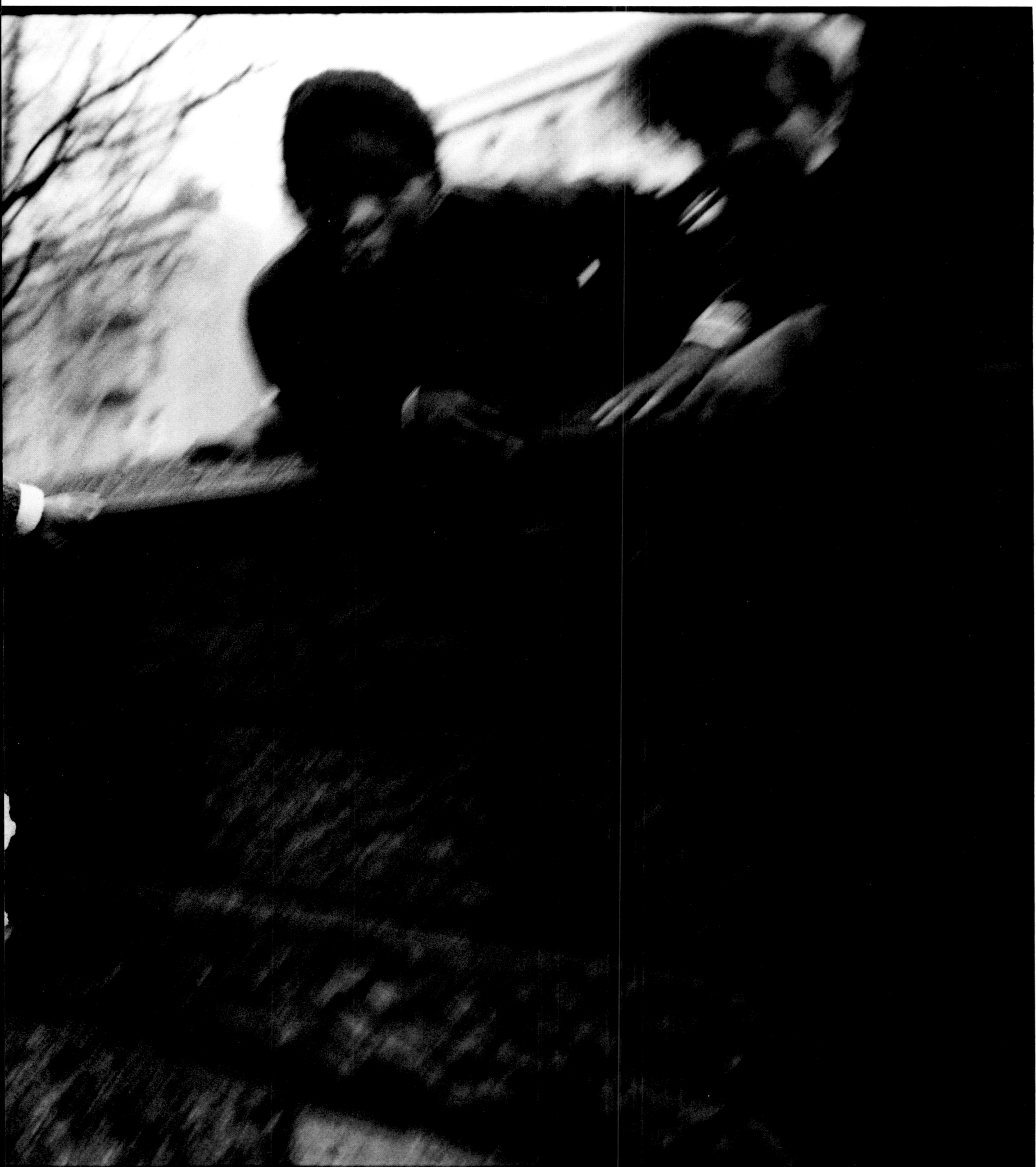

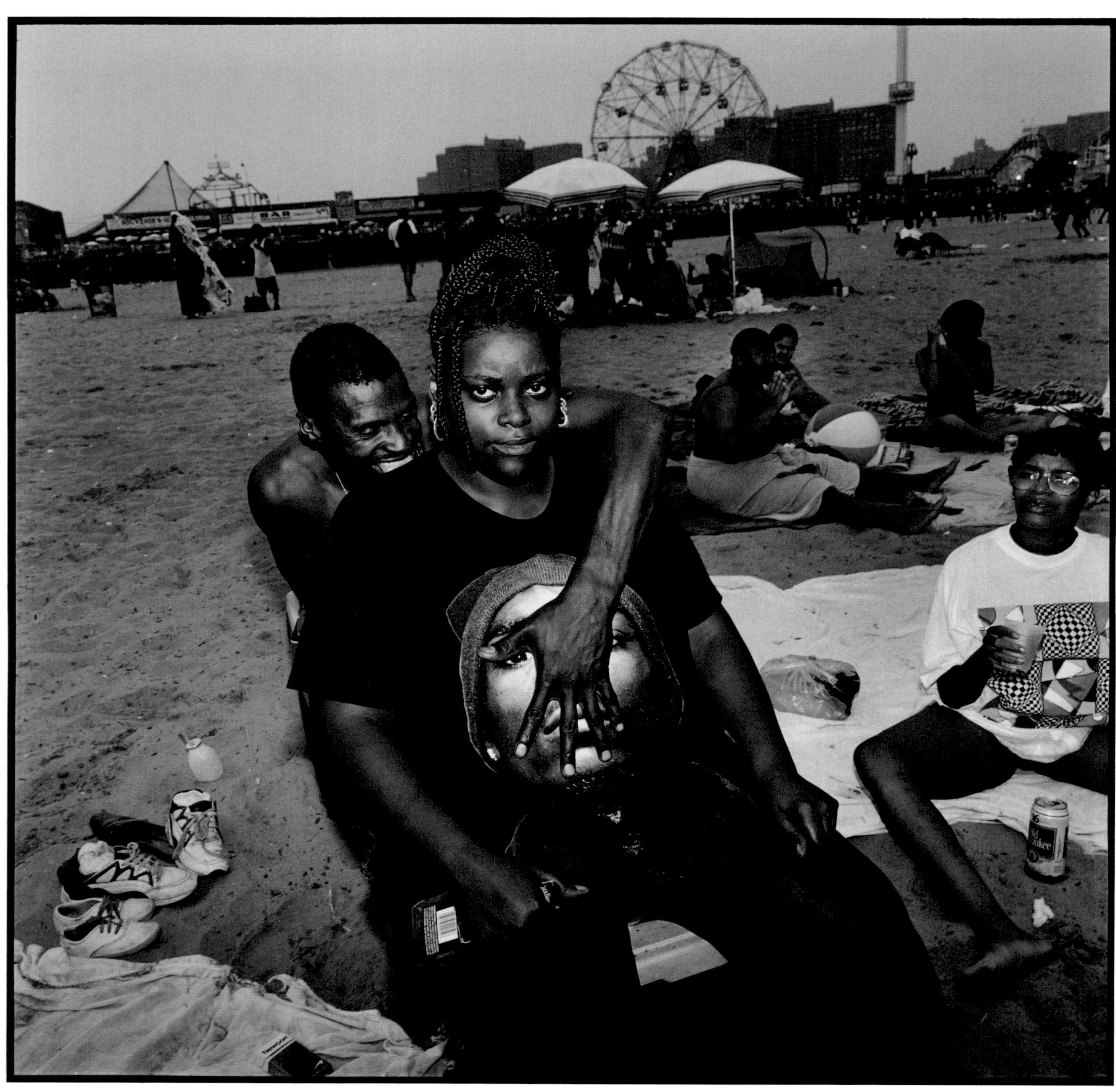

Coney Island, Brooklyn, New York, 1994

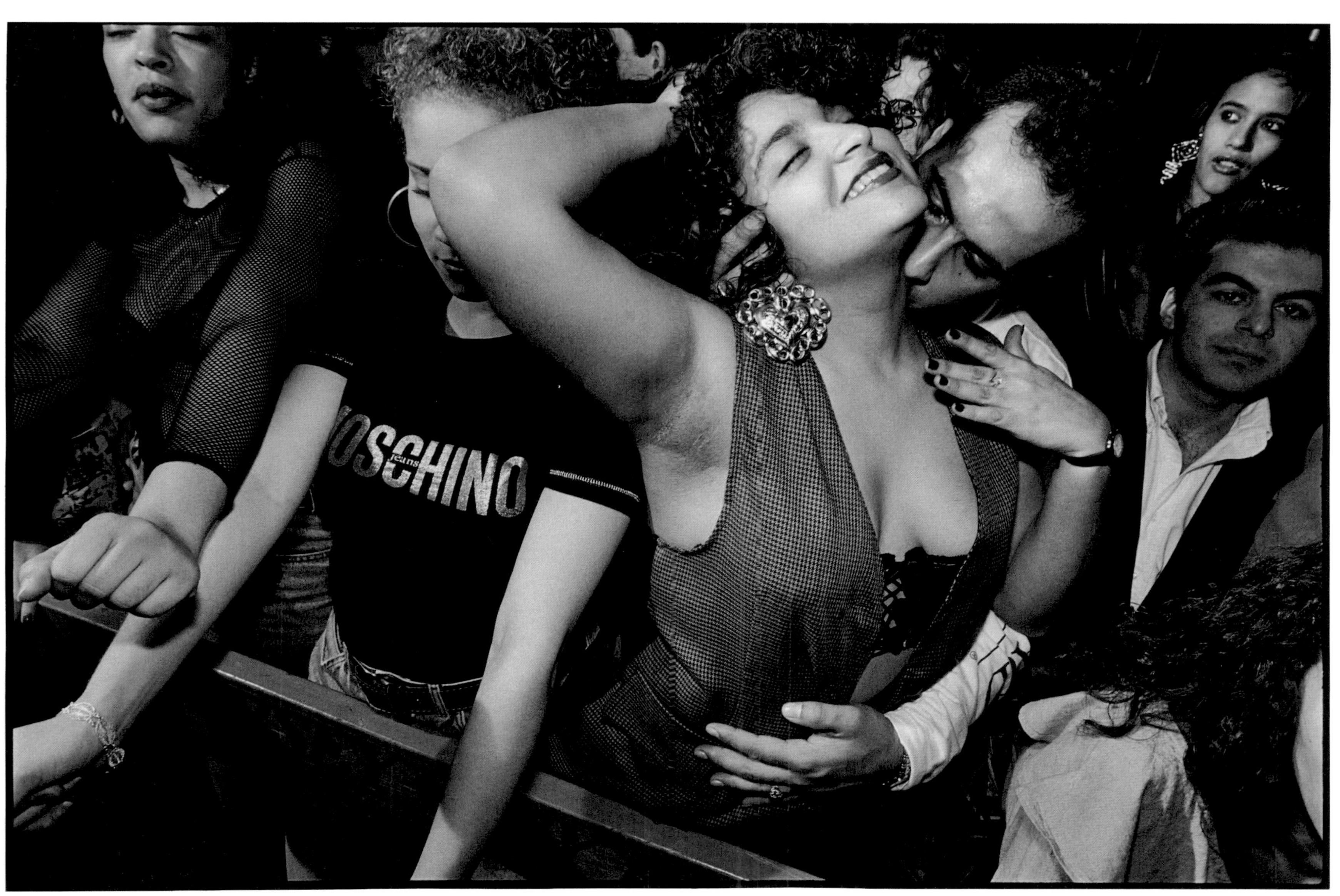

Marky Mark concert, Jersey City, New Jersey, 1993

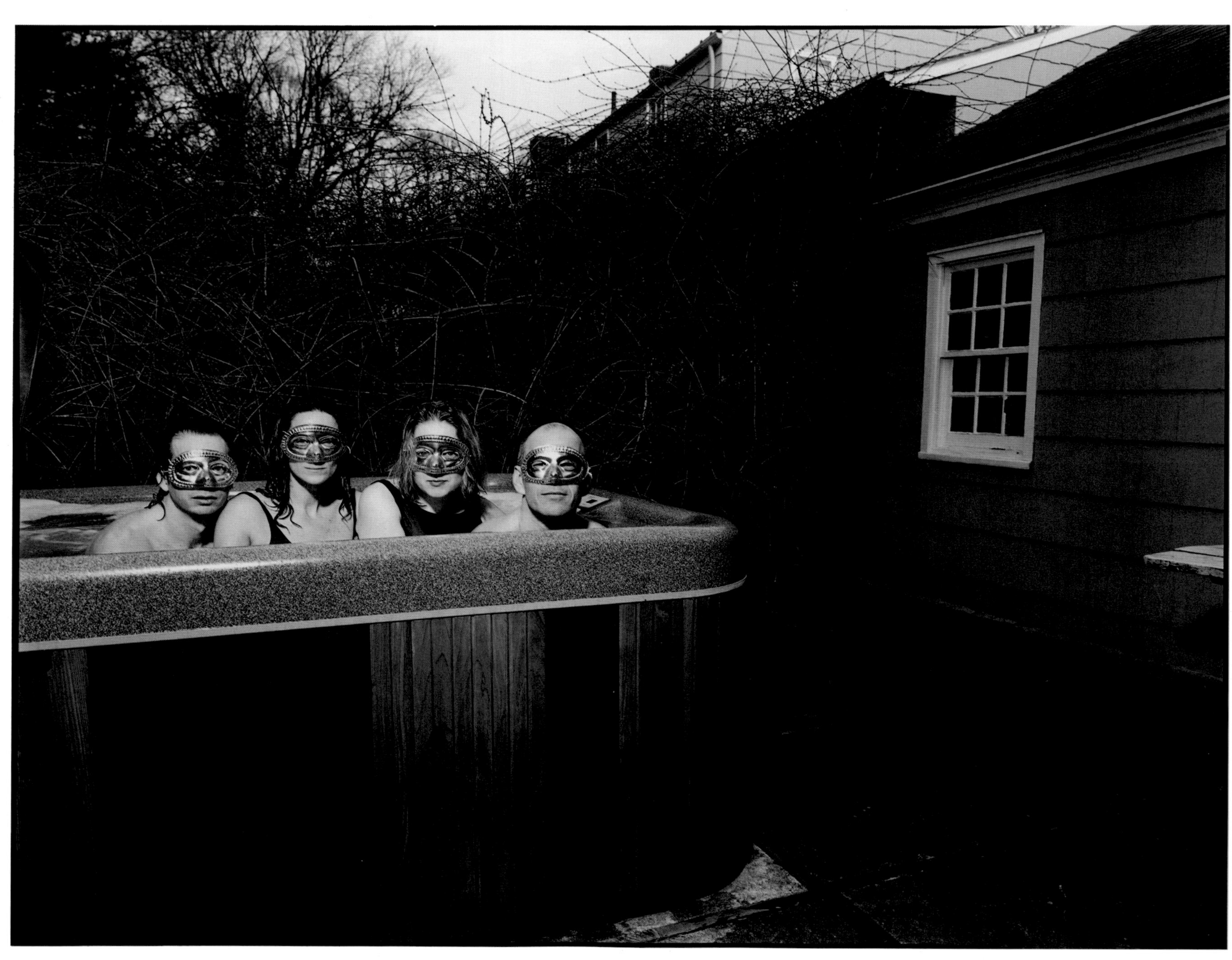

Hot tub, West Orange, New Jersey, 1999

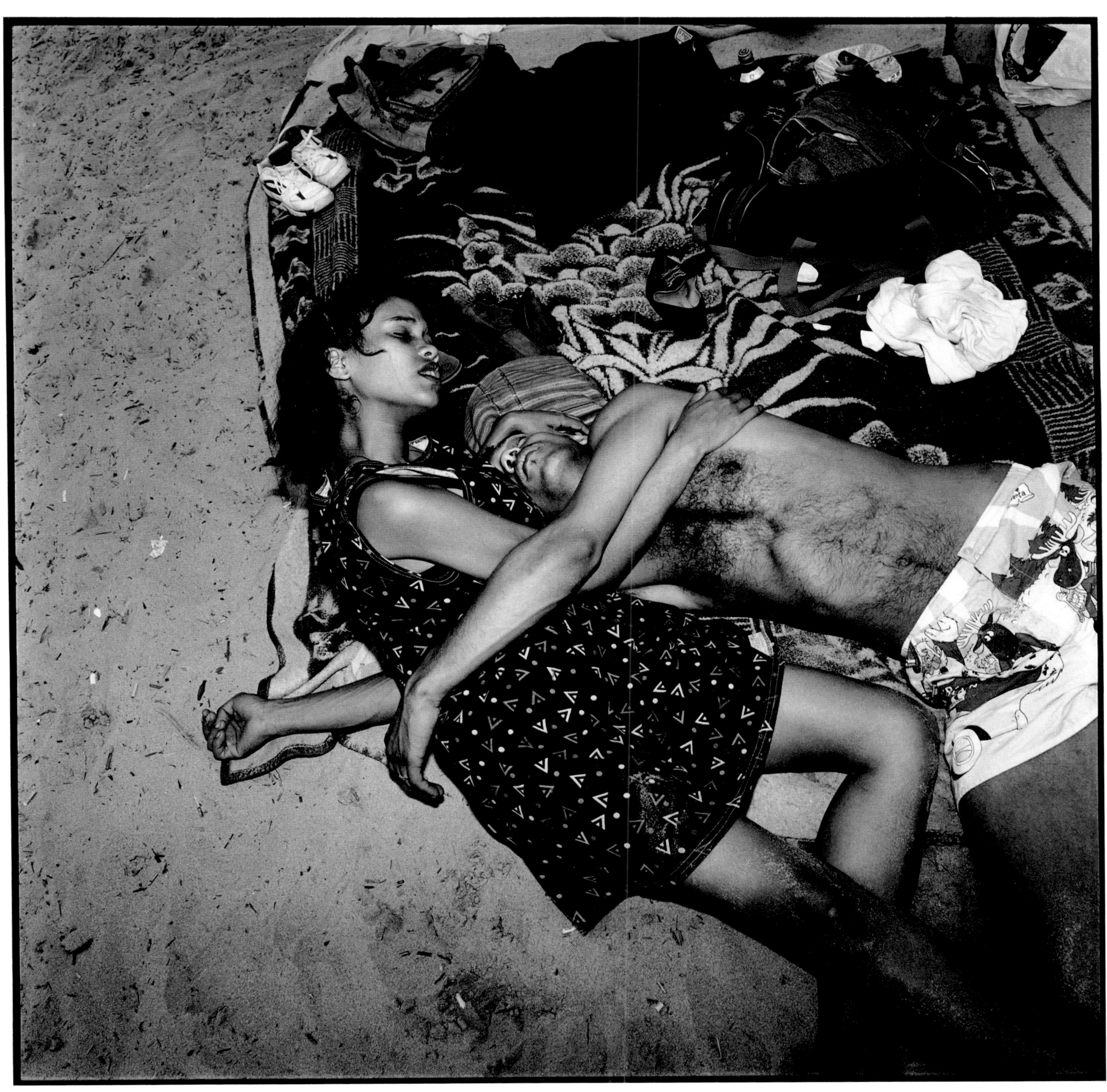

Coney Island, Brooklyn, New York, 1994

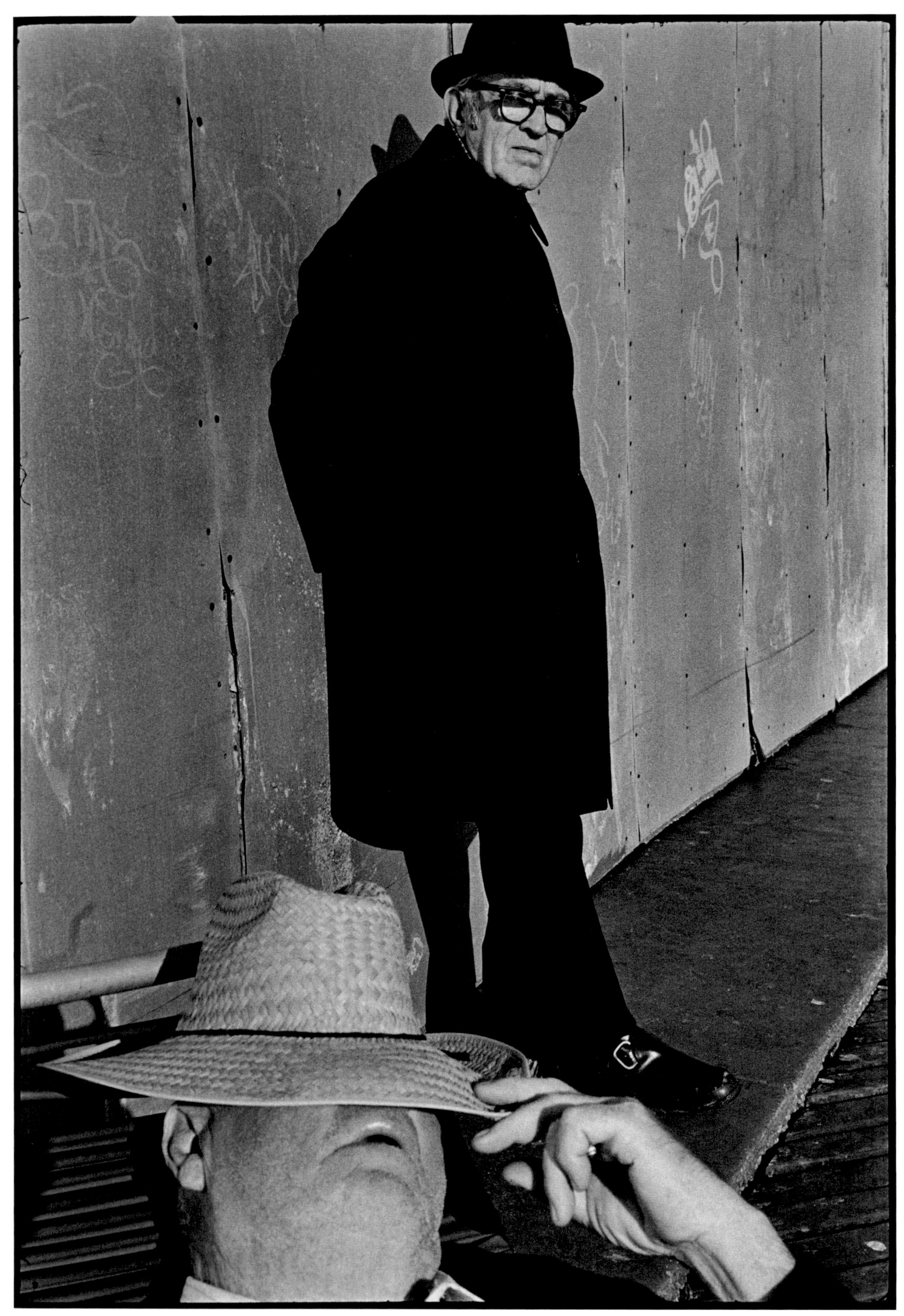

Winter, Coney Island, Brooklyn, New York, 1974

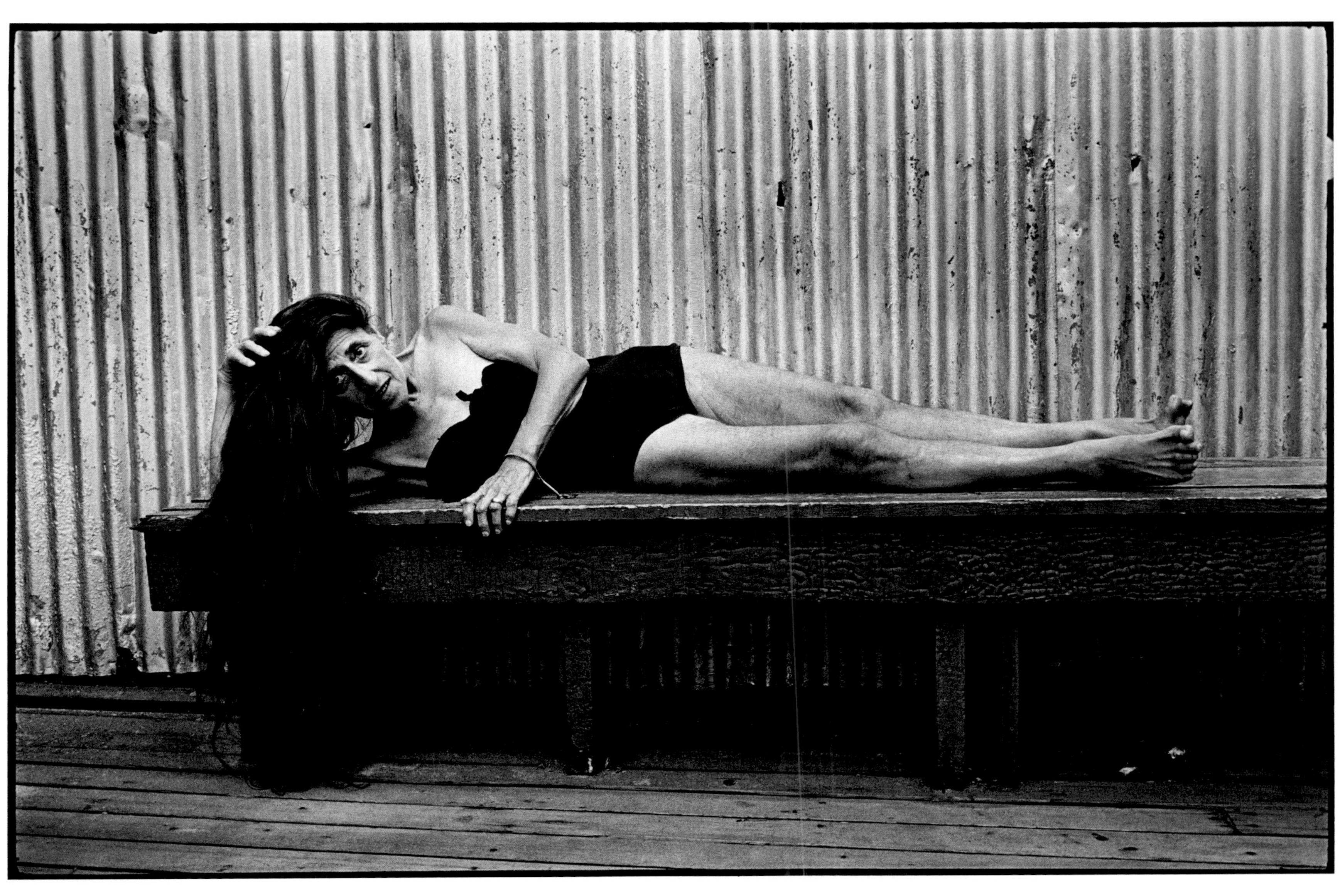

Summer, Coney Island, Brooklyn, New York, 1974

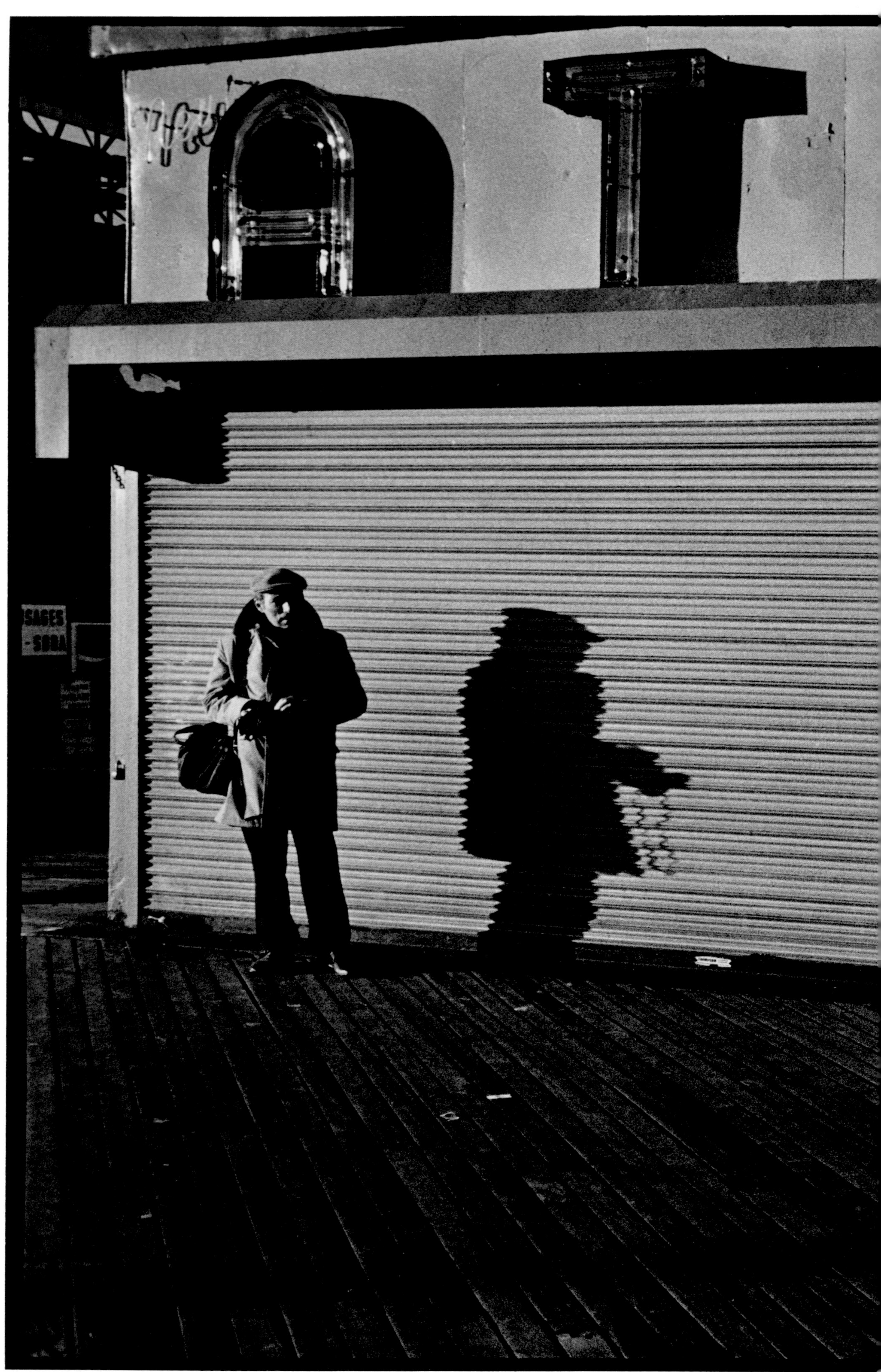

Winter, Coney Island,
Brooklyn, New York, 1974

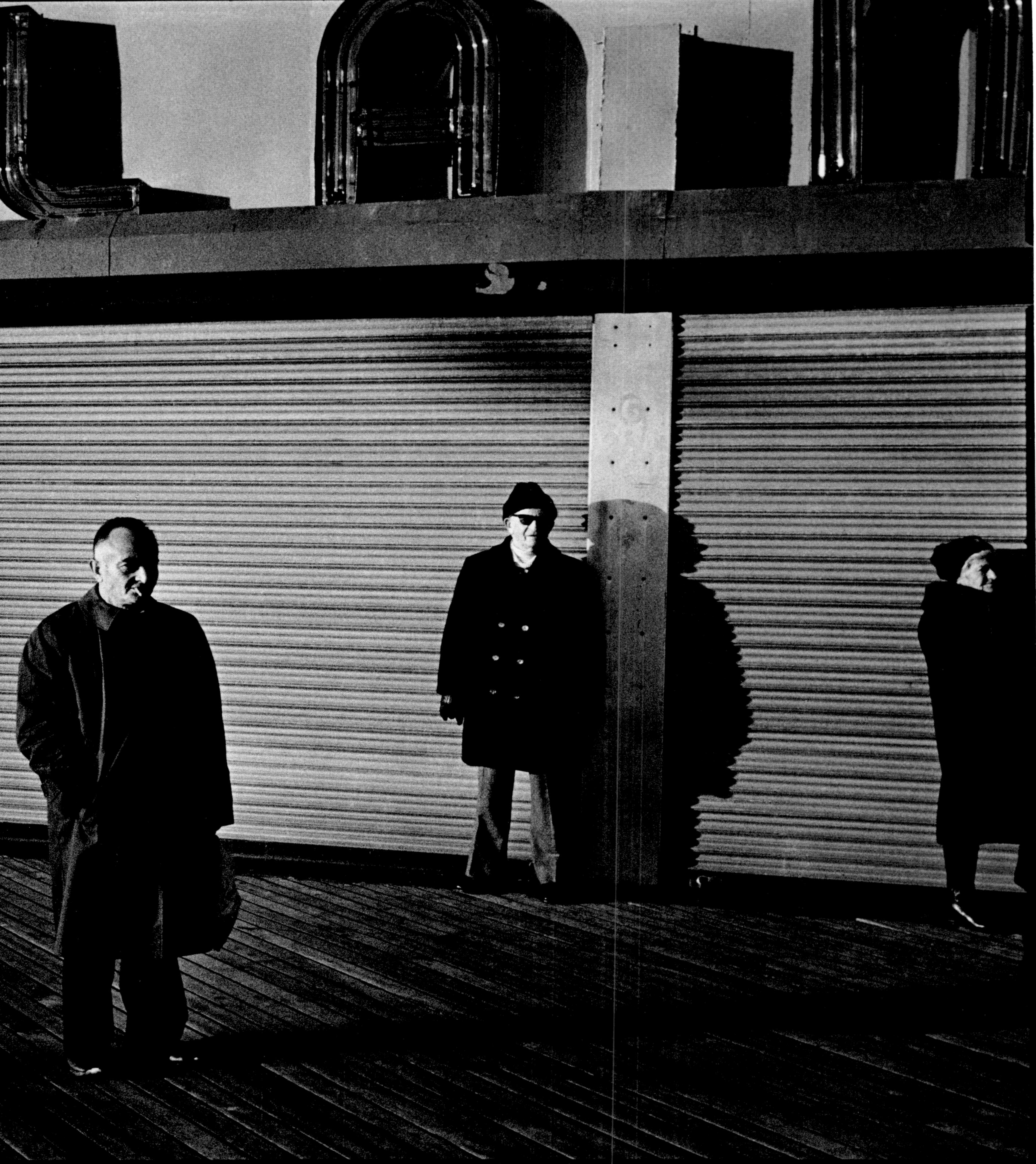

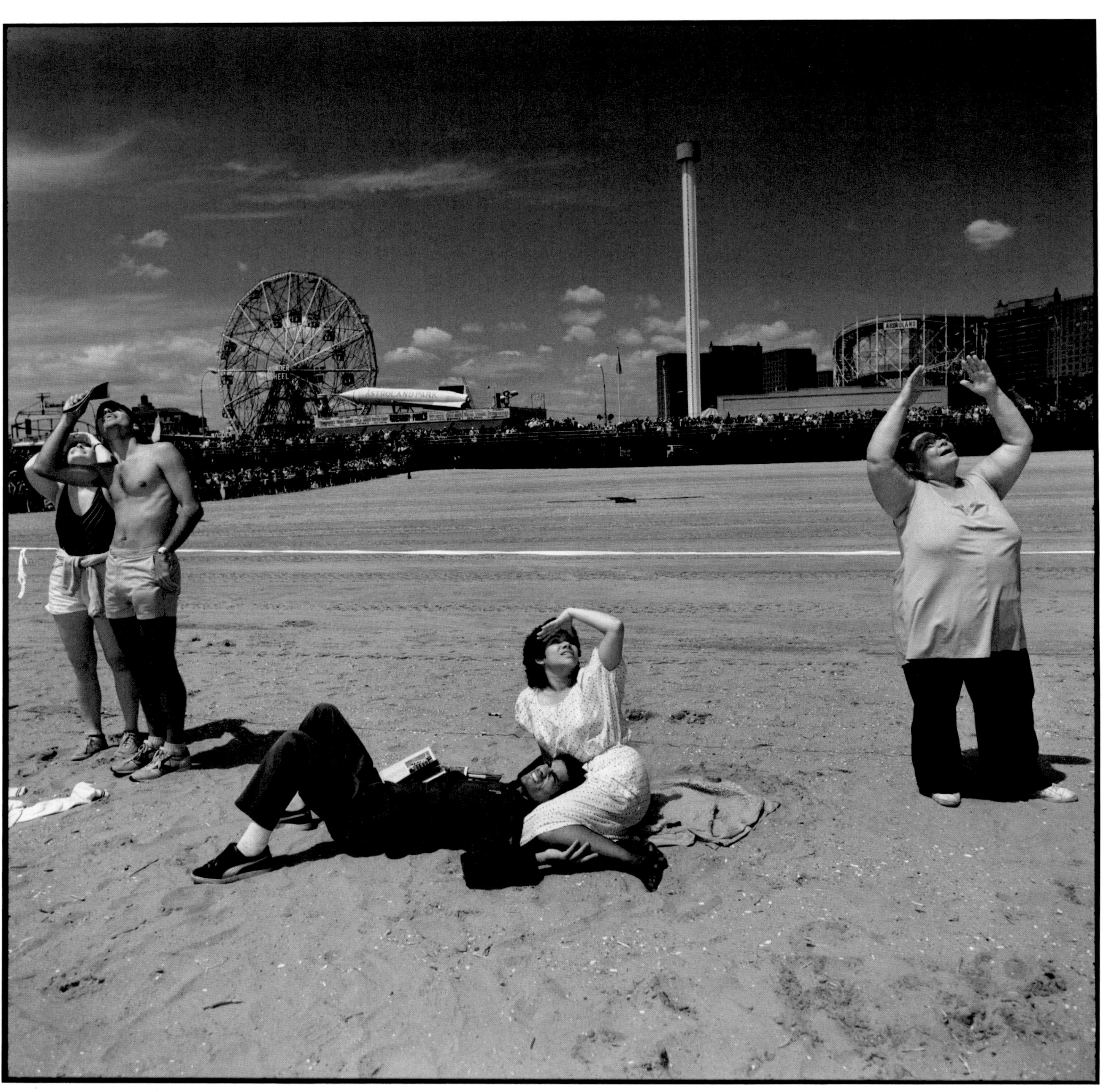

Coney Island, Brooklyn, New York, 1983

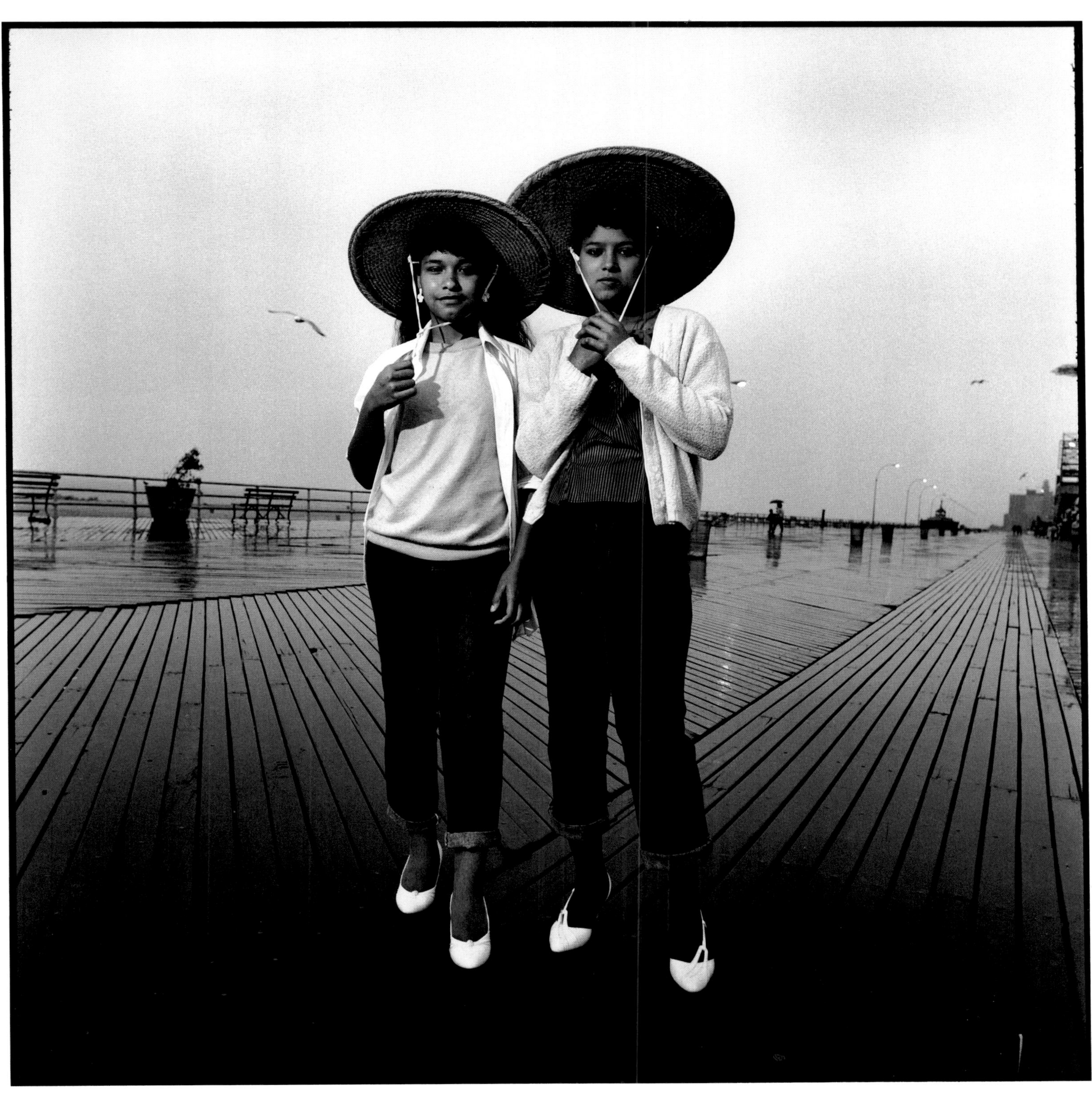

Two girls with hats, Coney Island, Brooklyn, New York, 1983

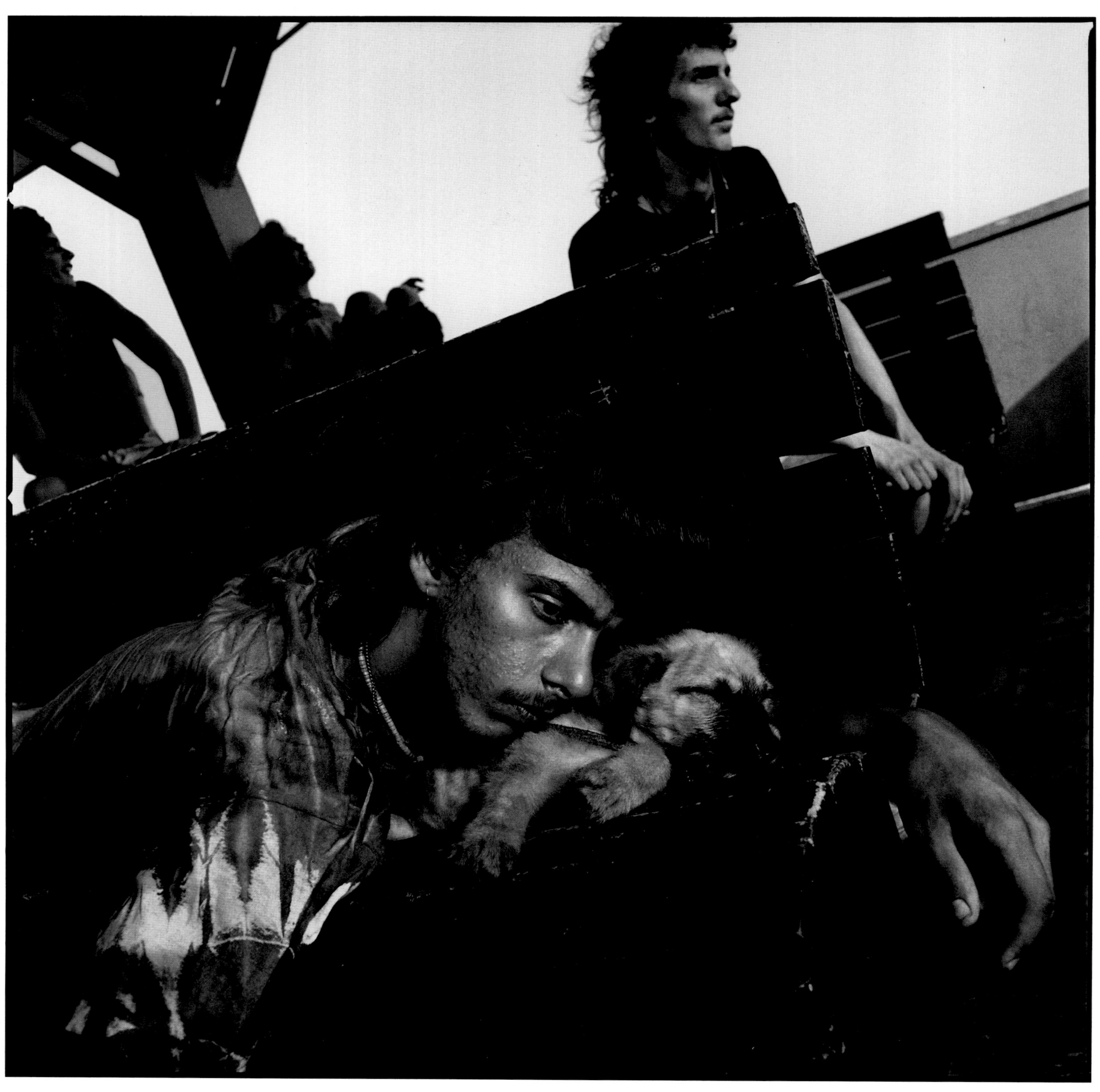

Boy with a puppy, Wildwood, New Jersey, 1991

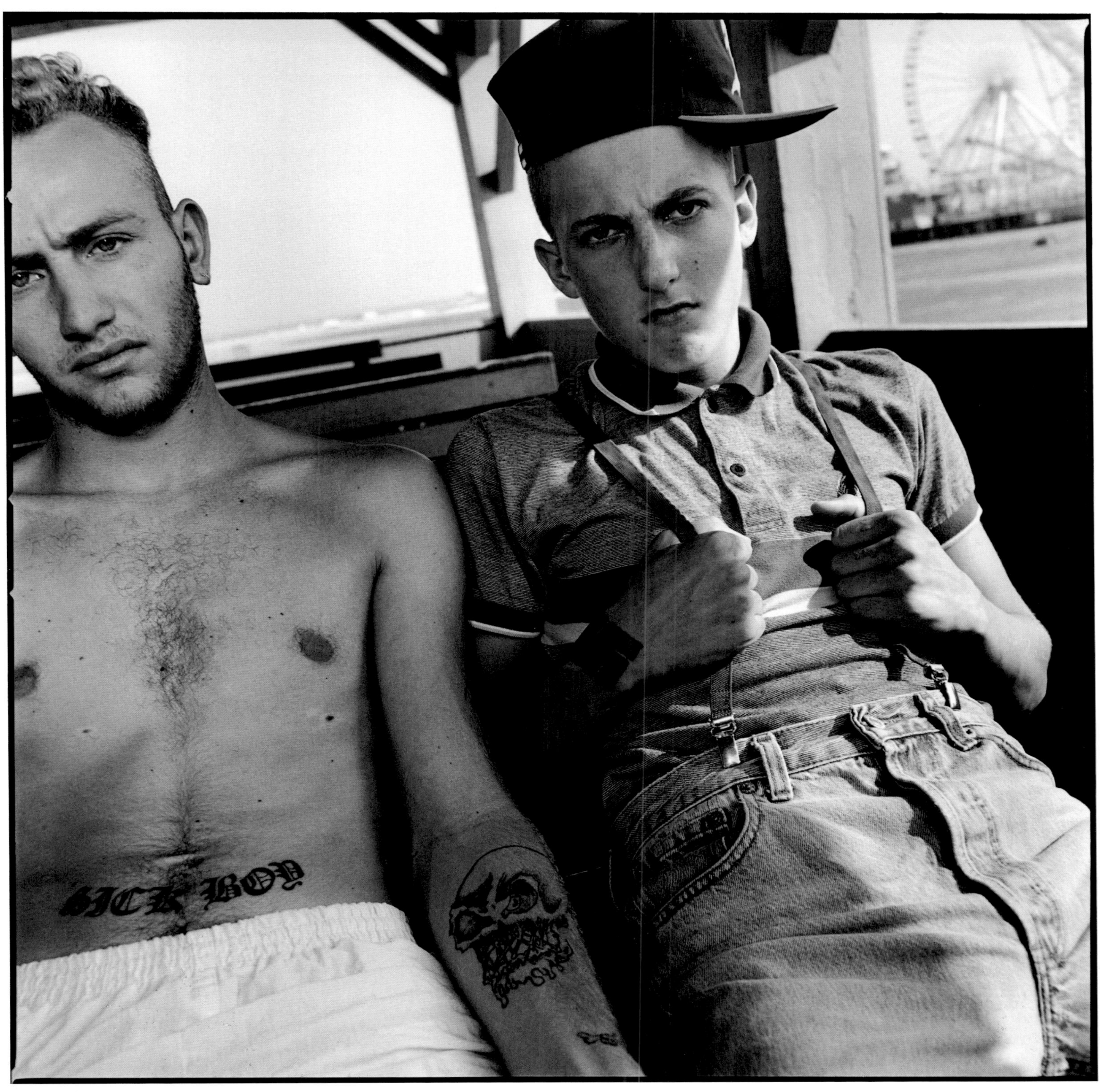

Wildwood, New Jersey, 1991

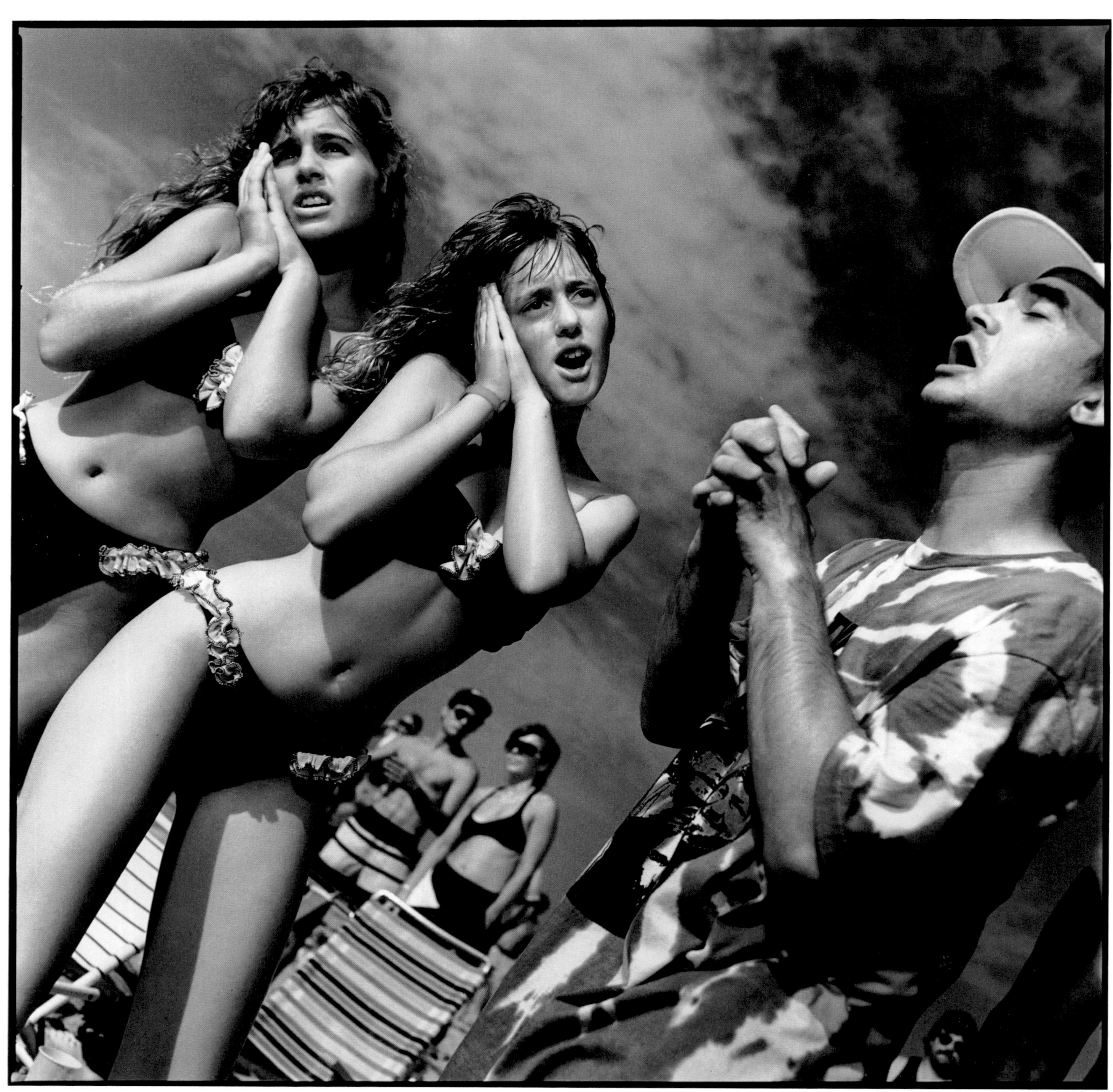

Concert, Wildwood, New Jersey, 1991

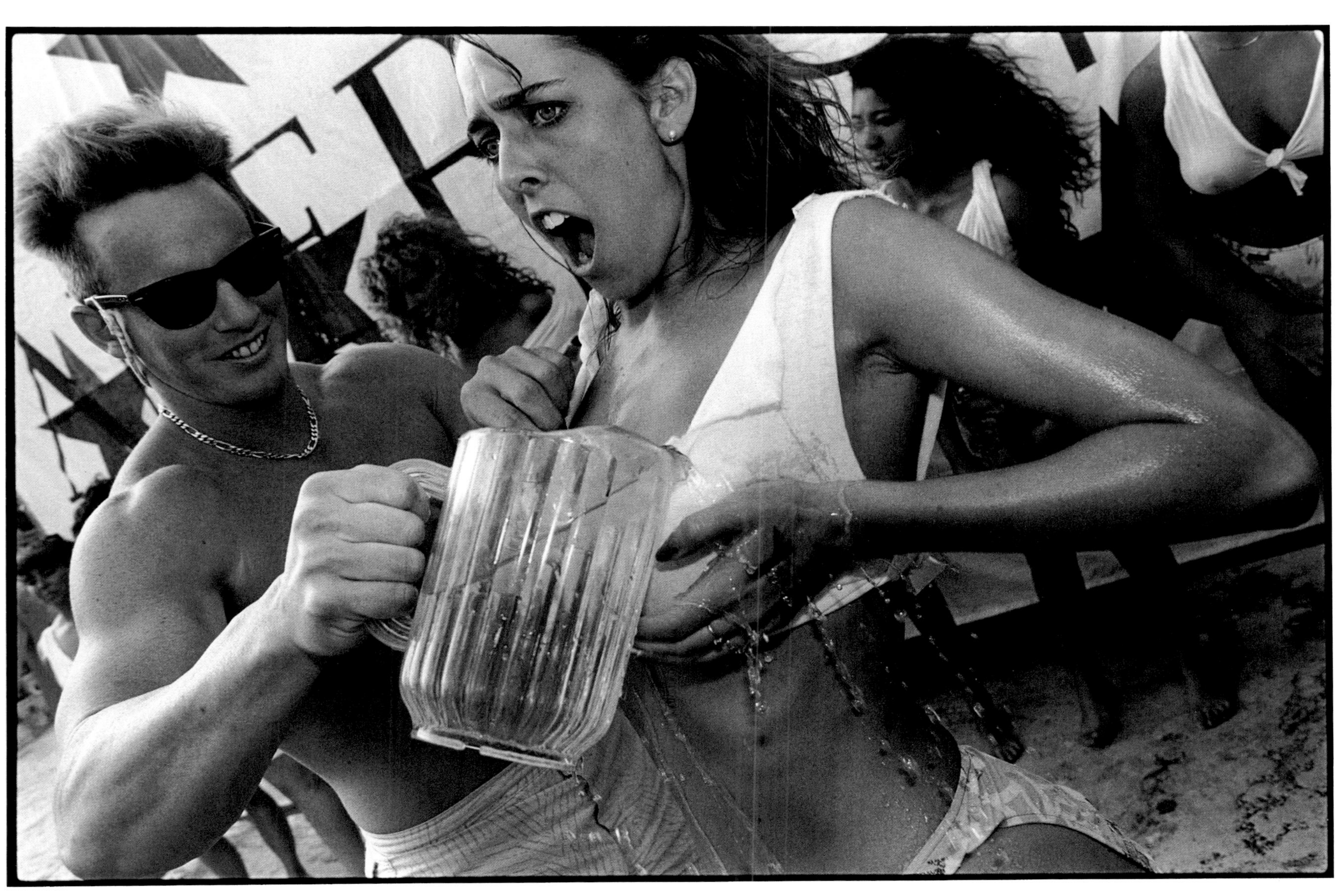

Wet t-shirt contest, Spring Break, Daytona Beach, Florida, 1991

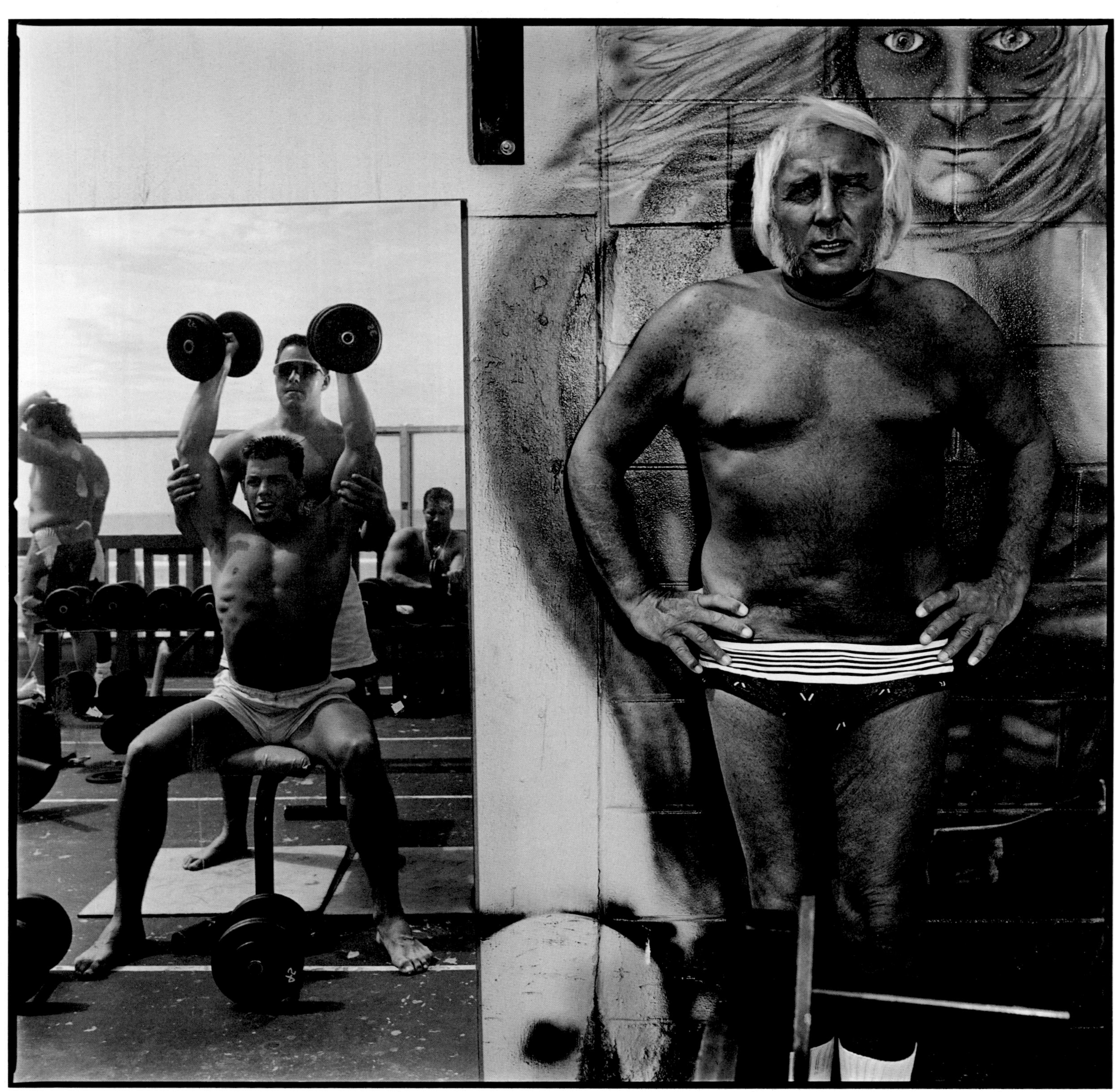

Bodybuilder, Daytona Beach, Florida, 1991

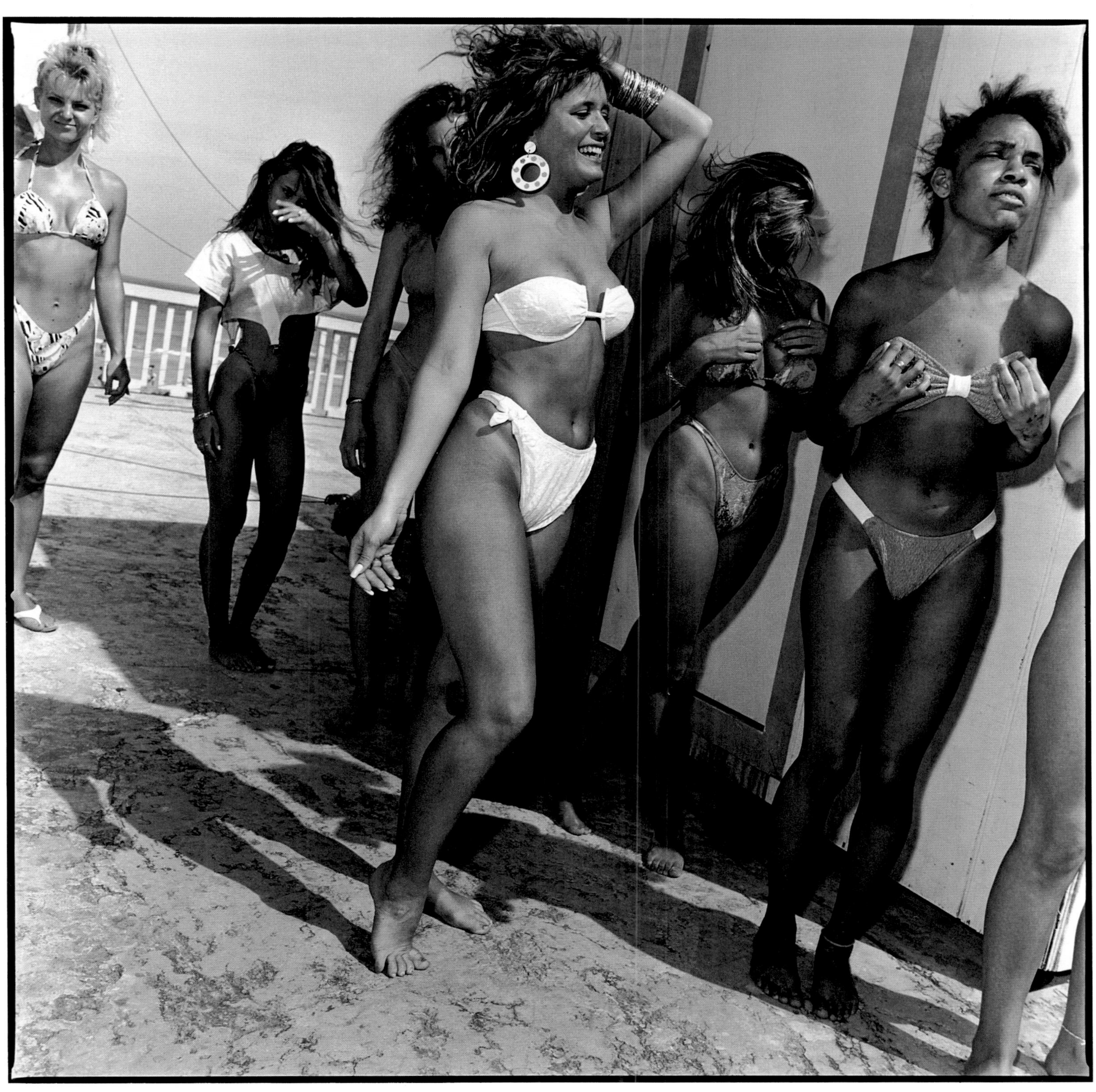

Beauty contest, Spring Break, Daytona Beach, Florida, 1991

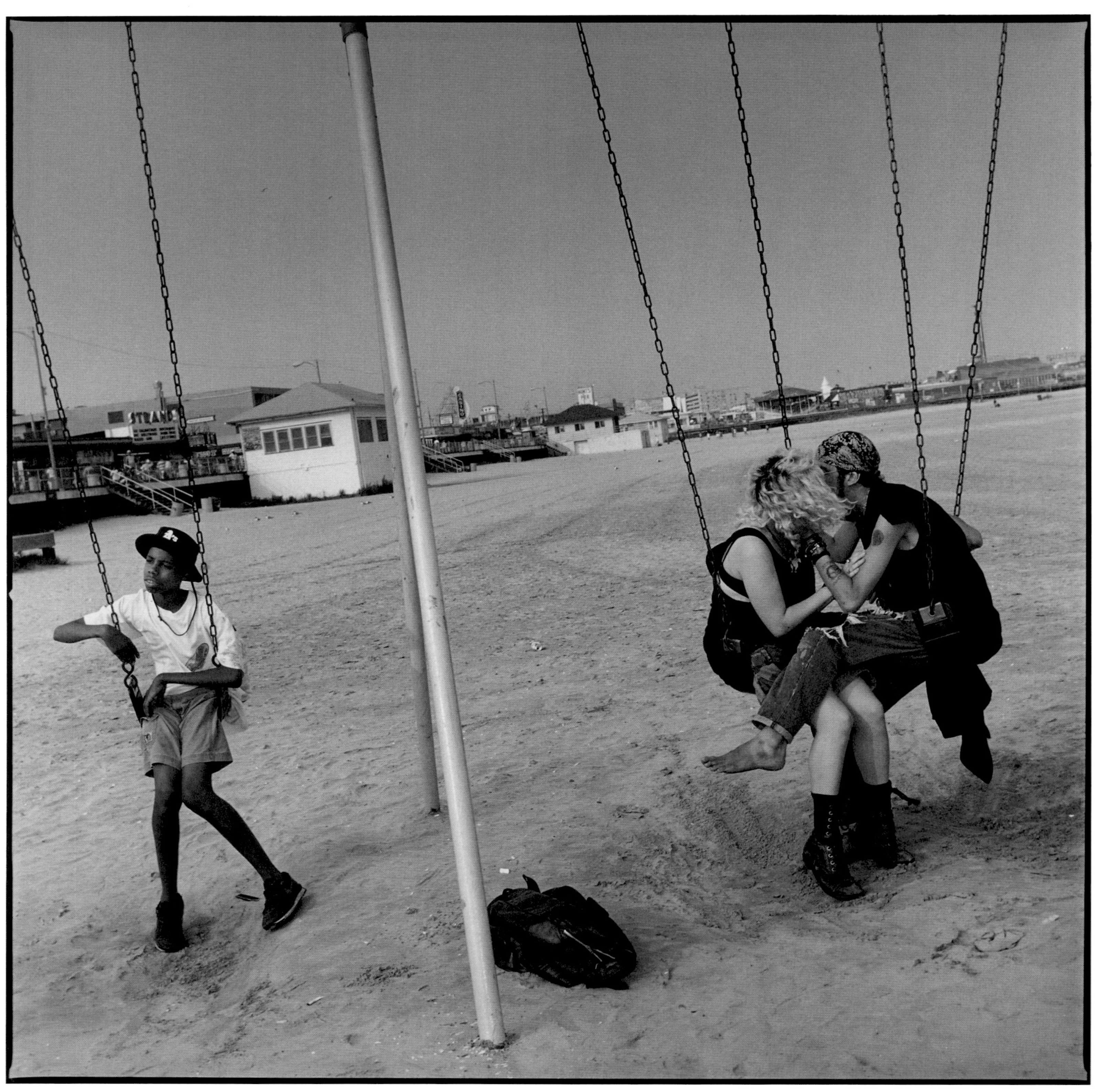

Wildwood, New Jersey, 1991

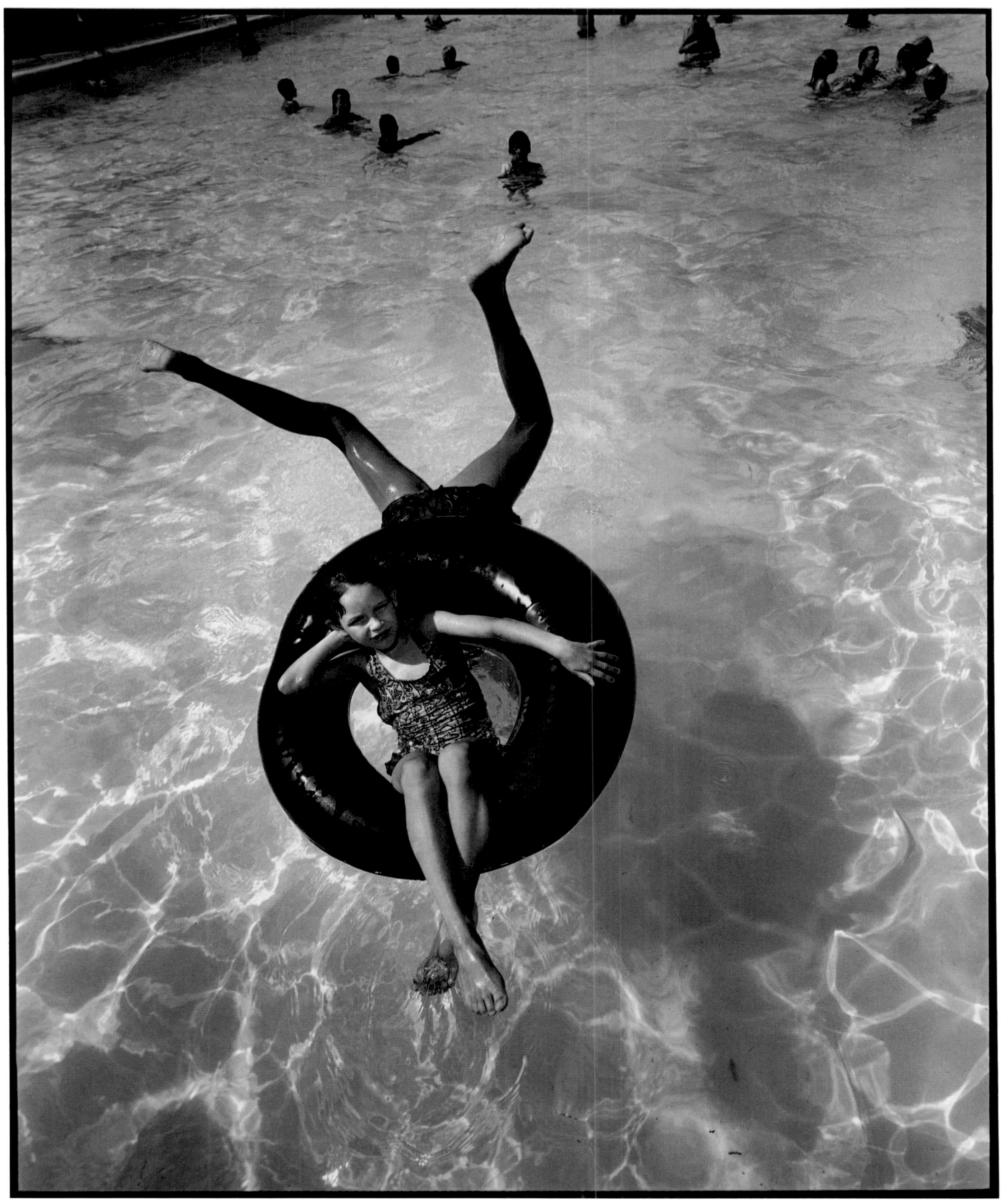

Russell, Kansas, 1996

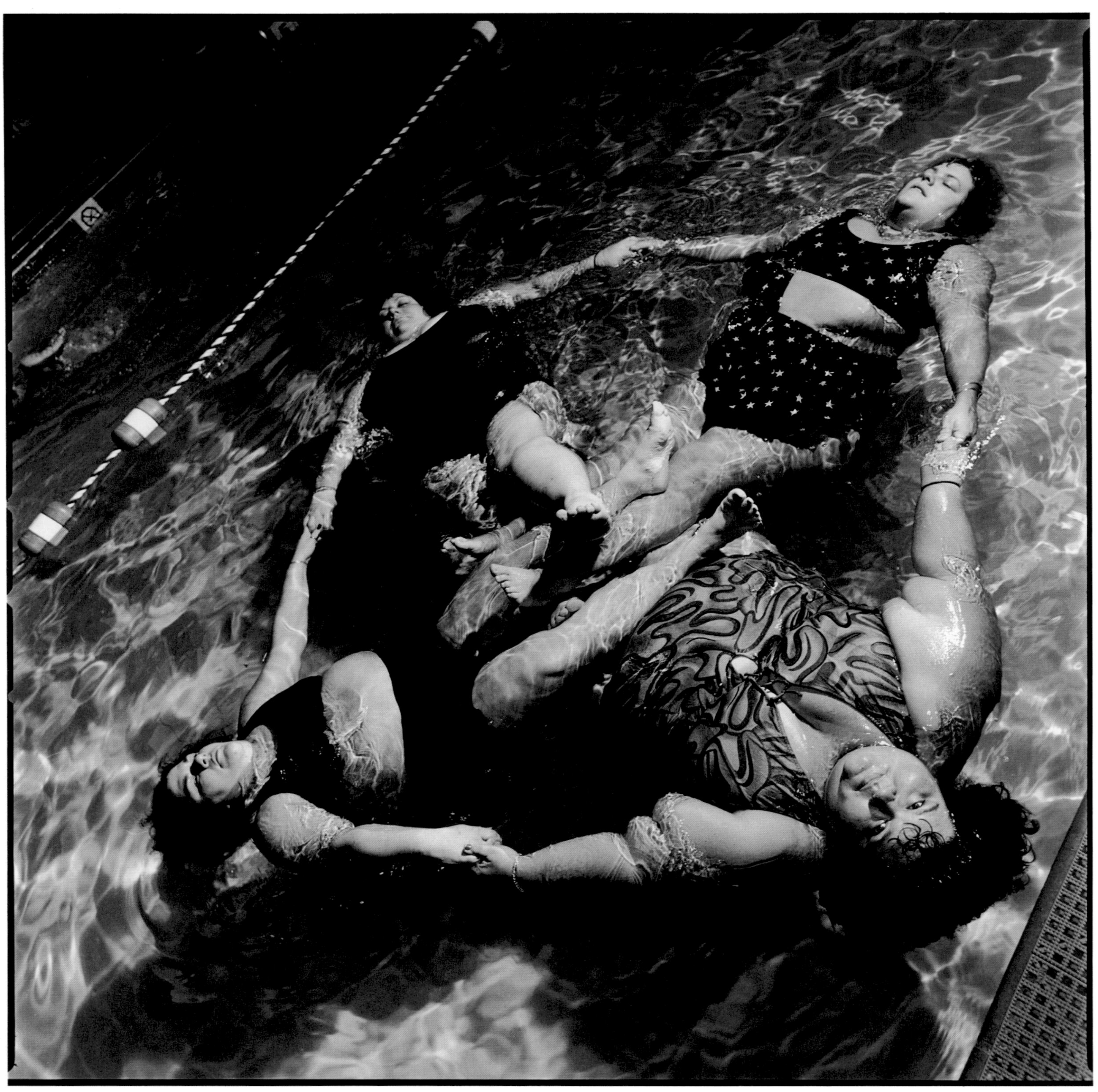

National Association to Advance Fat Acceptance, Big and Beautiful New Year's Eve party, Long Island, New York, 1996

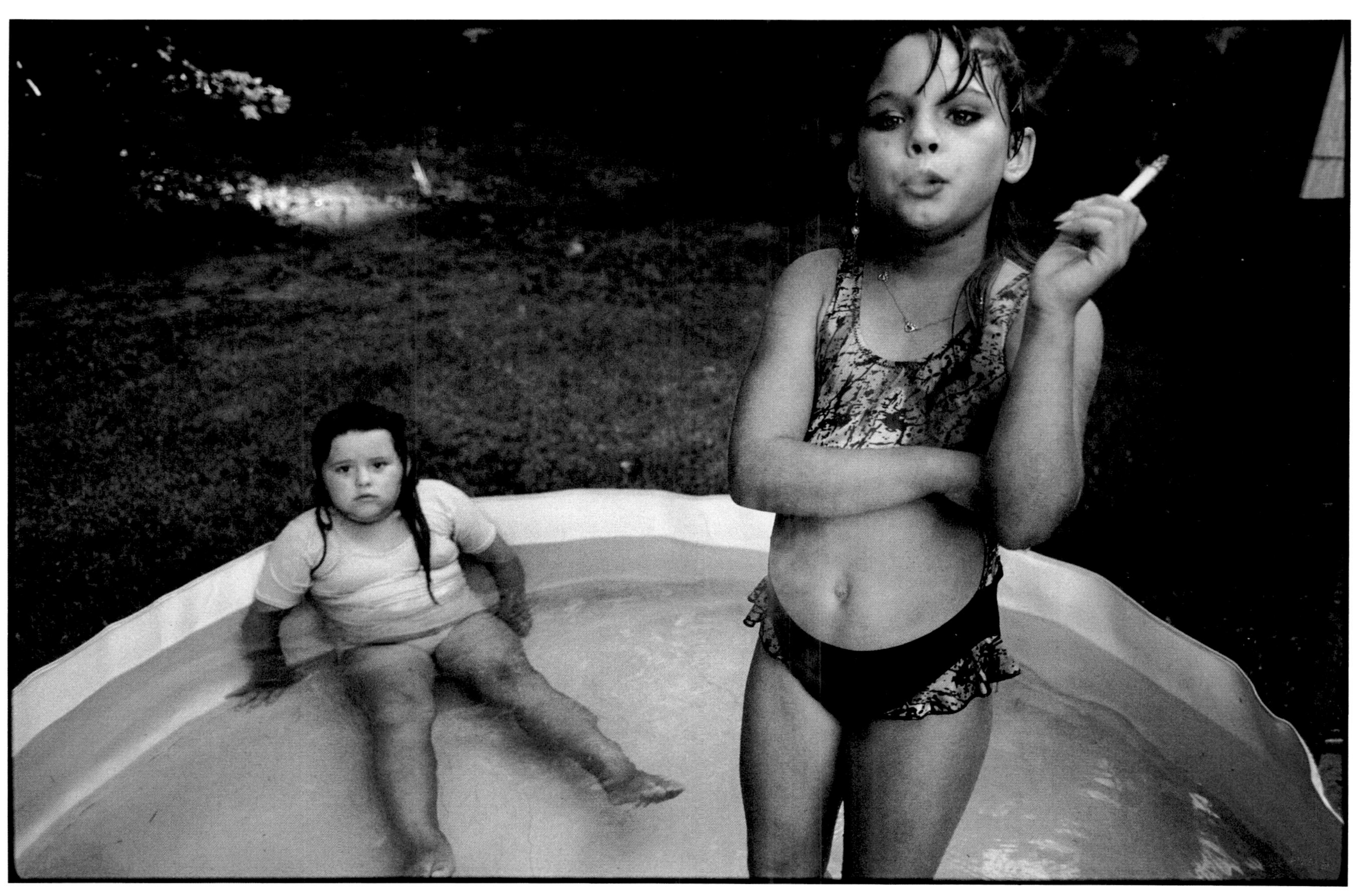

Amanda and her cousin Amy, Valdese, North Carolina, 1990

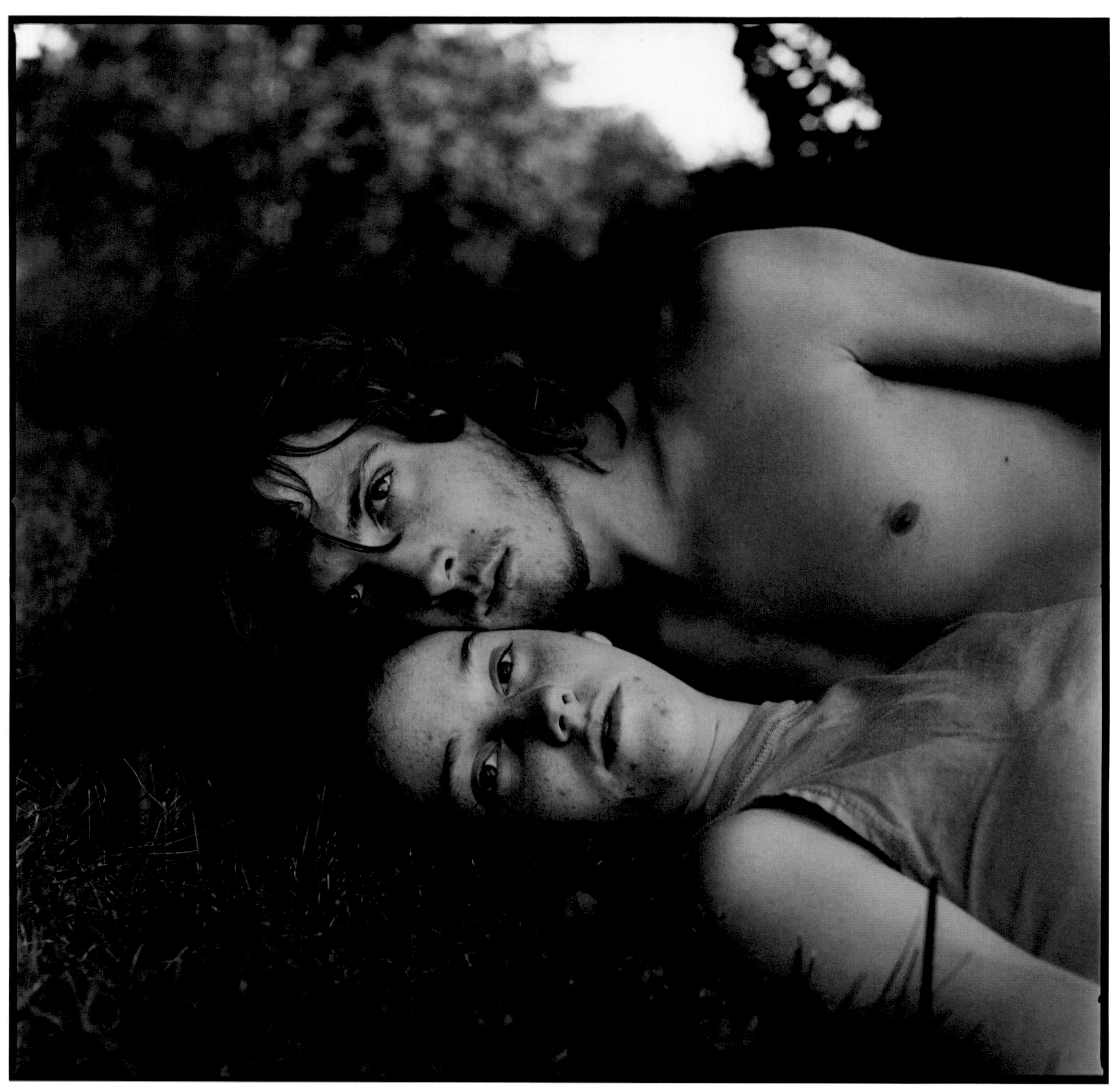

James and Natasha Gurley, Valdese, North Carolina, 1990

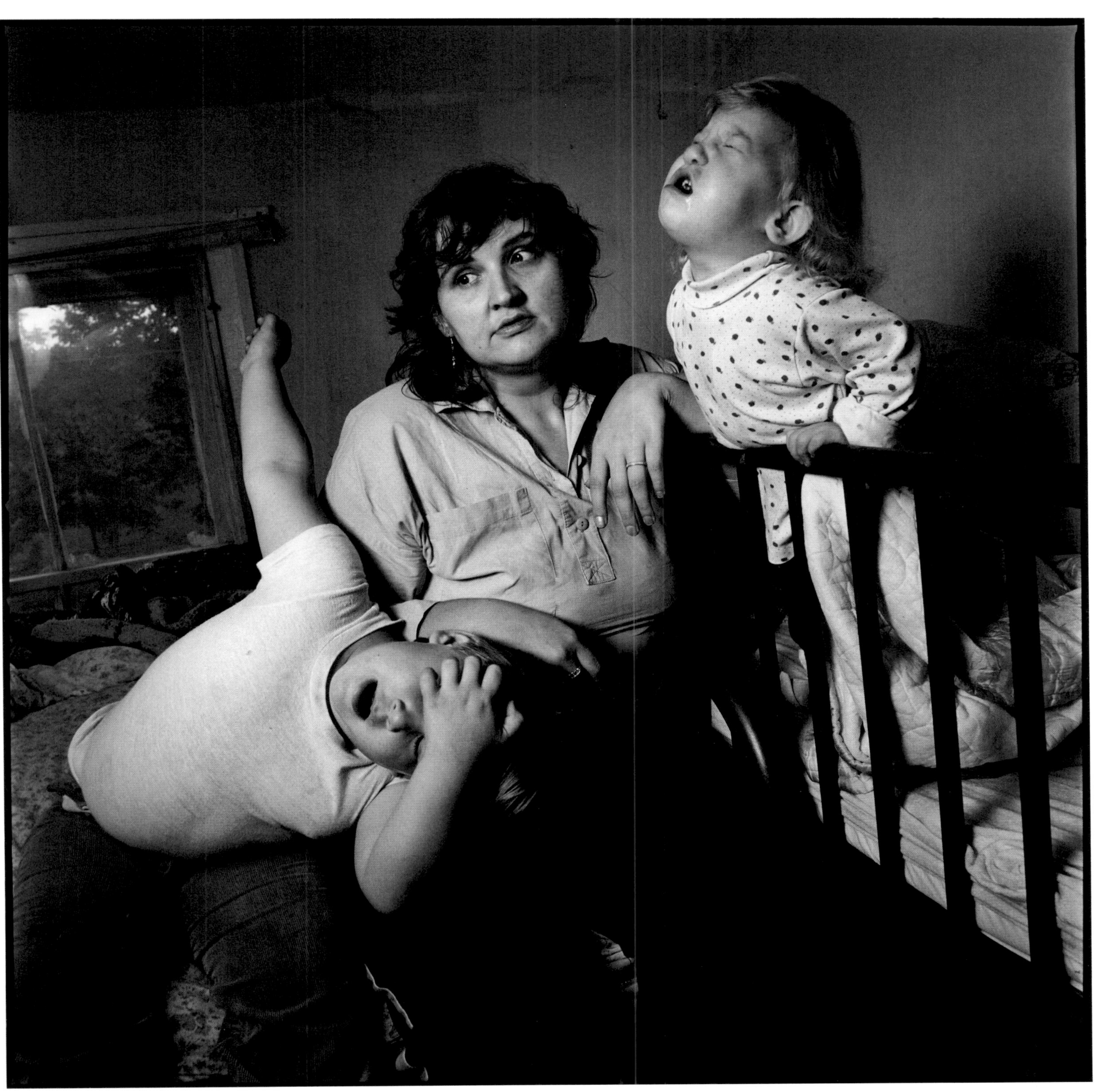

Tamy-Lu Riley with Roland and Kristina, Belfast, Maine, 1990

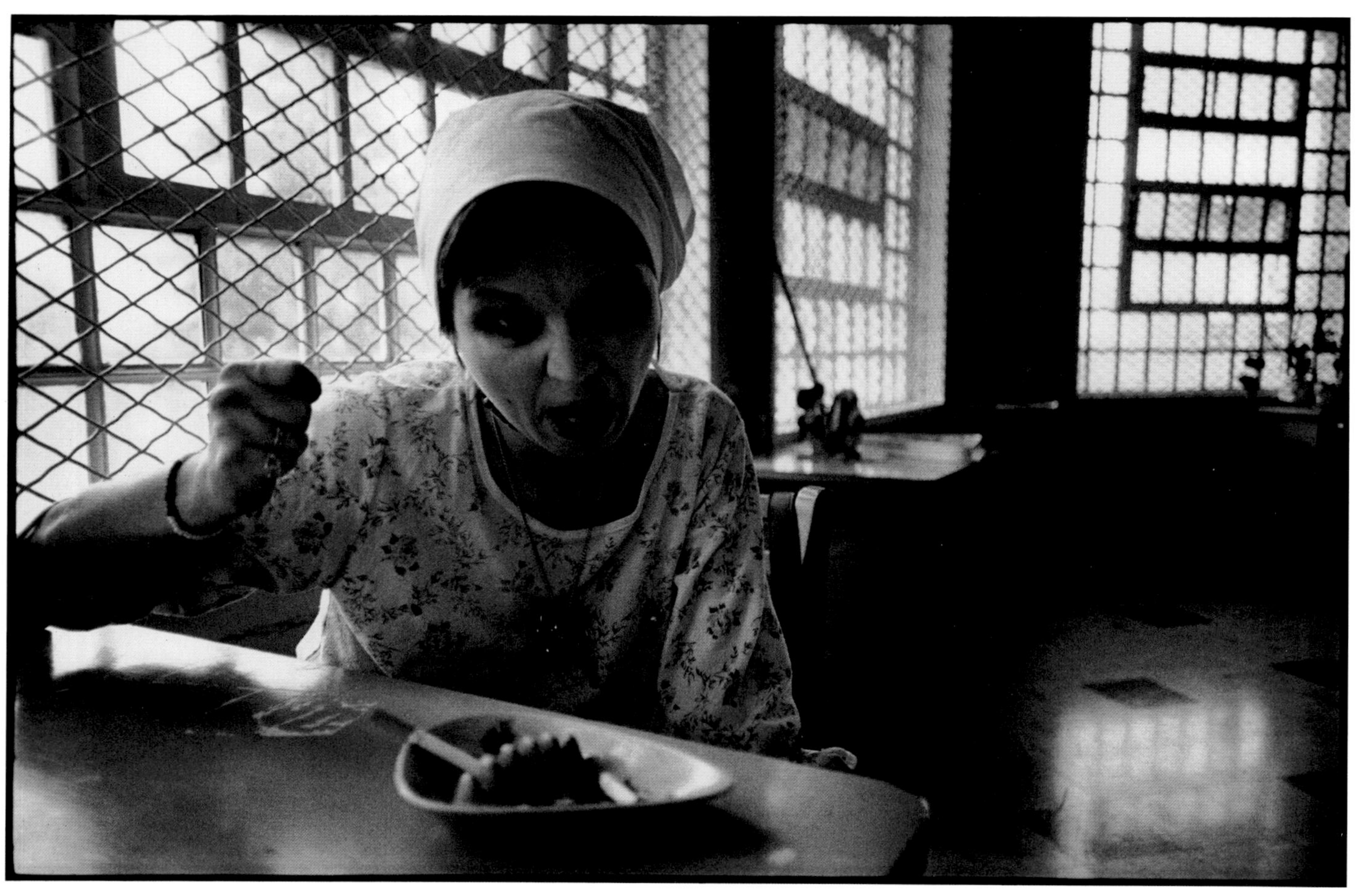

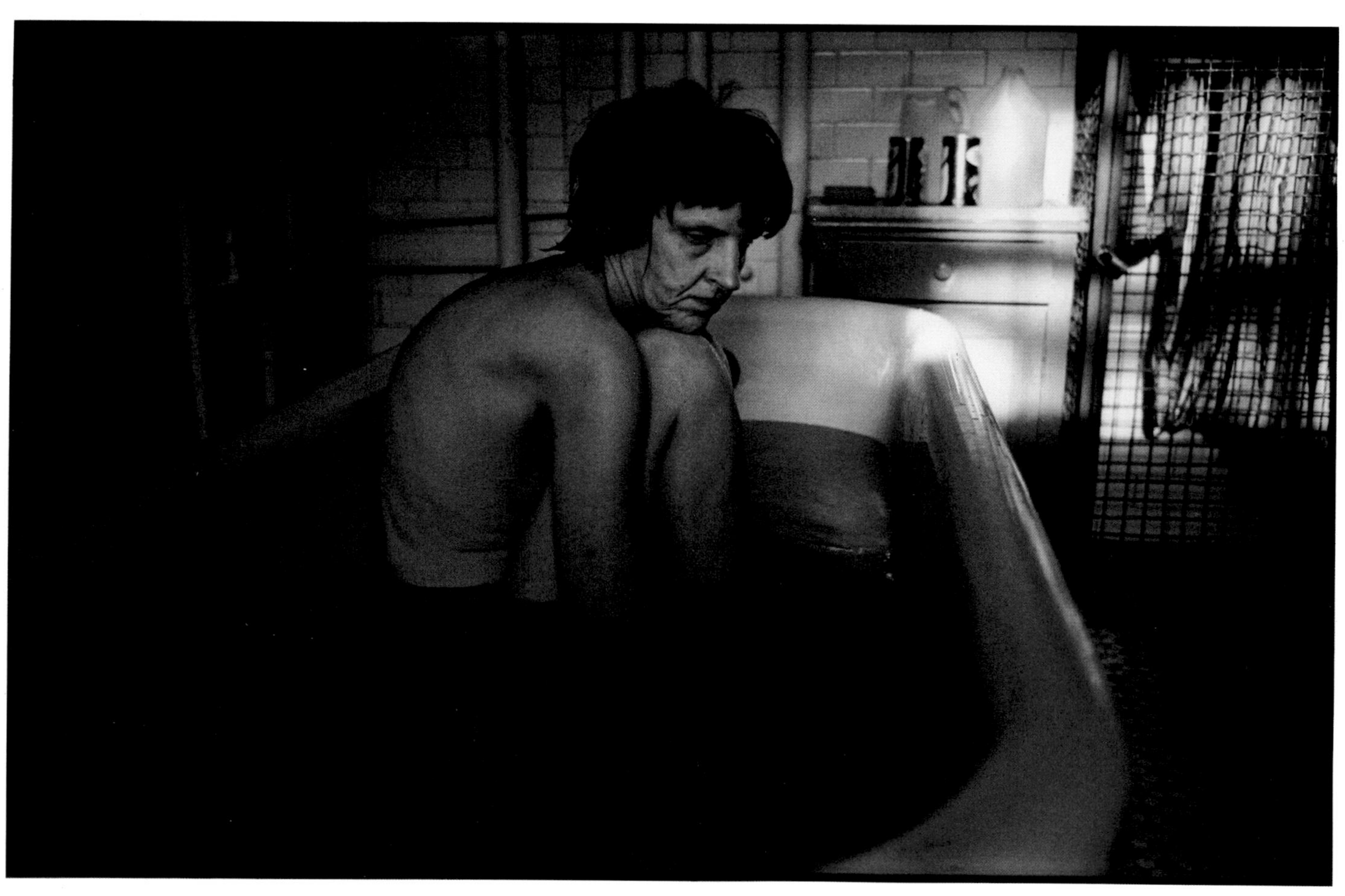

top: Mona, angry, Ward 81, Salem, Oregon, 1976
bottom: Mary Frances in the tub, Ward 81, Salem, Oregon, 1976

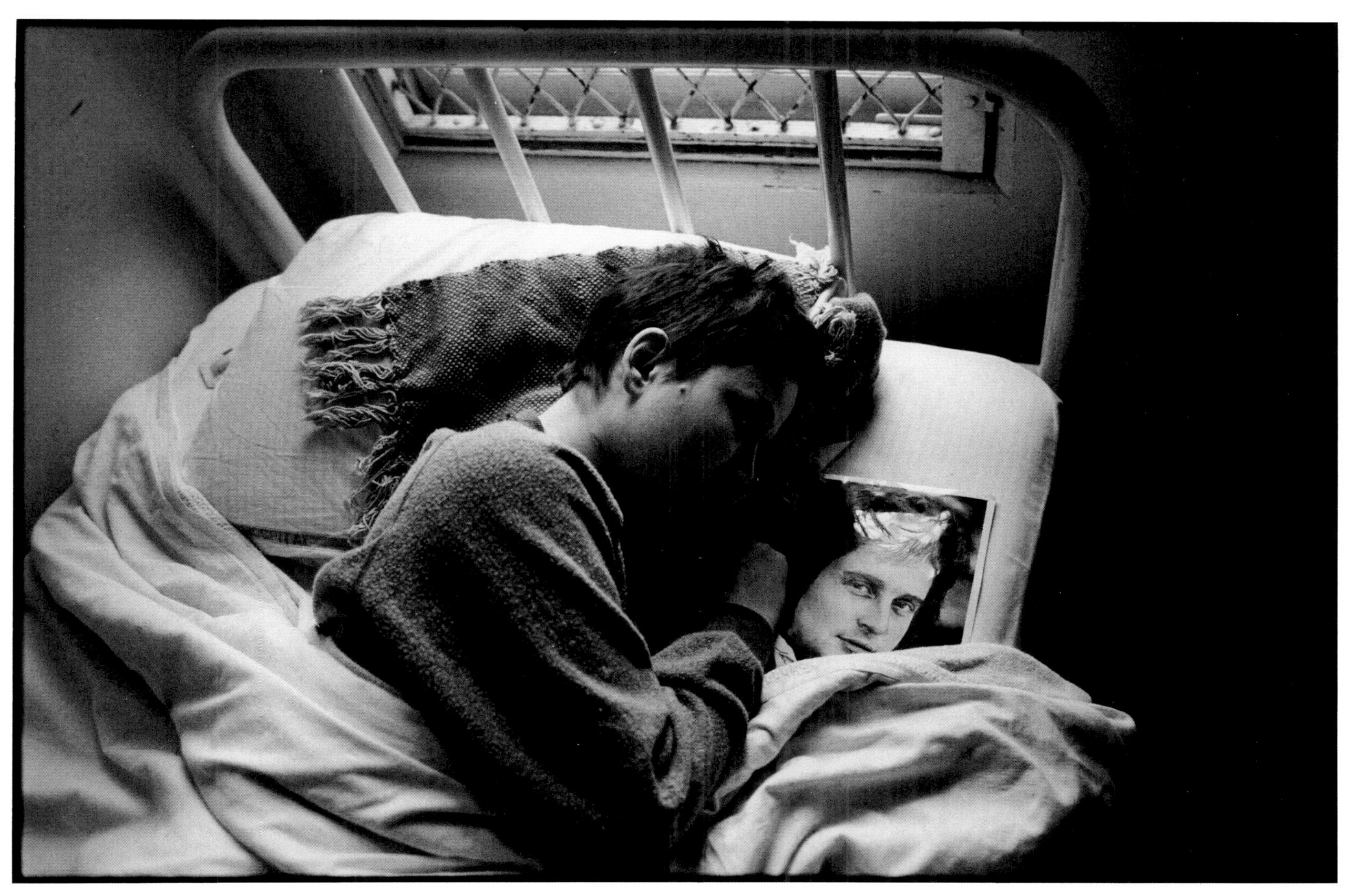

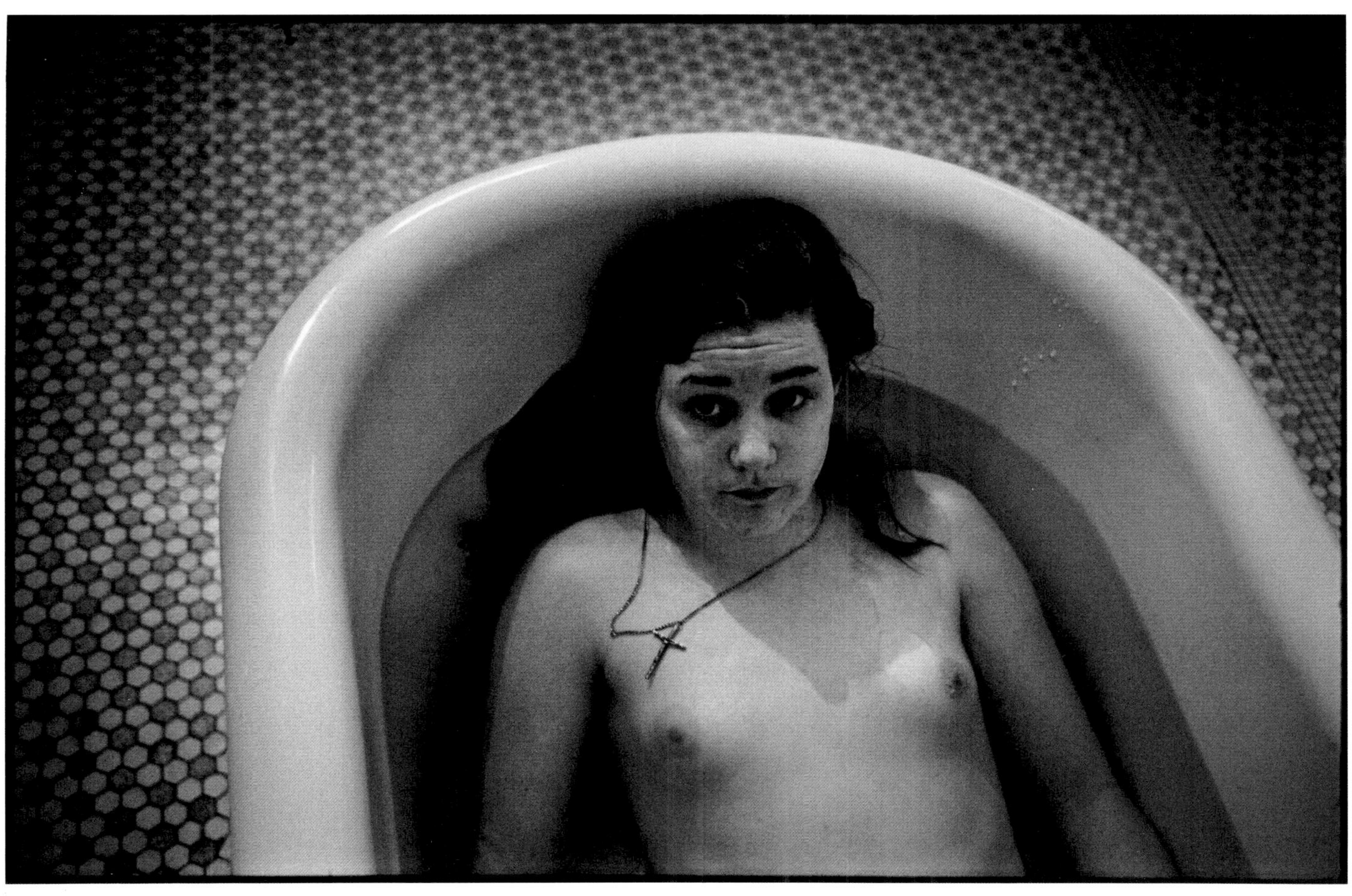

top: Mona with Michael Douglas's picture, Ward 81, Salem, Oregon, 1976
bottom: Laurie in the tub, Ward 81, Salem, Oregon, 1976

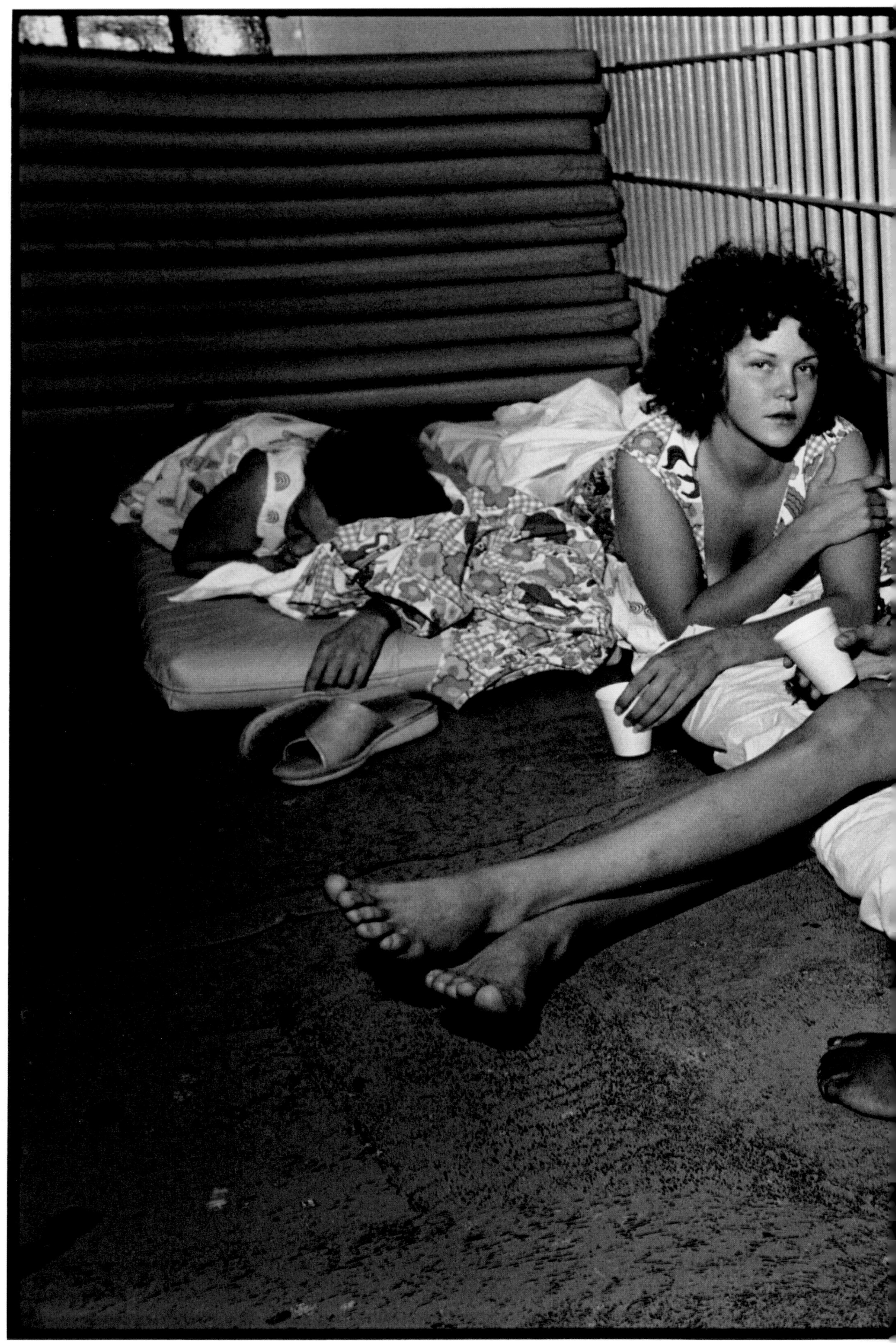

Jail, Houston, Texas, 1977

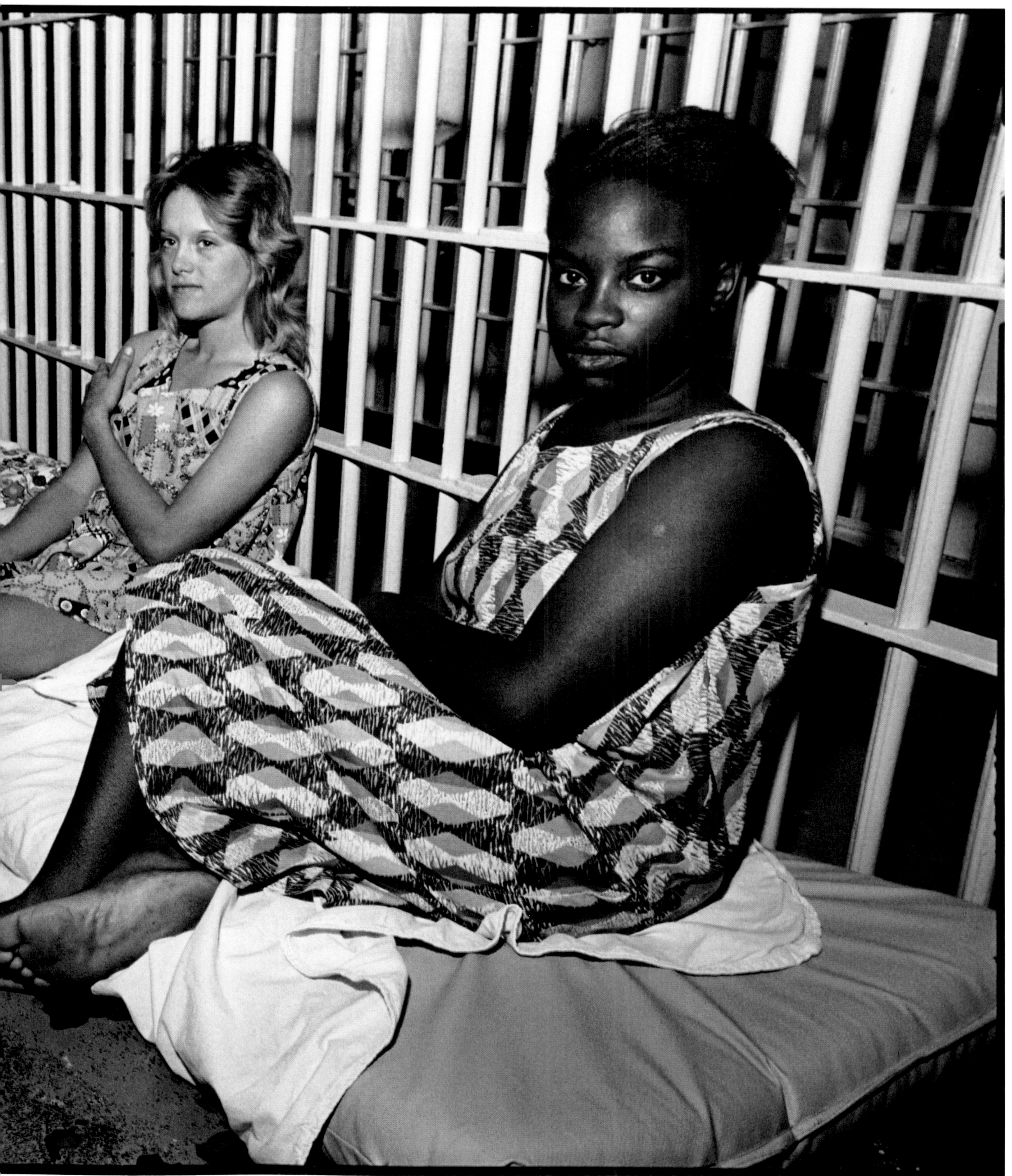

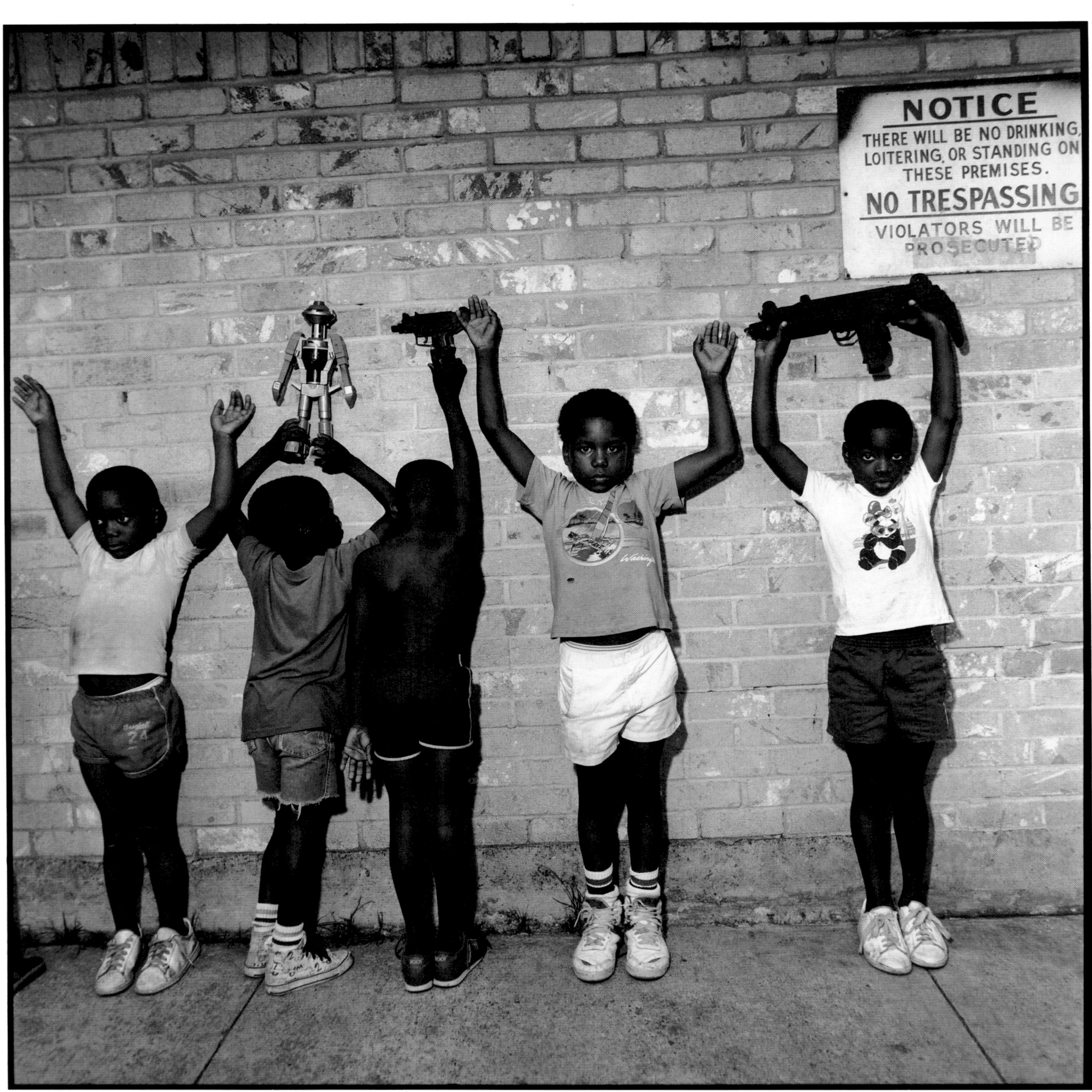

Children playing gangsters, South Dallas, Texas, 1988

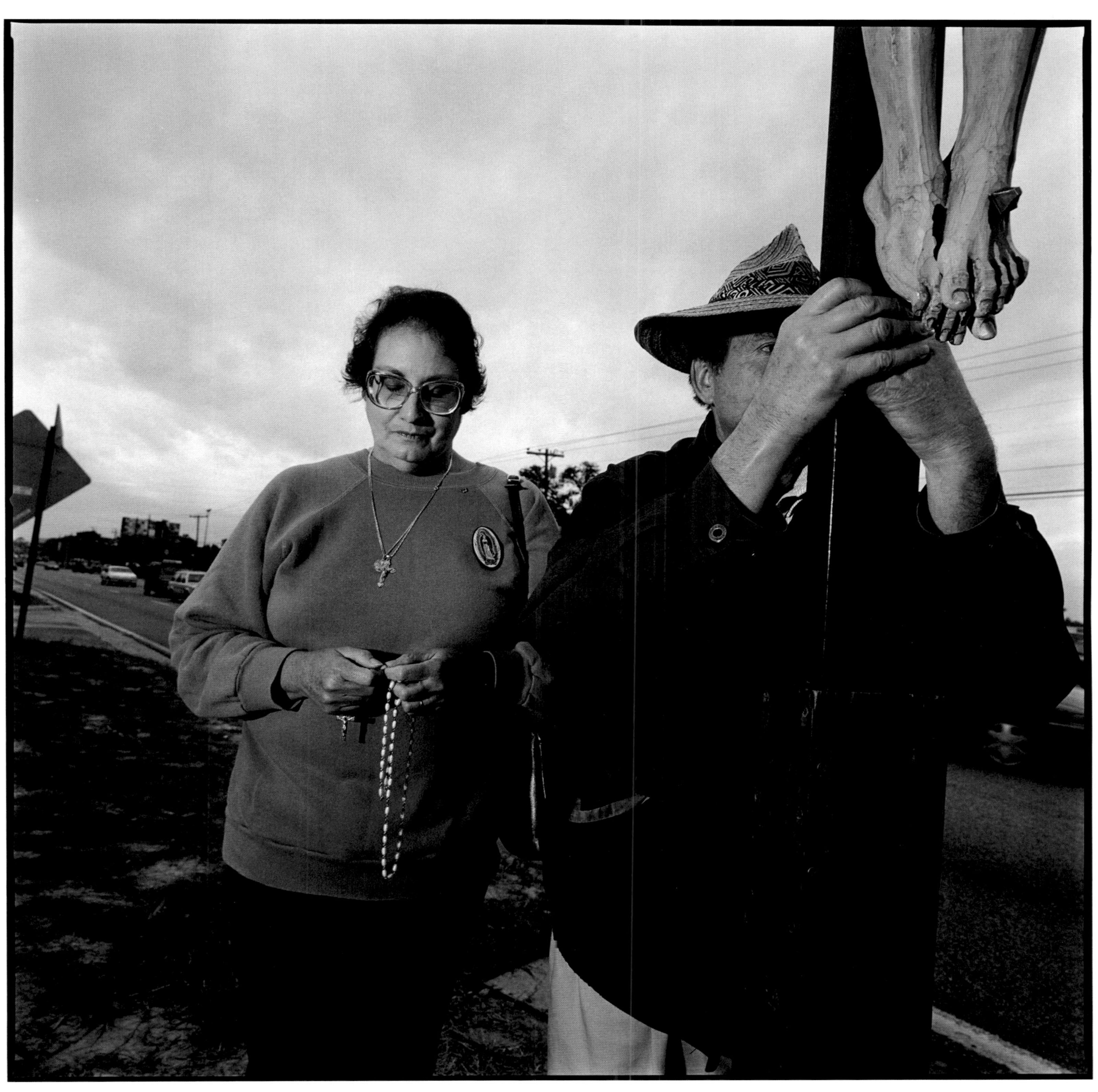

Anti-abortion rally, Per sacola, Florida, 1993

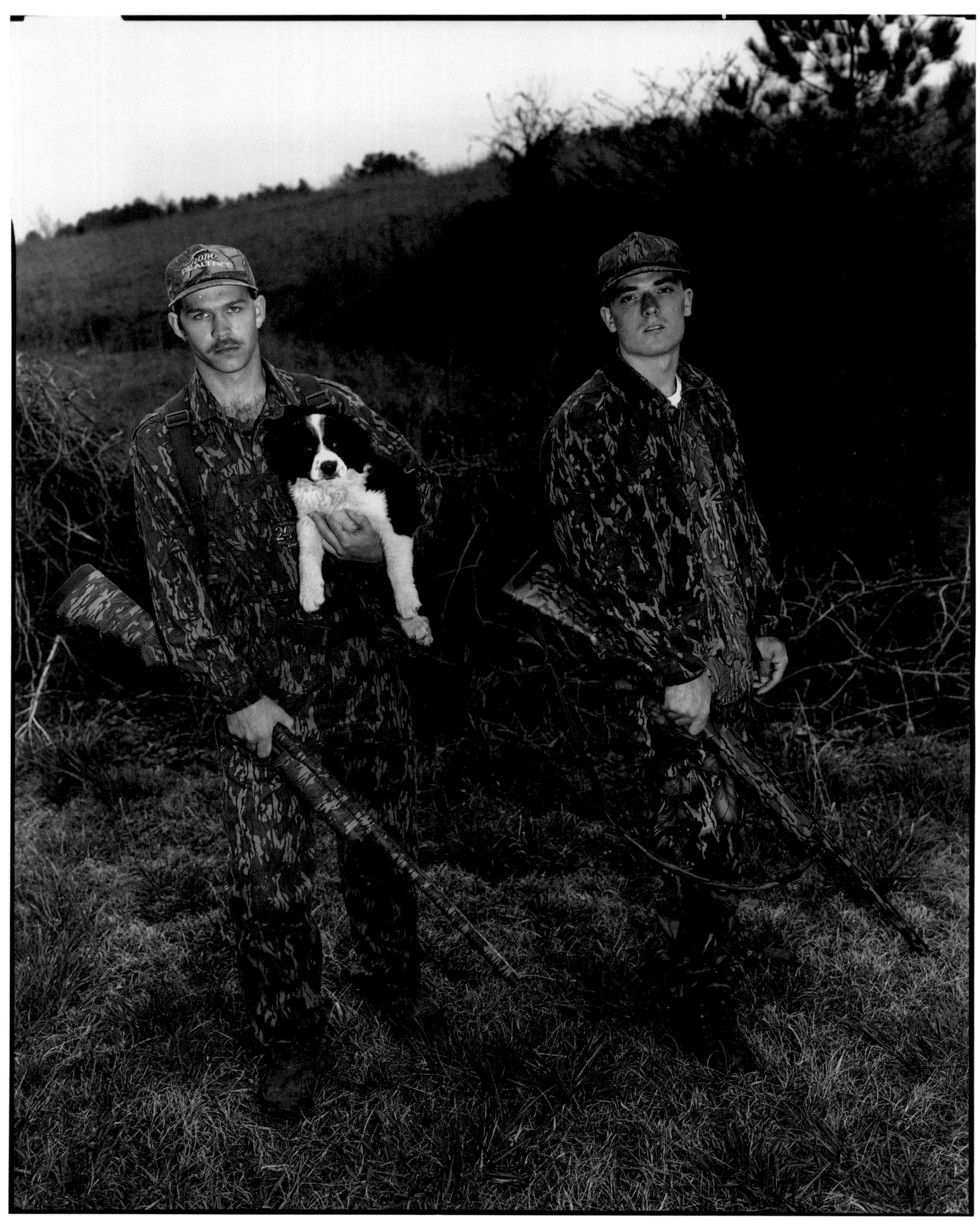

Bryant Heard and James Gilbert, Randolph County, Alabama, 1995

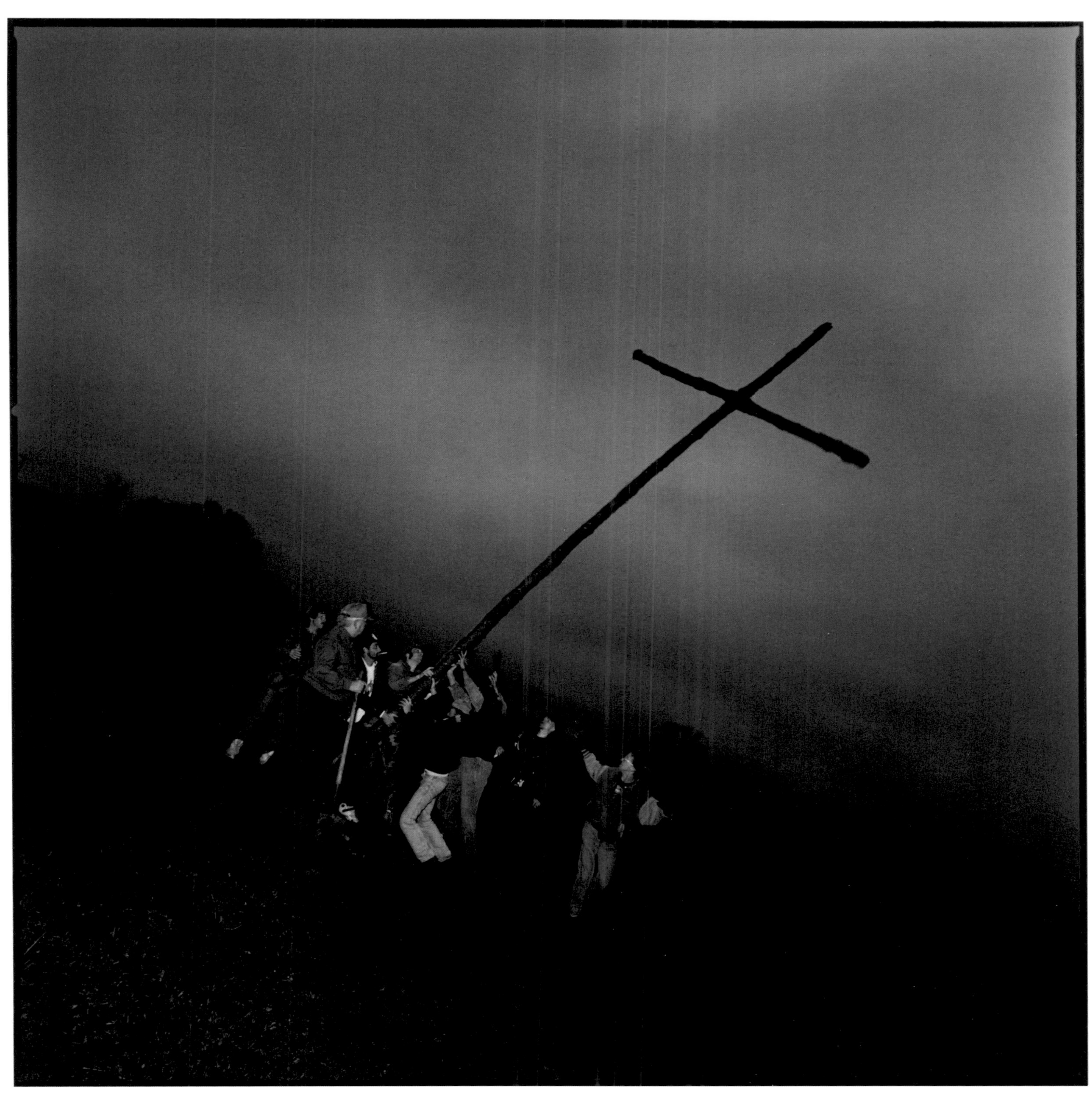

KKK rally, Polaski, Tennessee, 1994

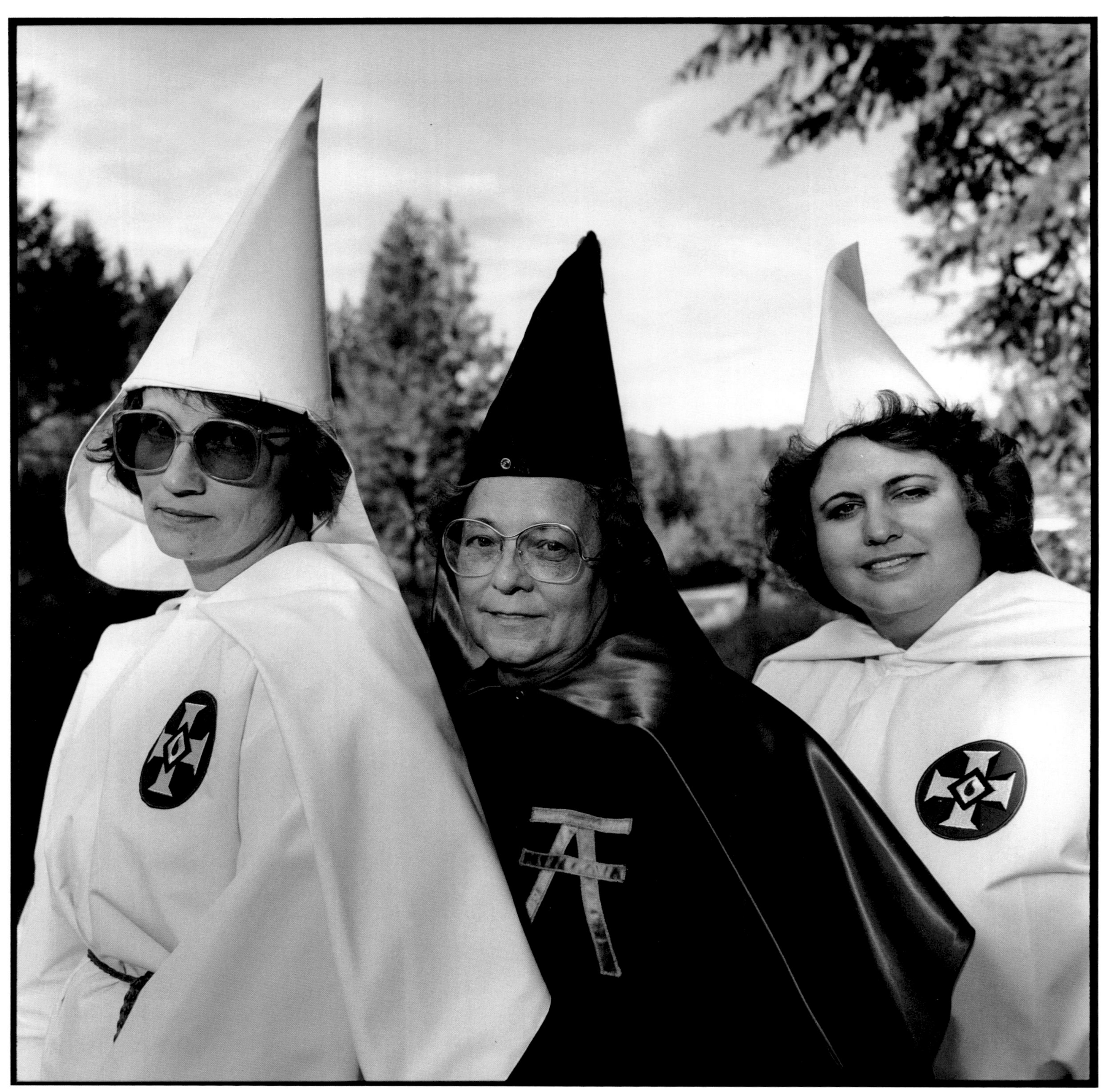

Aryan Nations, Hayden Lake, Idaho, 1986

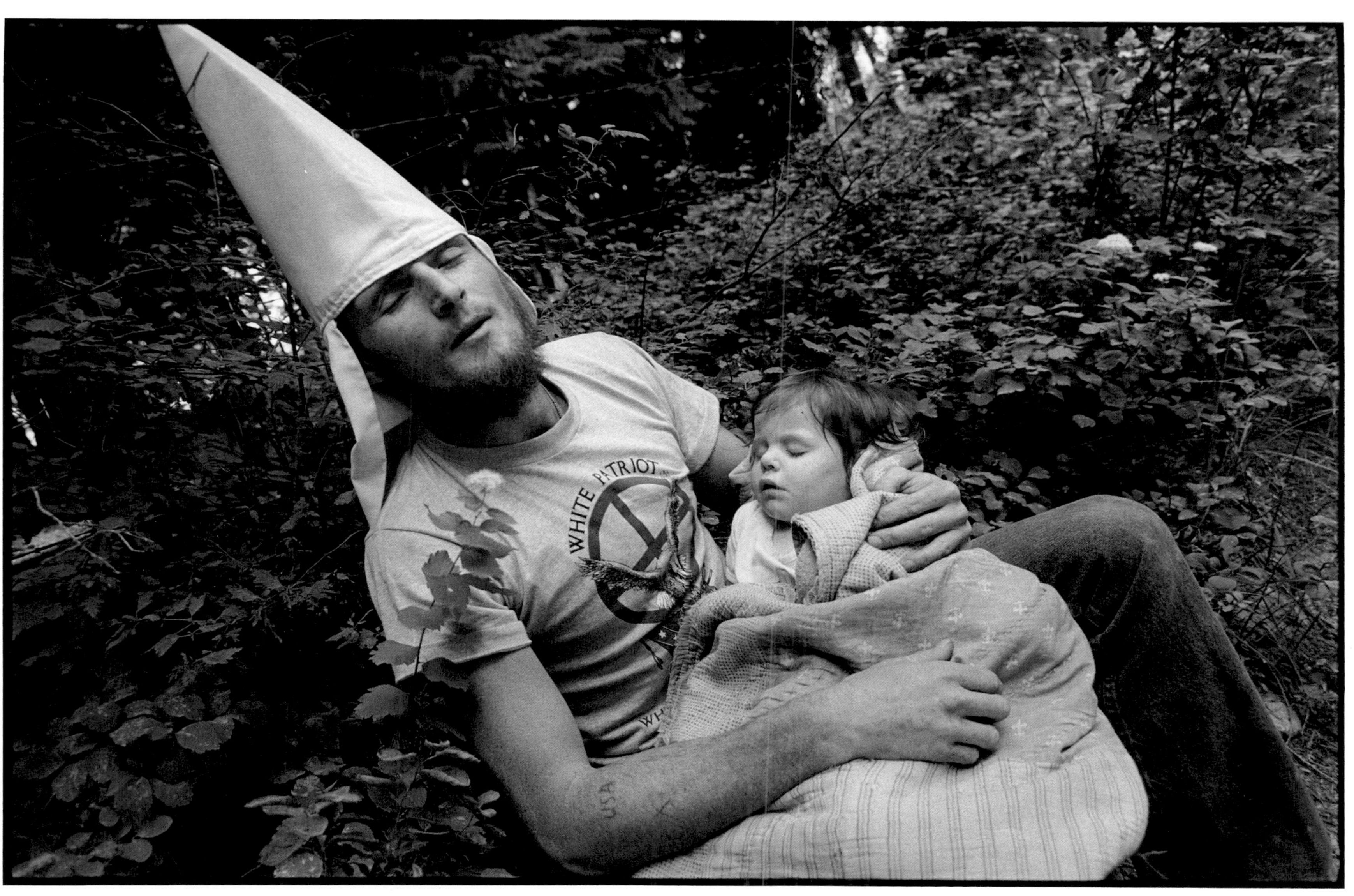

Father and daughter, Aryan Nations, Hayden Lake, Idaho, 1986

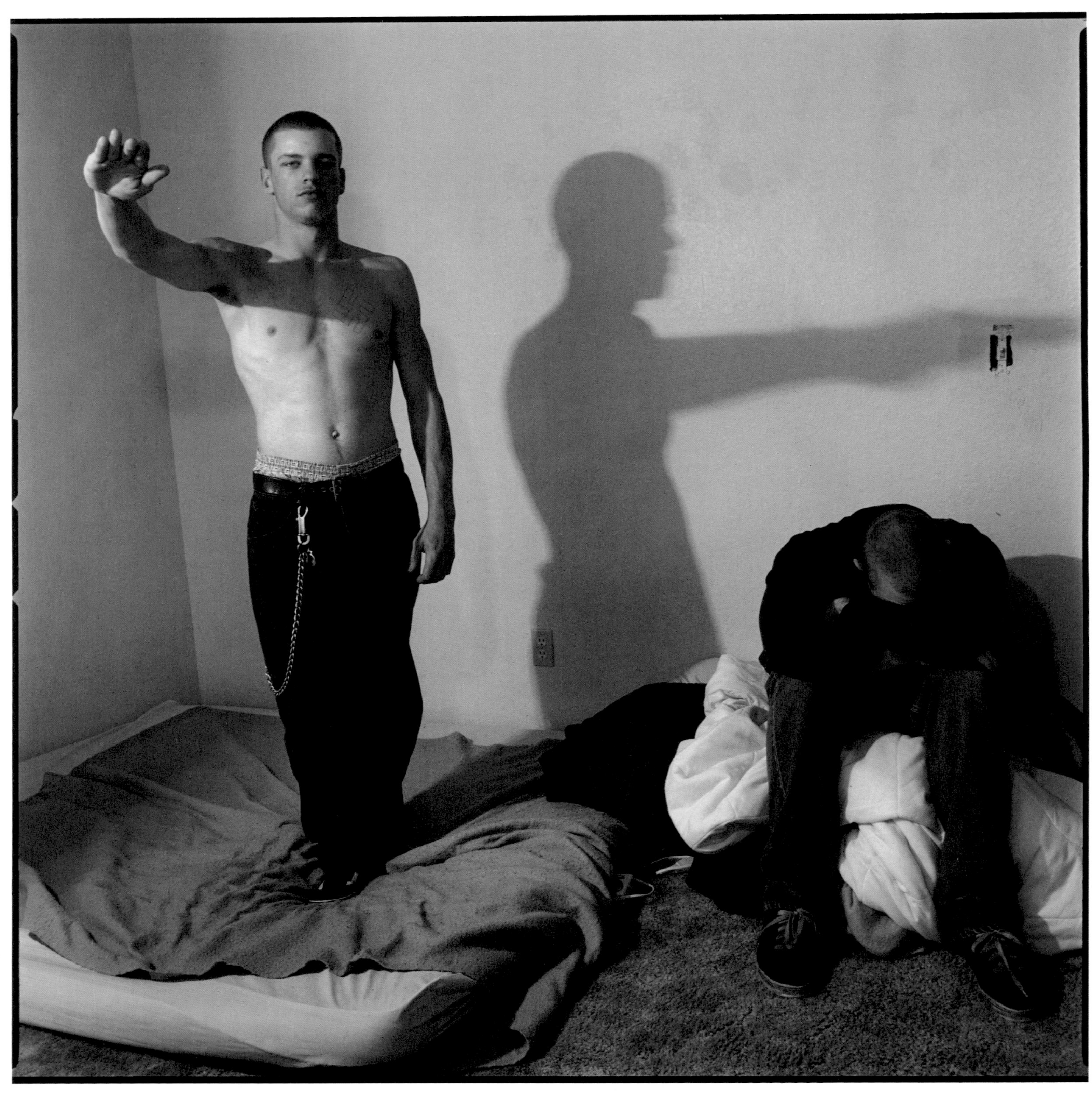

Tim Malone and fellow gang member, Antelope Valley, California, 1997

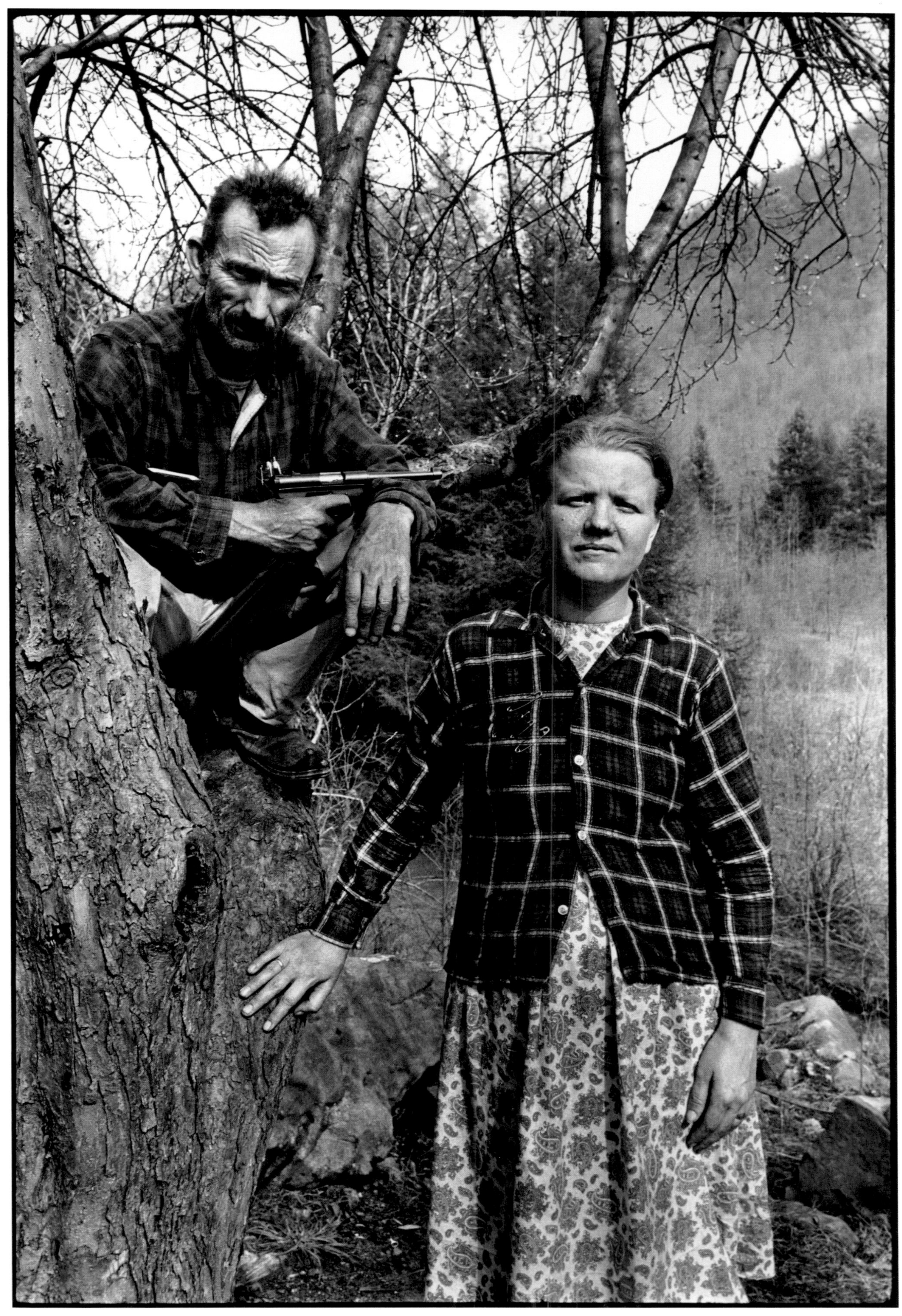

Husband and wife, Harlan County, Kentucky, 1971

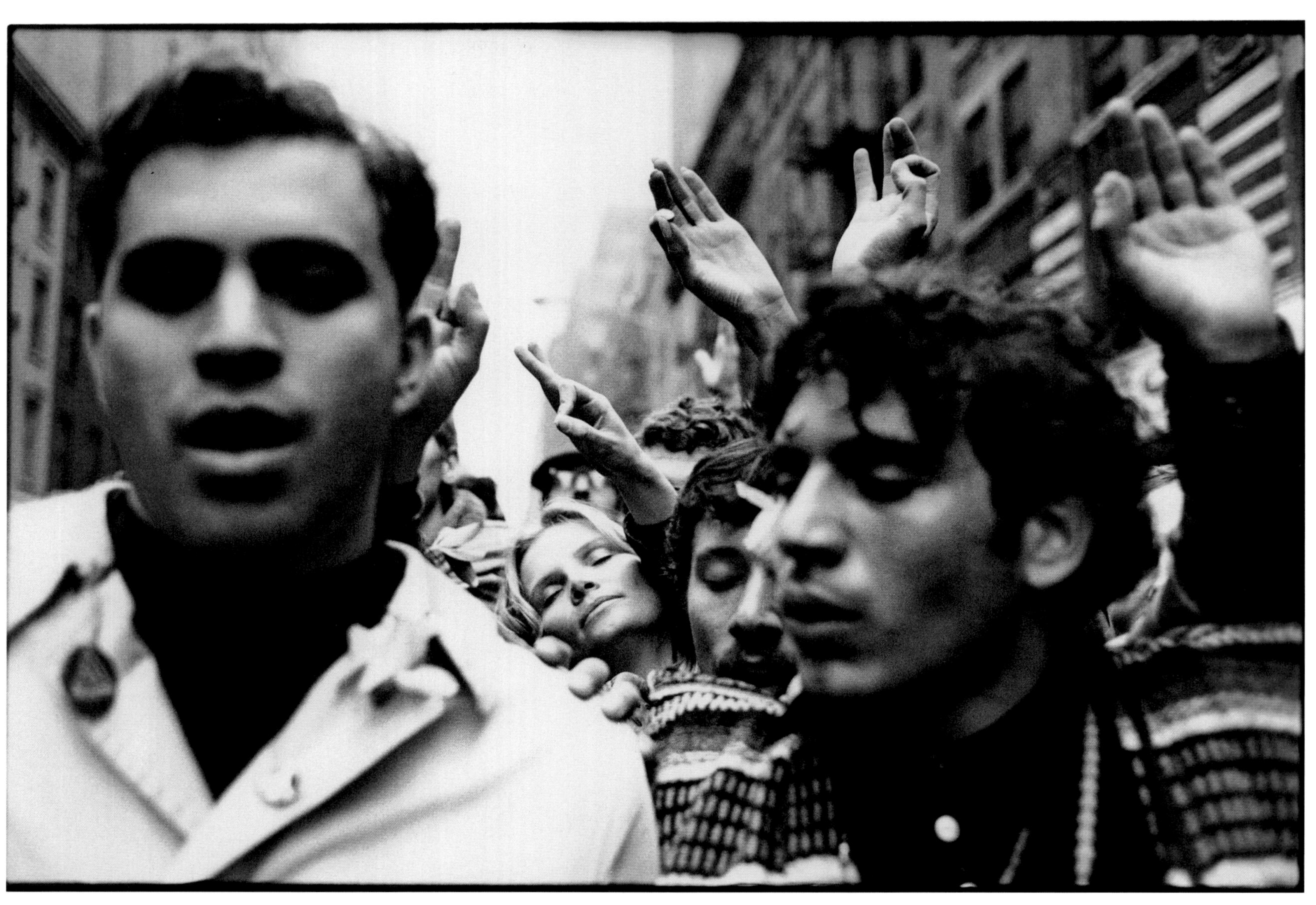

Anti–Vietnam War demonstration, New York City, 1968

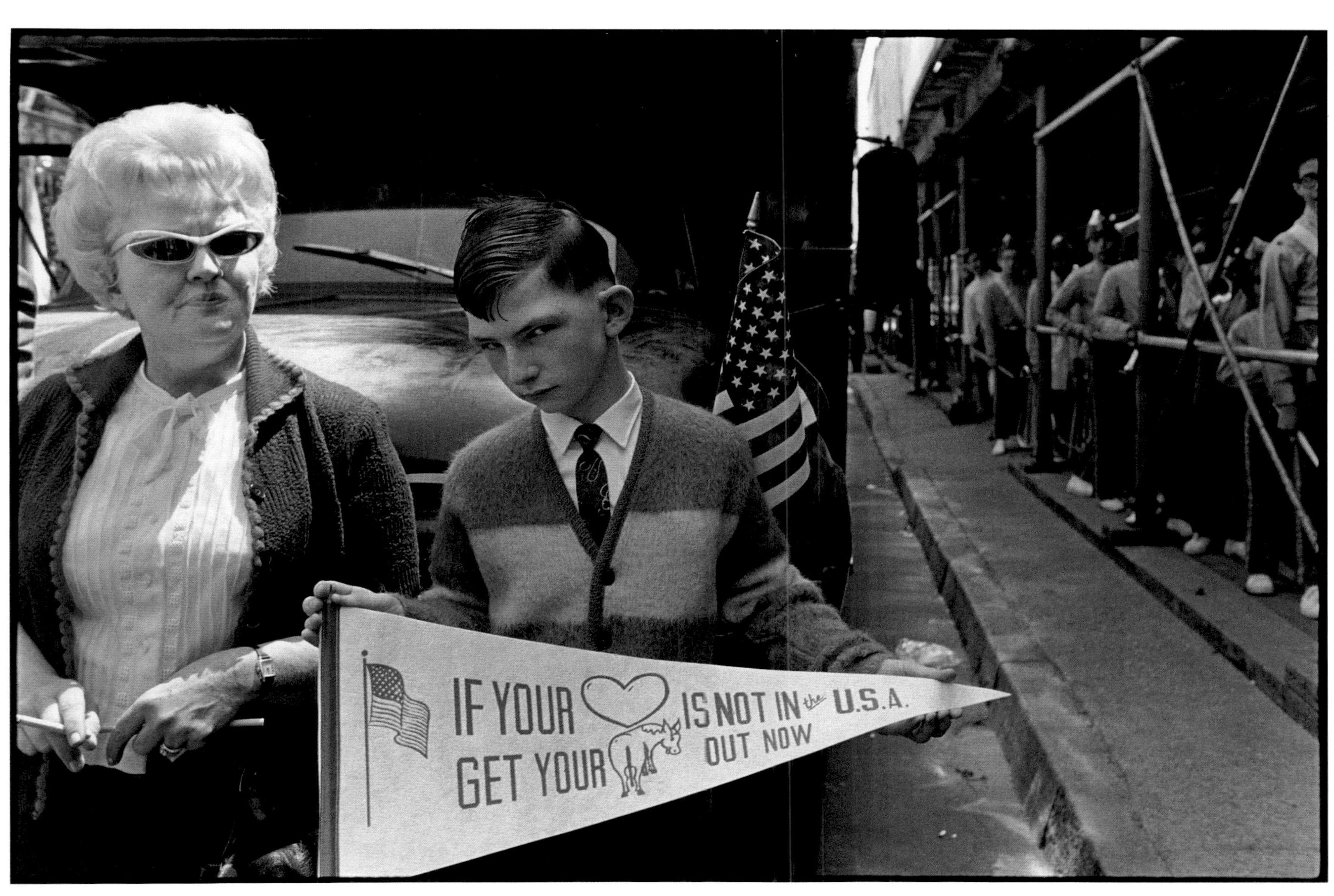

Pro–Vietnam War parade, New York City, 1968

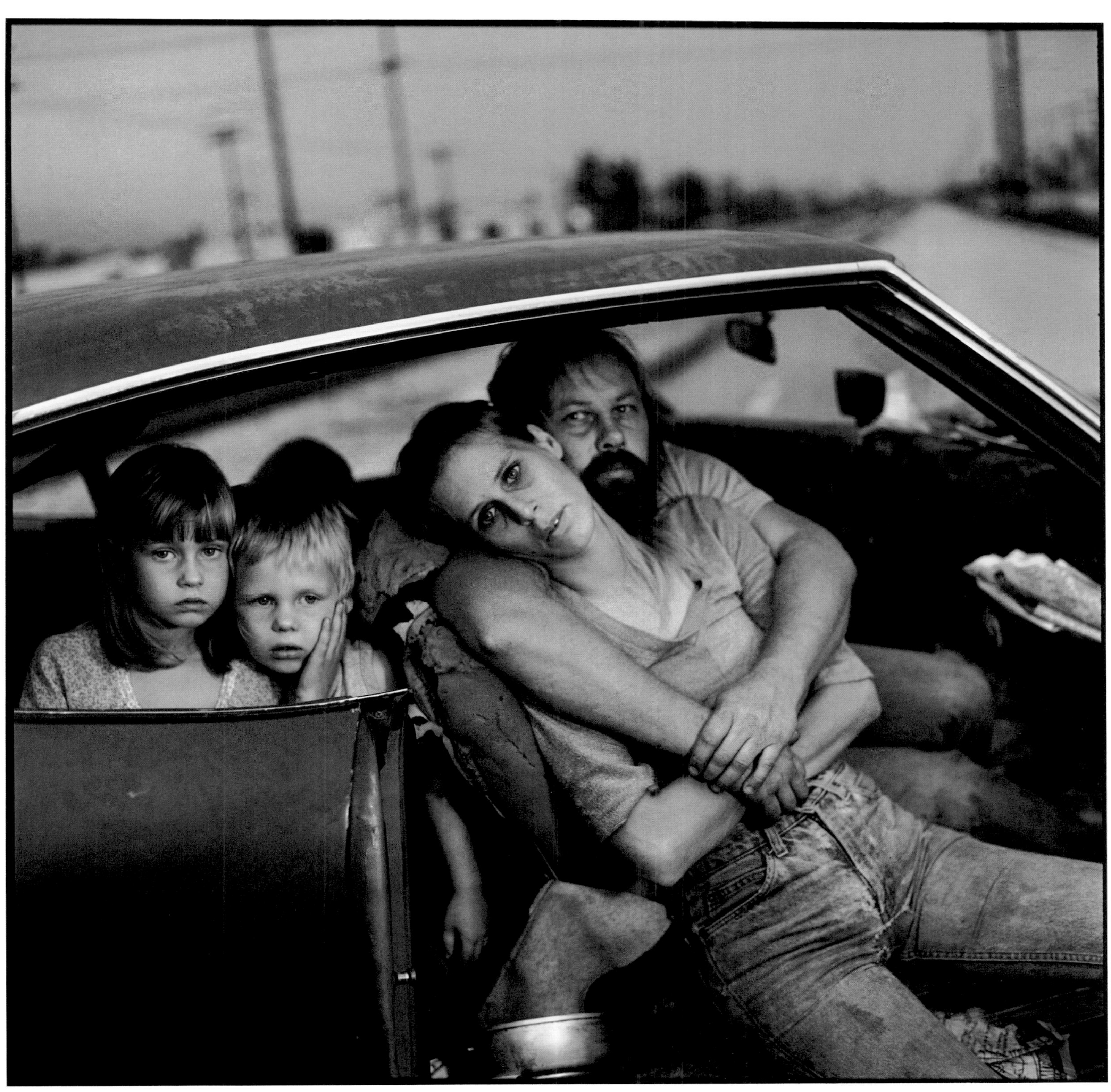

The Damm family in their car, Los Angeles, California, 1987

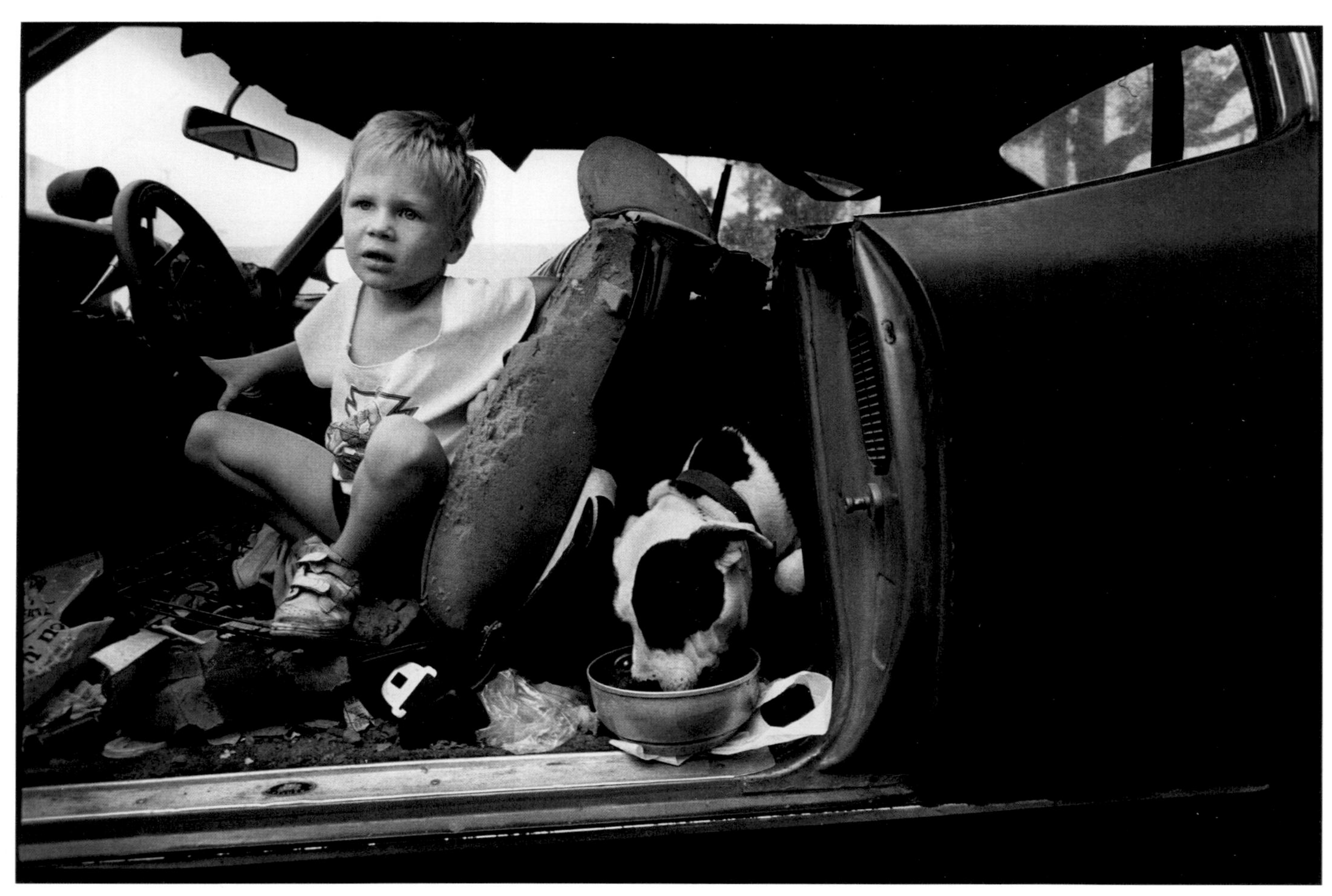

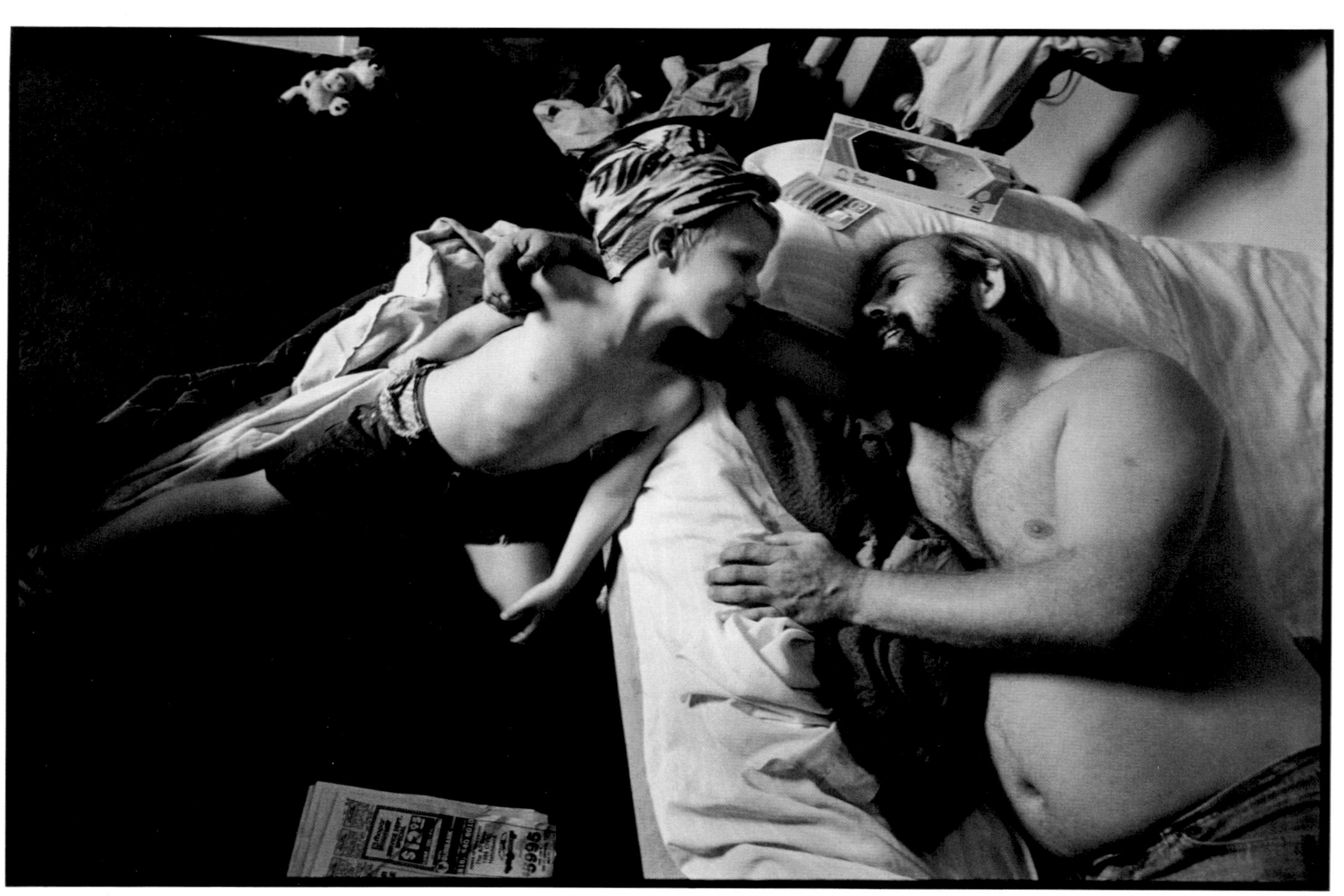

top: Jesse with his dog, Runtley, Los Angeles, California, 1987
bottom: Jesse and Dean Damm, Los Angeles, California, 1987

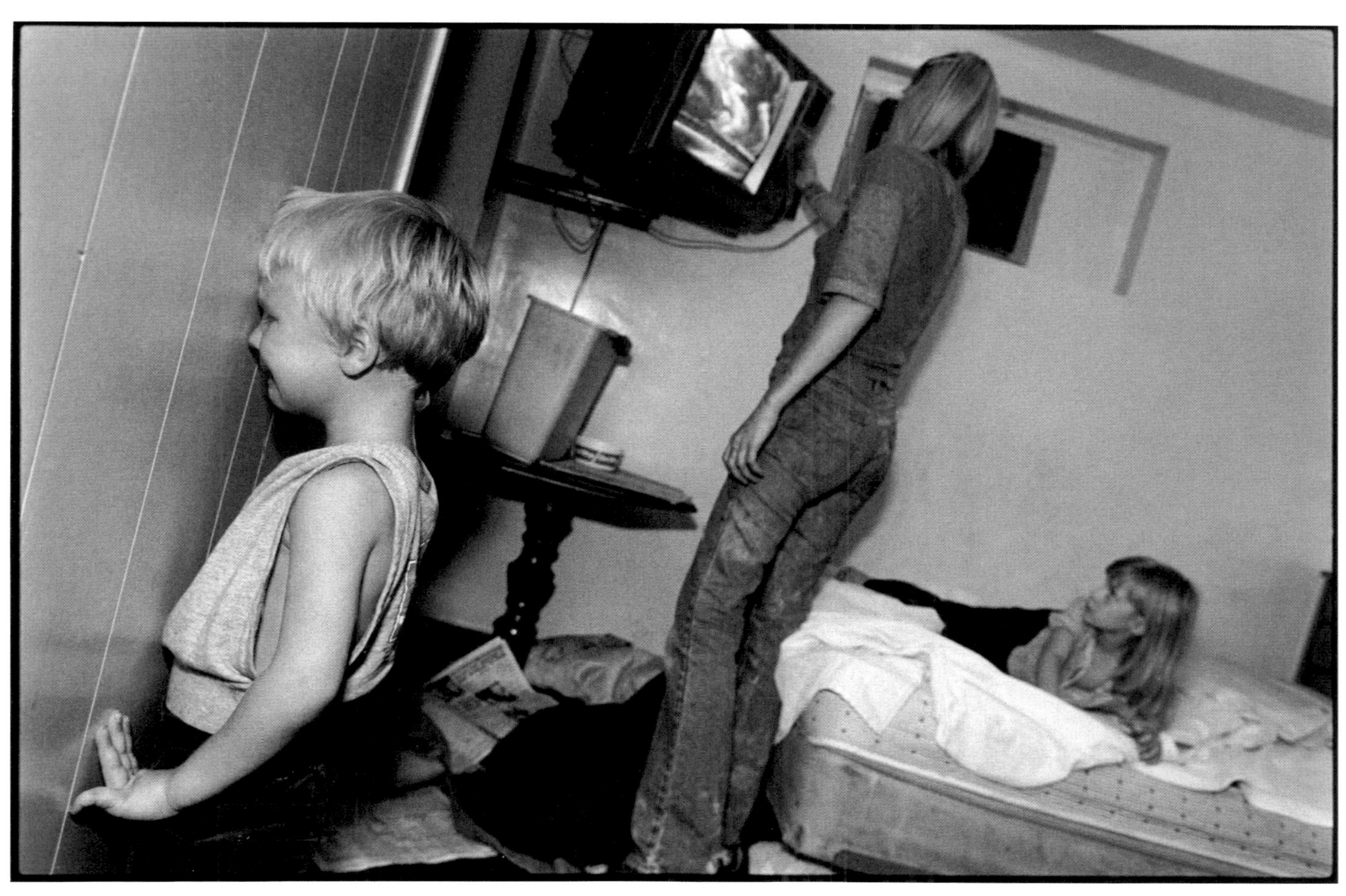

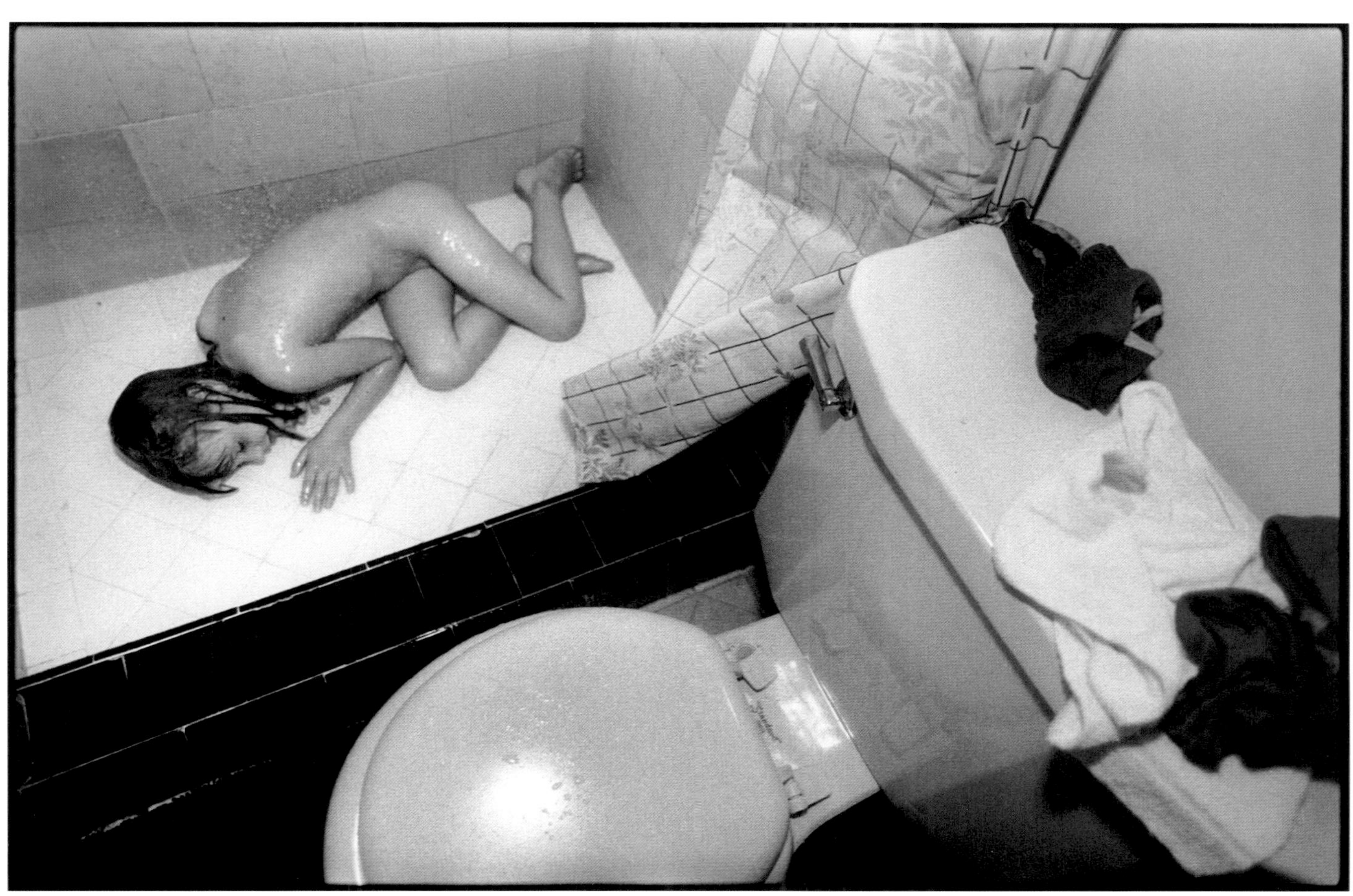

top: Jesse, Linda, and Crissy, Los Angeles, California, 1987
bottom: Crissy in a motel shower, Los Angeles, California, 1987

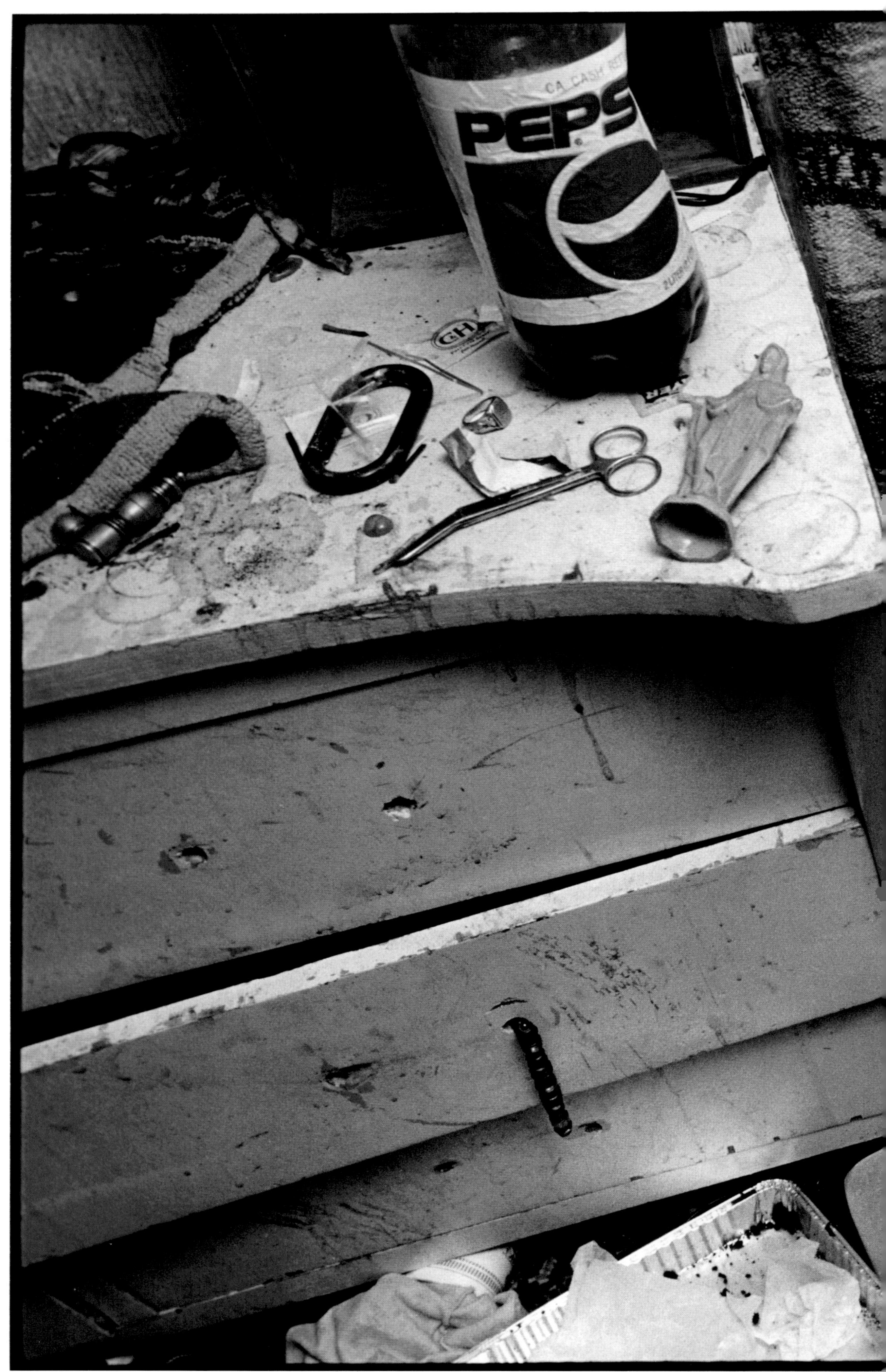

Crissy, Dean, and Linda Damm,
Llano, California, 1994

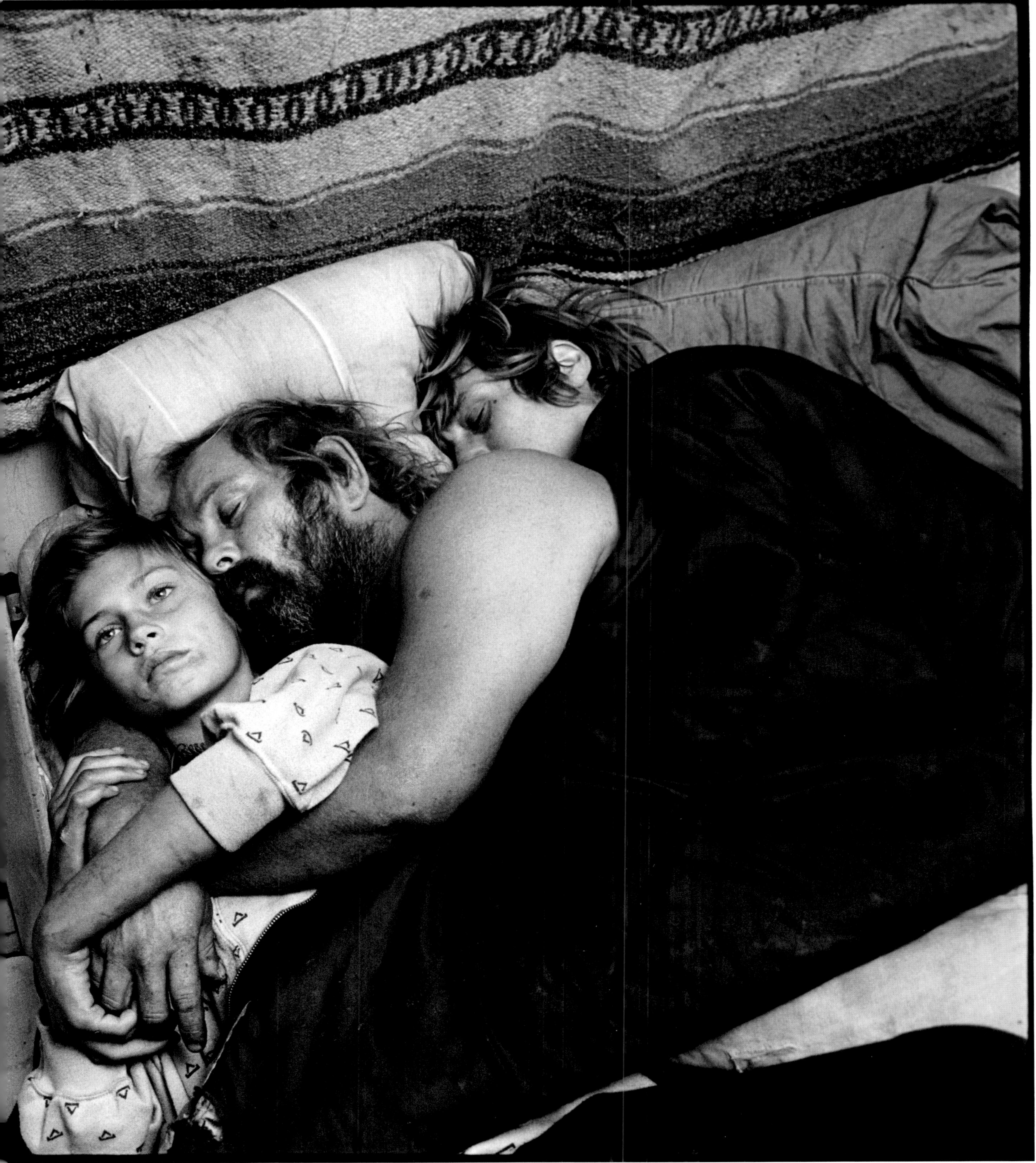

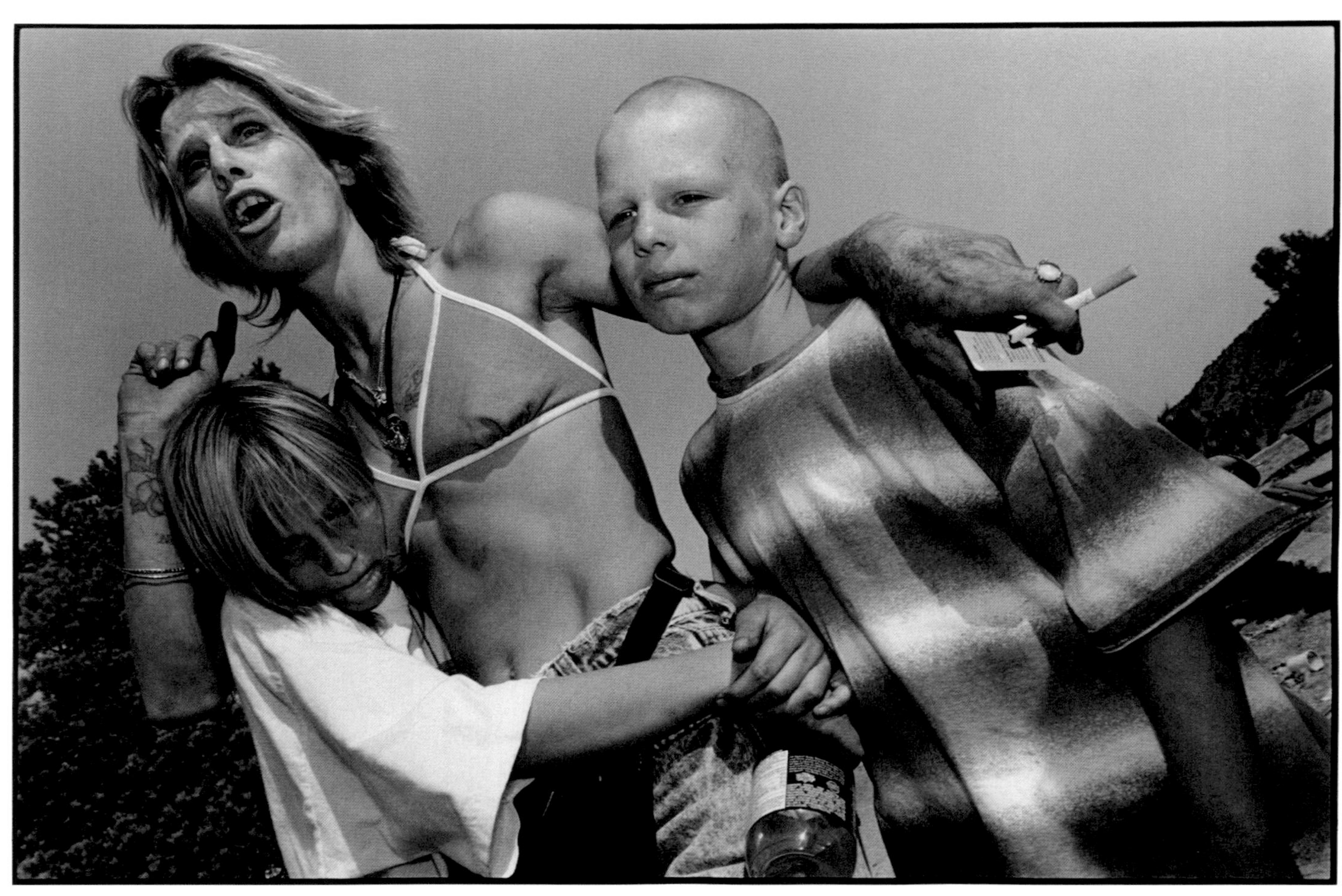

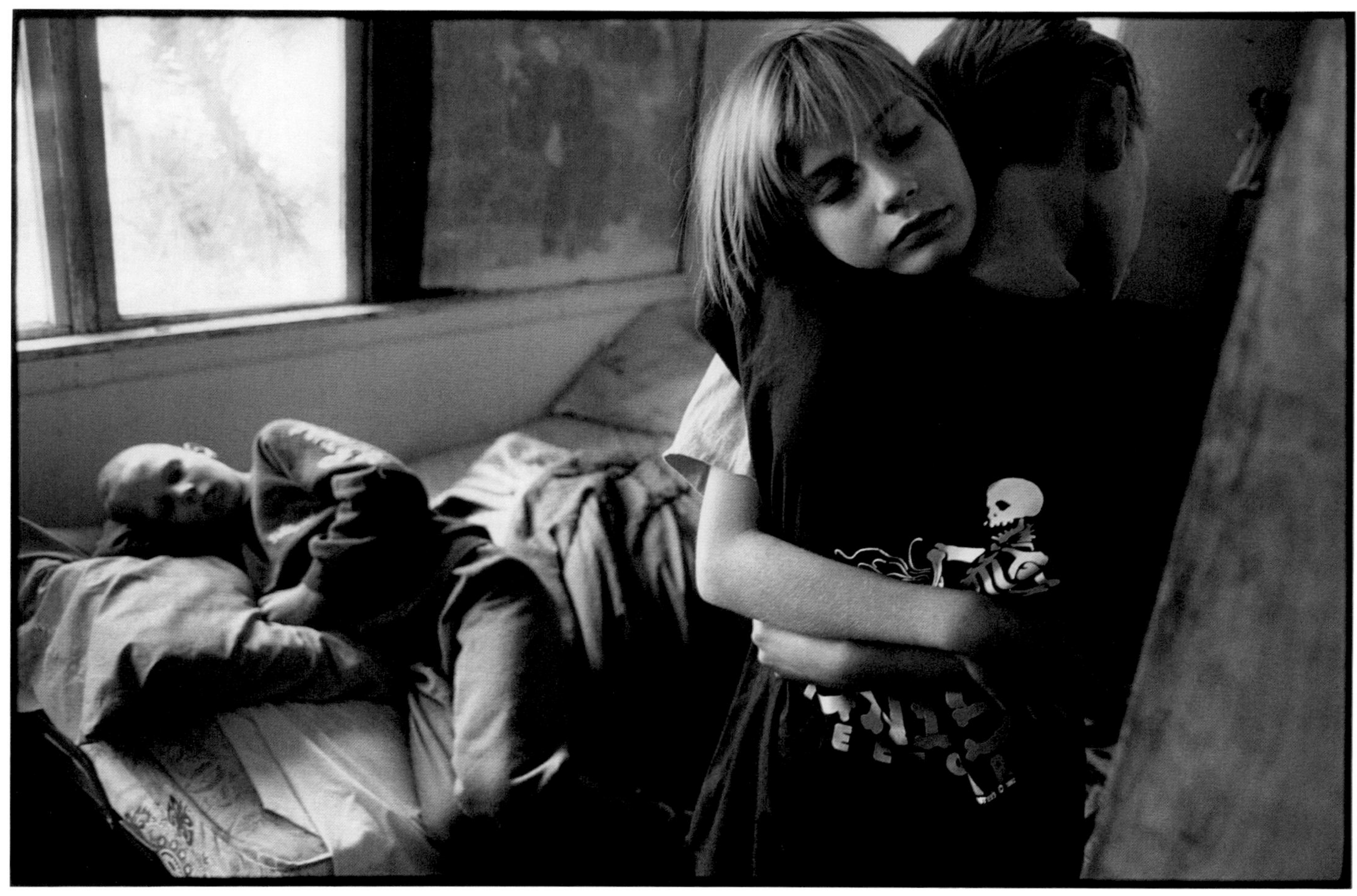

top: Crissy, Linda, and Jesse, Llano, California, 1994
bottom: Jesse, Crissy, and Adam, Llano, California, 1994

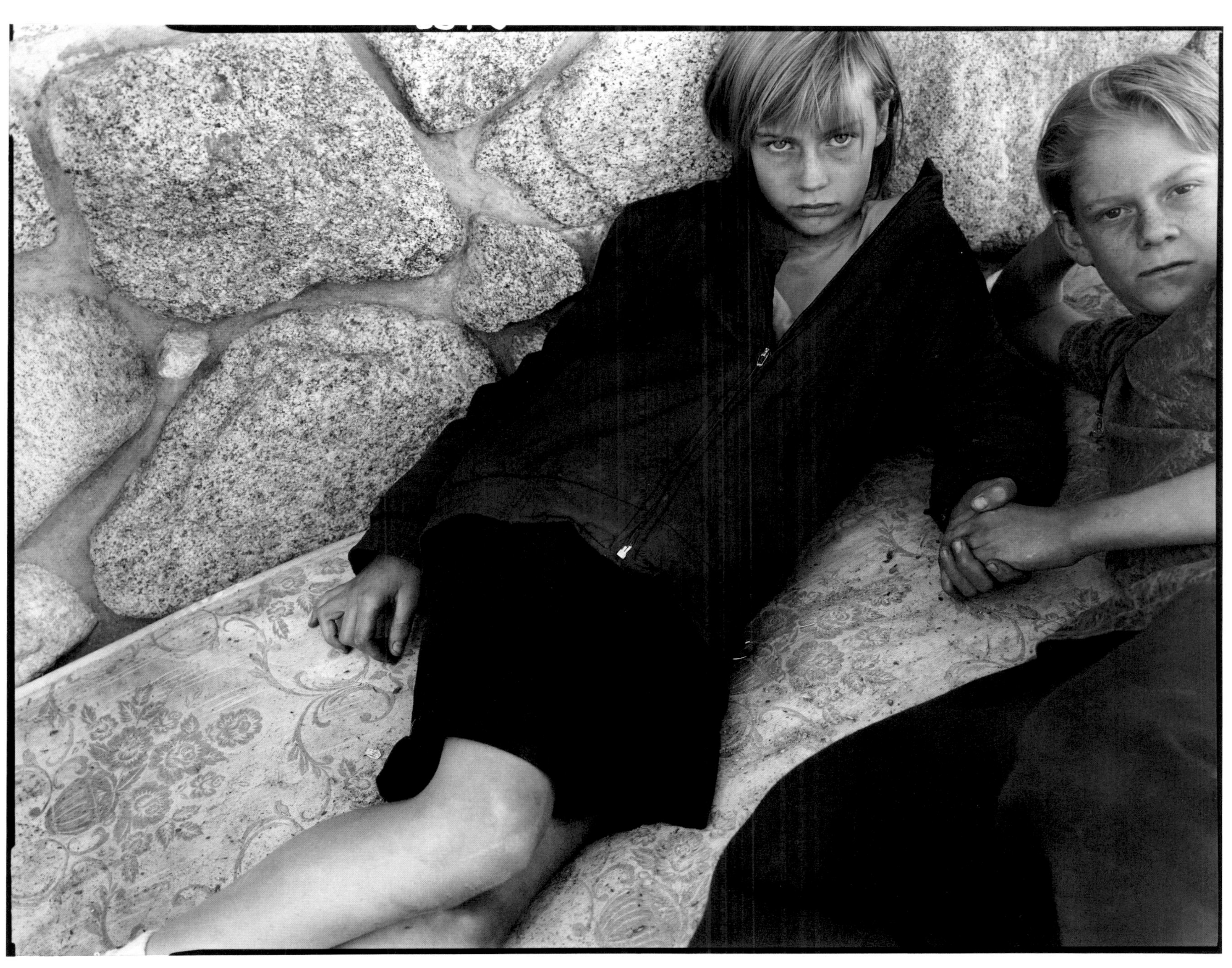

Crissy Damm and Adam Johnson. Llano, California, 1994

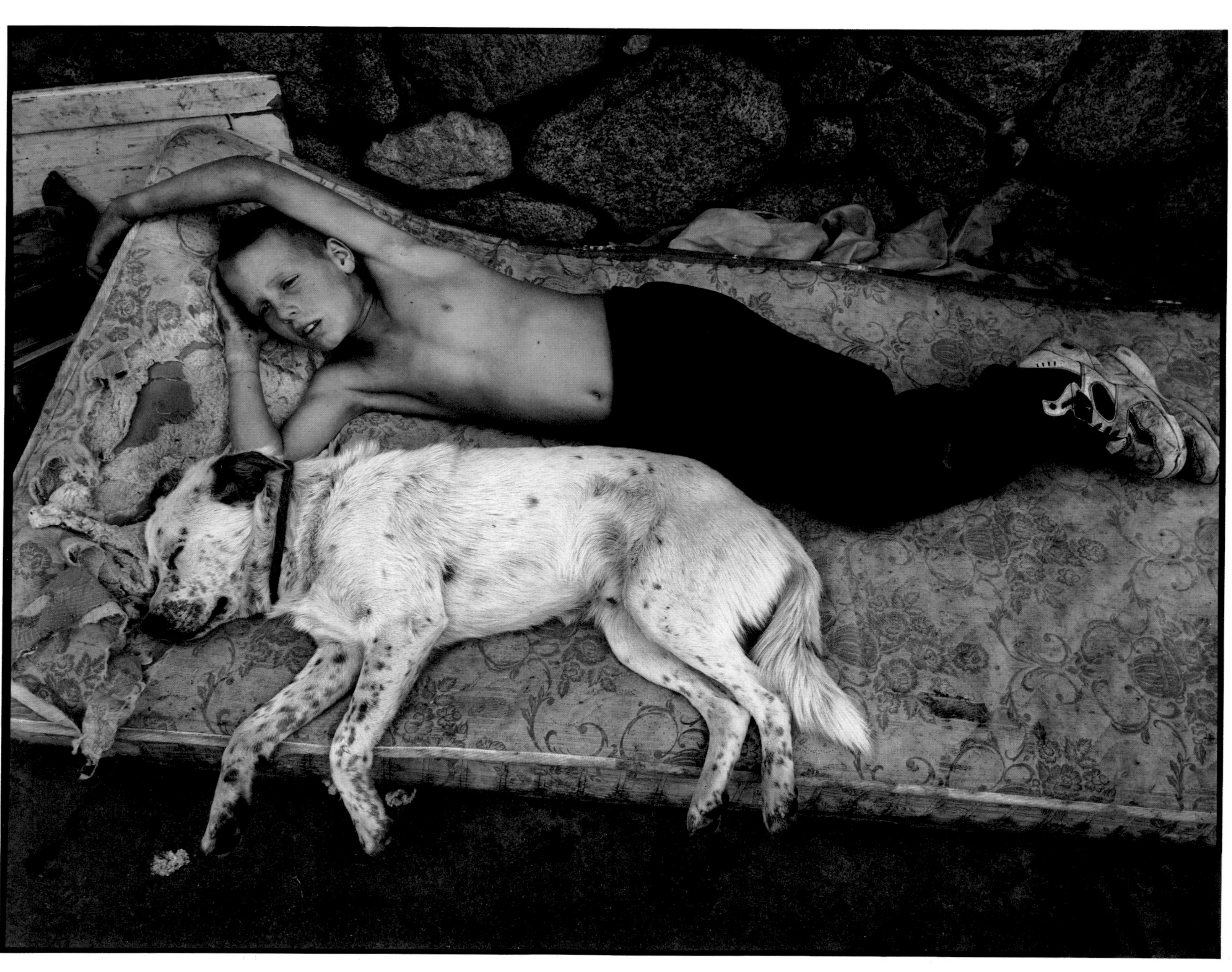

Jesse Damm and Nick, Llano, California, 1994

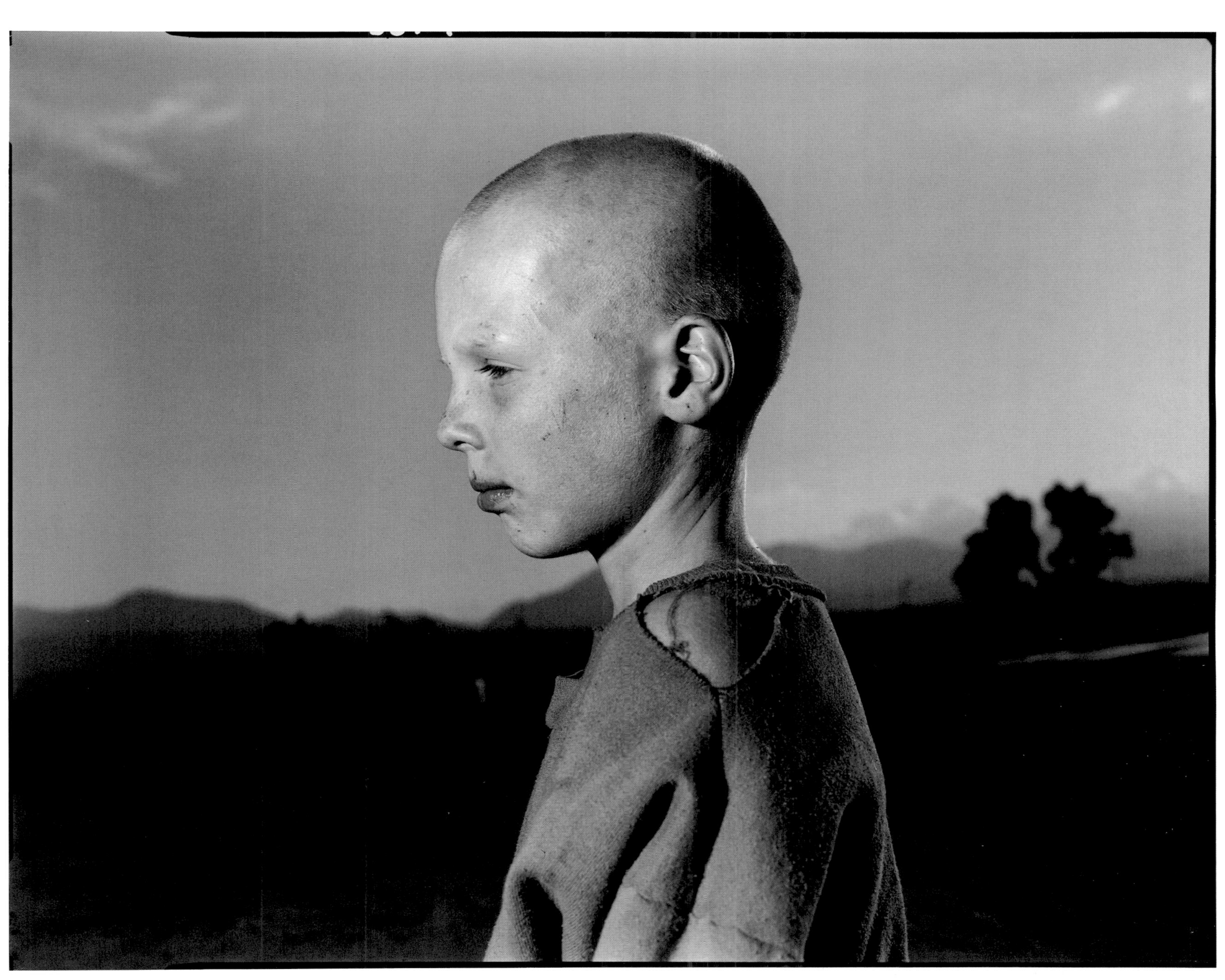

Jesse Damm, Llano, California, 1994

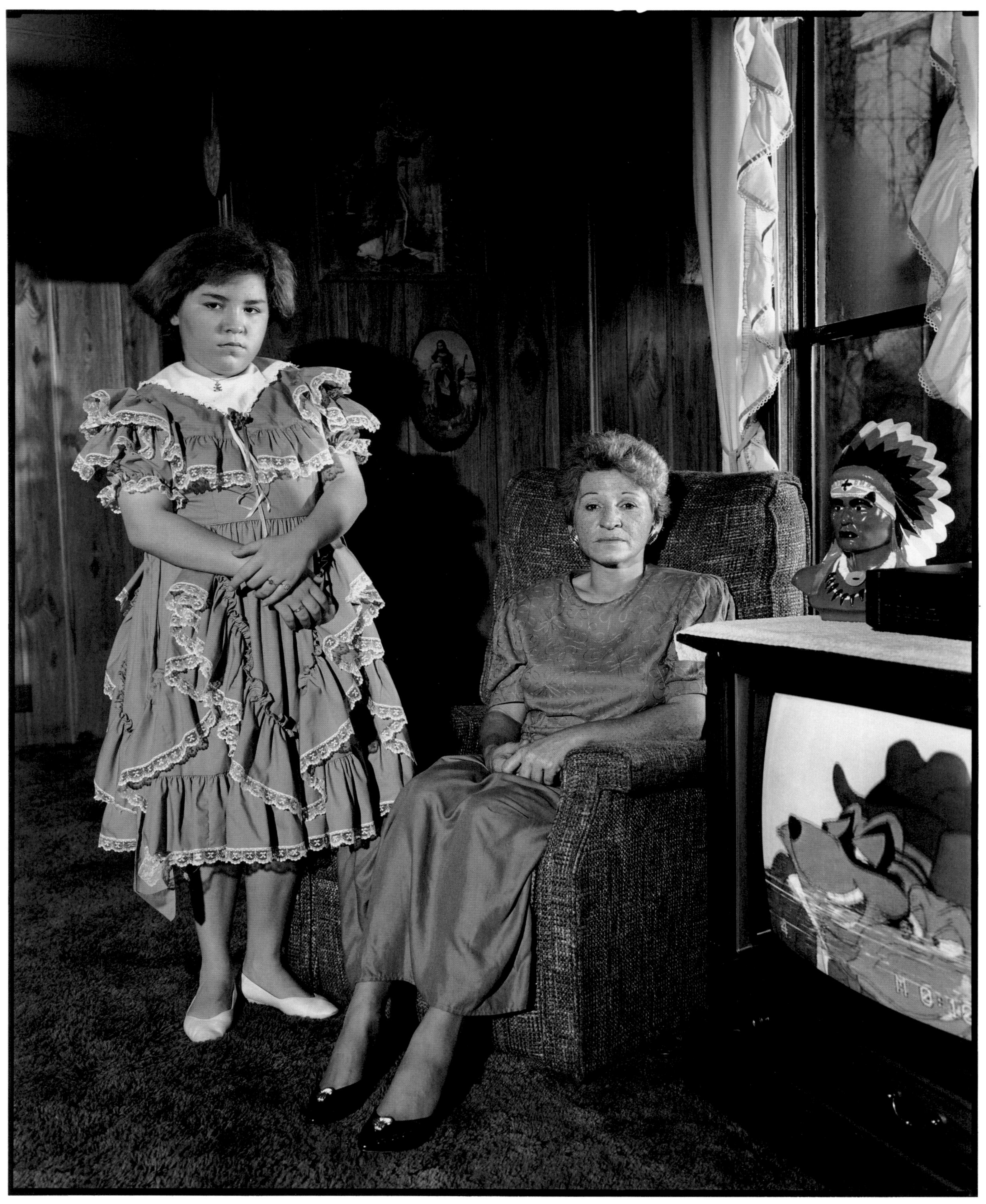

Chrystal and Virginia Demery, Lumberton, North Carolina, 1994

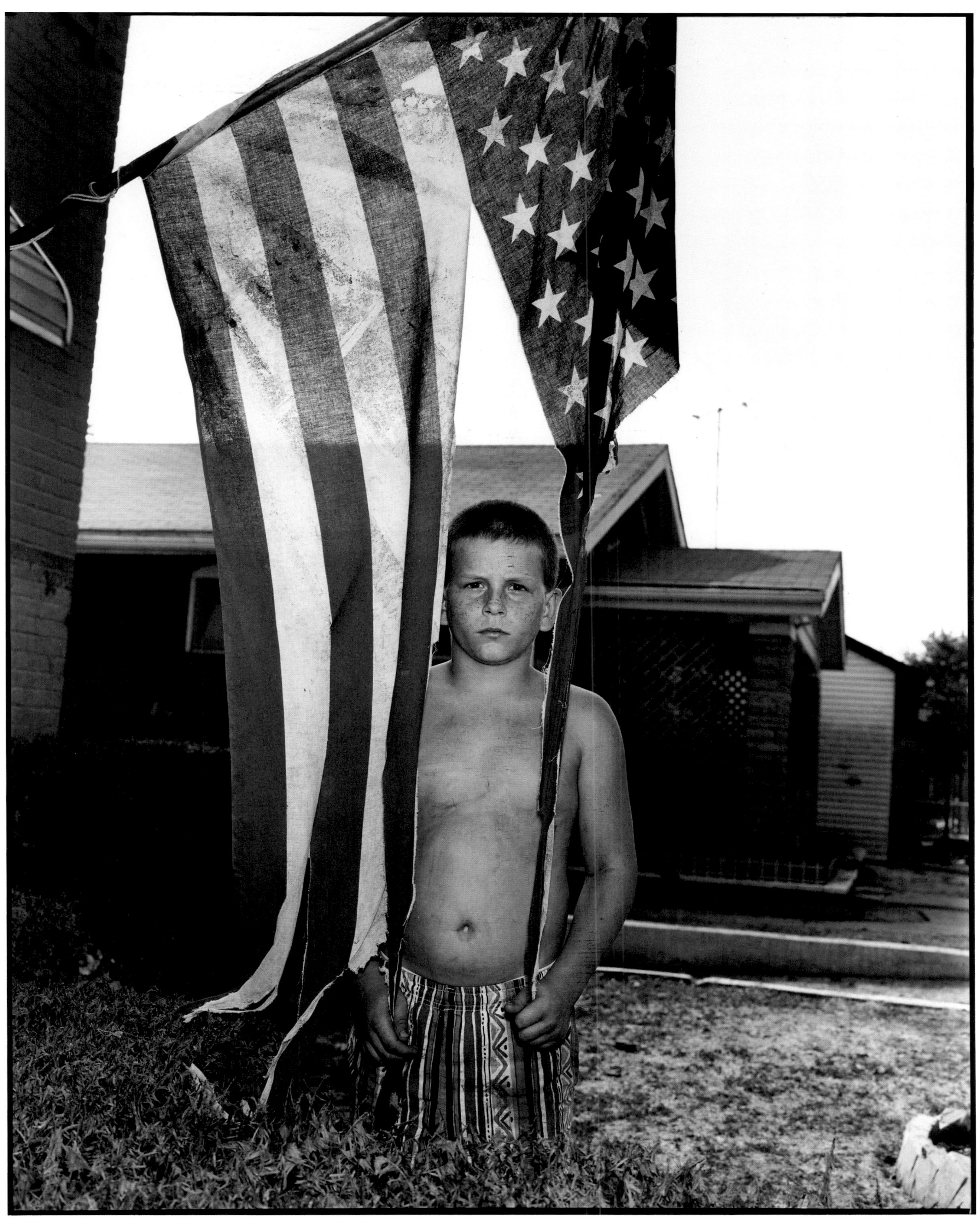

Hurstie Laxton after the flood, St. Louis, Missouri, 1993

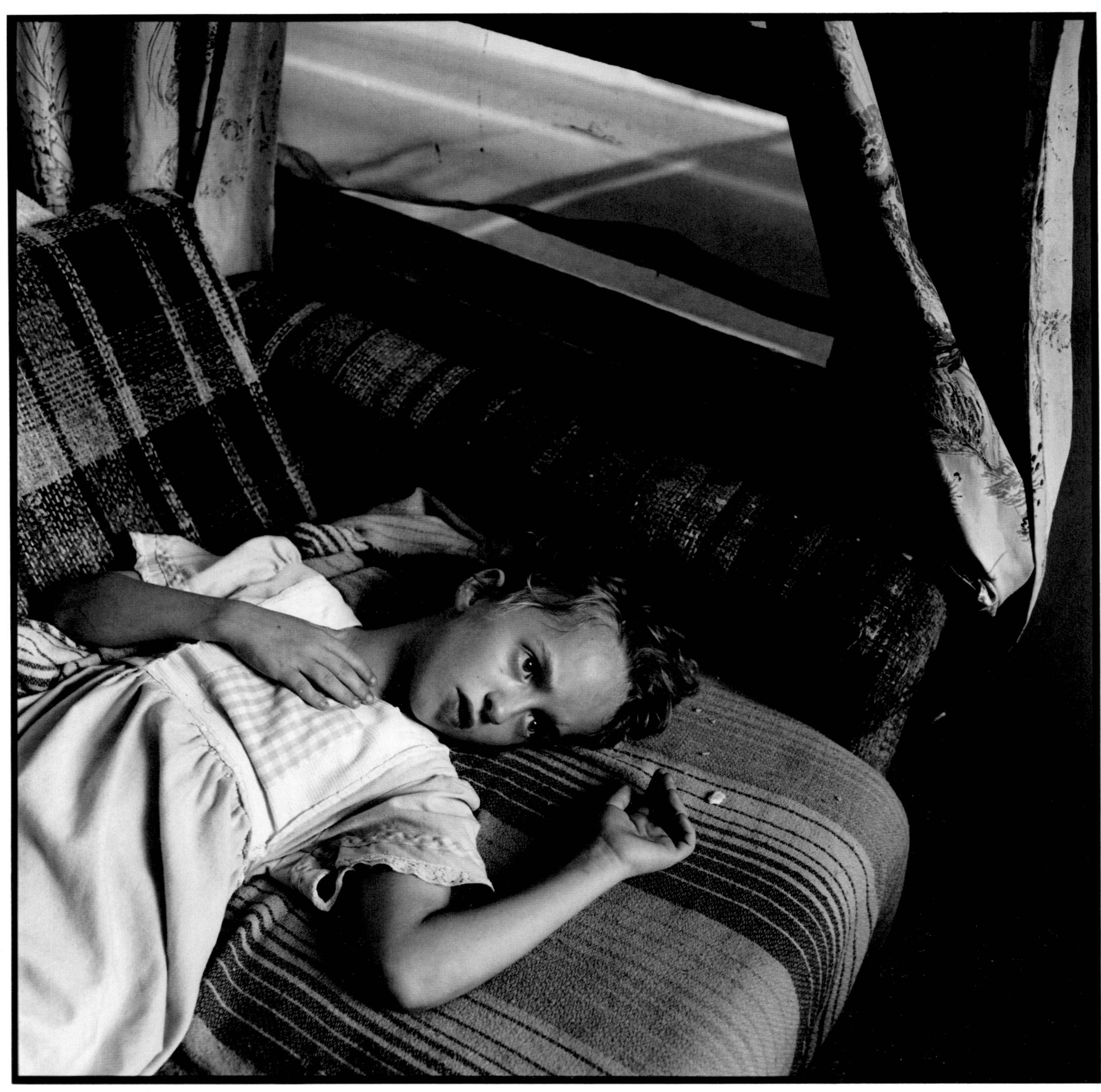

Carrie Copas, Portsmouth, Ohio, 1989

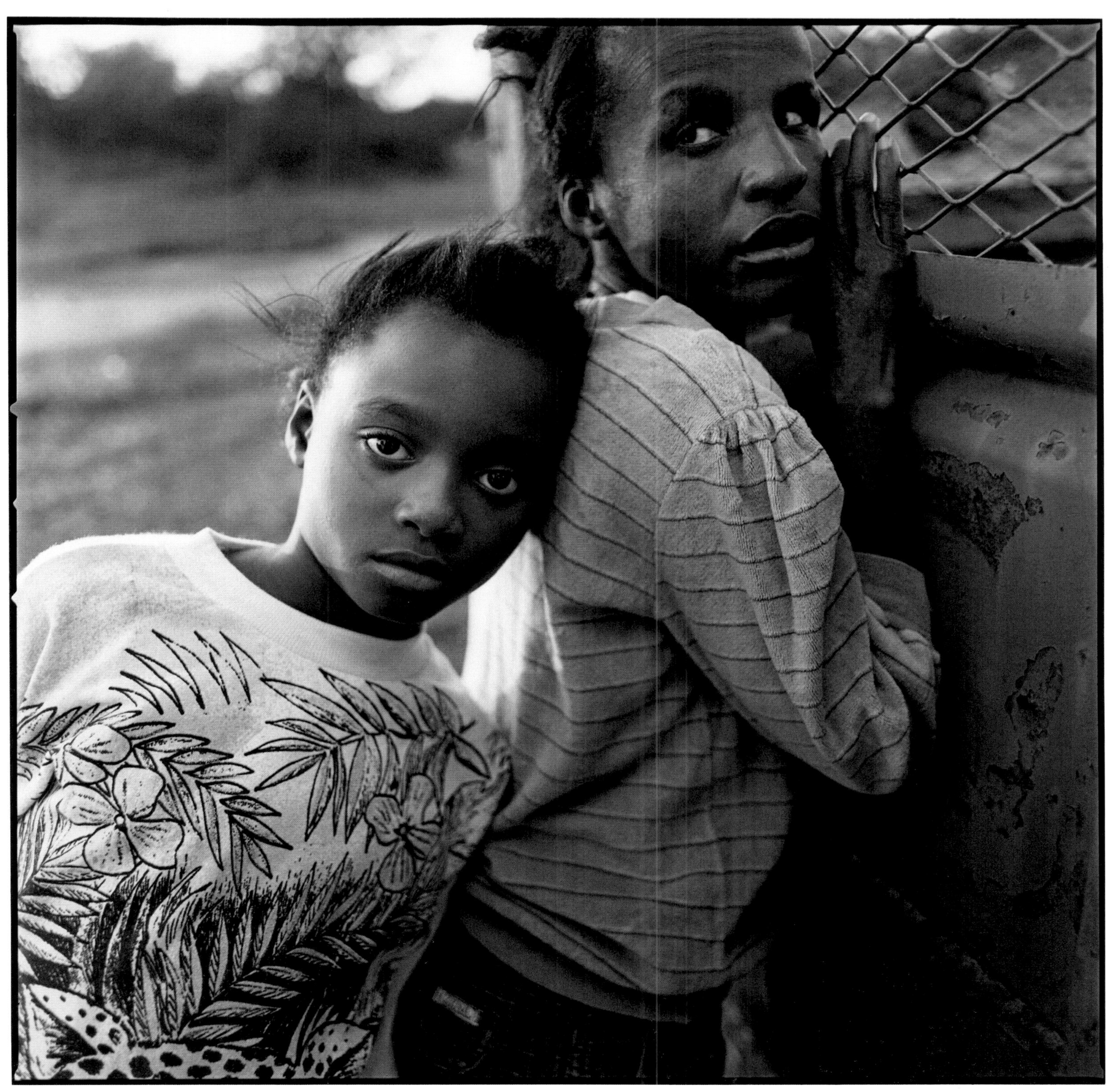

Mother and daughter, Clarksdale, Mississippi, 1990

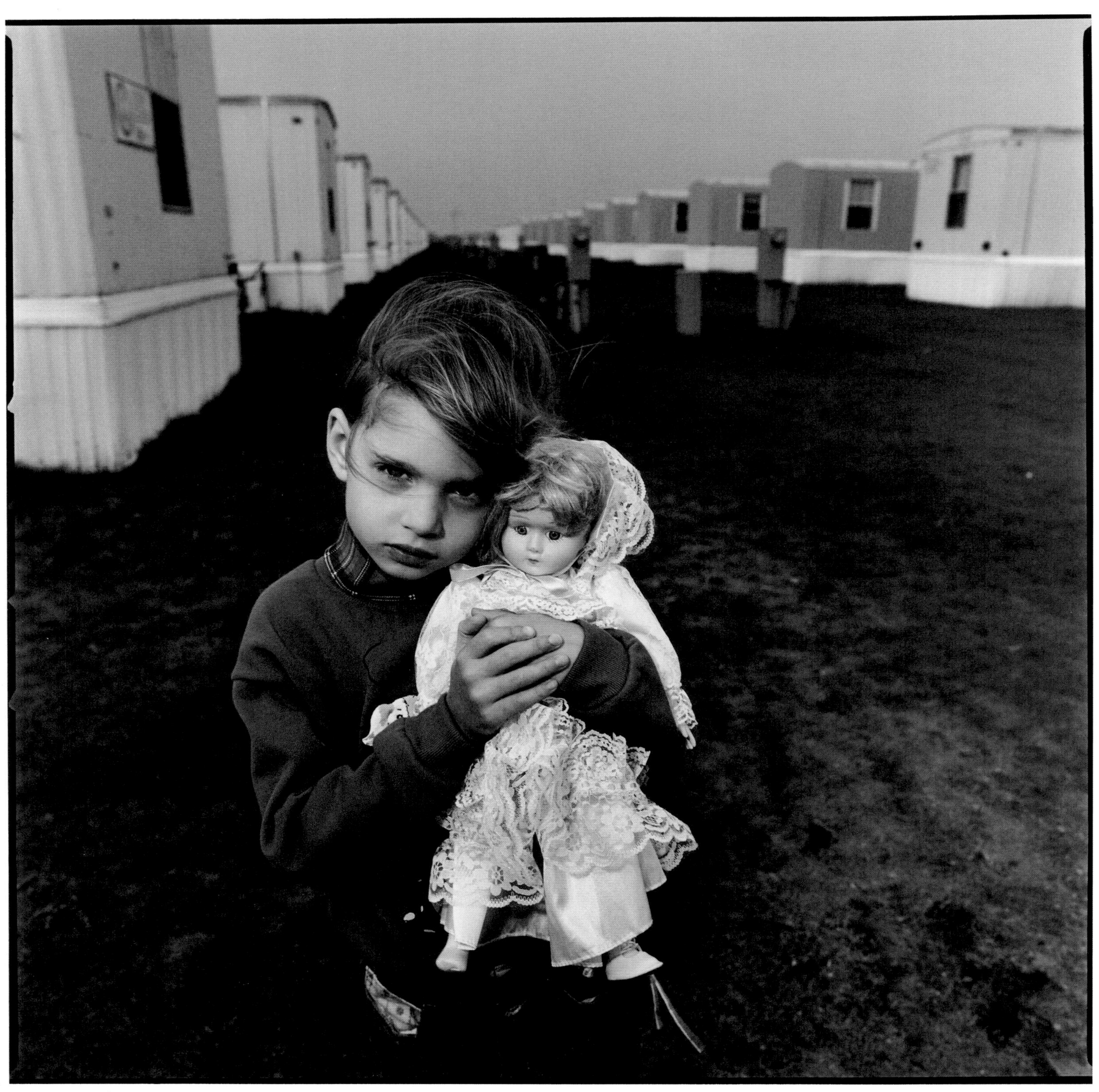

Breann Benedict, government flood housing, Grand Forks, North Dakota, 1997

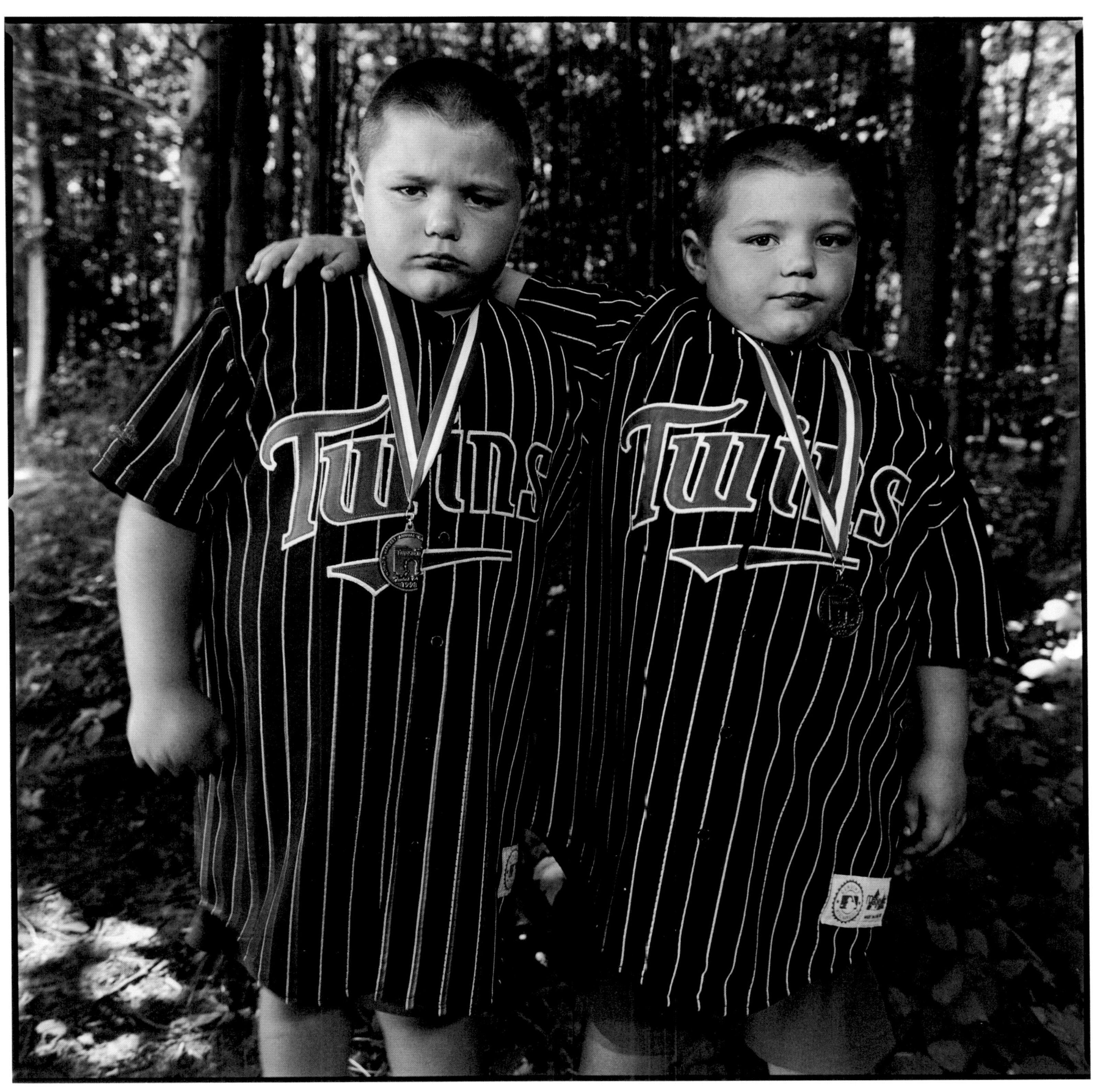

Spencer and Skyler Szbkowski, Twinsburg, Ohio, 1998

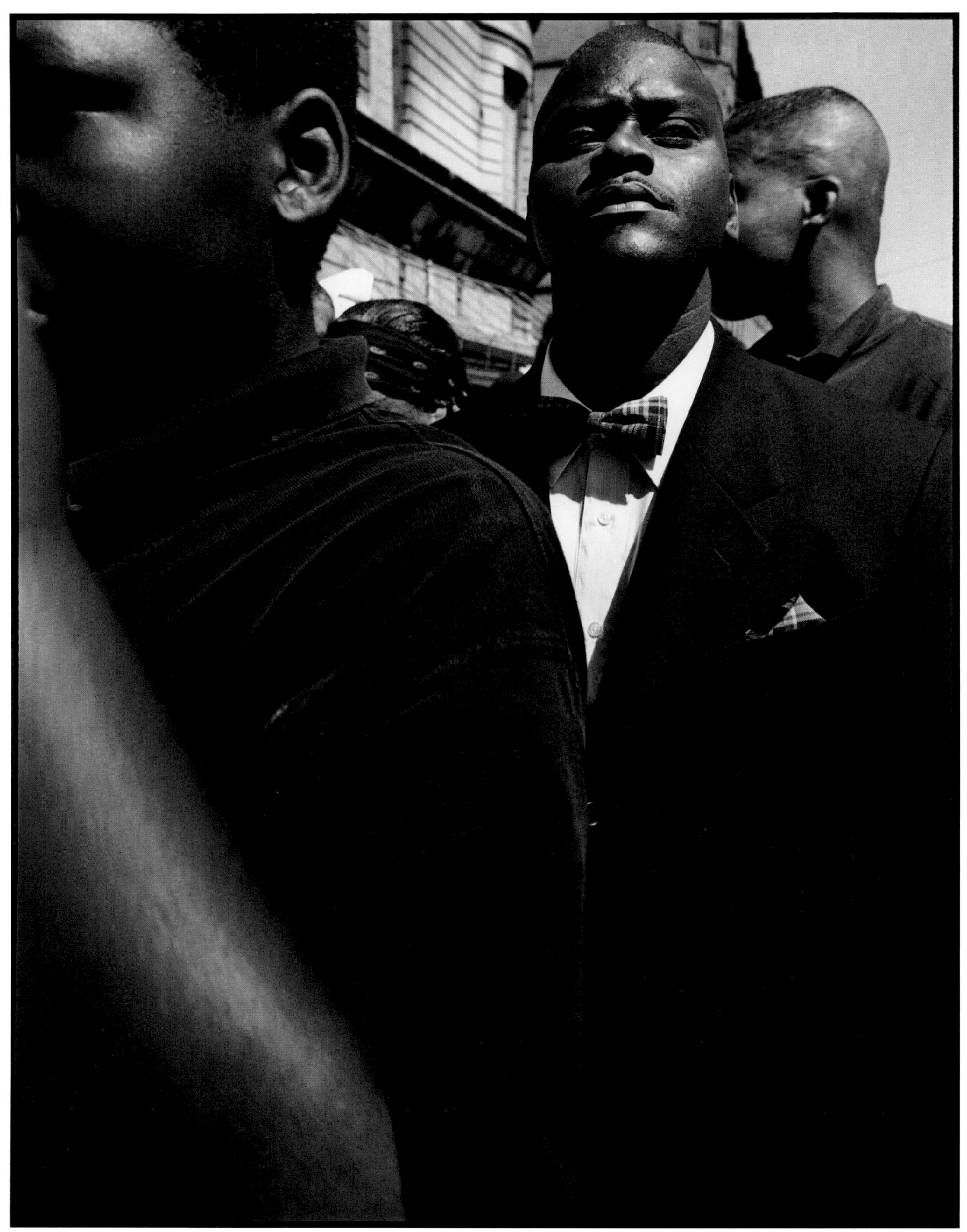

Million Youth March, Harlem, New York City, 1998

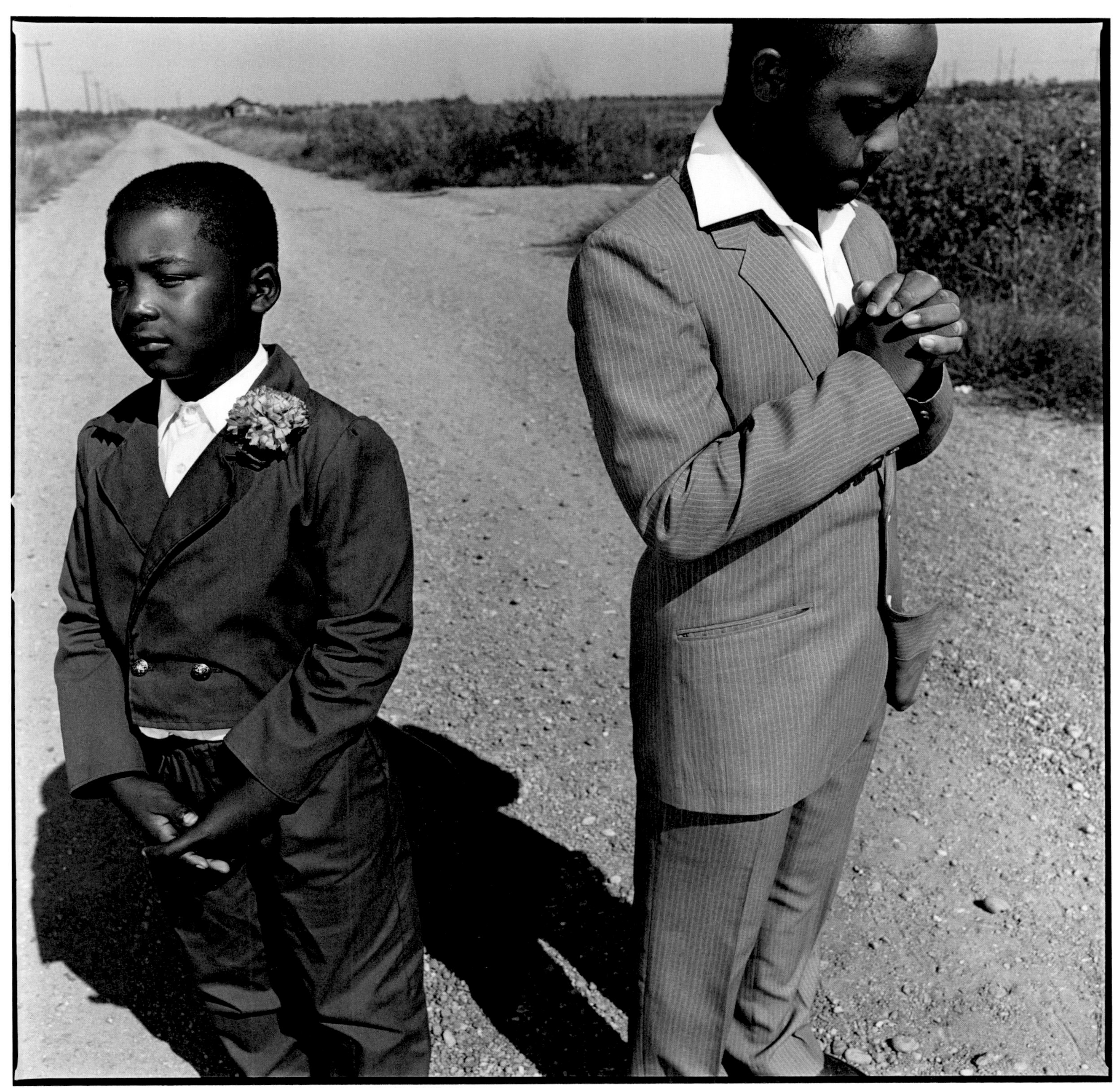

Brothers going to church, Tunica. Mississippi, 1990

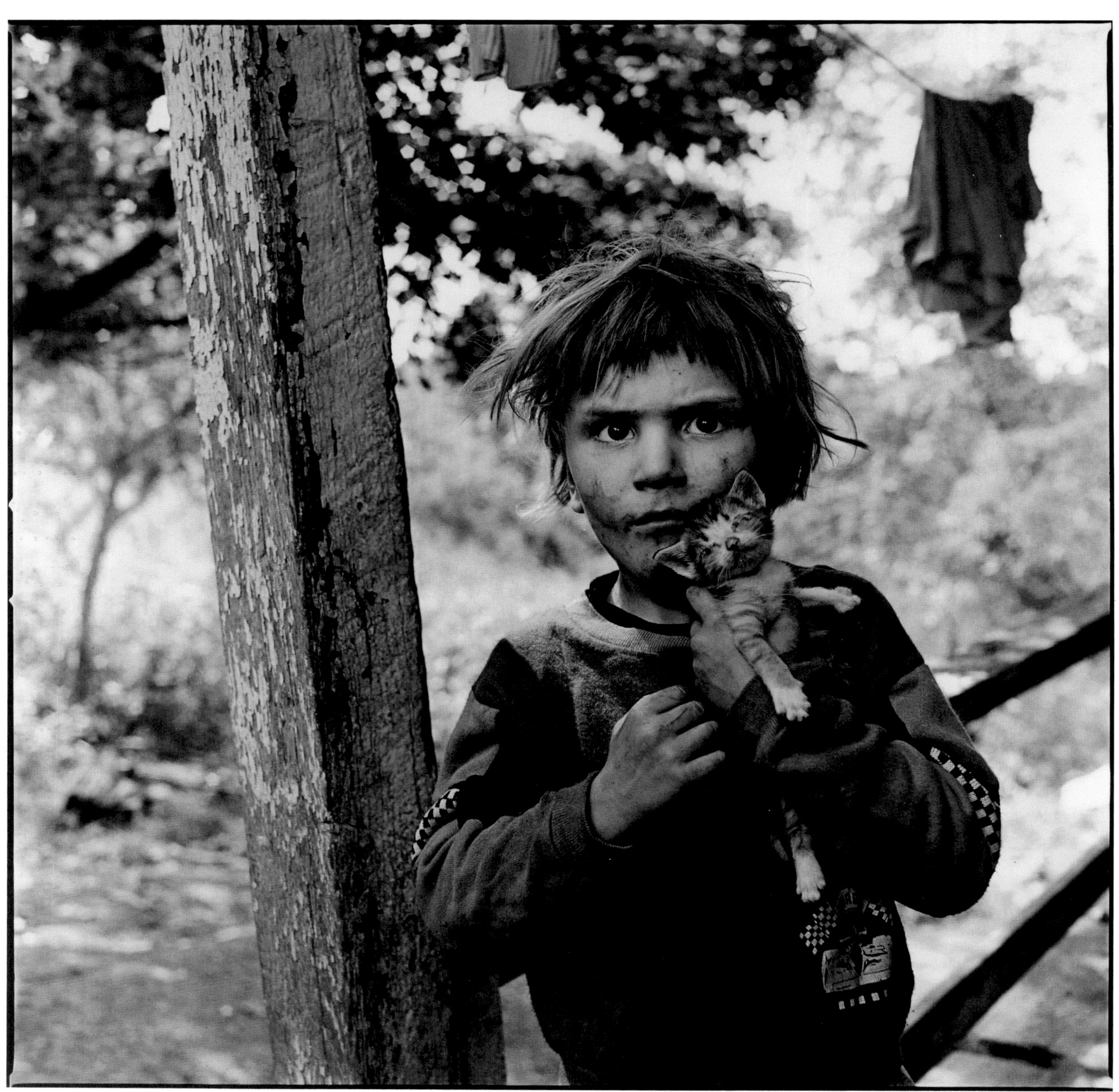

Christopher with his kitten, Sandgap, Kentucky, 1990

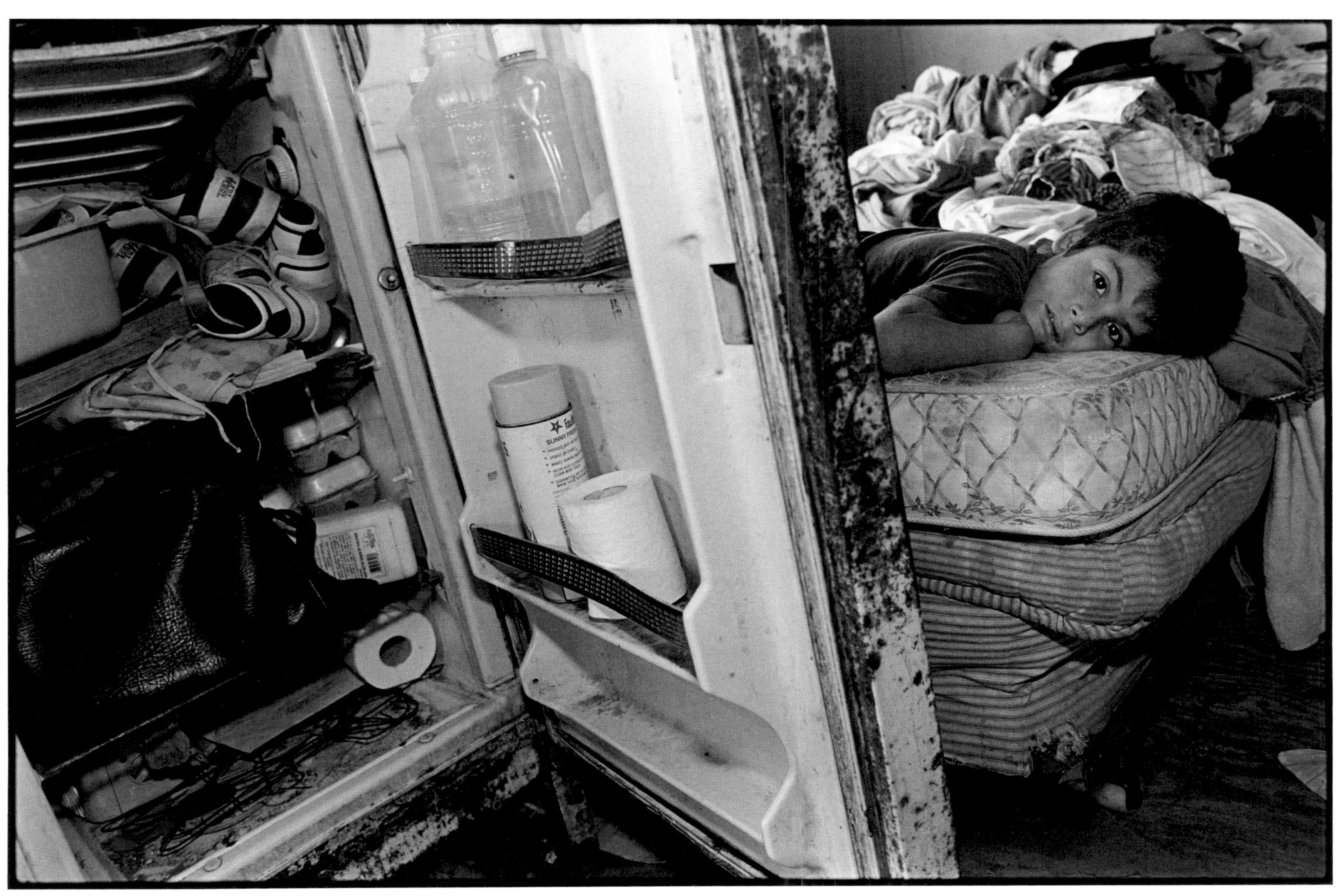

Nestor, Mission, Texas, 1990

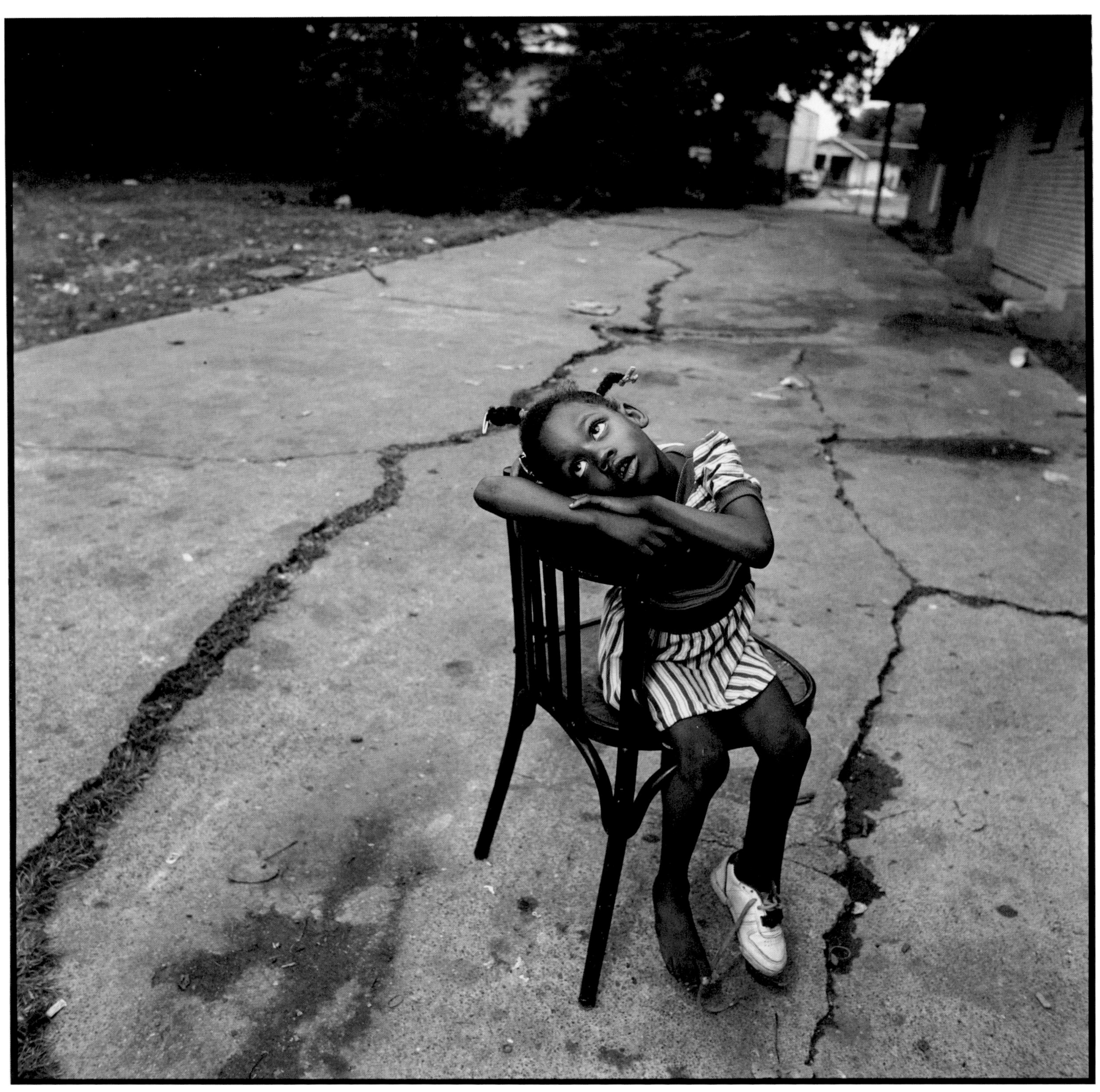

Lakiesha, South Dallas, Texas, 1988

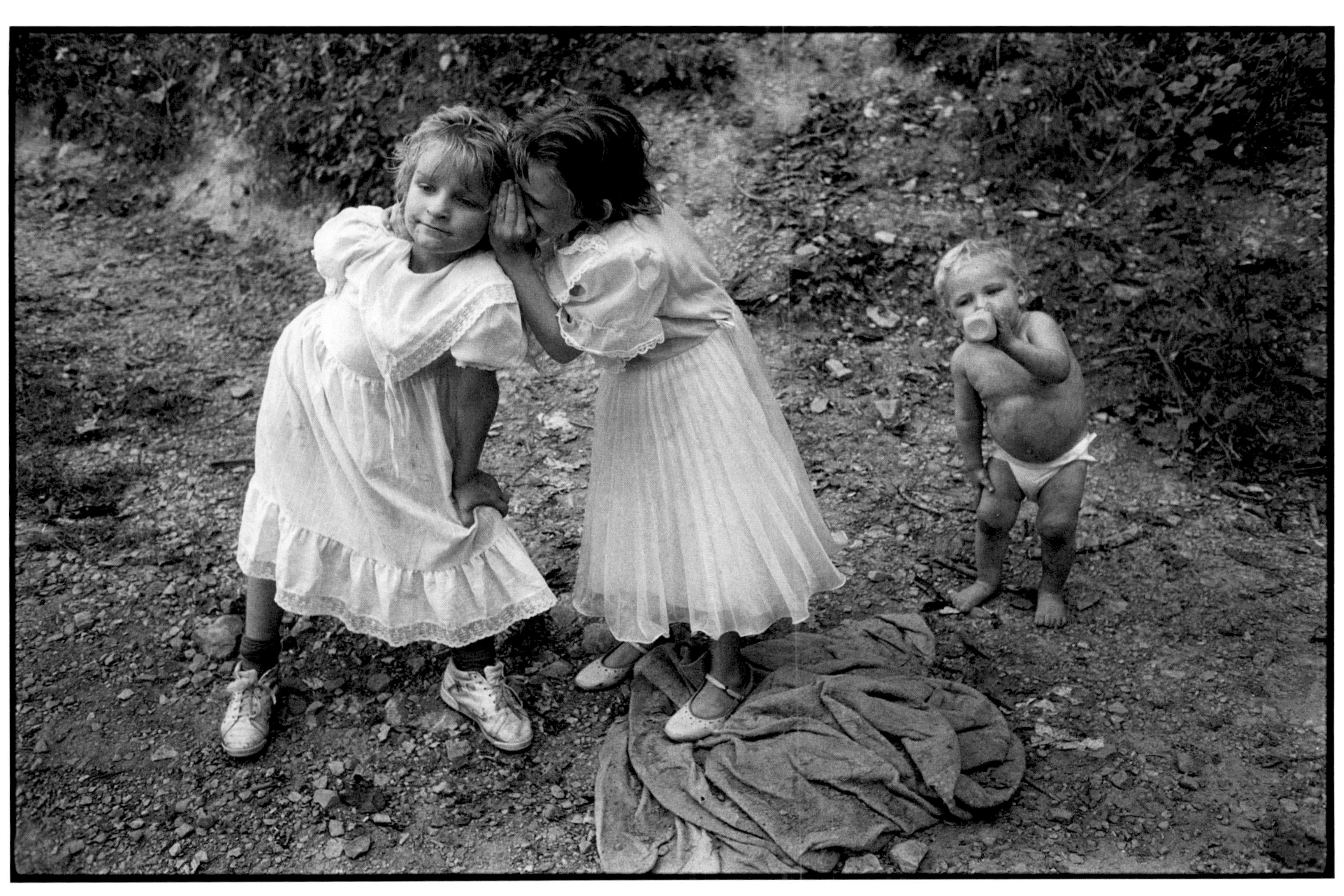

McKee, Kentucky, 1990

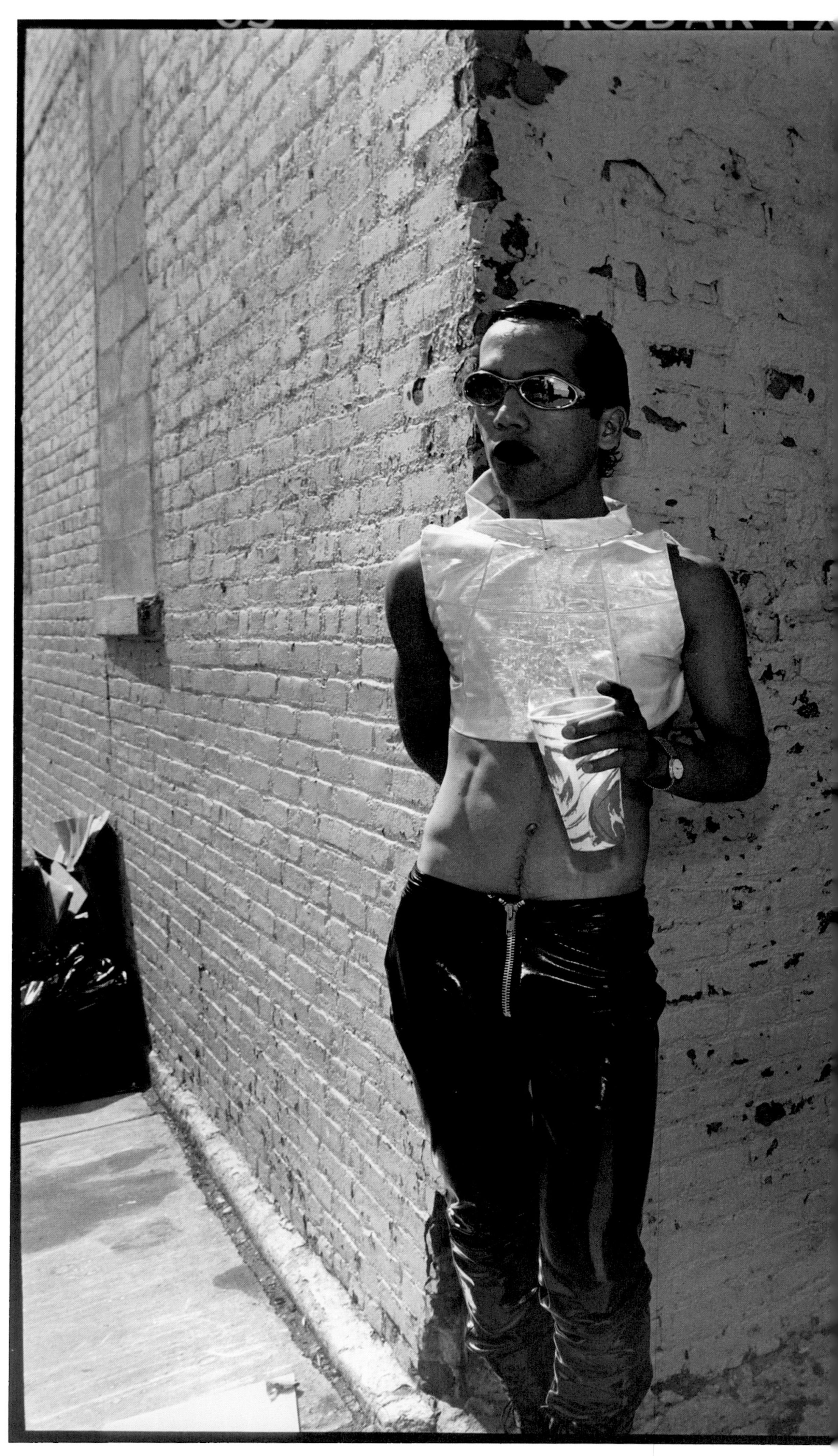

Gay Pride parade, New York City, 1997

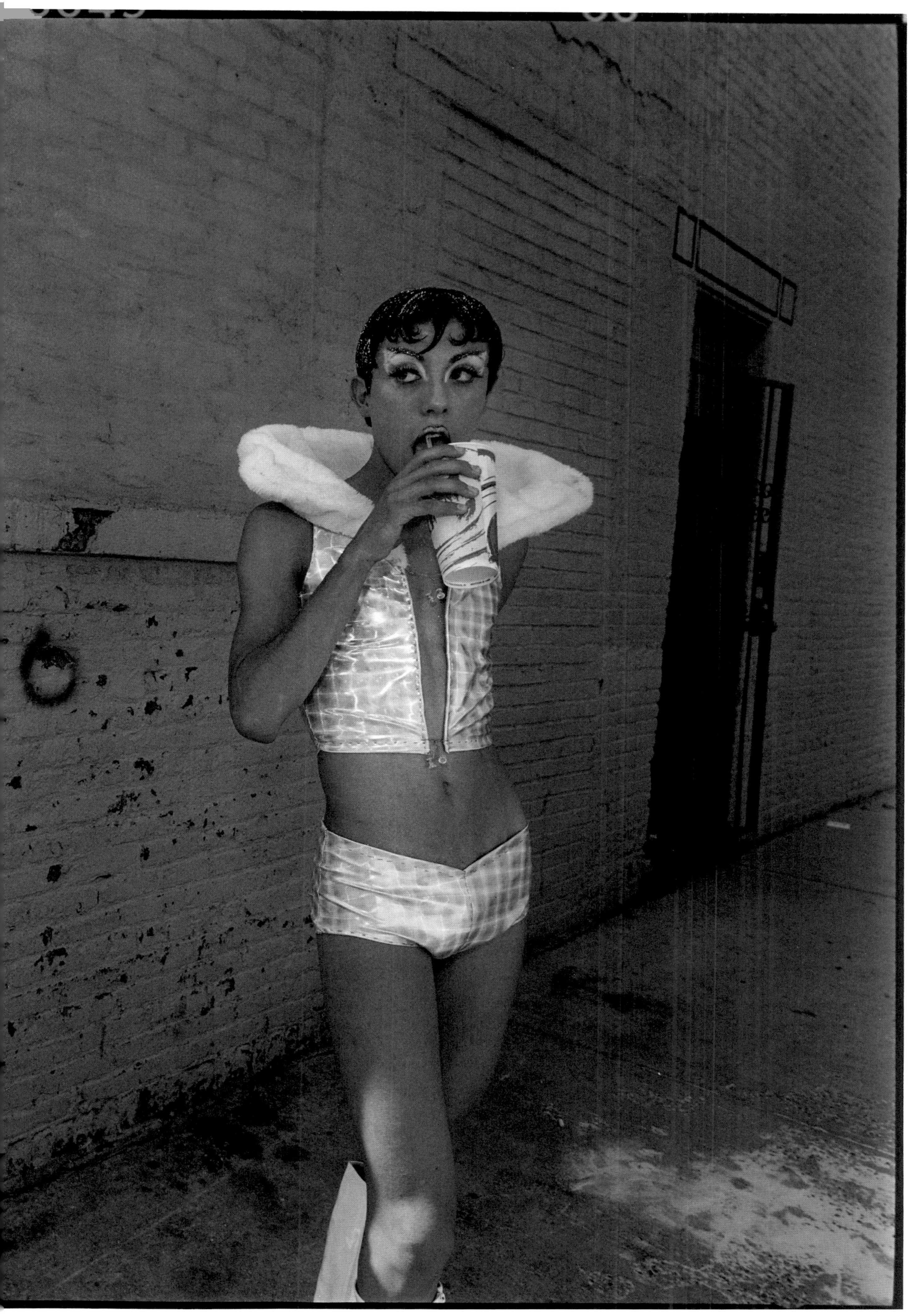

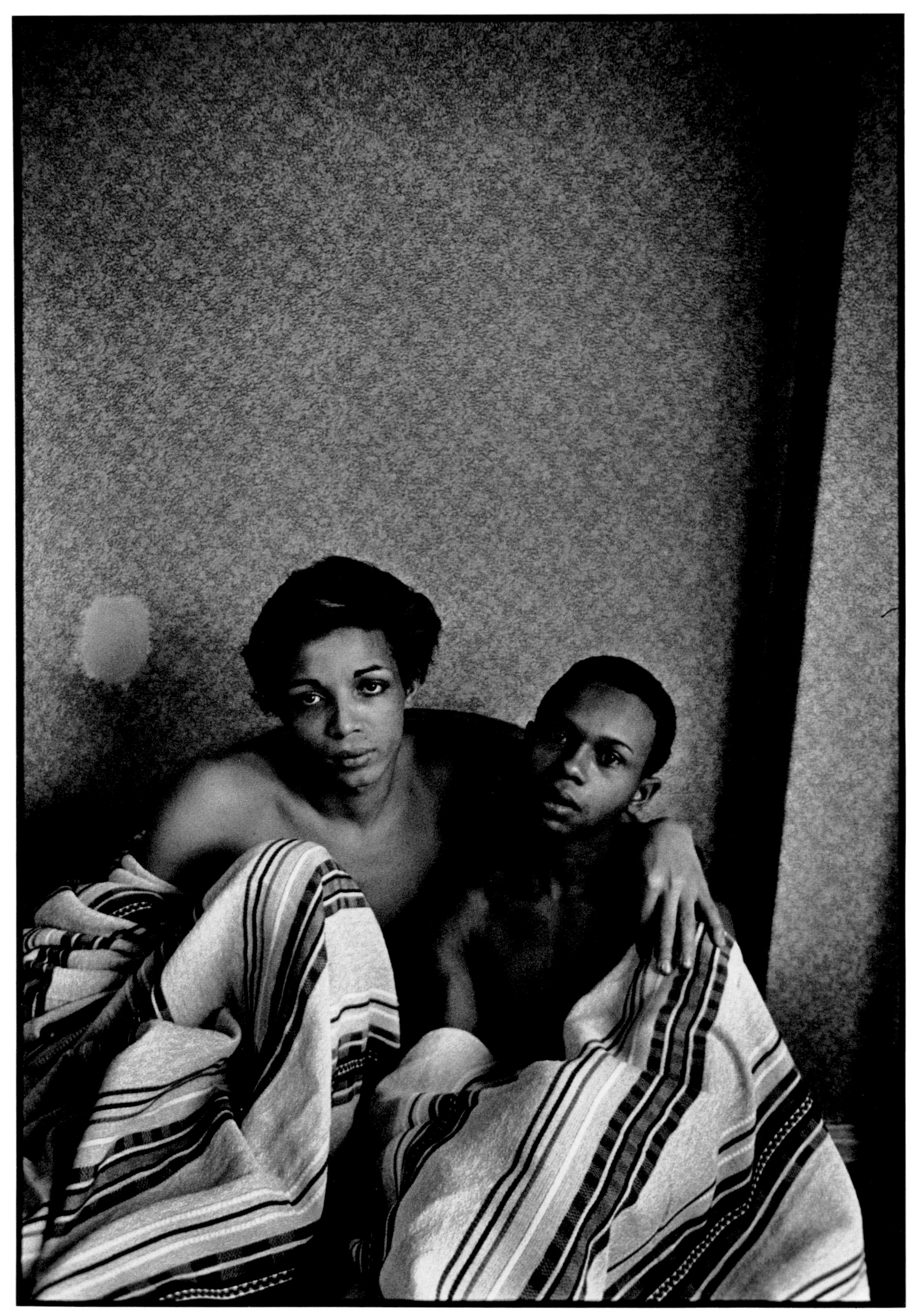

Transvestite couple in their hotel room, Broadway Hotel, New York City, 1968

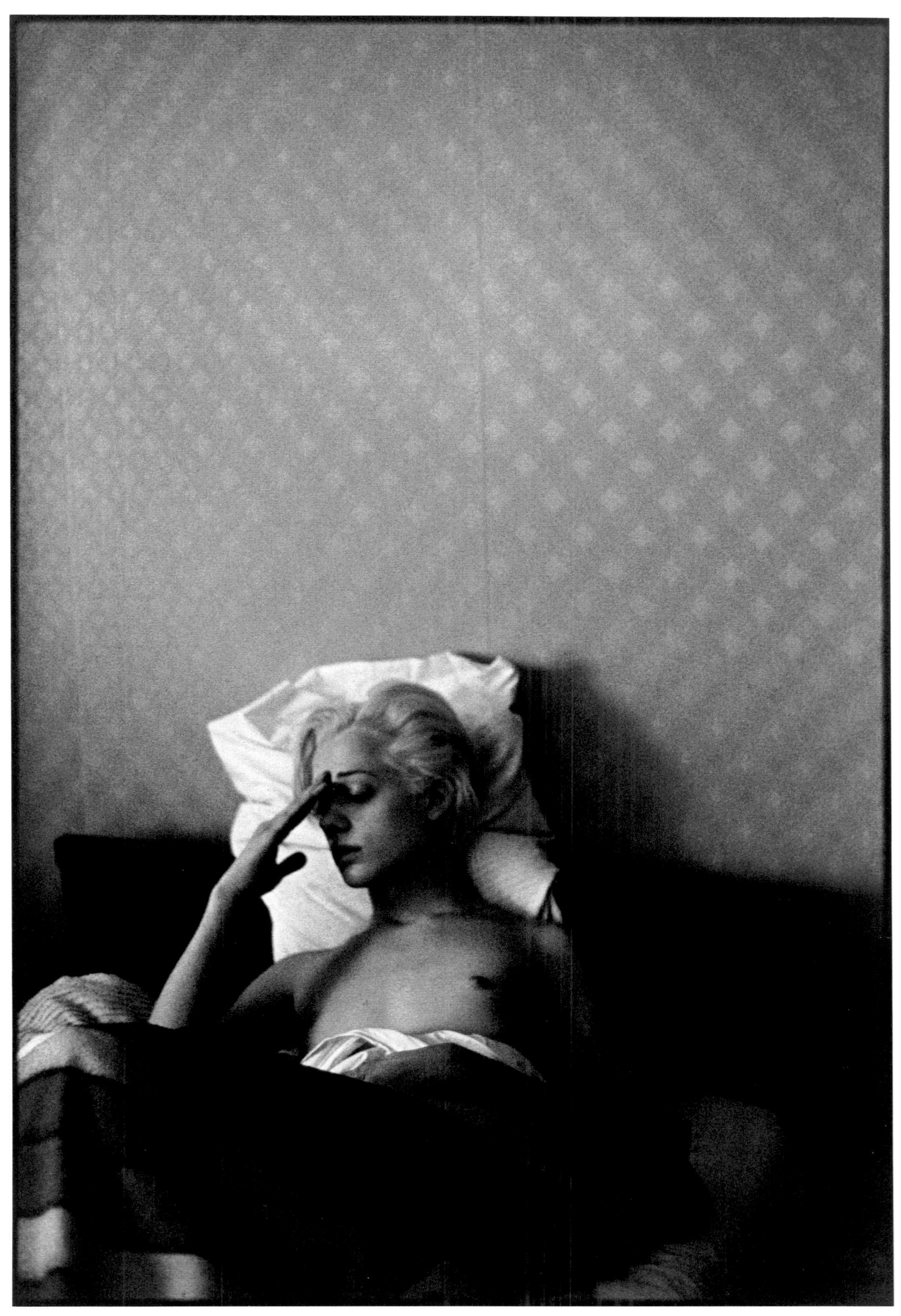

Transvestite in her hotel room, New Yo-k City, 1968

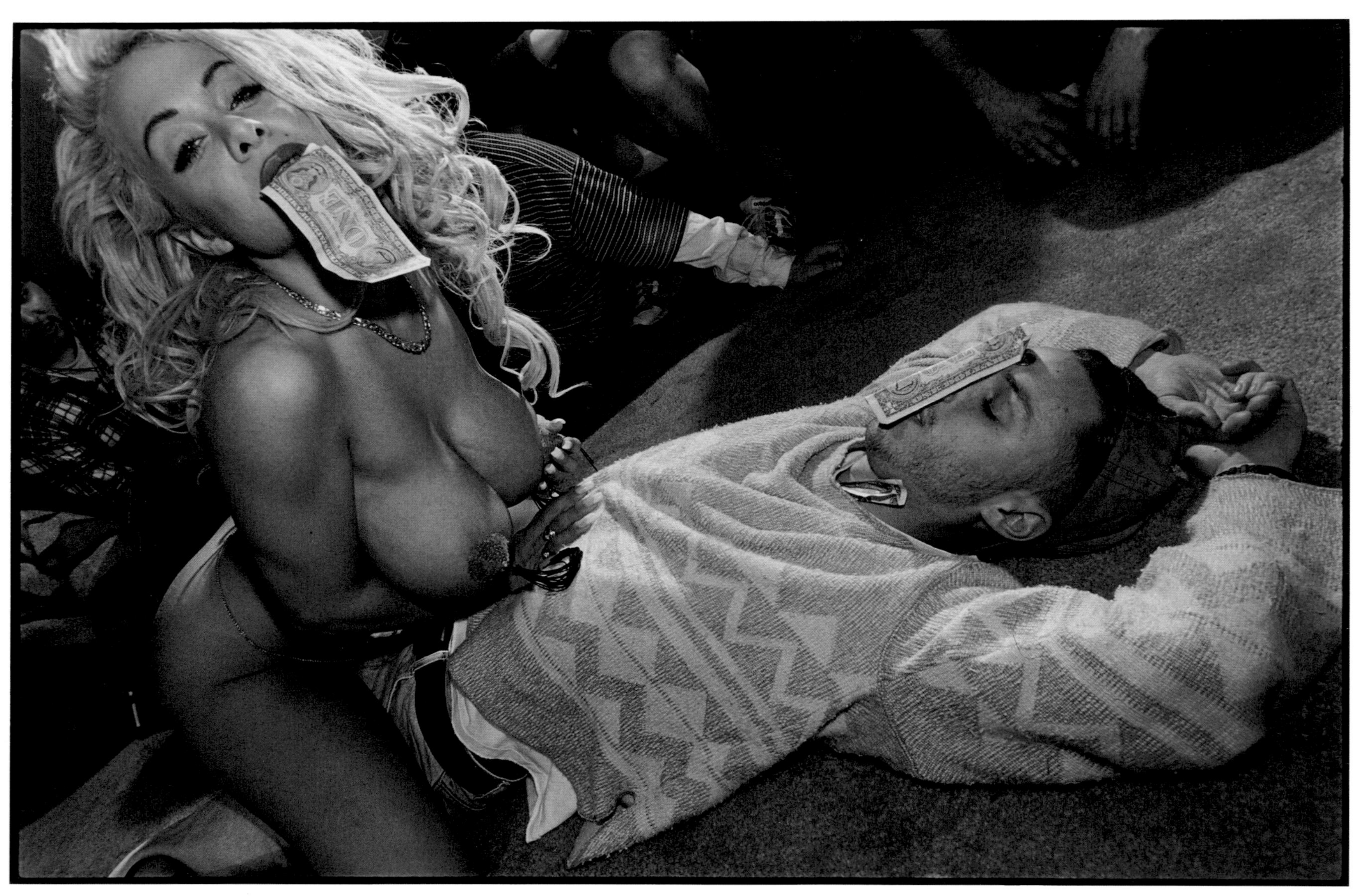

Stacy Cotugno at a frat party, Maryland, 1996

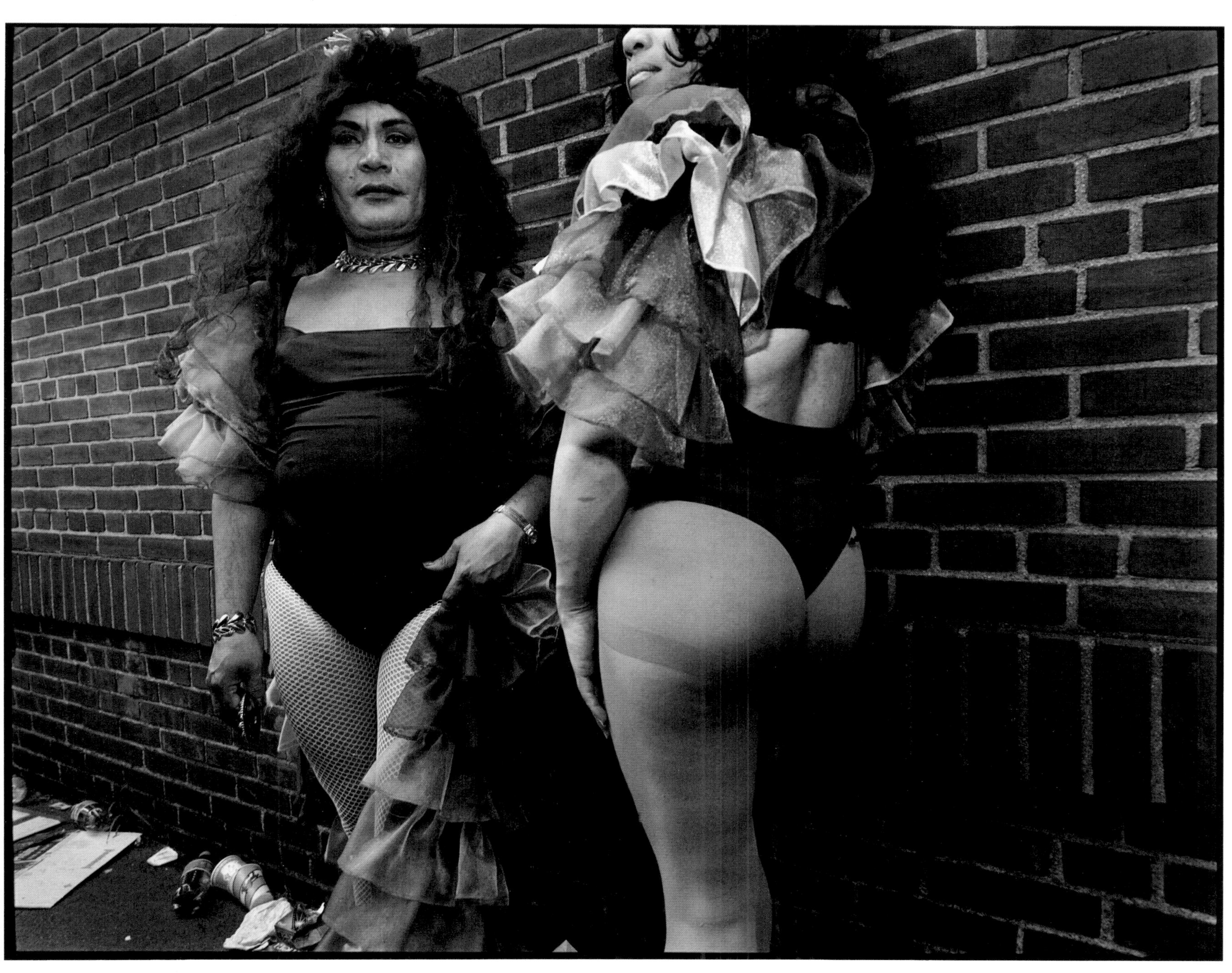

Gay Pride parade, New York City, 1997

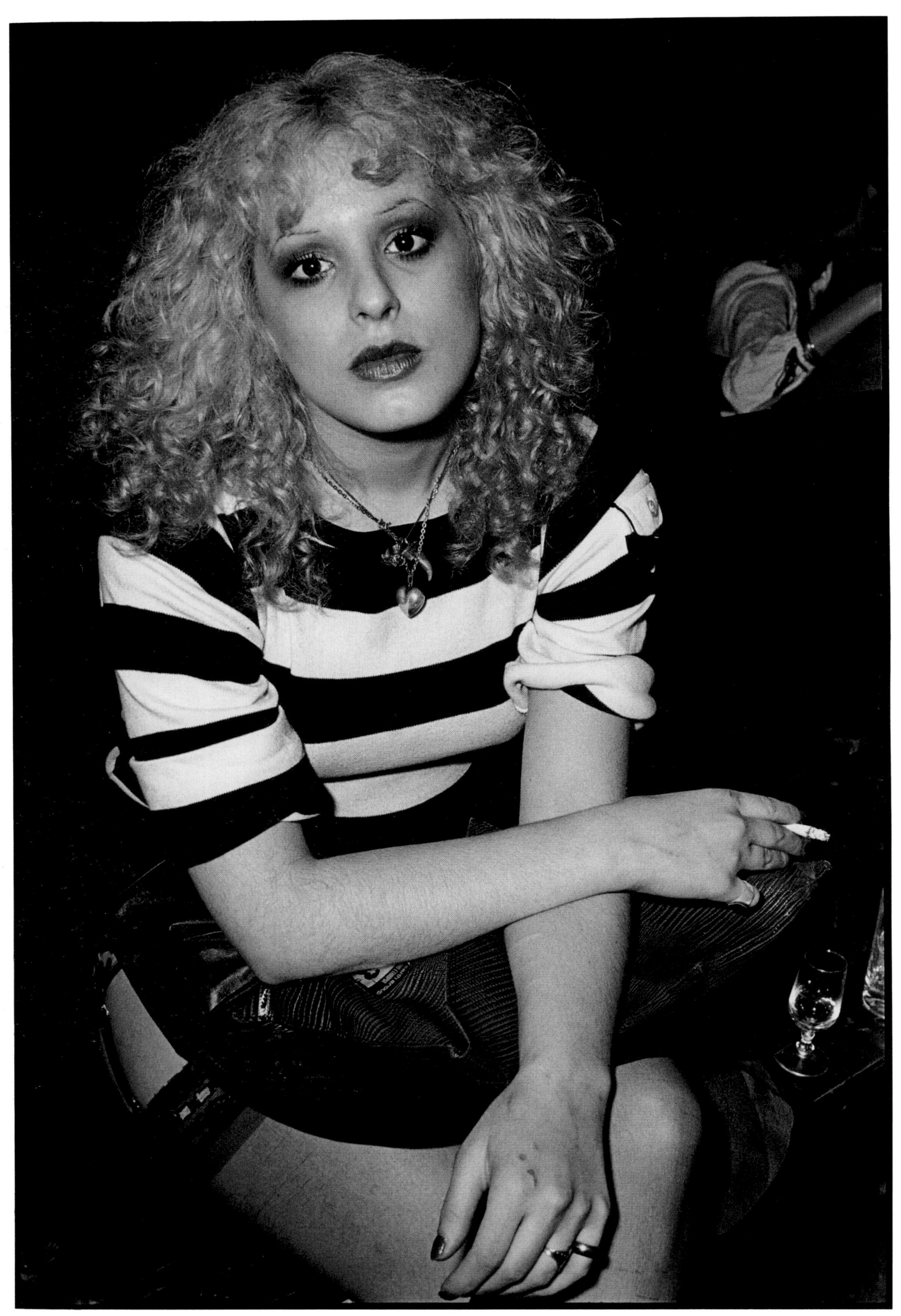

Nancy Spungen, New York City, 1977

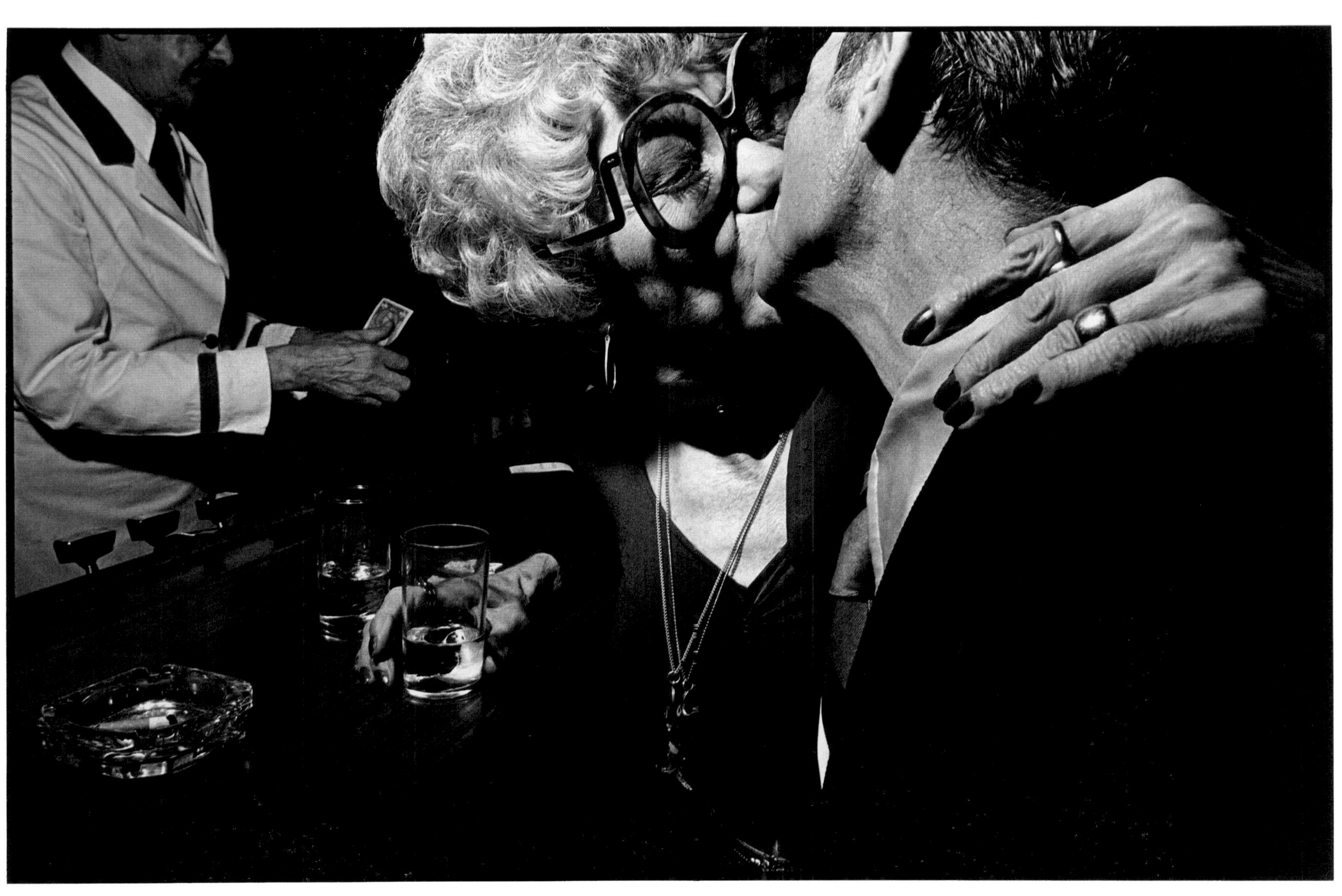

Older couple in a bar, New York City, 1977

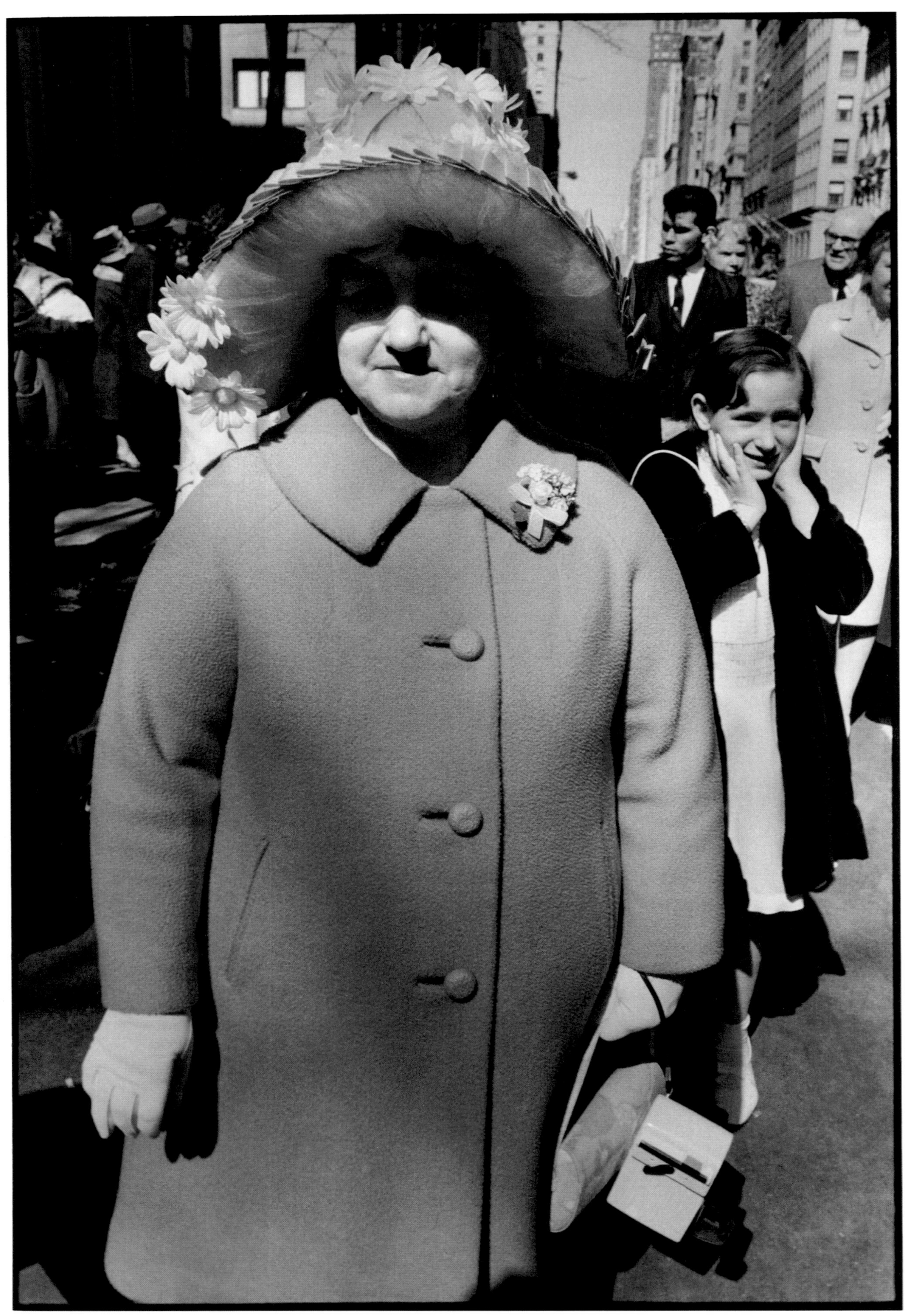

Easter parade, New York City, 1969

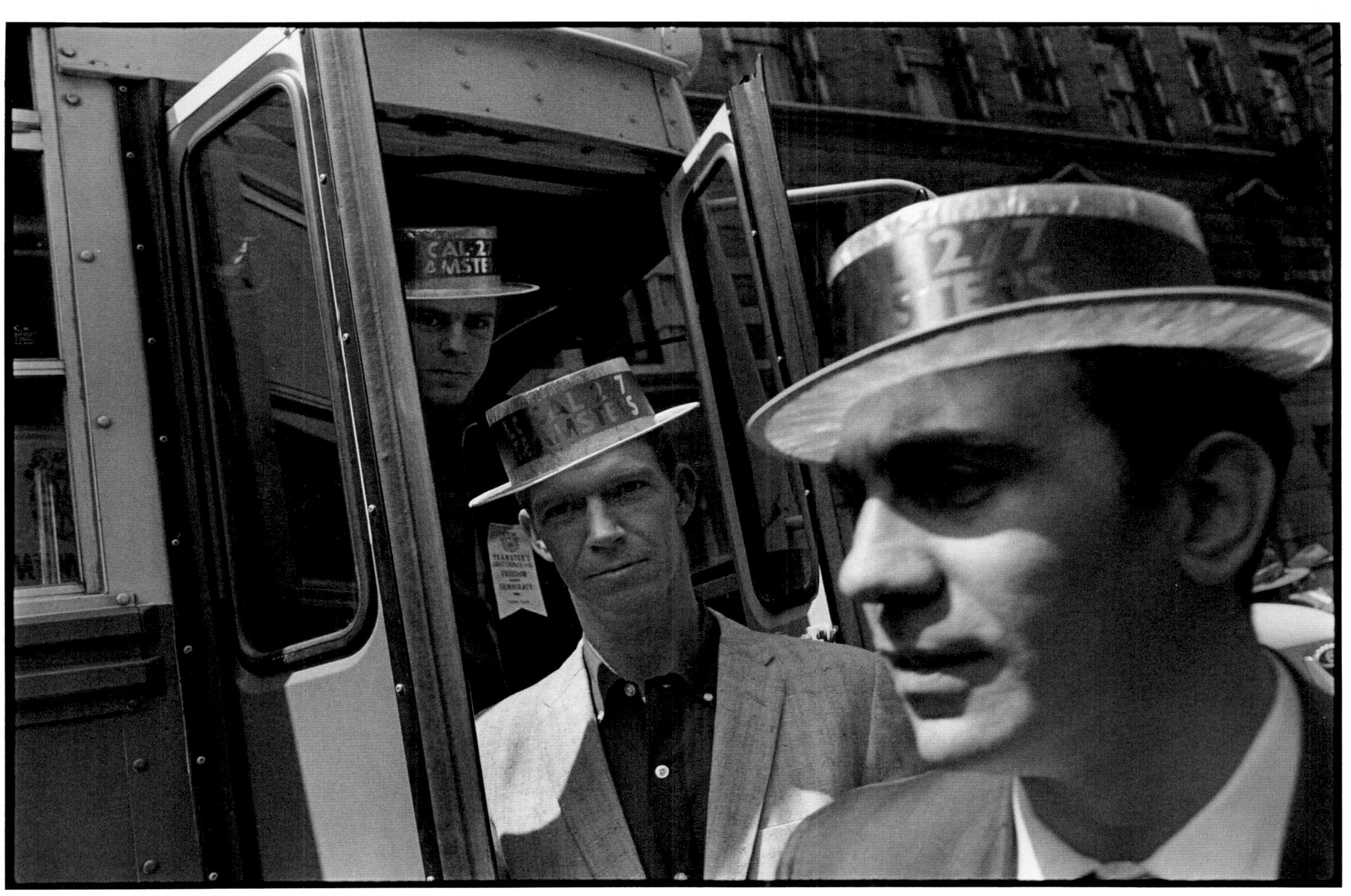

Pro–Vietnam War parade, New York City, 1968

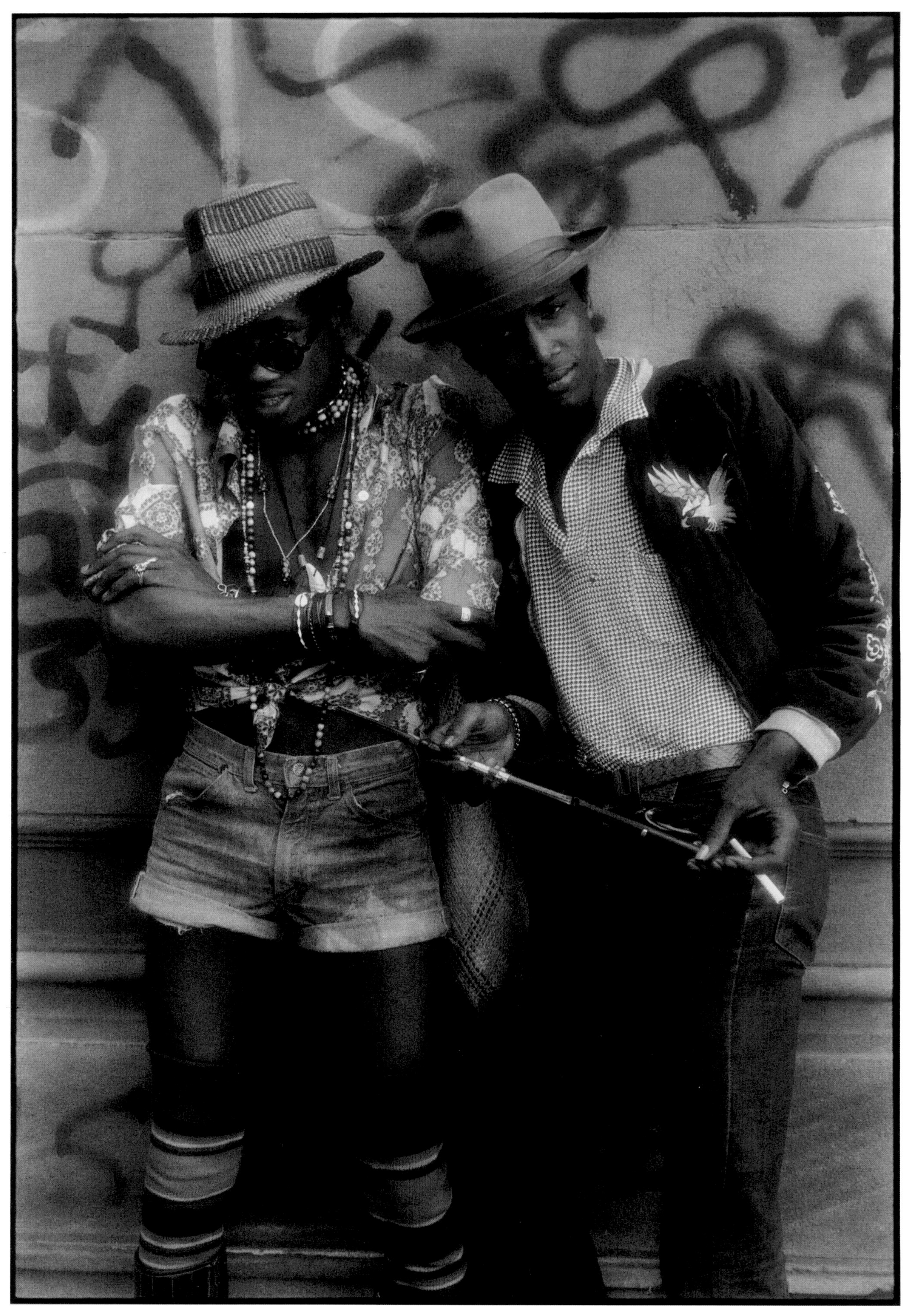

Dressed-up boys, Central Park, New York City, 1968

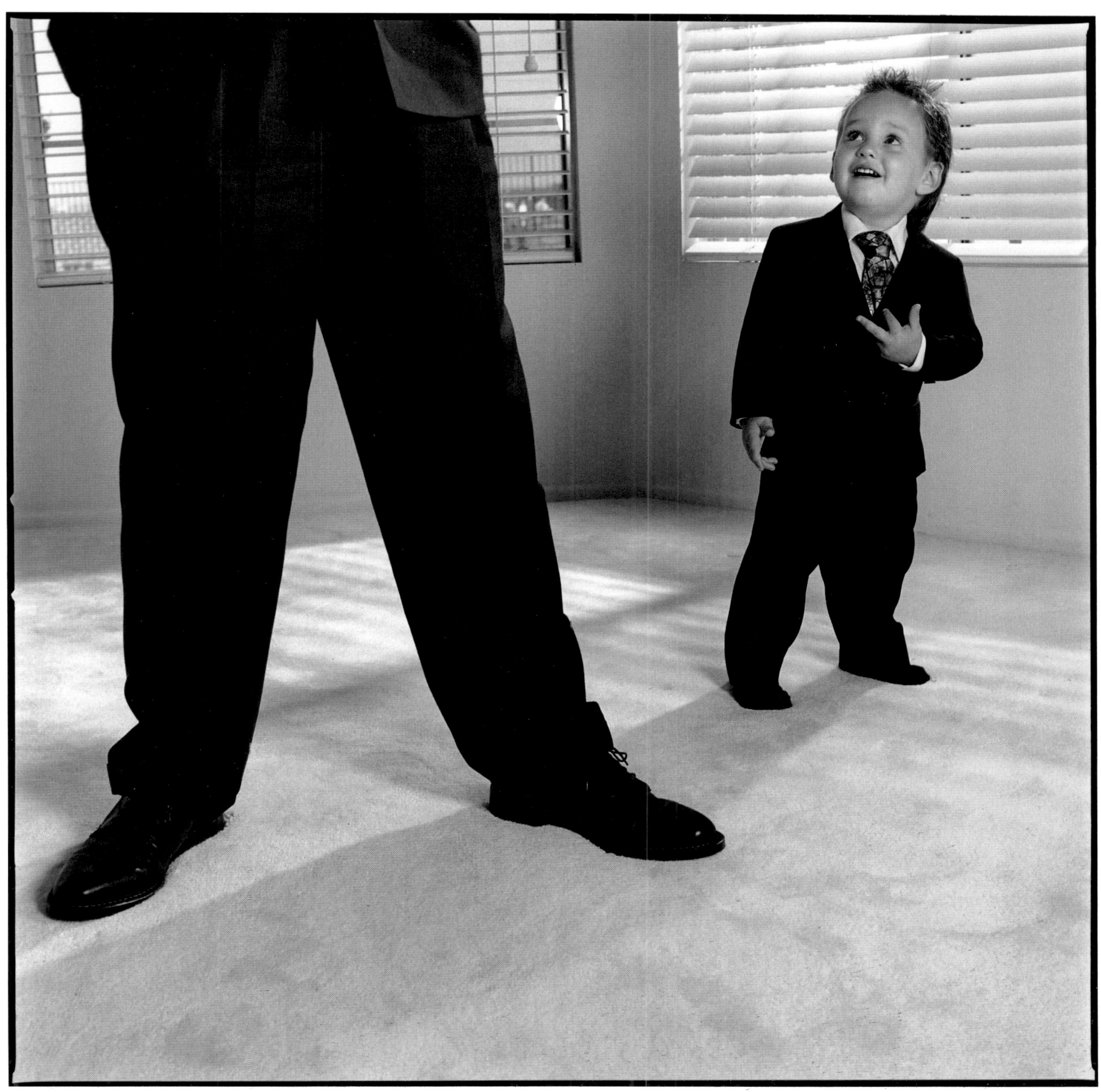

Clinton Albright and his father, Santa Clarita, California, 1992

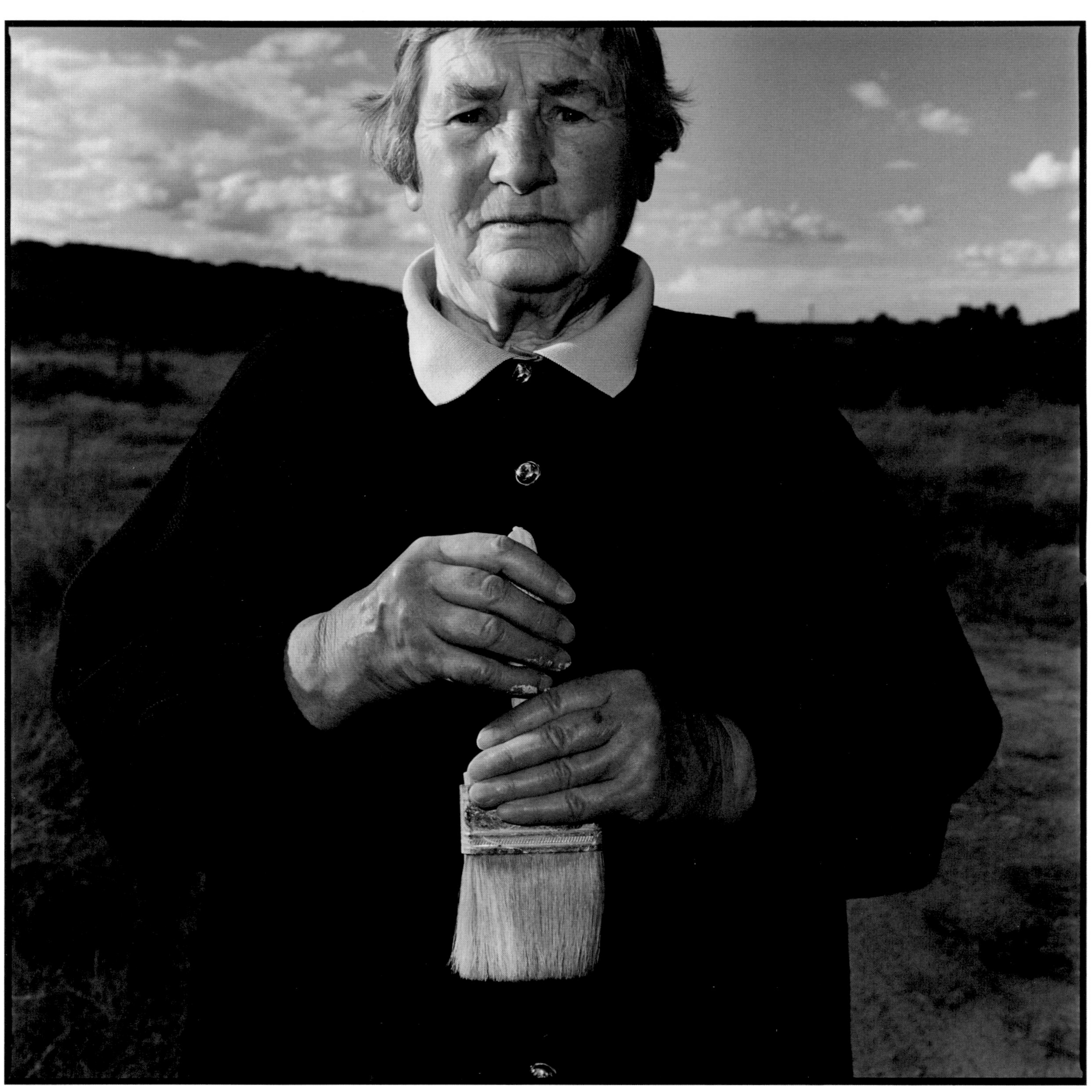

Agnes Martin, Galisteo, New Mexico, 1992

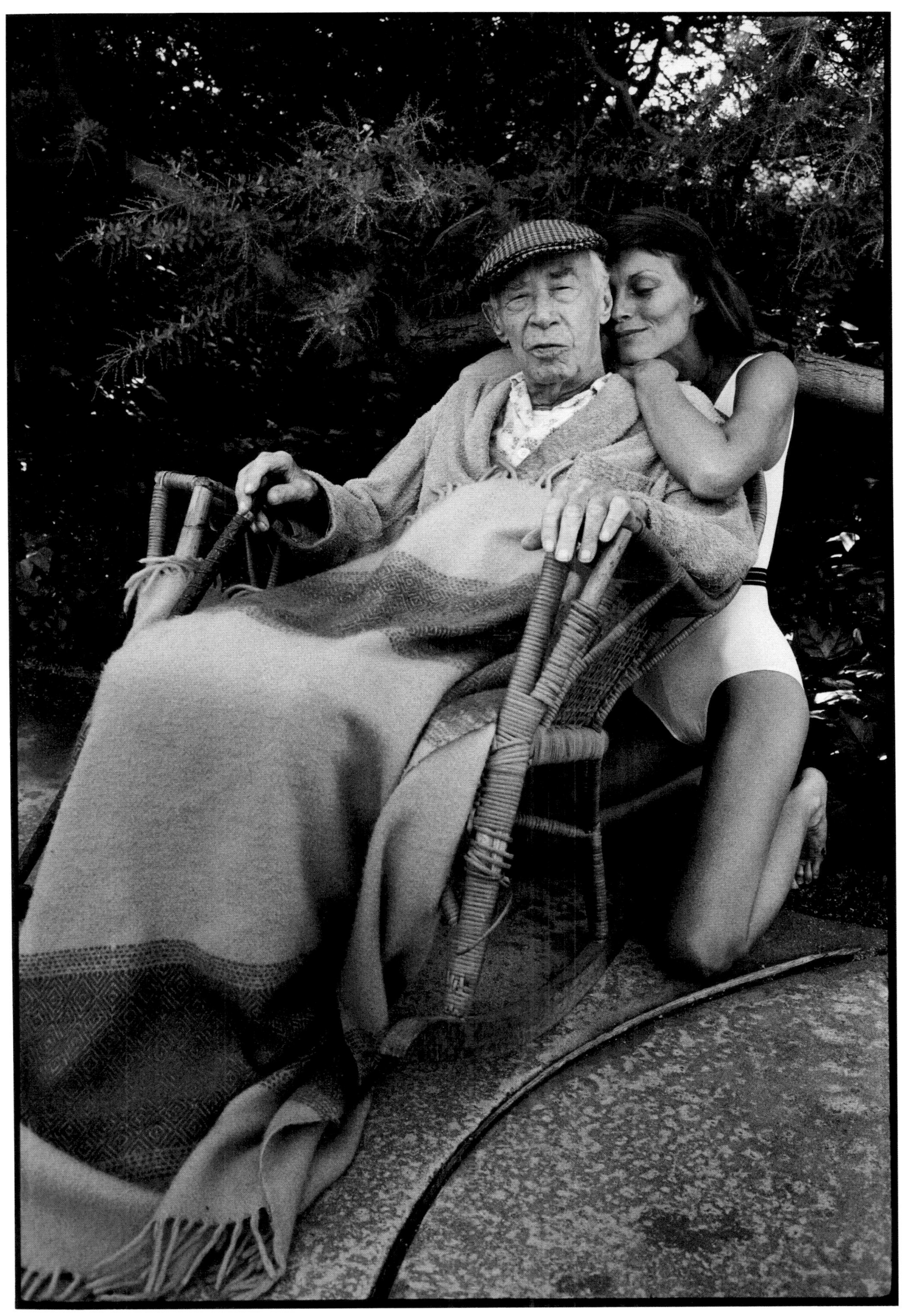

Henry Miller and Twinka, Pacific Palisades, California, 1975

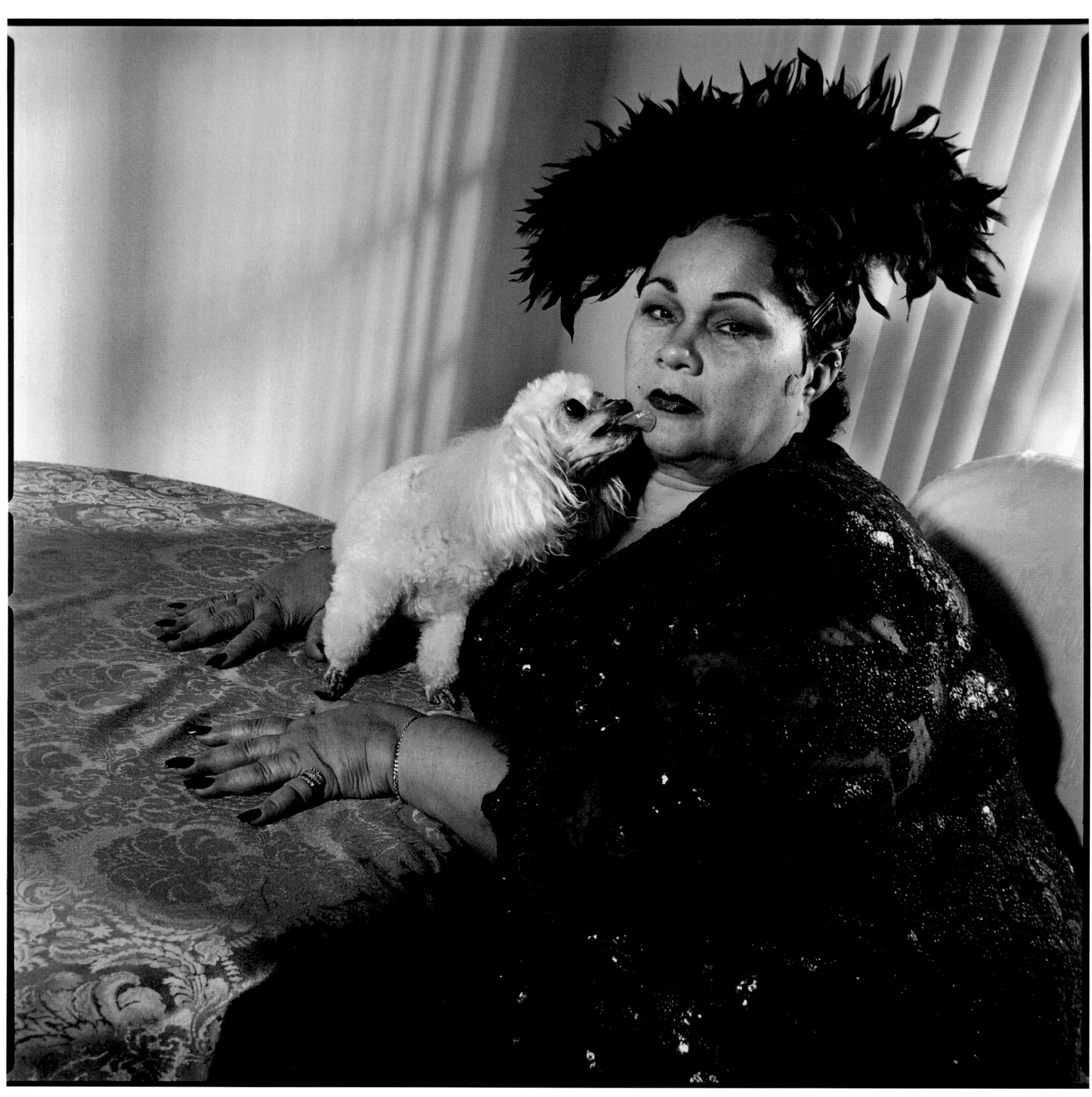

Etta James and Strappy, Riverside, California, 1997

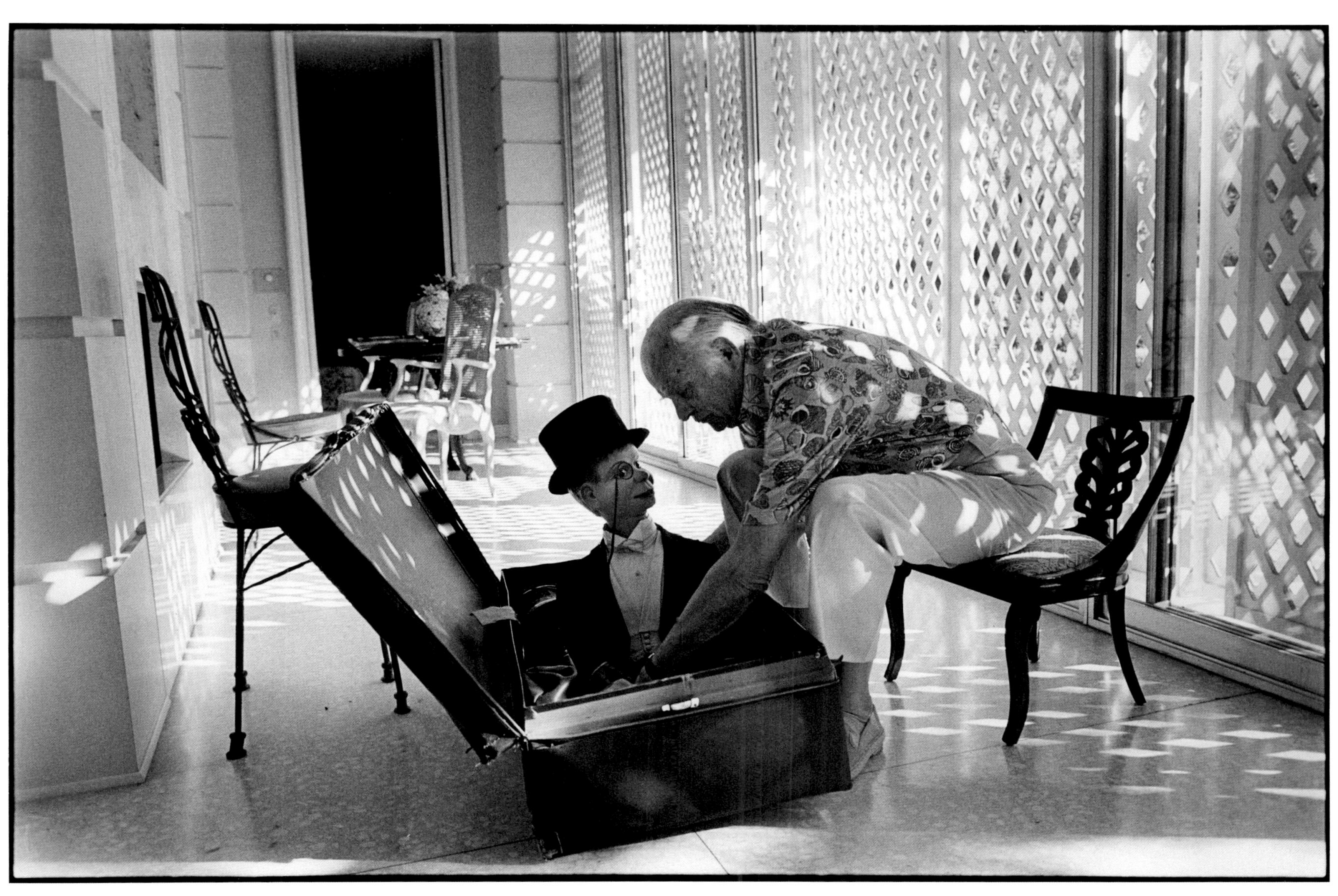

Edgar Bergen and Charlie McCarthy, Los Angeles, California, 1978

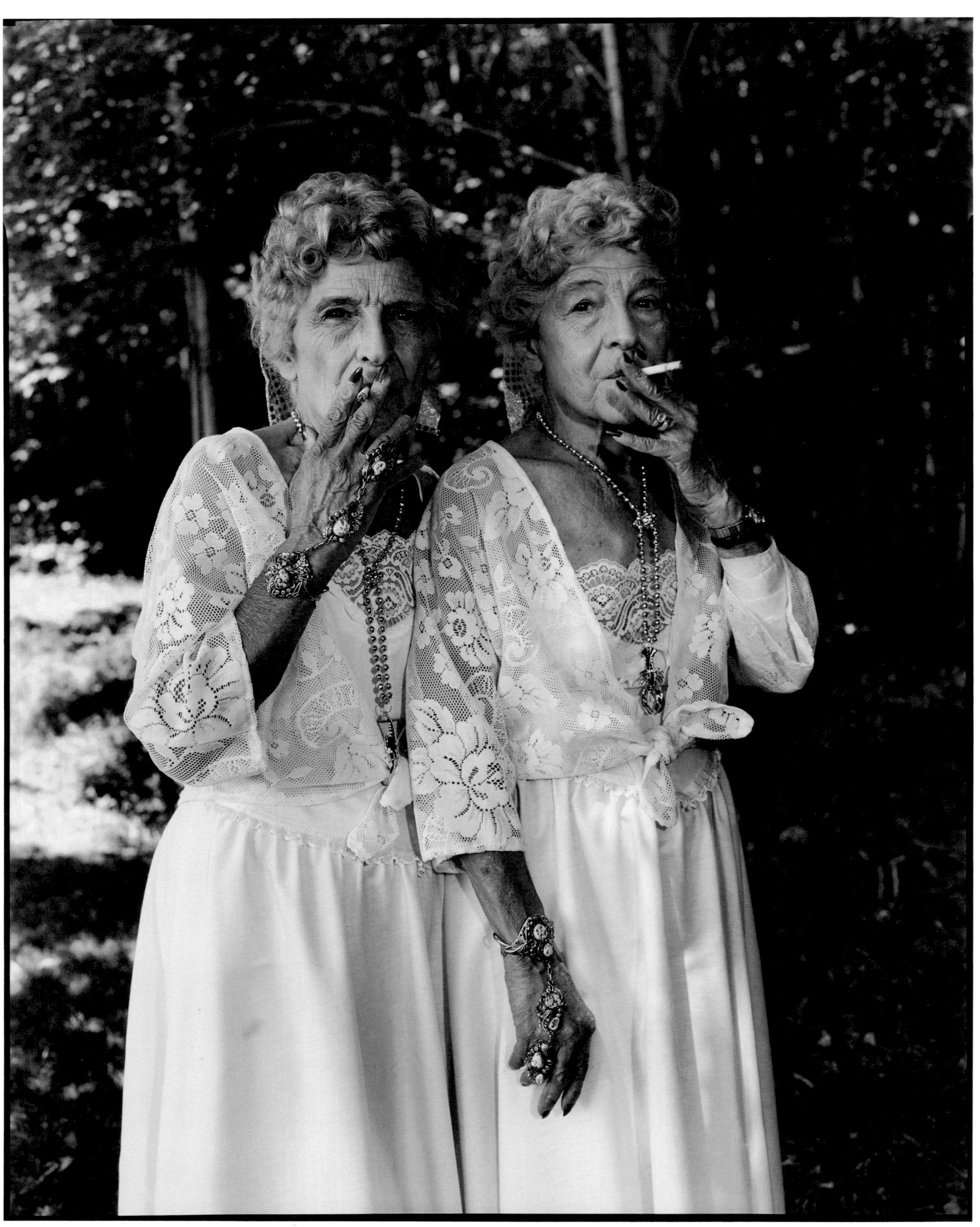

Sue Gallo Baugher and Faye Gallo, Twinsburg, Ohio, 1998

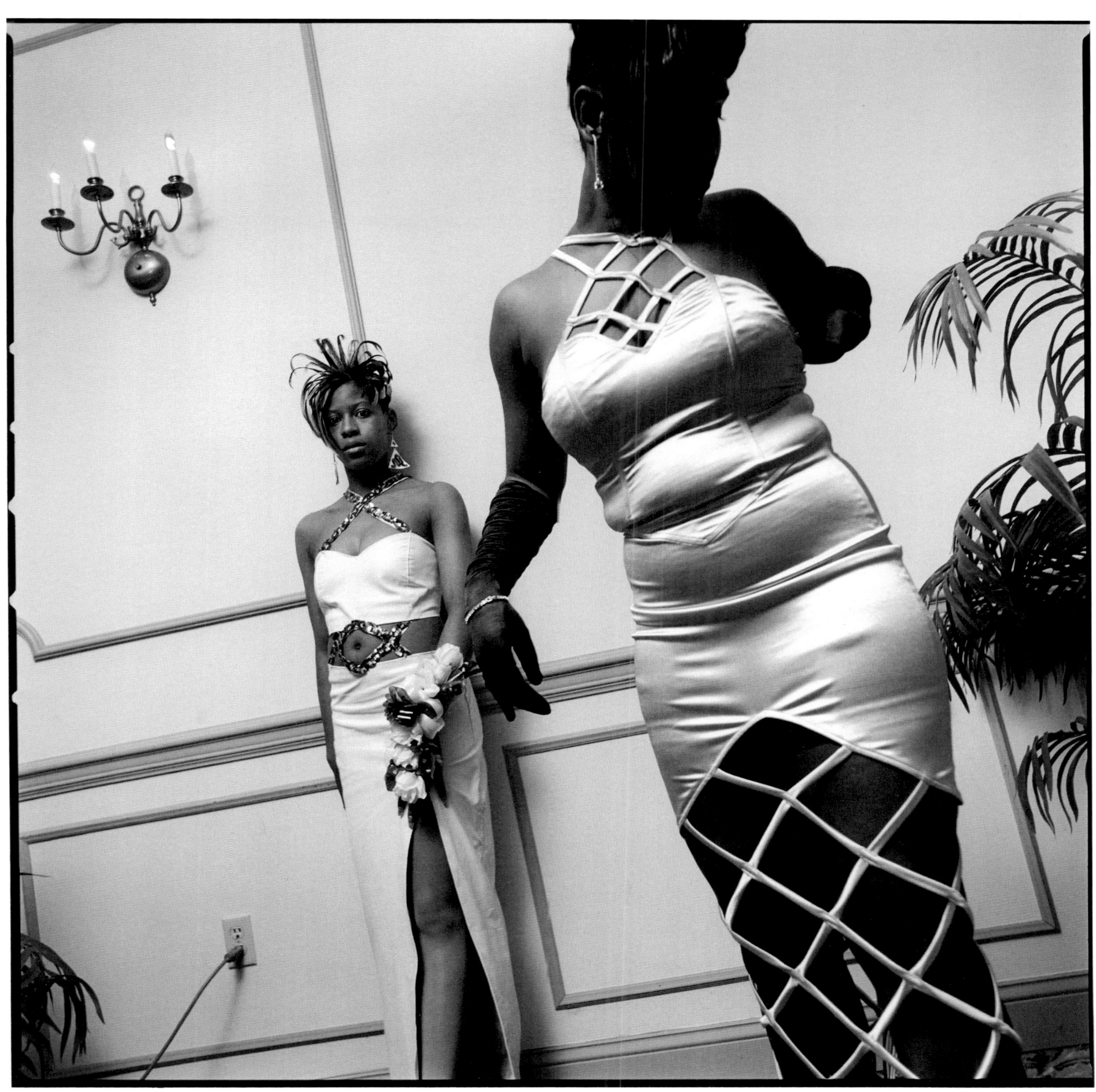

Senior Prom, Pittsburgh, Pennsylvania, 1995

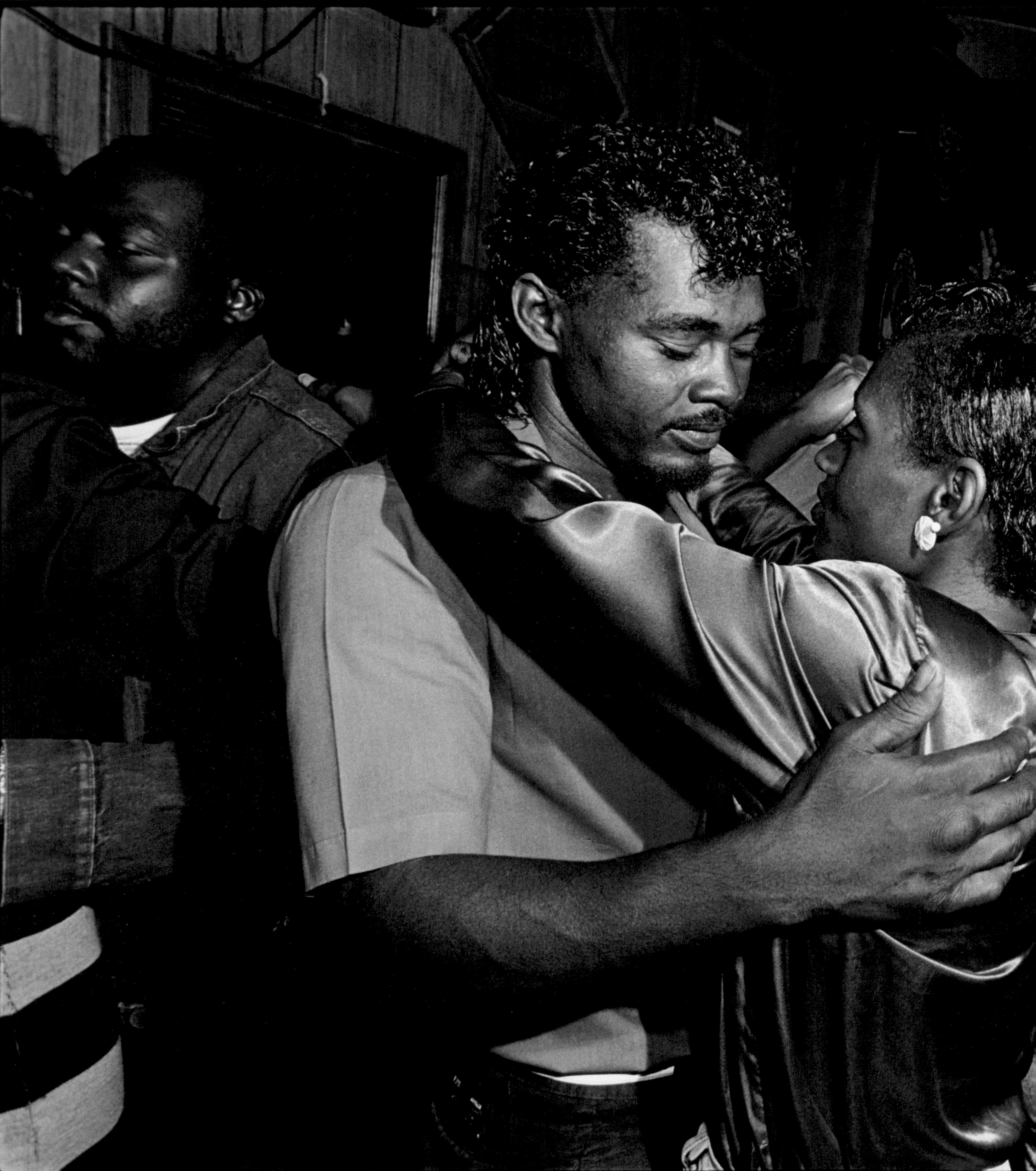

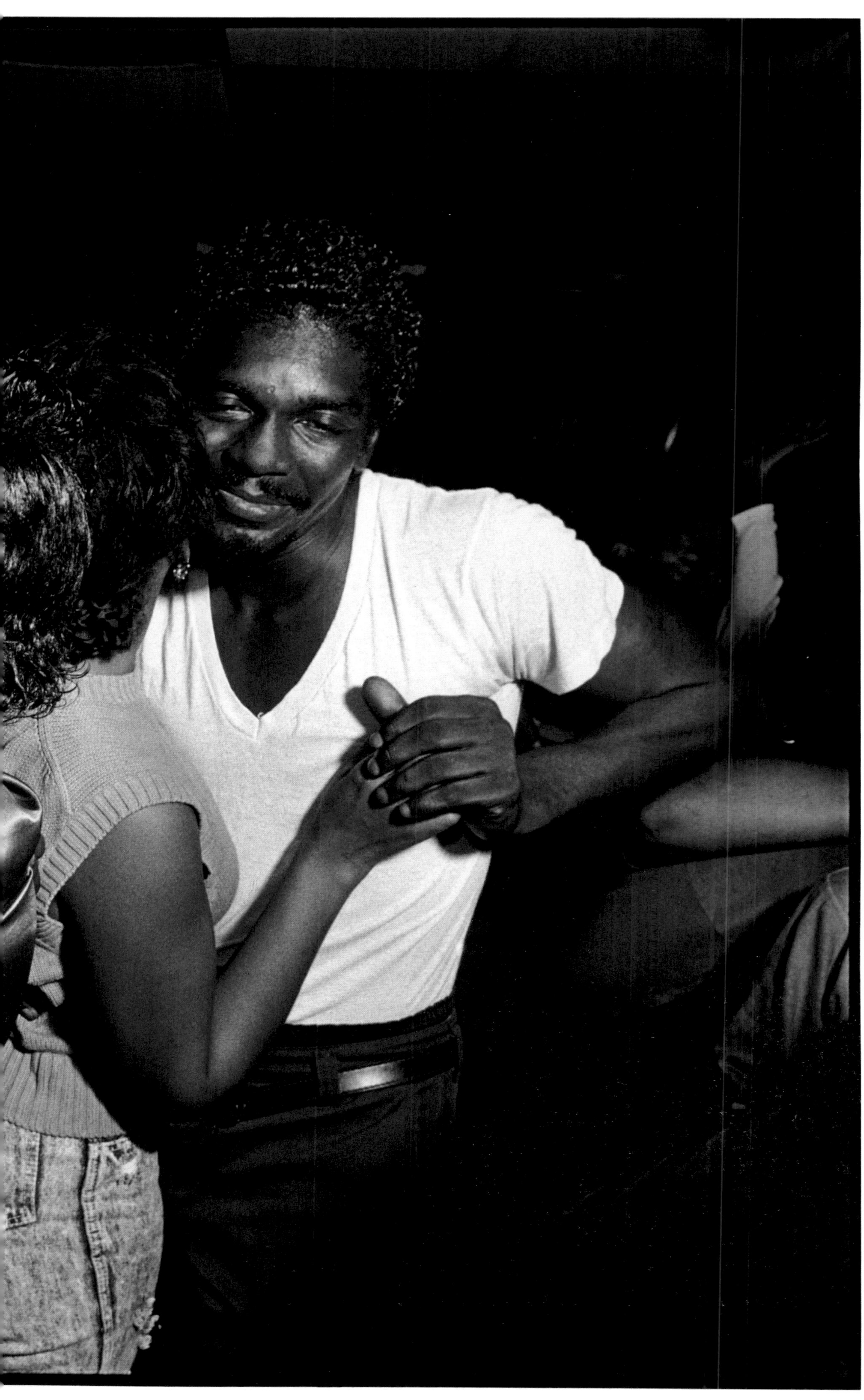

Nightclub off of
Highway 61, Mississippi, 1990

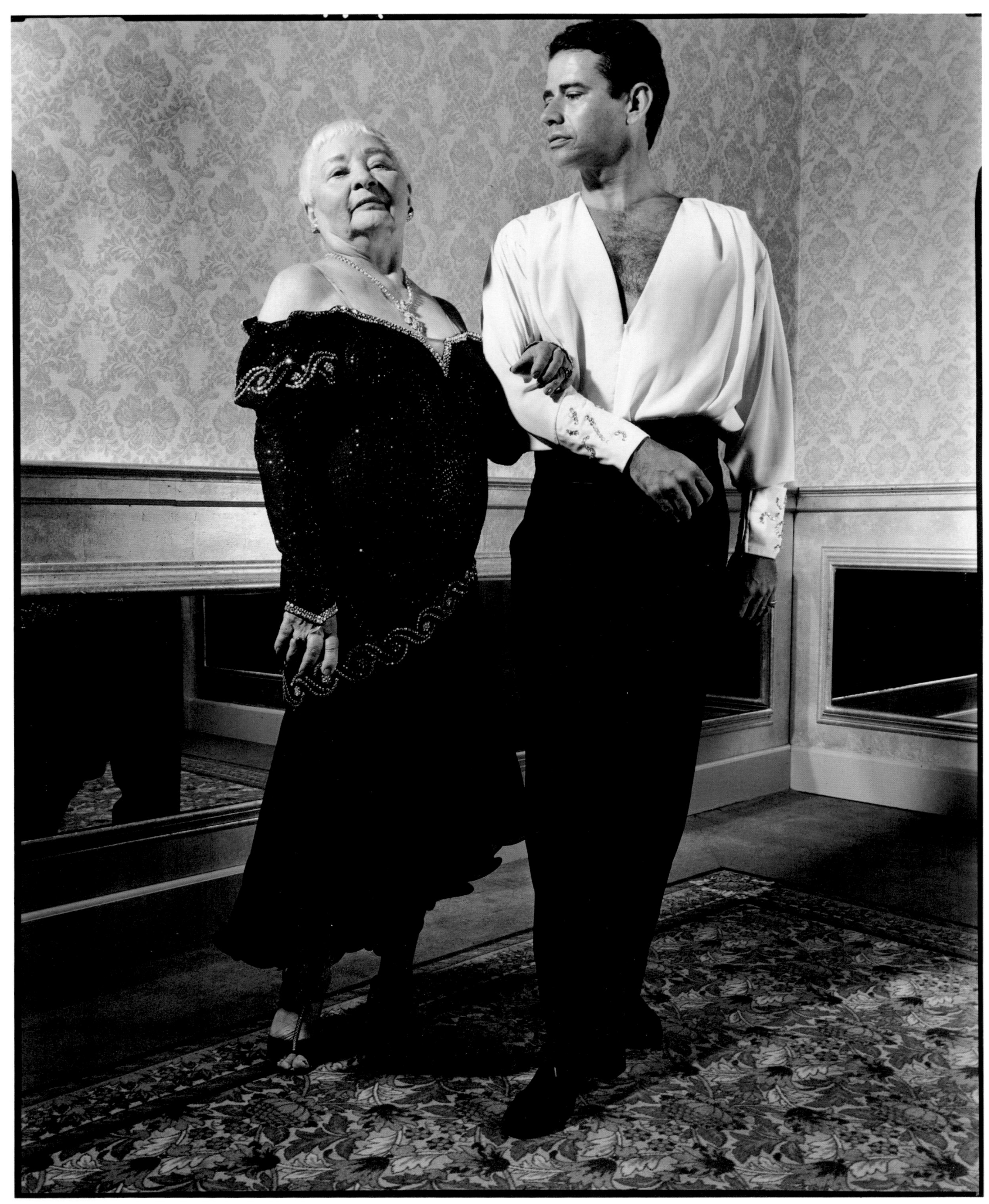

Daphne Klein and Daniel Maloney, Hilton Hotel Dance Showcase, Boca Raton, Florida, 1993

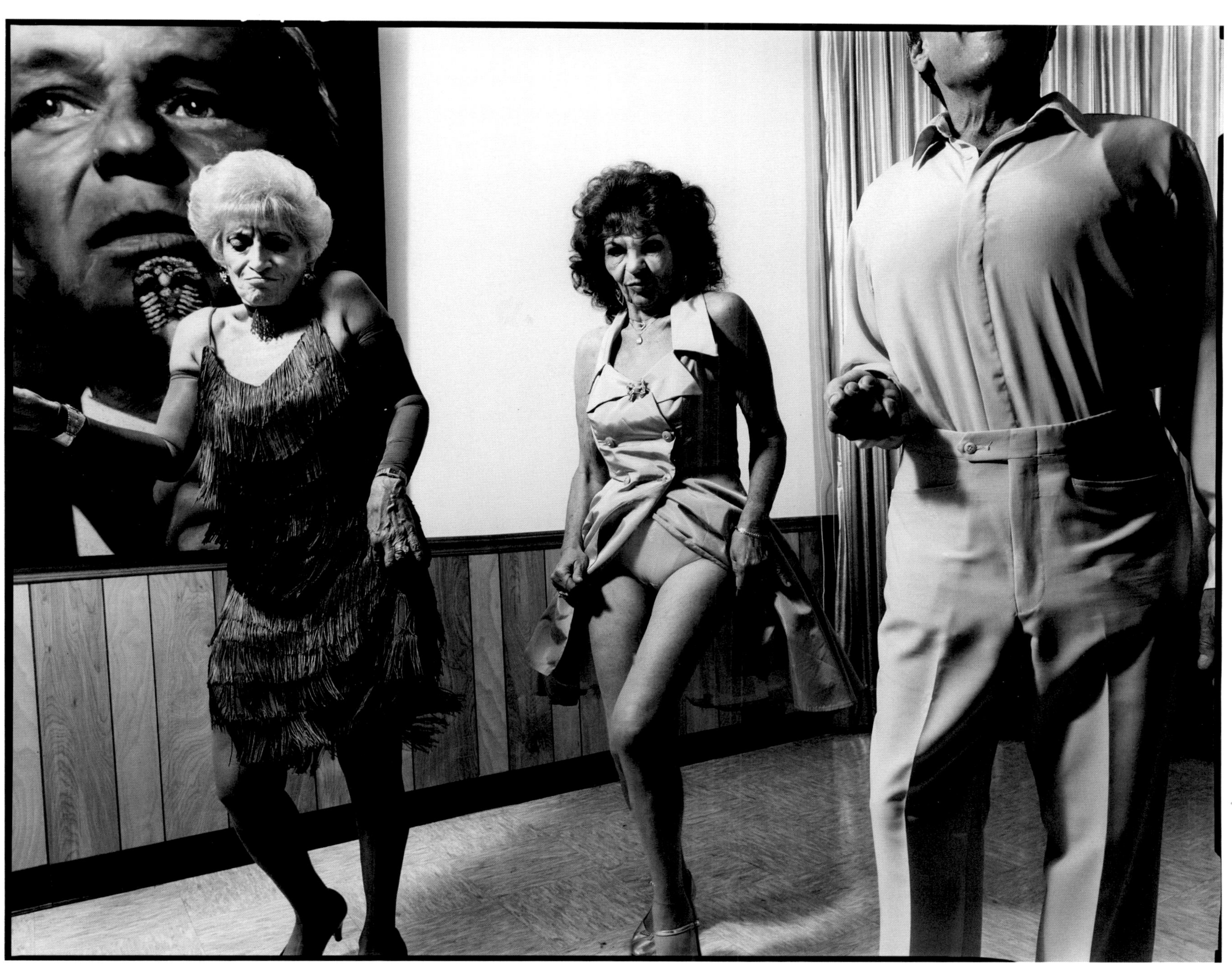

Vera Antinoro, Rhoda Camporato, and Murray Goldman, Luigi's Italian American Club, Miami, Florida, 1993

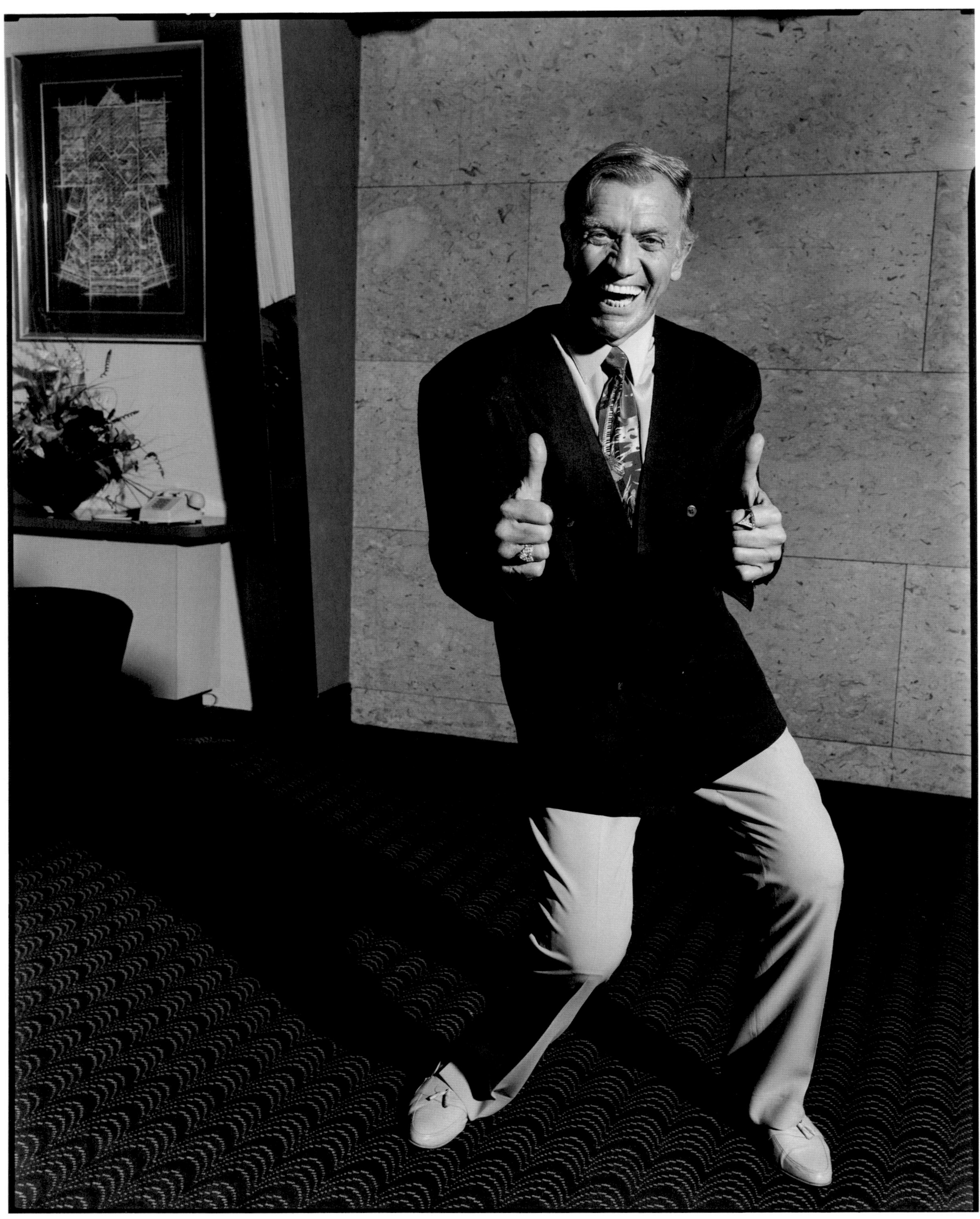

Lucky Kargo, professional ballroom dancer, Sun Spa, Miami, Florida, 1993

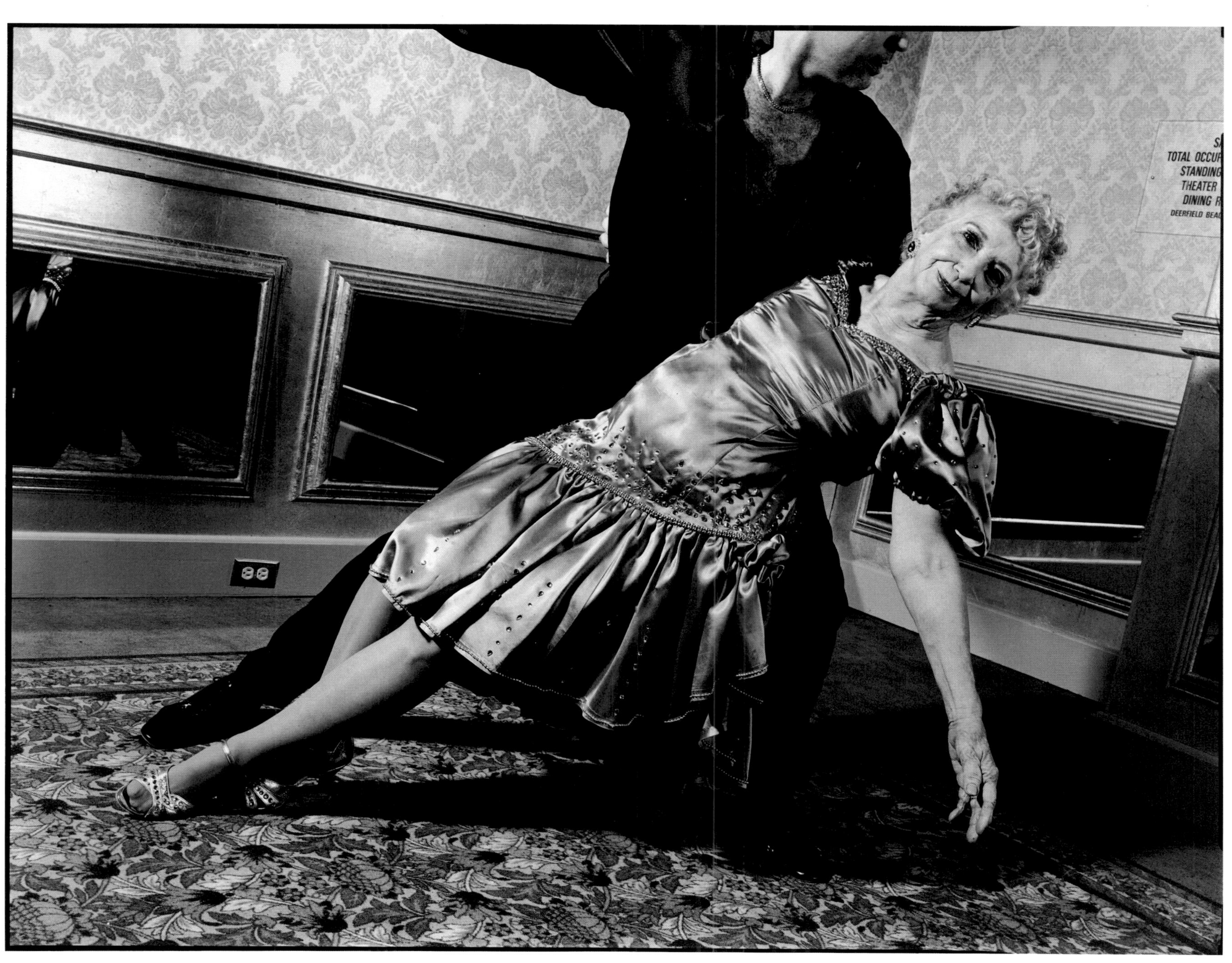

Jerry Hill and Margaret Sell, Hilton Hotel Dance Showcase, Boca Raton, Florida, 1993

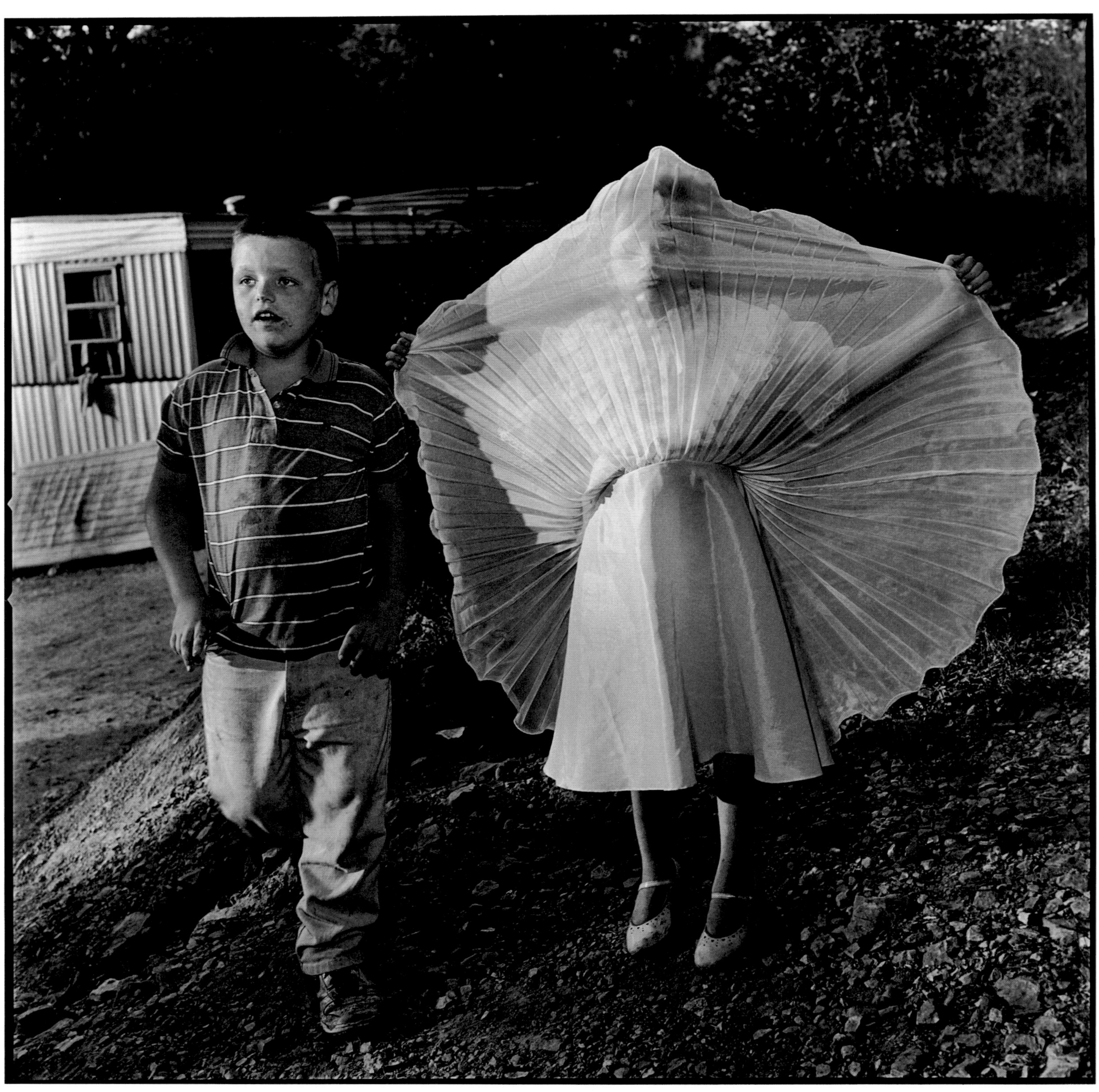

Jeff Gilman and Stacy Spivey, McKee, Kentucky, 1990

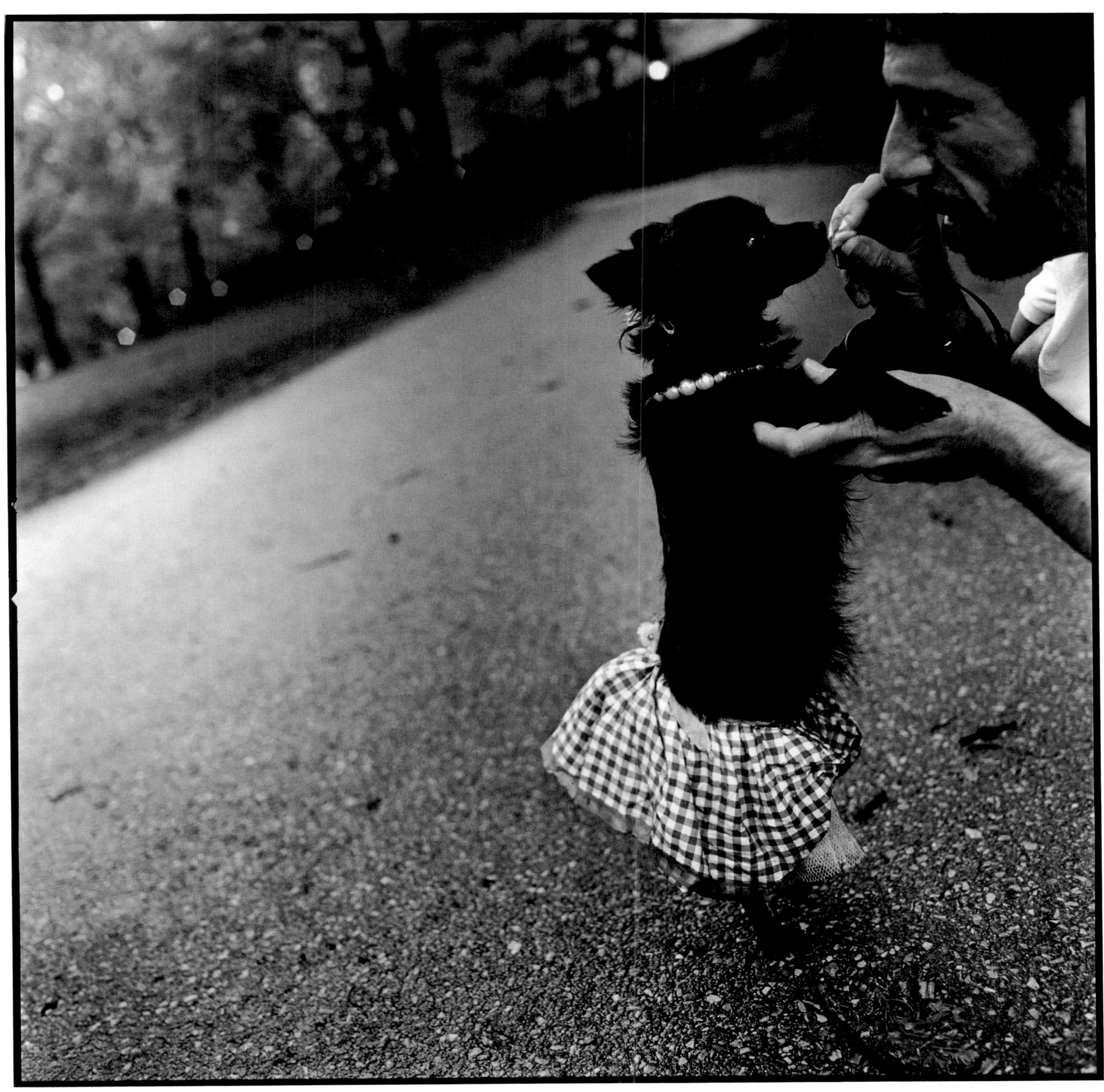

Paws Walk, New York City, 1994

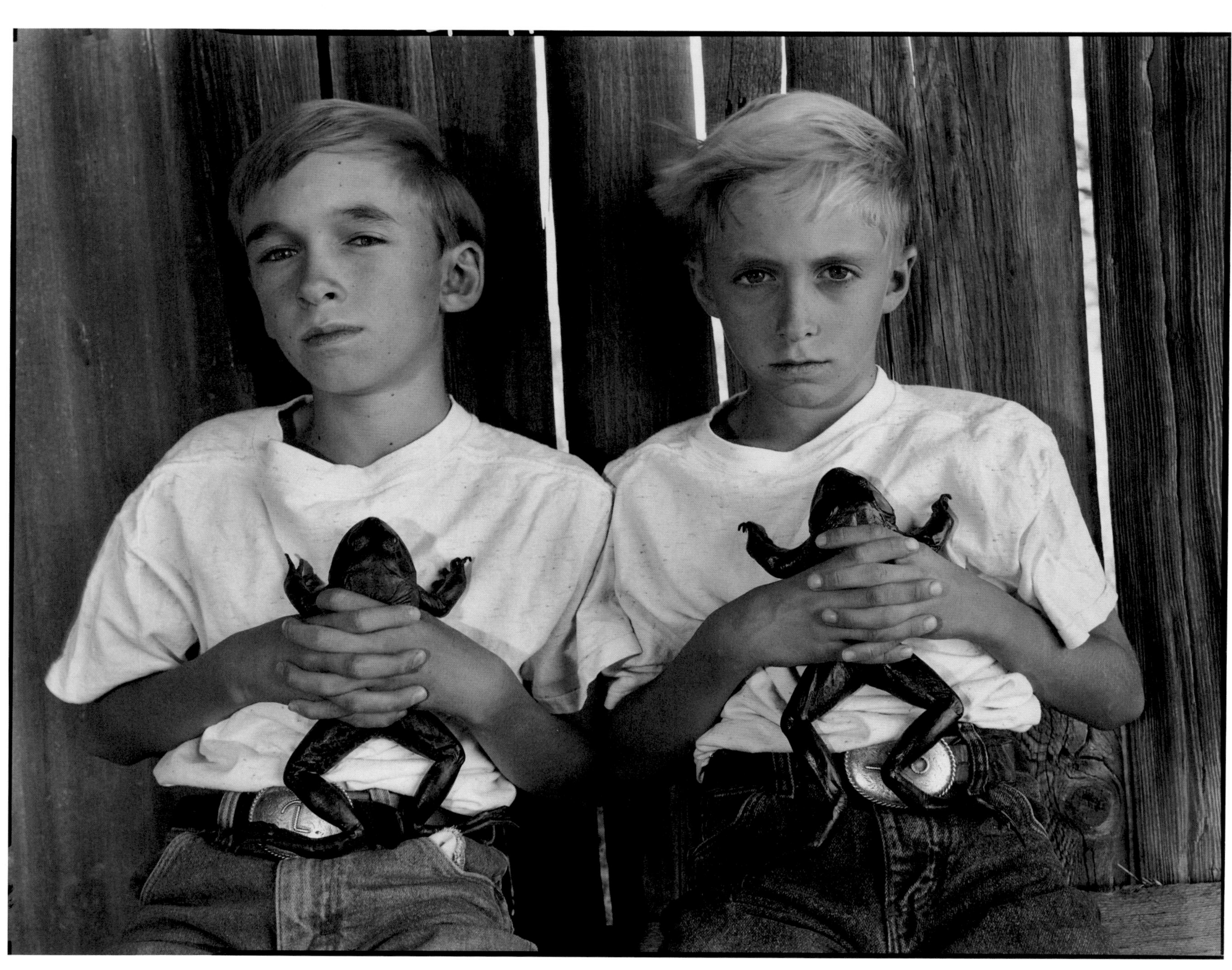

Mike and Chris Magoffin, San Bernadino Valley, Arizona, 1995

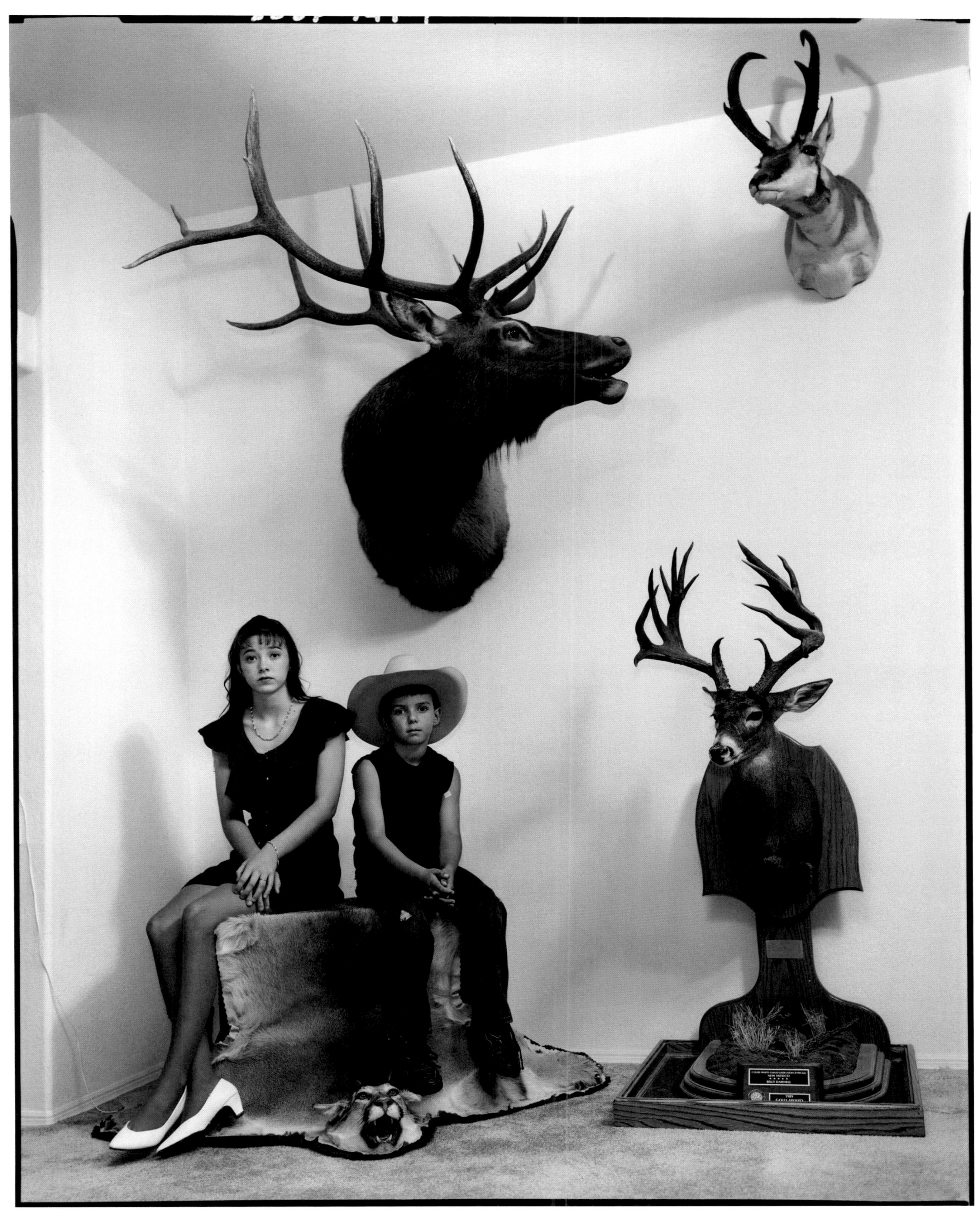

Jamie Diaz and Jesse Darnell, Animas Valley, New Mexico, 1995

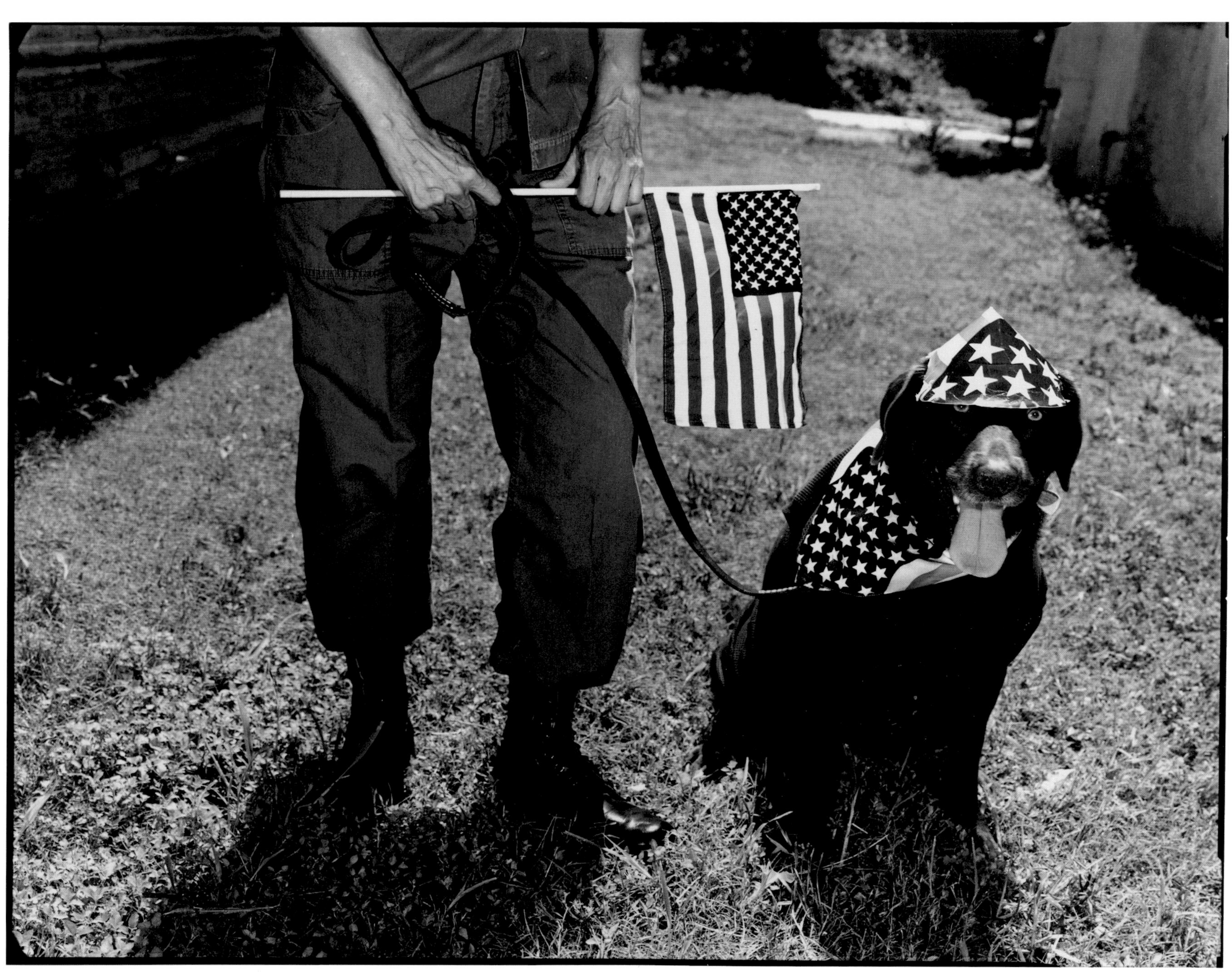

Champion Mocha of Oz, Leakey, Texas, 1991

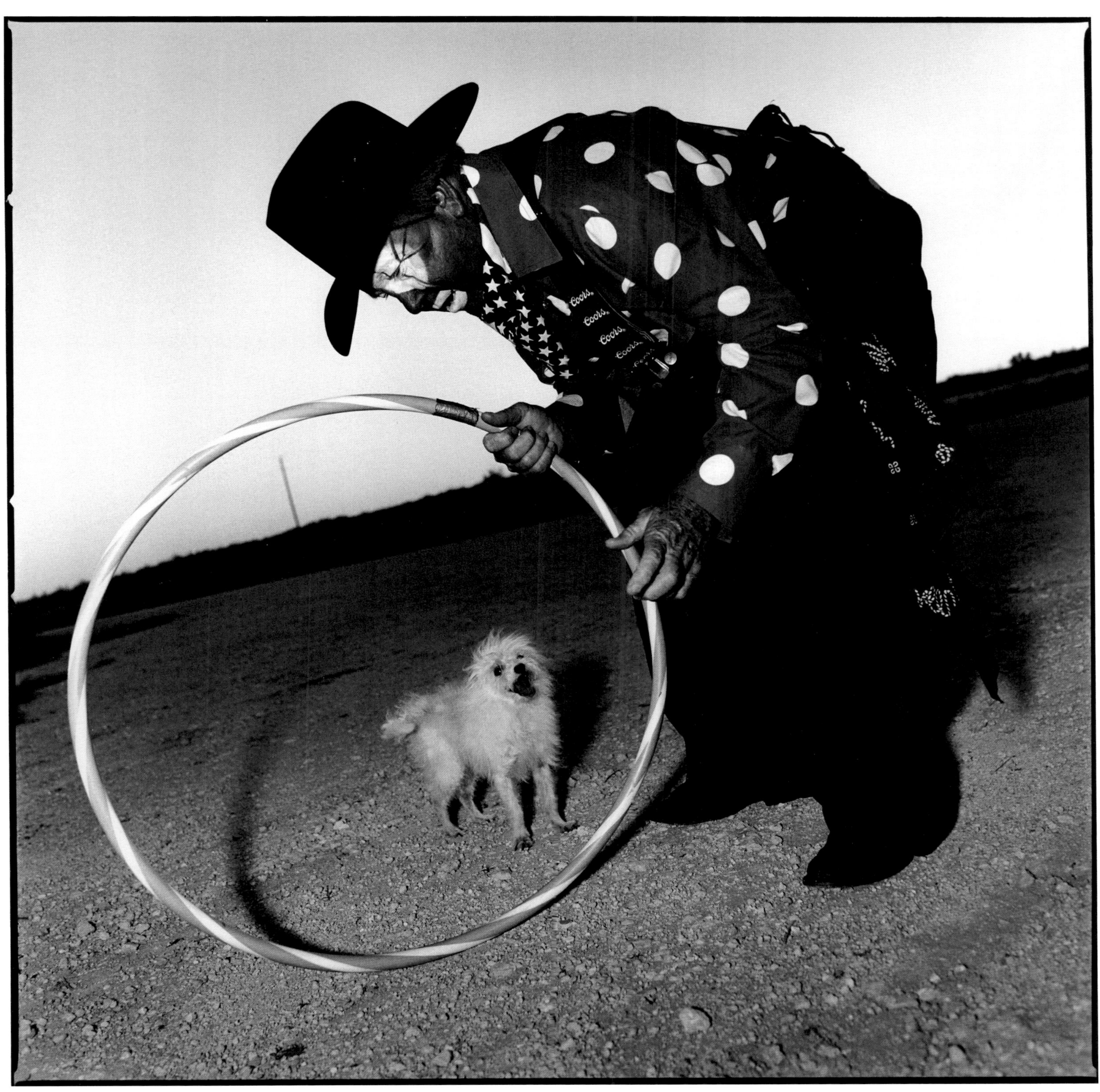

Rodeo clown, Quail Dobbs and Phyllis, Rock Springs, Texas, 1991

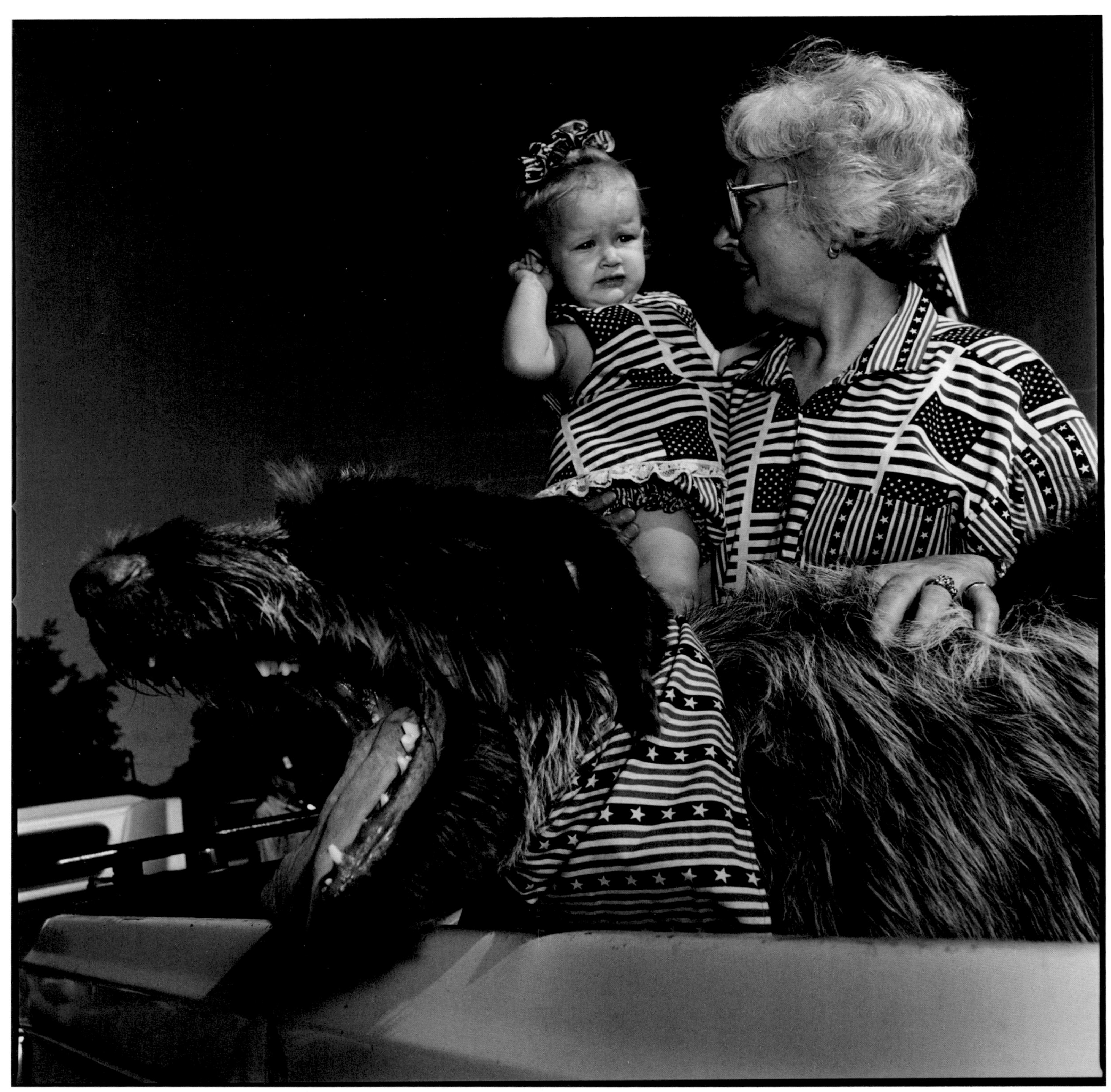

Rodeo, Leakey, Texas, 1991

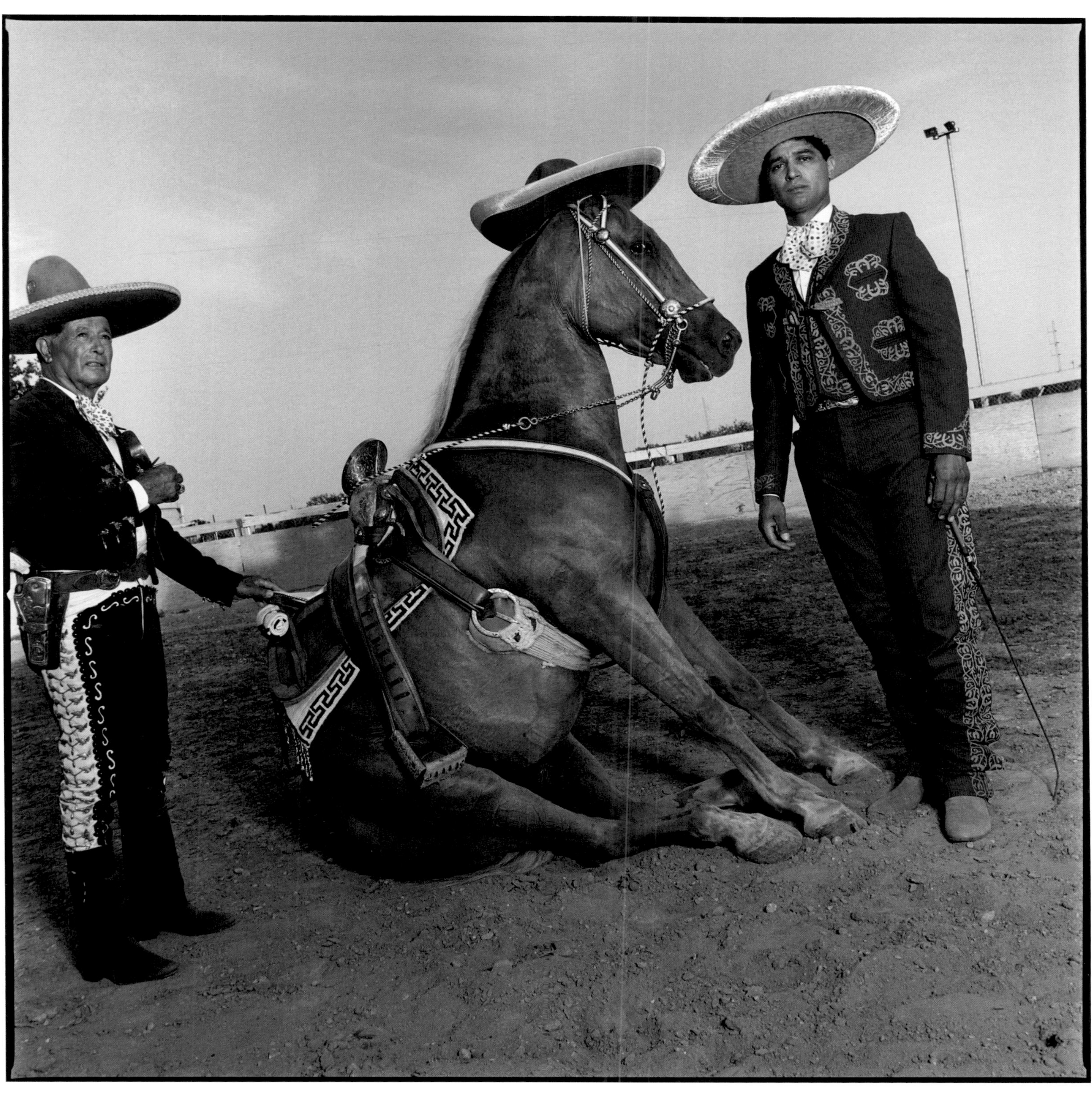

Jose "Pepe" Diaz and son Jerry with their horse, Rock Springs Rodeo, San Antonio, Texas, 1991

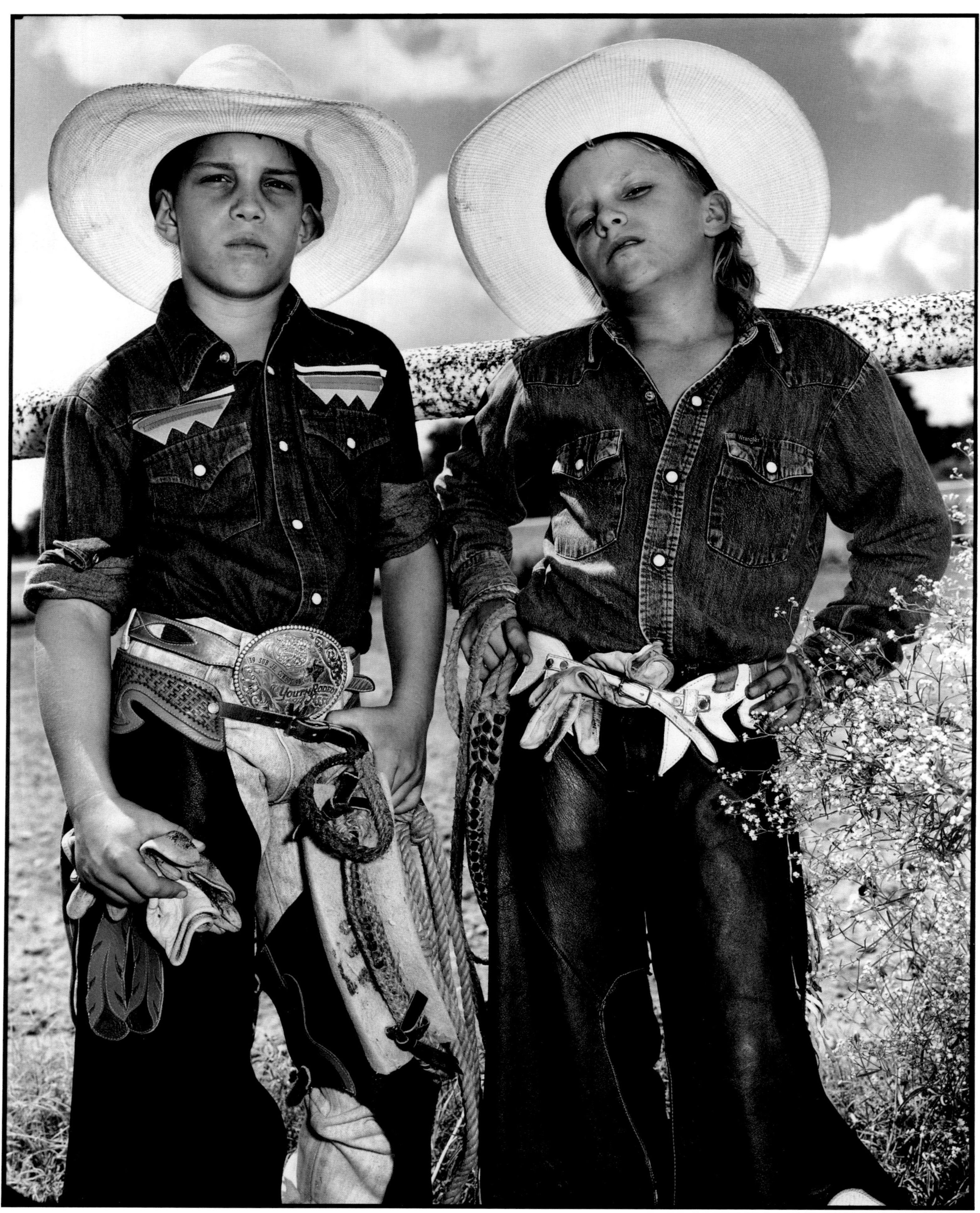

Bull riders Craig Scarmardo and Cheyloh Mather, Boerne Rodeo, Texas, 1991

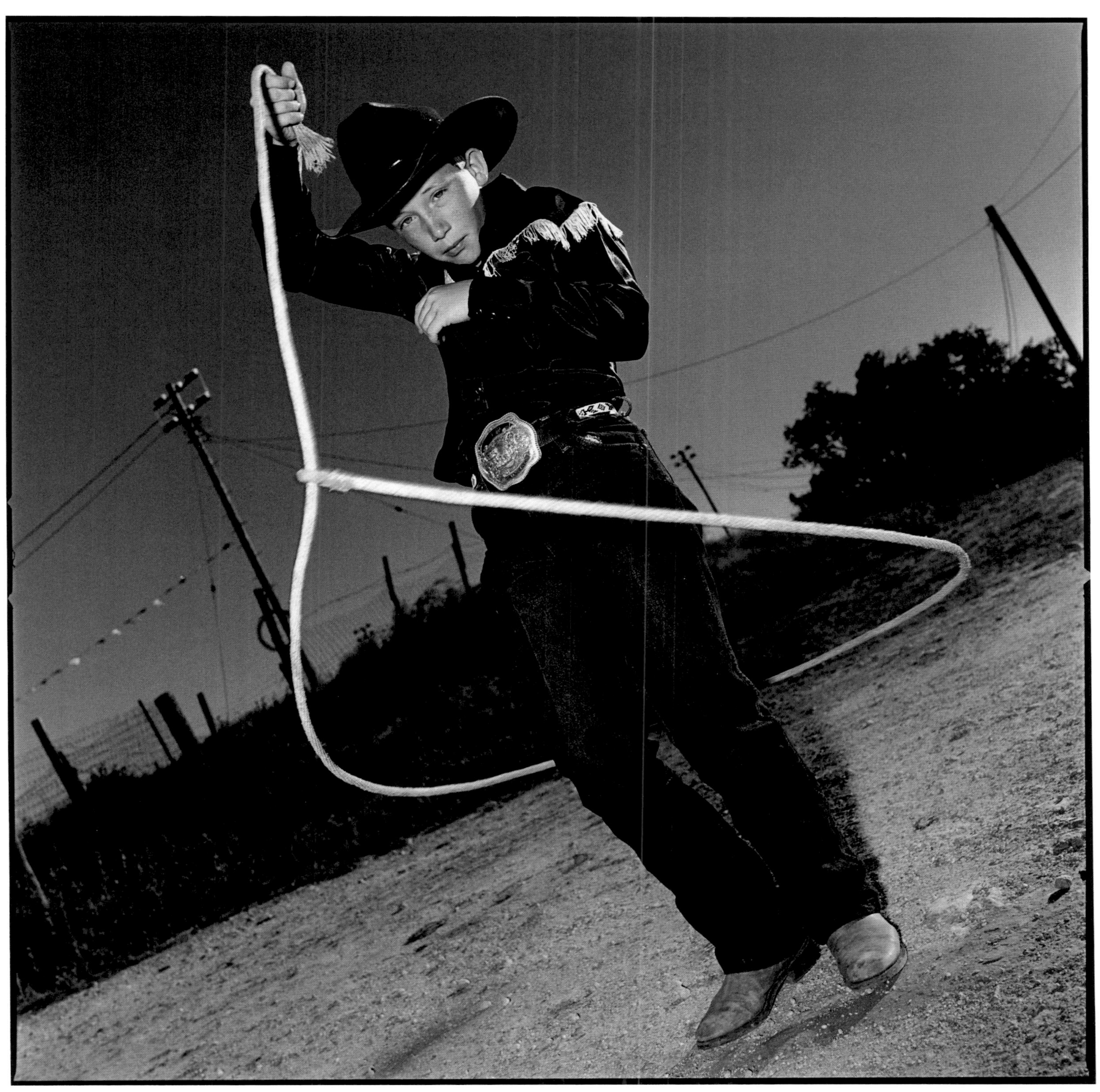

Arles Pearce, Big Spring Rodeo, Texas, 1991

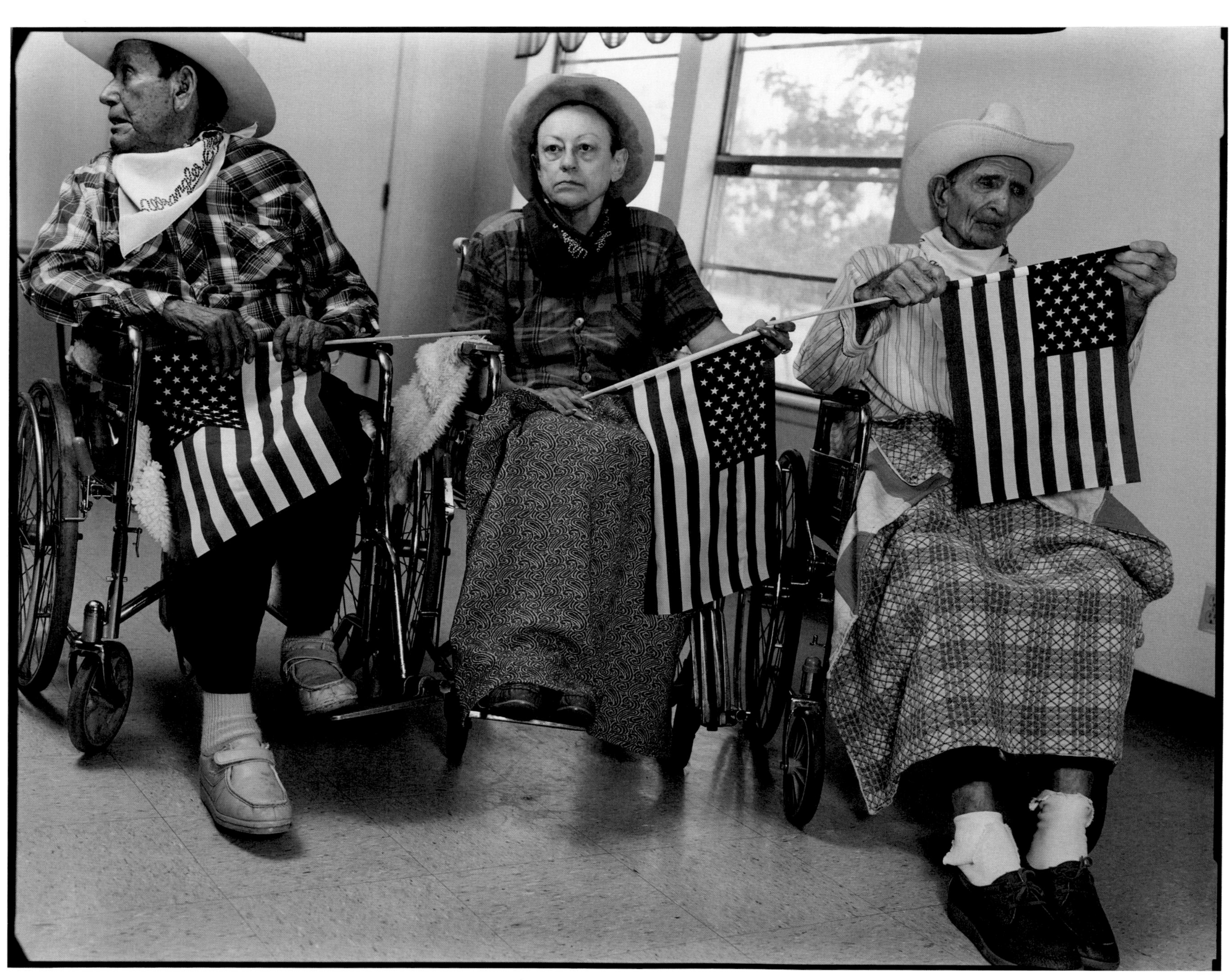

Retired rodeo performers, Leakey, Texas, 1991

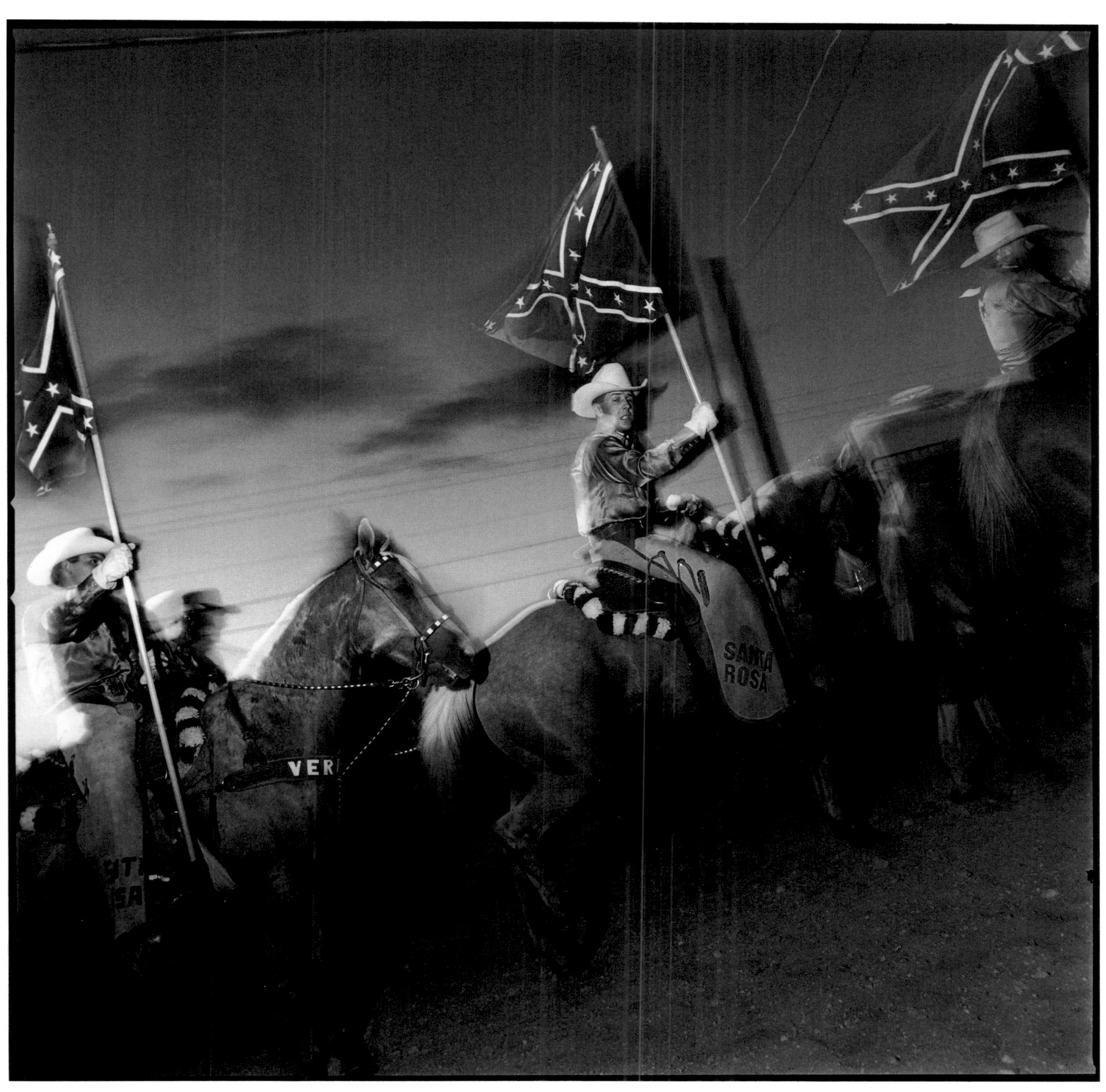

Big Spring Rodeo, Texas, 1991

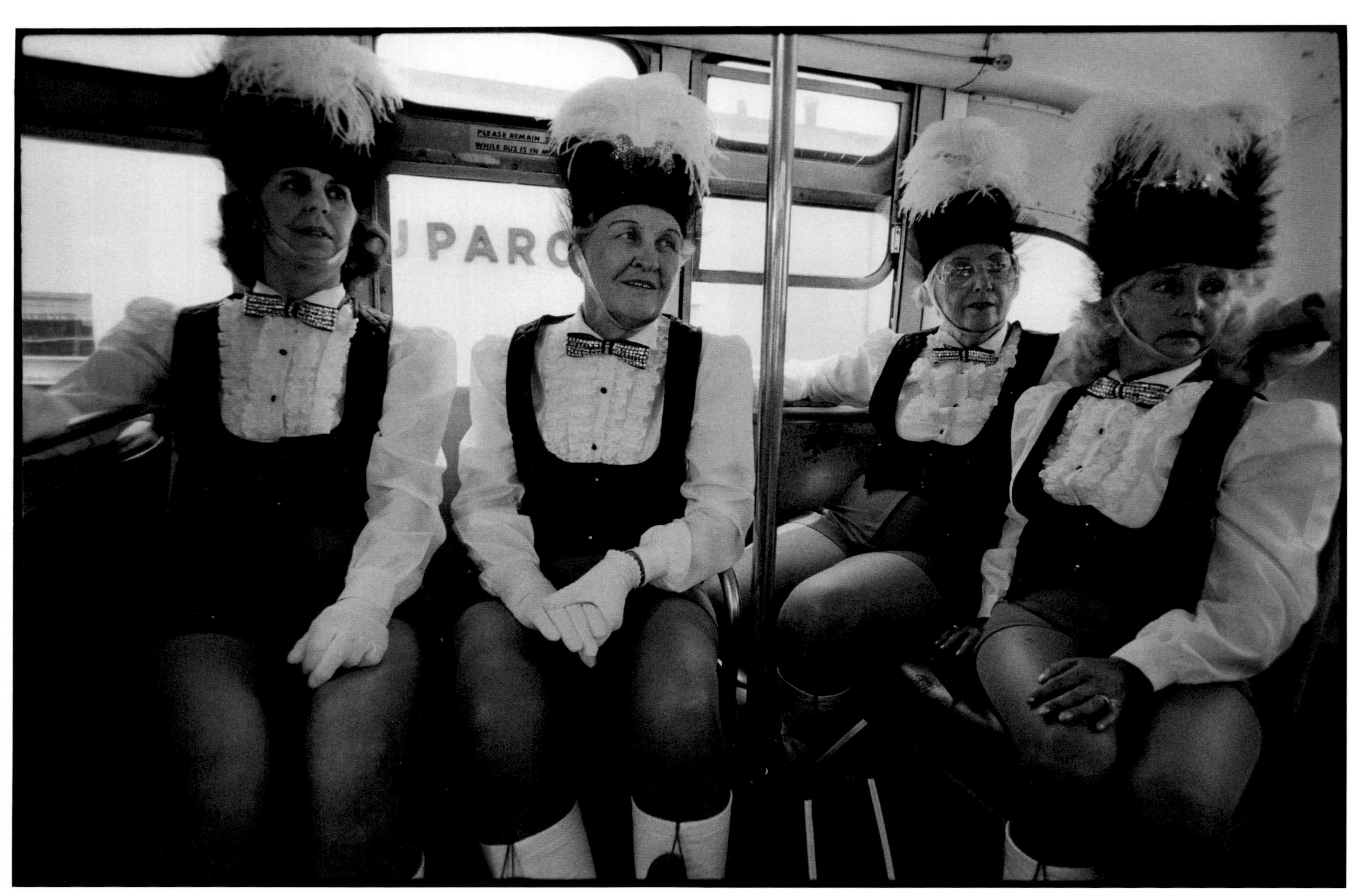

Dance class, St. Petersburg, Florida, 1986

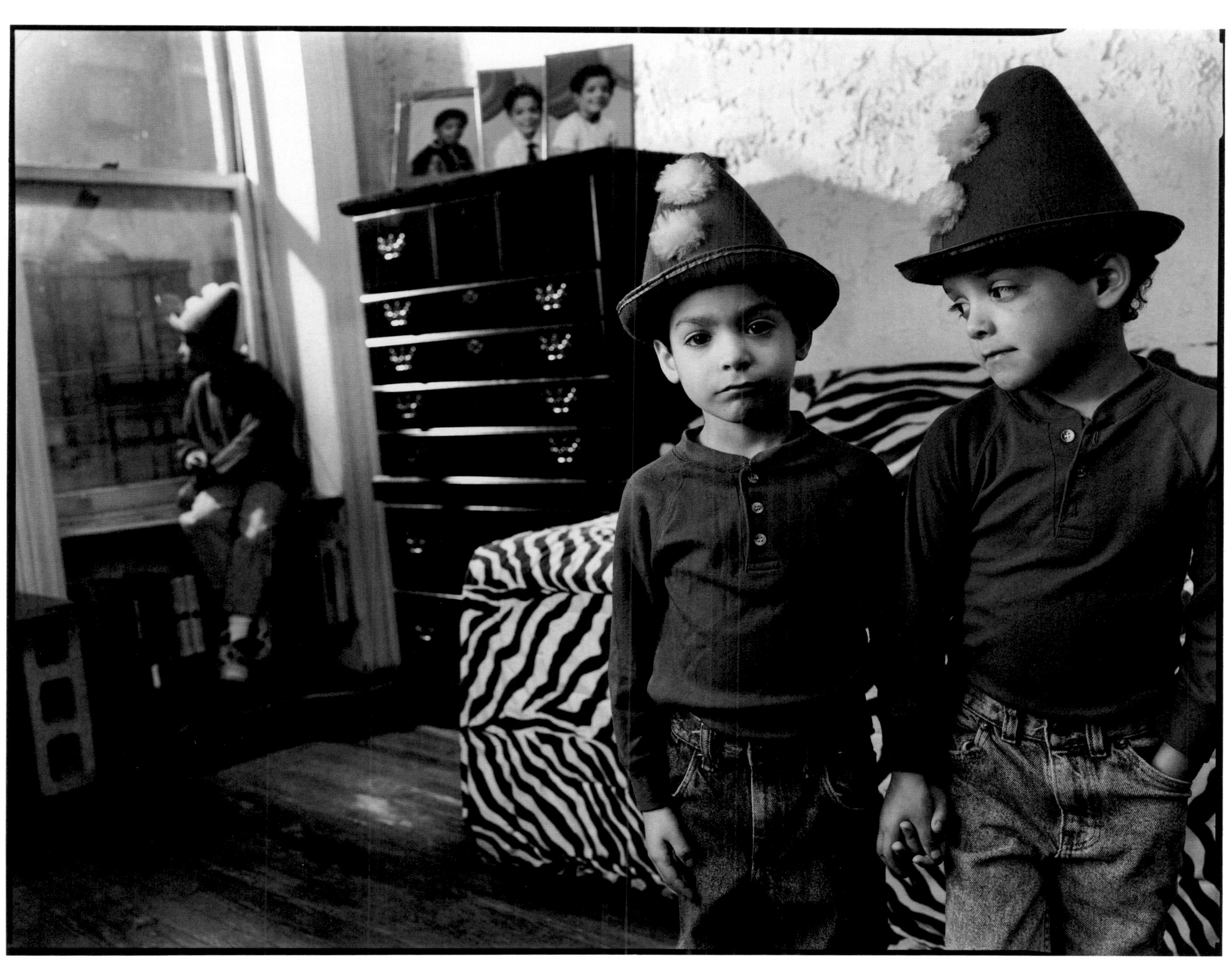

Adopted children, New York Ci-y, 1993

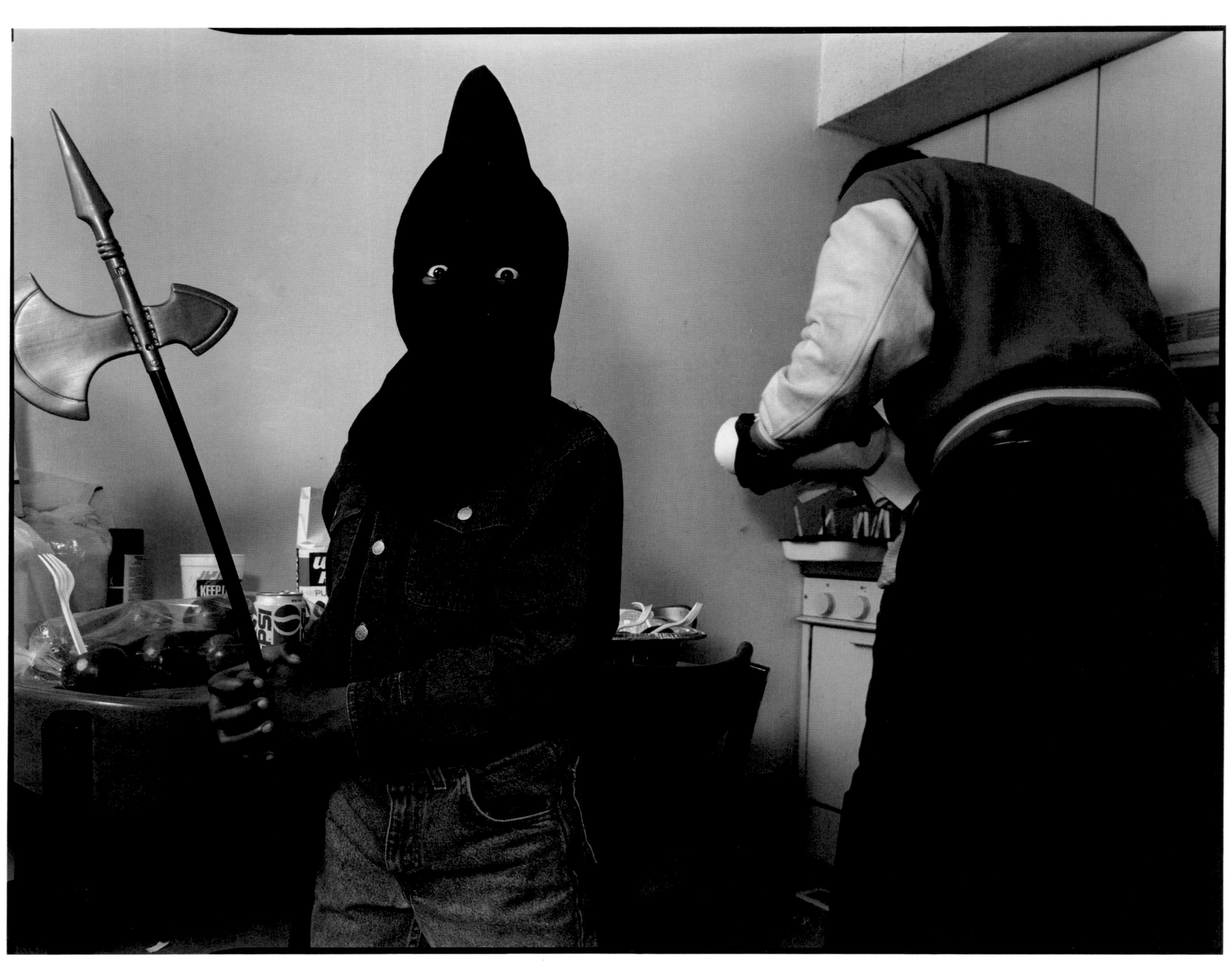

Edward Simmons, Halloween, South Bronx H.E.L.P. Shelter, New York, 1993

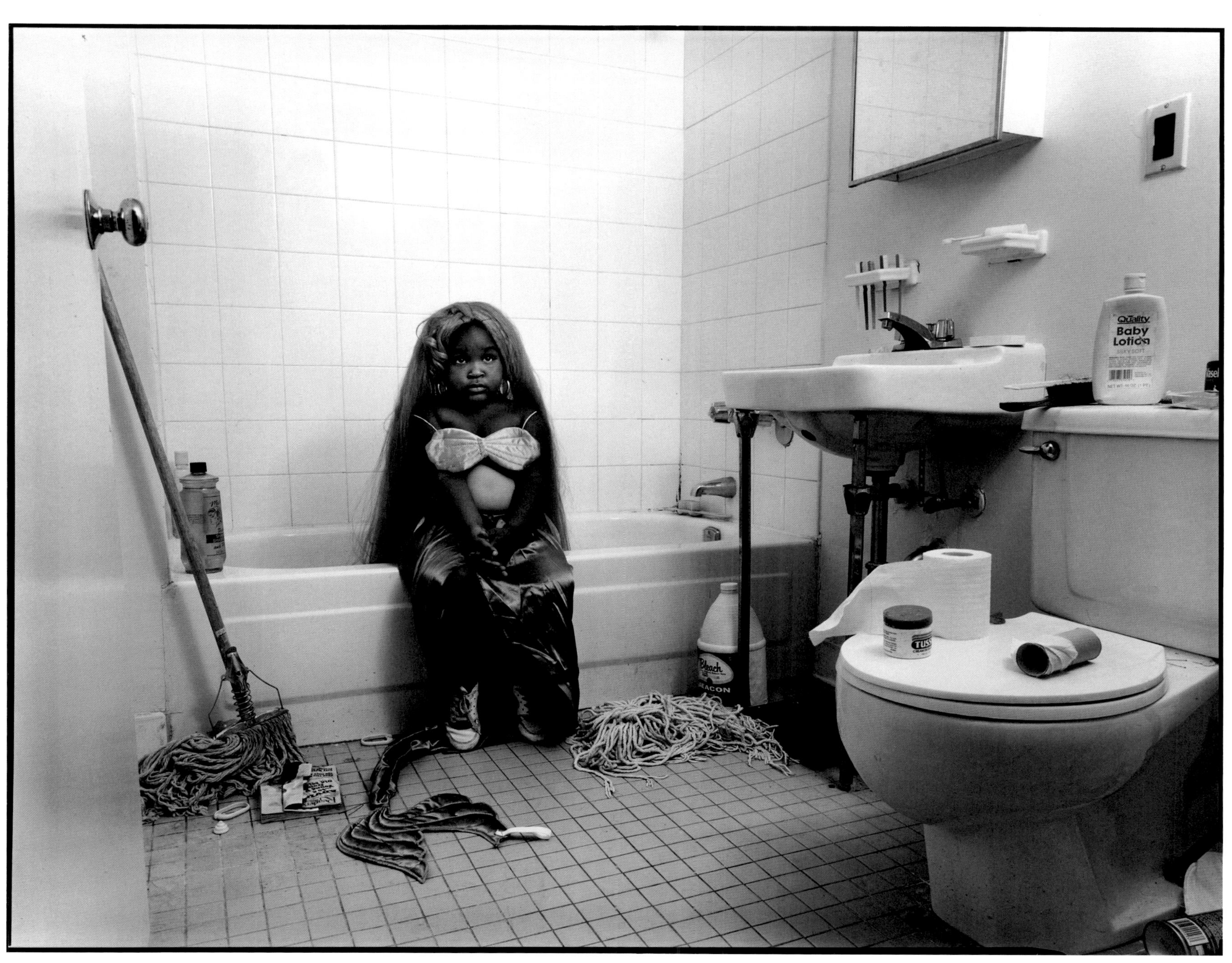

Diamond Settles, Halloween, South Bronx H.E.L.P. Shelter, New York, 1993

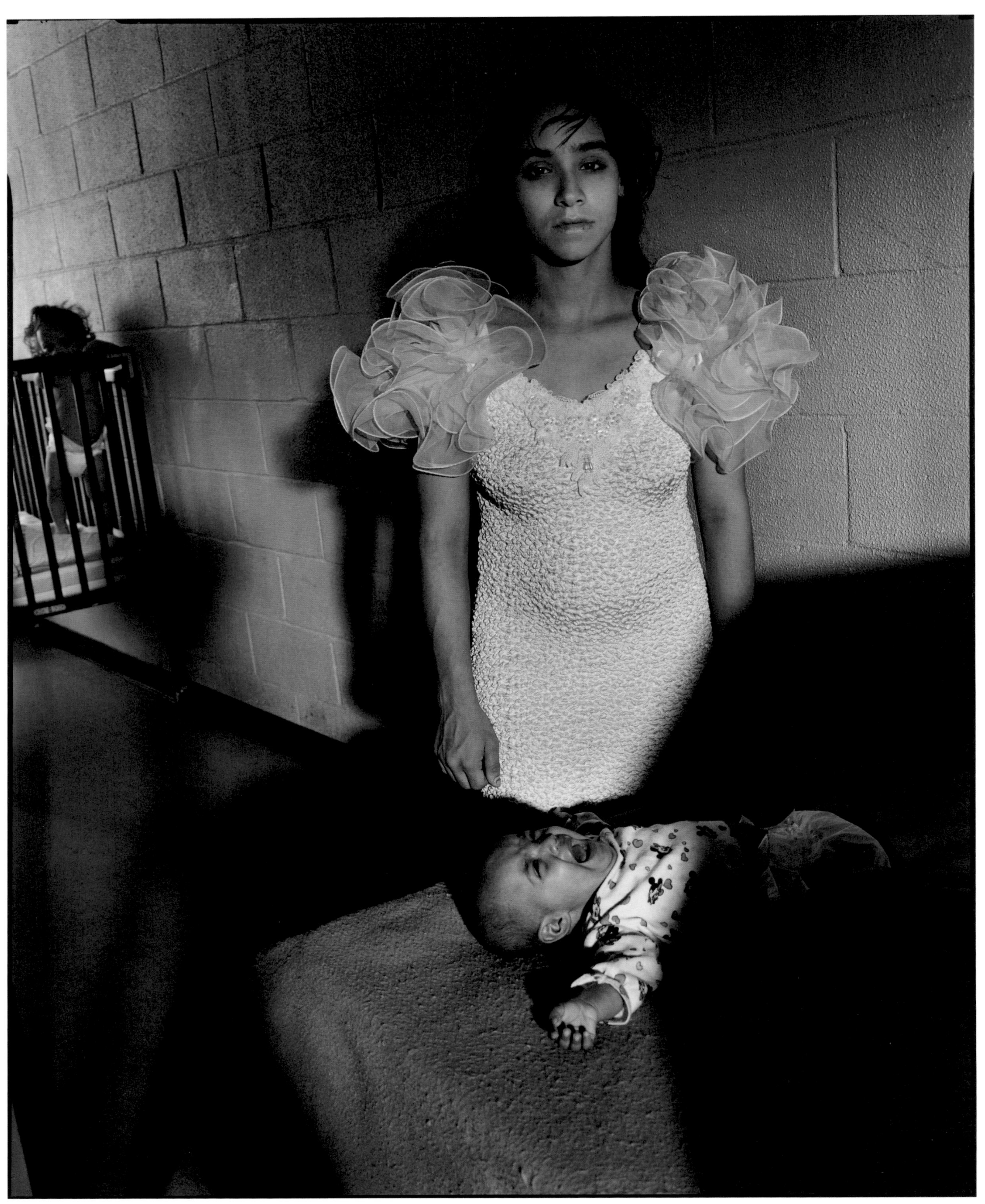

Nellie Torres with her children, Yasmine and Bianca, South Bronx H.E.L.P. Shelter, New York, 1993

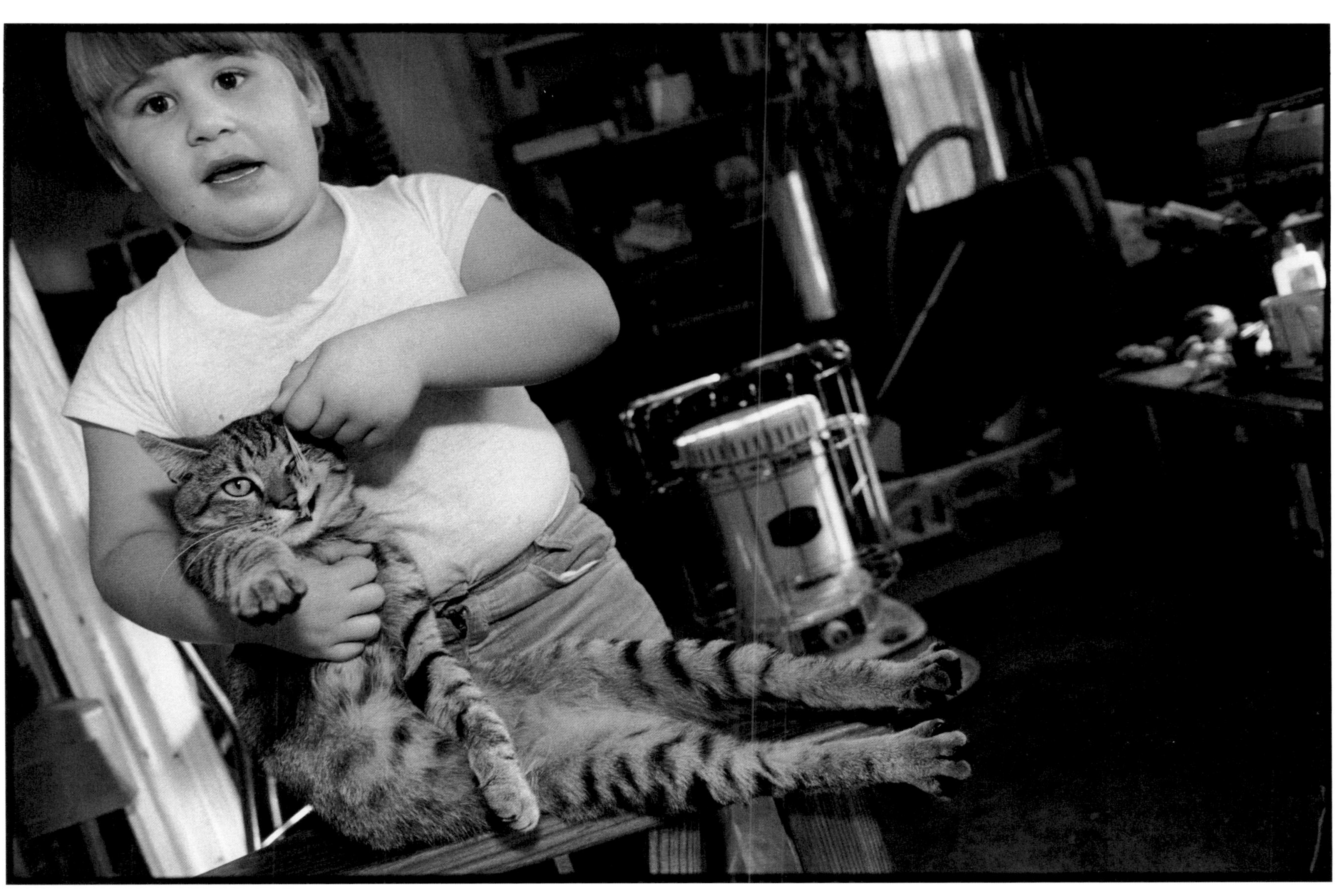

Roland Riley pulling his cat's whiskers, Belfast, Maine, 1990

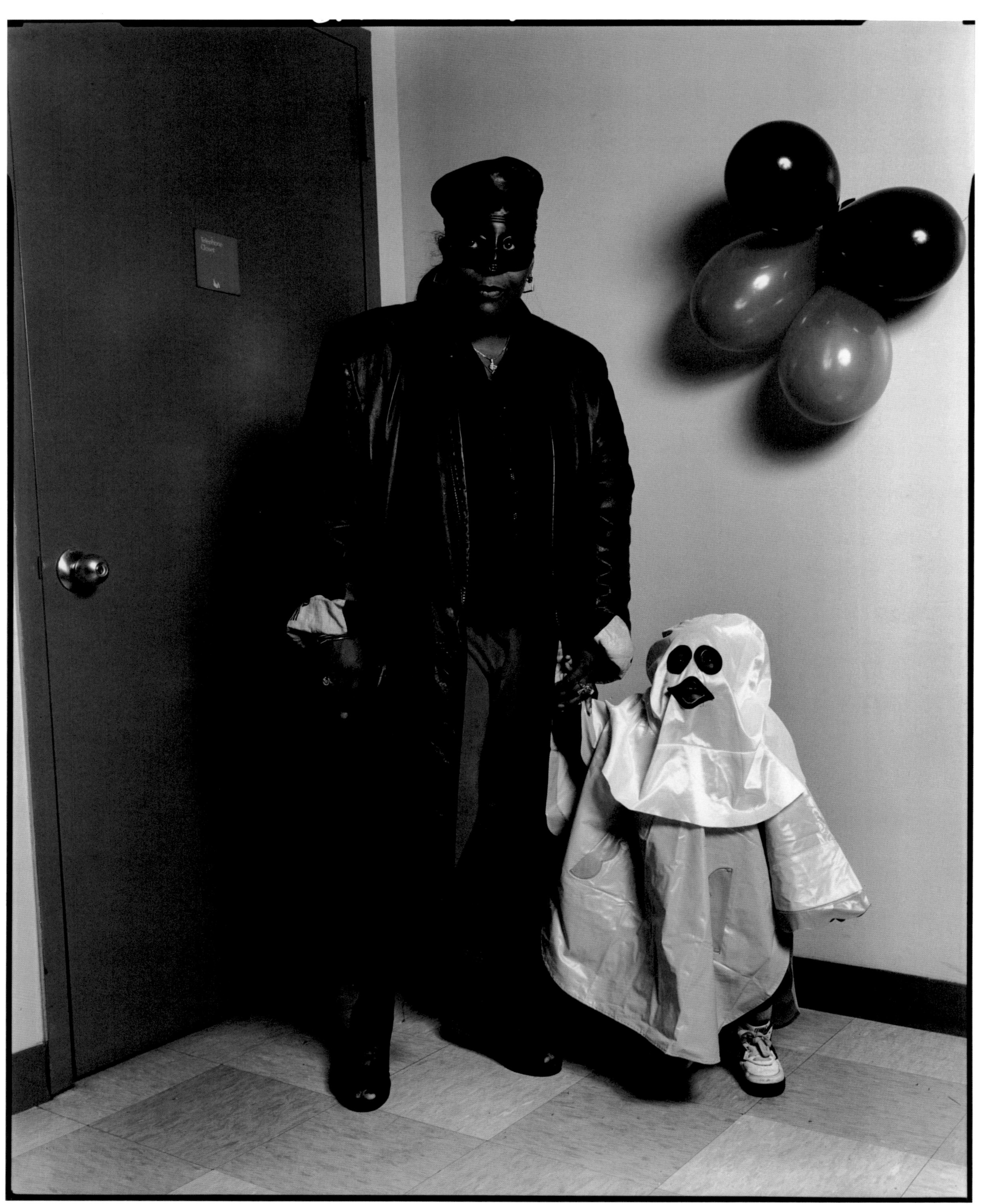

Robin and Azizuddin Clark, Halloween, South Bronx H.E.L.P. Shelter, New York, 1993

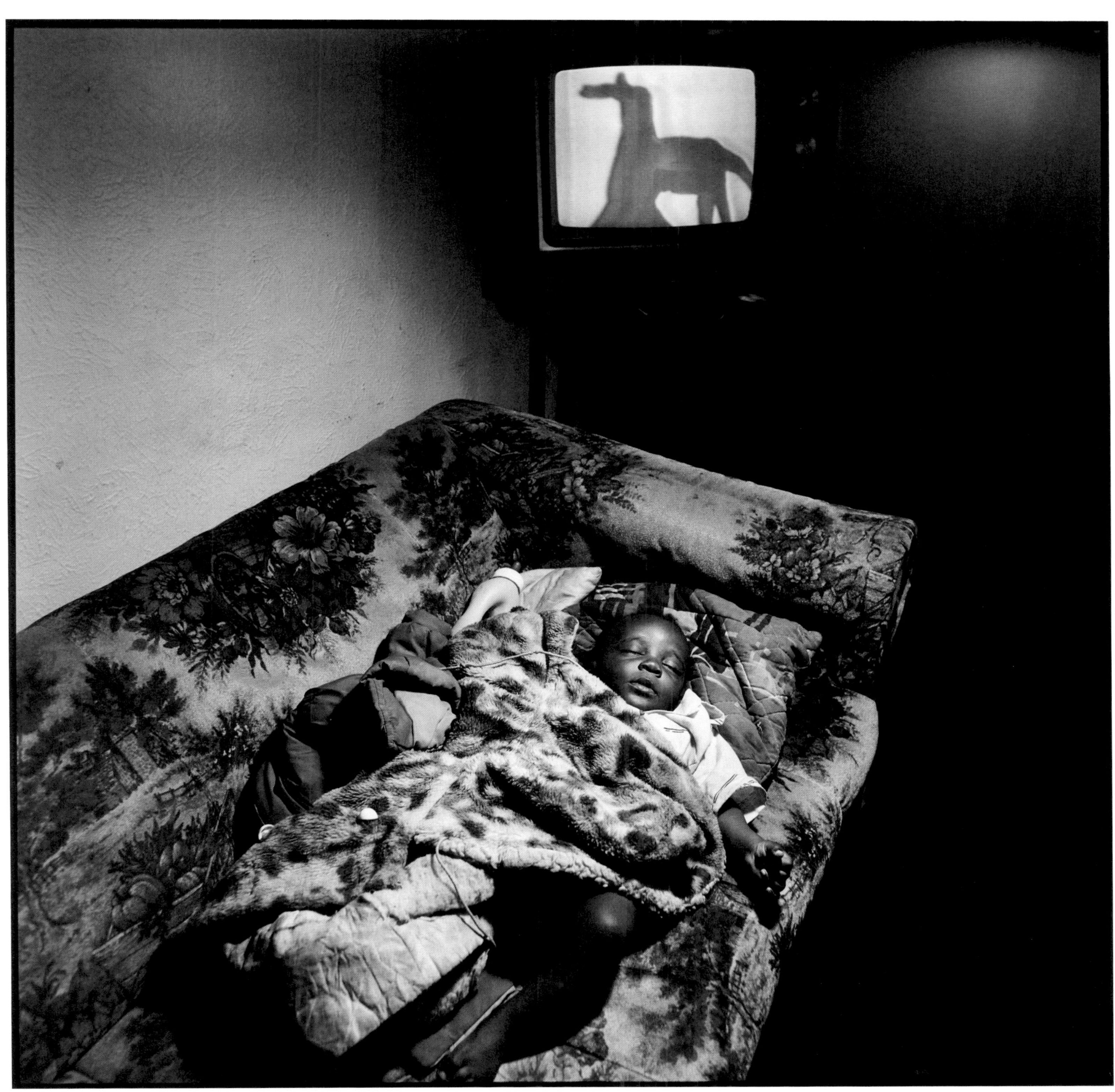

Lakiesha Rudd, South Dallas, Texas, 1988

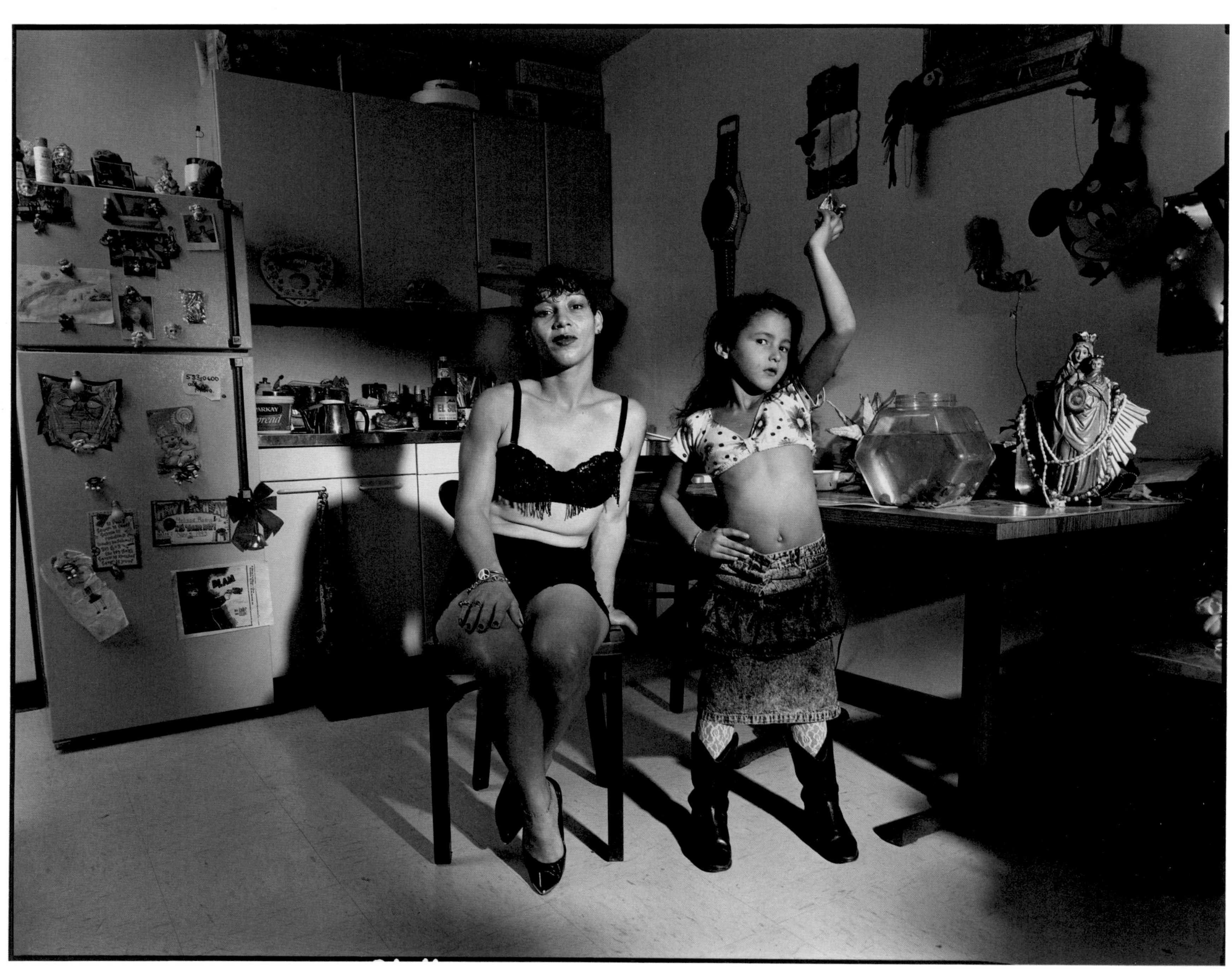

South Bronx H.E.L.P. Shelter, New York, 1993

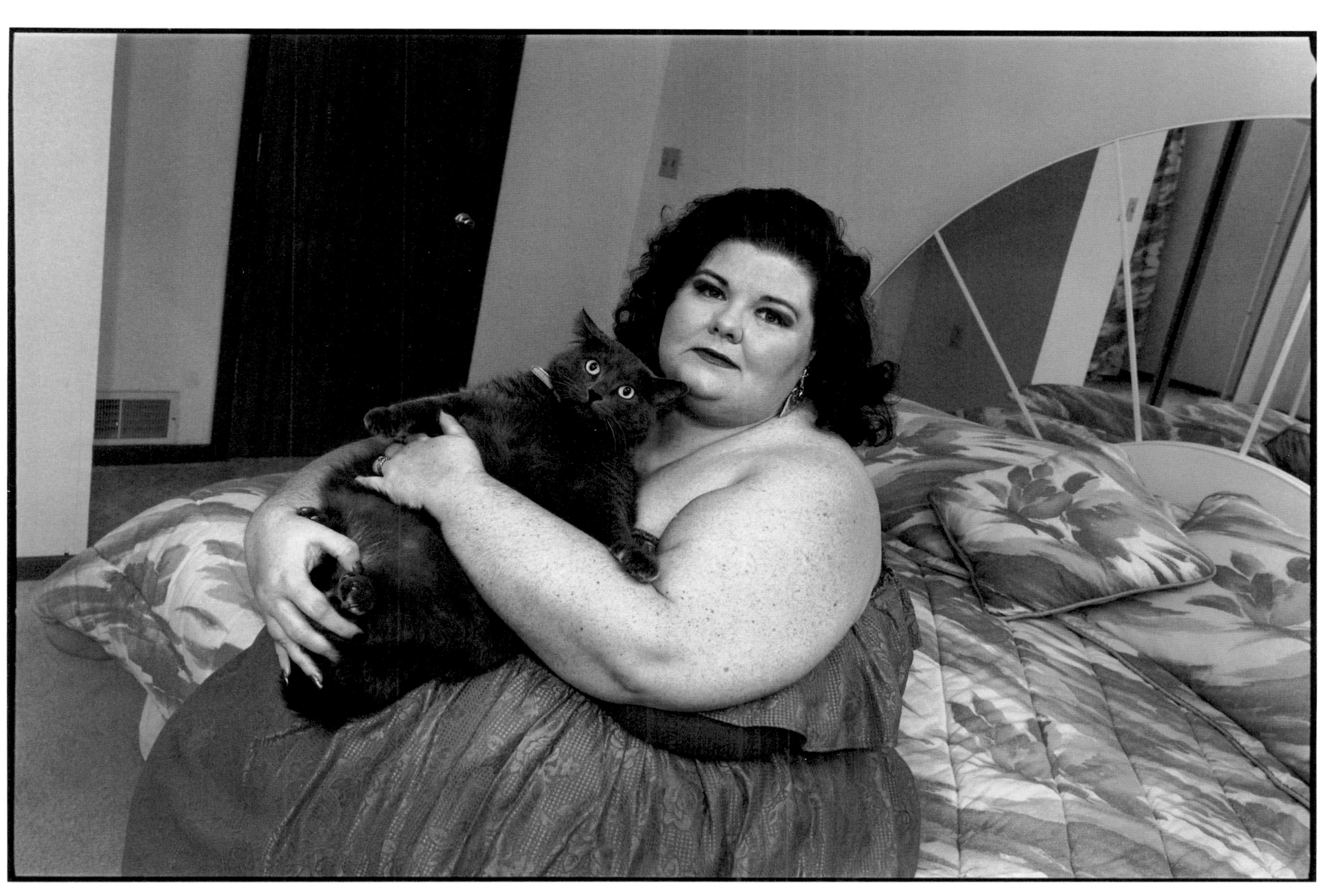

Sherry Collins Eckert with Madame Butterfly, Afton, Missouri, 1995

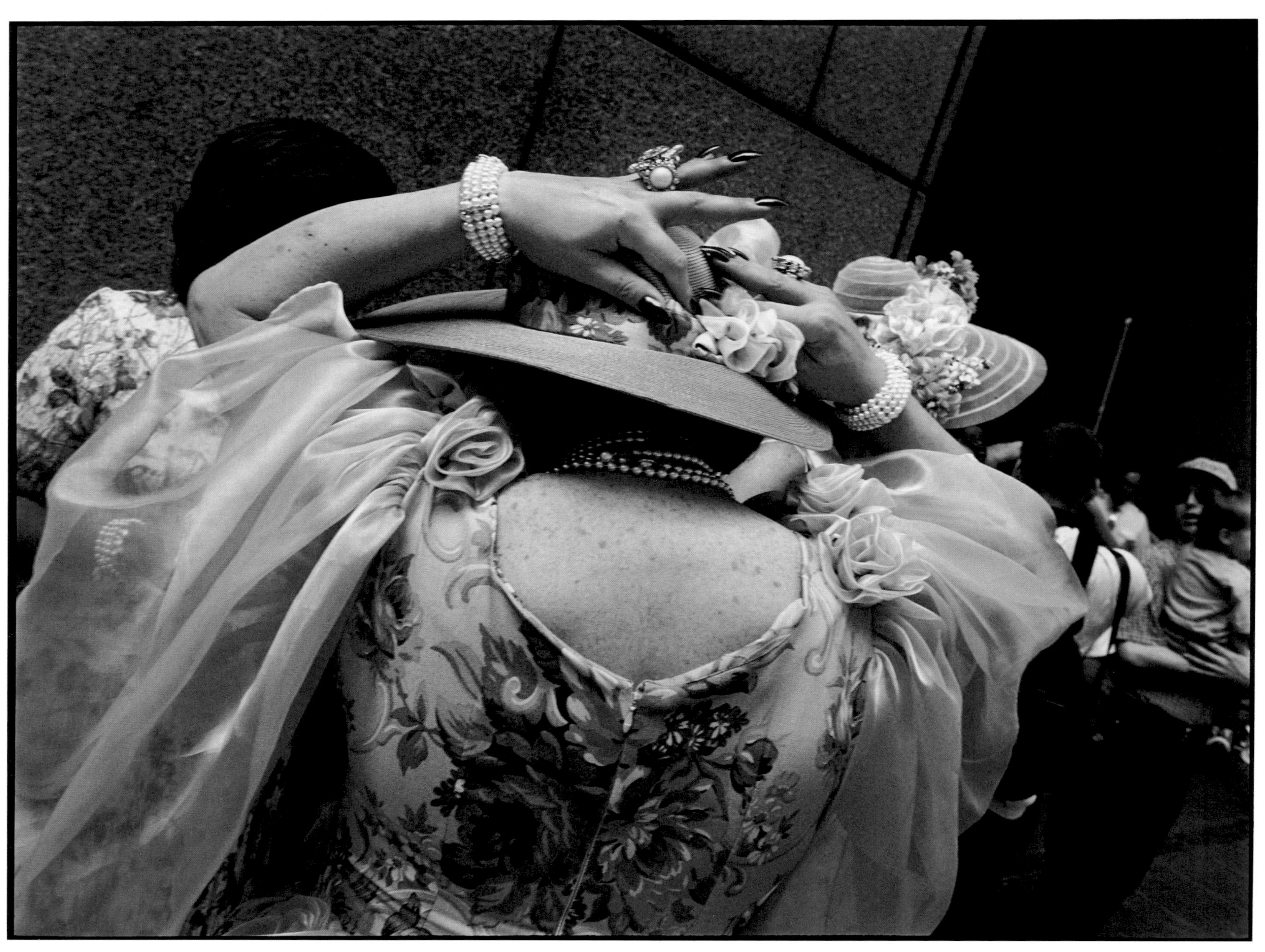

Gay Pride parade, New York City, 1998

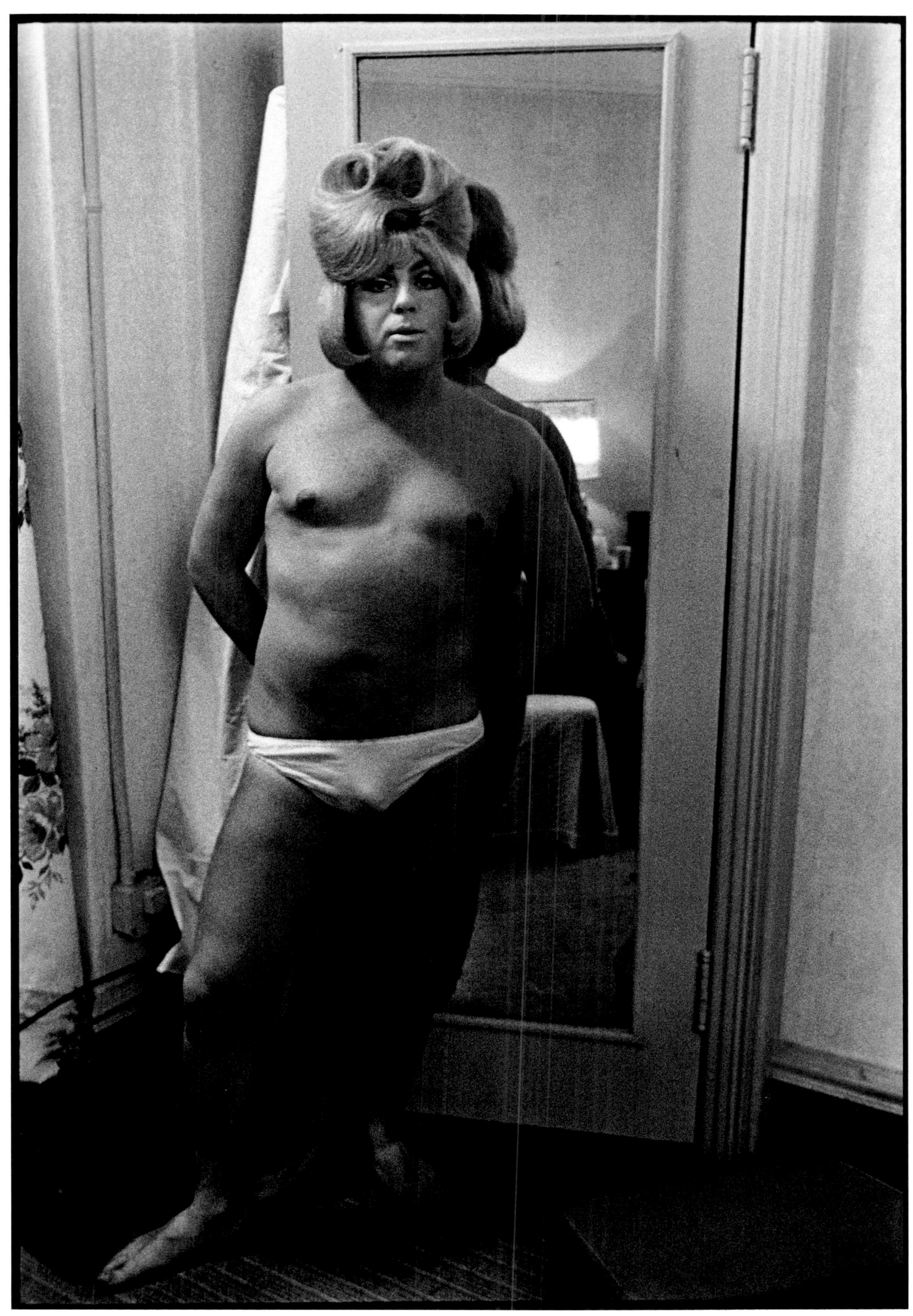

Transvestite getting ready for a contest, New York City, 1968

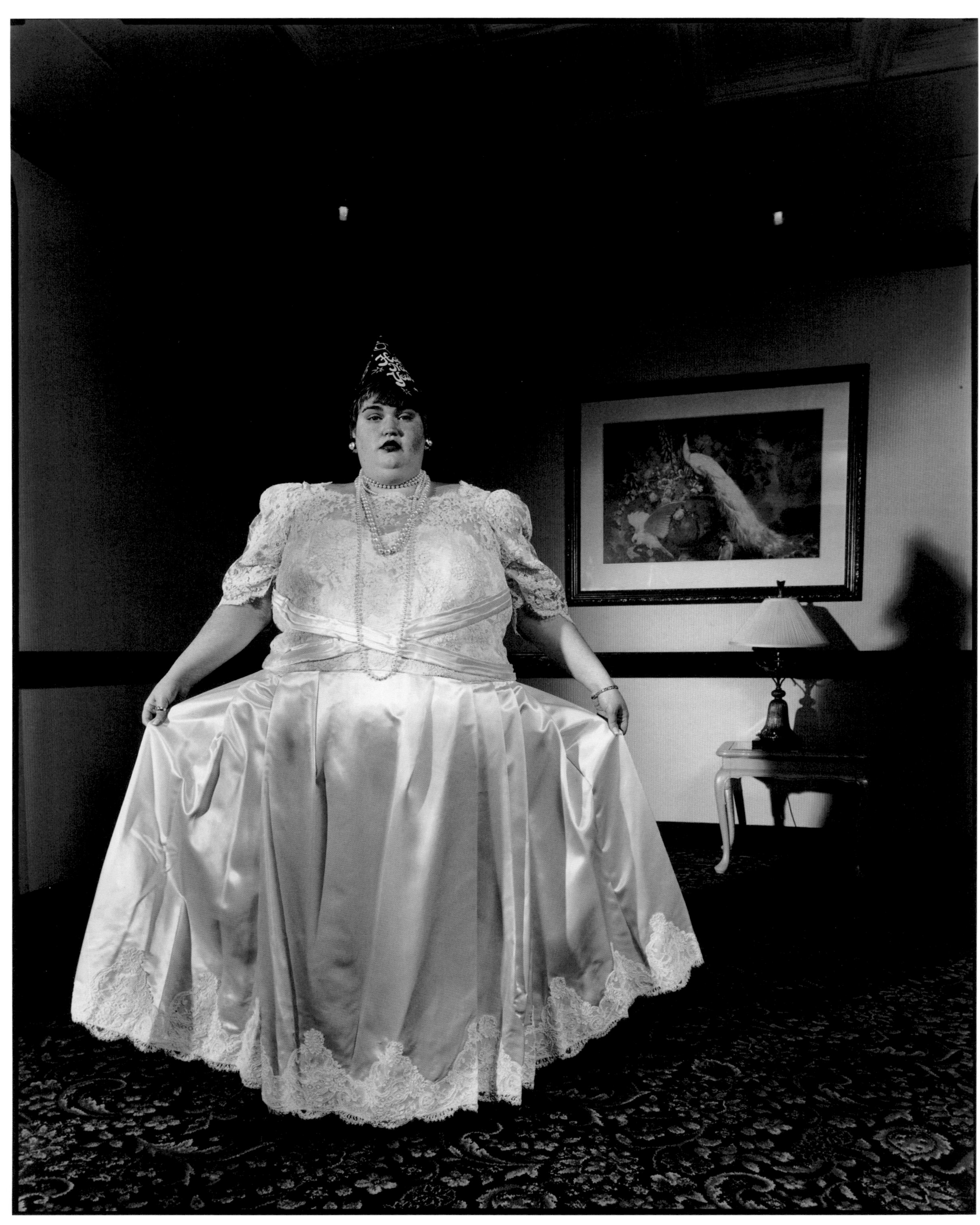

Julie d'Aquili, National Association to Advance Fat Acceptance, Big and Beautiful New Year's Eve party, Long Island, New York, 1995

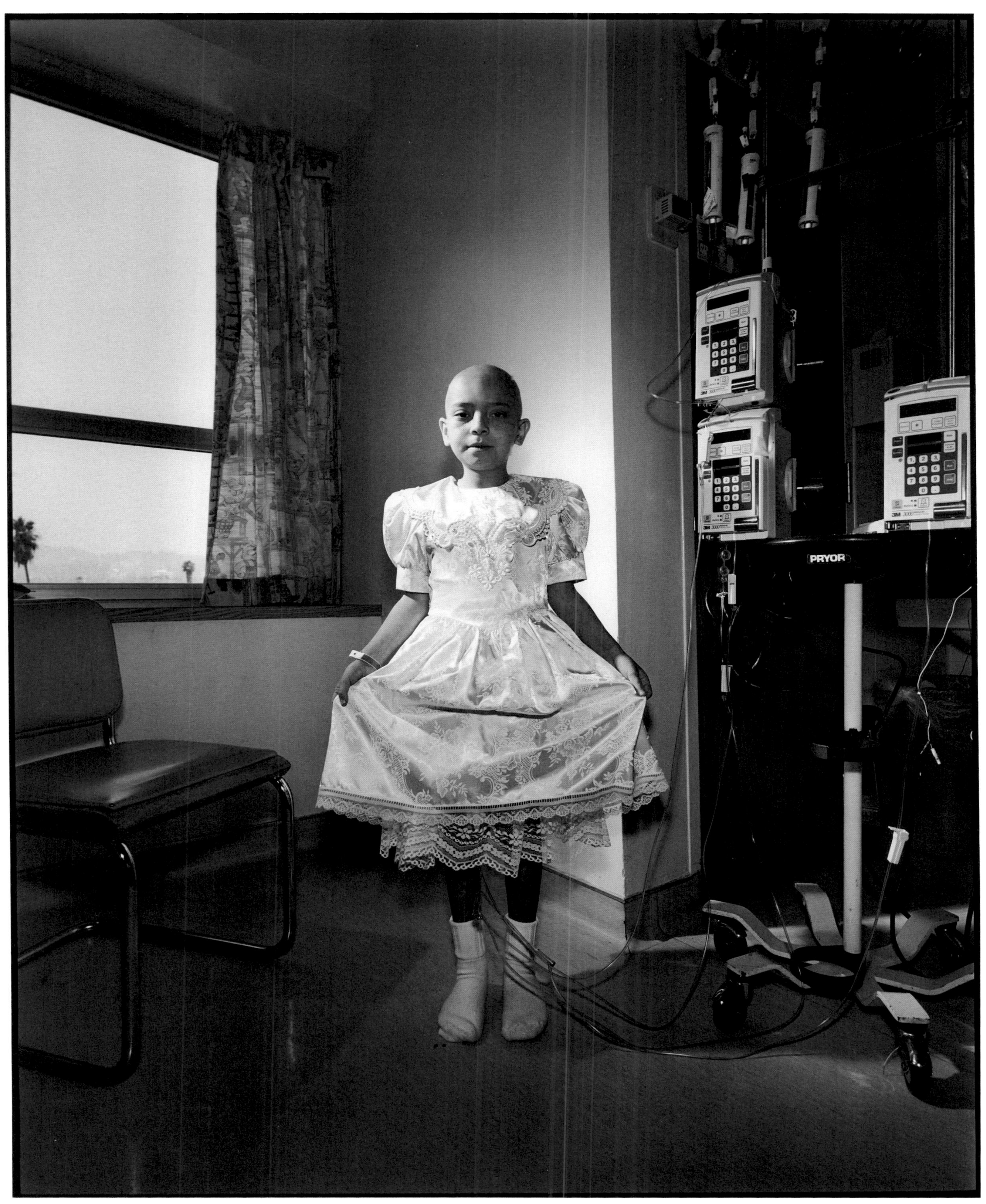

Cynthia Galves, Children's Hospital, Los Angeles, California, 1996

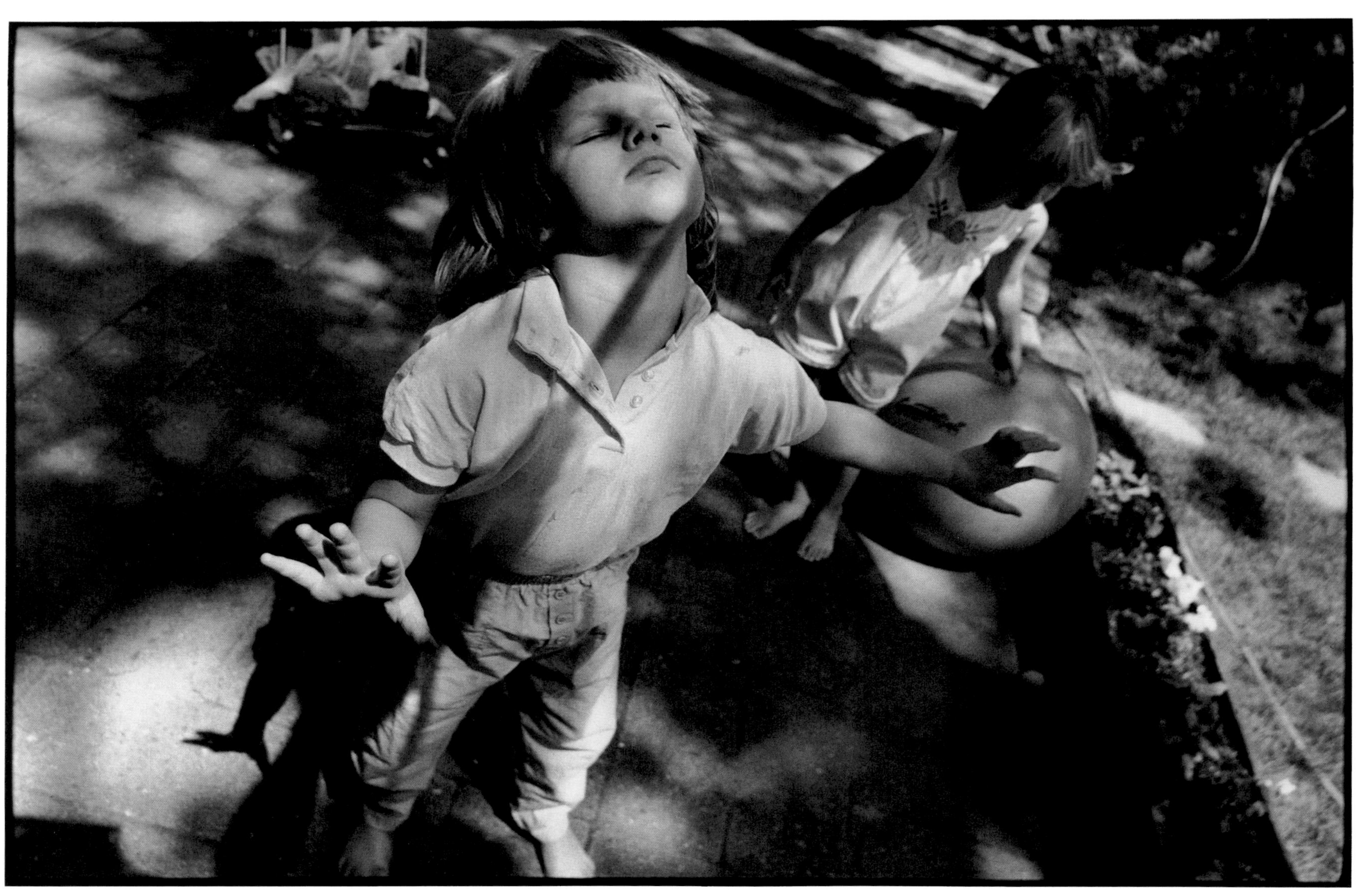

Lindsay, deaf and blind child, Watertown, Massachusetts, 1990

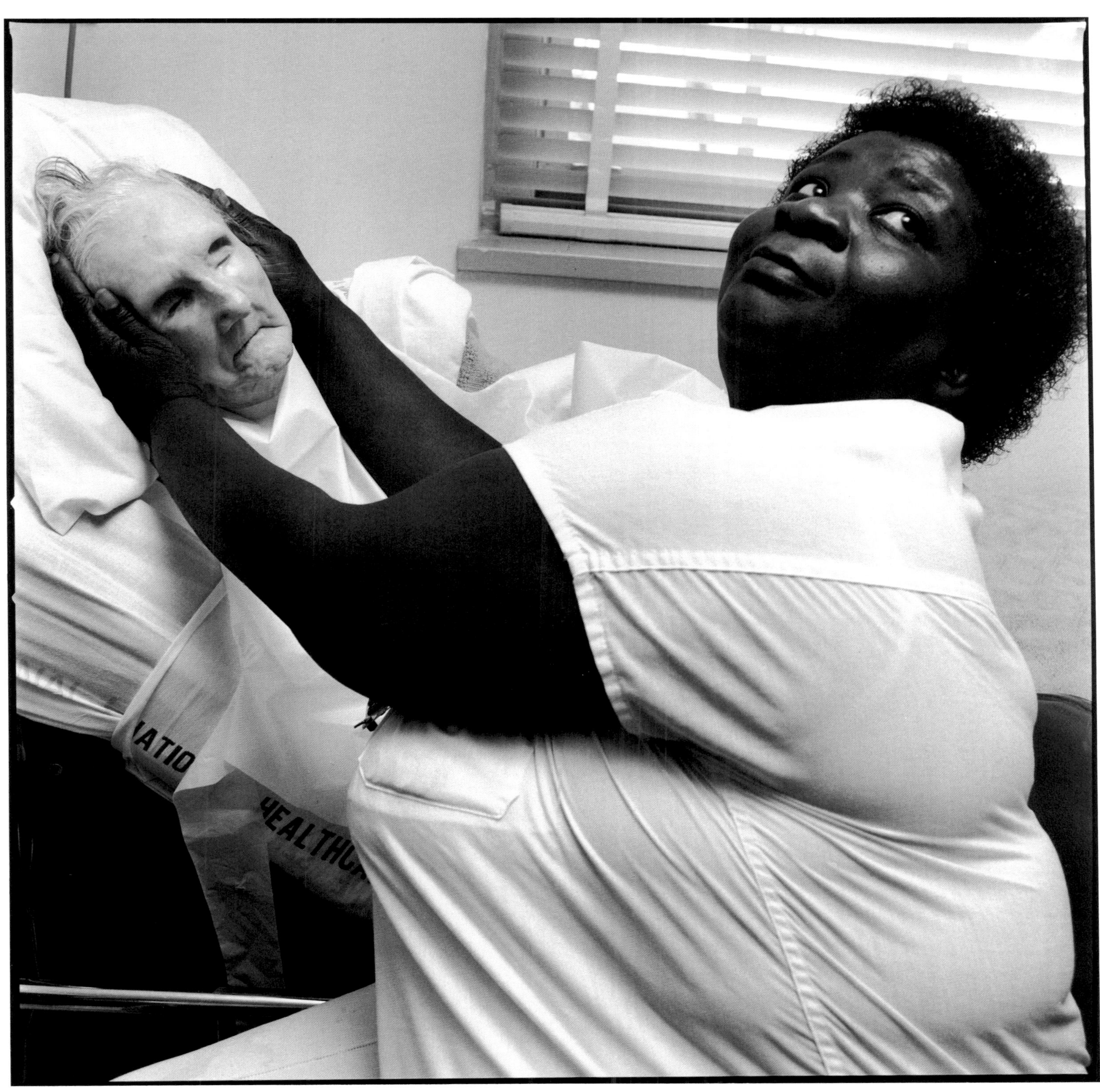

Leprosy patient with her nurse, National Har sen’s Disease Center, Carville, Louisiana, 1990

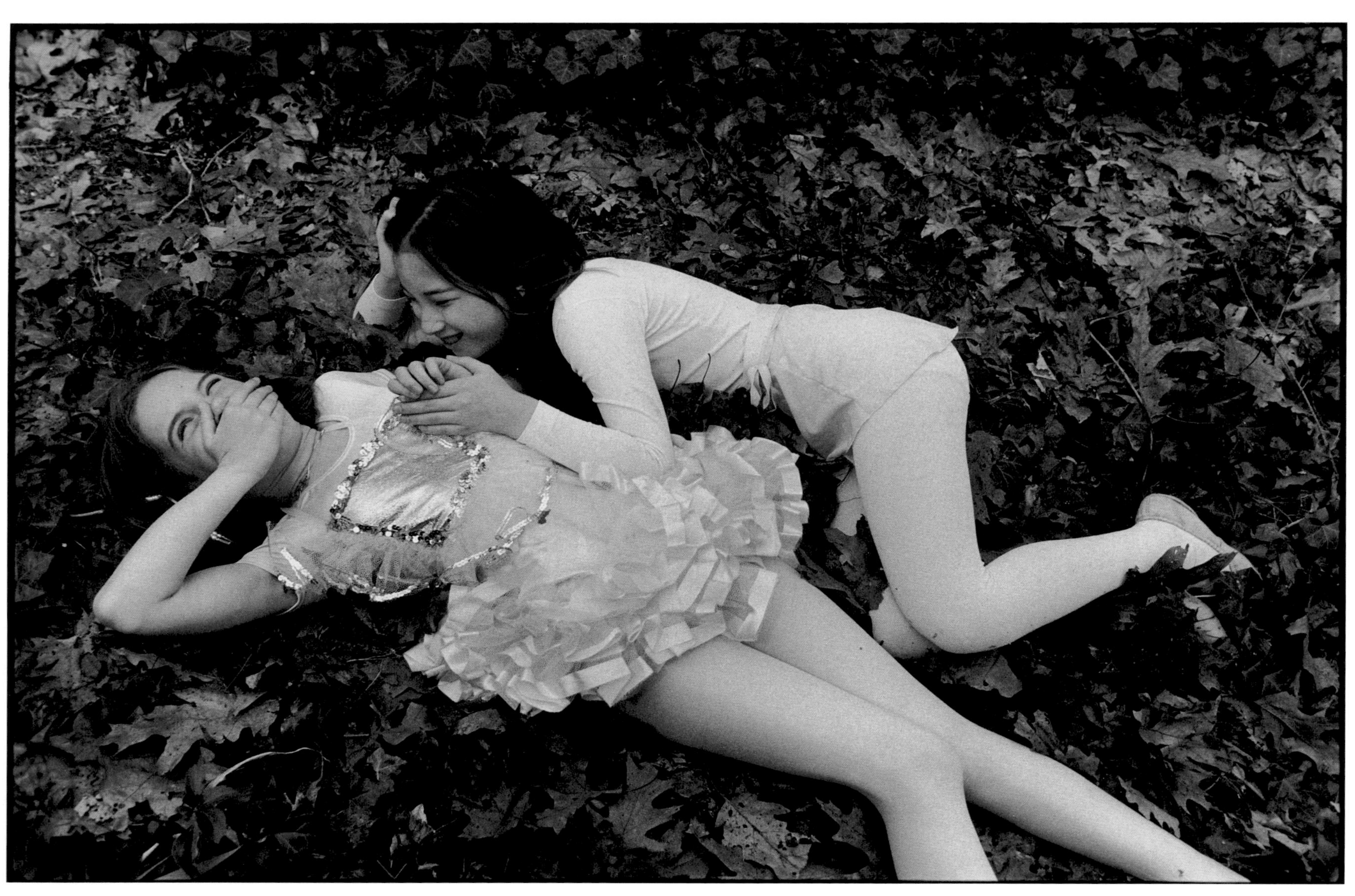

Katy and Ema, West Cornwall, Connecticut, 1987

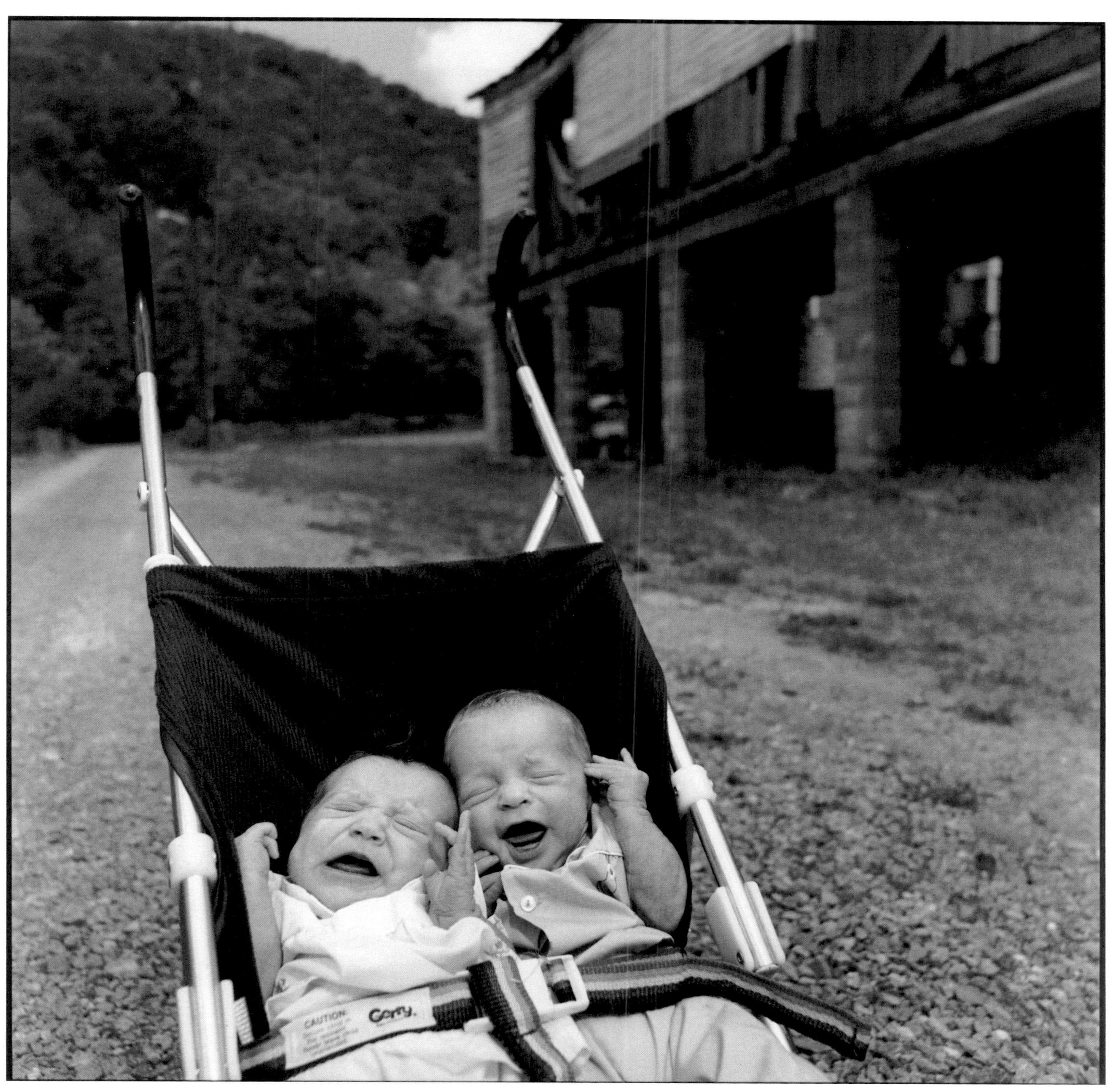

Crying twins, Middlesboro, Kentucky, 1988

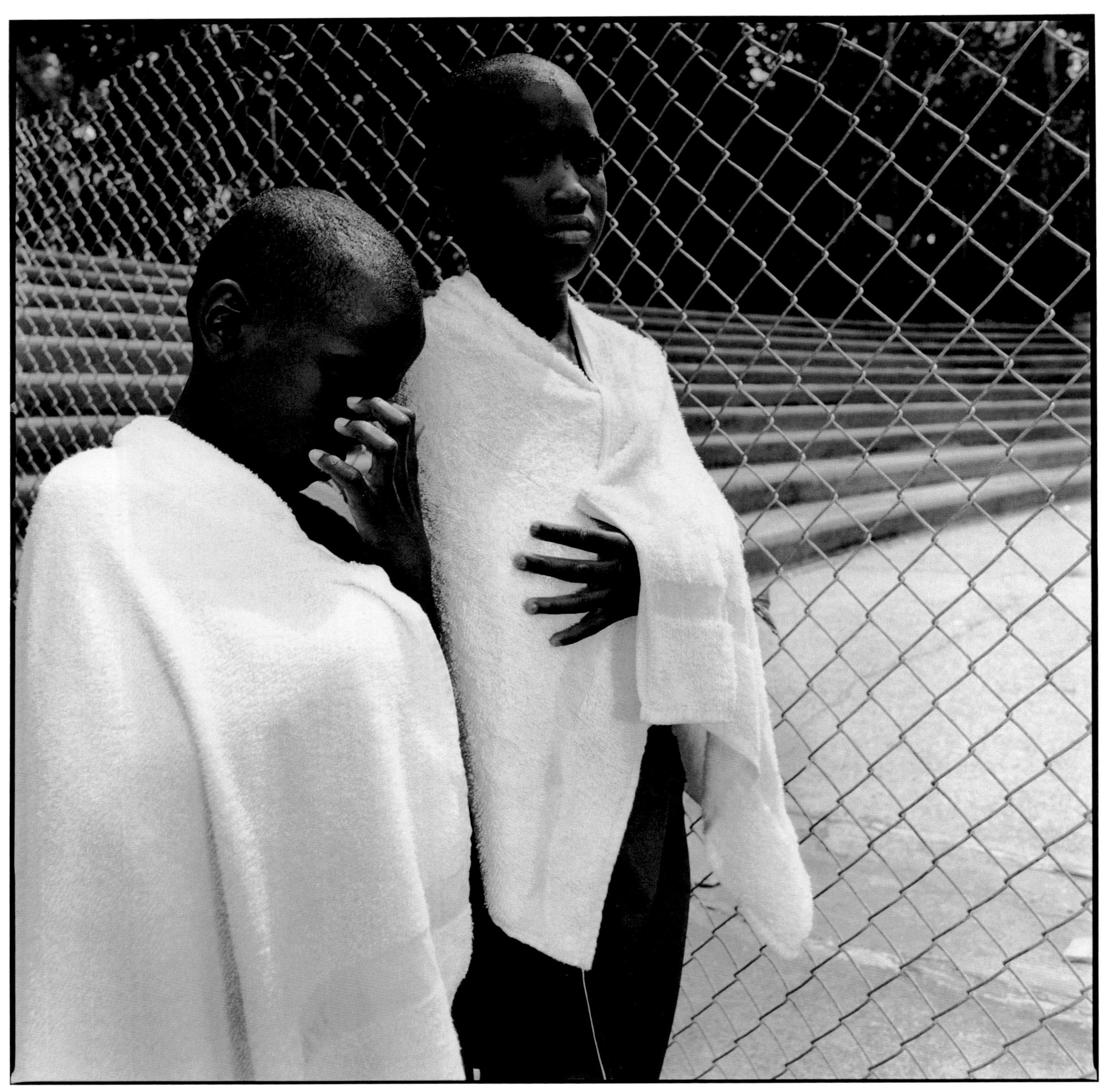

H.E.L.P. Shelter children, Tyrone Jackson and Kevin Crumel, Astoria Pool, Queens, New York, 1993

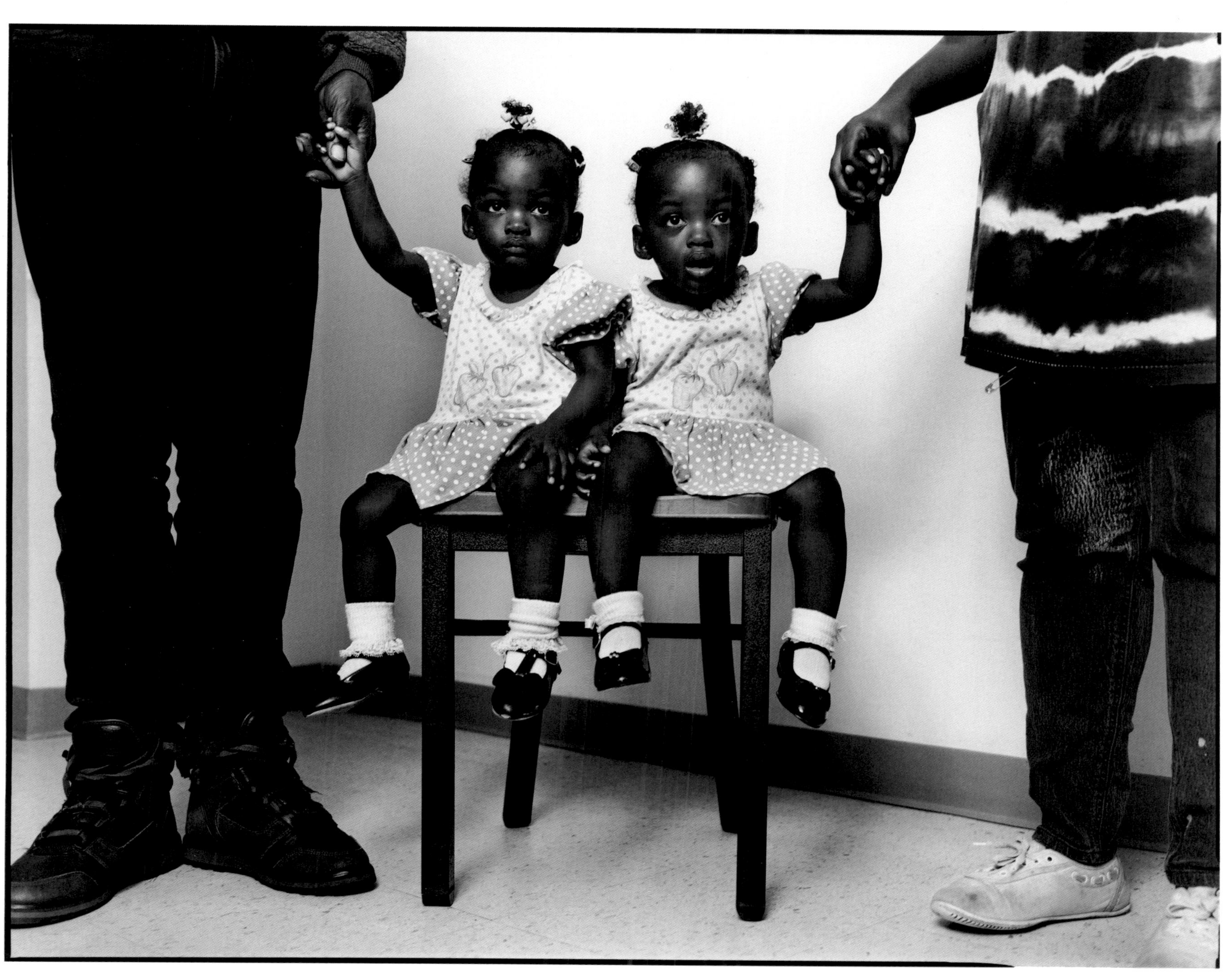

Vashira and Tashira Hargrove, twins, H.E.L.P. Shelter, Suffolk, New York, 1993

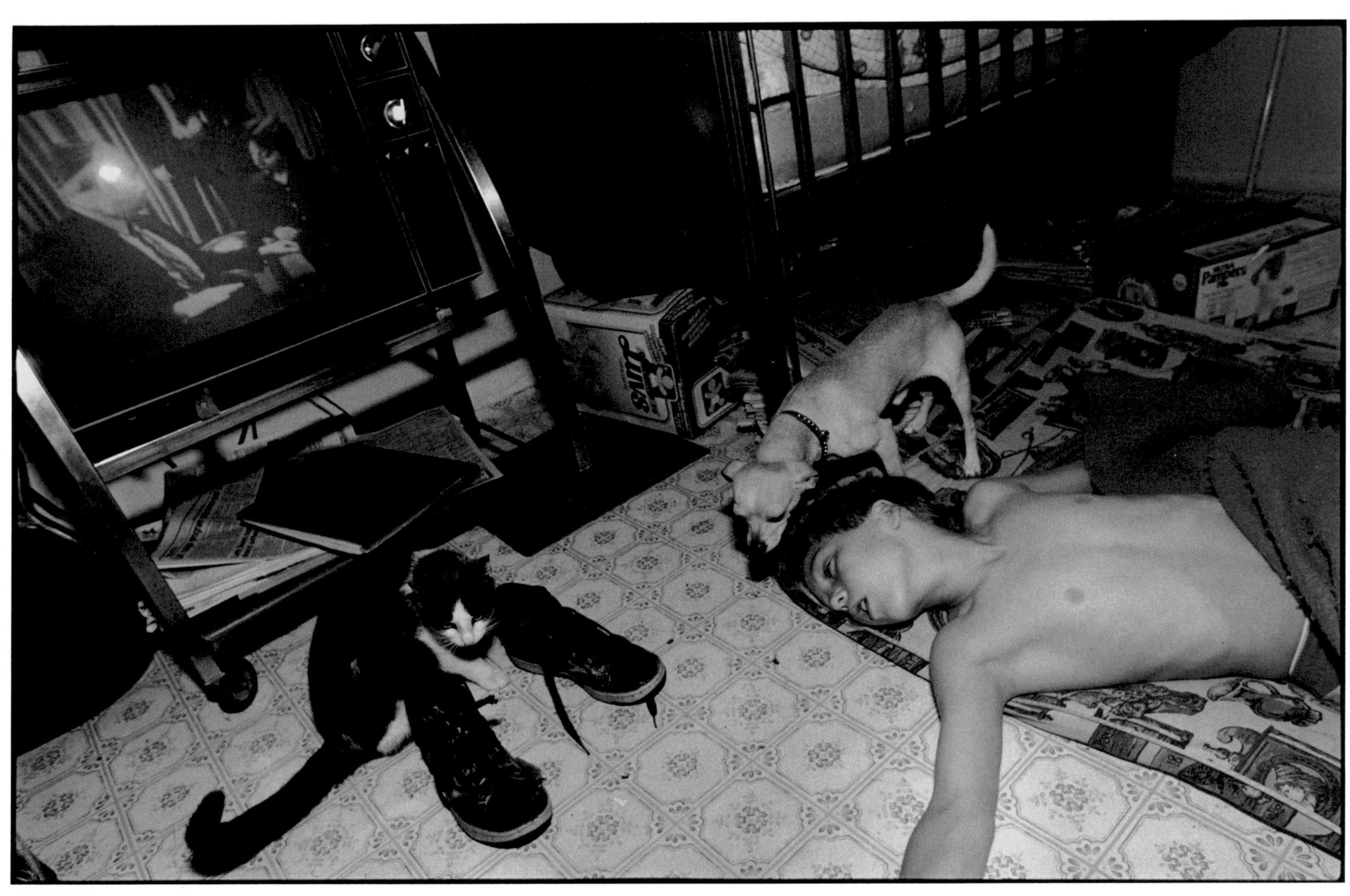

Chuck, Portsmouth, Ohio, 1998

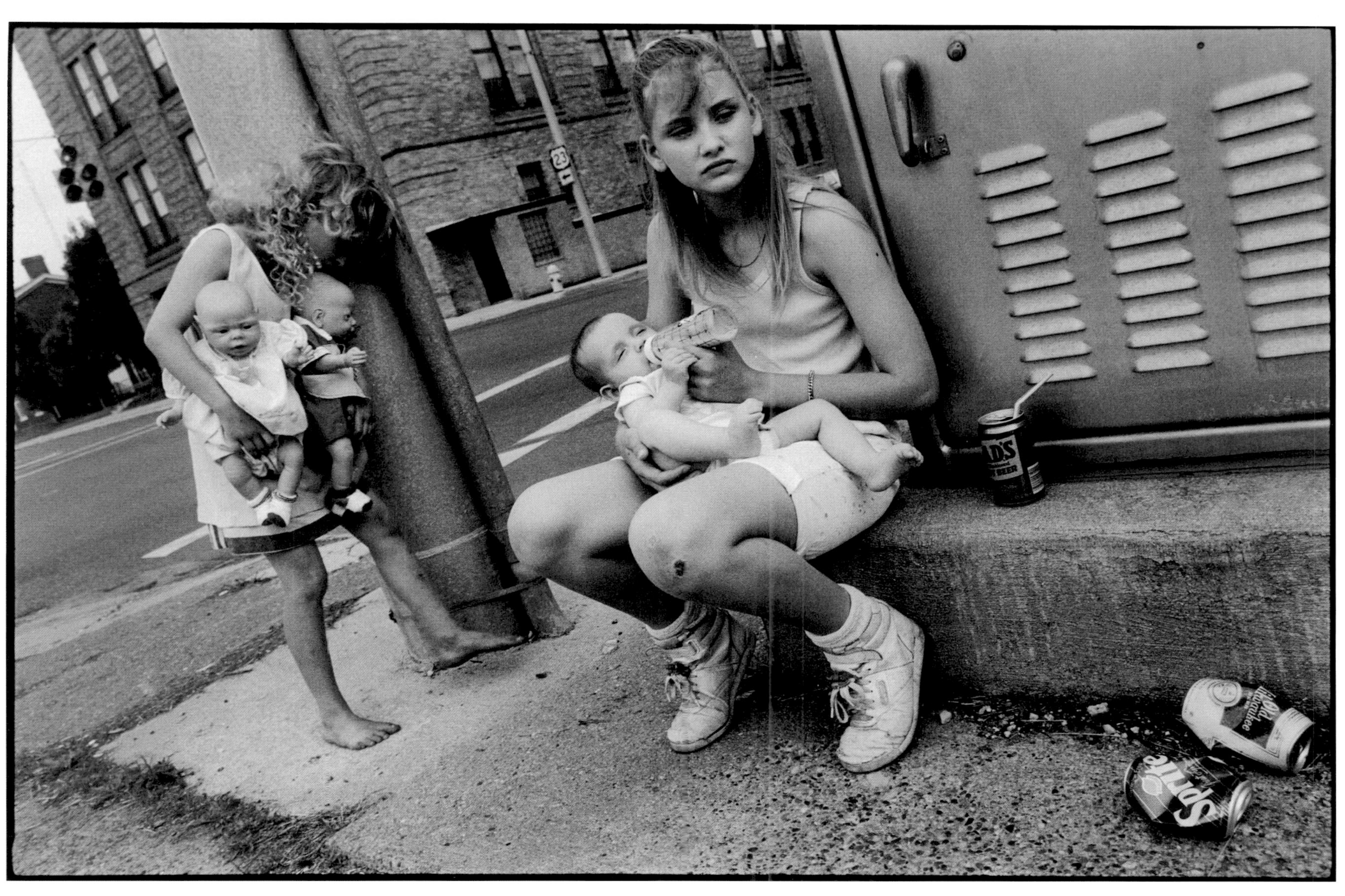

Jennifer, Tiffany, and Carrie, Portsmouth, Ohio, 1989

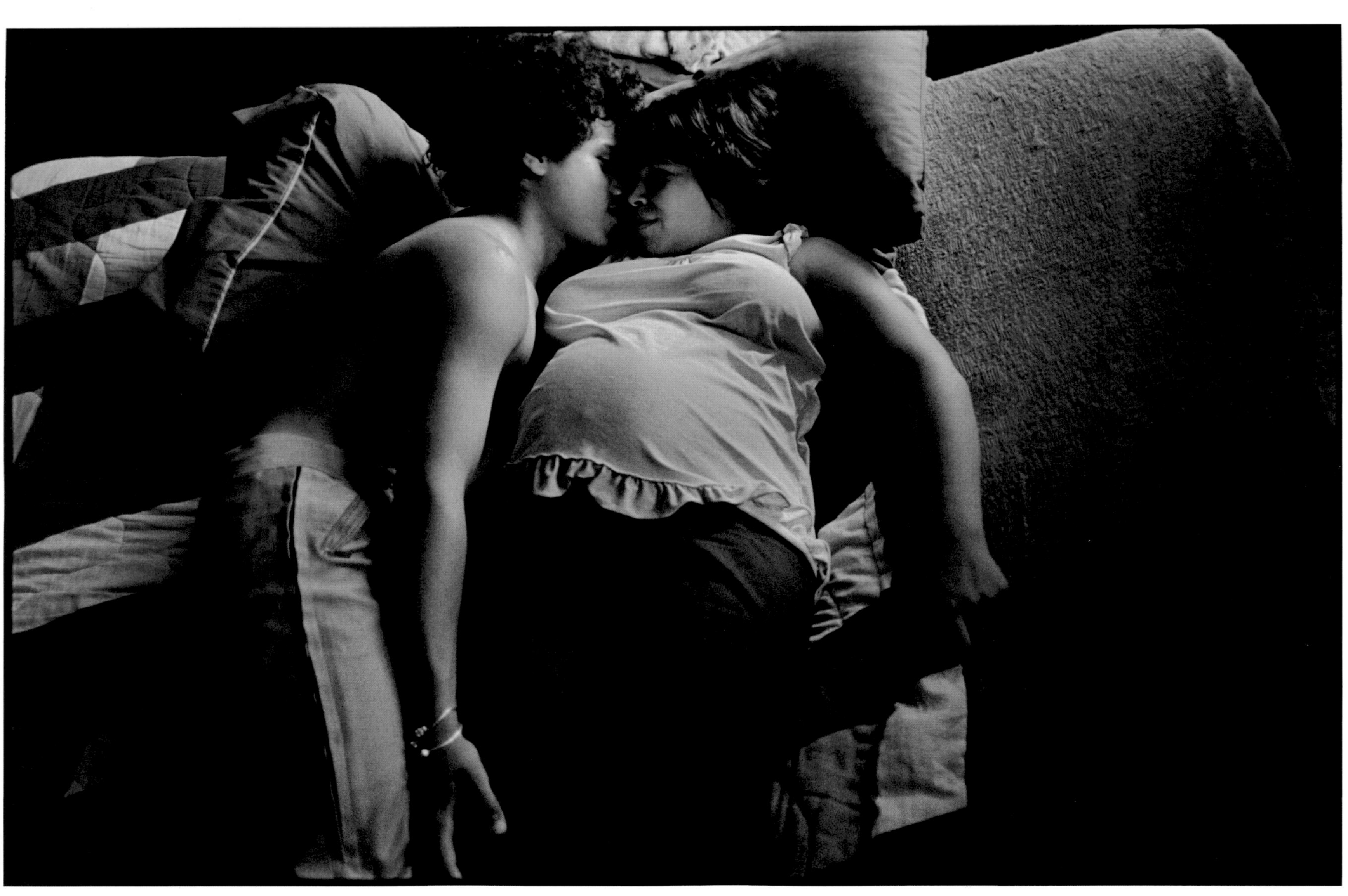

Jeanette and Victor, Brooklyn, New York, 1979

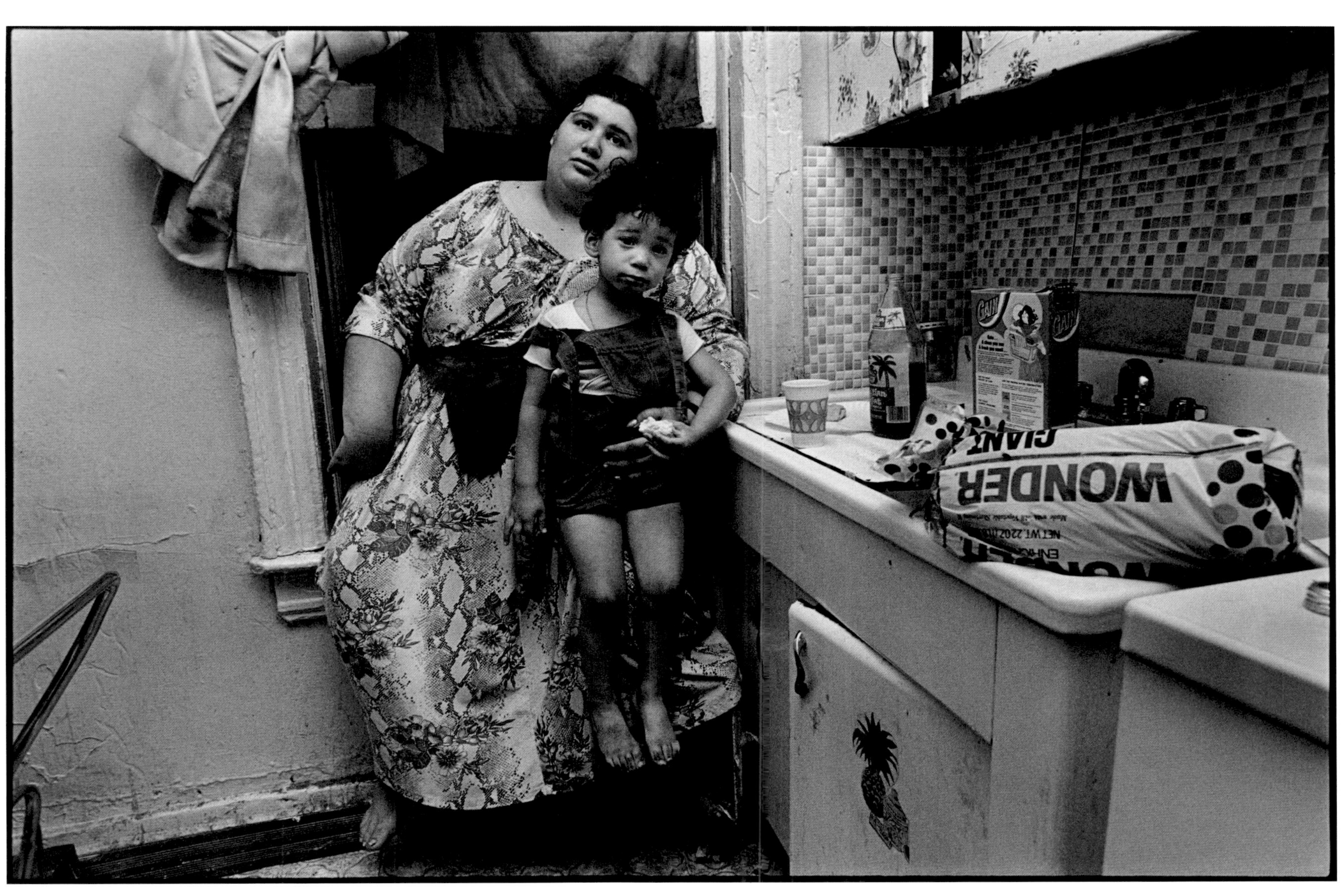

Jeanette's neighbors in their kitchen, Brooklyn, New York, 1979

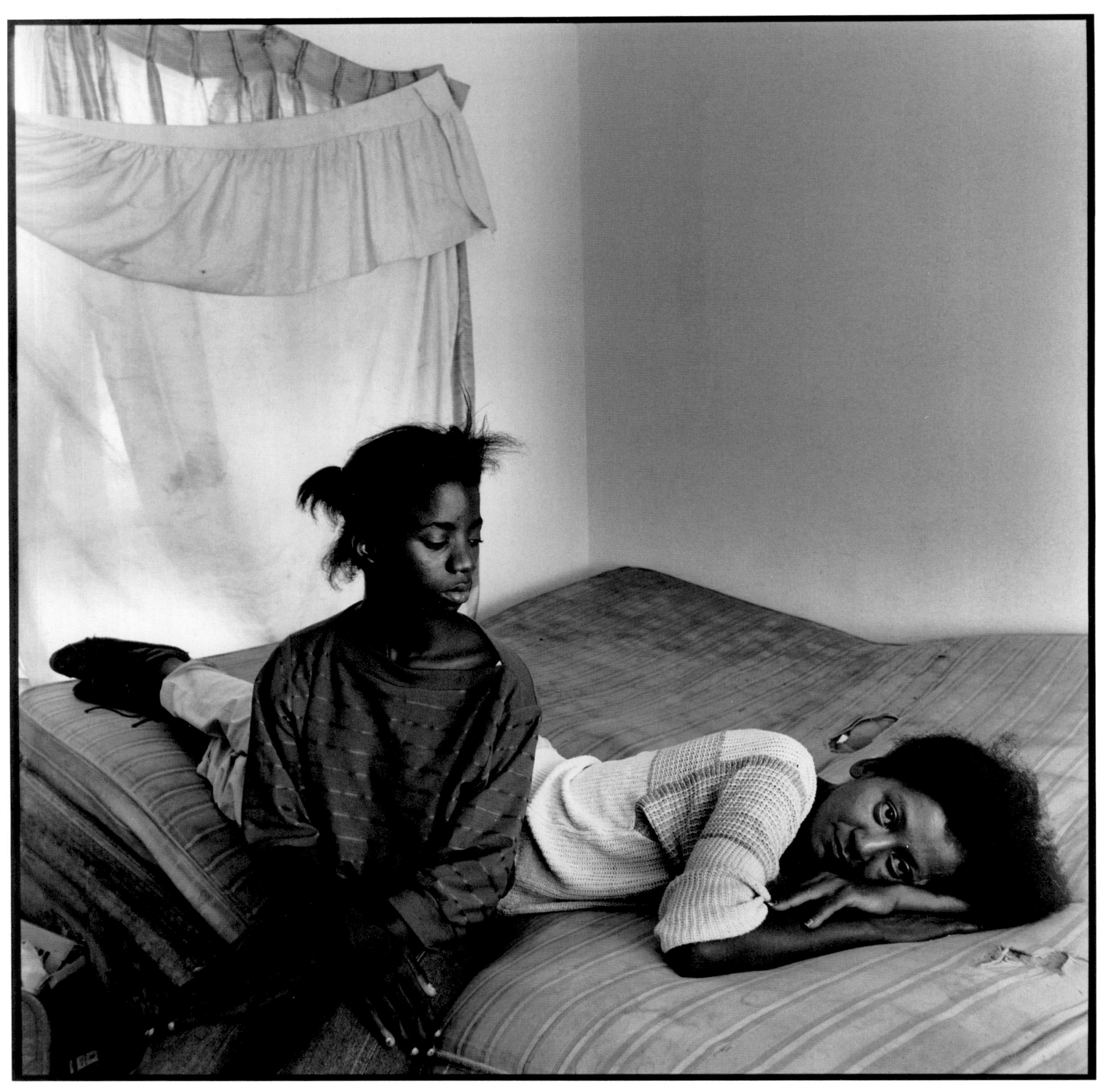

Joanne and Charlene Rudd, South Dallas, Texas, 1988

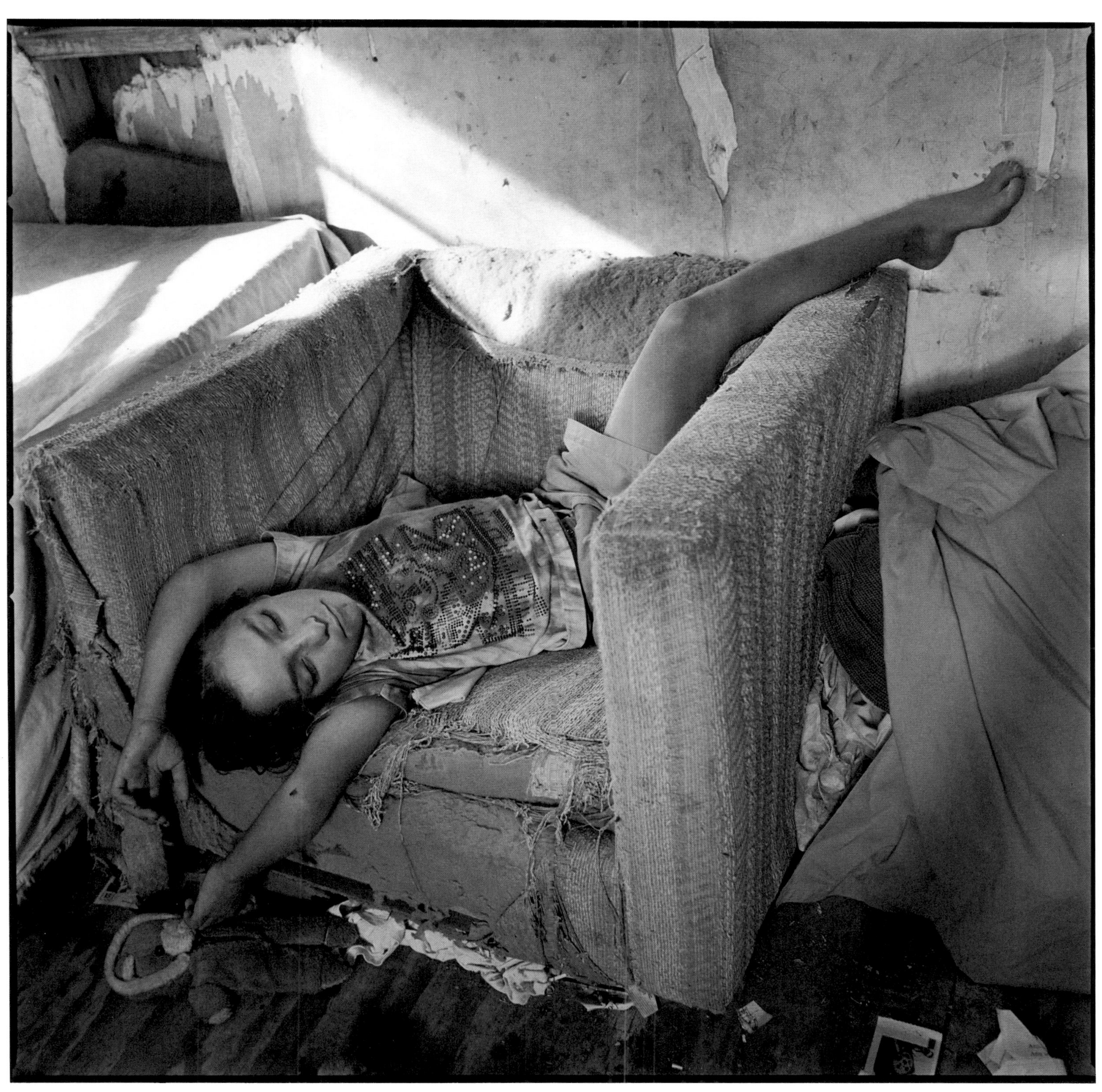

Vicky, Mission, Texas, 1990

AUTOBIO POEM

LA SHAWNDREA
Helpful, kind, fair, good listener,
Sister of Keanna, Daylon, Mikka,
Who loves pizza, ice cream, fruit,
Who feels funny, unselfish, lucky,
Who finds happiness in myself, my family, and going on vacation,
Who needs love from my family, people to like me and to learn in school,
Who gives loyalty, friendship, and understanding,
Who fears losing a member of my family, not being able to live with my
Mom, and someone breaking in my house,
Who would like to see a castle, Disneyland, or Disneyworld,
Who enjoys the outdoors, tag, and roller skating,
Who likes to wear shorts, Nike shoes, jogging pants,
Resident of Seattle, 10th Avenue SW,
BLACKWELL
November 1996

Tiny's daughter, La Shawndrea Blackwell, wrote this poem when she was nine years old.

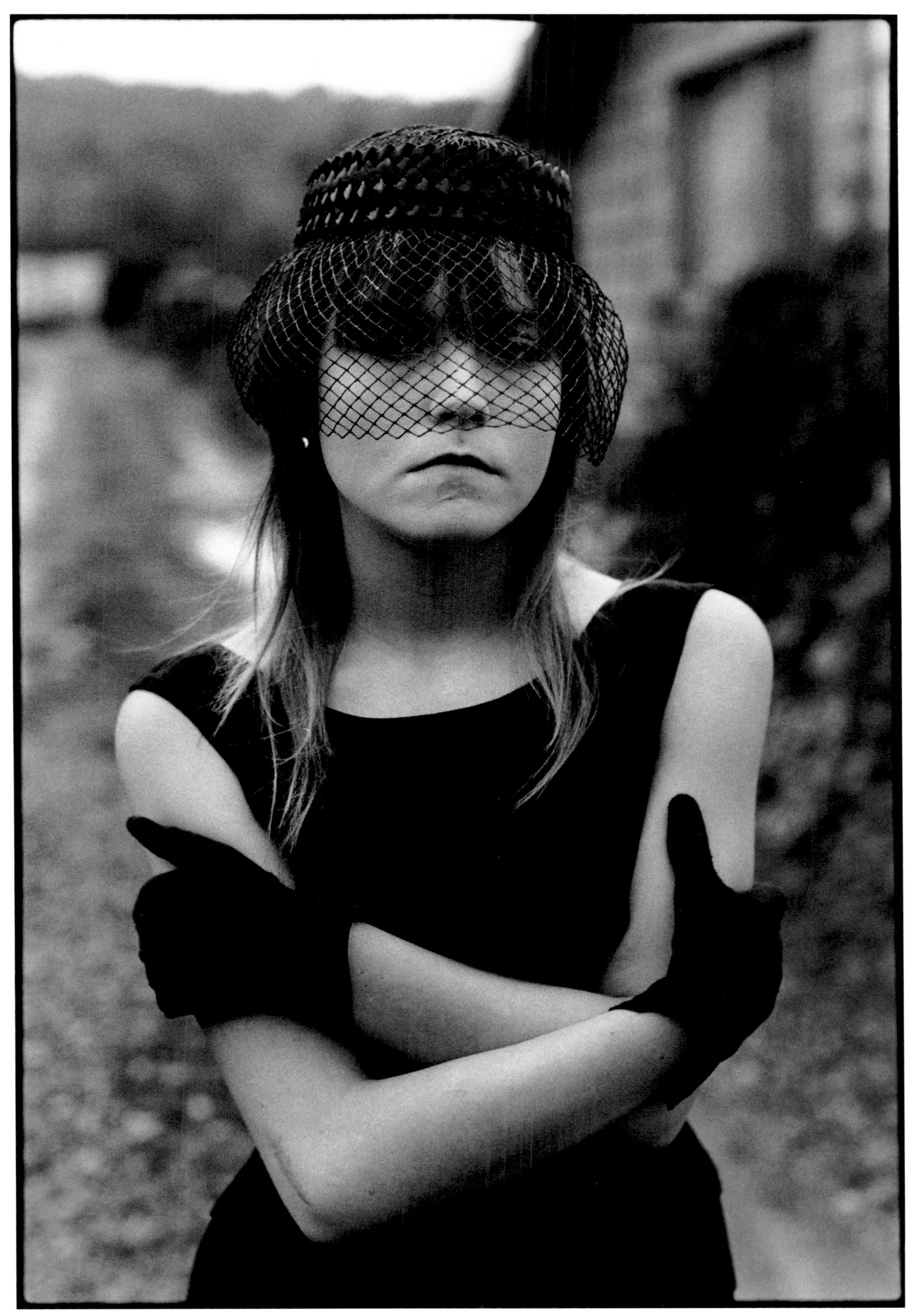

Tiny in her Halloween costume, Seattle, Washington, 1983

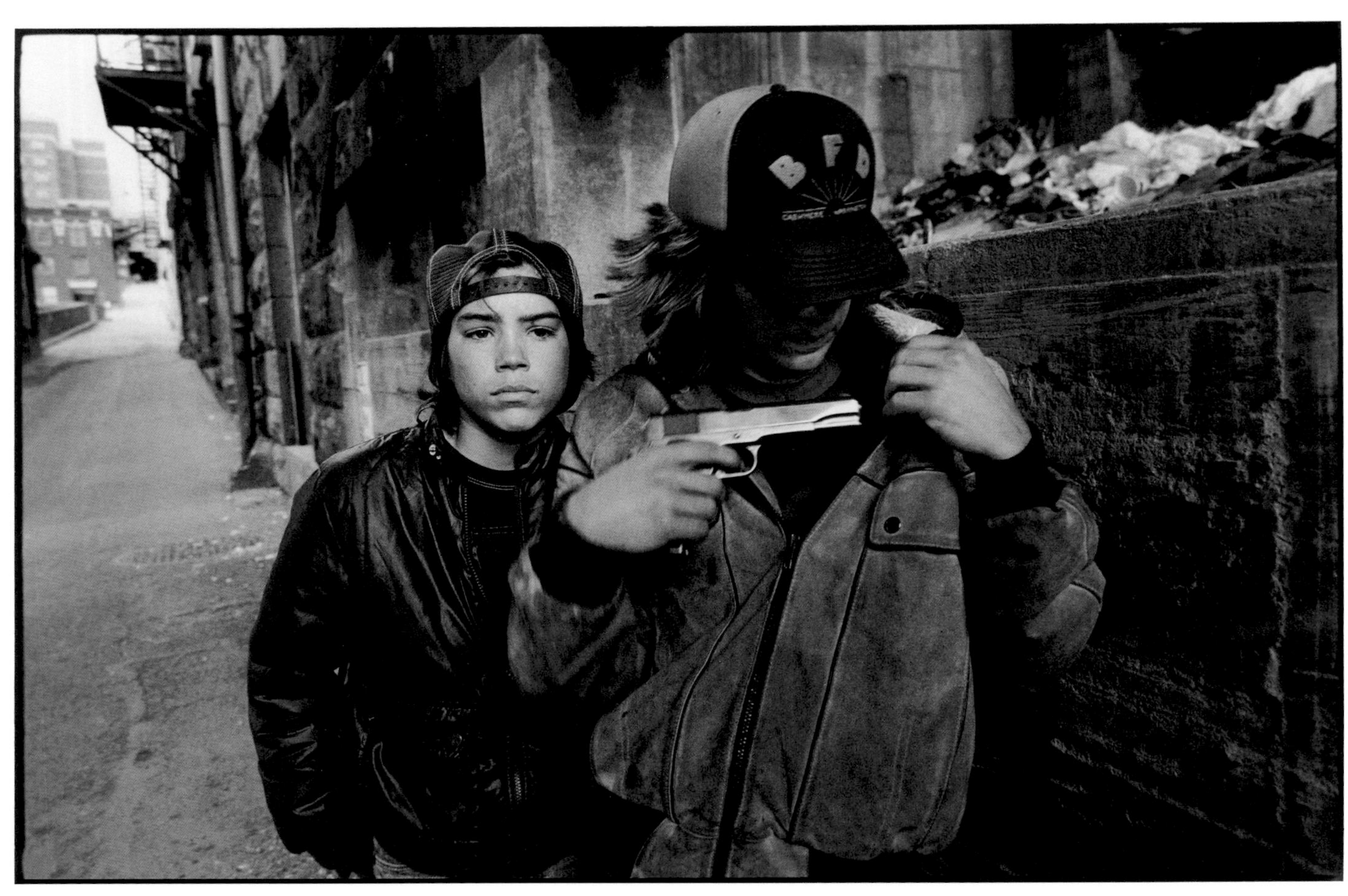

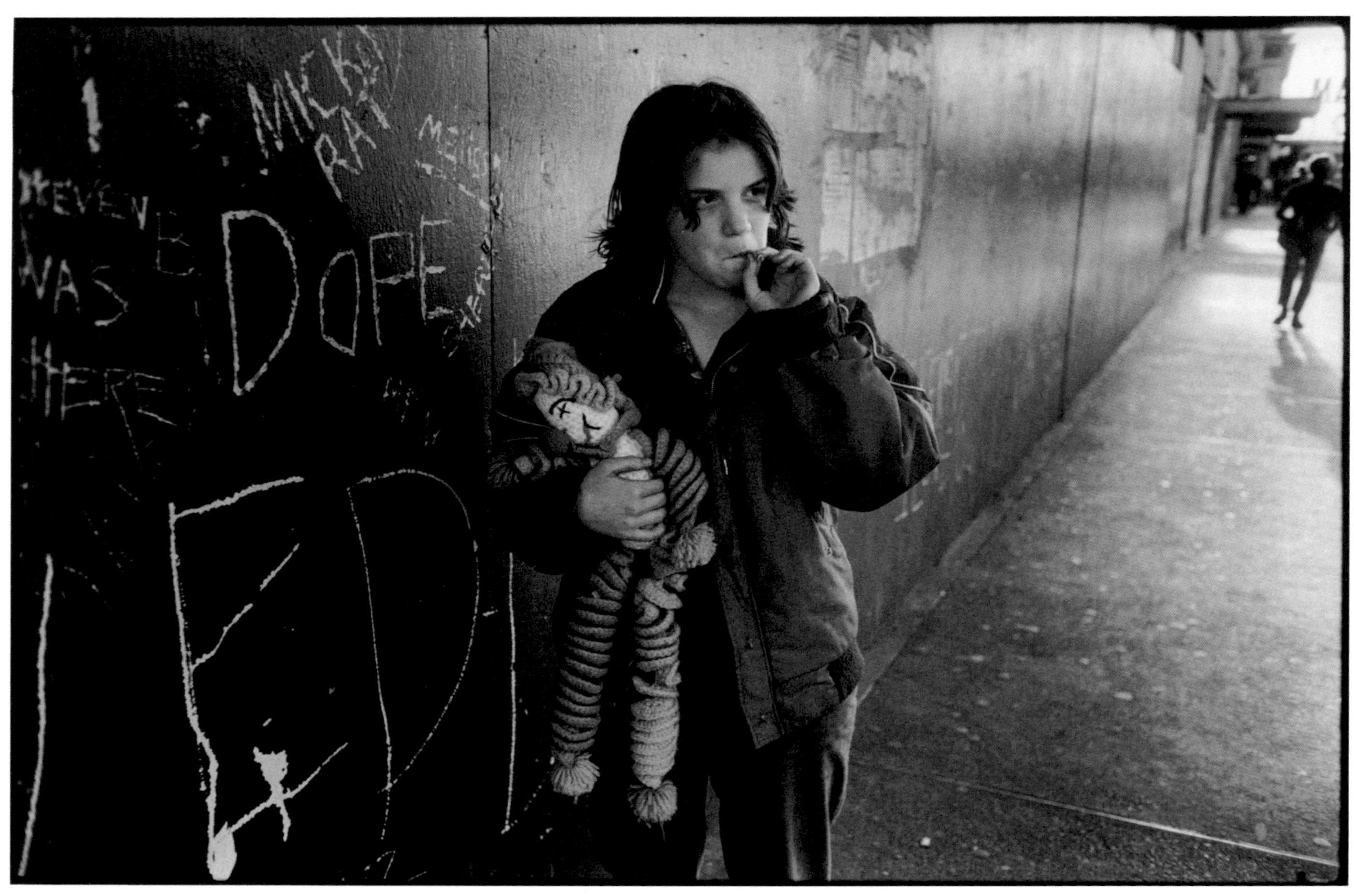

top: "Rat" and Mike with a gun, Seattle, Washington, 1983
bottom: Lillie with her rag doll, Seattle, Washington, 1983

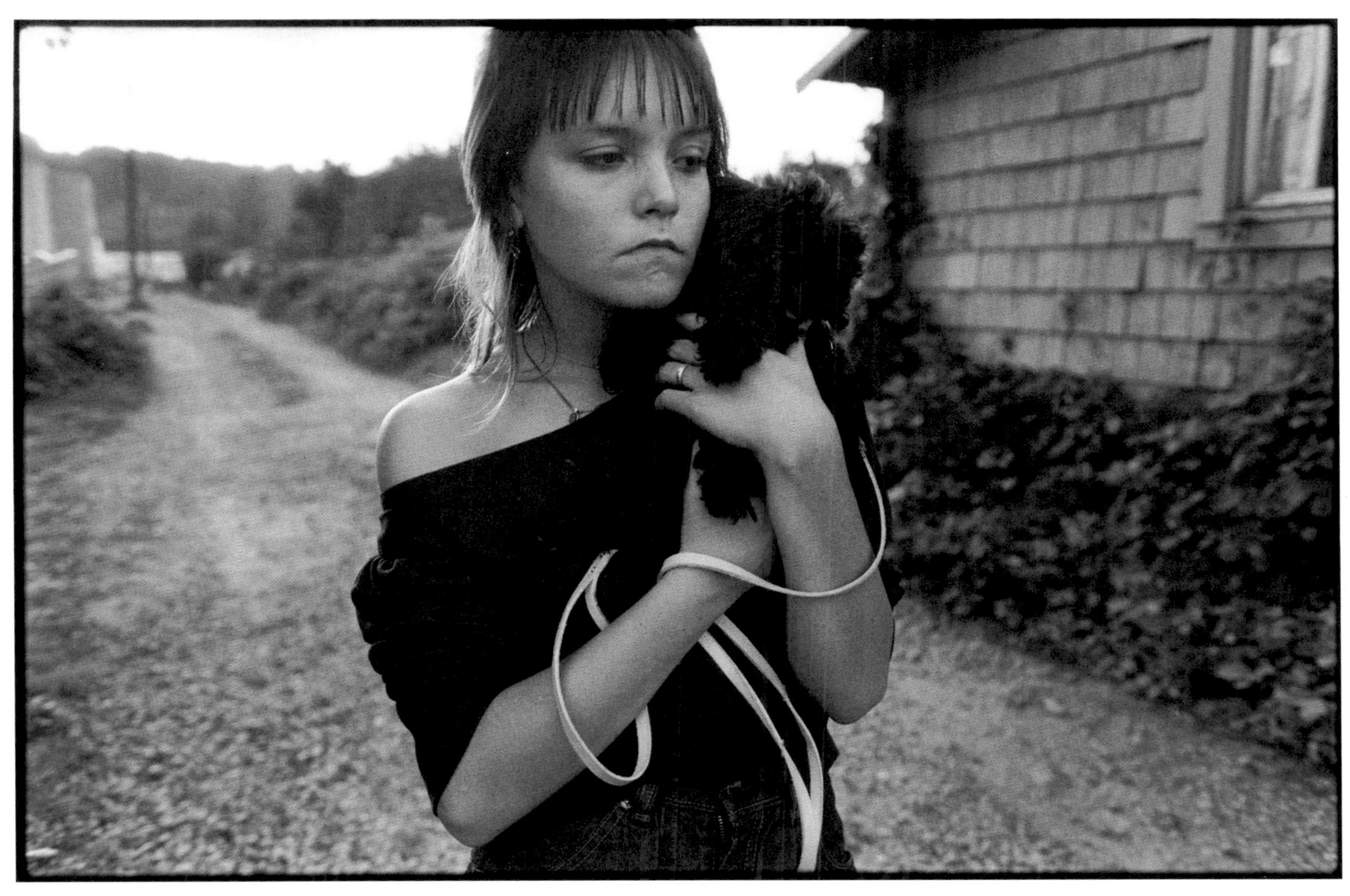

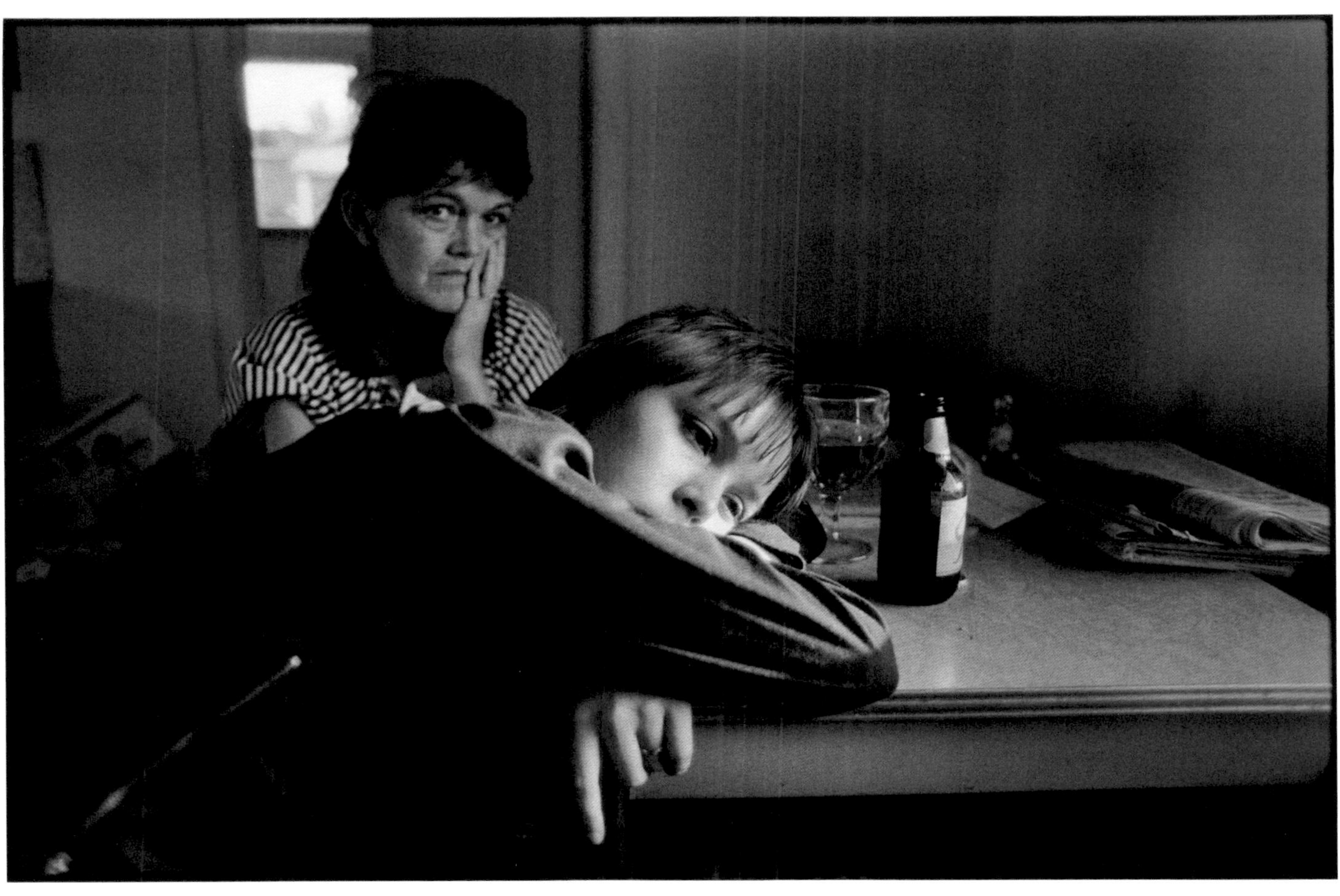

top: Tiny with Papas, Seattle, Washington, 1983
bottom: Tiny and her mother, Pat, Seattle, Washington, 1983

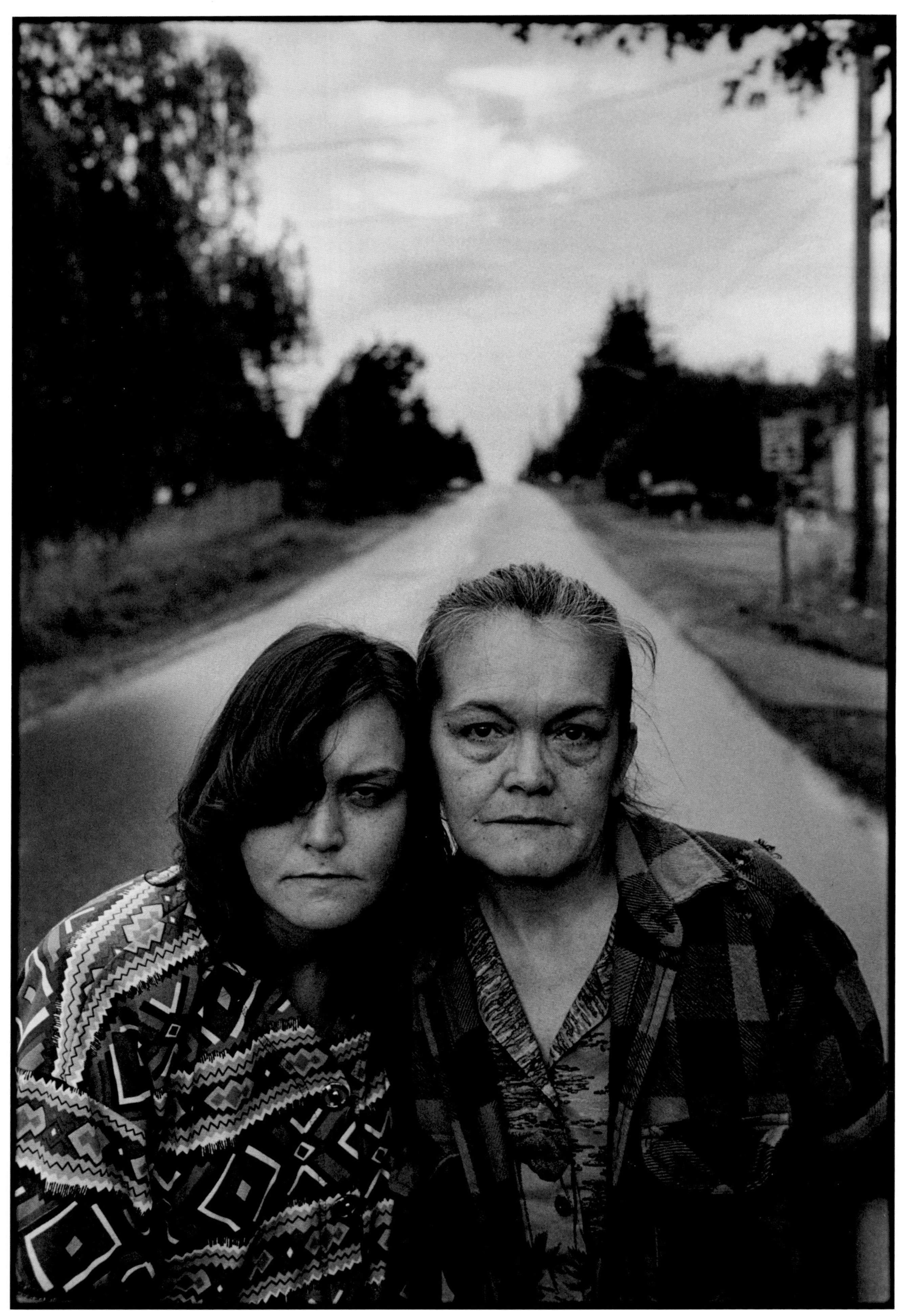

Tiny and her mother, Pat, Seattle, Washington, 1993

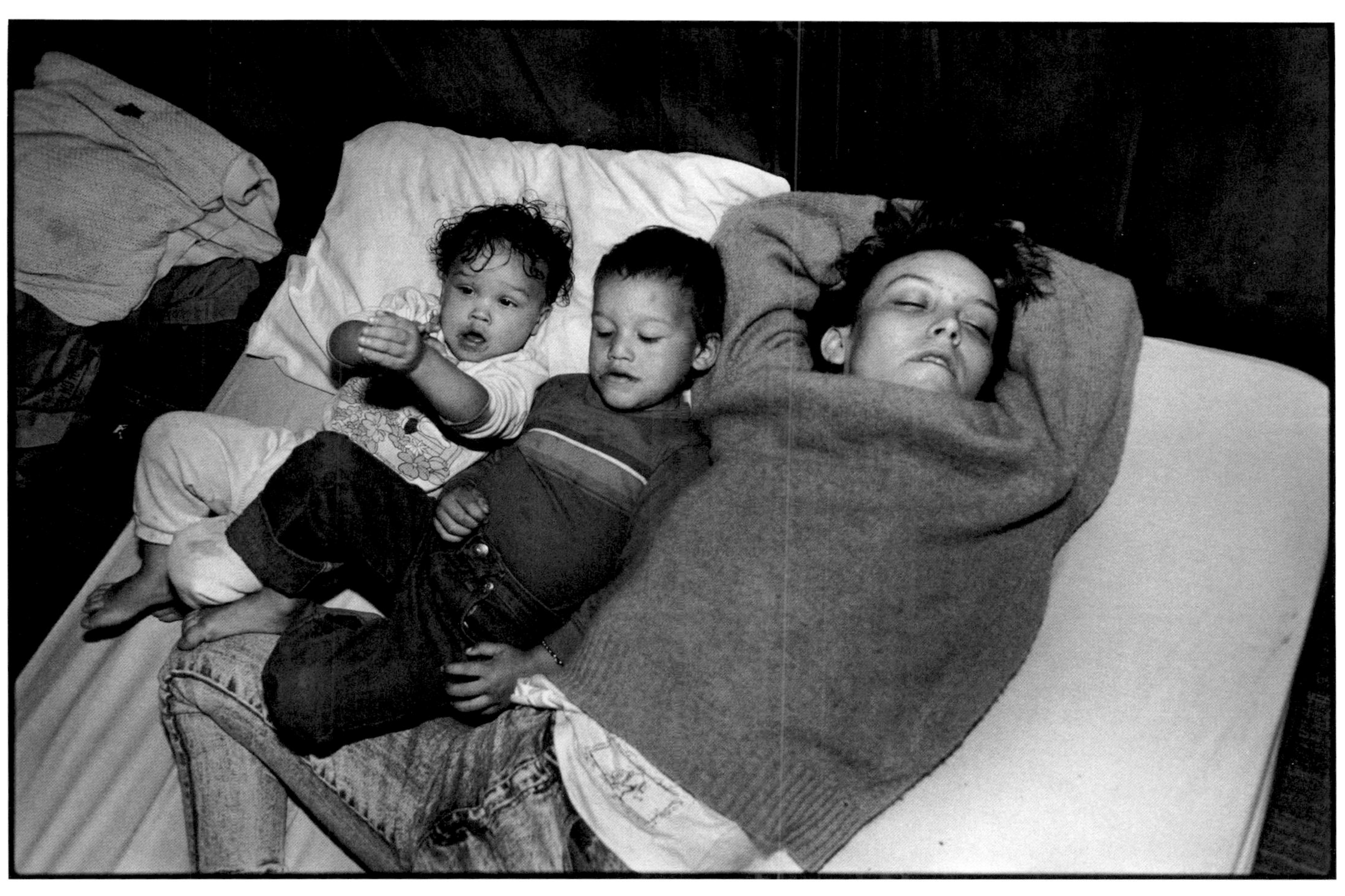

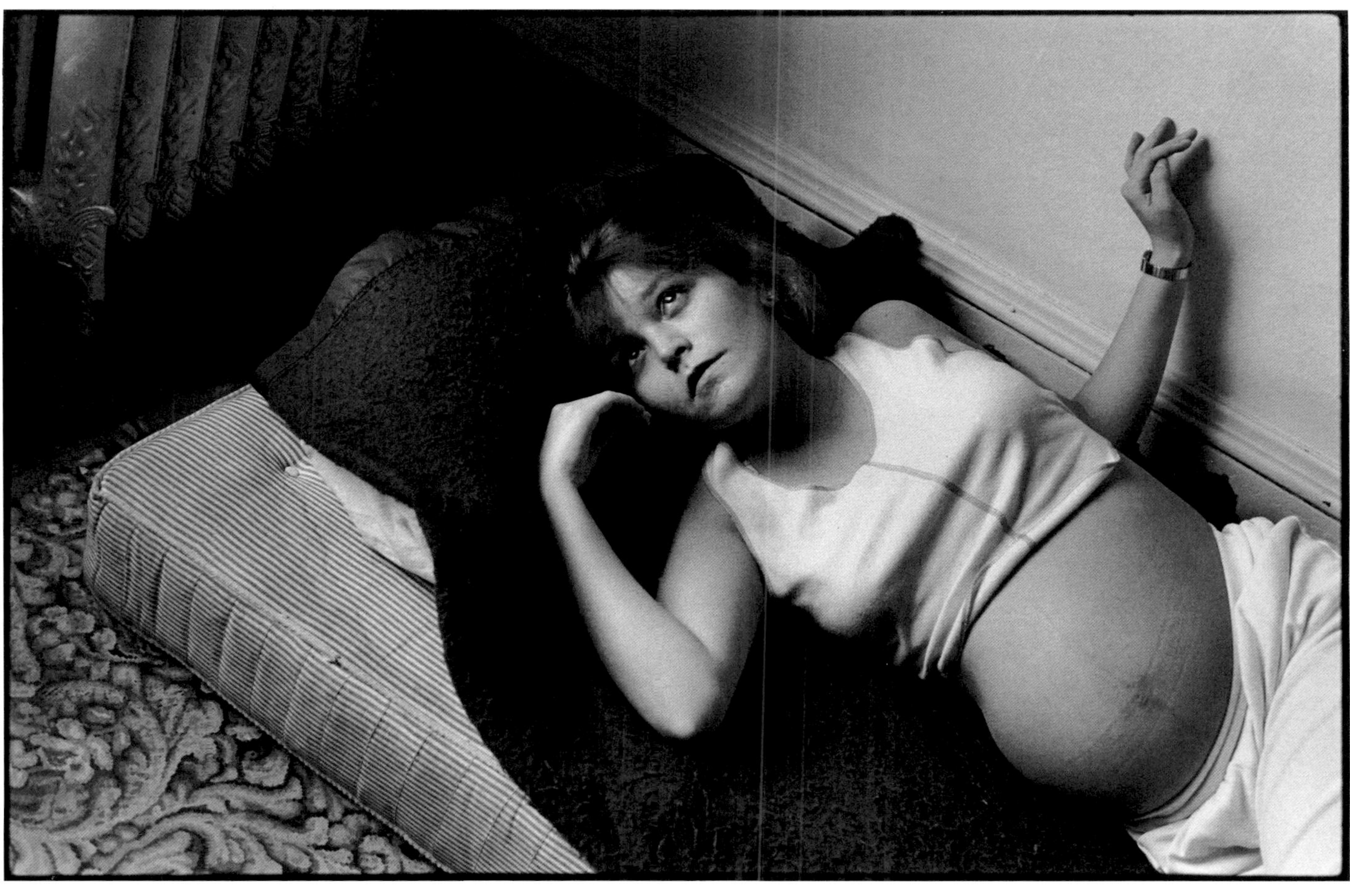

top: La Shawndrea, Daylon, and Tiny, Seattle, Washington, 1989
bottom: Tiny, pregnant, Seattle, Washington, 1985

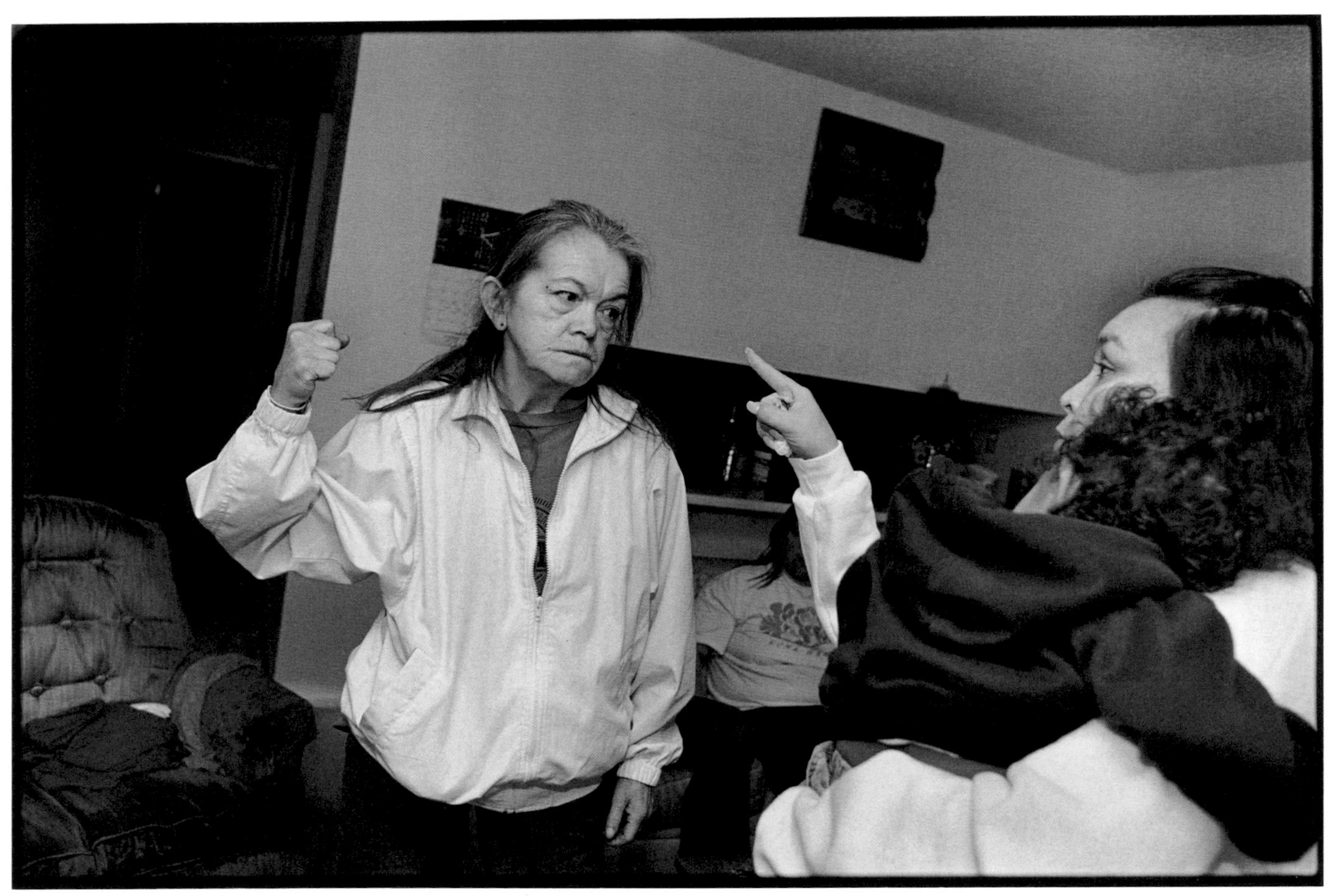

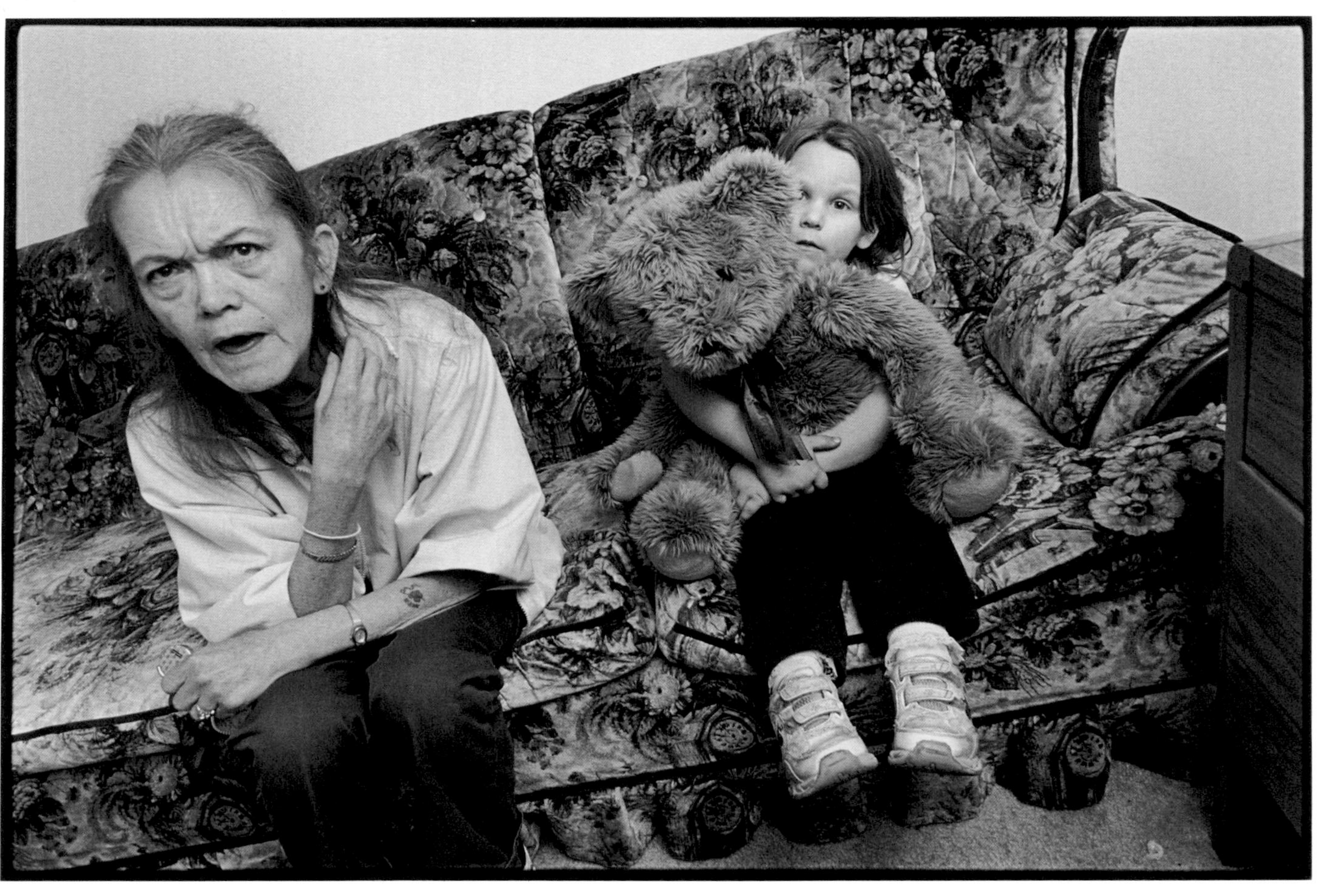

top: Tiny and her mother fighting, Seattle, Washington, 1999
bottom: Pat and Rachel, Seattle, Washington, 1999

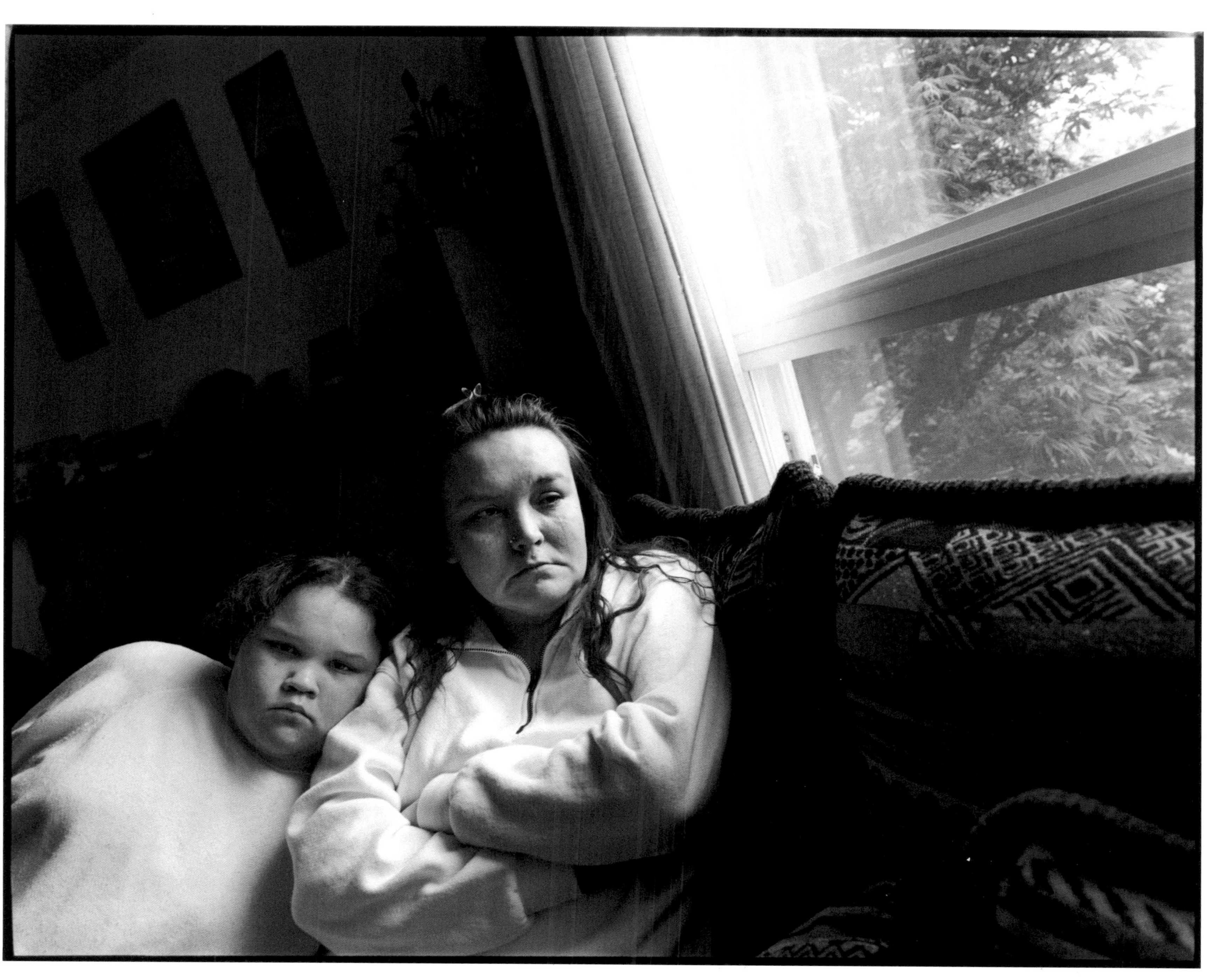

La Shawndrea with Tiny crying, Seattle, Washington, 1999

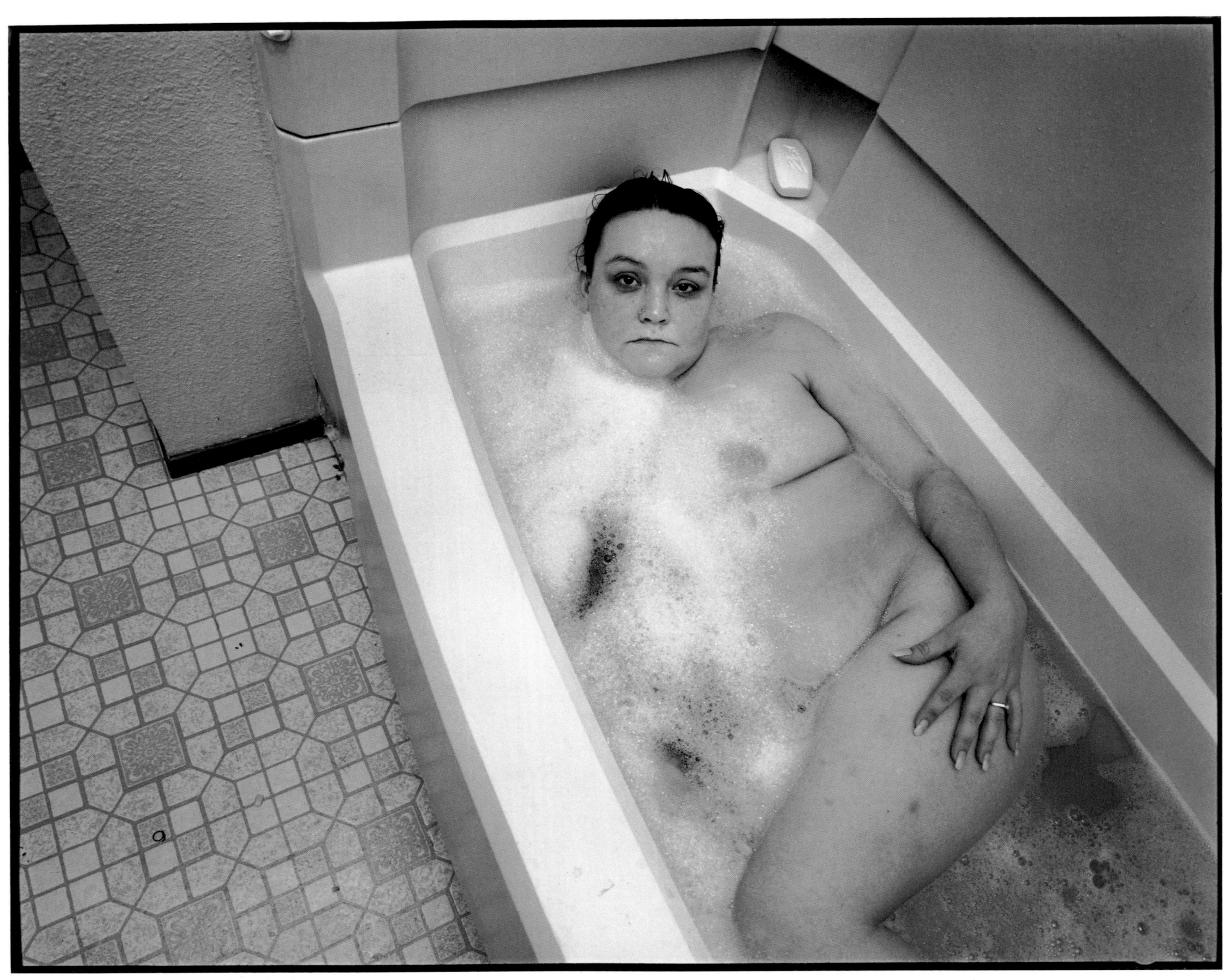

Tiny in her tub, Seattle, Washington, 1999

AFTERWORD

Looking back, my work in America strikes me now as being a long and blessed journey—a journey that has taken me from one end of this country to the other many times and allowed me to enter into the lives of countless people. From the extremely poor to the very rich I have been a witness to some of the things that make this country so extraordinary. I have photographed people at baby beauty pageants and in singles' bars; at twins' conventions and Ku Klux Klan gatherings. I have crossed paths with some wonderful people and some terrible ones. One thing is for sure, for all of its ups and downs, it has always been an incredible adventure. You can find everything in this country—anything goes, and anything can happen. My travels through America have defined my vision as a photographer.

In my work, I am guided by what moves and surprises me. Photographs can be enigmatic. They sometimes work because of what is included in the frame, and sometimes because of what is not. There's no formula for taking pictures. It's a mysterious process; an endless challenge. Ideas for projects are constantly unfolding and possibilities reveal themselves around every corner. The trick is to be open enough to recognize them the moment they appear and driven enough to pursue them.

I started photographing in the early sixties when I was a student at the Annenberg School for Communications. From my first day out on the street with a camera, I knew that was it: I was going to be a photographer. That childhood sense of excitement has never left me, nor has my enjoyment of the contact with people that photography gives me. Taking pictures can be a contradiction because the camera at once facilitates that connection with the subject and at the same time provides a necessary distance. Sometimes my work focuses on aspects of life that are very difficult. When the camera is between me and the subject, it often shields me from a grim reality while allowing me access to otherwise impenetrable worlds.

In the early 1970s I worked on Milos Forman's film *One Flew Over the Cuckoo's Nest* making still photographs. While the film was being made Dr. Dean Brooks, who was the head of Oregon State Hospital, gave me a tour of the facilities. The patients in Ward 81, the hospital's maximum-security women's ward, fascinated me and I returned to photograph there two years after the film ended. This experience profoundly changed the way I approach my work. Since then, many of my books, like *Ward 81*, *Falkland Road*, *Streetwise*, or *Indian Circus,* have concentrated on a small group of people who live in a clearly defined area. This provides an anchor allowing me to return day after day to explore the group and to intimately document their rituals, customs, and lives.

I try to spend as much time as possible on a project to build a rapport with my subjects. Intimacy is very important in my photographs. Being a woman is often an advantage in enabling me to achieve this intimacy because people, especially strangers, are less threatened by women. In Ward 81, the women had to know and trust me before they would allow me to enter their painful lives. As a woman, I was able to photograph the patients bathing and witness the most personal details of their lives. Tiny, from *Streetwise*, was able to relate to me in part because I am a woman. The men in her life were mostly customers and she had a different relationship with them. The prostitutes in Bombay were much more open to me for the same reason. And the extremely macho Dean Damm would have definitely been threatened by the presence of a man taking photographs of his family.

I photographed the Damm family twice, first in 1987 and then again in 1994. As it turned out, both times were pivotal moments in their lives. In 1987 Linda, Dean, Jesse, and Crissy had just been thrown out of a shelter. Sometimes they stayed in a motel for the weekend, if Social Services could arrange it, but mostly they all lived in their car. Seven years later, they were again desperate, squatting in an abandoned ranch. Jesse and Crissy were twelve and thirteen and not attending school. There were two more children, Ashley, six; and Summer, four. Linda and Dean were heavily into drugs, and consumed by the mounting pressures in their lives. I was able to locate the Damms the second time because, like Tiny, I gave them my phone number and they would call collect now and then to tell me what was happening in their lives. Photographing the same people over many years can be a very intense experience.

I much prefer to photograph people I care about. Often, the subjects of my photographs have become my friends. To develop any degree of trust with someone, a photographer must be very honest. Photographing the Ku Klux Klan was difficult as they were so paranoid and didn't really trust me. (Perhaps they sensed that I didn't accept their beliefs and that I felt uncomfortable.)
A photographer has to take control of the situation. Whether the subjects are unknown or very famous, they need to have confidence in the photographer. With documentary projects, my subjects know from the outset that they will be spending a lot of time with me. It is not always easy to find people who can be so open with their lives in the presence of a camera. Young teenagers are interesting to photograph since they are often much less inhibited than adults and allow you to see just who they are.

Tiny (from *Streetwise*) was twelve years old when we met and was completely candid and open in front of the camera—except for the very first time I saw her and took her picture in a parking lot (she thought I was the police, screamed and ran away). Once we got past that, Tiny was totally herself. Now, eighteen years later, she still loves being photographed. We met again recently—it had been about five years since we last saw each other. She is now a single mother with five children all by different fathers. She is still beautiful. For the first time since I have known her we related to each other as adults and peers. Her own children are wonderful. I especially bonded with twelve-year-old Shawnee (La Shawndrea) and was deeply moved by her autobiographical poem, which I have included in this book. Tiny's life is so difficult. She tries very hard to make it work and yet she essentially survives on welfare. Still, Tiny has many dreams. They are not as grand as they were when she was twelve "I wanna be really rich . . . and live on a farm with a bunch of horses, which is my main best animal . . . and have three yachts or more . . . and diamonds and jewels and all that stuff." At thirty, she wishes for a man to treat her well and take care of her and, like any mother, she wishes for a better life for her children (of course she would still like to be rich one day). Watching her grow and change over time, getting to know her children continues to be a privilege for me, a unique experience of trust and understanding that has only grown over time.

From my earliest days as a photographer, many of my subjects have been on the edge of or outside the mainstream of our culture. Some of them were pushed over the edge due to painful circumstances and some of them manage to survive even with the most unspeakable and unjust obstacles placed in their lives. I've always tried to let my photographs be a voice for people who have less of an opportunity to speak for themselves.

In the mid-sixties, at the start of my career, magazines were like sponsors or patrons. Documentary work was a major part of magazines. In those days my magazine work and my personal work often overlapped. Now that's changed. Documentary assignments are almost nonexistent. These days the money to support myself and my personal work comes primarily from portraiture assignments for magazines, some commercial work, and teaching. Still, with assignments, I always try to find the quirkiness in my subjects, to go beyond clichés and discover the common human element that connects people all over the world.

I like to think that my photographs stand on their own as singular images. In that sense, I am not really a photo-essayist. I am always thinking about making pictures that speak for themselves. A great picture has to go beyond the literal subject matter. In the way that poetry is beautiful and emotional in its abstraction, photographs have to be a little abstract, too. Ultimately, I want my photographs to move people.

Looking back on this journey through America I would not change a thing. Without photography my life would have been unimaginably different. For one thing, I would have missed meeting all of these amazing people who shaped my life. I am very grateful and looking forward to many more years of making photographs as the odyssey is not yet over.

Mary Ellen Mark, June 9, 1999

MARY ELLEN MARK: AMERICAN ODYSSEY
IS MADE POSSIBLE BY THE GENEROUS SUPPORT OF
ANNETTE AND JACK FRIEDLAND
LYNNE AND HAROLD HONICKMAN
MARION BOULTON STROUD

ADDITIONAL SUPPORT WAS PROVIDED BY
SONDRA GILMAN AND CELSO GONZALEZ-FALLA
THE BUHL FOUNDATION, NEW YORK

MARY ELLEN MARK WISHES TO ACKNOWLEDGE FOR SUPPORT OF THIS PHOTOGRAPHIC WORK:
AMBASSADOR WALTER ANNENBERG; KODAK PROFESSIONAL NORDEN/BE NE LUX,
BJÖRN WESSTRÖM; HASSELBLAD USA, TONY CORBELL AND SKIP COHEN;
HASSELBLAD CENTER FOR PHOTOGRAPHY; ERNA AND VICTOR HASSELBLAD
FOUNDATION; VICTOR HASSELBLAD AB, BENGT FORSSBEACK;
HASSE PERSSON; ERNST WILDI; CANON USA INC.

ACKNOWLEDGMENTS

Throughout my career as a photographer there have been certain people who I consider mentors—people whose belief in and support of my work have enabled me to undertake this incredible journey.

Ambassador Walter Annenberg was the first of these people. In 1963 he gave me a scholarship to the Annenberg School for Communications and because of this, I discovered that photography was my life's passion. I am very fortunate and grateful to have had the opportunities that the Annenberg School afforded me. I want to thank Ambassador Annenberg and Kathleen Jamieson, Dean of the Annenberg School, for their continuous encouragement and support.

Barbara Kurgan, Terri Barbero, Cameron Baird, Julie Claire, Sandra Wong, Stephanie Cunningham, Joanne Roe, and Meredith Lue have all worked in my studio. Their friendship, encouragement, and assistance have allowed me to concentrate on making my photographs. I have also been lucky to have had wonderful interns who have generously given their time.

I am very grateful to the countless photo editors and art directors who, over the years, have given me the opportunity to photograph so many fascinating people and situations. They gave me the chance to make many of the pictures in this book. Too many years and too many assignments have gone by for me to thank each person individually.

I very much appreciate the hard work and dedication of the assistants who have worked with me over the years and have been invaluable in the making of my pictures. Their dedication and hard work are extraordinary. Here also, there are too many to name.

Sarah Jenkins and Lesley Yudelson made the beautiful silver prints that allowed Robert Hennessey to make the perfect separations for Stevan Baron to work with on press.

Without the ingenious work of Anna Roma and Michael Dalton, who wrote the computer program that runs both my studio and library, I would still be working out of legal boxes.

Melissa Harris from Aperture was a wonderful editor to collaborate with on this book. And Wendy Byrne the designer had the perfect vision. My gratitude to Michael Hoffman for believing in *American Odyssey* and making it a reality.

And of course I want to thank my husband, Martin Bell, whose brilliant eye and invaluable advice mean everything to me.

I consider myself very fortunate indeed in having had the wonderful life that photography has given me. Over the years I have met and photographed so many special people and they have generously allowed me to enter their lives. My deepest thanks to all of you who trusted me and allowed me to take your picture.

Library of Congress Catalog Card Number: 99-64609
Hardcover ISBN: 0-89381-880-1
Paperback ISBN: 0-89381-887-9

Tritone separations by Bob Hennessey
Printed and bound by L.E.G.O., Vicenza, Italy

The Staff at Aperture for *Mary Ellen Mark: American Odyssey* is:
Michael E. Hoffman, *Executive Director*
Melissa Harris, *Editor*
Stevan A. Baron, *Production Director*
Helen Marra, *Production Manager*
Wendy Byrne, *Designer*
Lesley A. Martin, *Managing Editor*
Phyllis Thompson Reid, *Associate Editor*
Tamara McCaw, *Editorial Assistant*
Elaine Schnoor, *Production Work-Scholar*

Aperture Foundation publishes a periodical, books, and portfolios of fine photography and presents world-class exhibitions to communicate with serious photographers and creative people everywhere. Catalogs are available upon request.

First edition
10 9 8 7 6 5 4 3 2 1

Aperture Book Center and Customer Service:
P.O. Box M, Millerton, NY 12546.
Phone: (518) 789-9003. Fax: (518) 789-3394.
Toll-free: (800) 929-2323.
E-mail: customerservice@aperture.org

Aperture Foundation, including bookstore and Burden Gallery: 20 East 23rd Street, New York, NY 10010.
Phone: (212) 505-5555, ext. 300.
Fax: (212) 979-7759. E-mail: info@aperture.org

Visit Aperture's website: http://www.aperture.org

Aperture Foundation books are distributed internationally through:

CANADA: General/Irwin Publishing Co., Ltd., 325 Humber College Blvd., Etobicoke, Ontario, M9W 7C3, Fax: (416) 213-1917.

UNITED KINGDOM, SCANDINAVIA, AND CONTINENTAL EUROPE: Robert Hale, Ltd., Clerkenwell House, 45–47 Clerkenwell Green, London, United Kingdom, EC1R OHT, Fax: (44) 171-490-4958.

NETHERLANDS, BELGIUM, AND LUXEMBURG: Nilsson & Lamm, BV, Pampuslaan 212–214, P.O. Box 195, 1382 JS Weesp, Fax: (31) 29-441-5054.

AUSTRALIA: Tower Books Pty. Ltd., Unit 9/19 Rodborough Road, Frenchs Forest, Sydney, New South Wales, Australia, Fax: (61) 2-9975-5599.

NEW ZEALAND: Southern Publishers Group, 22 Burleigh Street, Grafton, Auckland, New Zealand, Fax: (64) 9-309-6170.

INDIA: TBI Publishers, 46, Housing Project, South Extension Part-I, New Delhi 110049, India, Fax: (91) 11-461-0576.

For international magazine subscription orders to the periodical *Aperture*, contact Aperture International Subscription Service, P.O. Box 14, Harold Hill, Romford, RM3 8EQ, United Kingdom. One year: $50.00. Price subject to change.

To subscribe to the periodical *Aperture* in the U.S.A. write Aperture, P.O. Box 3000, Denville, NJ 07834. Toll-free: (800) 783-4903. One year: $40.00. Two years: $66.00.

RAGNAR KJARTANSSON

EPIC WASTE OF LOVE AND UNDERSTANDING

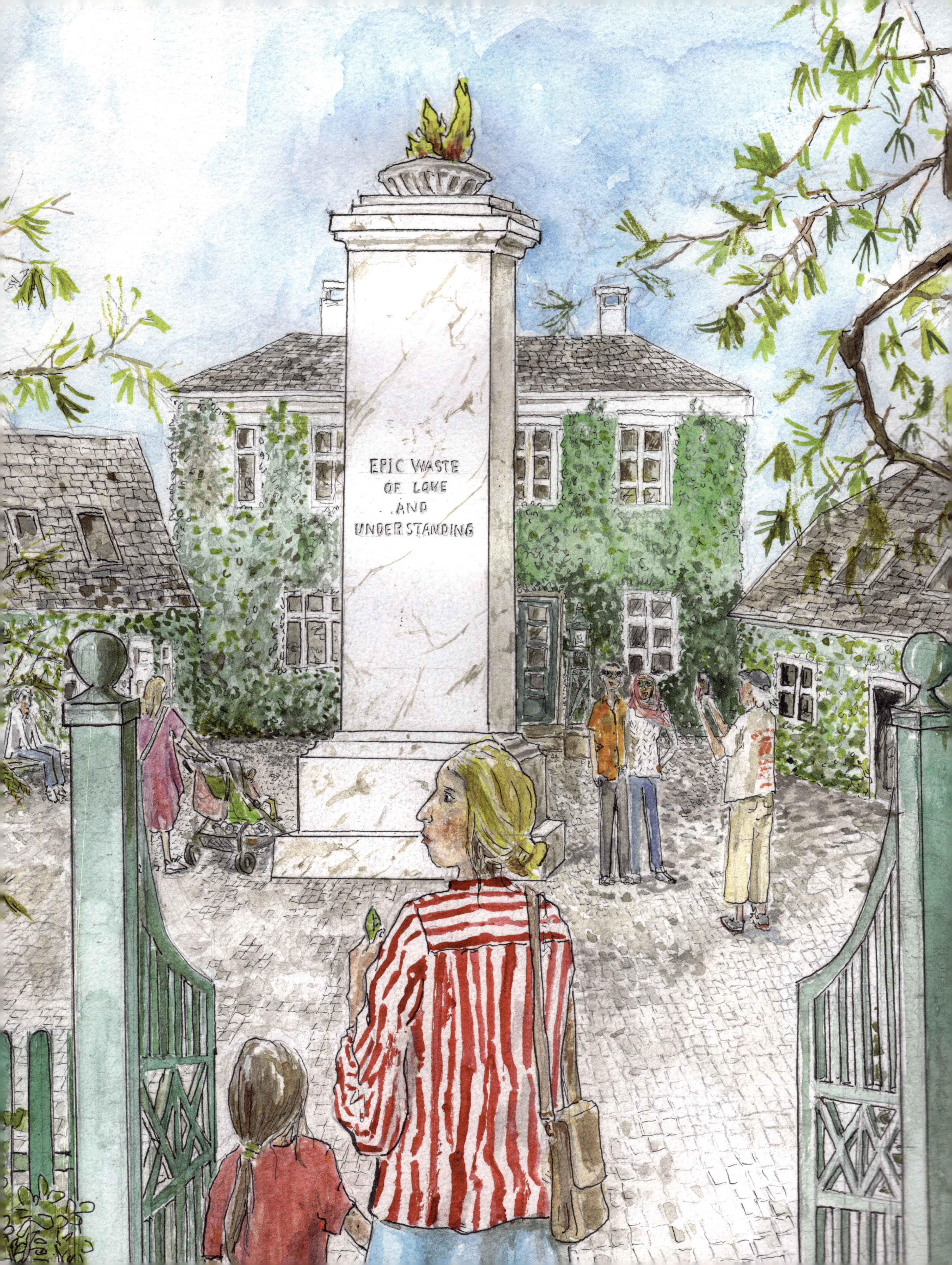
EPIC WASTE
OF LOVE
AND
UNDERSTANDING

CONTENTS

Opposite page: *Epic Waste of Love and Understanding* in front of the Old Villa at Louisiana Museum of Modern Art, drawing by Ragnar Kjartansson, 2023

PREFACE

By Tine Colstrup and Poul Erik Tøjner

The works of Icelandic artist Ragnar Kjartansson (born 1976) embody a loving, humorous and critical dialogue with Western culture – our self-understanding, our cliches, our myths, melancholy, confusion, hope and absurdities. Kjartansson's engagement with the world is as political as it is emotional, and with precision, his works quiver ambiguously between existential and political gravity and poppy lightness; between the tragic and the comic, which can – literally, we've seen it time and again – make audiences both laugh and cry.

Epic Waste of Love and Understanding is the first retrospective presentation of Kjartansson in Scandinavia. It encompasses 20 years of work in a selection that includes several of the artist's best-known projects as well as lesser-known early works and three entirely new pieces created for the exhibition. The non-chronological structure of the exhibition is directly reflected in this publication; works appear in the same order as we encounter them at the Louisiana, where they interact with one another – thematically, visually, sonically – not least in the rooms where several works are installed together.

With an anchor in performance art, Kjartansson operates freely across all media, and the exhibition presents sculpture, painting, works on paper, live performance as well as single-channel video works and large multiscreen installations with music, song and dance. Due to the variety in medium, a Ragnar Kjartansson exhibition can look like a group show at first glance, but core methods and themes remain consistent. The cultural cliche is Kjartansson's ultimate raw material, and he often uses repetition as a method to maintain, scrutinise and pressure test a simple, seemingly banal motif, inviting us to look, listen, chuckle and think again, and then again. Within that process, even the most seemingly superficial and pathetic can metamorphose into seriousness.

Throughout the exhibition, as in the artist's oeuvre, runs a seam of nuanced reflections on masculinity. For Kjartansson, it was initially feminist (performance) art's investigations of identity and gender cliches that became the decisive impulse for his own consistent engagement with these themes and the related power structures. Carolee Schneemann and Marina Abramović are among the artists he often singles out as major inspirational forces. His own performative practice began to take shape when he attended the art academy in Reykjavik (1997-2001). And while the performance art pioneers of the 1960s-1970s embody one set of foremothers – and forefathers – his own parents embody another. With parents working as actors, directors and playwrights Kjartansson grew up in the theatre, surrounded by all its repetitions of lines, role-playing, costumes, pathos formulas and painted

Opposite page: From the opening of the exhibition. Ragnar Kjartansson performing in the museum's park on the porch of the Old Villa, Louisiana Museum of Modern Art, 9 June 2023

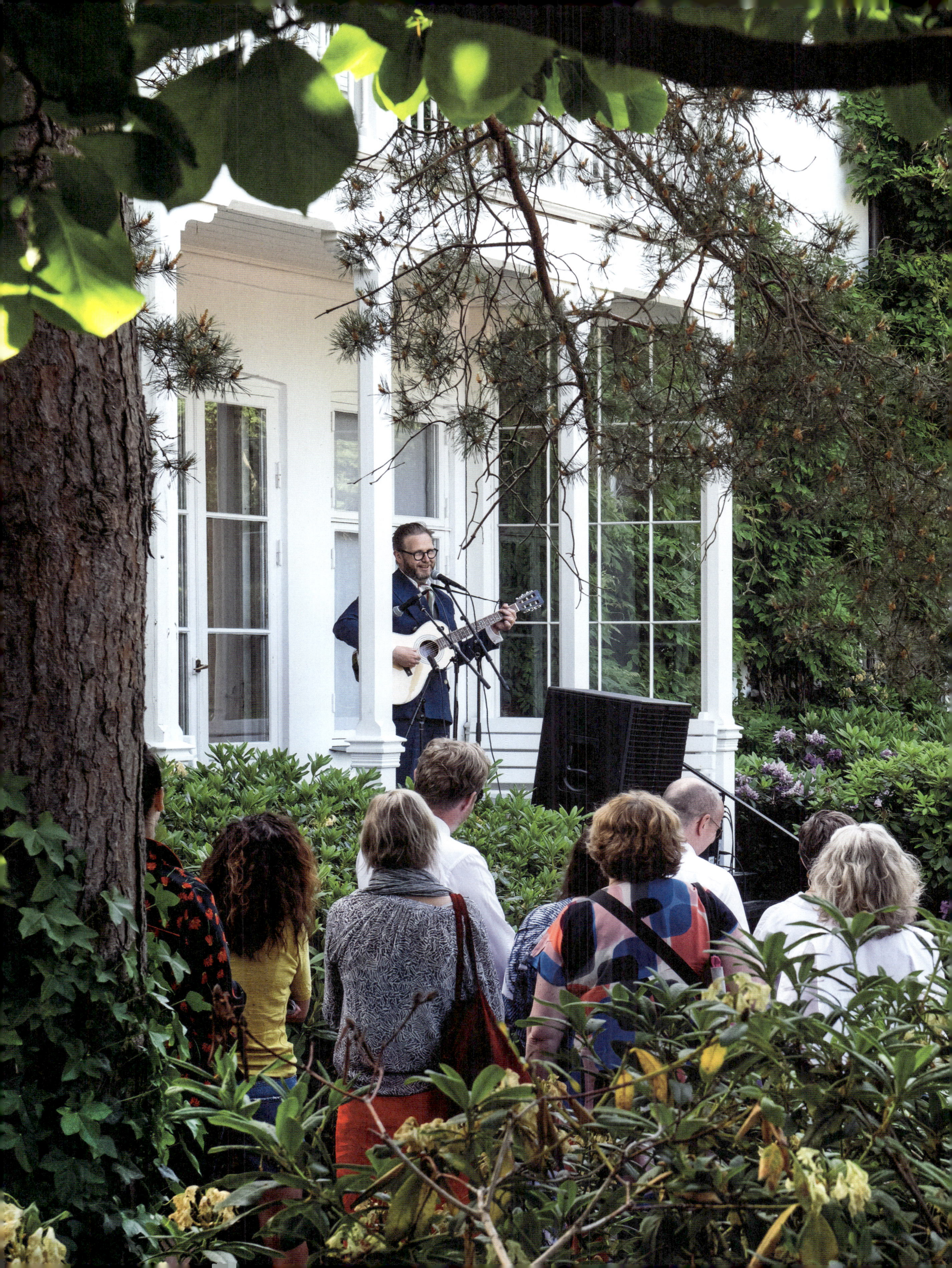

sets. He of course also played theatre himself, and in his fascination with dressing up, staging and dramatic effects, he for a while insisted – much to his family's amazement – on being an altar boy in the Roman Catholic church in Reykjavik. He later stepped onto the stage as a singer and guitarist in several bands. Kjartansson's practice is flavoured by all of the above, and in the works he once and again mixes references and formal devices drawn from the performing arts, classical literature, visual art, music history, pop culture as well as his immediate surroundings and his family.

Gradually, as world events unfolded around the curation of the Louisiana exhibition, not only masculinity became an increasingly central theme in the selection of works. The exhibition is very much a manifestation of the profound political engagement from which Kjartansson's work emerges. The remains of a so-called *Führerloge* made for Adolf Hitler in Berlin in 1941 are displayed alongside the filmed reenactments of two violent attacks on a painting that took place in Moscow in 1913 and 2018. The painting by Ukrainian painter Ilya Repin (1844-1930) depicts the autocratic Russian ruler Ivan the Terrible the moment he realises that he has killed his own son. Aggressive masculinity and geopolitics become two sides of the same coin – as is also the case in the works dealing with Denmark's historic colonial rule over the artist's homeland, Iceland. And, while the subjects are presented in the typically Kjartanssonian way as absurd scenes in the great, human comedy, the seriousness is unmistakable.

When viewed through a political lens, one can clearly see the critical commentary embedded in the oeuvre. The piece *The End – Venezia* (2009), for example, can be seen as a response to the macho capitalism that led Iceland into financial ruin in 2008. And it becomes crystal clear that the new, filmed performance piece created for the exhibition, *Hvad har vi dog gjort for at ha' det så godt* (What have we done to deserve this (2023)), is a hilarious but also rather stinging satire on the privilege blindness that can lurk in Scandinavia and the West in general. Kjartansson masters the art of grasping the wondrous moments of life and the world and their translation into an artistic form, which is precise and distinct yet open enough to accommodate a multitude of complicated topics and readings at the same time.

Poul Erik Tøjner, Director

Tine Colstrup, Curator

Thank you!

For the decisive support that enabled us to realise the exhibition we thank the C.L. David Foundation and Collection, and we thank Myndlistarsjóður / the Icelandic Visual Arts Fund for additional support.

We are also thankful for the encouragement and support that we received from Börkur Arnarson and everyone at i8 Gallery in Reykjavik and Roland Augustine, Lawrence Luhring and the rest of the team at Luhring Augustine in New York.

Our gratitude also goes to all of the writers who contributed great texts and insights for this publication, making it a varied mix of reflections and perspectives on Kjartansson's work.

An exhibition of this kind, including newly produced works in different media, would be impossible to realise without the care and expertise of numerous people from across many fields. We thank everyone who has contributed in one way or another, including not least the formidable and dedicated team at the Louisiana and the team of performers who will perform *Bangemand* (Scaredman) throughout the exhibition period.

We express our heartfelt thanks to the artist and his team: thank you very much Ragnar Kjartansson, Ingibjörg Sigurjónsdóttir, Christopher McDonald and Lilja Gunnarsdóttir. It has been an utmost pleasure to collaborate with you and benefit from your trust, your good spirits and generous dedication towards the exhibition and the catalogue. Second to none.

For their generous contributions to the exhibition, we thank private and institutional lenders who have all met the project with kindness and enthusiasm:

AMA Collection, Venezia
The Art Institute of Chicago
De Pont museum, Tilburg
Fondazione Sandretto Re Rebaudengo, Torino
Hirshhorn Museum and Sculpture Garden,
Smithsonian Institution, Washington, D.C.
i8 Gallery, Reykjavik
Luhring Augustine, New York
Migros Museum für Gegenwartskunst, Zürich
National Gallery of Iceland, Reykjavik
We also thank the private collectors and lenders who wish to remain anonymous.

On the occasion of the exhibition, a video interview was recorded in the artist's studio in Reykjavik in May 2023, which can be found online on Louisiana Channel – along with earlier interviews with the artist – under the title *I'm Not An Authentic Human Being*.

Opposite page: Photos taken during the preparation of the exhibition as well as from the opening

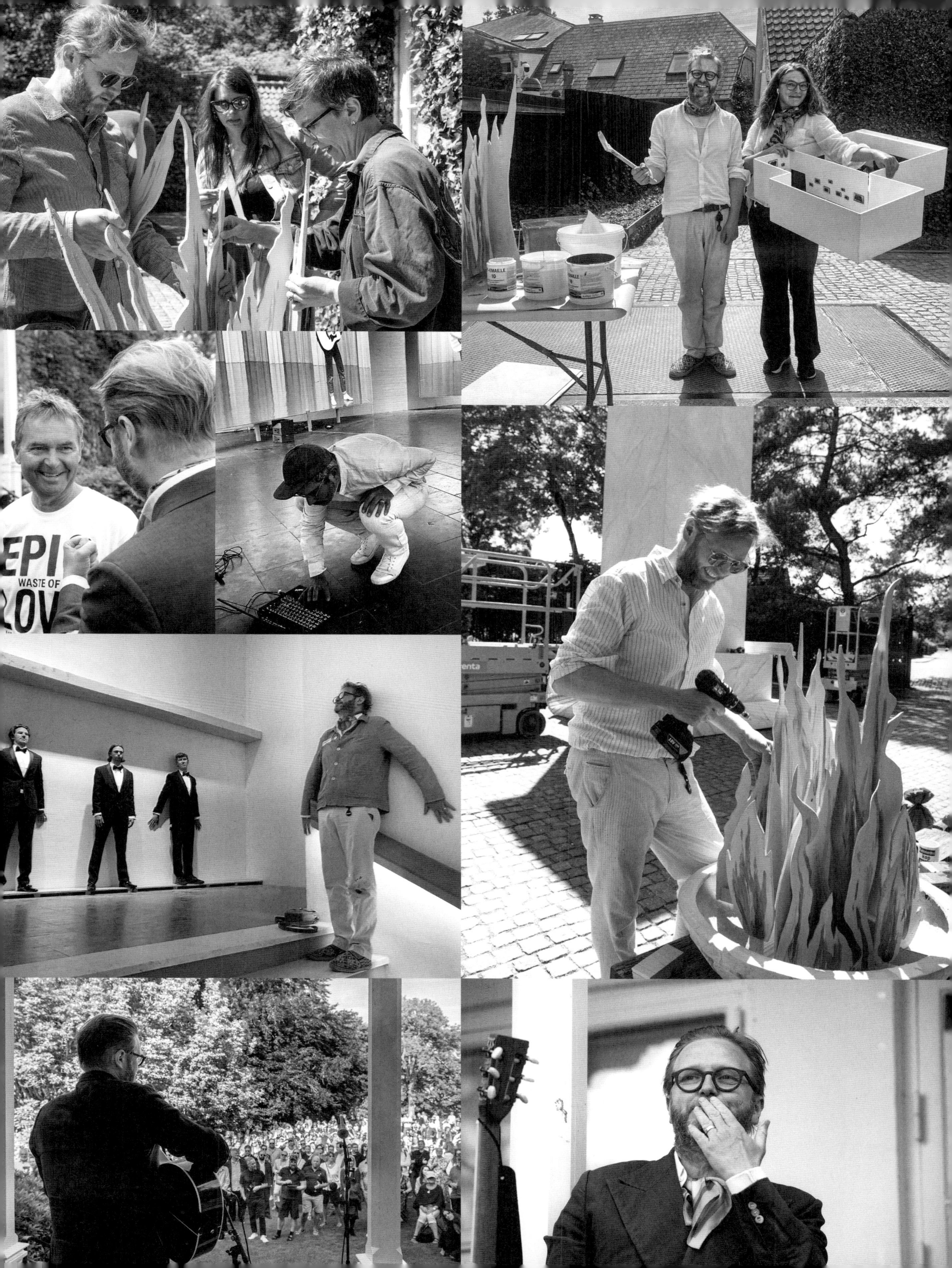
WASTE OF

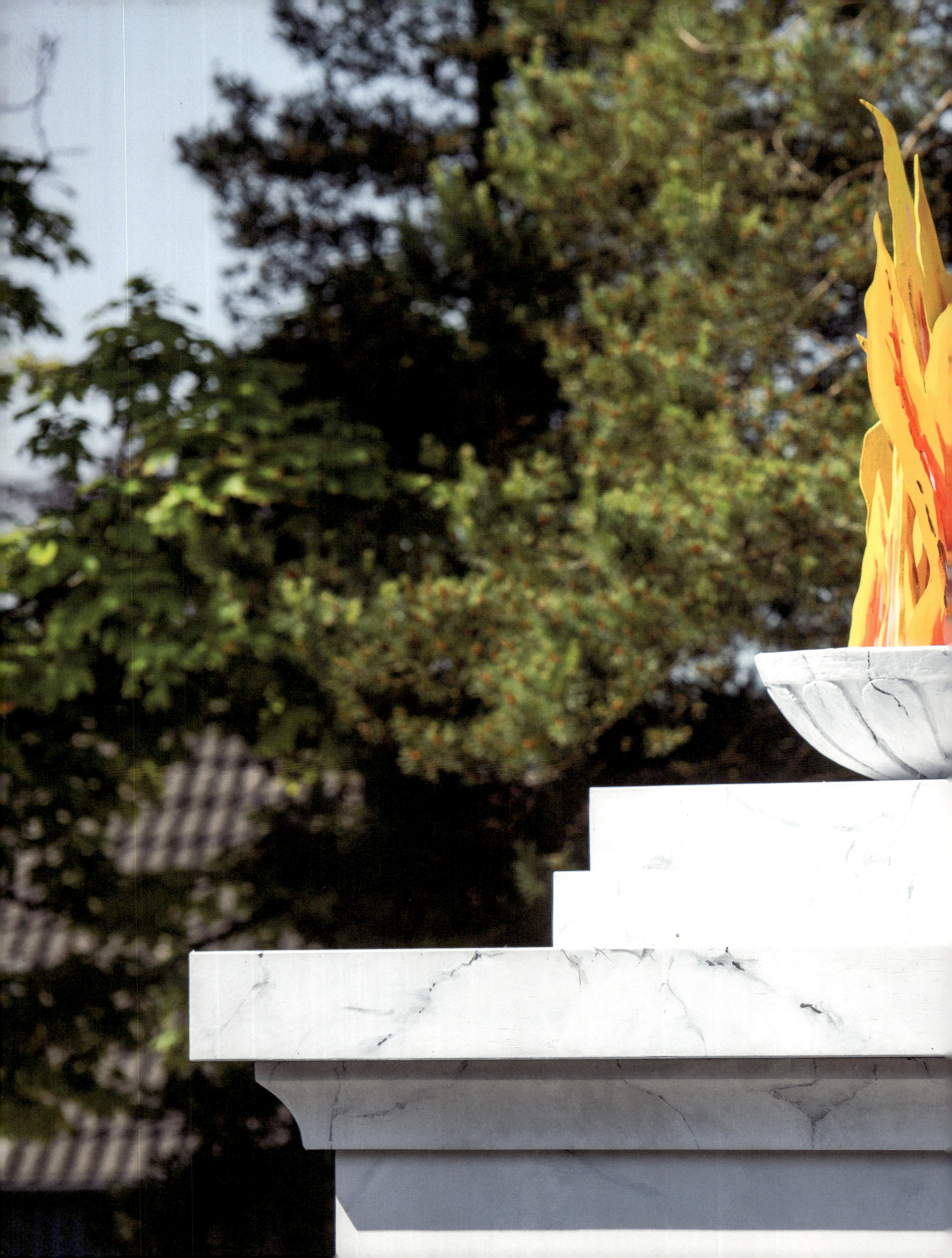

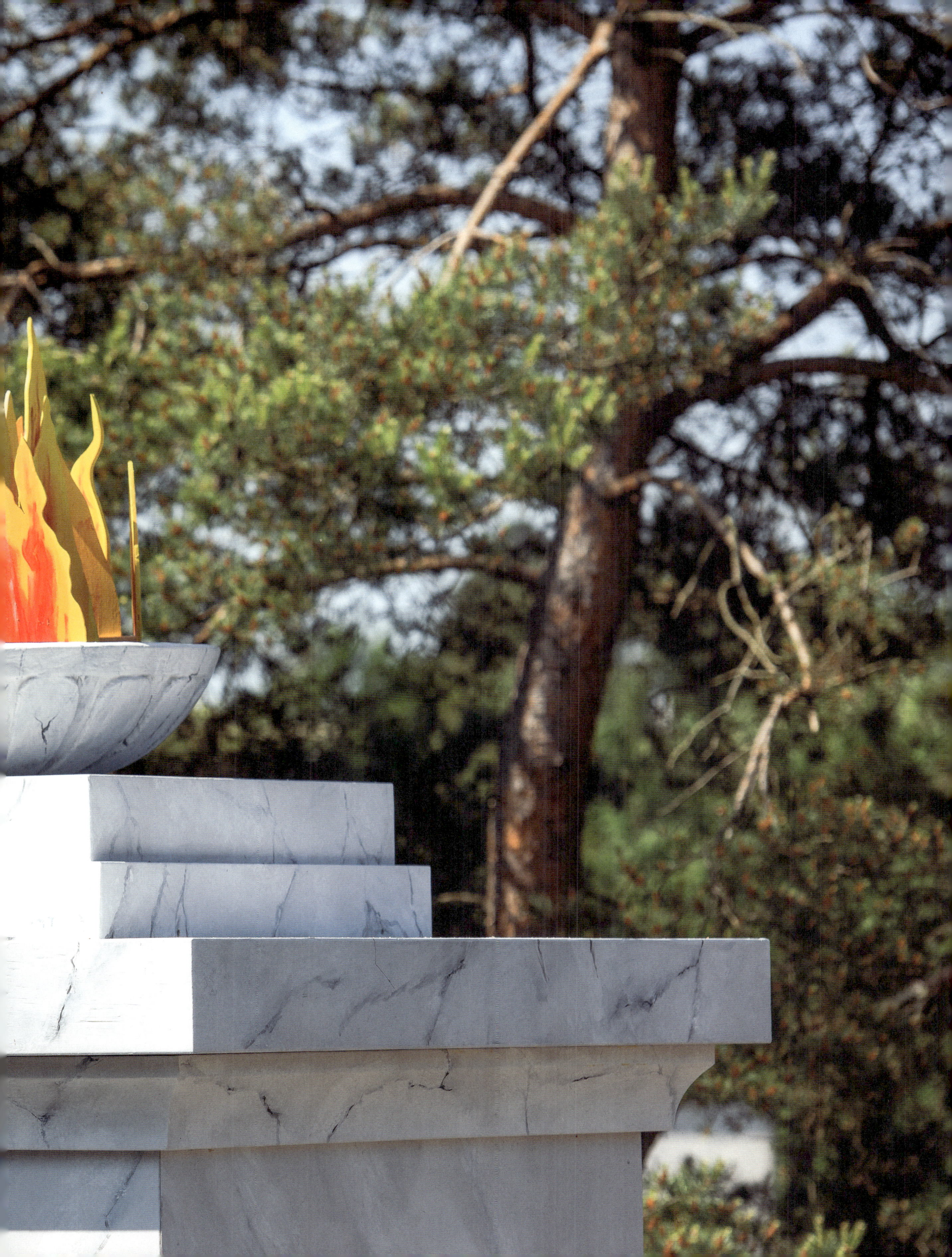

EPIC WASTE OF LOVE AND UNDERSTANDING — 2023

Plywood and paint
230 × 600 × 230 cm
Courtesy of the artist, Luhring Augustine, New York, and i8 Gallery, Reykjavik

By Tine Colstrup

The monument was created for the exhibition at the Louisiana where it is placed in front of the entrance to the museum. It is constructed of plywood and takes on the unmistakable character of a faux marble theatre set, replete with a painted eternal flame on the top. It mimics a classic monument of the kind erected to commemorate important figures or historical events. Kjartansson has created a monument to an "epic waste of love and understanding". The phrase is taken from an argument the artist and his wife had at home in their kitchen. In monumental form, it stands as an almost too grandiose poetic-pathetic statement on the striking squandering of love and empathy found in the crisis and conflicts of history and the present day, and in our relationships with each other and the world.

TINE COLSTRUP is curator at Louisiana Museum of Modern Art and curated *Epic Waste of Love and Understanding*.

Opposite page and the previous spread: Installation views, Louisiana Museum of Modern Art, 2023

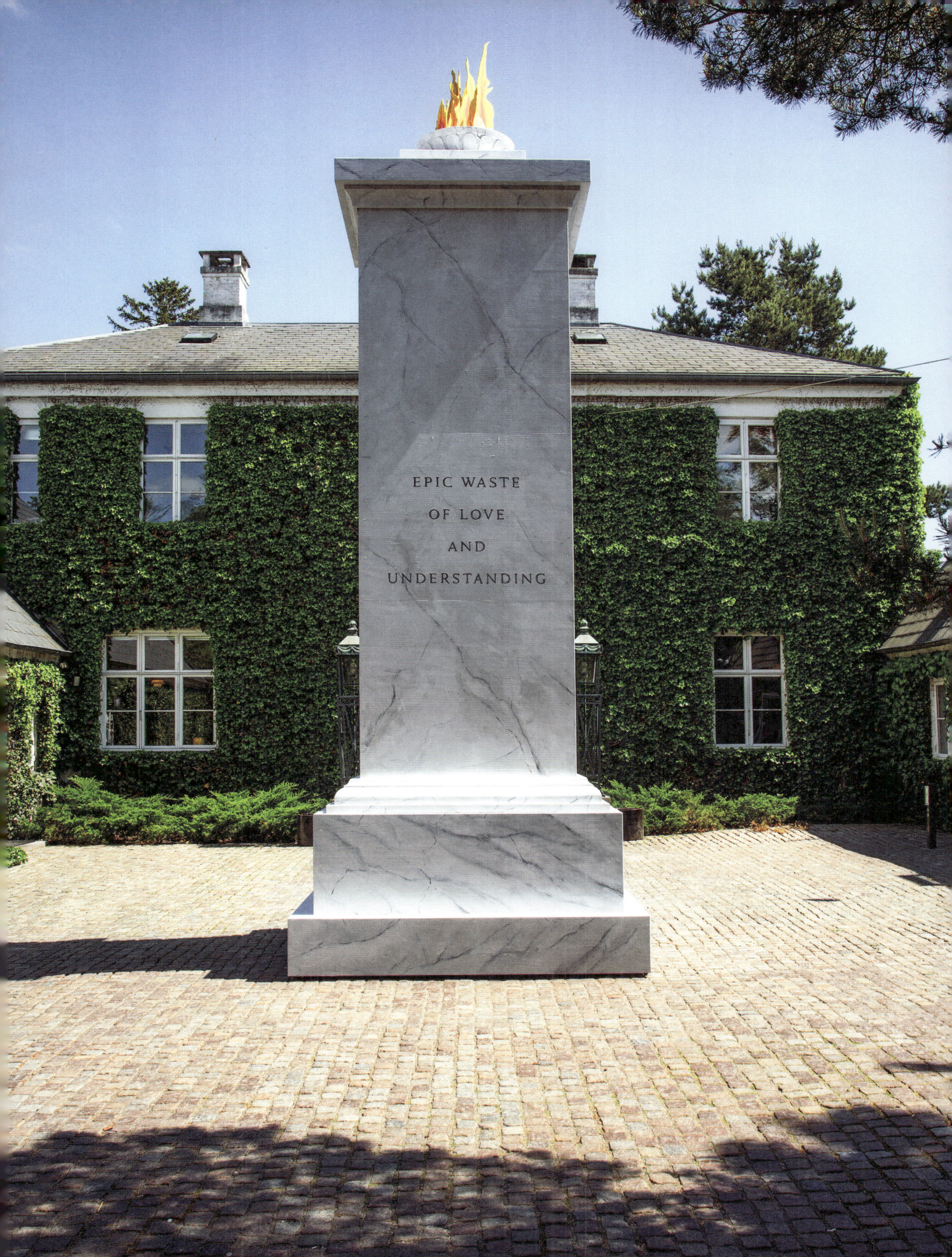
EPIC WASTE
OF LOVE
AND
UNDERSTANDING

GUILT AND FEAR — 2022

Porcelain salt and pepper shakers
Dimensions variable
Courtesy of the artist, Luhring Augustine, New York, and i8 Gallery, Reykjavik

Theaster Gates in conversation with Ragnar Kjartansson

Theaster Gates: Ragnar, you made the decision to make a ceramic multiple. Can you talk about why ceramics, why clay, seemed important for this project?

Ragnar Kjartansson: The piece is just two salt and pepper shakers. One called "Guilt", the other called "Fear". The idea just came like a "pling". I was having a conversation with a friend. I had done a piece, where everything within it was very fragile; all the morals of it and all this art-world tension of 'whose story is it to tell', etc. And she was talking about the mood in general and the mood in New York and said, "Oh, it's all just soaked in guilt and fear." And I remember instantly thinking, I want to make this kind of white porcelain multiple of salt and pepper shakers with guilt and fear. And just play with the idea of porcelain and all its cultural connotations.

TG: The innuendo of porcelain.

RK: Oh, yeah. Innuendo is sort of the substance of art, I would say.

TG: If you were going to add a third thing to guilt and fear, you would probably add something that has to do with envy or assumption or rumour. But I love that these two words are a reflection by another artist who is offering some of her insight as to the state of the art world, which is often the state of the world.

RK: Yeah, totally.

TG: They connect.

RK: And I was also thinking a lot about the positive effects of guilt and fear. Because we're always told like, "Oh, don't have any fear and, fuck guilt and all that stuff." But it is the essence of empathy and progress in so many ways.

TG: In the US, the absence of guilt and fear is what led to the storming of the Capitol [2021].

RK: So it was basically a comment on a mood. I mean, I was in New York, in 2021, the pandemic was ending. But everything was just really soaked in guilt and fear.

TG: Yeah. It's also reasonable that the project that we had going in Moscow in 2022 was a kind of precursive moment where Russia, the superpower, was kind of declaring itself to be such, and I could tell that that kind of national, or governmental, position was led with fear.

RK: Absolutely. And that was just fear of one man.

TG: But imagine fear of an invisible disease or fear of an invisible virus. And the gaslighting and all those things that are happening now. Some people deserve to be made to feel guilty [*laughs*].

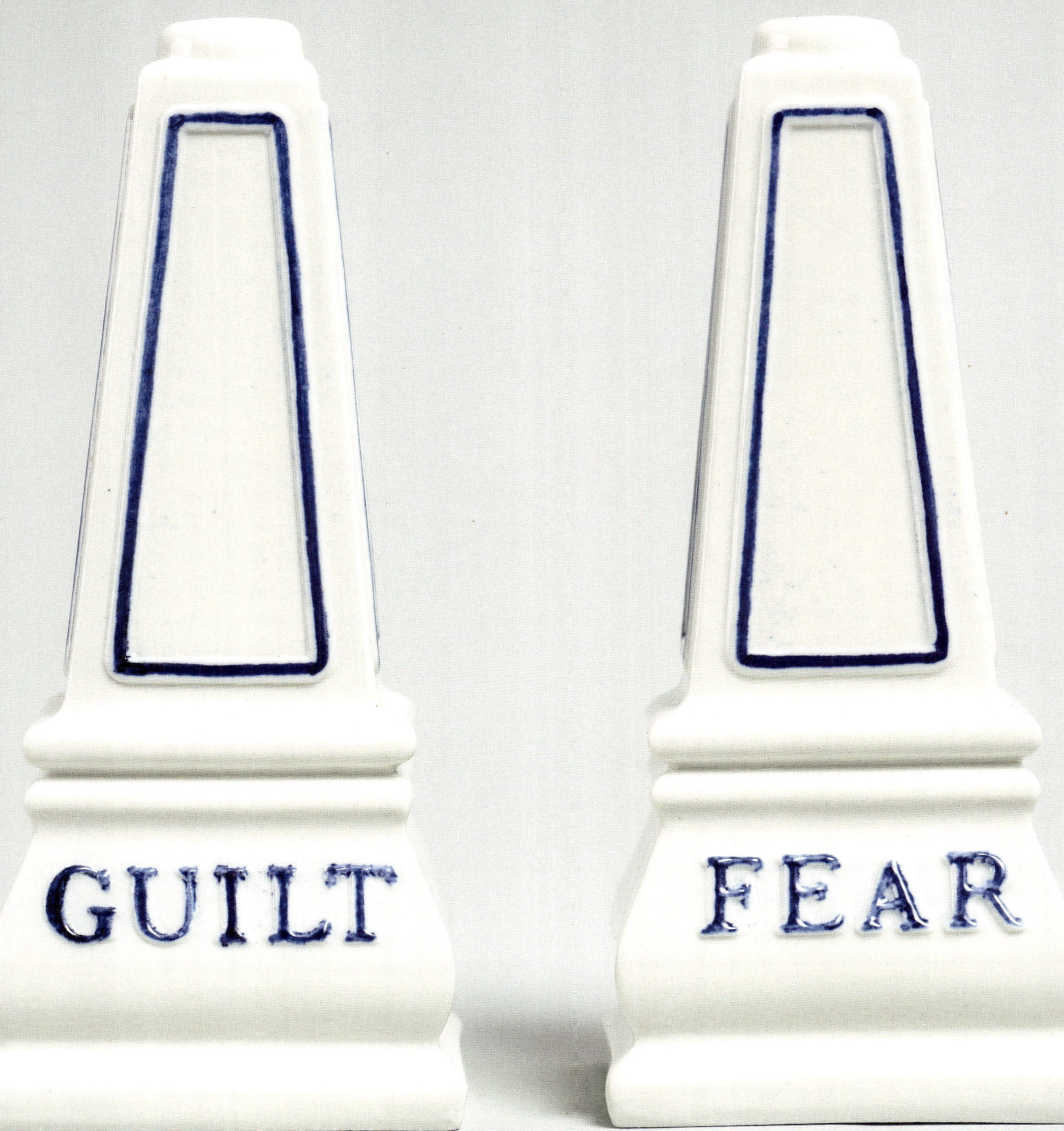
GUILT
FEAR

RK: Totally [*laughs too*].

TG: But being guilty and having guilt are a little bit different.

RK: Absolutely. I was thinking about it a lot, because the feeling I was trying to tap into was also the post-MeToo and post-Black Lives Matter guilt and fear. Everything was also soaked in both a positive part of it and a weird hypocrisy.

TG: One of the things that I really thought about over the years was when people would try to align me with one political arts or artistic canon or another. But I don't need positionality. Because often positionality is the thing that leads to zealousness. And that leads to judgment. And I don't need to judge someone else's position because I have such an absolute position. I'm just making. If I want to do something with a vacant building, I'm going to do it, or with the varying resources or people I have access to, I'm going to share it. I don't need someone to say, "Oh, well, he's doing that because he's sided with this camp." Because I really do think that is the beginning of an unnecessary hegemonic device. No, no, no, no. We're family! We try to do good things together.

RK: I totally agree with you. I think that is the attitude of progress, actually. Then we can have real progress.

TG: If you catch me while I'm drinking – I learned this from you – if you catch me while I'm drinking, and I say something like, "I think education should be free." Which I probably would. And if a conservative comes back and says, "It shouldn't be free for everyone, it should be free for those who really deserve it." Then you can get into a debate about who deserves free education. I want to have that debate.

RK: All debate is good. Absolutely. And I deeply believe in it. I've been thinking so much about the progress that was made here in Iceland with the women's party. They started it in 1983, and Iceland basically became a very feminist country just because the women's party got into parliament. And they got in by being funny and open and getting everybody involved. You know, you really have to get the enemy involved.

TG: Yeah, man.

RK: So that things actually happen. But if you're always just blocking everybody out, nothing happens. I think that's the bliss for the status quo.

TG: It is interesting that you say that because it feels like your approach to making overall has been with intelligence, with a touch of humour and candour and self-critique. And this way of making makes room for others to imagine that they can fit inside of the work. That the work is relating to them, even if it's totally different from anything they've ever seen. There's an honesty and a sincerity. And I think that that's really hard to do. But I wanted you to talk about the approach to some of these things that are just at the cusp of political rage; you still approach it with nuance, salt and pepper shakers. Can you talk about this approach of 'I'm not going to take myself too seriously', but then you turn that into art. How do you do that?

RK: I am just in awe of the politics going through everything in our lives.

TG: Yeah. Yeah!

RK: And that's also something I really love about the 21st century. You often hear artists go like, "Oh, you can't say anything, you can't do anything, blah, blah, blah." But of course, you can. And after having worked in totalitarian countries where people cannot say anything for real! I just roll my eyes when I hear that. There is a huge difference from being scolded on Twitter and sent to prison. Well, and this sense of not being serious about what's serious? I think it's just coming from trying to be honest about things. Everything is just totally soaked in tension, and I'm just so interested in it. That's what I also love about our time: things are constantly being deconstructed.

TG: Yeah.

RK: And these huge political issues just end up being these porcelain salt and pepper shakers. Where you try to deal with our emotions, our fears and guilt, but also colonialism and whatnot. Iceland was a colony of Denmark, and for me Danish porcelain is like the ultimate elegance. I thought I was a proper human being when I could first afford a set of porcelain plates, you know.

TG: Tell me more about that. About your history with ceramics. And the truth of Icelandic occupation.

The following spread: Installation view, Louisiana Museum of Modern Art, 2023

RK: Well, I've always been totally in awe of ceramics because I was raised with a grandfather who was really a pioneer in ceramics in Iceland. I'm his namesake; he was Ragnar Kjartansson [1923-1988]. And when I started being an artist, people who love his work would contact my grandmother and say, "There's some clown destroying the good name of Ragnar Kjartansson. We have to stop this!" And my grandmother was like, "I'm sorry, there's nothing we can do. He's our grandson. And we had no idea he was going to be an artist; he just has this name."

TG: That's great!

RK: So, I was always fascinated with all this. Because ceramics to us seem like a cute division of art; it has this assumption of being close to earth and all that stuff. But my granddad was a disciple of Guðmundur frá Miðdal (1893-1968), who was not only the pioneer of ceramics in Iceland, but he was also a Nazi. He was an outdoorsman, so my grandfather, who was his assistant, would go on trips around the highlands with him and some SS guys as a teenager. And it's ... really disturbing. My grandfather was far from being a Nazi – he was a total Commie arty kind of dude – but he had this experience in his youth. And then there is my aunt, Inga Ragnarsdóttir (born 1955), who is also a ceramicist and a sculptor. Talking about ceramics and materials and traditions with her is always a feast. There are all these connections. But my granddad started his pottery studio, and it became really an avant-garde hub in Reykjavik, and a lot of the artists who would become the Fluxus artists in Iceland were working there. And then this Swiss guy called Dieter Roth (1930-1998) came over.

TG: Wow!

RK: My granddad and Dieter would make ceramics together and Dieter made a kind of very modernist, full-on ceramics, and he created all their visual presentation in his gorgeous graphic design. My grandfather's ceramics studio really became a kind of arty haven. I was talking to Björn Roth [born 1961], the son of Dieter Roth. And you know, we know Dieter Roth as this great artist of chaos and explosion, but Björn said, "You have to remember that when Dieter came to Iceland, he was a purist modernist who didn't drink, he didn't read novels, and he only believed in functional stuff." And then he met my grandfather, who was a guitar-playing kind of screaming party man. And Dieter just went into the chaos of his pottery studio and never ever looked back.

TG: Ragnar, you're saying that your grandfather turned Dieter Roth out?

RK: That was what Björn Roth told me. And I had never thought that there was this kind of connection. But it makes sense.

TG: I love that, bro! I've often said that modernism began with ceramics. Look at Herbert Read (1893-1968) one of the great British writers and poets. He thought about the plastic arts, sculpture, and how, in a way, we couldn't have gotten to the modernist art forms or Míro if we didn't have additive plastic studio practices; that clay in that sense is precursive to the thing we understand is modernism.

RK: Ah, so that from clay you understand functionalism? It's so hands on?

TG: Yeah, and that you can get from craft to the sculptural form. Take your pick: Henry Moore, Calder, Picasso. You could get to a form and refine it and refine it and refine it. I'd like to think that clay is at the root of revolutionary practices. And this story between Ragnar Sr. and Dieter Roth is another of these moments; like Peter Voulkos (1924-2002) at Black Mountain College. Where you come in straight and then a revolution happens within the material that just explodes your imagination.

RK: Totally. And I love that in the studio they were dealing with these tensions of modernism, and Dieter exploded as an artist. But then my grandfather ... looked into the abyss of the non-form of modernism and just got scared. He went into bed and lay there for two years. He had been this hardcore modernist looking for the truth of the form, but he got out of bed and became a social realist, making sculptures of cows and sailors. There's a memorial for a sailor in every town in Iceland made by my grandfather. But they always continued being friends and Dieter really respected this because he was all about truth in art. Like, "Okay, if this is your truth to become a social realist, I totally respect that."

TG: I love that. I also love that you're from this lineage that holds intention, ideas and materials. It's not restricted to just performance or just sculpture or bad drawings or bad painting [*both laugh*]. And now ceramics is hot.

RK: It's super-hot [*both laugh*].

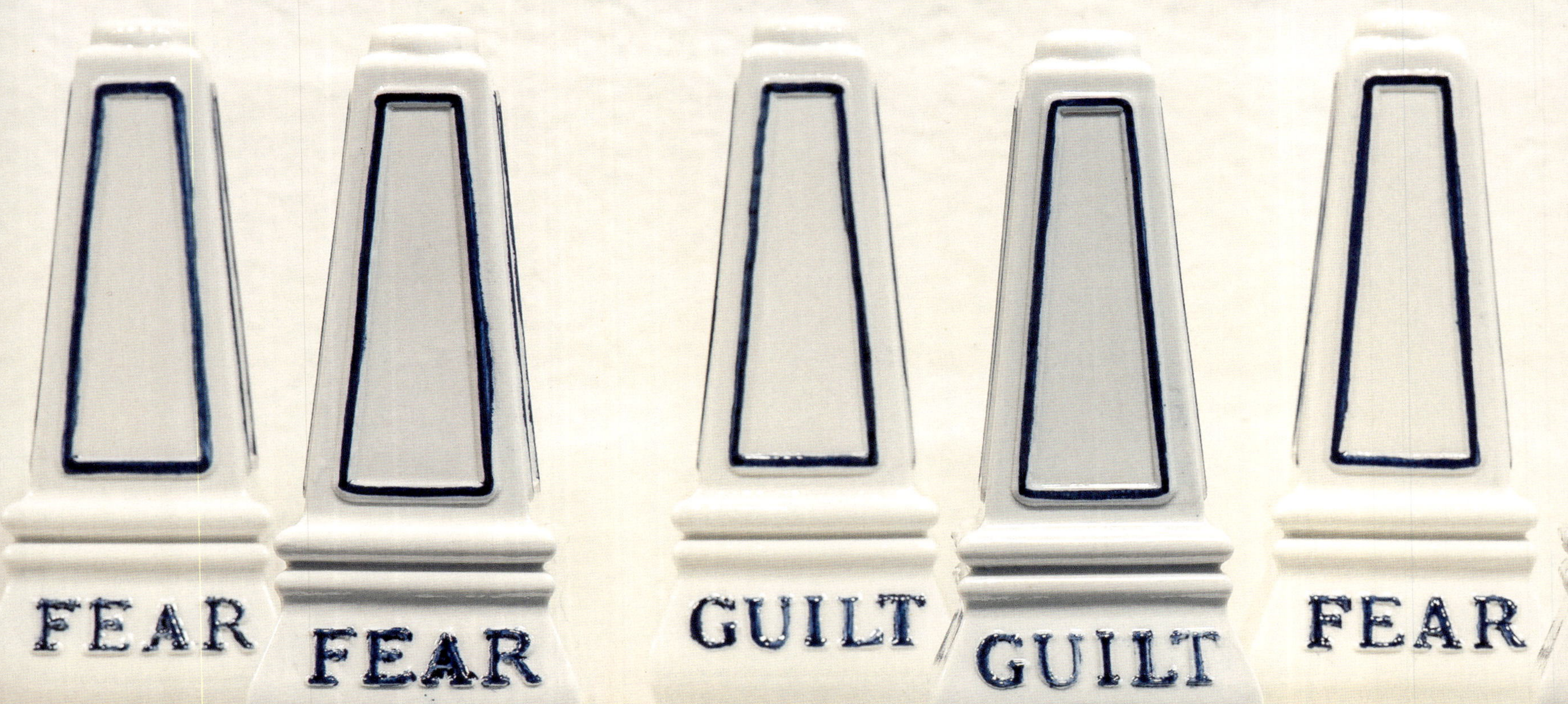
FEAR
FEAR
GUILT
GUILT
FEAR

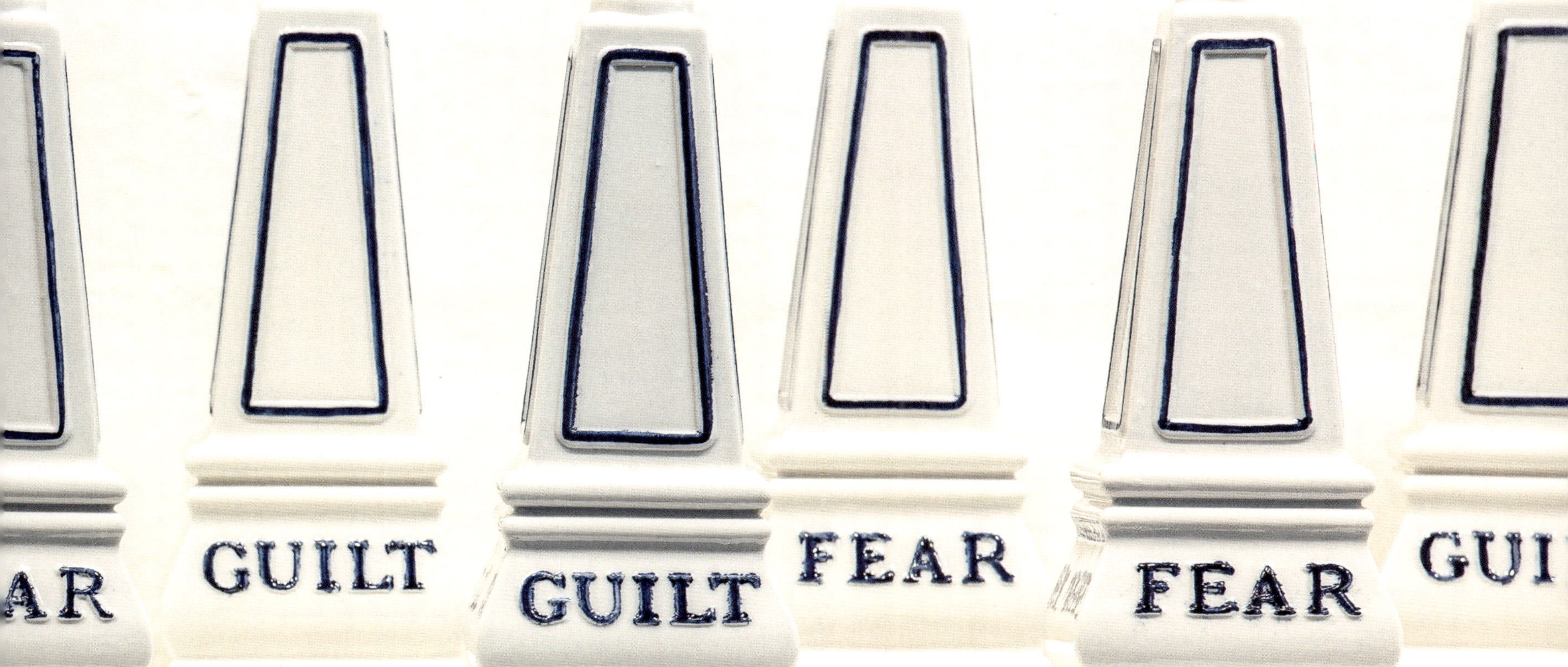
GUILT
GUILT
FEAR
FEAR

TG: And people are like, "What made you get into ceramics?" Well, I didn't come to clay as a contemporary artist looking for myself. I started in ceramics. And my self kept growing. But I never divorced who I am. This is back to the burden of trying to be post-colonial. If the thing that I learned was 'contemporary, white American ceramics', how can I ingest that? Add to it? Without being oppressed by it, but internalise it and turn it into what I needed to be to be great? And I spend time with potters around the world, saying, "Oh, this isn't American ceramics, this isn't white ceramics, this is people's ability." And I fuck with people's ability, I'm interested in that. And I want to applaud you for having courage to mess with something that can be so specific in terms of its own boutique tradition within art.

RK: I mess with it. Sometimes I make ceramics for Christmas presents and stuff, but I have never made it as an art practice. Except this piece, which I made in collaboration with this awesome porcelain specialist, Marlies Crooijmans at Fabrique Céramique in the Netherlands. It had to be deep European porcelain, you know. And what you were referring to, when you started studying ceramics, and "Okay, it's like white American heritage?" I always like to think of this kind of ultimate whiteness of porcelain. It's so super European in a way. But no, no, it's Chinese and it's basically European cultural appropriation. And I just find that so amazing. But porcelain has this kind of similar ultimate whiteness as a Polo Ralph Lauren sweater worn across the shoulders, you know.

TG: What you are articulating right now is that one way of imagining ceramics, is that the history of ceramics in Europe has been the pursuit of whiteness. And it's like, where do you find the whitest white? You actually find it in China ... No matter how white the Brits want to be, the best they'll get is a Chinese vase. So, you had to do all these things to lighten the complexion of the ceramics?

RK: And brutal lightness. I love the idea of brutal lightness. It is so important, I think.

TG: Yeah. Can you describe the piece?

RK: It's hundreds of "Guilt and Fear" salt and pepper shakers side by side through a whole hallway in the Louisiana. Just a line of couples in the hundreds of "Guilt and Fear", "Guilt and Fear". I like the poetry of it. When you walk past it, it's just "Guilt and Fear", "Guilt and Fear", "Guilt and Fear", "Guilt and Fear".

TG: I should do the *Guilt and Fear* performance!

RK: Definitely [*laughs*]. So it's almost like a heartbeat when you walk past it, like [*saying it rhythmically*] "Guilt and Fear", "Guilt and Fear", "Guilt and Fear", "Guilt and Fear", "Guilt and Fear", "Guilt and Fear", "Guilt and Fear", "Guilt and Fear". And then they are just there, ready to be guilt and fear, ready for domestic use.

TG: They're ready for Christmas presents. You can give them to all of Iceland [*both laugh*]. To all your friends and enemies.

RK: Yes, absolutely. We all share the same thing: guilt and fear.

TG: Ragnar, it is this idea of the current state of things turned into a form. And what is in every kitchen? Guilt and fear. You know, guilt and fear is as common as salt and pepper. I really love that as a poetic move for your first formal project, but I remember being on a train with you, and you had on a very elegantly tailored suit. Can you talk about the ways that craft is a part of your life?

RK: I would say it's just a kick. I am just so into it. It's not fetish, it's just a kick to be around well-crafted things. And the idea of craftsmanship? I just find it very, very beautiful. I went to a housewife school in Iceland.

TG: Oh?

RK: Yeah. It was called the Home Economics School of Reykjavik, but it used to be called the Housewives School of Reykjavik. And I went there basically to appreciate and understand especially feminine craftsmanship like knitting and sewing and all that stuff; the craft that goes into when your grandmother gives you a sweater. Which has been so belittled. So, just from that I learned to appreciate craftsmanship a lot; like the kick of being in a well-tailored suit; all the work that goes into it. The deep mystery of sewing and stitching. It's just fantastic. And it goes to everything, of course, like pottery or a car; the craftmanship of a car. I love that stuff. And what I learned from the headmistress of the housewife school was this philosophy: "It's expensive to buy cheap."

TG: Oh, yeah, absolutely. "Buy once in a hundred years."

RK: And it's also very environmentally true that we should use stuff that is well-made and take care of it and preserve. It's really a matter of environmental urgency. Talking like this is very kind of sounding like King Charles, which is hilarious [*both laugh*].

TG: I love that, because I just keep going back to the metaphor of salt and pepper, like, "Oh, guilt and fear? You run out of it." The salt and pepper shakers have a limited amount of guilt and fear and then you have to refill it. CNN, Fox News ... it is the constant refilling of guilt and fear.

RK: Yeah. It's like the morning brief, "Okay, we have to refill our containers today, what do we do?"

TG: "Two men killed, car bombing, carjacking." You realise that part of our media is strategically, consistently feeding us content in a way that makes us total aliens from each other.

RK: Total aliens from each other. I think in our hearts we are sick and media and tech companies benefit from that. There was an interview with Cardi B (born 1992) where she was talking politics in a super sharp way, I've been quoting it so much, she said, "I'm a Bernie girl, but Trump's going to win. Because people vote with their hearts, not with their minds. And in their hearts, people are racists." It's so wisely said. And it applies to all politics. What's in the heart? The mind says, "Distribute wealth, secure good health care, good education." And all these things are really important, but they're boring. The heart just wants to hate something and someone.

TG: And a person raised in capitalism never wants to lose their position. You know, if you're receiving one of something means that I had five of that thing and now I'll have four, this shit scares people to no end. The equity gap. It's like, could we solve hunger? I think we could. But we have guilt and fear. Guilt and fear.

Having an exhibition at the Louisiana is a big deal. It's a gift. Can you talk a little bit about what you are wanting the *Guilt and Fear* piece within the larger show to do?

RK: There's going to be a big sculpture outside the museum, which is in a kind of similar classical shape as the salt and pepper shakers. Because I always connect these classical shapes with Bertel Thorvaldsen (1770-1844), the Icelandic-Danish sculptor of the 19th century, who was super classical and one of the many, many things Denmark and Iceland have in common. It's going to look like a marble monument, like these sculptor's sculptures of a First World War memorial. But it's just made out of plywood and painted as marble. It's also the title piece of the show: *Epic Waste of Love and Understanding*. It was something that Ingibjörg, my wife, said to me when we were arguing, and I was just like, "That was a good sentence!"

TG: Yeah. Like, "Baby, I'm sorry. I love you. I am stealing that. Recognise it with love and understanding."

RK: Yeah. So a lot of the show, which I make with Tine, the curator, is very personal. It's about my stand in the world as who I am, but also what I am. I take a lot of my practice from the feminist artists who deal with the identity of the artist. And I find it fascinating that my identity is the problem. I am the middle-aged white artist guy. And I find this culture and the evilness and beauty of it so fascinating. So I'm hoping that the show becomes both personal and generates feelings, gut feelings. And that it becomes a show about the complexities of Western culture, both positive and negative.

In all my works there are these uneasy politics. I find everything so ambiguous, and this work is at the start of the show, and it's really a sort of a prelude, like the start of an opera [*he sings some notes*]. It's like, "Okay, here I am. This is the opera starting based on guilt and fear, guilt and fear, guilt and fear." So that's what I'm hoping for. And also for me, it's fun to show in the Louisiana because it's like I'm going to show in the capital. You know, it's still like Copenhagen is the capital of Iceland; we got independence in 1944, but there is this kind of feeling about it.

And then there are a few pieces dealing with the Icelandic-Danish relationship and the complexities of it. Man, I'm really raised with this idea that we are victims of Danish colonialism. But, you know, when you look at history, maybe it wasn't that bad. Because historically it's mostly Icelandic landowners who were torturing people, basically, and the Danish king always trying to go, "Okay, please, please, please be kind. You know, remember, human life is important, etc." So I hope that these ideas are all going to somehow ambiguously shine through. And *Guilt and Fear* is a very important factor in that. With the idea of the material, the porcelain and the Delft blue and then the repetition ... Turning something complex into form.

TG: Well, I have to admit that the project, which takes this kind of current sentiment and gives it form, is inspiring to me. And encouraging. It kind of makes me want to stay in the studio. And I think it's going to be an important piece for kids who study ceramics and who study contemporary practices to know that they can be poetic even within the craft. So thank you. Thank you. Thank you. Thank you. And thank you for this conversation. I just hope you turned the tape recorder on.

THEASTER GATES is an American artist, social innovator and professor in the Department of Visual Arts at the University of Chicago. Originally trained as a ceramicist, Gates translates the intricacies of objecthood and Blackness through space theory, land development, sculpture and performance.

This conversation took place via Zoom in May 2023.

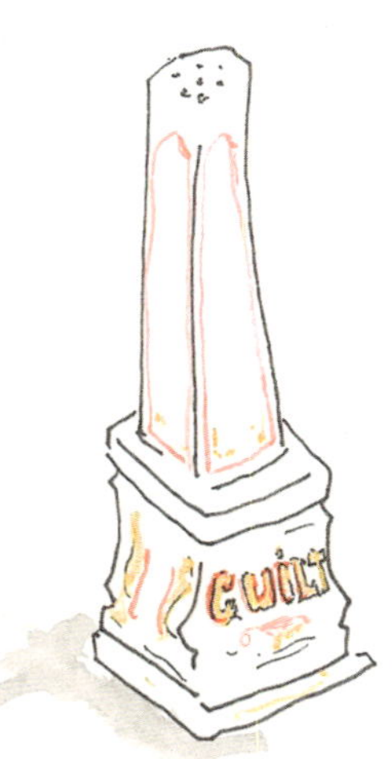

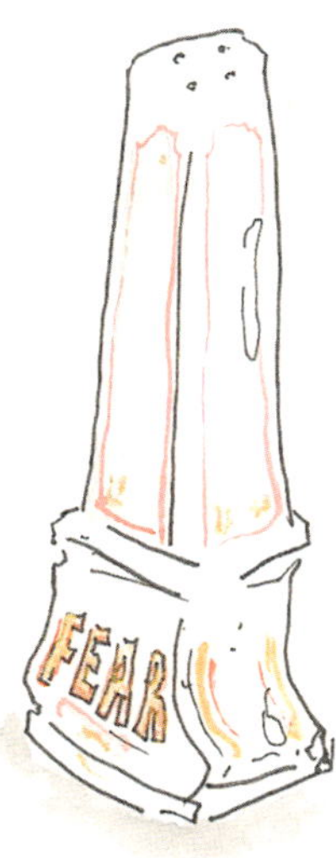

Drawing by Ragnar Kjartansson, 2021
Opposite page and following spread: Installation views, Louisiana Museum of Modern Art, 2023

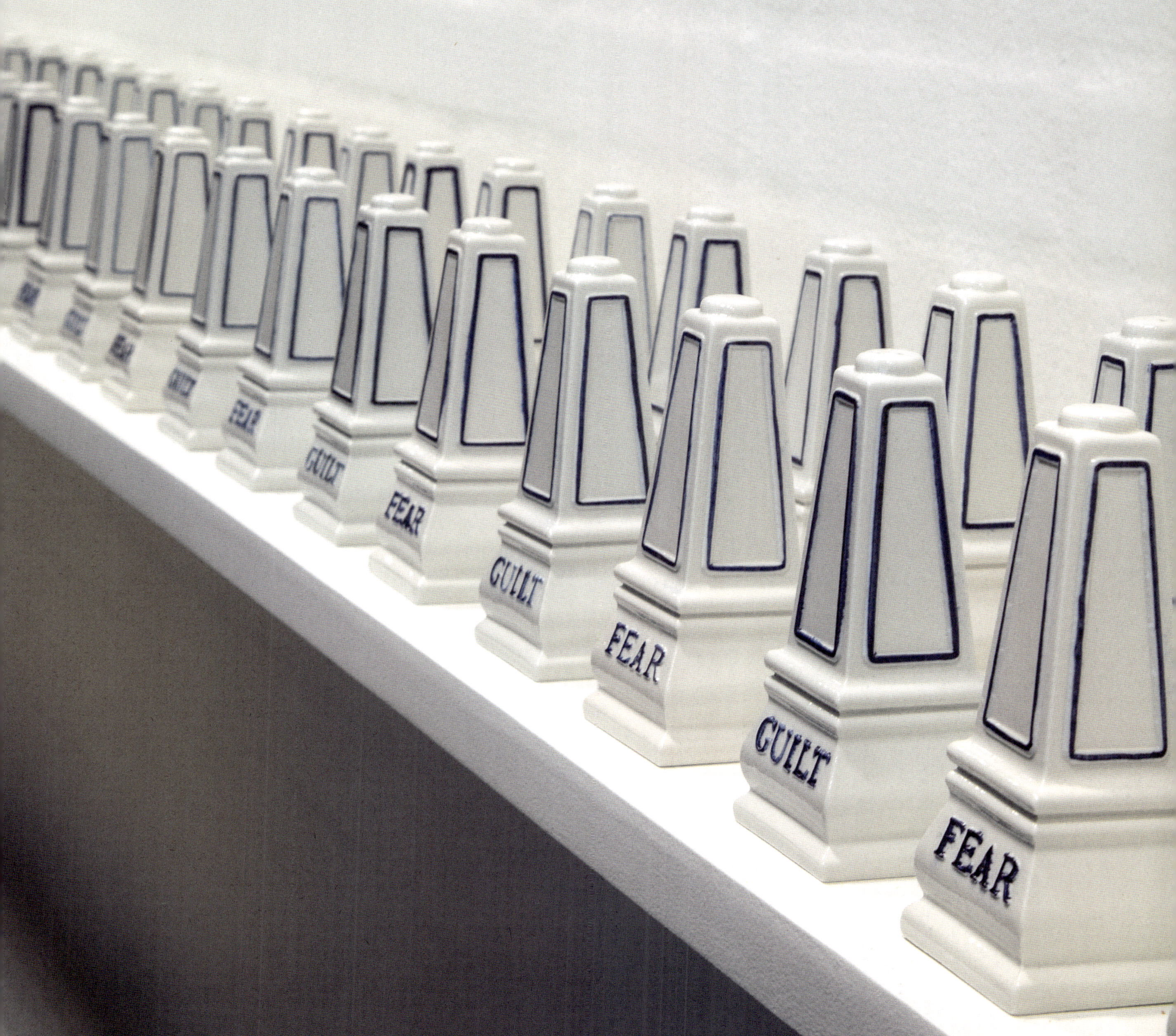
FEAR
GUILT
FEAR
GUILT
FEAR
GUILT
FEAR

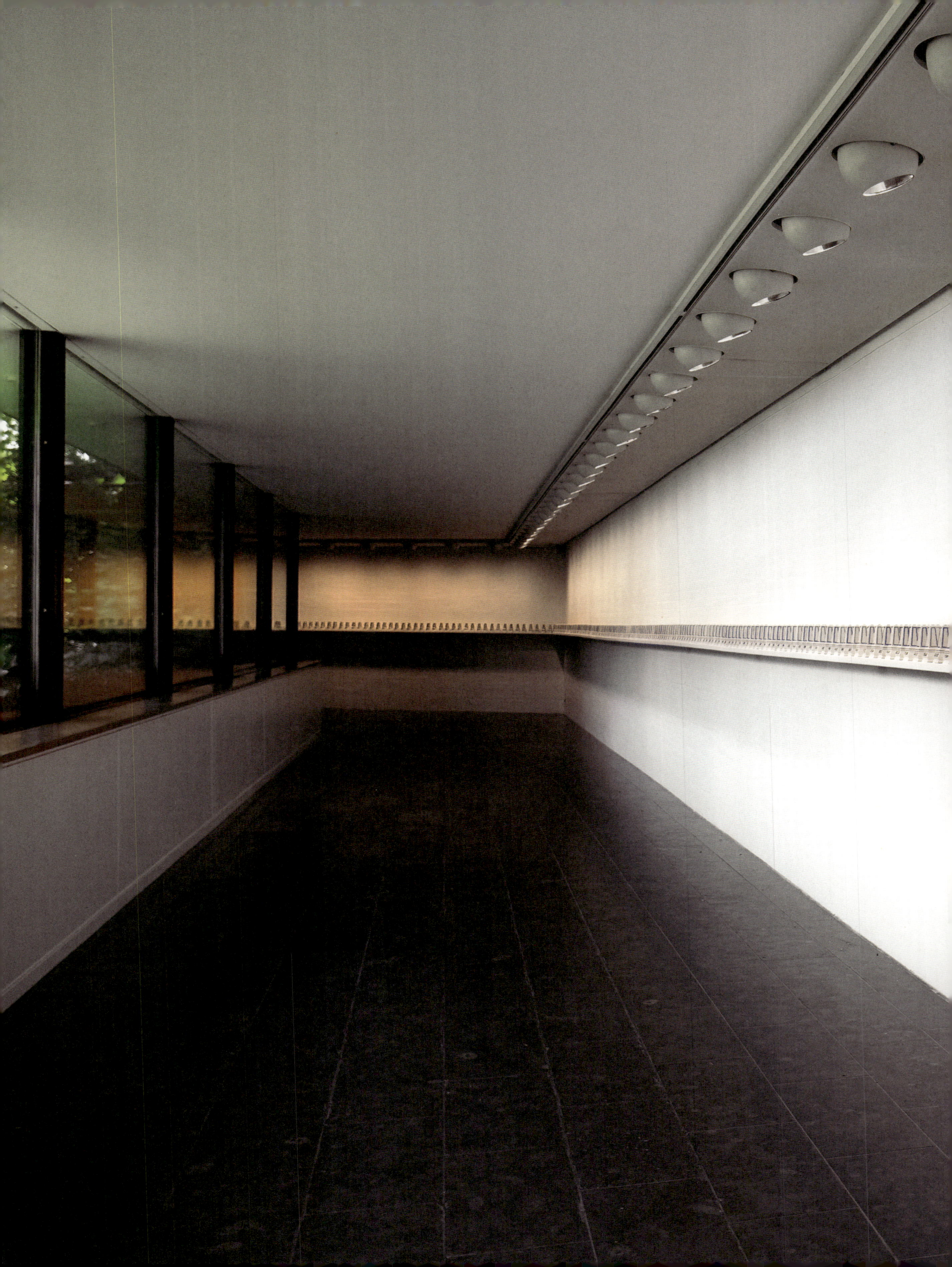

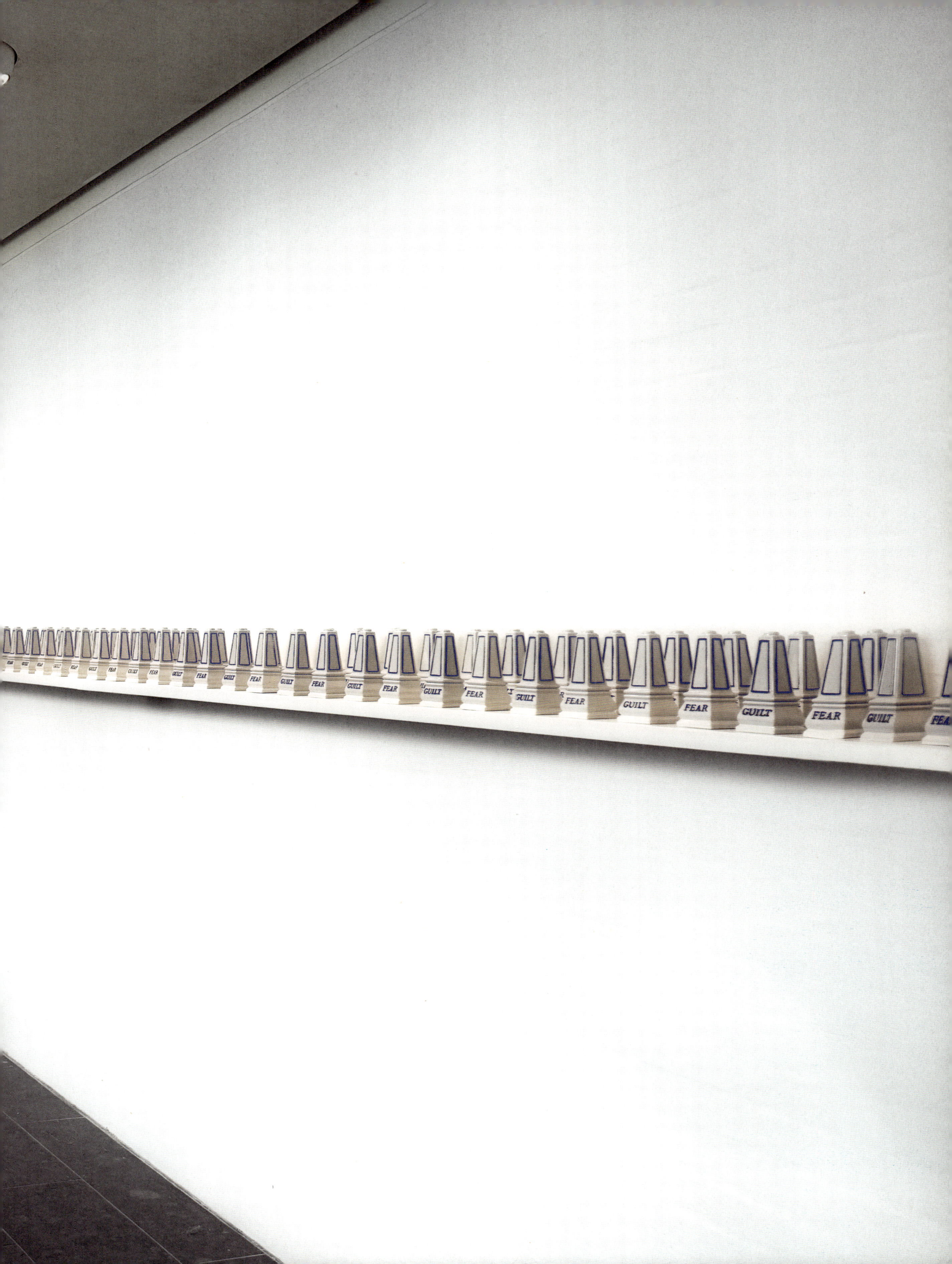
FEAR
GUILT
FEAR
GUILT
FEAR
GUILT
FEAR
GUILT
FEAR
GUILT
FEAR
GUILT

ME AND MY MOTHER — 2000/2005/2010/2015*/2020

Single-channel videos
Durations: 2000: 7:07 min. / 2005: 3:40 min. / 2010: 20 min. / 2015: 20:25 min. / 2020: 10:38 min.
Hirshhorn Museum and Sculpture Garden, Smithsonian Institution, Washington, D.C.,
Joseph H. Hirshhorn Purchase Fund, 2018
*Louisiana Museum of Modern Art, Humlebæk
Acquired with funding from Museumsfonden af 7. december 1966

By Pejk Malinovski

Ragnar's work has always inspired me – it makes me think and smile and want to make work myself.

In January 2020, I travelled to Iceland to make a radio documentary about Ragnar and his mother Guðrún and the strange video piece they've been creating over the past 20 years. I wanted to get to the bottom of this spitting business.

But I never got to the bottom of it, because the spitting business has no bottom. And I won't even attempt to get anywhere near the bottom here. Instead, I'll tell you about the flying cake.

A few days before I was supposed to fly to Iceland, Ragnar had written to me to cancel the whole thing. His mother had been sick for a month and wasn't up for it after all. I decided to go anyway, to record interviews with each of them separately. I wanted to talk to Guðrún about her childhood, about her life in the theatre, about her relationship with Ragnar, her youngest child. And I wanted to interview Ragnar about growing up in the theatre, what it was like to be backstage in the hurly-burly of costumes and props and actors and extras (Ragnar himself played a number of parts as a child and toured with his mother). Both of them were so incredibly warm and welcoming and shared many intimate stories, and during the days I was recording these audio interviews Guðrún felt better and decided to go ahead with the filming.

On a Thursday morning Ragnar, smiling broadly under a big fur hat, picked me up at a cafe and we headed over to Guðrún's house to film the fifth installment of *Me and My Mother*.

[*Car door slamming, gentle wind*]

Ragnar [*mumbling to himself*]: I think it's one trip with bakery goods and one trip with shirts and suits ...

[*Plane flying overhead ... microphone handling noise*]

Pejk: Testing, one-two, one-two.

Ragnar: Is it working?

On the way we stopped at the dry cleaner's and Ragnar picked up four different suits (always good to have options), then we did a little interview in his soundproof Volvo. Ragnar was excited that his mother had agreed to film. It had been a long month of sickness and so he said that it felt weirdly glamorous to do it now.

Pejk: All right, let's do it.

[*Fumbling with bags, boom pole gets bonked*]

Ragnar: Rock and Roll. [*Car door opens*]

Opposite page: Stills from *Me and my Mother*, 2000 (top) and 2005 (bottom)

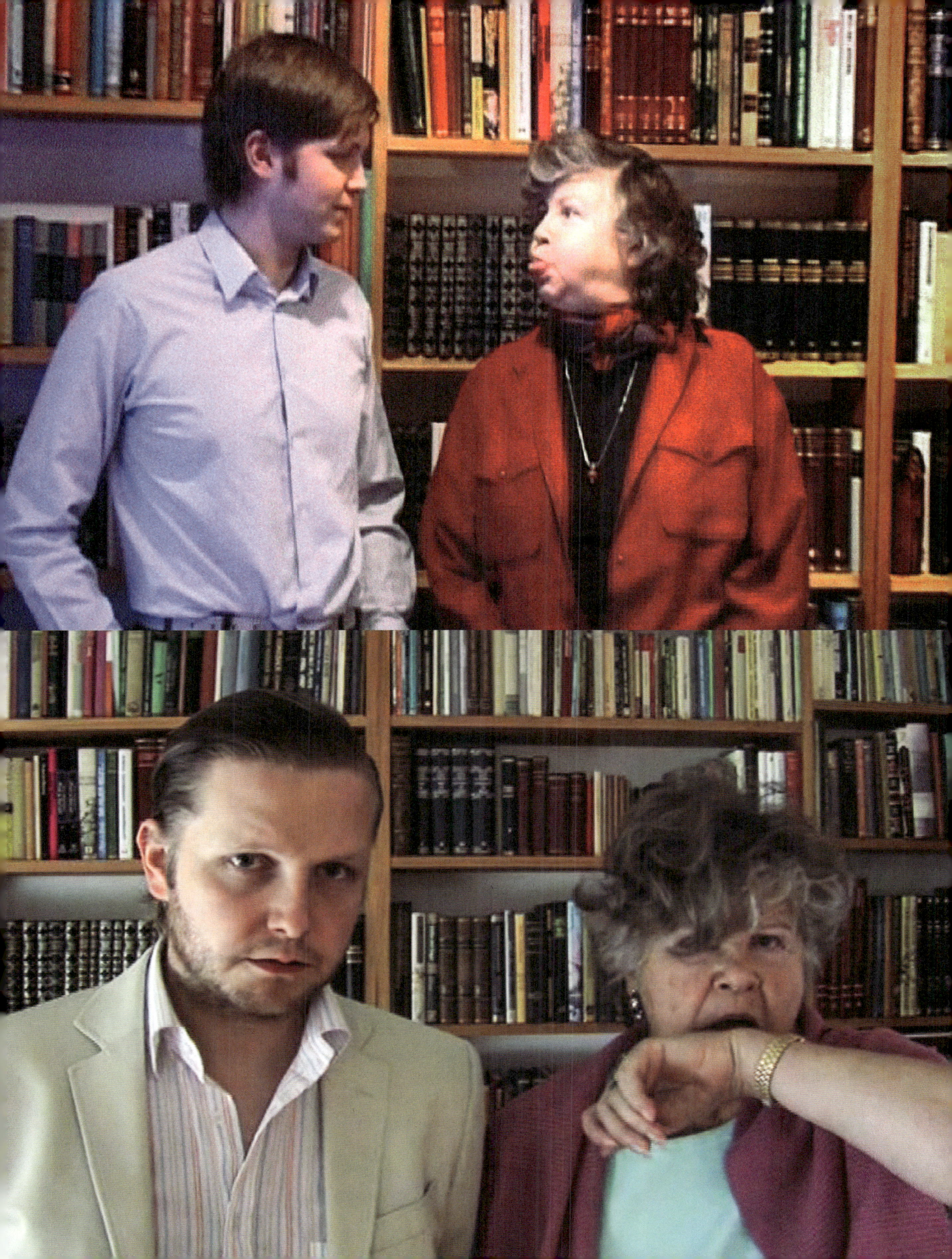

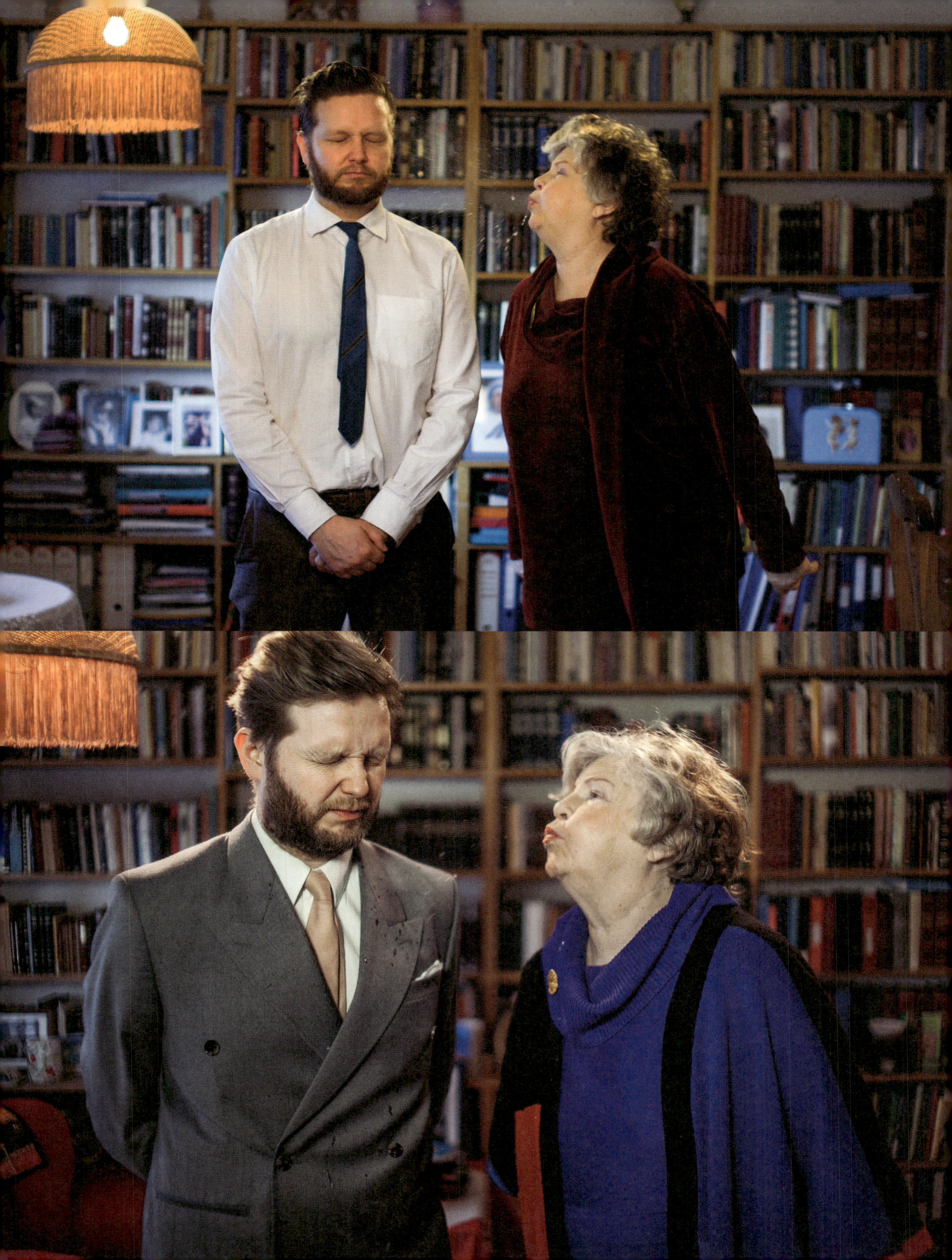

[*Squeaky footsteps on compact snow*]

We step out onto the bright, icy sidewalk, Ragnar has decided to try to carry the suits and the bakery goods in one trip, but after the first couple of steps he seems to lose his footing. He takes a couple of quick dance steps on the spot, like someone in a silent film, and during this panicked foxtrot, the cake box slips out of his hands and flies through the air, soaring in a big, beautiful arch until it lands on the sidewalk.

[*Sound of paper rustling*]

Ragnar [*screaming*]: Aaaaaaaalo!

[*Cardboard box landing on icy sidewalk, sliding to a rest*]

We hobble after it and lean in over the confectionery box, baffled to find that the cake, a meticulously decorated piece of pastry art, is completely intact.

Pejk: Oh, wow!

Ragnar [*laughing*]: The cake fell, but it's OK.

Pejk: It landed perfectly! Oh my god.

Ragnar [*laughing*]: I think that was a good sign. The cake fell but it's ok.

[*Footsteps, wind, laughter*]

When I look back on it now, this moment of giddy astonishment is emblematic of my time with Ragnar and my feelings about his life and art. Everything comes together so effortlessly, and even the mistakes, the accidents, are perfect; they couldn't have been planned if you'd tried. Maybe that's a theater thing. And if so, it must come from his mom, Guðrún.

[*Footsteps ascending concrete staircase, knock on wooden door, door opening*]

Ragnar: Hello!

Guðrún: Hallo, *elskling*.

Ragnar: Here I come with Pejk.

[*Door slamming shut behind us*]

Pejk: Hello Guðrún, nice to see you.

Guðrún: Nice to see you.

Ragnar: We were outside, the cake fell, but it landed perfectly.

Guðrún: Good. That means it will be terrific.

The crew filed in slowly, each one a sweetheart. They were chatting eagerly, like an old band getting back together. Lights were set, sound and camera started rolling and then suddenly all was quiet and Guðrún began spitting. I was right there in front of them, pointing my boom just out of the frame and it was intense to behold the power of Guðrún, to see her unfolding her craft in service of her son, giving life and meaning to his work, like Atum the ancient Egyptian God, who gave birth by spit.

But in a way the twelve minutes the performance lasted seemed the least eventful of the day. As soon as it was over, everyone flocked to the kitchen: plates and cutlery and cups were clinking, salmon, sausage, and cheese was brought to the table, coffee and juice were poured. Ragnar's gallerist, his partner – the artist Ingibjörg Sigurjónsdóttir – his daughters Zíta and Sólveig Katrín, the crew, everyone sat down for the celebratory lunch. Guðrún at the head of the table, Ragnar freshly showered. Eager chatter and roaring laughter, conversations about politics, religion, literature, anecdotes about who might or might not have been found having sex in a garage during a recent party. And in the middle of it all stood the beautiful cake.

PEJK MALINOVSKI is a Danish documentarian and poet. Featuring interviews with Guðrún Ásmundsdóttir and Ragnar Kjartansson, find his documentary *My Mother and Me* (2020) on https://www.bbc.co.uk/programmes/m000gvpl

Opposite page: Stills from *Me and my Mother*, 2010 (top) and 2015 (bottom).
The following spread: Still from *Me and my Mother*, 2020

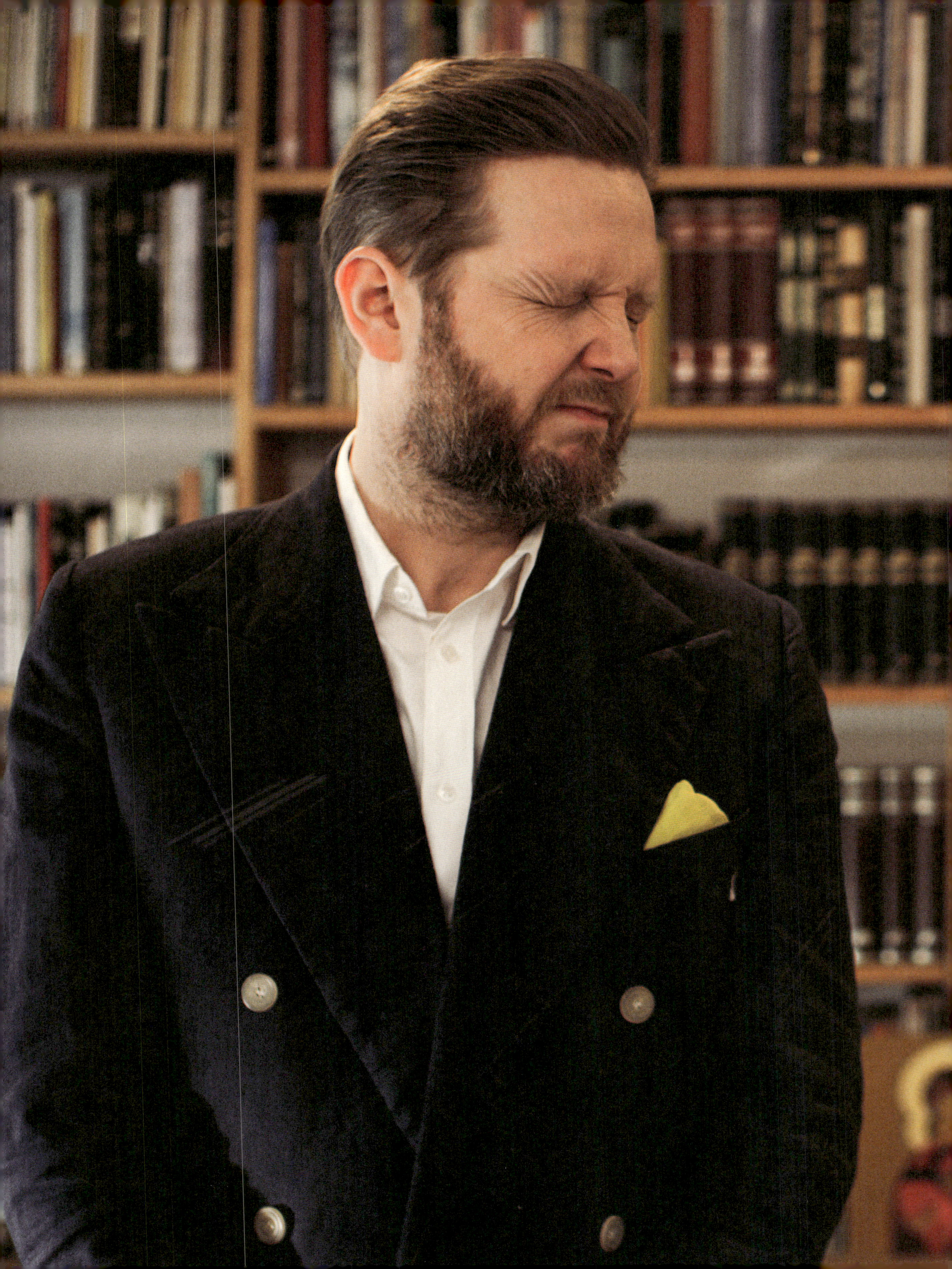

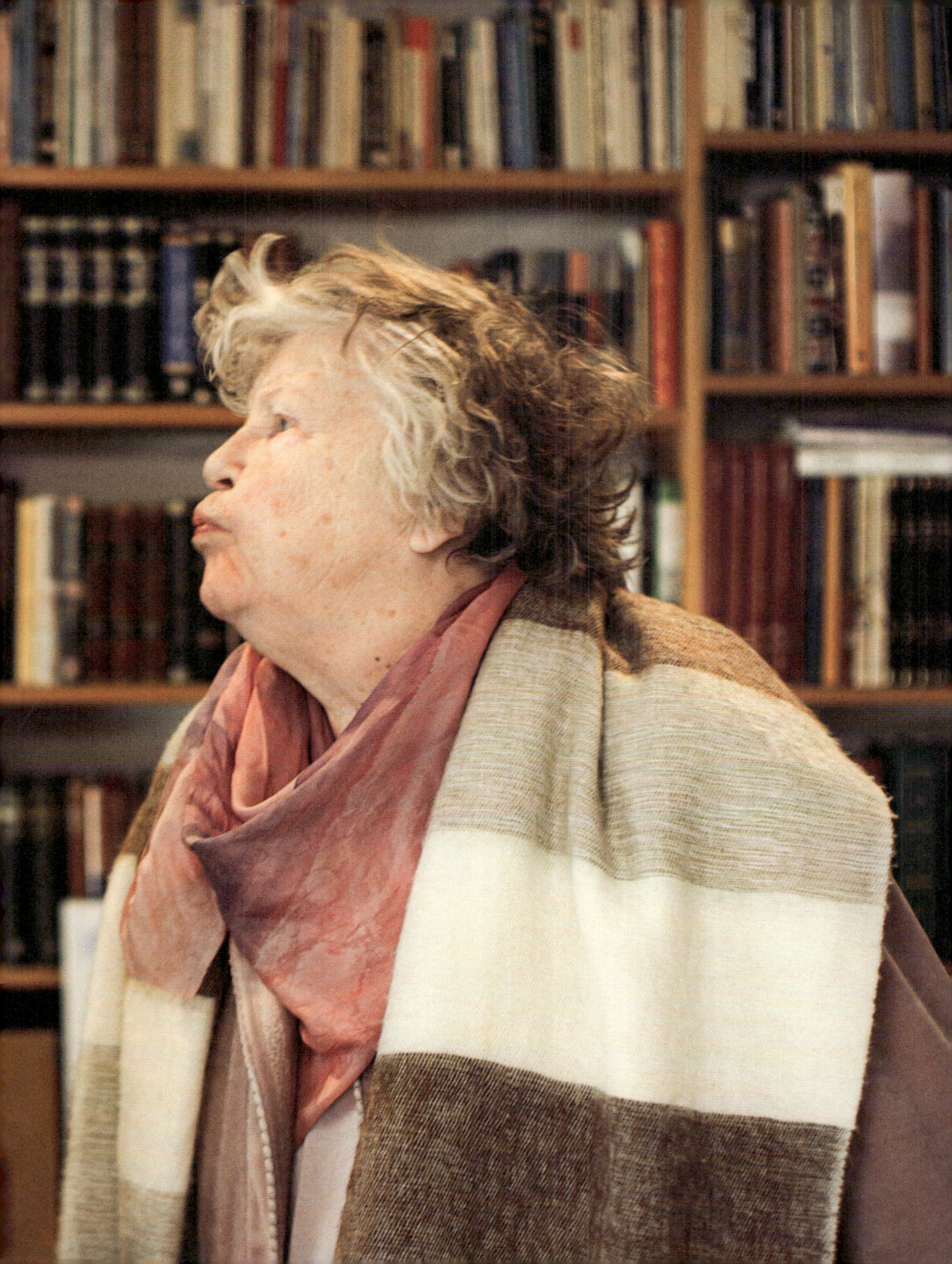

MERCY — 2004

Single-channel video
Duration: 62:30 min.
National Gallery of Iceland, Reykjavik

By Tine Colstrup

Alone with his guitar in front of a video camera, the artist repeats the same question for an hour: "Oh, why do I keep on hurting you?" The question is as simple as it is complex, and Kjartansson leaves it hanging in the air like a trance-inducing mantra, balanced in tension between superficiality and sincerity.

The artist has taken on the role of a classic crooner modelled on figures such as Johnny Cash (1932-2003) and Elvis Presley (1935-1977), mustering all of the enigmatic spirit of melancholy, guilt and self-absorption found in rich abundance in the country music genre. A dialogue with Western culture's masculine identity cliches and sensitivity codes – not least as they have been formulated throughout music history – runs as a *leitmotif* through Kjartansson's work.

Repetition is one of the methods he employs most frequently. A single, distilled motif is adhered to so that it can be seen and heard and considered again and again. Why do I keep on hurting you?

TINE COLSTRUP is curator at Louisiana Museum of Modern Art and curated *Epic Waste of Love and Understanding.*

Opposite and next page: Stills from *Mercy*, 2004
The following page: Installation view, Louisiana Museum of Modern Art, 2023

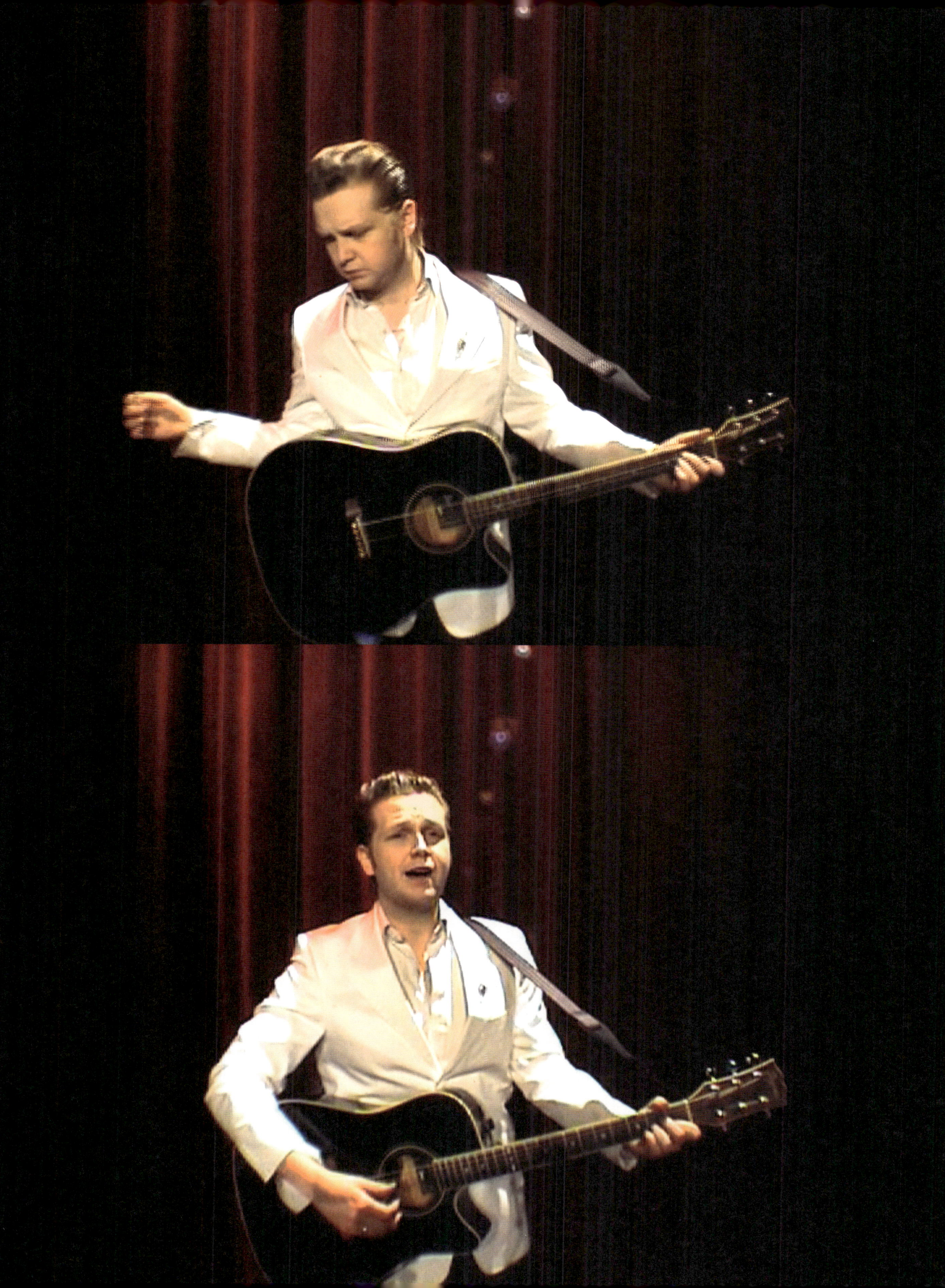

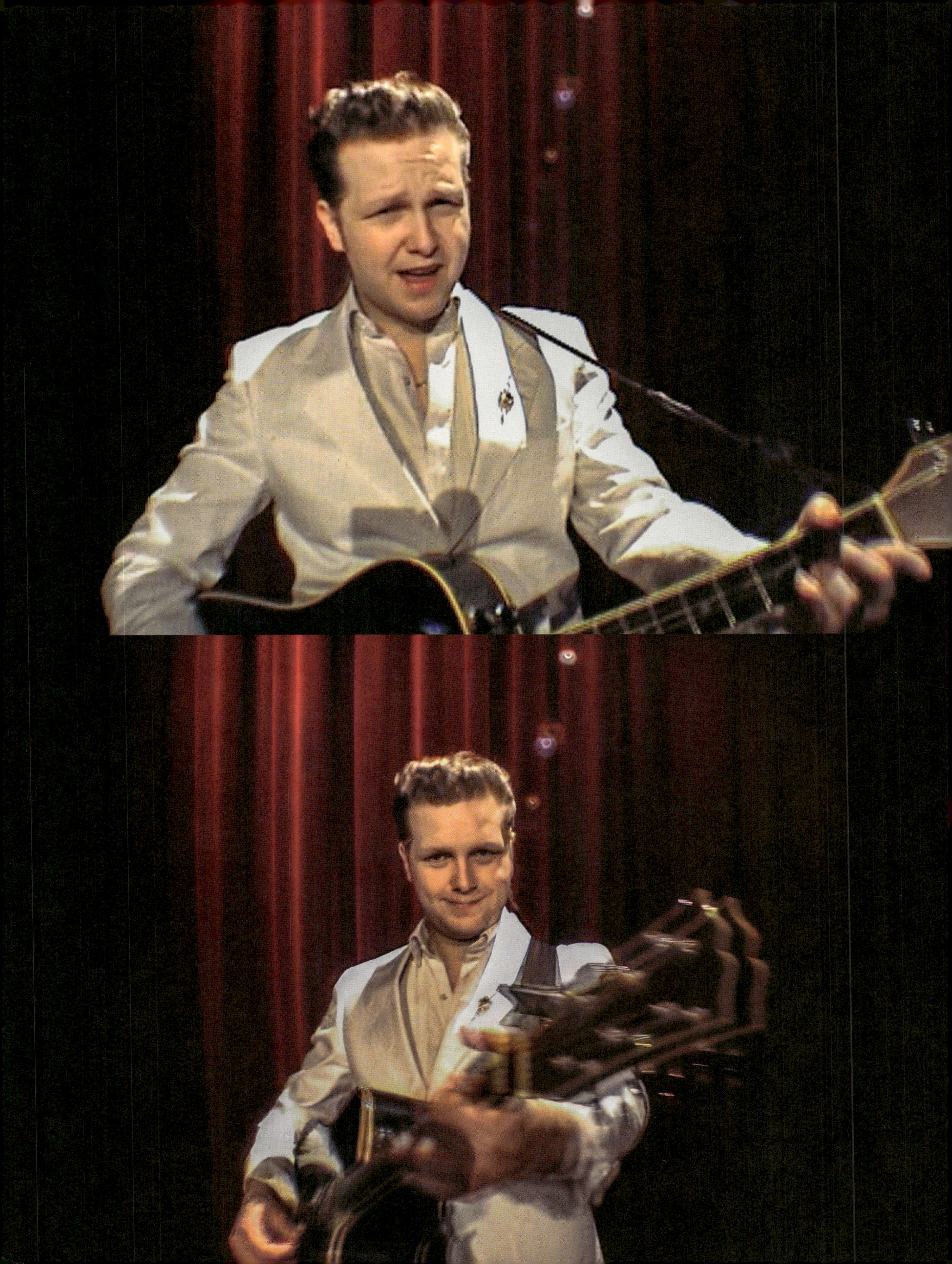

Oh, why do I keep on hurting you

Rep. ad lib.

Ragnar Kjartansson. *Mercy,* 2004

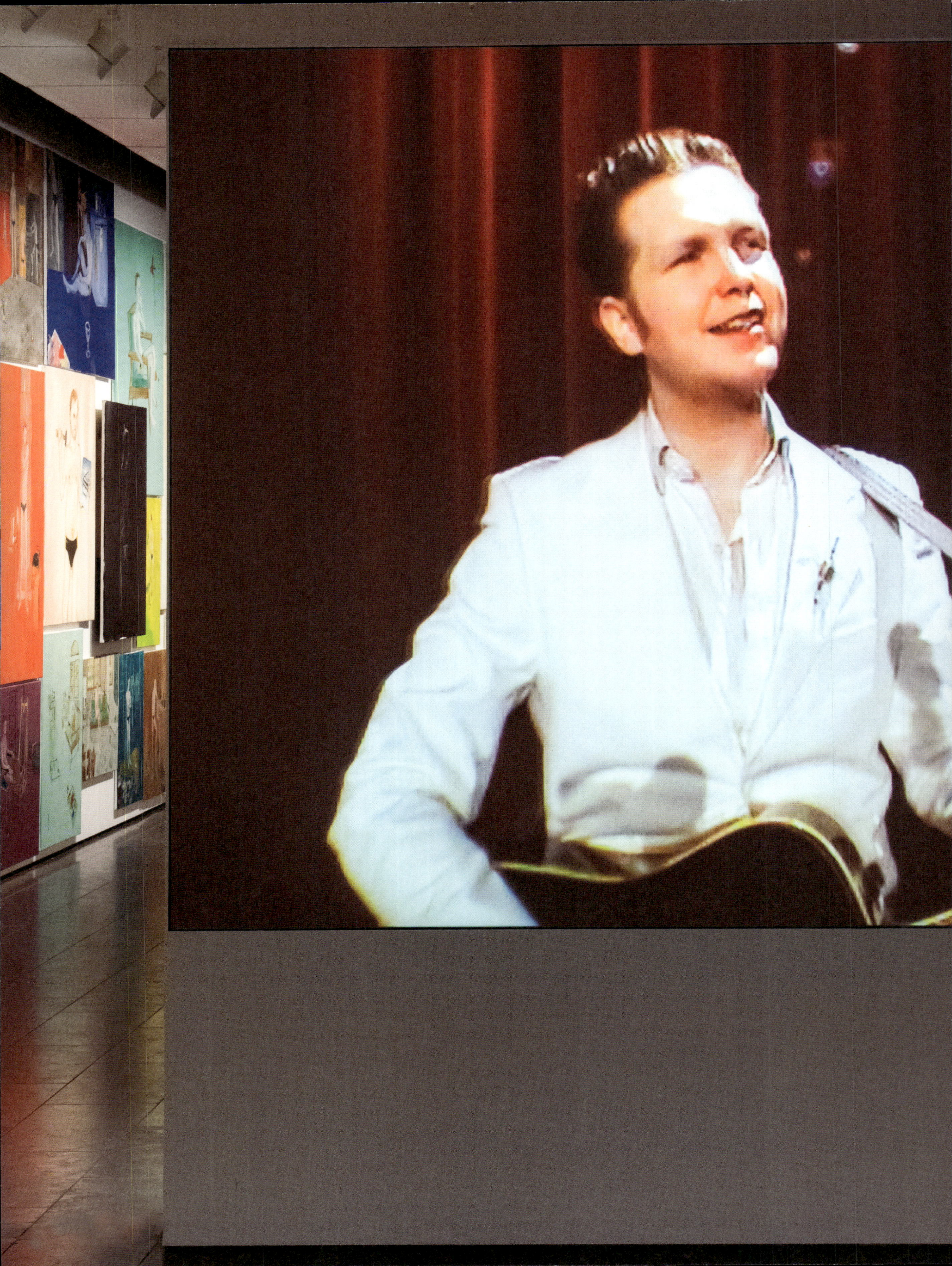

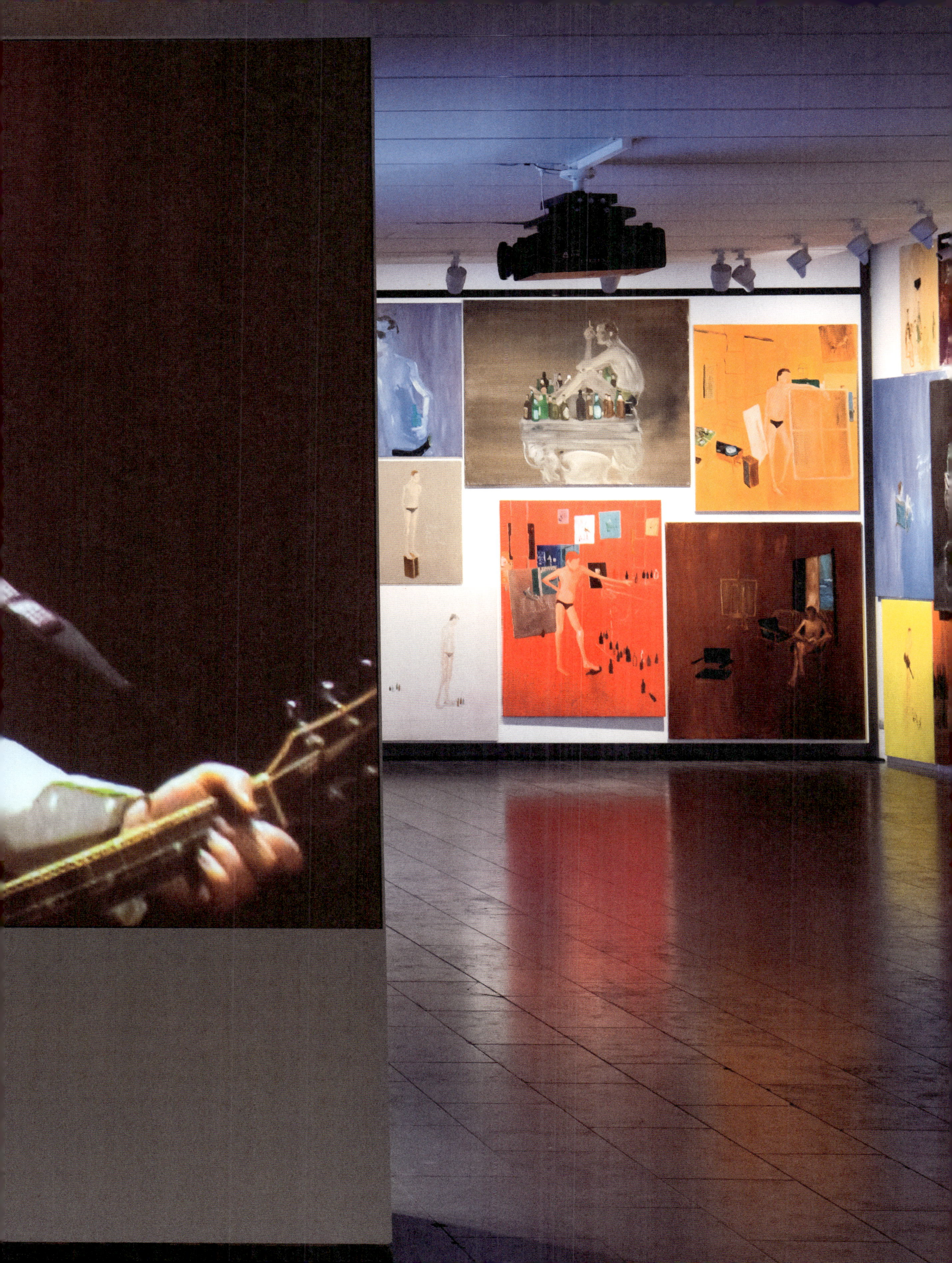

THE END – VENEZIA — 2009

Oil on canvas
144 paintings
Dimensions variable
Performed at the Icelandic Pavilion during the 53rd Venice Biennale, 14 June – 22 November, daily for six hours
Commissioned by the Center for Icelandic Art, Reykjavik
Fondazione Sandretto Re Rebaudengo, Torino

MAN DIES BUT BEAUTY DOES NOT

By Auður Ava Ólafsdóttir

Unlike many contemporary artists, Ragnar Kjartansson is not afraid of big ideas, even huge ones like beauty, death, time or God. He also does not shy away from working with big emotions rooted in romanticism, human solitude, *weltschmerz*, tragedy and the sublime.

The beauty of Ragnar's work is closely linked to the knowledge of man's mortality and the impermanence of all things. The question that lies at the heart of many of his works is whether man can forget that he is dying, that his imminent end is around the corner, by creating something bigger than himself, something magnificent. We can call it beauty, and if it is big enough, it can eliminate the pain and fear for a brief moment. The beauty in Ragnar's work relates to Western culture's concepts of beauty; it is a kind of distilled beauty or essence of beauty with a plaintive undertone of longing. At the same time, the artist is aware of the fact that beauty, or rather the perception of beauty is a *survivor kit* for the viewers – their way of constantly postponing the end. In this way the melancholy of the artist and the viewer converge on the idea that what is beautiful is also sad.

In this context, the title of Ragnar's work at the 2009 Venice Biennale, *The End*, seemed perfectly logical. And this is despite the obvious paradox that Ragnar was the youngest artist ever to be chosen by Iceland to participate in the Biennale, since he was only 31 years old when he got the call, and was therefore in a way at the starting point of his career.

Ragnar is an unusually multi-layered visual artist in that his imaginary world encompasses many art forms, music, theatre, film and literature, as well as art history. When one bears in mind that few places in the world of Western culture connect the elements of beauty, decay, death and the end as eloquently as Venice does, it is safe to expect an interesting encounter between a sinking city and an artist – that the artist and the place will in some way mirror each other. Thomas Mann's novella from 1912 about the relationship between art and life, *Death in Venice*, certainly comes to mind, as well as Visconti's film of the same title from 1971, but also Byron's years of exile in the city and the poems of romantic poets such as Shelley and Wordsworth, who spent long periods in Venice in the first half of the 19th century, not to mention artists who died there, such as Wagner, Diaghilev, Ezra Pound and Stravinsky and others who contracted the plague there and died from it later, like Dante. One should also not forget that Ragnar worked on the preparation of this work in the middle of the great economic meltdown in Iceland in the autumn of 2008, and says himself that "the hopelessness and gloom of the collapse was reflected in the work".* In that connection, it should be pointed out that the Icelandic title, *Endalokin* has a

Opposite page: Installation view, Louisiana Museum of Modern Art, 2023

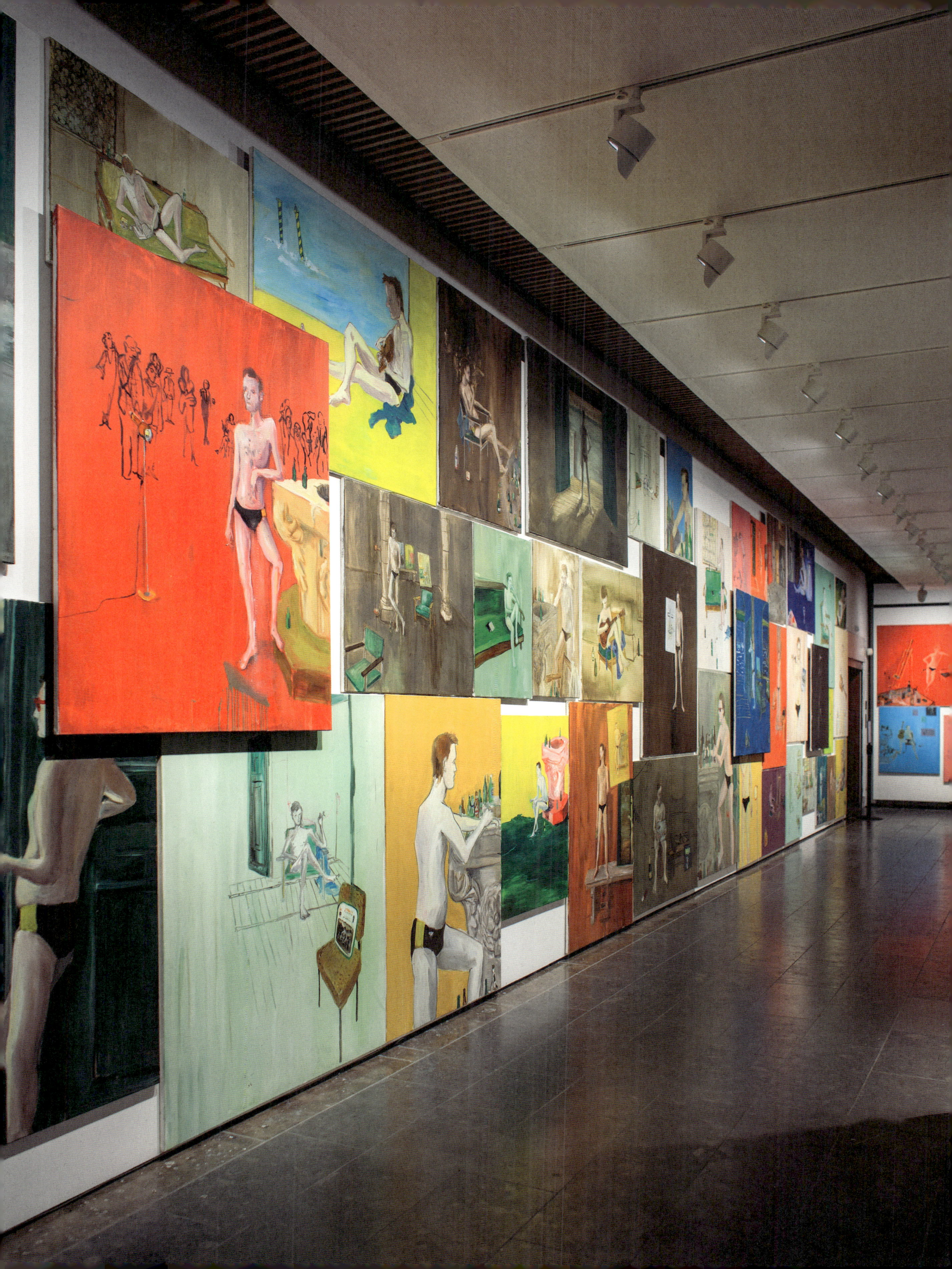

more apocalyptic feel to it than its English translation *The End*, which people also associate with the big screen where it is often preceded by the adjective *happy* as in *Happy End*.

Although one could have assumed in advance that a place as steeped in significance as Venice would inevitably have manifested itself in Ragnar's work and that he is well versed in putting himself on stage, I think few expected the artist to leave himself so personally exposed for the duration of this six-month-long performance.

The work in the Icelandic pavilion in Palazzo Bianchi Michiel on the Grand Canal was divided into two sections: in one part of the pavilion there was a large video and music installation on five screens, projecting a beautiful white winter landscape in the Rocky Mountains in Canada, where Ragnar in the company of another man played various instruments, including a grand piano, outdoors at a temperature of minus 30 degrees. The other part of the pavilion had been set up as a painter's studio and Ragnar was standing there as some kind of a *showcase* in the role of an artist inside his own work of art, working at an easel for six hours a day, throughout the opening hours of the Biennale, from the 14th of June to the 22nd of November 2009, painting oil portraits of his model, a young man dressed in nothing but Speedo swimming trunks. Although it is almost impossible to imagine a more extreme contrast than the Rocky Mountains at minus 30 degrees and Venice in a summer heat wave, one could say that romantic concepts of the tragic fate of the artist and the sublime connect both parts of the exhibition. The studio was actually an open set that hundreds of spectators visited every day to watch the staging of the myth of the male painter who stands by his easel in a white shirt, a bohemian who drinks and smokes as he works. (It was no coincidence that Dylan Thomas' books were scattered around the studio). However, it is by no means possible to reduce the output of this exhibition to the 144 portraits of the model that the artist painted during this period and are owned by an Italian art collector in Turin. Rather, it is much more appropriate to liken the work to a living sculpture that changed from day to day, as the exhibition period progressed, paintings accumulated on the walls, and empty beer bottles multiplied.

Time is a fundamental concept in all of Ragnar's work and in *The End* he uses various methods to stage time. First of all, the time element of the work resides in the long period in which it is a *work in progress* and the incredible endurance of an artist who puts himself on stage together with his model in a challenging role. Every morning the painter walks to the easel and begins a new work in an eternal cycle of *repetitions*, a key component in Ragnar's conceptual world and his quest to defer the inevitable end. It is also blatantly clear that the time of art history is built into the work in the centuries-long act of painting a portrait of a model. First and foremost, though, the time element of the work resides in the viewer's experience, which is consistent with Ragnar's fundamental notion that art is the experience of art, that beauty is not an object, but an experience of beauty. Mingled into that experience there is the smell of turpentine, the clammy heat and the damp odour of the canals, but also the effects of the surrounding water that flooded the floor of the studio several times and the strange unearthly light that envelops everything in Venice and plays a large part in creating a sense of timelessness. But the viewers will never experience the work as a whole, never see the whole picture, but only a fragment of a work, because they are in the middle of a process, where something has happened before and something will happen after they are gone. The viewer therefore does not know how the work "ends". The fragment in which the viewer is always present is equivalent to the moment, which I suspect is Ragnar's favourite unit of time. That is the eternal now, constantly repeating itself. By dwelling in the moment, one forgets that the end is near. Salvation is to be found in art. Man dies but beauty is immortal.

AUÐUR AVA ÓLAFSDÓTTIR is an Icelandic author.

* *Morgunblaðið* newspaper, 8 November 2009

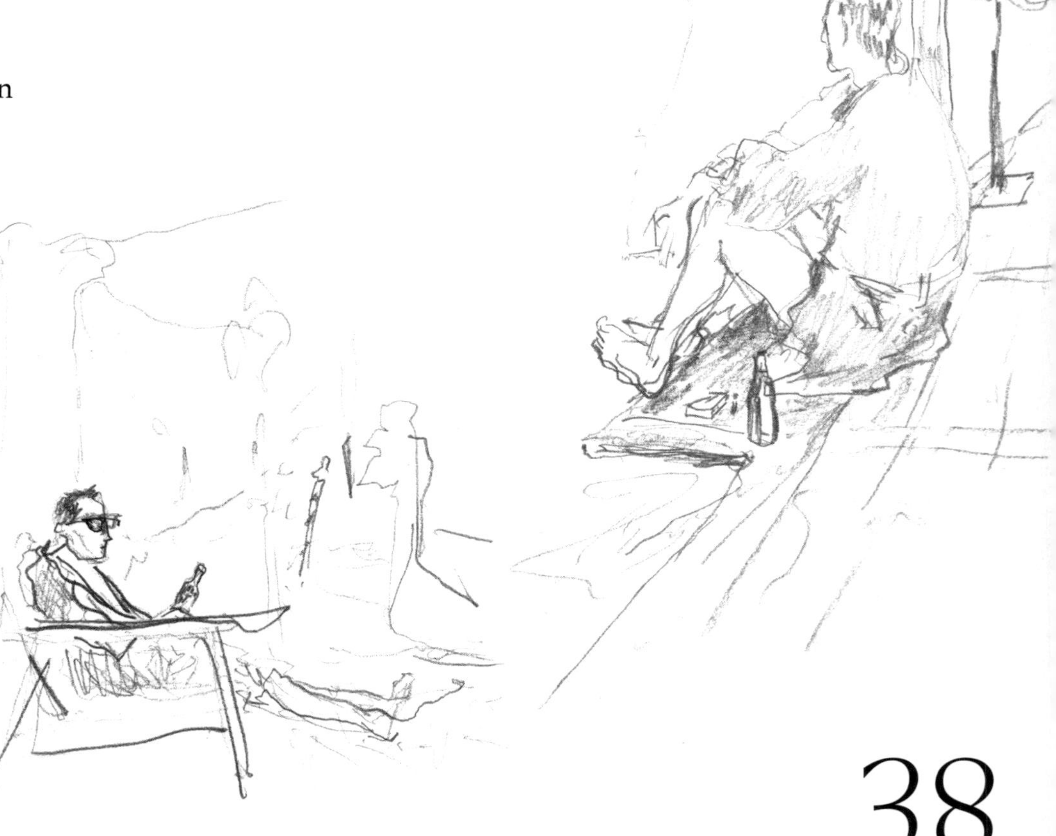

Drawings by Ragnar Kjartanssson, 2009
Opposite page: Installation views, Venice Biennale, 2009
The following spreads: Installation views, Louisiana Museum of Modern Art, 2023

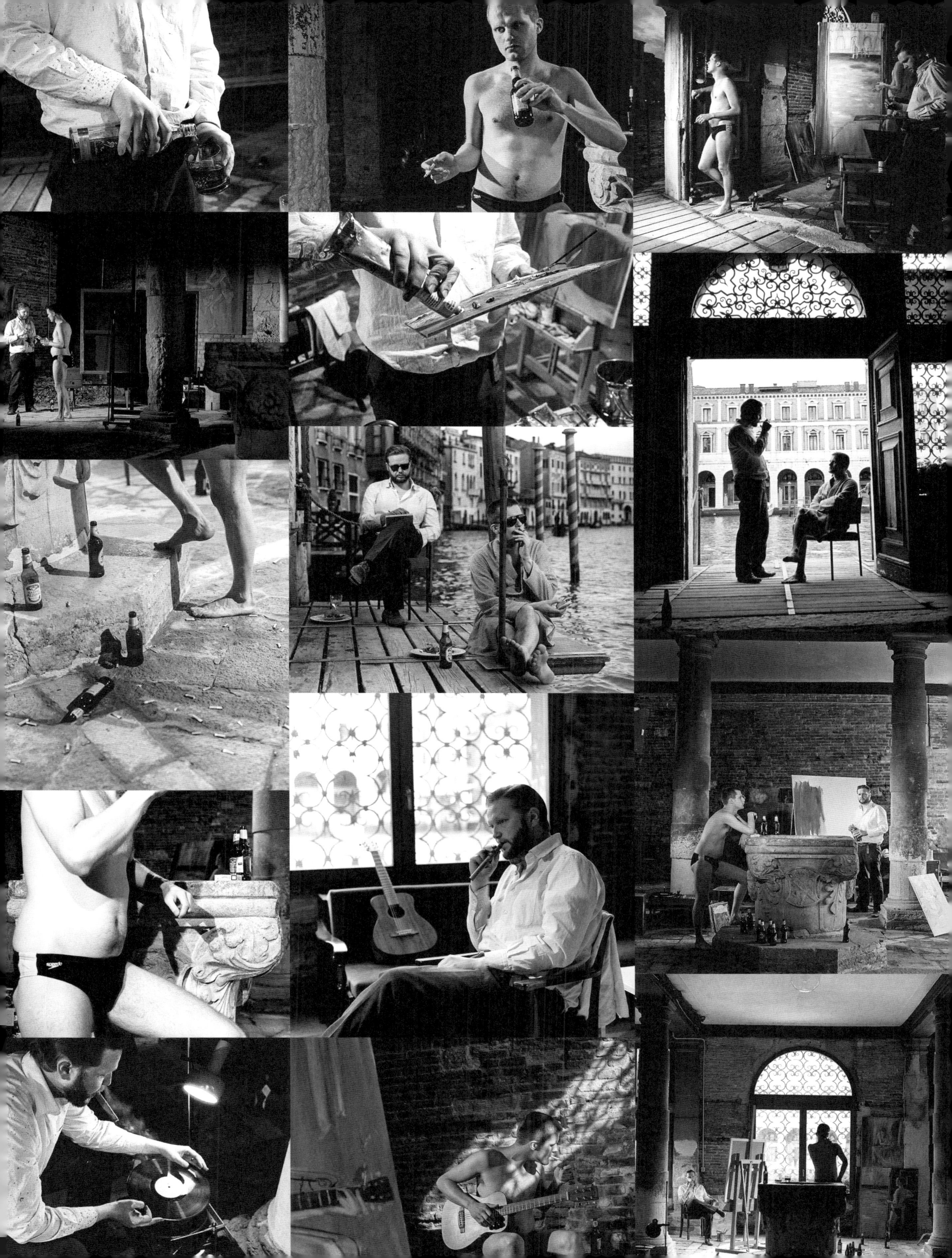
speedo

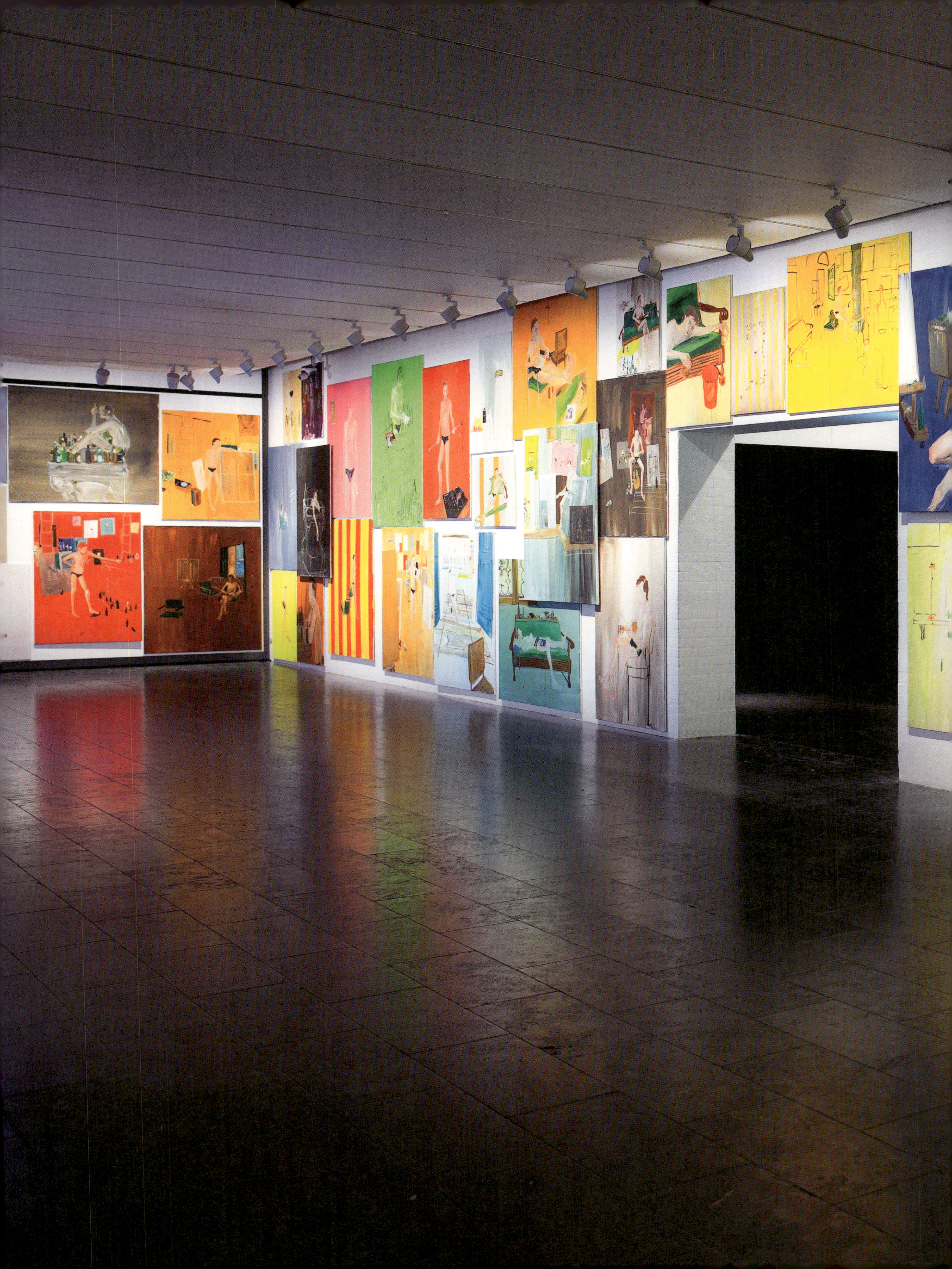

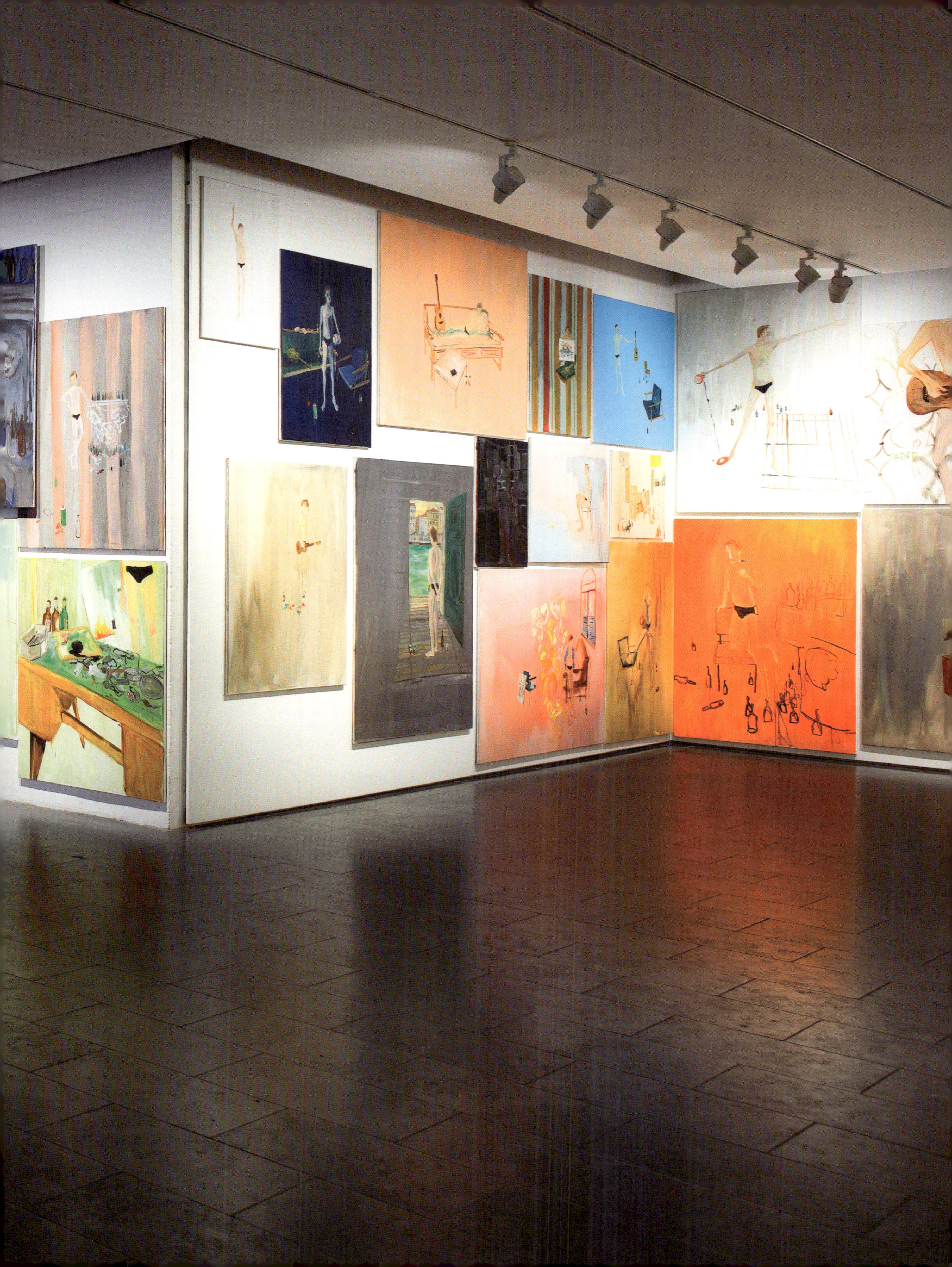
FADER

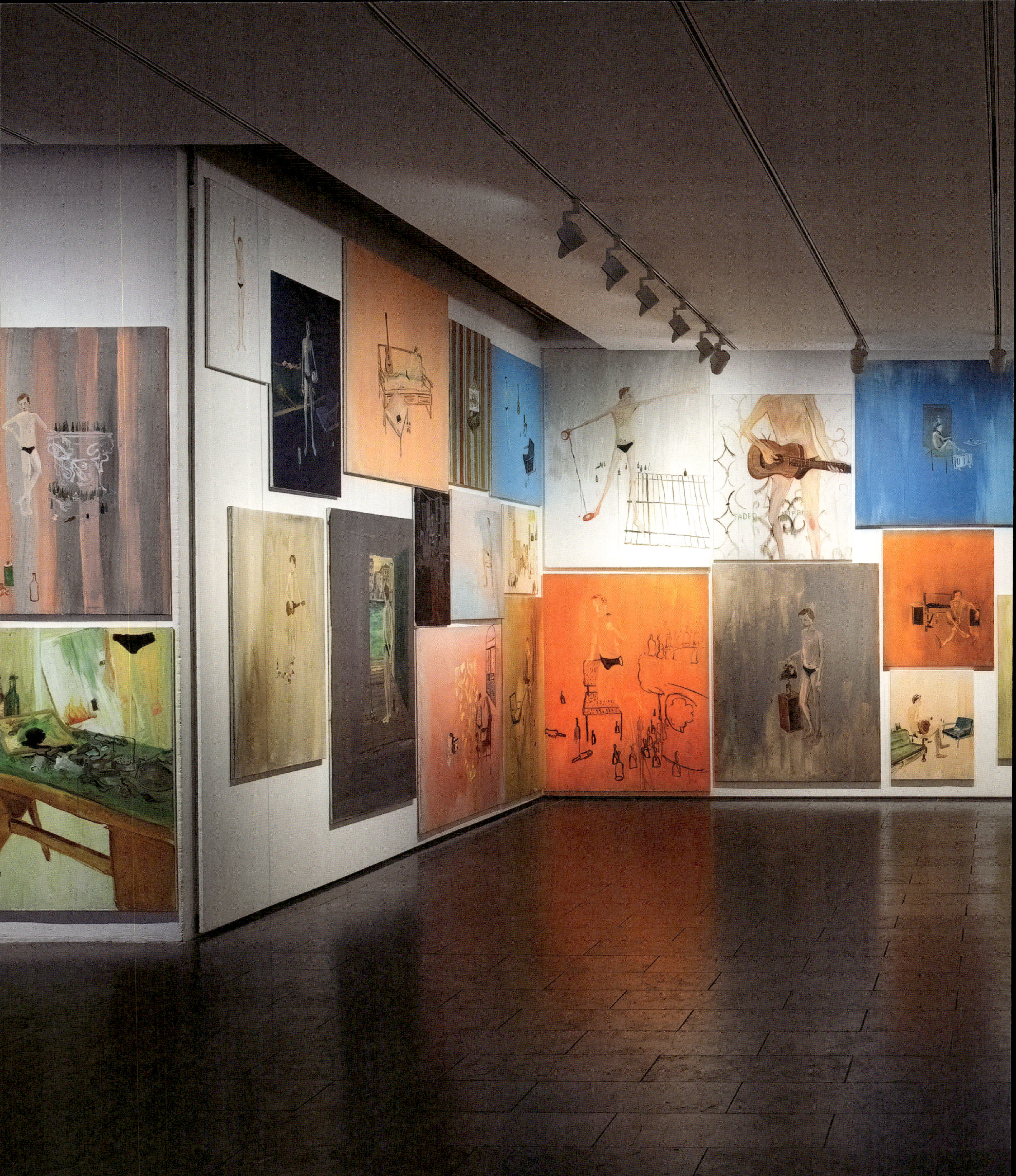
FADED

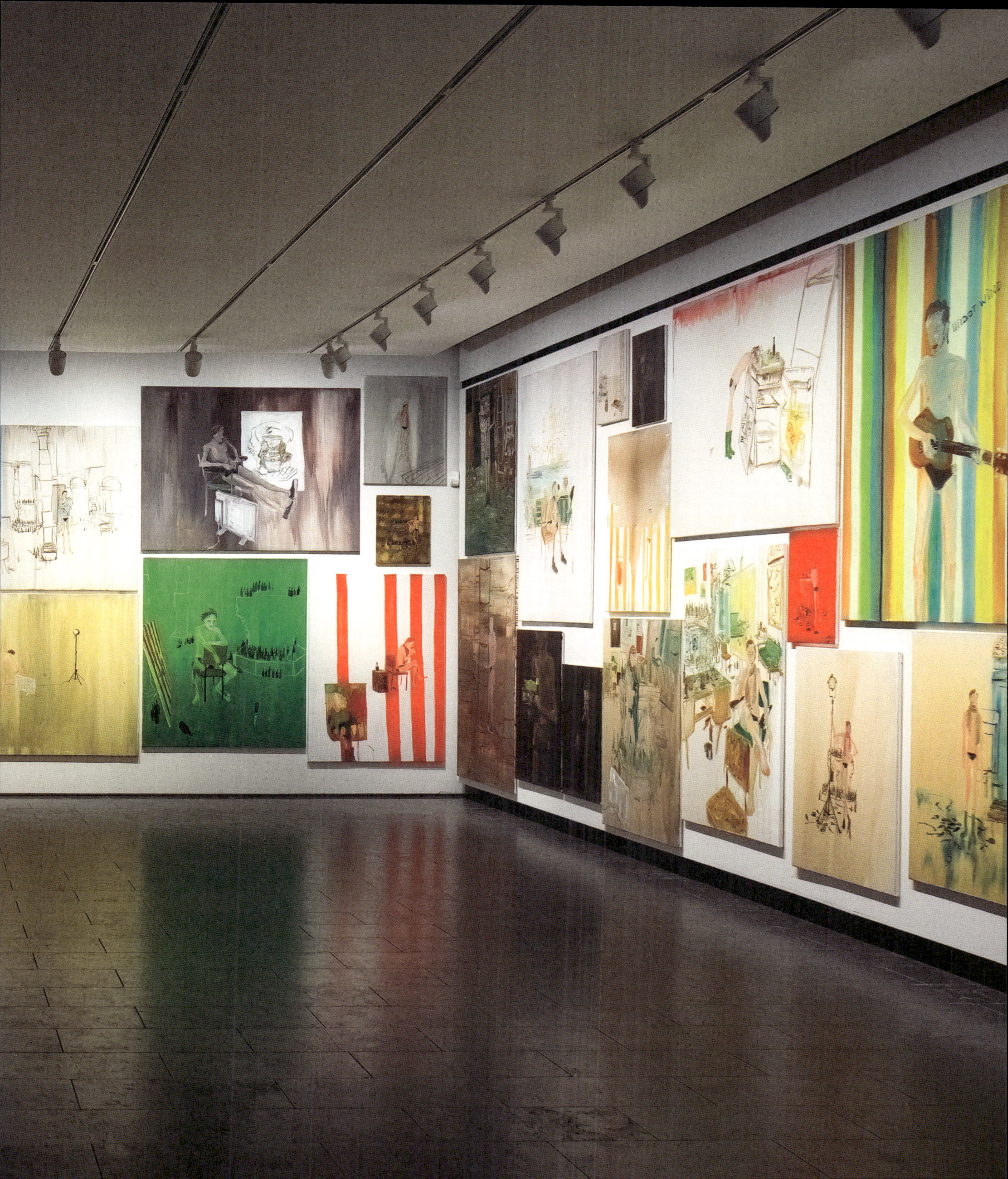

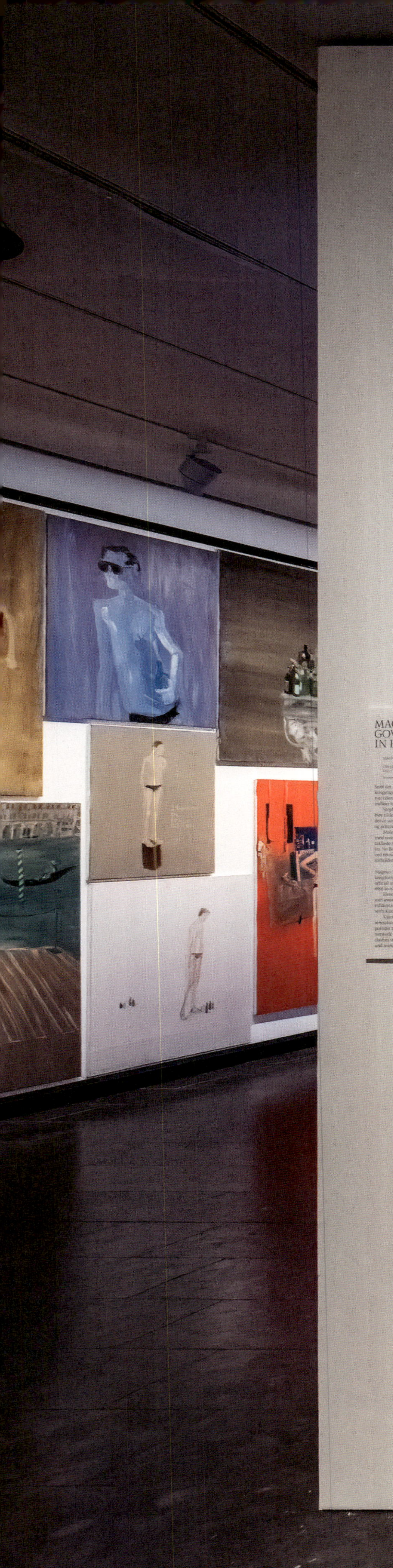

MAGNÚS STEPHENSEN,
GOVERNOR-GENERAL
IN FULL REGALIA

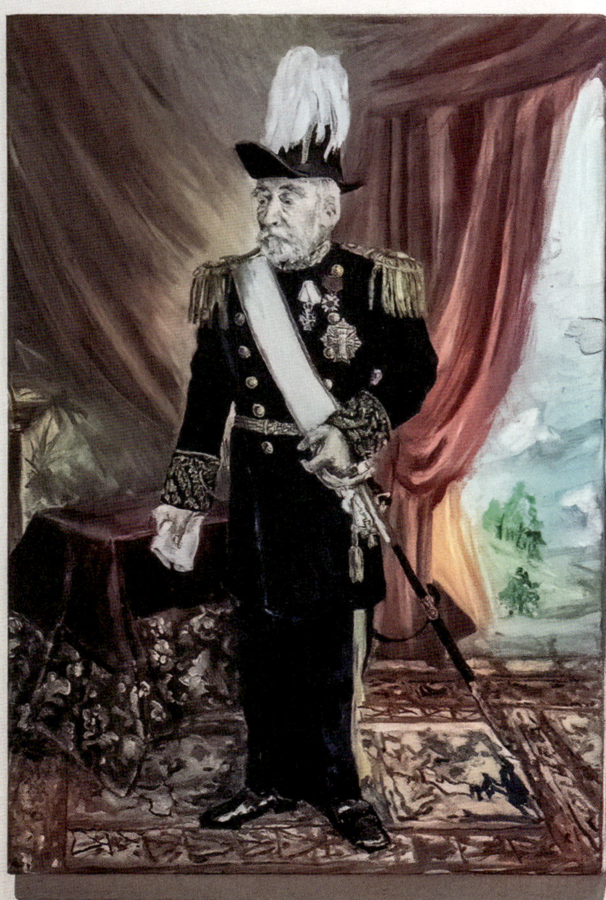

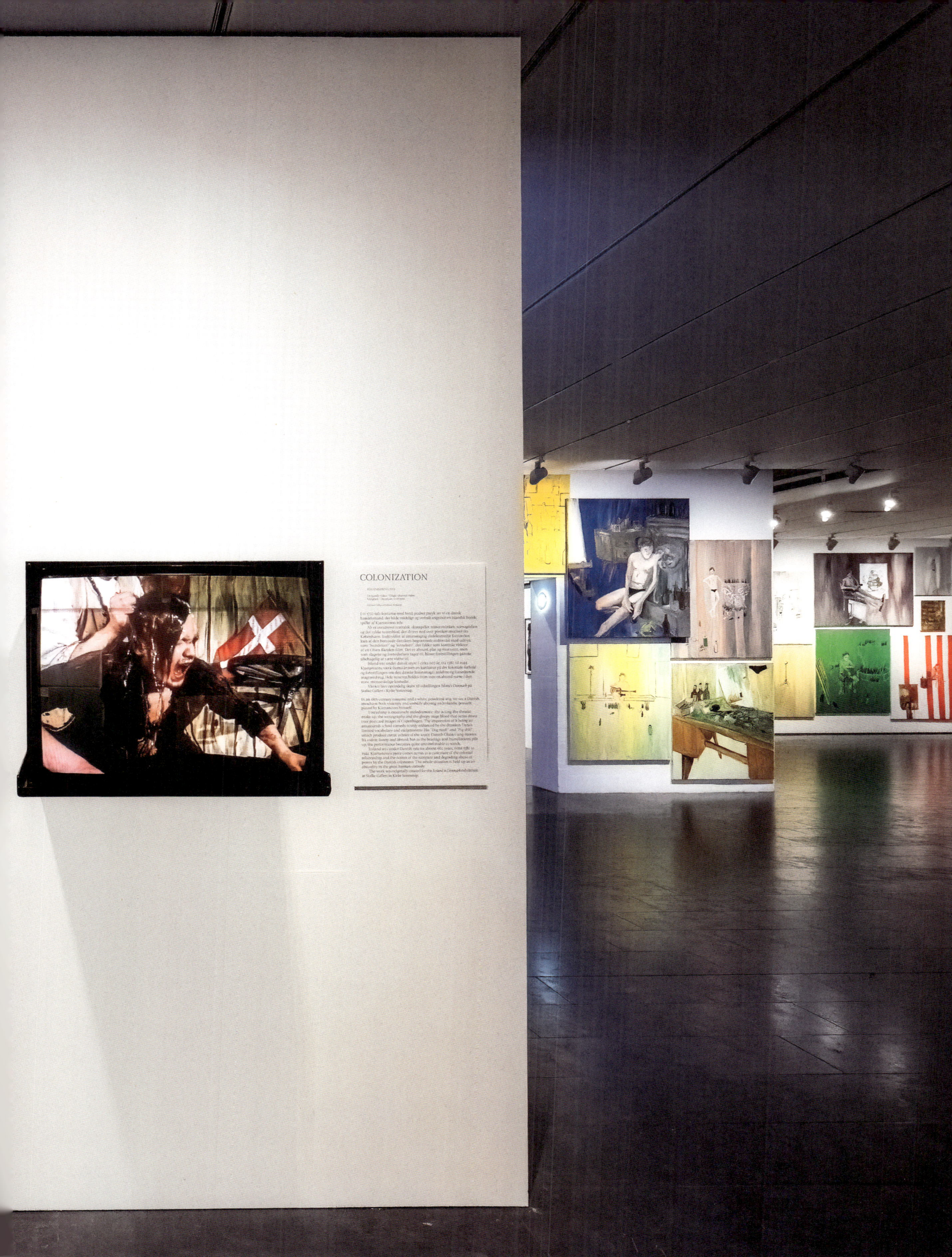
COLONIZATION

MAGNÚS STEPHENSEN, GOVERNOR-GENERAL IN FULL REGALIA — 2021

Oil on canvas
120.5 × 80 × 2.5 cm
Private collection, Reykjavik

By Vera Sóley Illugadóttir

Iceland was more or less under Danish rule from 1380 to 1944. In 1871, Denmark passed new laws aiming to clarify the standing of Iceland within the Danish realm, introducing the office of *landshöfðingi* (governor-general) to run Iceland according to orders from Copenhagen.

Magnús Stephensen (1836-1917) was a public servant, judge and member of Alþingi (Parliament House), and the third, last and longest-serving governor-general, in office from 1886 to 1904, the year Iceland achieved home rule and the governor-general post was abolished.

The portrait of Magnús Stephensen was requested by a financial company, whose headquarters are situated in Næpan (The Turnip), an unusual house Magnús built for himself in central Reykjavik after retiring. In return for the portait, the financial company agreed to Ragnar's request to pay the legal fees of a group of young Icelandic activists, arrested for protesting the deportations of asylum seekers.

The photo on which Ragnar's portrait is based was likely taken towards the end of Magnús's reign. Magnús wears a pompous uniform adorned with several large medals. Despite this, he looks dejected. Perhaps faced with the inevitable loss of his position as chief of the land, as well as this impressive uniform? (Did he use that handkerchief to wipe a tear from his eye?)

Or is it the look of a man who for years was caught between two poles, juggling to maintain the trust of both his superiors in Denmark and countrymen in Iceland fighting for increased independence. In reality, it is believed Magnús sympathised quite a lot with the Icelandic independence movement, and it is likely that he resented having to speak against it as a representative of the Danish state.

Magnús was despite all this really quite an industrious governor and a colourful one, not just in clothing. But in his last speech he almost apologised for his 18 years in office, and what he described as his lack of iniative and ideals. He even admitted he never really wanted the job in the first place.

VERA SÓLEY ILLUGADÓTTIR is an Icelandic journalist, programme coordinator and host on the history radio show *Í ljósi sögunnar* (In light of History) on the RÚV (The Icelandic National Broadcasting Service – Ríkisútvarpið). She holds a BA degree in Middle Eastern Studies.

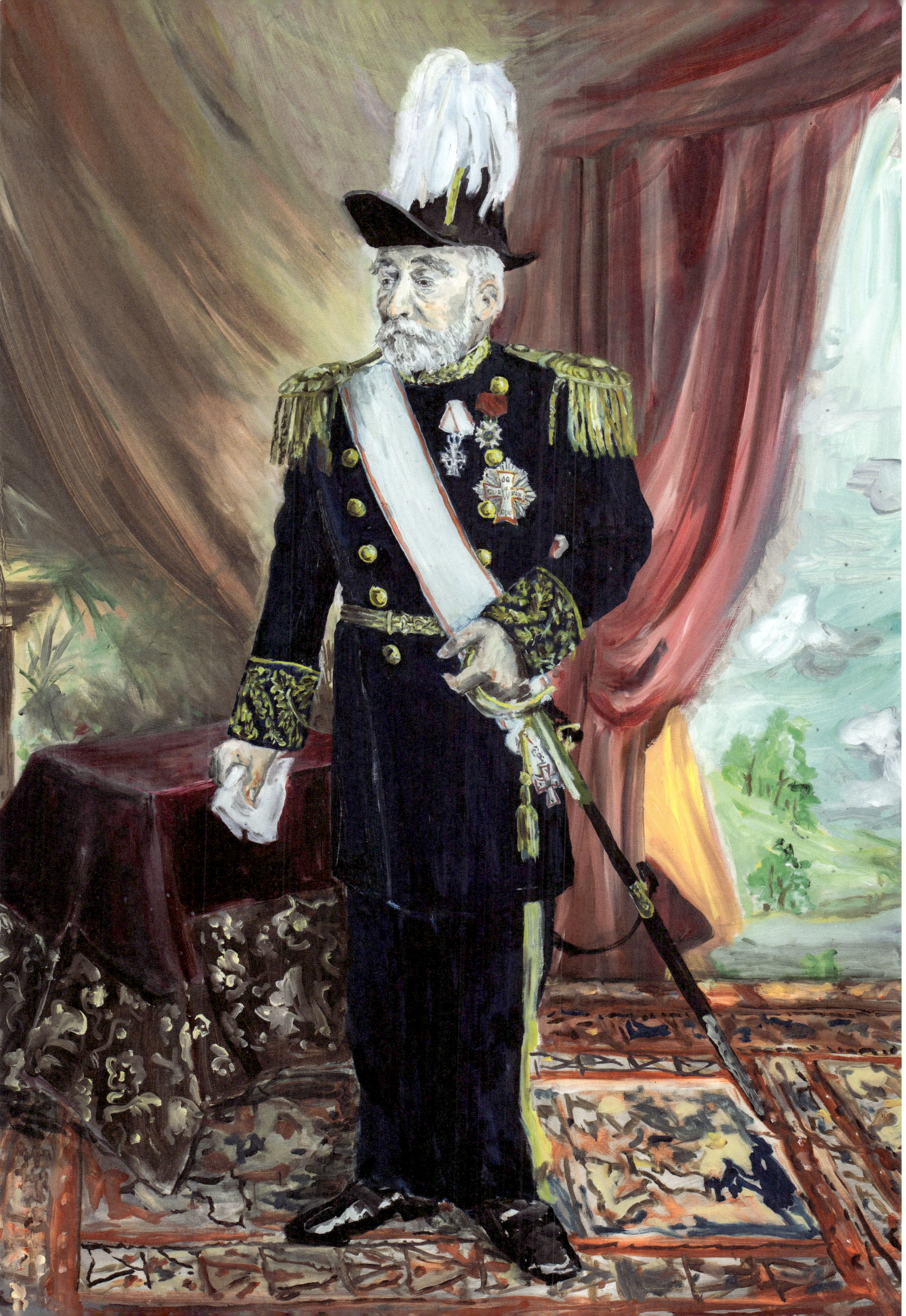

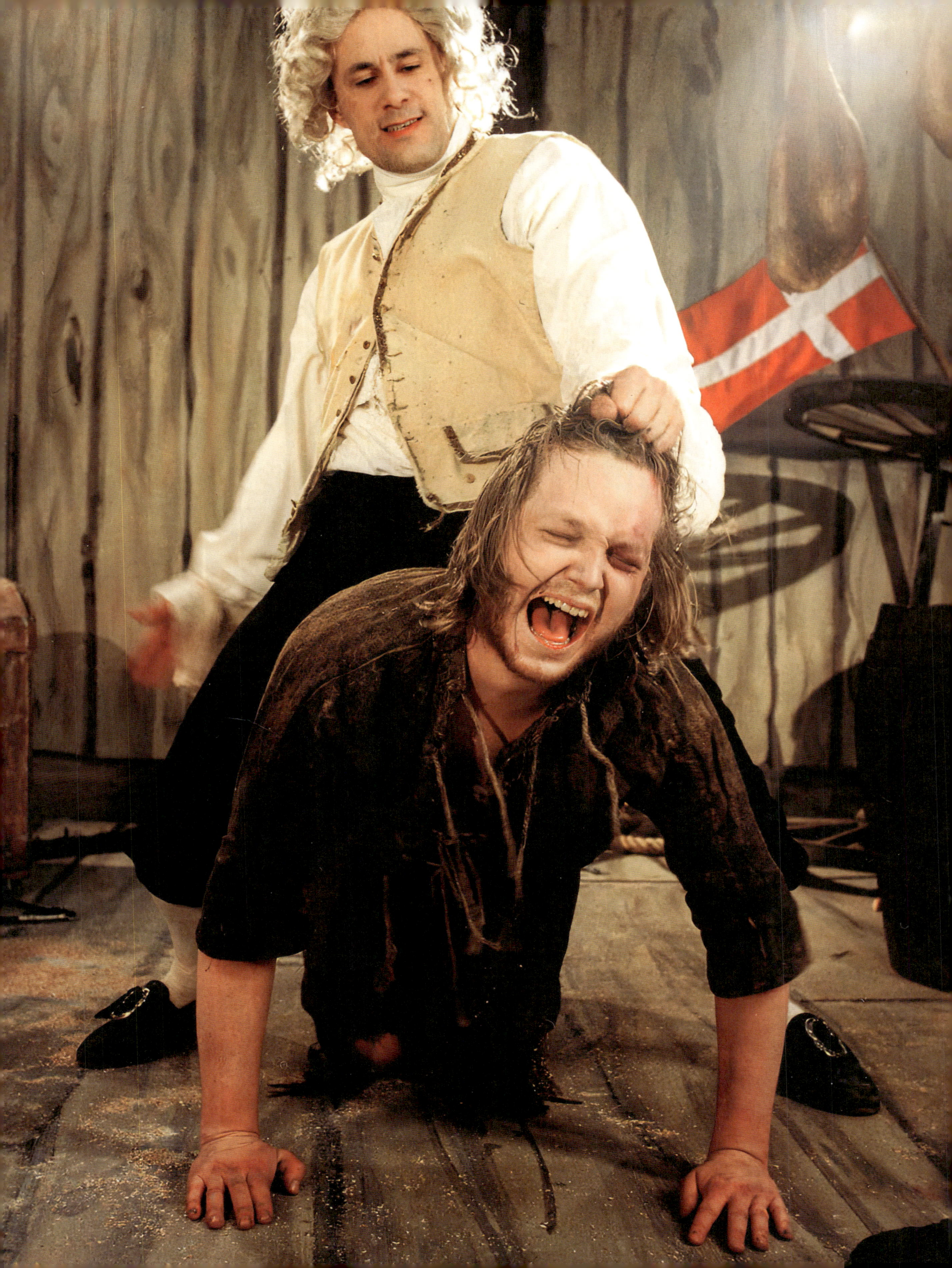

COLONIZATION — 2003

Single-channel video
Duration: 12:08 min.
National Gallery of Iceland, Reykjavik

By Vera Sóley Illugadóttir

The scene is instantly quite humorous. The violence and the dramatic images of blood-soaked Danish landmarks. And there is just something about the Danish language inherently funny to Icelandic people, I think. Especially when performed by other Icelanders, as here, with a choice of words inspired by the 'naive' 1970 Danish movie language from the golden age of Nordisk Film (Nordic Film) as seen in the movie series *Olsen Banden* (The Olsen Gang).

On view is a Danish merchant, cruelly berating and beating a poor Icelandic peasant. But did Icelanders really suffer such extreme cruelties by their Danish overlords?

The scene certainly aligns with the stories Icelandic children were told for decades about the injustices of Danish colonial rule (c. 1380-1944). Most famously, the trade monopoly imposed on Iceland by Denmark in the 17th and 18th centuries, which allowed Danish merchants to ship their absolutely worst products to Iceland. Rotten flour, teeming with maggots. Probably beat Icelanders bloody as well.

Although in reality, there was only one recorded instance of rotten flour being sent to Iceland during the monopoly years – in 1767, after a particularly bad harvest. And the merchants responsible ended up having to pay a considerable amount to Iceland in compensation, money which was later used to build a school in Reykjavik.

And was Iceland even ever a Danish colony, really? This is a matter which has been debated for centuries and still is. Even during Danish rule, Danes and Icelanders both were often unsure of the precise status of the island with regards to Denmark, and what to call this distant possession. Was Iceland *provins* or *biland* or *koloni* (province, extra land, colony)?

The term *koloni* was actually rarely if ever used to refer to Iceland in the Danish system. Proud (and often quite racist) Icelanders at the time certainly preferred to think of themselves as somehow above other colonial subjects of Denmark – even while they simultaneously craved independence and complained about monopolies, maggots and other Danish injustices. White Icelanders had, in their own opinion, to be a rank above 'uncivilised' colonials such as the Inuit of Greenland (although foreign visitors to Iceland in centuries past usually did not find the local population to be particularily civilised!).

A notorious example of this thinking is the colonial exhibition held in Tivoli in Copenhagen in the summer of 1905. The exhibition was put

Opposite page: From the recordings of *Colonization*, 2003

on to showcase local crafts from Danish-held areas abroad: the Danish West Indies, Greenland, the Faroe Islands and Iceland.

The idea to exhibit Icelandic culture alongside that of Black West Indians and Inuit (the peoples that actually suffered the worst cruelties and injustices by Danes) caused a scandal among Icelanders in Copenhagen, who complained loudly. No way, they said, could Icelanders appear next to such *skrælingjar* (barbarians). Exhibition organisers eventually had to make several concessions to appease offended Icelanders and try to make sure no visitors would equate Iceland and the 'true colonies' of the West Indies and Greenland.

It's unlikely that many Icelanders today really see themselves as postcolonial subjects. But the stories of maggots and other Danish cruelties do remain – perhaps especially when Icelanders need a bigger bad guy on which to blame their historical misfortunes.

VERA SÓLEY ILLUGADÓTTIR is an Icelandic journalist, programme coordinator and host on the history radio show *Í ljósi sögunnar* (In light of History) on the RÚV (The Icelandic National Broadcasting Service – Ríkisútvarpið). She holds a BA degree in Middle Eastern studies.

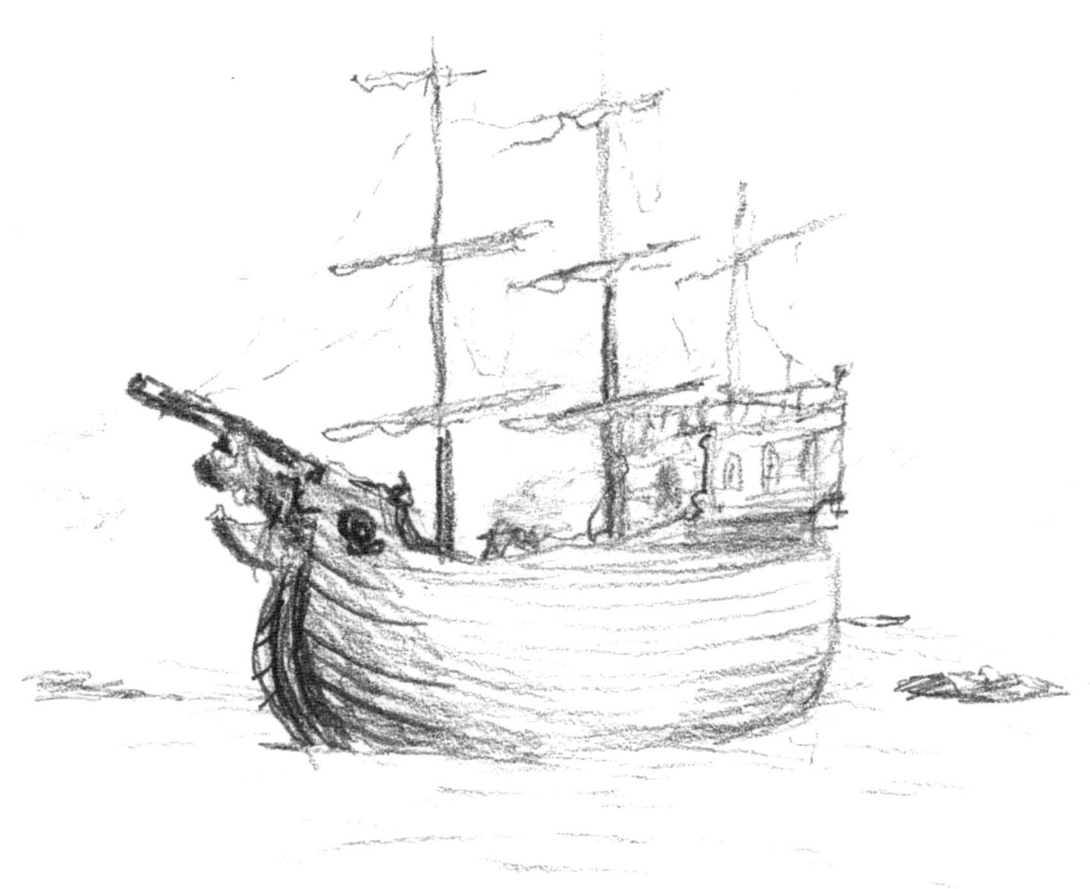

Drawing by Ragnar Kjartansson, 2003
Opposite page: From the recordings of *Colonization*, 2003

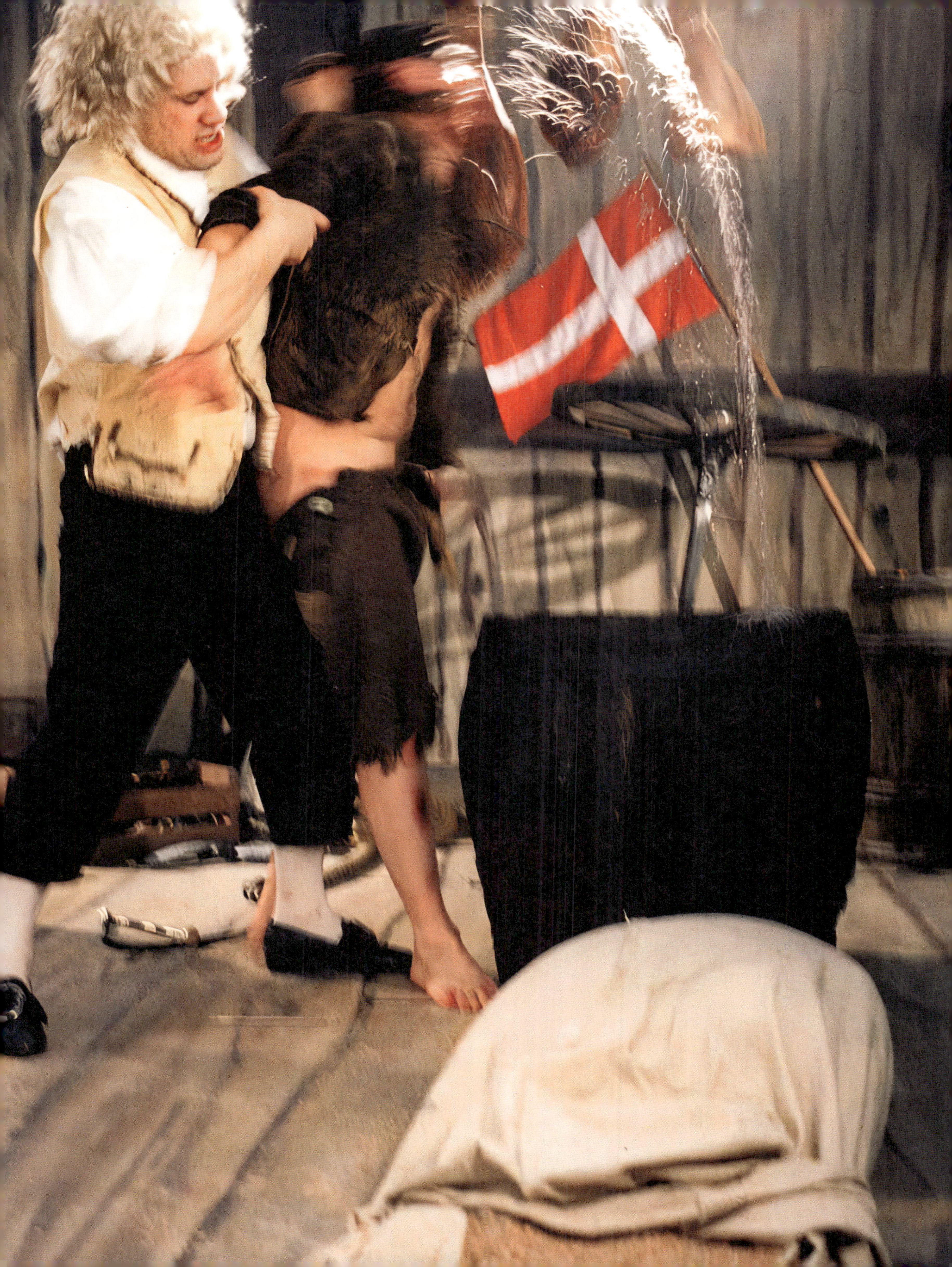

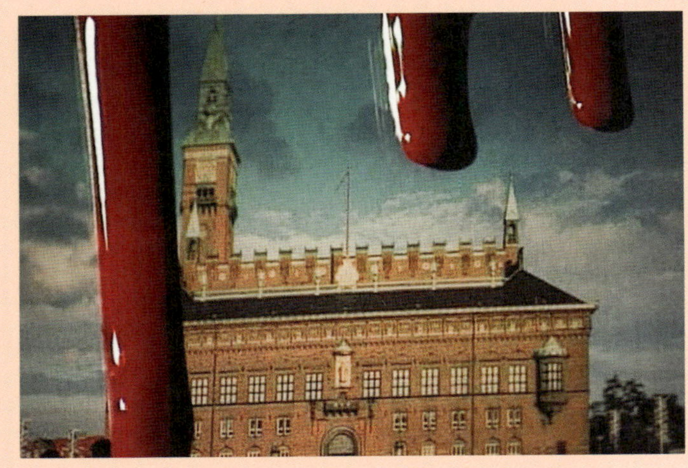

[Stillbillede af Marmorkirken bag dryppende blod]

DANSKER *[står]*

ISLÆNDING *[sidder/ligger]*

DANSKER *[giver* ISLÆNDING *lussinger, slag og spark]*: Du har stjålet nok fra mig, din lille tyv, din slapsvans. Dit møgsvin.

DANSKER *[hopper på* ISLÆNDING*]*: Satans islænding. Du snyder, du snyder, du snyder!

DANSKER *[snerrer]*

ISLÆNDING *[klynker]*

DANSKER: Din lille satan, dit lille møgsvin. Din hundelort. Svinelort. Svinelort!

[Pause]

ISLÆNDING *[trækker vejret heftigt]*

DANSKER *[slår* ISLÆNDING *med flad hånd oven i hovedet]*: Hundelort. Satans islænding.

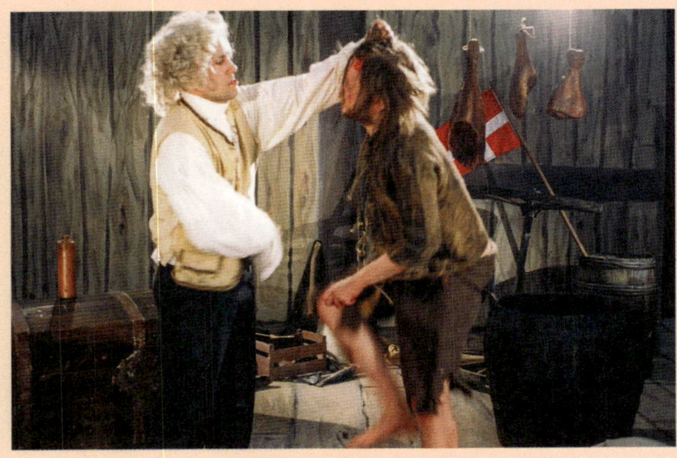

[Stillbillede af Københavns Rådhus. Kunstigt blod driver ned over billedet]

ISLÆNDING *[er lænet forover op ad en tønde, bukserne trukket ned]*

DANSKER *[pisker de blottede baller, griner]*: Du, svin. Dit lille svin. Ja, uh! Du keder mig.

ISLÆNDING *[klynker]*

DANSKER *[slår og pisker]*: Dit lille møgsvin. Islandske svin. Satans islænding. Svinepels. Svinelort. Svinelort. Satans islænding, ja!

ISLÆNDING *[hulker]*

DANSKER *[slikker på sine fingre, klasker* ISLÆNDING *bagi]*: Din svinepest. Svinelort. Din ... hundelort.

ISLÆNDING *[ømmer sig]*

DANSKER *[drikker af en flaske]*: Islandske lort. Du har stjålet nok fra mig.

DANSKER *[slikker på sine fingre, klasker* ISLÆNDING *bagi]*: Din satans islænding. Møgsvin. Ja. Ulidelige slapsvans. Utyske. Satans. Svinelort. Altså. Du satans svinelort. Utyske. Du har stjålet nok fra mig. Arh. Ja. Arh.

[Pause]

DANSKER: Altså. Du keder mig.

ISLÆNDING *[vånder sig, vil hive bukserne op, vakler]*

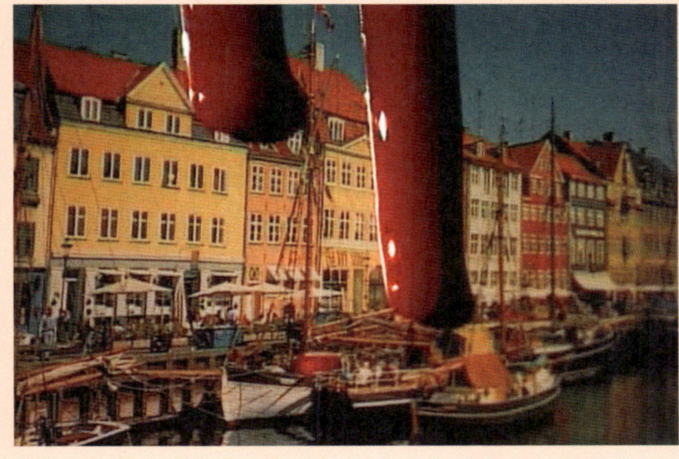

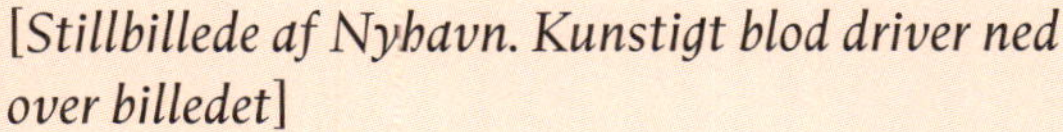

[Stillbillede af Nyhavn. Kunstigt blod driver ned over billedet]

DANSKER [*holder* ISLÆNDINGs *hoved under vand i en tønde*]

[*Druknelyde*]

DANSKER [*tørrer sine hænder af i* ISLÆNDINGs *tøj*]

ISLÆNDING [*puster ud, får vejret*]

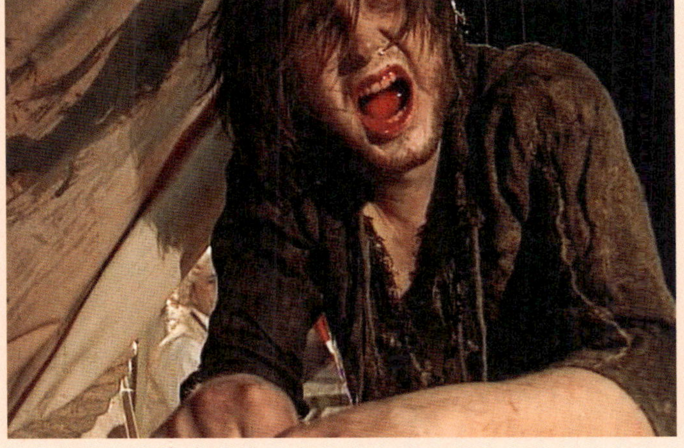

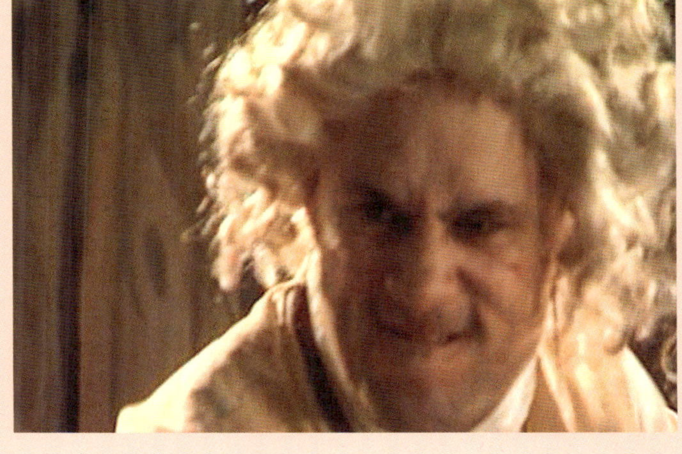

[Stillbillede af Den lille havfrue. Kunstigt blod driver ned over billedet]

DANSKER [*smadrer trækasser i hovedet på* ISLÆNDING]

DANSKER [*drikker fra en flaske og hælder noget af flaskens indhold i håret på* ISLÆNDING, *der afværger og klynker*]

DANSKER [*går frem og tilbage med Dannebrog, sparker* ISLÆNDING *i ryggen*]

ISLÆNDING [*på gulvet, spiser havregryn af sin hånd*]

DANSKER [*spytter*]

[*Harke- og spyttelyde*]

DANSKER [*banker ISLÆNDING med et stykke træ*]

ISLÆNDING [*spiser*]

[Stillbillede af Marmorkirken. Kunstigt blod driver ned over billedet]

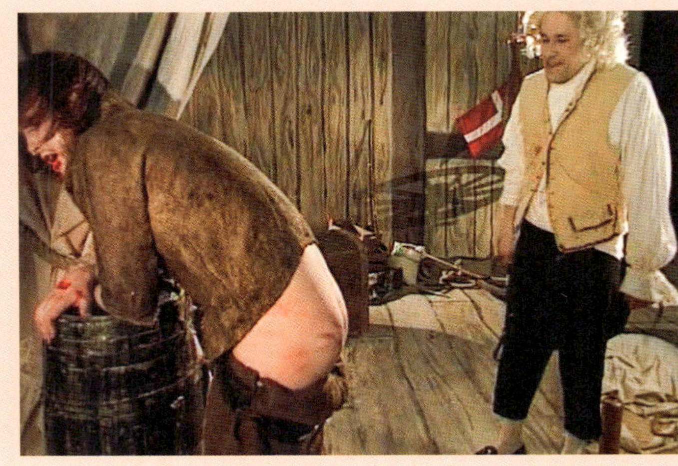

Ragnar Kjartansson. *Colonization*, 2003. Danish transcript and stills

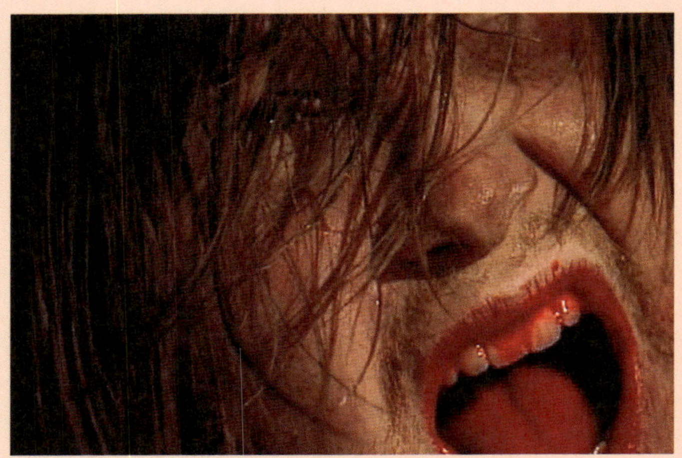

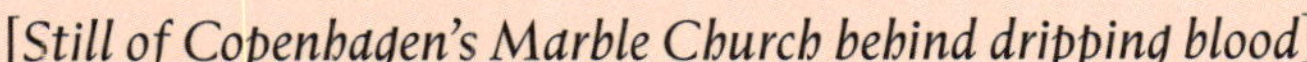

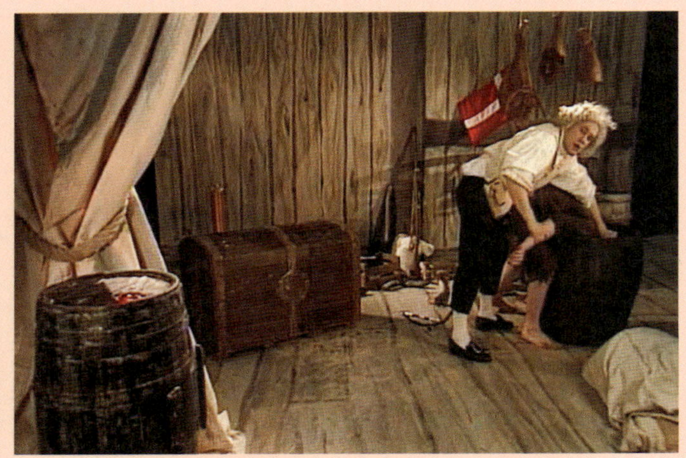

[Still of Copenhagen's Marble Church behind dripping blood]

DANE *[standing]*

ICELANDER *[sitting/reclining]*

DANE *[slaps, beats and kicks the* ICELANDER*]*: You've stolen enough from me, you little thief, you wimp. You dirty swine.

DANE *[jumps up and down on the* ICELANDER*]*: Goddam Icelander. You cheat, you cheat, you cheat!

DANE *[growling]*

ICELANDER *[whimpering]*

DANE: You little devil, you little swine. Dog shit. Pig shit. Pig shit!

[Beat]

ICELANDER *[breathing heavily]*

DANE *[strikes the* ICELANDER *on top of the head with an open hand]*: Dog shit. Fucking Icelander.

[Still of Copenhagen City Hall. Fake blood oozes down the image]

ICELANDER *[leans over a barrel with his trousers down]*

DANE *[whips the* ICELANDER'S *bared buttocks, laughing]*: You pig. You little pig. Yes, ooh! You bore me.

ICELANDER *[whimpering]*

DANE *[beating, whipping]*: You dirty, little swine. Icelandic pig. Fucking Icelander. Hog. Pig shit. Pig shit. Damn Icelander, yes!

ICELANDER *[sobbing]*

DANE *[licks his fingers, smacks the* ICELANDER'S *bottom]*: You swine fever. Pig shit. You ... dog shit.

ICELANDER *[wincing]*

DANE *[drinks from a bottle]*: Icelandic shit. You've stolen enough from me.

DANE *[licks his fingers, smacks the* ICELANDER'S *bottom]*: You fucking Icelander. Dirty swine. Yes. Unbearable wimp. Filthy animal. Fuck. Pig shit. Fucking pig shit. Filthy animal. You've stolen enough from me. Ah. Yes. Ah.

[Beat]

DANE: That's it. You bore me.

ICELANDER *[moaning, pulls up his trousers, staggers]*

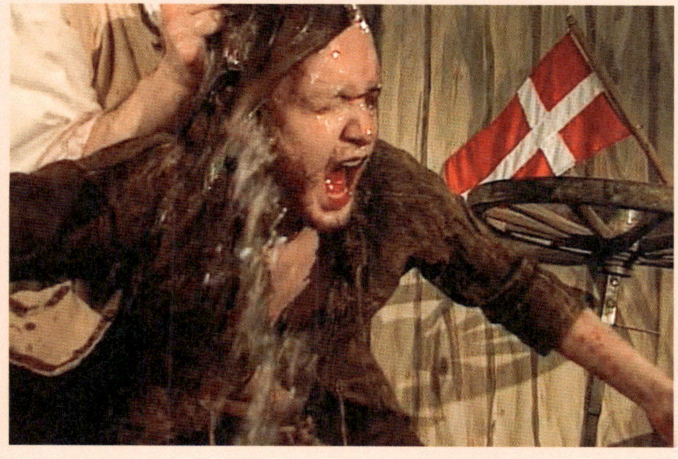

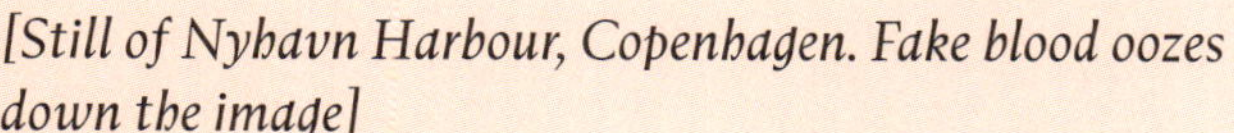

[Still of Nyhavn Harbour, Copenhagen. Fake blood oozes down the image]

DANE *[holds the* ICELANDER'S *head underwater in a barrel]*

[Sounds of drowning]

DANE *[wipes his hands on the* ICELANDER'S *clothes]*

ICELANDER *[gasping, catches his breath]*

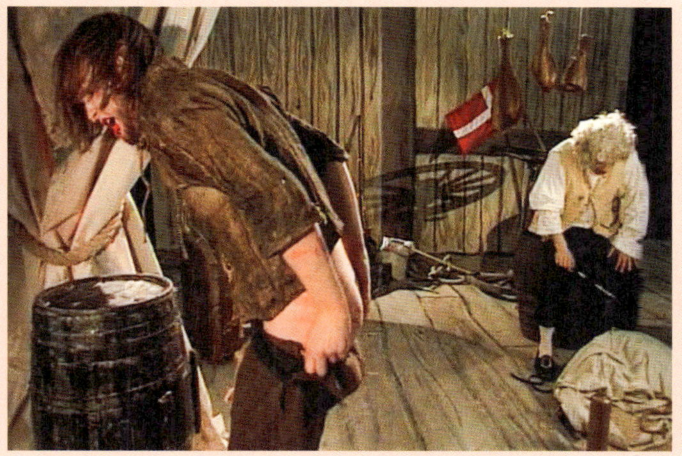

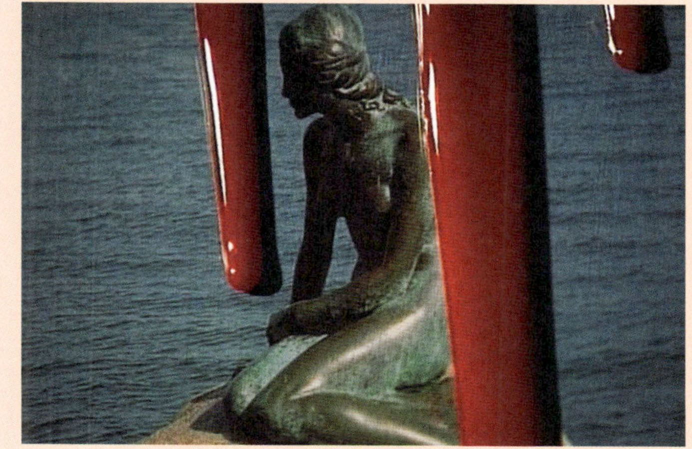

[Still of the Little Mermaid, Copenhagen. Fake blood oozes down the image]

DANE *[smashes wooden crates over the* ICELANDER'S *head]*

DANE *[drinks from a bottle, pours liquid from the bottle on the hair of the* ICELANDER, *who parries and whimpers]*

DANE *[paces back and forth with the Danish national flag, the Dannebrog, kicks the* ICELANDER *in the back]*

ICELANDER *[on the floor, eating rolled oats from one hand]*

DANE *[spits]*

[Hawking and spitting noises]

DANE *[beats the* ICELANDER *with a piece of wood]*

ICELANDER *[eating]*

[Still of the Marble Church. Fake blood oozes down the image]

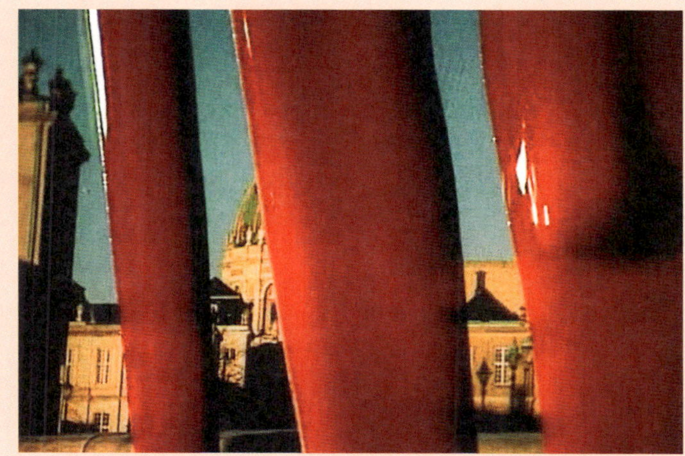

Ragnar Kjartansson. *Colonization*, 2003. English transcript and stills

GUILT TRIP — 2007

Single-channel video
Duration: 10:24 min.
Courtesy of the artist, Luhring Augustine, New York, and i8 Gallery, Reykjavik

KILLING STARS, excerpt from _Ragnar by Memory, Part 1_, 2013

By Roni Horn

A man with a rifle and a plastic bag arrives. Dressed for the cold, he stands in a seemingly endless snow-covered landscape. It's just a man surrounded in white and nothing else. Every move he makes is accompanied by the noisy, brittle sound of cold plastic and the scrunch of the snow.

He looks up. He's pointing his rifle. Nothing. But he sees something.

He shoots. At what? Nothing? A star? Maybe it's a star. Maybe, but I can't see it. He looks around again still pointing his rifle and bam! Another shot. Another star? Bam again. Another star? Maybe. Perhaps the stars are falling – invisible and silent in the dull white atmosphere and invisible again in the whiteness of the snow. Perhaps the stars are lying in the snow – accumulating like other flakes.

Or maybe the stars have melted the snow and silently, invisibly replaced it with their own look-alike whiteness. Or perhaps the stars were extinguished; the coldness of the snow finally subduing their heat, offering yet another form of invisibility.

RONI HORN is an artist and writer.

Opposite page: From the recordings of *Guilt Trip*, 2007
The following spreads: From the recordings of *Guilt Trip*, 2007, and an installation view, Louisiana Museum of Modern Art, 2023

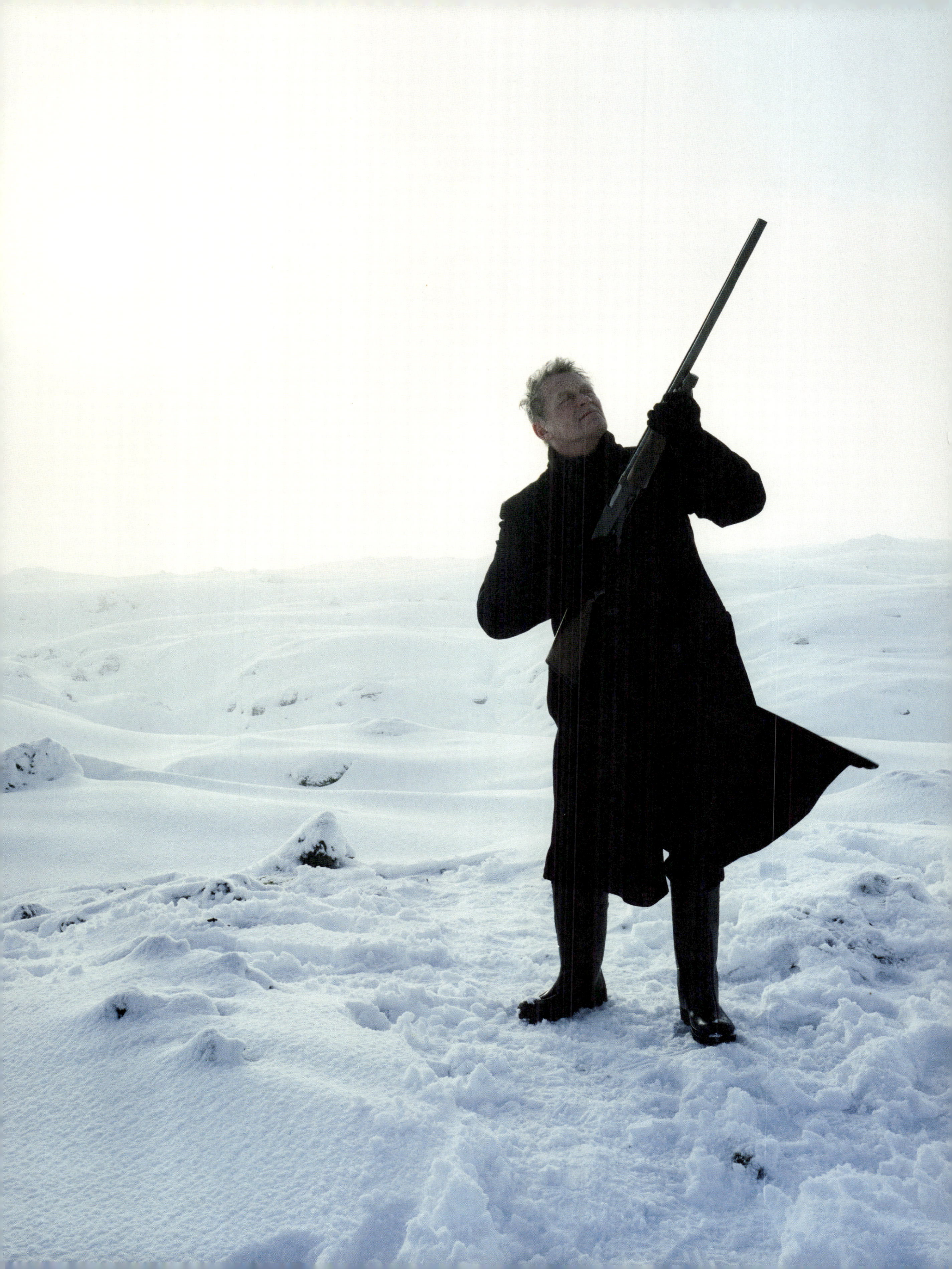

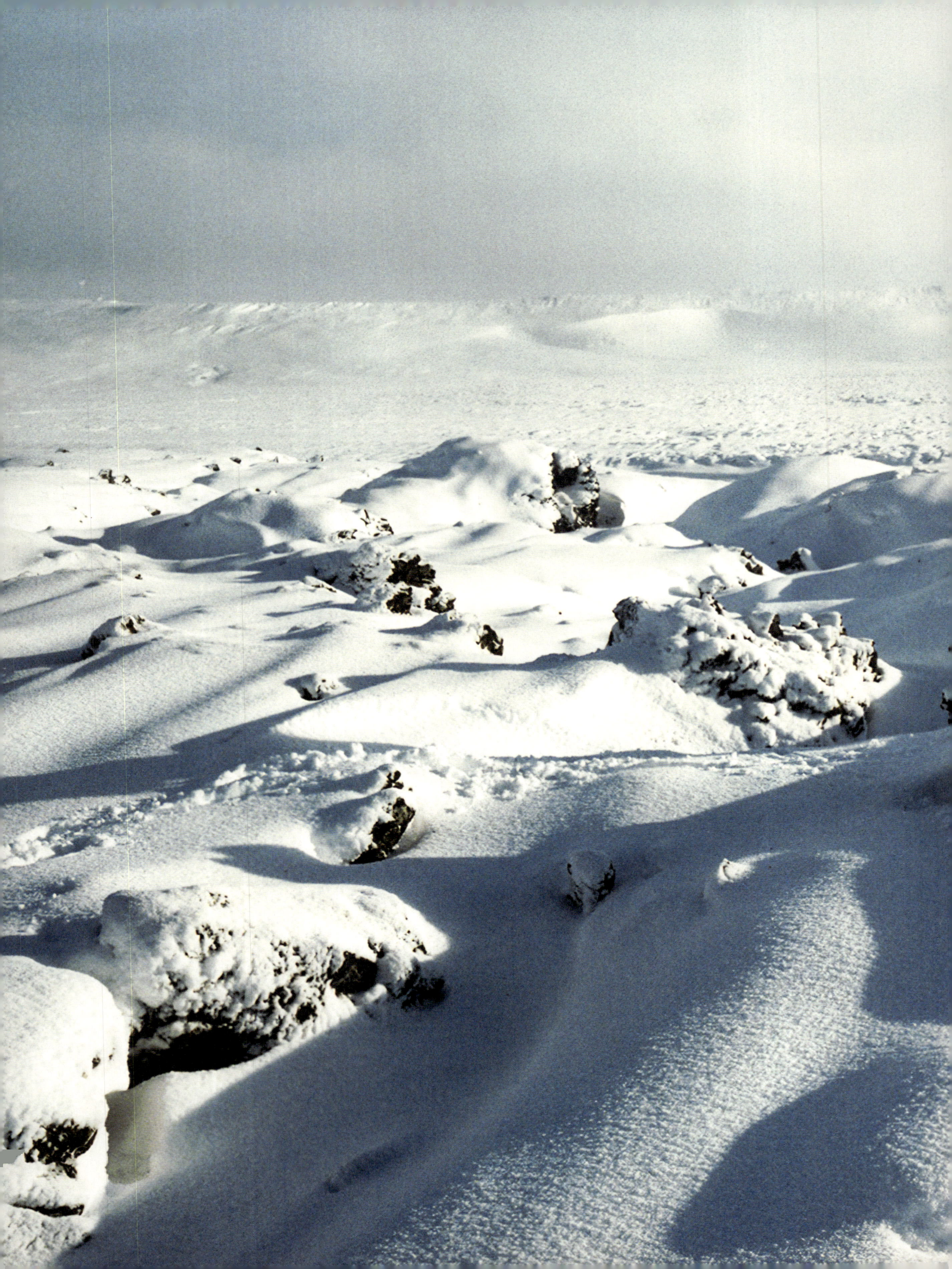

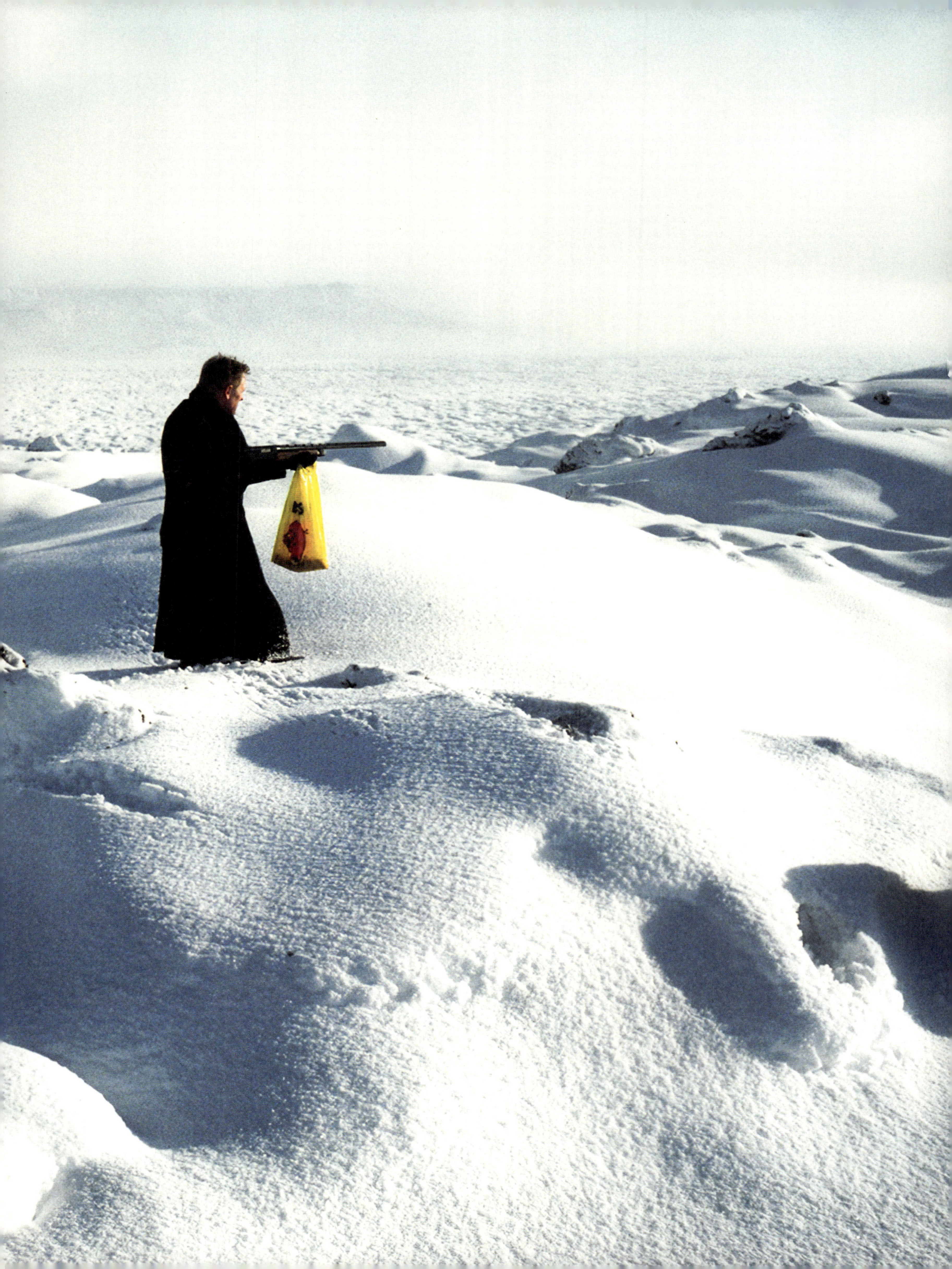

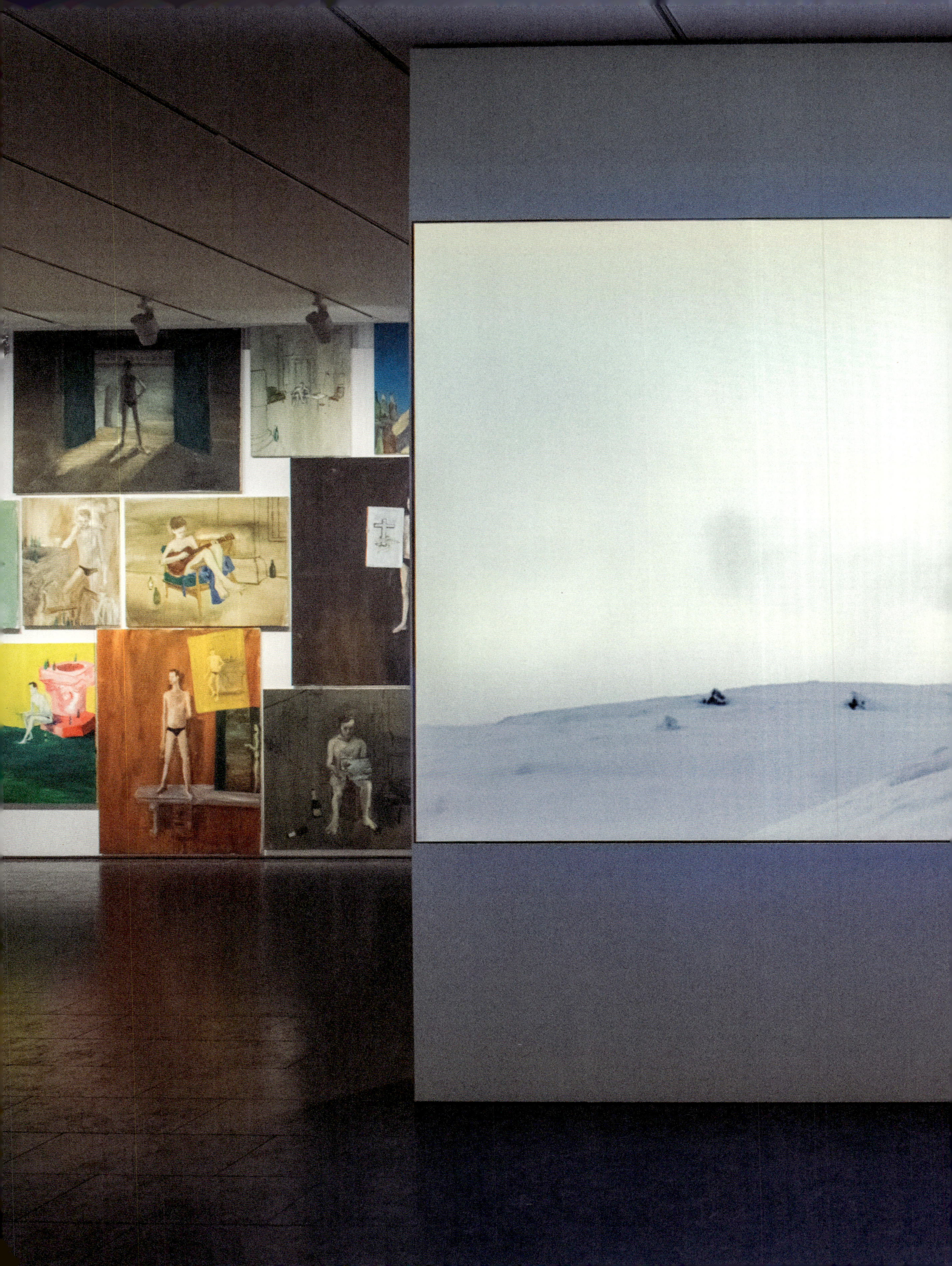

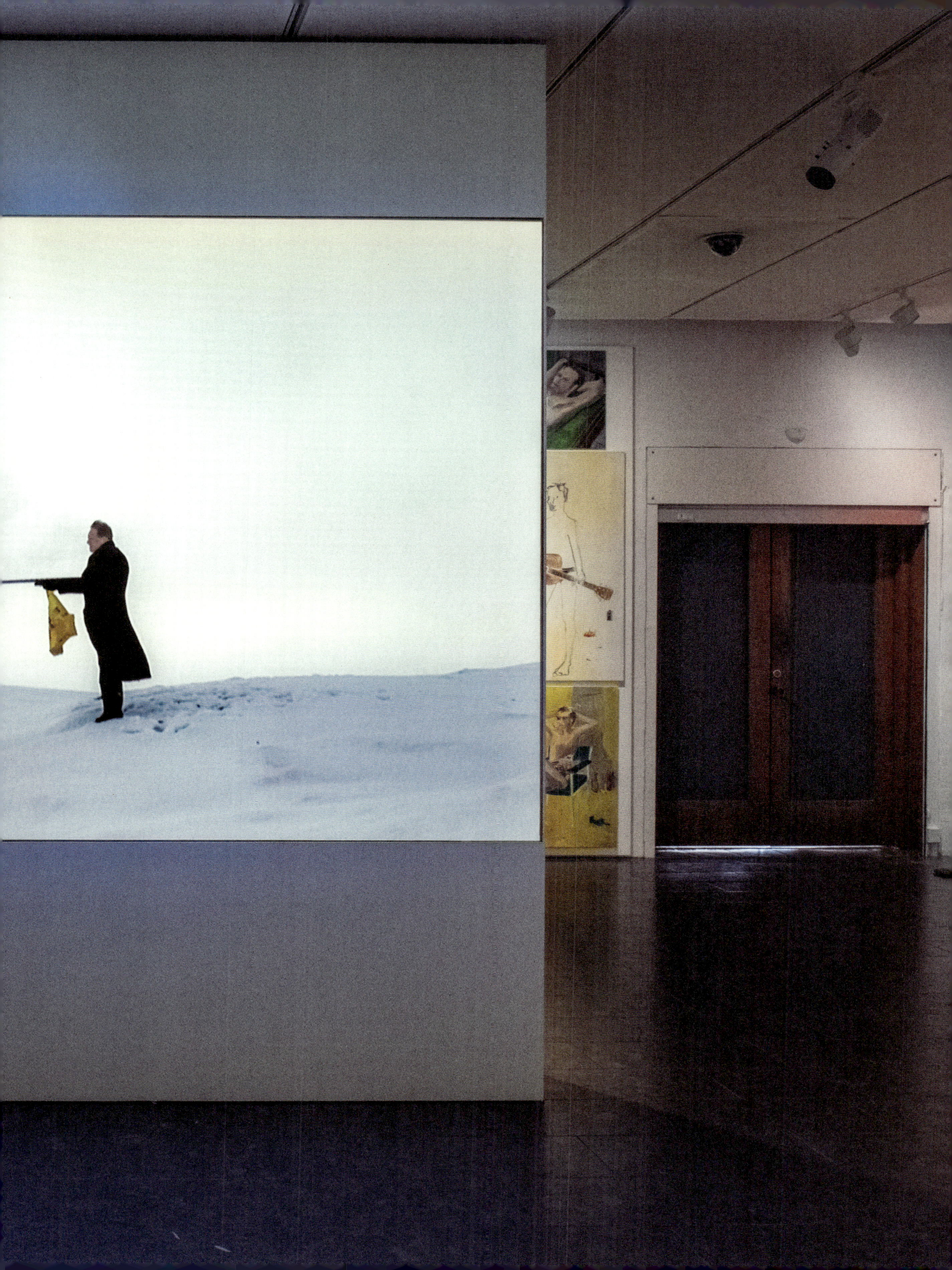

DIE NACHT DER HOCHZEIT — 2022/2023

Courtesy of the artist, Luhring Augustine, New York, and i8 Gallery, Reykjavik
Private collection, New York
collection De Pont museum, Tilburg

By Ragnar Helgi Ólafsson

The name is not the object named. Hardly anyone disputes this nowadays. By most accounts, Alfred Korzybski (1879-1950) settled the matter conclusively in his address to the International Congress in New Orleans in 1931. At that occasion, Alfred used, for the first time, the phrase (now on everyone's lips) to demonstrate the fact, "The map is not the territory". This seems undisputed even if, to some of us, it is still a mystery how a sentence made up of words could be used to prove such a thing. Still, we see no option but to conclude that a painting of the night sky is not the night sky.

*

Sometimes we (as in "I") find it hard to choose the right anniversary presents for ourselves, let alone for others. A lot of energy is squandered on this. A self-made painting of the night sky was, for a long time, Ragnar Kjartansson's 'standard issue' wedding gift to close friends. In that practical sense, these paintings are a one-stop shop. Ragnar settled the matter of wedding gifts once and for all. Effortless in both its banality and genuineness, no decision need to be made. An elegant solution to a complicated conundrum.

*

In recent weeks, we have stared at Ragnar Kjartansson's skies of the wedding night for much longer than we have looked at that which it claims to portray. Poetry is a swollen finger pointing at the moon, they say. Judging by hours spent, we are forced to draw the conclusion that of the two, we are more interested in the finger.

*

Of course, these night skies are only watercolours washed onto sheets of paper. They are small, not big; flat, not domed. The fact that we know that they are maps of a certain night sky (as opposed to the night sky in general) does the heavy lifting. In that light, these are not only skies but no normal ones at that. The skies of the night of the big day are endless in their vastness above the bed of the couple on their wedding night. Here, evidently, all the clocks have stopped ticking. The set, even if made of crudely painted plywood, is self-sufficient and, against all odds itching with poetry. This hour is of the liminal variety, we are told. A course has been set, but no boat has yet sailed. At this point, sea charts are superfluous ("we will never need them"); all thought of low-lying skerries and sunken rocks ("plainly absurd.") Sometimes – and usually against all our driven instincts – many of us can't help but feel that these intermezzos are the best of times. Anticipation tends to exceed the outcome, whatever the latter turns out to be – like the walk from the bus stop to the party: checking into the kiosk for cigarettes, noticing the squeak of one's sneakers, feeling the no-breeze in spring. Everything is expectant with

Opposite page: *Die Nacht der Hochzeit* (detail), 2022

anticipation of undefined happenings. While you are walking up the stairs, sniffing out the base drum pounding its way through your friend's door on the 3rd floor ... up until the moment you open that door: Anything is possible, not as in "many possible outcomes", but rather in the sense of plain undefined potentiality. The moment things start to happen (a door is opened, makeup removed, a tie loosened, dress unbuttoned), the clocks start ticking again ... at this point, potentiality shifts into sets of possibilities, which one by one then mutate into choices. On the night of the wedding, no one can imagine a quarrel over dirty laundry, just as no one is really thinking about happiness.

*

Flames painted on plywood won't burn your swollen finger, but they will burn if doused with gasoline and set alight.

*

I once overheard a conversation between two of Ragnar's friends who happened to be single at the time. They were talking about orchestrating marriages of convenience involving the two of them.

A: ... how else can I come to own a piece of the night sky?

B: But what happens to the *Night of the Wedding* in case of divorce? Which of the two gets to keep it?

A: Would you really want to keep it?

B: Maybe it reverts back to the artist.

*

As so often with Ragnar Kjartansson's art, *Die Nacht der Hochzeit* is a swollen finger pointing towards the sublime in the disguise of an overblown joke. Or is it the other way around? It's hard to say since none of the fakery is hidden. The perspective on the action is always that of the stagehand, not of the spectator. The scene doesn't really look like a bedroom on a wedding night. However, it very much looks like props, fabricated scenery trying in vain to give the impression of a bedroom on a wedding night.

*

We often stare at swollen fingers and frequently marvel at well-made maps. We probably do this more often than we take the time to inspect the landscape that good maps (according to Alfred Korzybski) fail so elegantly to portray. It is in this no man's land between the sublime and the thoroughly banal that Ragnar Kjartansson so often places his works. The ridiculous grandiosity of the artwork's stated aim and the inherent, and at least half wilful, clumsiness of its execution makes us laugh – out loud, even. Humour is the trap door in Ragnar's work. It gives us the alibi we need. It supplies us with a fake mustache and silly glasses to travel incognito through crowds we would not dare to travel undisguised or at least not partially cloaked in irony.

*

Legend has it that Alfred Korzybski managed to find his way from Poland to New Orleans in the fall of 1931 without ever consulting a map.

*

We (as in "I") sometimes forget that art is not a riddle to be solved. The function of art isn't the fabrication of beauty but rather, simply a search for beauty. This is an inherently haphazard undertaking in that it cannot be conducted systematically since its aim is not really to find the thing sought after. Still – and rather unexpectedly – for it to yield anything of interest, the search has to be skillfully conducted, which in this case means it must take us by surprise, be somewhat bewildering and essentially laughable. This is why Ragnar's friends whisper among themselves about the possibility of a nominal marriage of convenience. "How else am I to acquire a piece of the night sky?" they joke. The speaker and the listener both know that what they really seek is, of course, not a painting of the night sky but the trap door concealed within it. At the moment of laughter, the map that we use to distinguish the finger from the moon, the sublime from the banal, the night sky from the painting of the night sky – that map itself – stumbles without warning onto centre stage and, for an instant, becomes the actual butt of the joke – right before it falls down yet another unmapped trap door.

RAGNAR HELGI ÓLAFSSON is an Icelandic author and poet. He studied philosophy and holds a master's degree in fine arts. He is also an artist and has exhibited with Ragnar Kjartansson.

Opposite page and the following spread: *Die Nacht der Hochzeit* (detail), 2023, and *Die Nacht der Hochzeit*, 2022
Following spreads: Installation views, Louisiana Museum of Modern Art, 2023

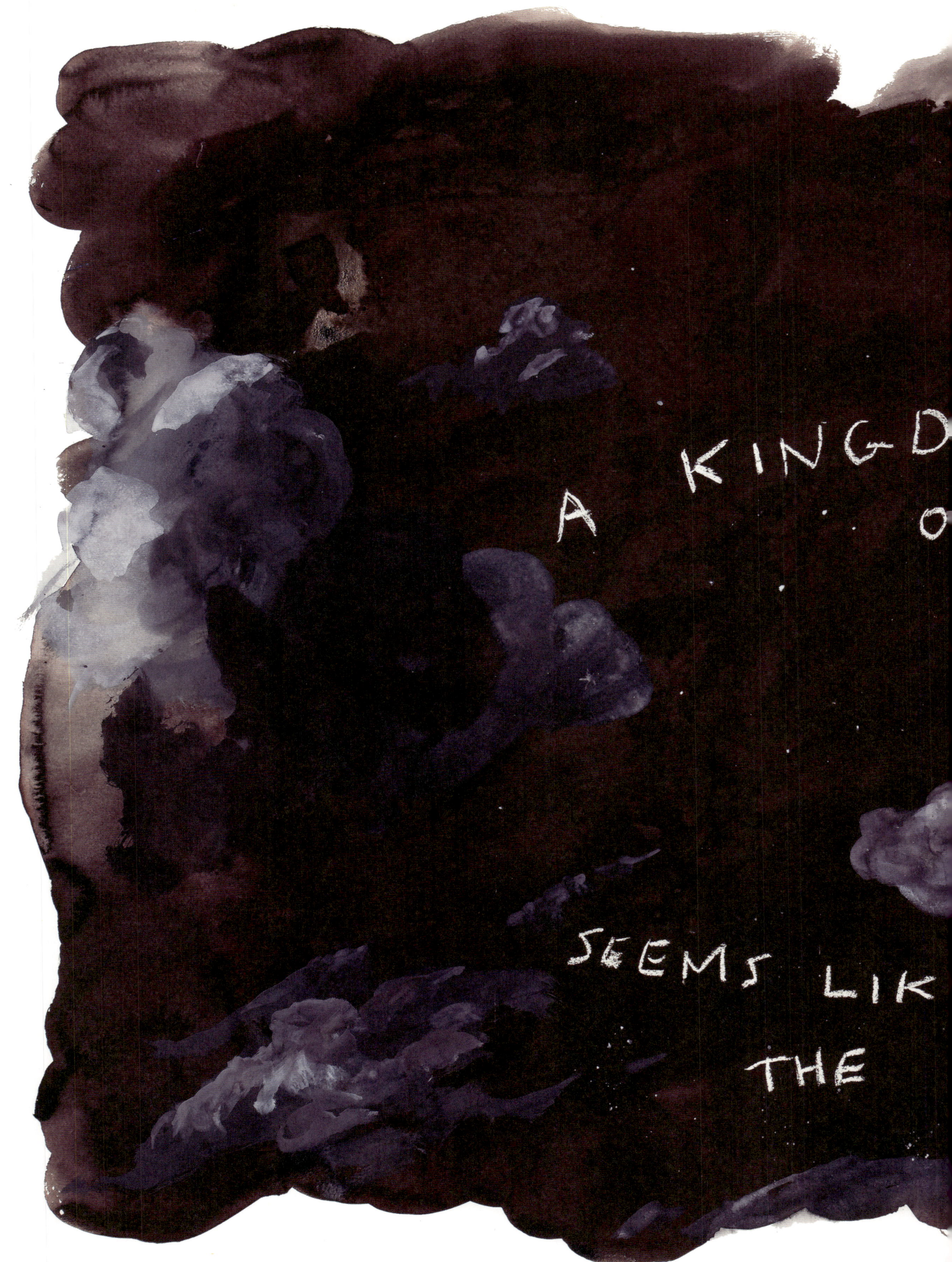
A KINGD
O
SEEMS LIK
THE

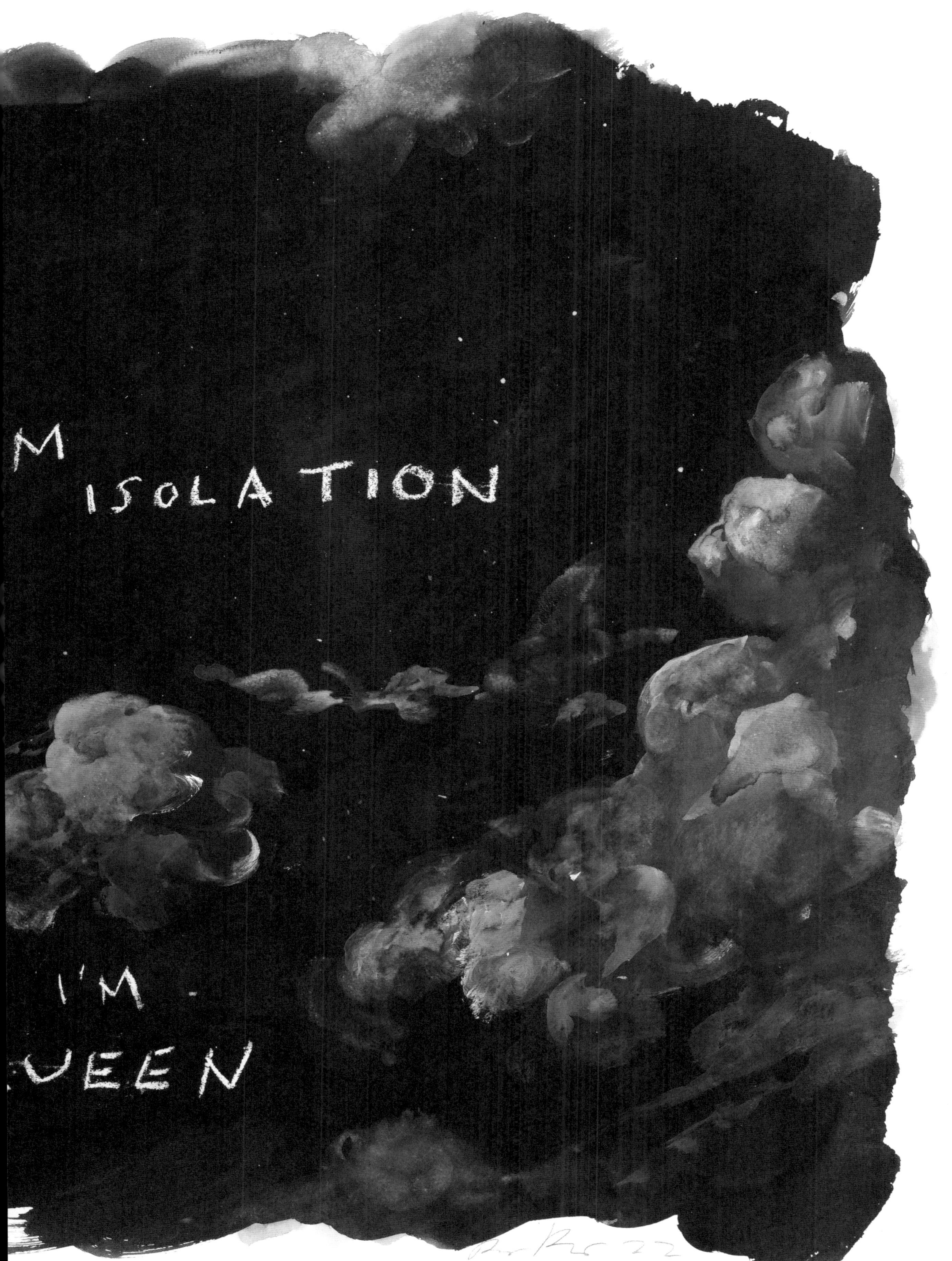
M
ISOLATION
I'M
UEEN

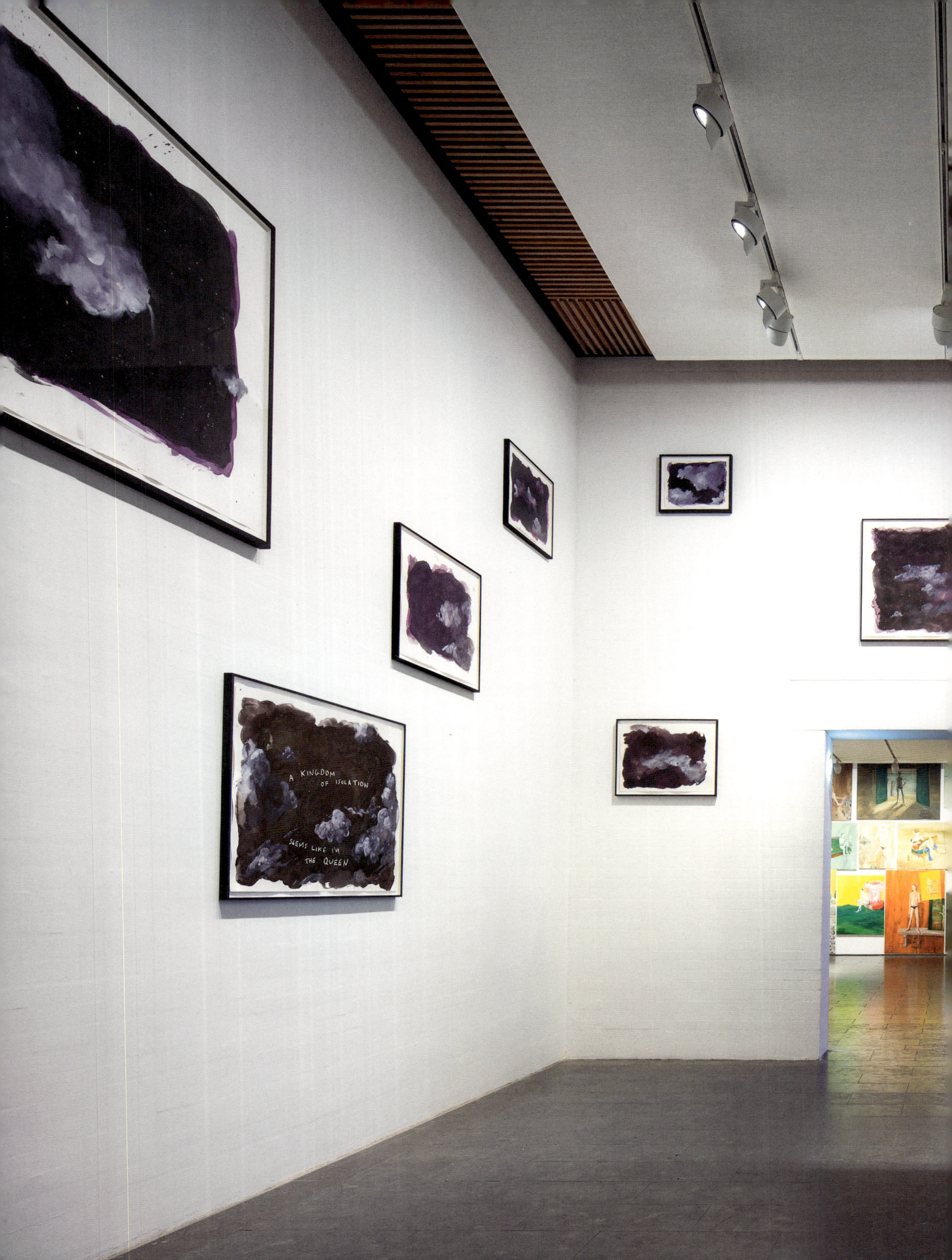
A KINGDOM
OF ISOLATION
SEEMS LIKE I'M
THE QUEEN

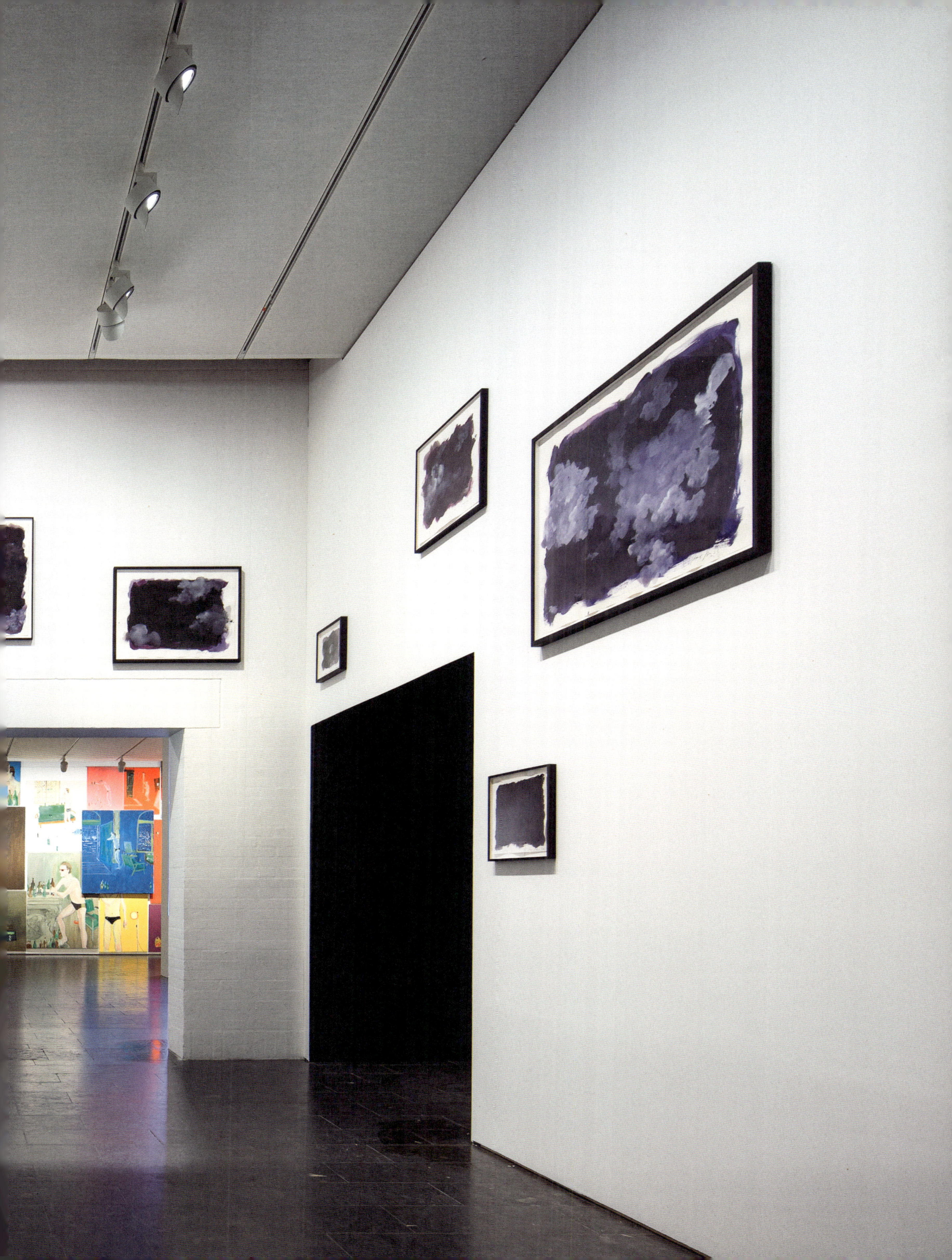

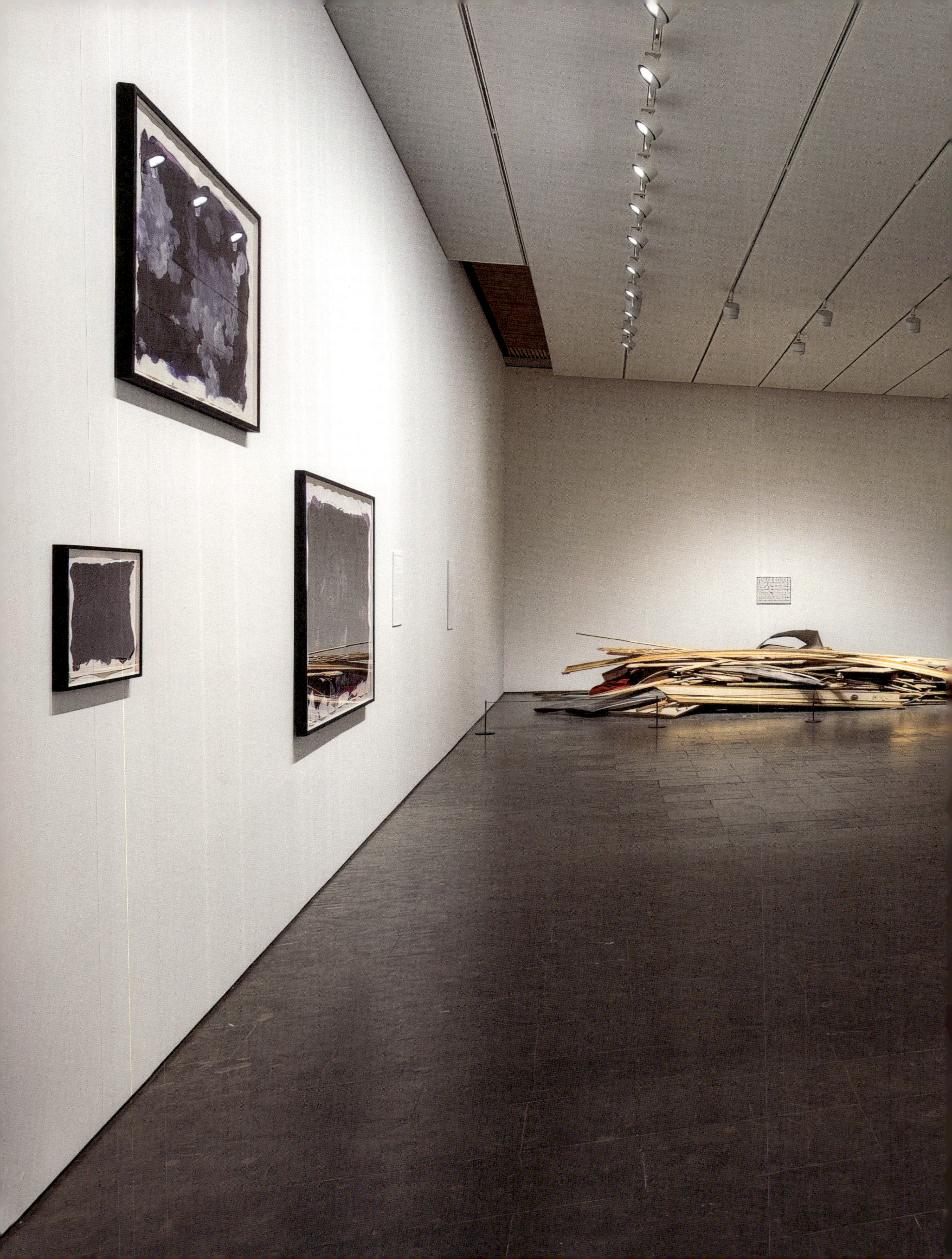

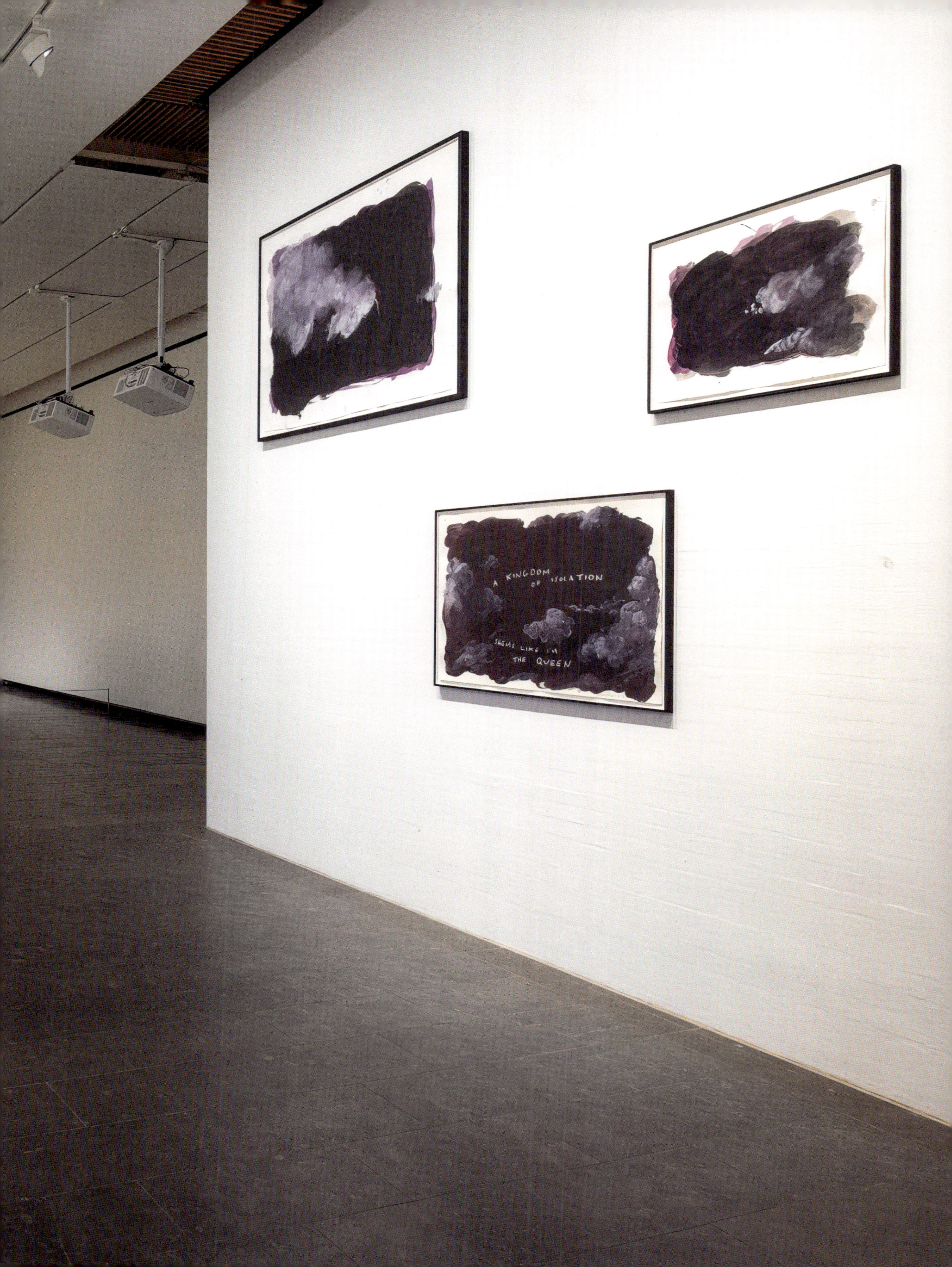
A KINGDOM OF ISOLATION
SEEMS LIKE I'M THE QUEEN

HITLER'S LOGE — 2006

Remains of a theatre loge, inscribed marble slab
Dimensions variable
National Gallery of Iceland, Reykjavik

By Tine Colstrup

The sculpture consists of the remains of what was known as a *Führerloge*: audience boxes built at the behest of Nazi leader Adolf Hitler (1889-1945) across an array of theatres and sports arenas in Germany. This one dates from 1941 and was built for the Admiralspalast theatre in Berlin. The Admiralspalast was close to the heart of the Nazi government and the *Führerbunker* and Hitler and his staff are said to have been frequent visitors. The theatre's programme featured variety and operetta performances, including Franz Lehár's (1870-1948) *The Merry Widow* (1905), Hitler's favourite operetta.

In 2006, two years before the financial collapse, Icelandic investors were buying up properties in Europe – in Copenhagen, for example, the Magasin du Nord department store and the iconic Hotel d'Angleterre. In that atmosphere, Icelandic actor and popstar Helgi Björns (born 1958) bought a derelict theatre in Berlin. Only then, during a major renovation of the theatre, the original Hitler interior was ripped out.

Kjartansson met Helgi Björns in his childhood, when they both performed on stage in a musical written by Kjartansson's father (Kjartan Ragnarsson, born 1945). Thus, the sculpture is an accumulation of demolition debris, geopolitical and personal histories. The artist has described the piece as "an evil pile of trash" that, "with the unpredictable ridiculousness of life", became part of his work. A marble slab next to the dilapidated symbol of power has a bone-dry explanation engraved:

ÉG HRINGDI
Í HELGA BJÖRNS
HANN ÚTVEGAÐI
MÉR STÚKU HITLERS
RAGNAR KJARTANSSON 2006

I CALLED
HELGI BJÖRNS
HE PROVIDED
ME WITH HITLER'S LOGE
RAGNAR KJARTANSSON 2006

TINE COLSTRUP is curator at Louisiana Museum of Modern Art and curated *Epic Waste of Love and Understanding*.

Opposite page and the following spread: Installation views, Louisiana Museum of Modern Art, 2023

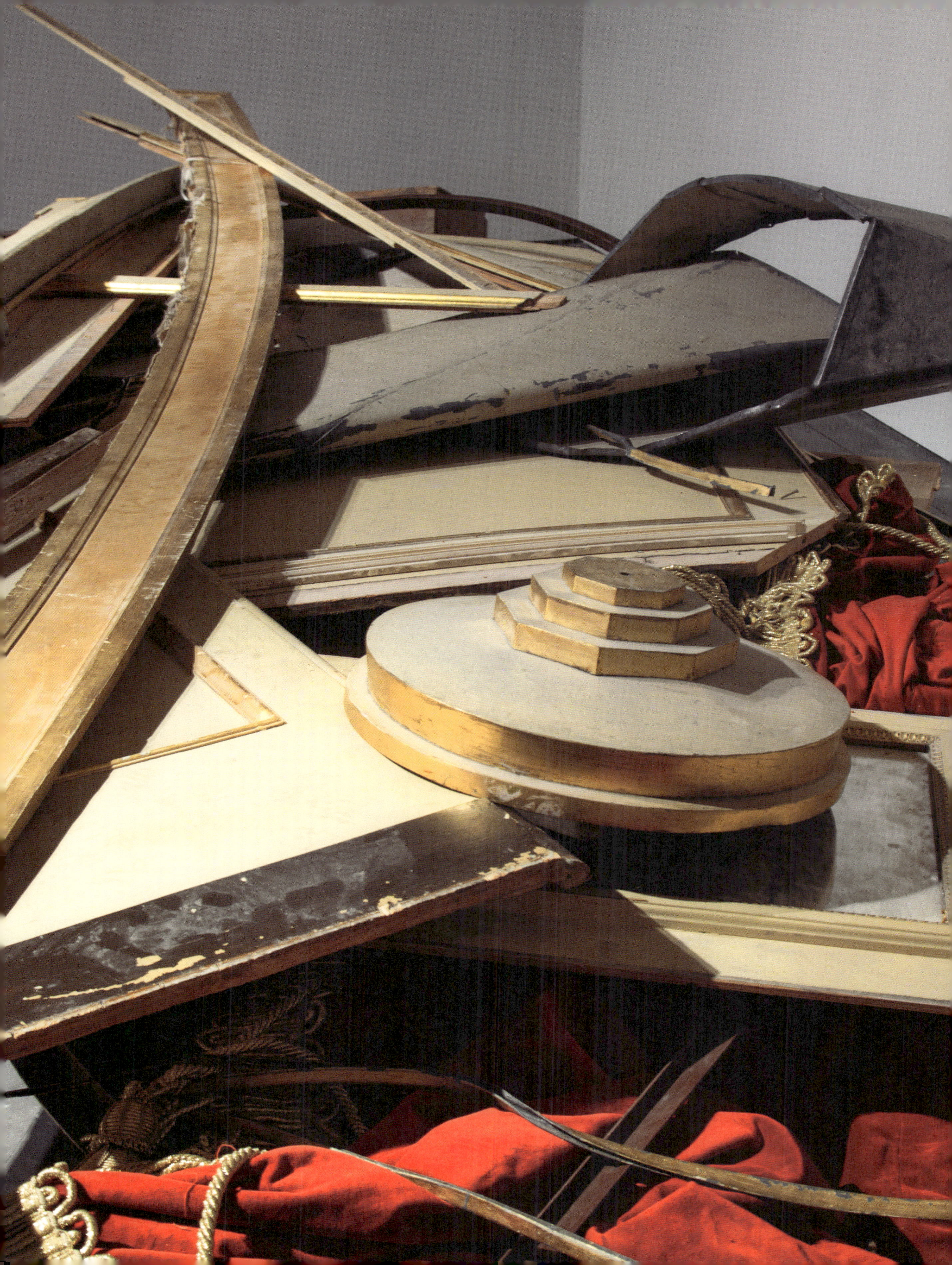

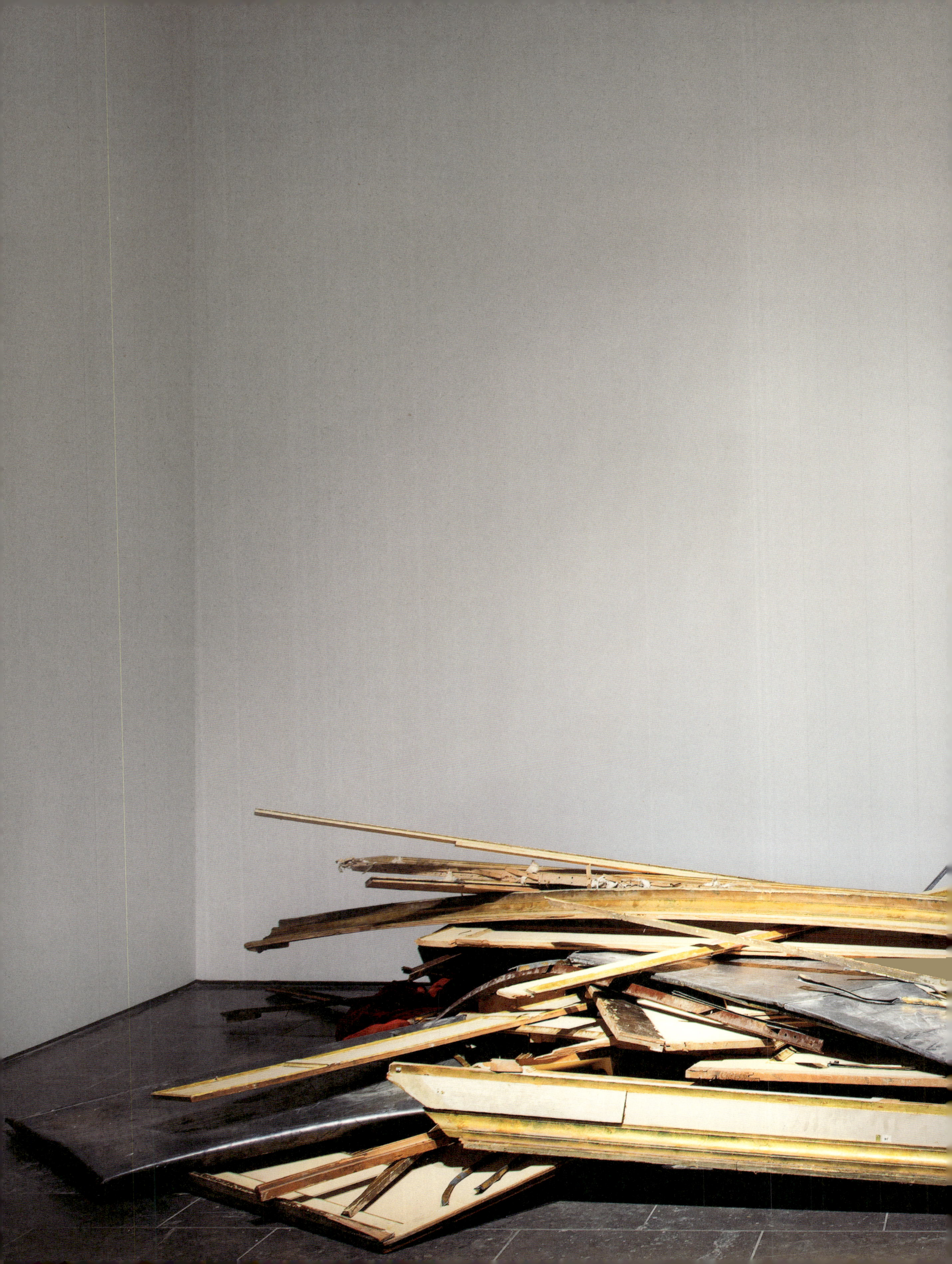

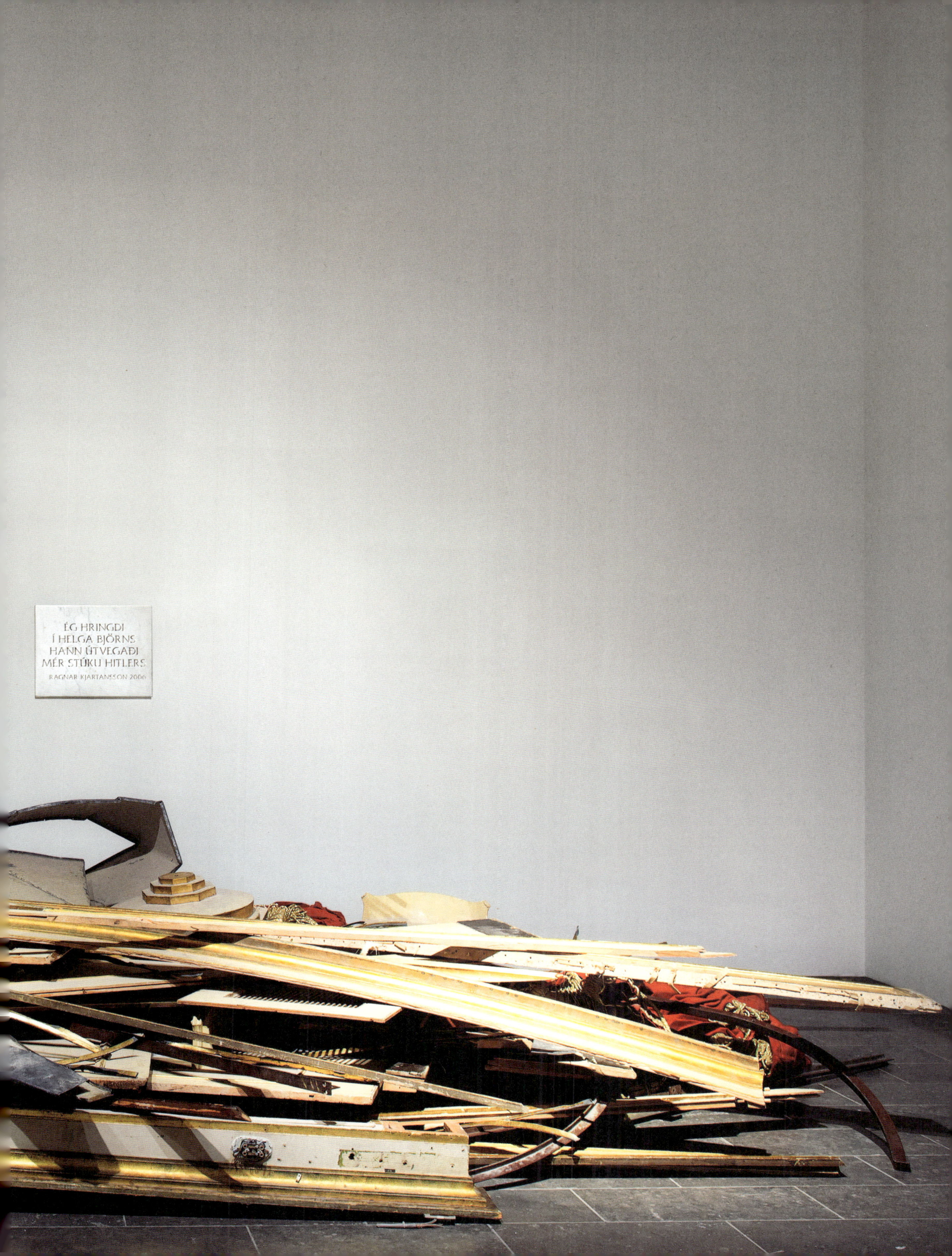

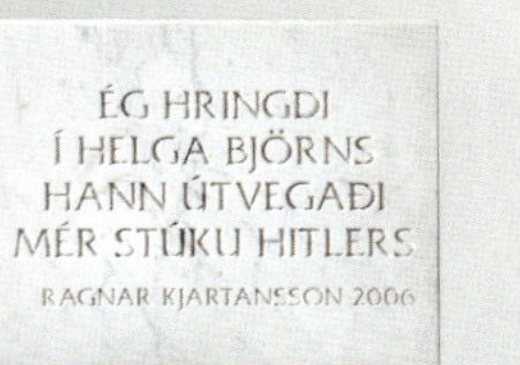
ÉG HRINGDI
Í HELGA BJÖRNS
HANN ÚTVEGAÐI
MÉR STÚKU HITLERS
RAGNAR KJARTANSSON 2006

TERRIBLE, TERRIBLE — 2021

Two-channel video
Duration: 3:30 min.
Commissioned by the V-A-C Foundation, Moscow
Courtesy of the artist, Luhring Augustine, New York, and i8 Gallery, Reykjavik

A conversation between Maria Alyokhina and Tine Colstrup

Tine Colstrup: Ragnar Kjartansson's piece *Terrible, Terrible* is a diptych of two videos that show reenactments of two actual, violent attacks on the same painting: *Ivan the Terrible and His Son Ivan on 16 November 1581*, painted in 1883-1885 by Ukrainian painter Ilya Repin (1844-1930). The two attacks on the painting happened almost exactly 100 years apart, in 1913 and 2018, in the Tretyakov Gallery in Moscow. Kjartansson re-staged and filmed them in his studio in Reykjavik in 2020.

Maria Alyokhina: Yes, Ragnar first showed me the piece in December 2021 in Moscow. I loved it, it's a really cool piece. I didn't even know about the attacks on the painting, but it's very interesting that they are similar but also very different, because they took place over a huge period of time and represent different parts of history. The first attacker in 1913 was an Old Believer, an icon painter, studying to be a priest, and he attacked the painting in a state of shock seeing the czar presented like this. He was a religiously motivated iconoclast. The second one a few years ago, in 2018, was a drunk nationalist, as far as I know. Both attacks were very emotionally driven, you could say.

TC: I wonder if you are familiar with Ilya Repin's painting? It is well-known in art history, where Repin is regarded as a central figure in Russian art. His Ukrainian roots are currently being highlighted in the West, however, and the information about his nationality is being changed in a number of museum records as we speak, due to the war. I assume that the painting is generally quite known in Russian culture?

MA: Yes, everyone kind of knows that it exist and many have seen it as a child at obligatory museum visits in school. As any other Moscow child who attended a public school I am familiar with this painting. But I only started to explore the history and context many years after when I began to read and re-read everything as I felt that something was wrong and unfair and there was a lot of injustice everywhere.

Ilya Repin lived in one of the most interesting periods of Russian history, and it's extremely interesting to watch historical changes through artworks. With this painting, *Ivan the Terrible*, it's perhaps not necessary to know Russian history in detail to sense what is going on, but some points are very cool to know. Most important is the personality of Ivan the Terrible (1530-1584) and the fact that his empire was one of the bloodiest empires in Russian history. He created this special organ called *Oprichnina* (a state police corps, ed.), who he more or less gave unlimited power. They were very violent; took territory; killed old people and aristocrats, and took their property. They did a lot of things rather

Opposite page: Stills from *Terrible, Terrible*, 2021 (left screen with the 1913 attack)

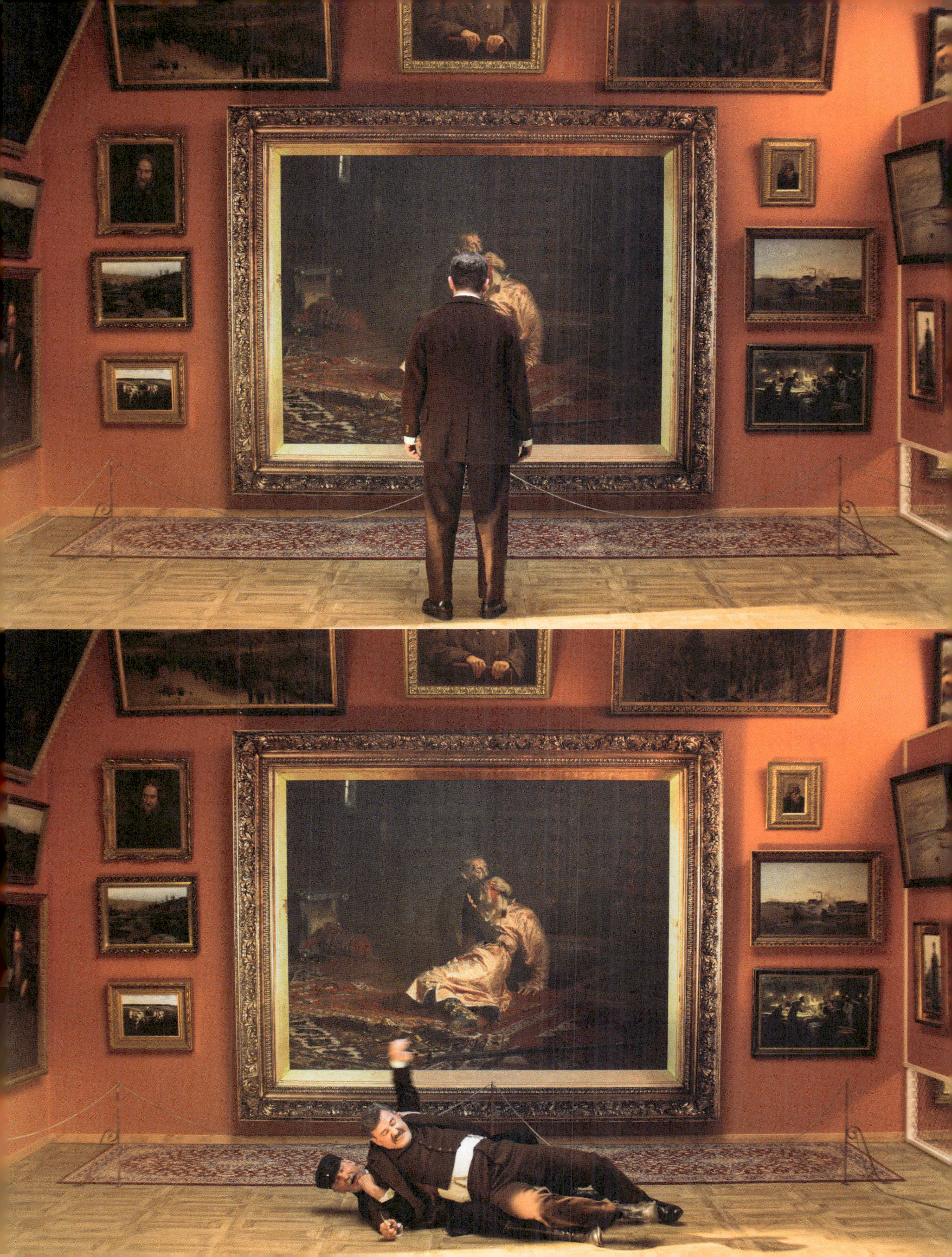

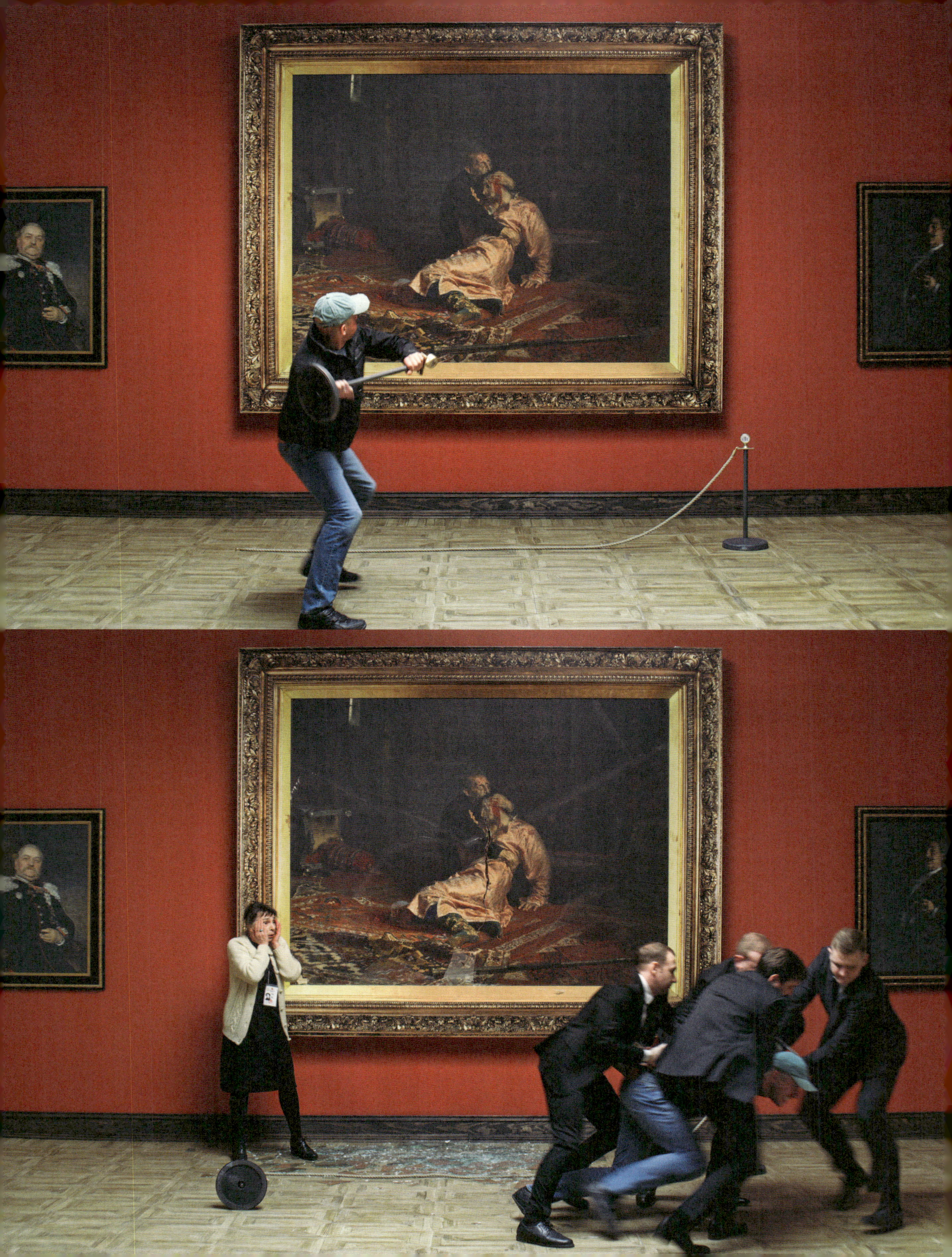

similar to what the Russian Secret Service is doing now ... The main thing about the *oprichniki*, the members of the *Oprichnina*, is basically this special power that Czar Ivan granted them, this special permission to do whatever they wanted, including public executions – which they did a lot. Ivan the Terrible is known to have been very paranoid and his personality is described as almost demonic. He was violent; he had several wives and was at times violent against women; and he had this staff or sceptre that could punch someone, literally to death. It is all captured in the painting by Repin. But it's an important fact that although Ivan was extremely paranoid he did not *want* to kill his son, for all that we know. It was probably an accident due to a fit of anger, and there is no theory in history that says that he actually intended to kill him.

TC: Why do you think it was important for Repin to paint this particular motif?

MA: Repin's own period of history, the end of the 19th century, was 40 years before the revolution where the Bolsheviks took the power. A really interesting time. Russia was very inspired by the French Revolution in 1789, and many people were trying to apply some Western traditions to Russia. Previously we had one liberal monarch, Alexander II (Emperor of Russia, 1855-1881), and he was killed by the anarchist People's Will movement in 1881, two years before Repin started his painting. In some notes Repin even said something like: "The time which I see now is so brutal that I should put this blood realism into my artworks." And he created this painting, which is extremely realistic, making a link between the past and his own time. And well, on a general note, Repin's painting is a quite cool representation of a dictator and how far they can go. In the painting, Ivan looks completely mad. Like an old dictator who has lost every last bit of his conscience.

TC: Ragnar has described how, when he was a child, his parents, who are both Icelandic theatre professionals, returned from a trip to Moscow and told him about the painting which had made an impression on them because it's so theatrical, dramatic and powerful. So powerful that someone had tried to 'kill it' with a knife, as his mother had described it. And well, since then it was attacked once more. He never saw the actual painting himself, but it makes great sense that he is fascinated by the two attacks which of course can be seen as repetitions of the painting's violent motif. A violent painting is violently attacked. In line with Ragnar's continuous explorations of masculinity this piece is also a crazy accumulation of masculine violence and destruction. Toxic.

MA: The personality of Ivan the Terrible was indeed very toxic! And it's quite obvious why this particular painting could become a magnet for violence. Do you know one of the most important current Russian authors, Vladimir Sorokin (born 1955)? His novel *Day of Oprichnik* is from 2006 but is set in Moscow in 2027. The protagonist is an employee of an *oprichnik* security organ inspired by Ivan the Terrible's. The book is an amazing dystopia! It's crazy how the story written by Sorokin 20 years ago now becomes real. And it's really important to know and remember who this czar was because he was one of the most brutal and top-level paranoid persons in Russian history.

TC: The violent activism represented in *Terrible, Terrible* is of a very different nature than your own with the Pussy Riot collective ...

MA: Yeah. We didn't attack paintings. We attacked *the sense* of paintings like this one by Repin! We work a lot with satire and like the idea of "Foolishness for Christ". The so-called *holy fools* date back to the medieval Russian empire where groups of people called themselves holy fools and considered themselves "innocent" before the eyes of God. They were making satirical jokes and actions about things which were officially forbidden to laugh about, but there was a silent agreement and they did not get punished. Pussy Riot was and is still, if not directly, playing with this idea and certainly points to a long historic tradition for satire as something quite important for our culture. At least that is how it began with Pussy Riot, and our *Punk Prayer* performance in the Christ the Saviour Cathedral in Moscow happened in a context of a very special vibe that was in the air in Russia in 2012. A spirit of hope, which a lot of people felt, and this spirit really inspired many different kinds of people to just open their personality and protest how they felt they needed to protest.

Today the times have changed completely. In the last ten years Russia went through a lot of actions of modern fascism. People are protesting without weapons, without any knives. They just have their bodies and hands. Members of Pussy Riot, including myself, suffered prison sentences for about three and a half years in total some years back. But now there are prison terms for nonviolent protesting for 20 years and more ... In Ukraine, in comparison,

Opposite page: Stills from *Terrible, Terrible*, 2021 (right screen with the 2018 attack)

they never had political prisoners. Ukraine never had dictators. Ukraine just never had the experience of what we had or what Belarus had and still has. It really changes people's minds, which is the most dangerous thing. Because you easily become familiar with obeying and following even the most crazy and violent rules – which, basically, are not even rules. It is as if George Orwell's (1903-1950), books became real – but in Eastern Europe, which is very strange!

TC: Would you also regard Ilya Repin's painting as a kind of allegory for what is going on now?

MA: I think there are a lot of similarities in the personalities of dictators all over the world. When they become old, they become extremely paranoid. They are surrounded by advisors who are very often the main thieves and the main executioners. Vladimir Putin (born 1952) is not an exception, of course. But Putin didn't create anything. In many ways he's just a grey nobody. Ivan the Terrible wasn't a grey nobody. He had a very strong, violent personality. Putin hasn't. But he wants to. And he has these role models like Joseph Stalin (1879-1953). He wants to follow the lead of these tyrants, which he promotes, and he spends Russian tax money to promote previous monarchs and dictators to make them more popular within the country. Because if they are popular, it's obviously more cool to say "I want to be like him".

TC: Is he doing the same with Ivan the Terrible?

MA: Well, that's too long ago in history. But Putin wants to be known as a collector of Russian territories – the territories that *he* considers to be Russia's. He has created a very crazy mix of "Soviet Union blessed by God" because he uses the church for the promotion of everything. Like Patriarch Kirill (born 1946) who promotes the Ukrainian war by saying "you should go to war and die because then you will go to heaven". We have a lot of priests who are making bizarre speeches, saying things like "it's better to die in the war than just die drunk in your flat". In their opinion, Russians don't have any third road, apparently! Amazing ... Very patriotic.

TC: *Terrible, Terrible* – is the title that Ragnar chose for his piece, in a repeated echo of the byname "Ivan the Terrible" which is common outside of Russia for Ivan IV, in English as well as in many other languages. I know that in Russian the term "terrible" is actually not used to refer to the monarch?

MA: Correct, we use different words. In Russian, it's not "terrible", it's grozny ("fearsome", "menacing" or "redoubtable", ed.). Think of the sound just before thunder or a heavy rainstorm: whodooo ... The word *grozny* is very connected with this sound which makes you aware. The meaning of *grozny* is basically like this sound. Whereas "terrible" implies that he was "extremely bad", his "bad" in Russian is just like "everyone should be aware and afraid". It's more like an enormous force of energy, and he was basically proud of being called *grozny*.

TC: What is his general image like in Russian history and culture today?

MA: I think in general Ivan the Terrible is regarded as the most brutal leader. There is a Grozny "fan club" consisting of Putin's closest supporters, like Konstantin Malofeev (born 1974) – an orthodox oligarch and main sponsor of the annexation of Crimea and the subsequent military invasion of Ukraine in 2014 – and Tikhon Shevkunov (born 1958) – Putin's priest, grey cardinal of orthodox Chekism – and many other figures. They build monuments and hold exhibitions promoting his cult – the cult of "the first anointed by God".

There is this widespread idea in Russia, that if a monarch is brutal he has his special reasons for it. There is a saying stating that a czar is innocent, and that all bad is due to his inner circle. It's a standing joke for many, of course, but at the same time many people really follow this idea. And even with Putin, you often hear things like, "he didn't know, they didn't tell him. It's the people around him, who are guilty. But he just did not know. We should tell him. We should tell him the truth. He will find the solution." *Very* Russian.

MARIA ALYOKHINA is a Russian member of the feminist punk collective Pussy Riot. She was sentenced to two years of imprisonment in August 2012 for her so-called "hooliganism motivated by religious hatred" following a Pussy Riot performance in Moscow's Cathedral of Christ the Saviour. In November 2022, the exhibition *Velvet Terrorism – Pussy Riot's Russia* opened at Kling & Bang in Reykjavik. The exhibition was created by Alyokhina and was curated by Dorothee Kirch, Ingibjörg Sigurjónsdóttir and Ragnar Kjartansson.

TINE COLSTRUP is curator at Louisiana Museum of Modern Art and curated *Epic Waste of Love and Understanding*.

This conversation took place via Zoom in March 2023.

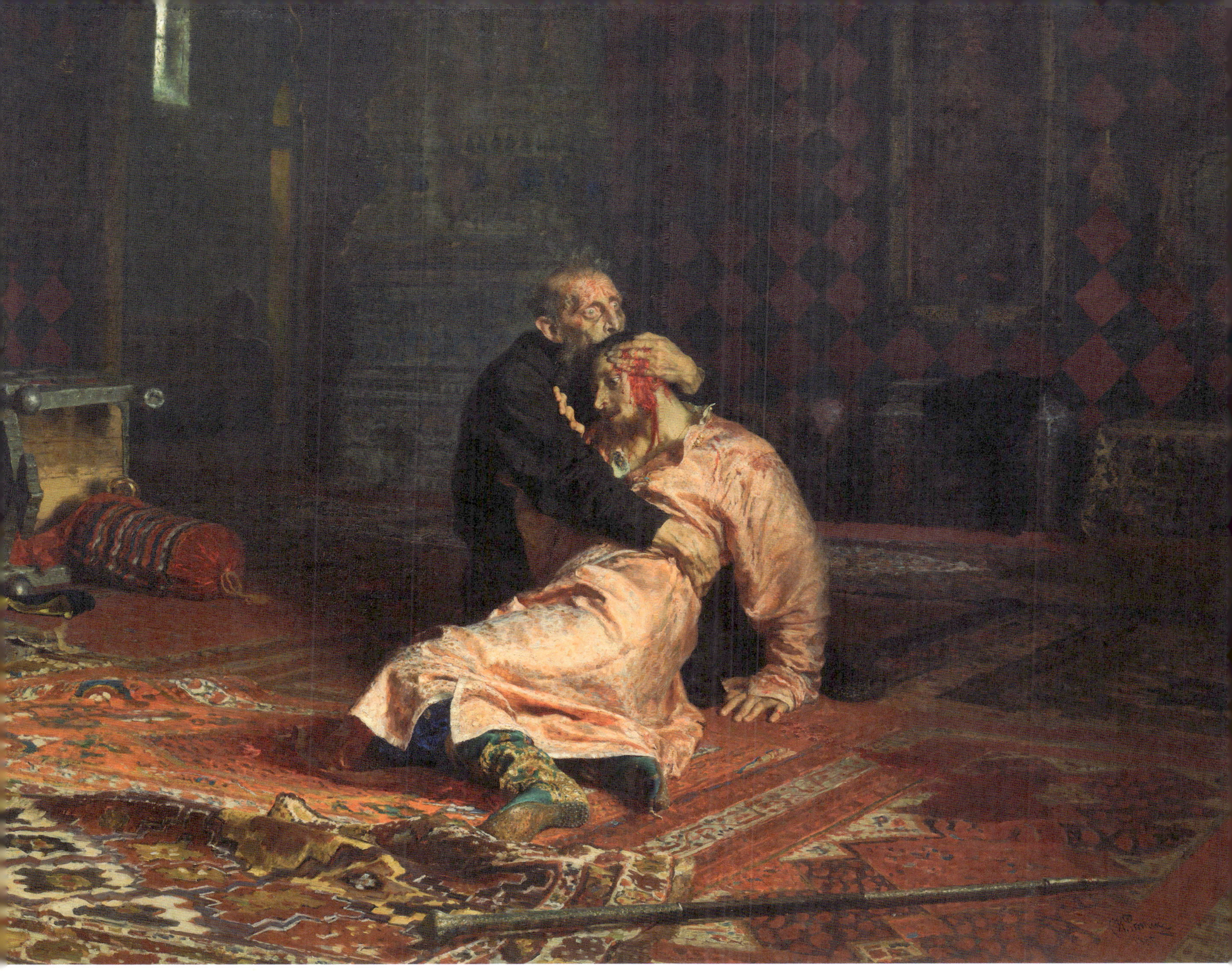

81

Ilya Repin: *Ivan the Terrible and His Son Ivan 16 November 1581*, 1883-1885. Tretyakov Gallery, Moscow

RAGNAR KJARTANSSON & THE NATIONAL

A LOT OF SORROW — 2013-2014

Single-channel video
Duration: 6:09 hr.
The performance took place at MoMA PS1, New York, as part of Sunday Sessions
The Art Institute of Chicago, purchased with funds provided by Stephanie Skestos Gabriele

Marina Abramović in conversation with Tine Colstrup

Tine Colstrup: The power of repetition ... For Kjartansson's work *A Lot of Sorrow* from 2013-2014 he asked the band The National to perform their 2010 song "Sorrow" over and over again for six hours straight at the MoMA PS1 venue in New York. Can you elaborate on the potential of sticking with one situation and just staying there for hours, sometimes days or months? It's a specialty of yours.

Marina Abramović: Well, this is really one of the oldest techniques from ancient civilisations' rituals of repetition. The repetition generates energy and that's essential to actually come to different states of mind. I often use this picture of opening and closing a door: you open the door, but you don't enter, you close the door, but you don't exit. You do this as long as possible, over and over again, for hours. It's a simple exercise, not just for a performance person but for anybody, as a method to explore how the door stops being a door and becomes space – between life and death, light and darkness, our universe. This simple repetition can completely open to something else. And that's one of the keys, that I've discovered in working with repetitions and performance. And not just me, but many other people.

Then there is the incredible power of long durational performances. In the long durational you can't pretend, you can't play, you have to show how vulnerable you are. We witness it in this piece, too. The facades wear off because they simply can't be kept up for very long. When you show this to the public they become supporting material – it becomes this new community, a bond between human beings that strengthens the action and the work and becomes a part of the situation. It's very powerful stuff. Repetition and long duration.

TC: Knowing that Ragnar cites you as an inspiration and knowing that you appreciate his work, I have been joyously thinking about this mutual respect despite the often radical difference in your approaches. Your own long durational performances are often clean, pure and spiritual, whereas *A Lot of Sorrow* is dirtier. Rock 'n' roll. The same goes for Kjartansson's 2009 piece *The End – Venezia*, where he painted a daily portrait of his friend whose costume was nothing but a pair of Speedos – 144 portraits in total. They were trashing themselves for six months, drinking beers, smoking cigarettes, playing a bit on the guitar, reading *Weltschmertz* literature, painting drunken paintings ... A proper long durational, but in the messy way!

MA: Ha ha, yes. If you look into rituals, there is a very famous sect in India called Aghori. It's based on doing everything completely opposite in comparison with most spiritual rituals. They are eating shit, performing rituals with corpses, using human sculls and bones for jewellery, drinking as much as they

Opposite page: From the recordings of *A Lot of Sorrow*, 2013-2014

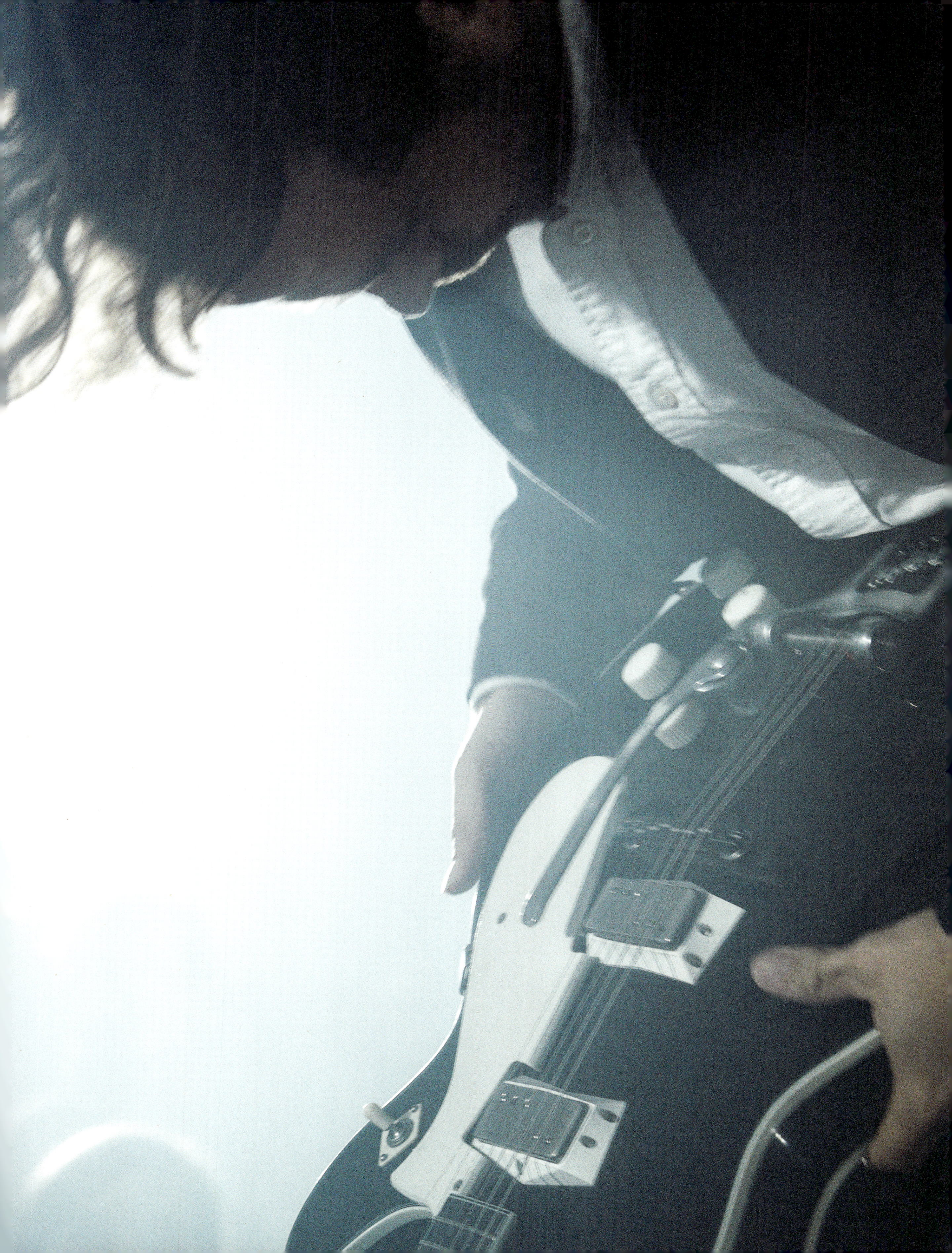

can. No kidding. Everything in this sect is based on excess. The excess of everything! But actually, the goal and the results are the same. You go on the other side – catharsis – with very different means, but with the same result. It's kind of mind-blowing. Part of the Aghori sect is that there is no judgment of bad and good. Of course there is no direct comparison, but when you mention the clean versus the messy this came to mind.

TC: It's interesting that both strategies can lead to the same thing. And well, the Apollonian and the Dionysian are poles in your own work as well. There is a lot of joy in Kjartansson's work, but *A Lot of Sorrow* is quite depressing. There is a melancholy note in so much of his work – do you recognise that?

MA: Yes, I'm very familiar with this because I come from the Slavic melancholy. Slavic people suffer all of their lives, they're never happy anywhere. There is this old, permanent melancholy. I mean, the movies and music in my culture are all based on the tradition of Russian literature ... And you have all of that Nordic melancholy! This melancholy is an incredibly important source for an artist. Nobody ever makes anything really good from happiness. The melancholy and the immersed suffering is such a key to be creative. You make the best works in this state of solitude, loneliness and melancholy after a love relationship breaks, right?

TC: In the 2004 piece *Mercy* Kjartansson is performing as this crooner cliche, alone with his guitar in front of the camera, repeating one line over and over again for an hour: "Oh, why do I keep on hurting you?" It's incredibly sad.

MA: This is so beautiful to me. This is why I love his works – exactly for that. His work is deeply emotional. And these emotions are travelling back and forth as part of the works. He finds the keys to emotions! This creates a bridge to the public. He shows his vulnerability, the public can show their own. And then that connection turns into celebration. Because what will you do with this vulnerability? You have to heal it. In a way, it's a kind of scream – a scream from pain, not from joy, although there is a lot of fun and happiness in his works, too. His works touch my heart – because of emotions, depression, melancholy, the whole package. I like Ragnar's freedom and incredible openness. He takes life in its fullness and deals with things as they are, good and bad.

TC: You and your generation formulated some very clear distinctions between "performance" and "theatre". Kjartansson has often talked about the difference between the two, and he does not buy it! He grew up in the theatre, as you know, with a mother who was an actress and a father who was a director, and much of his work is about the ambiguity between real and fake emotions and identities – with a profound disbelief that there is a clear border between performing and acting ...

MA: It's really interesting, the theatre was the complete enemy in the performance art circles in the 1970s. It generated a kind of distrust and hate amongst my generation. In theatre everything's fake, it's repetitive, you have to place somebody else on stage who isn't you, the audience is in the dark without direct contact to the performers and so on. But you know, while many in my generation probably stayed with the same opinion, I've changed completely. I have lots of repetition in my work and I started doing opera and theatre many years ago. After *The Great Wall Walk* in 1989, the last performance I made with Ulay (1943-2020), I made six theatre pieces called *Biography*, the last one of them was called *The Life and Death of Marina Abramović* by Robert Wilson (born 1941), who I in 2011 asked to direct my own life. So, I don't think theatre is fake at all.

I think it depends on how you take reality and what reality is. I'm thinking of an old Buddhist parable, where this king asks the biggest master of painting to paint a dragon. The king locks him up inside his castle until he's finished. Every month the king would come and check up on the painter, but the dragon keeps coming to nothing. And then finally one day the painter paints the dragon, and the king asks surprised, "How is it possible, that you've finally painted the dragon?" "It's simple", he answers, "I became the dragon." This idea of *becoming* is really the major thing in theatre – when you really get into the role you actually become what you're playing, and then there is no distinction anymore between what is fake and what is not. It's just not fake. I'm with Ragnar!

TC: You are quite familiar with Kjartansson's work – when did you meet it first?

MA: My first encounter with him was in Iceland. There I saw the spitting video with his mother for the first time (*Me and My Mother*, 2000-2020). To me it had nothing to do with theatre, to me

The following spread: From the recordings of *A Lot of Sorrow*, 2013-2014 this was absolutely pure performance – but then again, never mind the distinction. Then I saw him in 2009 in Venice at the Biennale where, as you just mentioned, he installed himself for six months in a studio, painting his friend's portrait every day. This piece was like walking into a small community, and Ragnar has this ability to create new art communities where everybody has a role and is doing it together. Much of his work comes out of this community building which is neither performance or theatre. I don't have a name for it and really do not want to label it either. His work is really a *Gesamtkunstwerk* – it is everything at once: painting, video, live performance and the kind of real situations that he embodies. That's what I like about it. And besides the melancholy there is this incredible humour and enjoyment that you don't see so much in art. You could just look at him sitting in that bath tub playing the guitar – surrounded by the community he created in *The Visitors* (2012) – over and over again!

TC: Speaking of humour and melancholy. We've just decided the title for the upcoming exhibition: *Epic Waste of Love and Understanding*. It's a sentence, that Ragnar's wife uttered during an argument at home in their kitchen ...

MA: "Epic waste of love" – beautiful!

TC: And full of a lot of sorrow! At the same time, however, the title is carved into a faux marble monument built of plywood, looking like a temporary and slightly too large theatre set. I read the title as a poetic headline summing up our long durational, repeated waste of love and understanding ... from our melting poles to the war in Ukraine ... War is a theme that pops up in the exhibition in several works, often indirectly. In your own work, war and violent powers are steady themes throughout – how do you actually see the role of art in times of war?

MA: I think it is so important not to react right away. In 2021 I created a 40-metre-long wall piece in Kyiv, Ukraine, called *Crystal Wall of Crying*. It's a monument for the Babyn Yar Holocaust Memorial Center, marking the 80th anniversary since the massacre in Babyn Yar in 1941, where more than 30,000 people – Jews – were killed. The Ukrainian president, Volodymyr Zelensky (born 1978), said in a speech, that these kinds of atrocities should never happen again. Just two months later, Russia bombed Kyiv. After the war broke out and bombs hit this very area, the wall became like a sacred spot to some people. People came there to pray, putting their heads and hearts against the wall. It makes me really emotional ... The piece went from being art to being a part of life.

I think that whatever you do right away will be like political art for a specific context. It easily becomes outdated and old. You have to figure out something that is of interest outside of the specific moment, something that can last and be relevant across time. To me the main example has always been Henri Matisse (1869-1954). During World War II, Matisse only painted flowers. That's it. You need the human spirit to create something totally different. I'm for the beauty. There's already so much horrible stuff happening, so many terrible images. Do you want to create more of this? I don't think so.

MARINA ABRAMOVIĆ is a Serbian-born performance artist living in the US.

TINE COLSTRUP is curator at Louisiana Museum of Modern Art and curated *Epic Waste of Love and Understanding*.

This conversation took place via Zoom in March 2023.

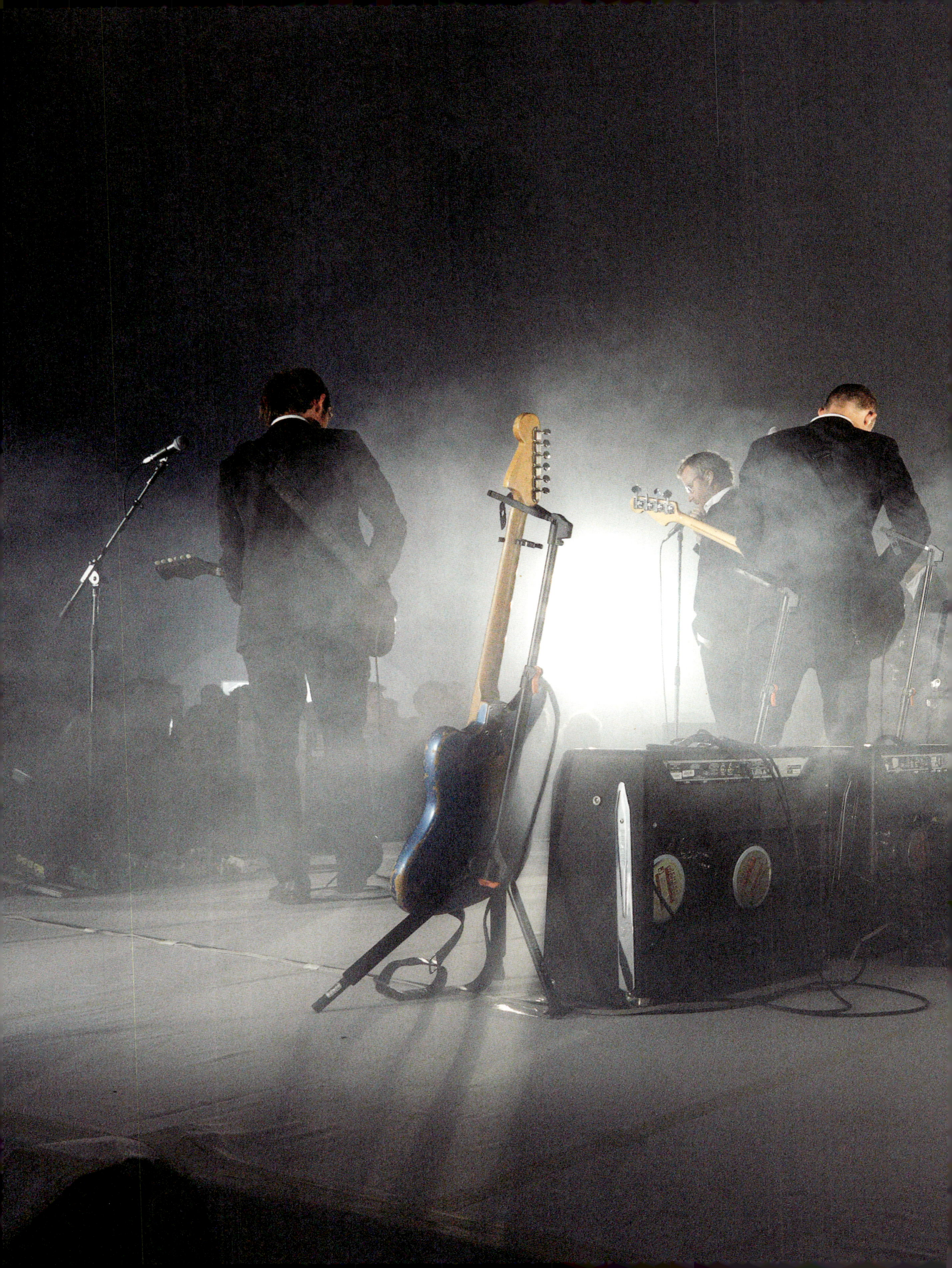

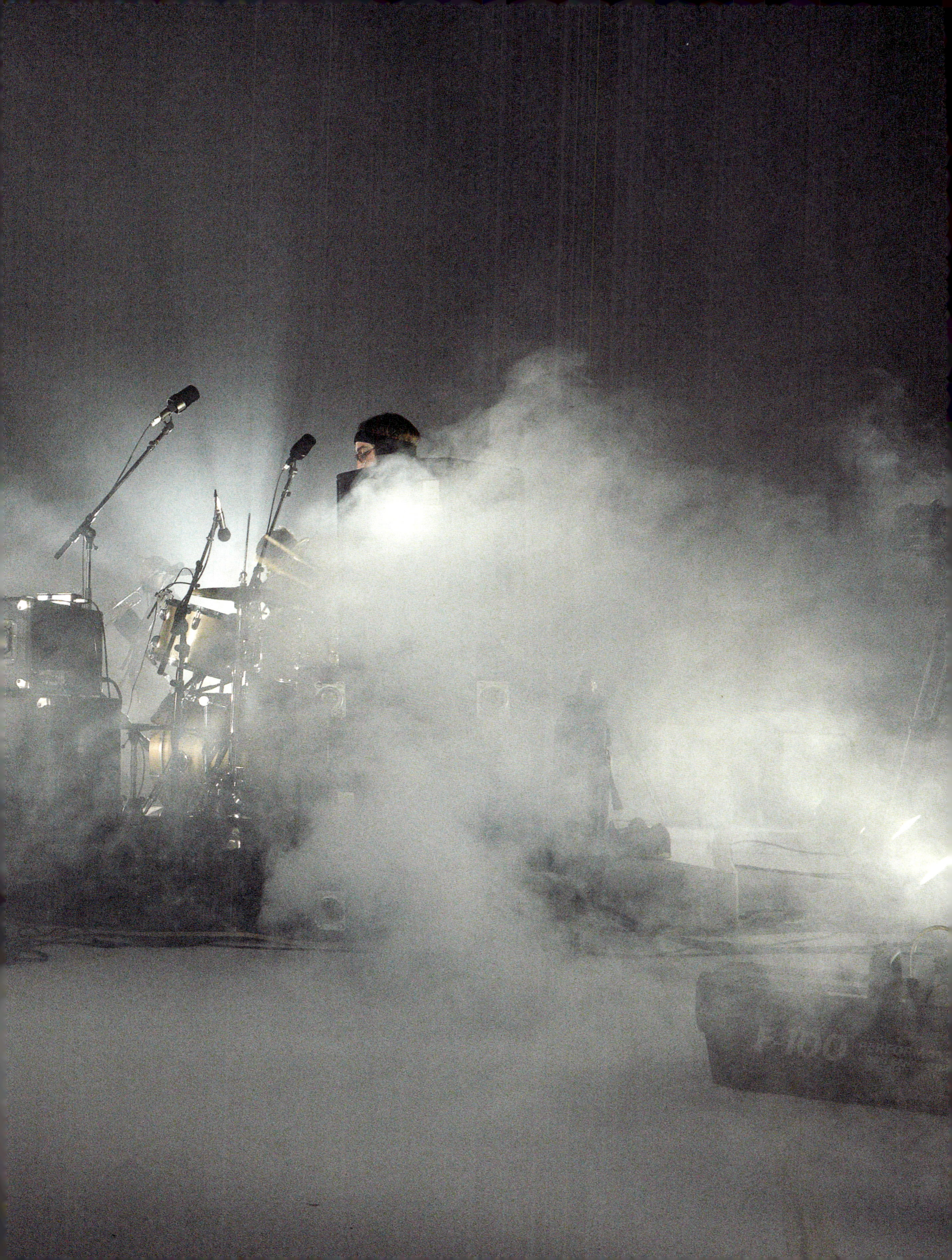

Sorrow found me when I was young
Sorrow waited, sorrow won
Sorrow they put me on the pill
It's in my honey, it's in my milk

Don't leave my hyper heart alone on the water
Cover me in rag and bone and sympathy
Cause I don't wanna get over you
I don't wanna get over you

Sorrow's my body on the waves
Sorrow's the girl inside my cake
I live in a city sorrow built
It's in my honey, it's in my milk

Don't leave my hyper heart alone on the water
Cover me in rag and bone and sympathy
Cause I don't wanna get over you
I don't wanna get over you

(oohs)

Don't leave my hyper heart alone on the water
Cover me in rag and bone and sympathy
Cause I don't wanna get over you
I don't wanna get over you

(oohs)

Sorrow. Composed by Aaron B. Dessner, lyrics by Matthew D. Berninger, 2010

Opposite page: From the recordings of *A Lot of Sorrow*, 2013-2014, with The National's set list for the six-hour performance at MoMA PS1, New York, 2013
The following spread: Installation view, Louisiana Museum of Modern Art, 2023

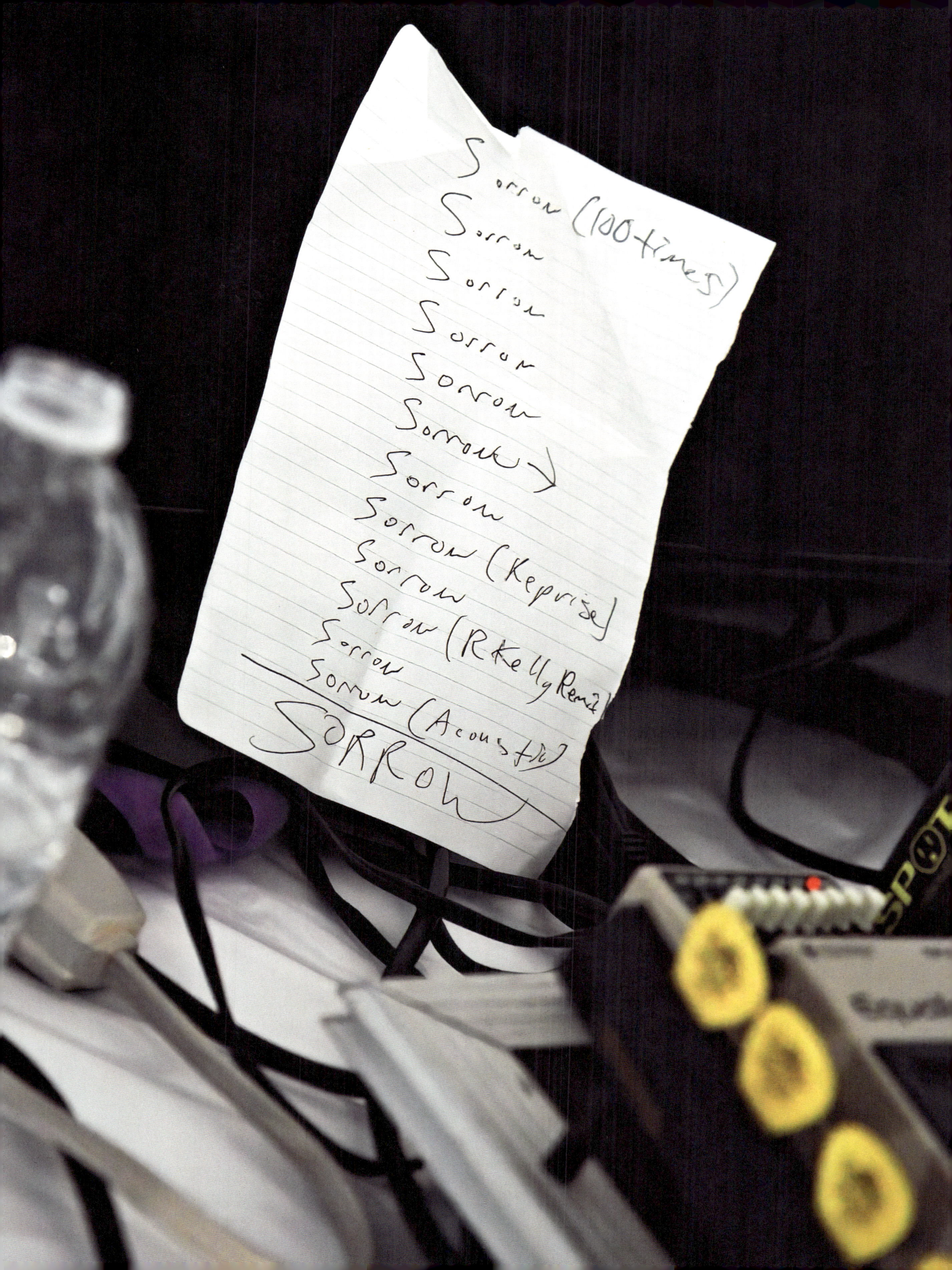

Sorrow (100 times)
Sorrow
Sorrow
Sorrow
Sorrow
Sorrow →
Sorrow
Sorrow (Reprise)
Sorrow
Sorrow (R Kelly Remi
Sorrow
Sorrow (Acoustic)
SORROW

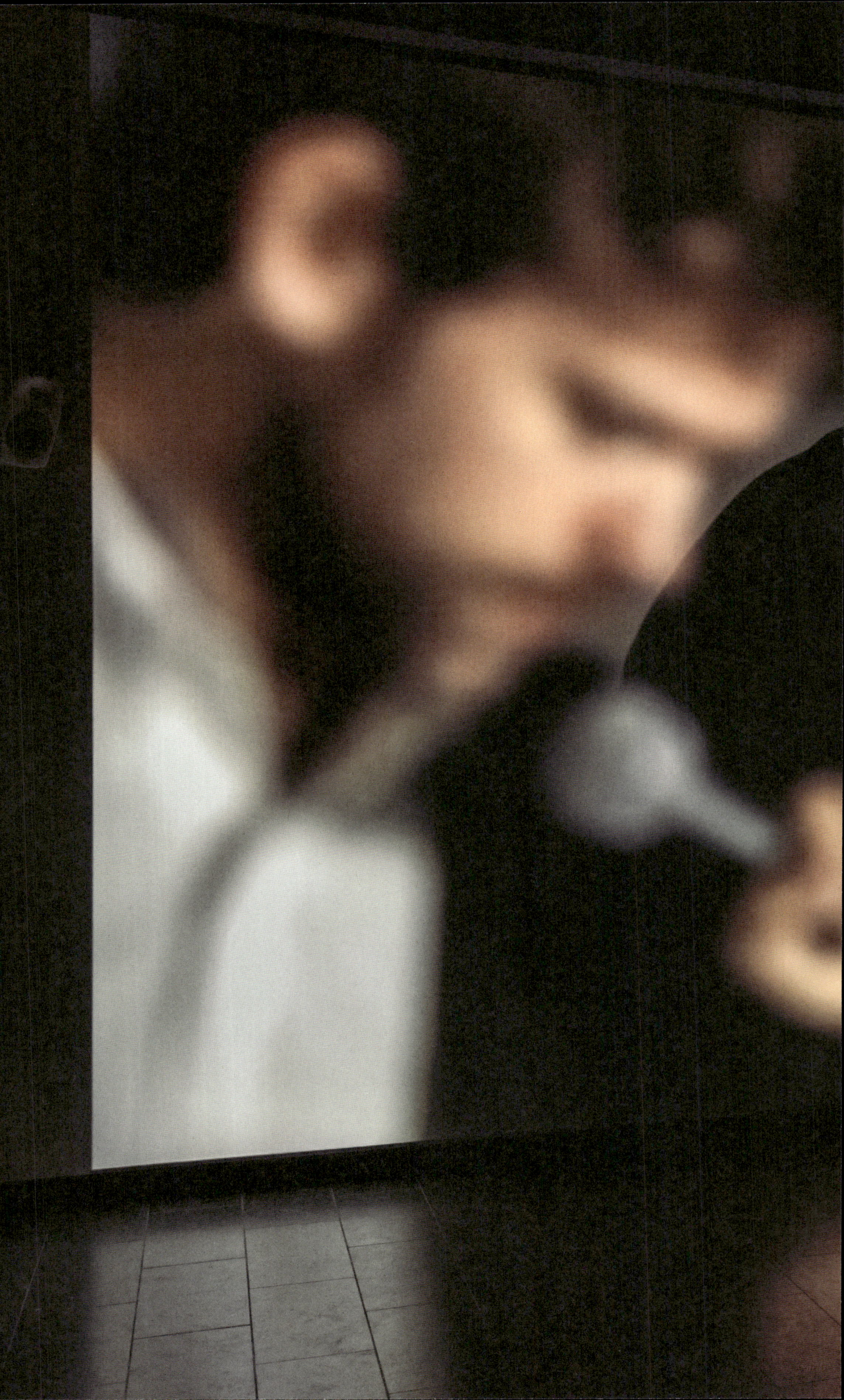

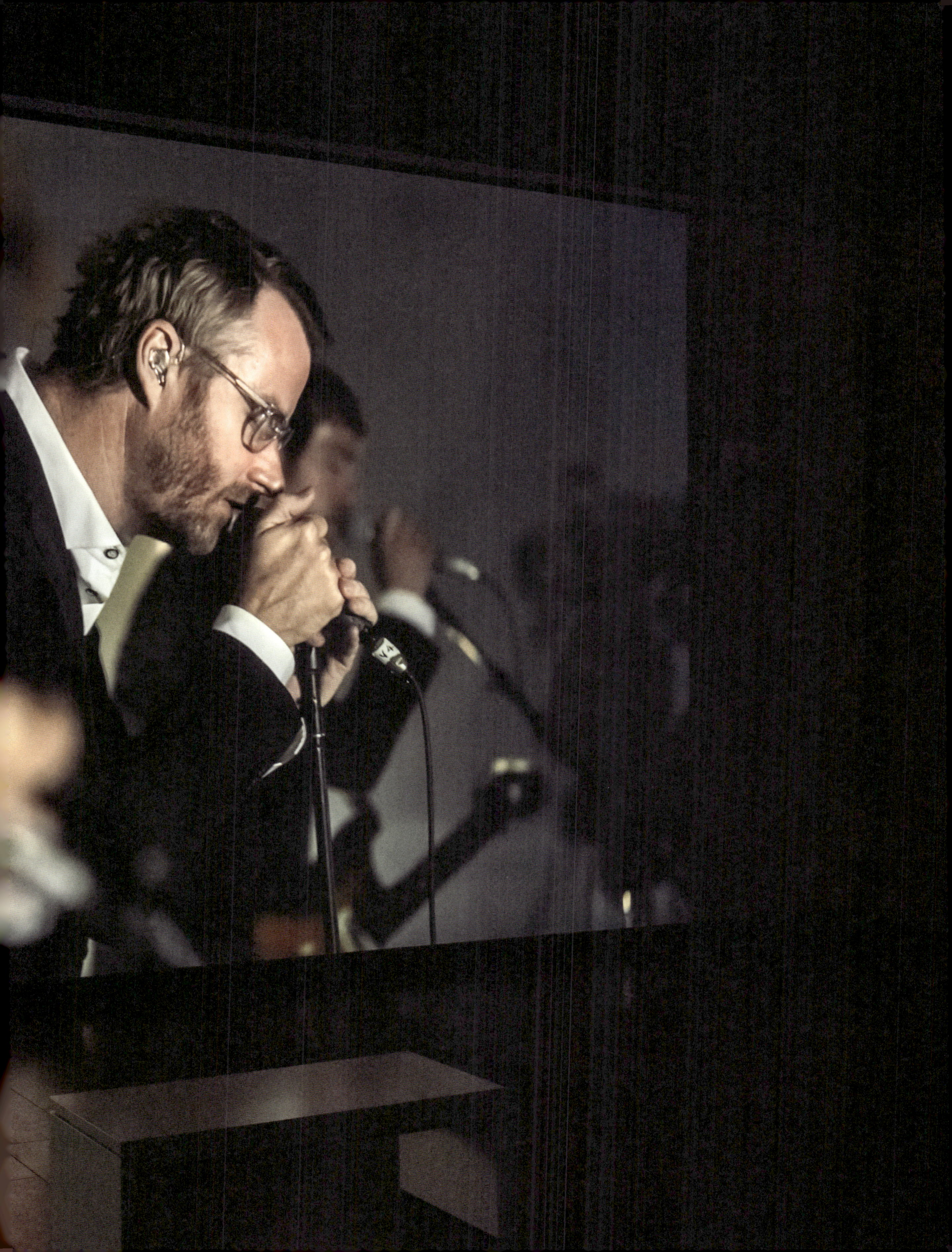

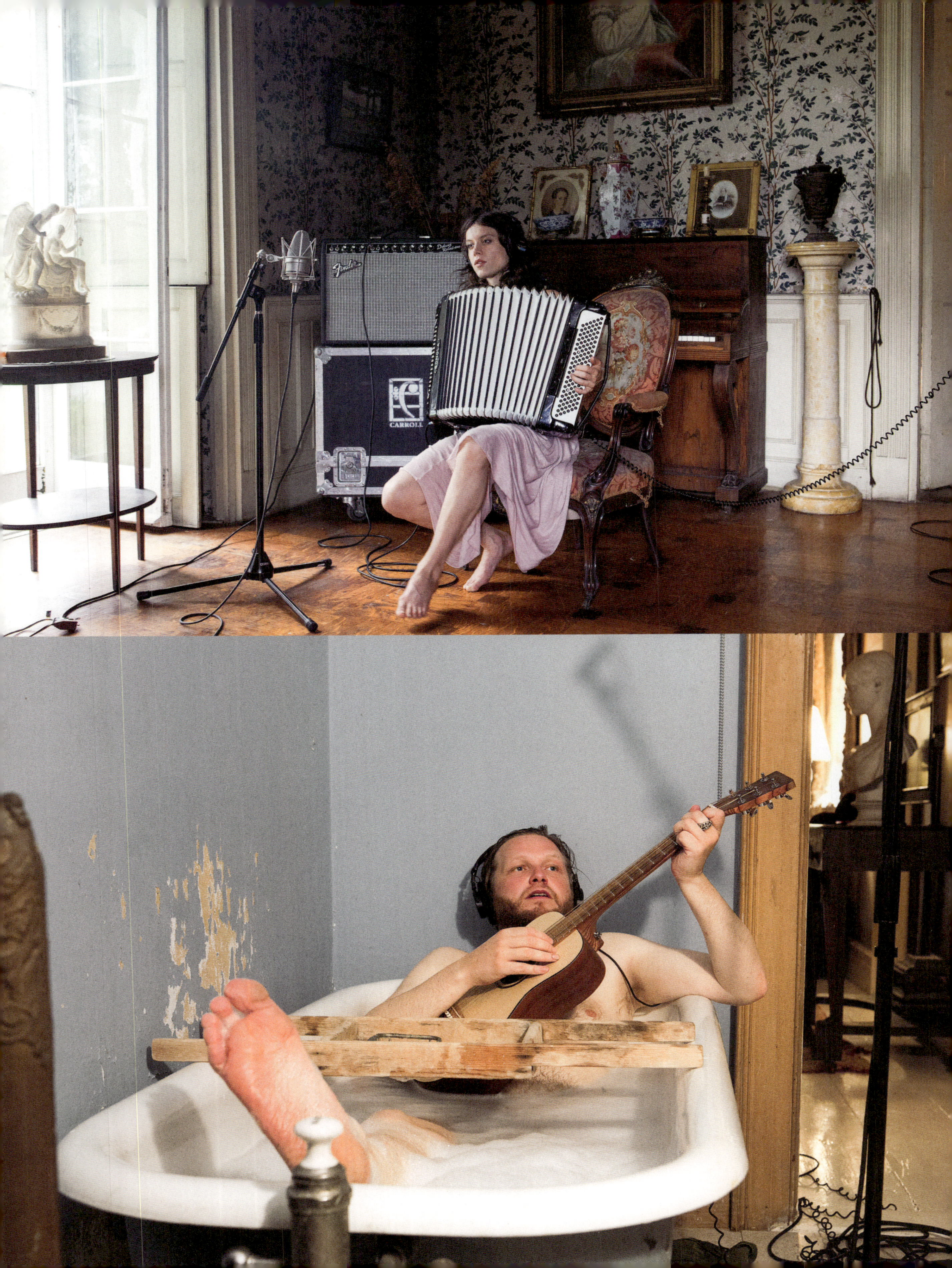
Fender
CARROLL

THE VISITORS — 2012

Nine-channel video installation
Duration: 64:00 min.
Commissioned Migros Museum für Gegenwartskunst, Zürich
Sammlung Migros Museum für Gegenwartskunst, Zürich

LINER NOTES

By Anne Carson

What are these people doing here? I wake up one morning and the house is full of visitors. The landlord has a tendency to invite. Where is he? Oh, off in the fields somewhere. Back for lunch no doubt, he likes his lunch. I listen at my door. Don't want to bump into visitors on the way to the bathroom. How many bathrooms are there? Five or six but only one I like. It is somewhat hidden, maybe visitors won't find it. All the bathrooms are somewhat hidden, maybe visitors won't find any of them and will go home. Meanwhile I look up "visitor" in *Roget's Thesaurus*, a handy reference tool I keep in my room.

Visitor (noun). caller, guest,
habitué (French), passenger,
transient, visitant,
newcomer, late comer,
Johnny-come-lately.
(see ARRIVAL)

See ARRIVAL? What about DEPARTURE? I feel a gust of disappointment, nonetheless reading *Roget's* has its usual calming effect. I am a mean and solitary person in general, somewhat autistic, kind of a pinchfist. But words give me hope and expansion – how they dangle their little roots in the past while blooming forward as if reaching out to us. And *Roget's* tidy pages, the beautifully ordered lists, all these analogical children of his lifelong reverie, do surely welcome words into our reasoning – blossom after blossom, nuance after nuance, implication after implication, slight difference after slight difference – it is the opposite of anarchy! No maybe not.

"I do not care for modern poetry. I do not care for music or astrology. I do not care for ceremonial." These, if we are to believe his patient, Hilda Doolittle, were the words of Freud one day in London when they were discussing psychic matters (the ray of healing), which he also did not care for. "We trapped each other", she says, "but his wings held." They let the telephone ring on and on. Why am I telling you this? Is it the opposite of anarchy? Probably not. I like to put a touch of Freud in everything, just to see what happens. Not much happened here but his wings held keeps bothering my mind. What did she mean by that?
(H.D. *Tribute to Freud*, 53)

Speaking of *Roget's*, I suppose you know why Roget himself made lists. Chronic mental instability in several members of his family including himself led him to seek what Freud might call a *coping mechanism:* compulsive activities like list-making can have a sedative effect on anxious natures. Roget made lists of lots of things, not just words, but posterity has not found much use for his tallies of plant life in the garden or the movements of the iris of his own eye. His *Thesaurus*, first printed 1852, enjoyed 28 reprintings in his lifetime. He lived to be 90

Opposite page: From the recordings of *The Visitors*, 2012

and dabbled in a variety of scientific researches, e.g. "Explanation of an optical deception in the appearance of the spokes of a wheel when seen through vertical apertures," a paper he presented to the Royal Society of London in 1824, thus more or less inventing the movies.

My fox veers homelessly between the familiar and the strange.

"Are you religious? Is this some kind of ritual?" I ask the Laughing Tyrant when I corner him in the kitchen later – I'd heard someone rummaging around down there, no doubt going for the jam, I had to intervene. Who cares how much gin they drink but I do like to keep the jam for the fox. "No," he says in his klippetty-klop little accent, "it is a 64-minute video to be shot simultaneously in 7 rooms of the house plus the front porch. We rehearse today and shoot tomorrow. Single take." I ask him what it's about and he says, "Sex, divorce, fighting, longing, realness, pretending." And when I say, "Oh, not jam?" we both laugh. His is a guilty laugh.

I don't understand, or trust much of Freudian psychic theory – still, what a sparky guy! "To gain control over fire man has to renounce the homosexually-tinged desire to put it out with a stream of piss," he confides in a footnote to *Civilization and Its Discontents*. Urination, elimination, excretion, miction, micturition, piddling.

Roget had no fox, no fox pocket. Even as a child he couldn't relax. He was compulsively neat and orderly. His first word list, compiled at age 8, would continue to be perfected till his death in 1869. He organised the first edition (1852) in 1,002 concepts. He looked at it, he paused. Then by reclassifying "absence of intellect" as a subcategory of "intellect" and "indiscrimination" as a subcategory of "choice", he pared it down to a clean 1,000.

I could have been a major artist but my drawing paper, kept under the mattress, gets wrinkled and folded wrong. Drawing nice lines is hard. I force my way over the bumps and knots, I loosen it out and sometimes join the human community. That is what a good drawing does – joining, release from the dead season of oneself. Yesterday I drew a man holding a fox. It wasn't any good but I will try again. When not drawing I am incongruous. Inappropriate, inapt, improper, incompatible, irreconcilable, inconsistent, unusual, warring, strange, alien.

Often I mean to be polite but just can't. There are, as I said, five or six bathrooms in the house but only one with an adequate and necessary bathtub. Imagine my surprise – I stumble in, the door not locked, there lies the Laughing Tyrant *in flagrante*, big naked guitar laid across his manly parts, big naked head flung back against the wall, big mouth agape with song, big naked white foot propped on the taps and projecting towards me exactly like the dead Saviour's foot in Mantegna's *Lamentation of Christ*, except we know from art history class that Mantegna had to scale down the size of Christ's foot to prevent it blocking our view of Christ's violently foreshortened legs, torso and face. No scale-down with this visitor – splayed out there in his headphones he laughs, he twangs, he flashes his blue eye-guns at me and cries, "One take! I love the tension!"

Hilda Doolittle's analytic experience began in Vienna in 1933. There were swastikas chalked onto the pavement all along the street to Freud's house. "No one brushed the swastikas out. It is not so easy to scrub death-head chalk marks from the pavement." Also there were rifles. "They were stacked neatly. They stood in bivouac formations at the street corners. It must have been the weekend ... The stacked rifles gave the streets a neat, finished effect, as of an 1860 print."
(H.D. *Tribute to Freud*, 59)

Well, these guys are no Eric Rohmer. Making some kind of movie (they claim) but they're all in different rooms playing instruments and singing, louder and louder and all at the same time until by late afternoon they're wailing like dinosaurs. Rohmer wore earplugs while shooting the nightclub scenes of *Full Moon In Paris*, a fine early film of his that (most people don't notice) has a fox in the corner of one scene. "Eric Rohmer" of course is a pseudonym – his real name being Maurice [something] – his mother never knew he made movies, she thought he was a high school teacher all his life. Why am I telling you this? Watch for the fox.

To enter the door of the drawing is uncanny.

Gazing out the basement window of his house on Bernard Street, London, one morning of 1820, Roget watched a man with a horse and cart passing by and noticed something important: that the spokes of the cart, seen through the vertical blinds of the window, appeared to be curved. He dashed up to the street and paid the man to drive back and forth several times while he took notes and made mathematical calculations. The retina of the human eye, he had discovered, typically sees a fast series of still images as a continuous movie.

Even though this is not my movie, not my unconscious, I feel a need to keep things tidy, orderly, sleek, prim, spruce, smart, trim, unscrambled.

Retreating from Christ's unforeshortened foot, I hide on the stairs. What a maelstrom in me. Am I imagining this or did the Laughing Tyrant really have headphones and a plugged-in guitar as he lay in the bath? Is this wise? Are we insured against electrocution? And what was he singing? Something like, "Fuck me again I fall into my jam and gin days" – what could that mean? Some kind of lunatic diet plan that keeps him healthy underwater? An era of his private religion? Code for world anarchy? Coping mechanism? Little did I know he was to dominate my bathtub for two further days. The fox opens and closes in my pocket. Tomorrow we will look for a door for him to enter my drawing.

Did I mention my admiration for Eric Rohmer? In adolescence I used to watch his movies with pencil and paper in hand, alert for quotes to use with older women. "Oh how he shattered the spirit world, as Pascal said of Archimedes," is a good one. Also I loved the way Jean-Louis Trintignant pronounced "boy scoot" and his awful haircut. Why am I telling you this? Because Eric Rohmer knew how to make a movie. Keep everybody in the same room, is a good first rule. Need I mention the opposite of anarchy.

And who is this woman in white satin undergarments wandering the house? Do they know her? They demur. Her whiteness makes me dream. She is always going out of rooms just as I come in, it's like living in the New Wave. I am a bachelor, I am mysterious.

A final detail for your mental image of Freud, him beating with his fist on Hilda Doolittle's analytic sofa saying, "I am an old man, you do not think it worth your while to love me!" Chaos, pandemonium, tumult, turmoil, turbulence, lawlessness, disorder, mob rule, anarchism. (H.D. *Tribute to Freud*, p. 62, 141)

Sneaking about the halls, eavesdropping, I learn a few things. They are from Iceland, these visitors, which explains a lot. Have you been to Iceland? I went once, I couldn't stay. There is nothing there but emptiness. A gigantic empty wind wails along the edge of every minute and tosses the odd dazed seabird out onto the empty beach. When you drive the single lonely highway a huge piece of emptiness drives along beside you and goes wherever you go, then piles up in your driveway at home on top of the emptinesses from other days. You see horses standing in the fields so soaked with emptiness they can't move, they've been there for years, they might as well be waterfalls. Of course all this exerts a psychic pressure on inhabitants – the whole soul frays. I made lists while I was there. Lists of national delusions e.g. the widespread belief that everyone in Iceland is named Ragnar (I attended parties where every single guest introduced himself to me by this name). I took photographs too but later at home found the emptiness had vanished from each one, leaving a tiny print. Paw-print, handprint, mouthprint, I can't tell.

The most uncanny thing about my fox is whether or not he will find the door.

I ask the Laughing Tyrant for his theory of *mimesis*. He answers, "My heart is a yacht!" perhaps quoting some 9th-century saga. There will be a lot of tidying up for me to do after they leave. You probably know the 17th-century George Herbert poem with the line, "Man stole the fruit but I must climb the tree." Not a Christian myself but I love these old figures of thought, the fruit, the tree, the forbidden, the ghastly boy who robs heaven. Is it possible to multiply ways of understanding without ranking them? Objectivity, subjectivity, the irruptions of others, their bad timing? Their pathos. Yes, certainly. No, not really. I go round and round this argument in my head. The fox is chewing off old bits of the fur behind his leg. His leg is beginning to look like Jean-Louis Trintignant's haircut.

My fox gets trembly when there are leavetakings. Finally it is the end. I see all the visitors' souls one by one slide back into their bodies and scamper off down a grassy slope to the river. The rooms of the house stand empty. Faint ticking or dripping sounds (they left the microphones on). A tech guy appears and switches off the microphones, the lights. He goes from room to room. I sit in the dark, I am patient. Later we will try the drawing again. The fox breathes with the night, with the stars. In and out he breathes.

which represents endurance to you, the sea or the land
both
the littoral zones
the land
just smile
the sea
the sea
the sea
the sea
the land
the sea

What is your philosophy of time
I am not familiar with this tool
what is your philosophy of time
colonization, time drops down its bars
what is your philosophy of time
the dog would like it
what is your philosophy of time
darker in the nights
what is your philosophy of time
the kind of pillow one does not worry about
what kind of pillow do you prefer
the sea
what kind of pillow do you prefer
any as long as I am entitled to tear it apart whenever it suits me
what kind of pillow do you prefer
you should feel sorry for them
what kind of pillow do you prefer
sexy
what kind of pillow do you prefer
my real hidden life
what kind of pillow do you prefer
I move past these feelings
what kind of pillow do you prefer
I am not familiar with this tool
what kind of pillow do you prefer
once I slept in a contrabass case
what kind of pillow do you prefer
no pillow

do you neaten your bed in the morning
why yes most almost always
why
because of my baby bunny she'd lay little poops all over
do you neaten your bed in the morning
yes
why
small ceremonies are good for the soul
do you neaten your bed in the morning
yes
once I slept in a contrabass case maybe I told you already
do you neaten your bed in the morning
no
why
I live alone
do you neaten your bed in the morning
sometimes
why
it has to do with Martin Luther
do you neaten your bed in the morning
yes
why
then I can walk tall into the day
do you neaten your bed in the morning
sometimes
why
I love you
do you neaten your bed in the morning
I try to
why
otherwise I get restless
do you neaten your bed in the morning
no
why
I will go do it now

How did he get out of the box?
Did I hear him scratching?
(H.D. Tribute to Freud, *128)*

how do you sustain morale during a long project
by loosing track
how do you sustain morale during a long project
put full faith in Ricky
how do you sustain morale during a long project
I hear Heraklitos whisper in the waves
how do you sustain morale during a long project
Lutherian guilt
how do you sustain morale during a long project
cigarettes and bourbon
how do you sustain morale during a long project
best thing is to smile
how do you sustain morale during a long project
pills can help
how do you sustain morale during a long project
breathe deep
how do you sustain morale during a long project
frozen orange juice
how do you sustain morale during a long project
reality was a mirage interrupting me
how do you sustain morale during a long project
dress dandy
how do you sustain morale during a long project
make God make us God
how do you sustain morale during a long project
no mirrors

how do you sustain morale during a long project
silky nightgown
how do you sustain morale during a long project
be a baby
how do you sustain morale during a long project
surrender
how do you sustain morale during a long project
Ricky!

what is your philosophy of time
I'm pretty sure we'll surrender
what is your philosophy of time
it is a way to travel
what is your philosophy of time
feel like in a giant chestnut
what is your philosophy of time
how it's sweet and how it moves
what is your philosophy of time
a shallow closet with narrow bench and a rope to pull you up
what is your philosophy of time
thin cradle of feathers
what is your philosophy of time
backwards is north
what is your philosophy of time
just smile
what is your philosophy of time
(as a noun) snare or lasso (as a verb) flick flip twirl
what is your philosophy of time
me and Doddi switching beds
what is your philosophy of time
power
what is your philosophy of time
for a year I made homemade toothpaste

do you like jam
yes
do you like the films of Eric Rohmer
don't know
do you like jam
not a fan
do you like the films of Eric Rohmer
I am curious now
do you like jam
very much
do you like the films of Eric Rohmer
sexy
do you like the films of Eric Rohmer
very much
do you like the films of Eric Rohmer
no idea
do you like jam
I do
do you like the films of Eric Rohmer
Love in the Afternoon is fantastic
do you like jam
yes when in need
do you like jam
nothing swampy please
do you like the films of Eric Rohmer
too sugary
do you like jam
I like watching paint dry
do you like the films of Eric Rohmer
Sorry
do you like the films of Eric Rohmer
no
do you like jam
it still leaves God untouched
do you like the films of Eric Rohmer
I find realistic techniques delightful
do you like jam
yes during the night
do you like the films of Eric Rohmer
don't know
do you like jam
it's in my thoughts a lot

ANNE CARSON is a Canadian poet, essayist and professor.

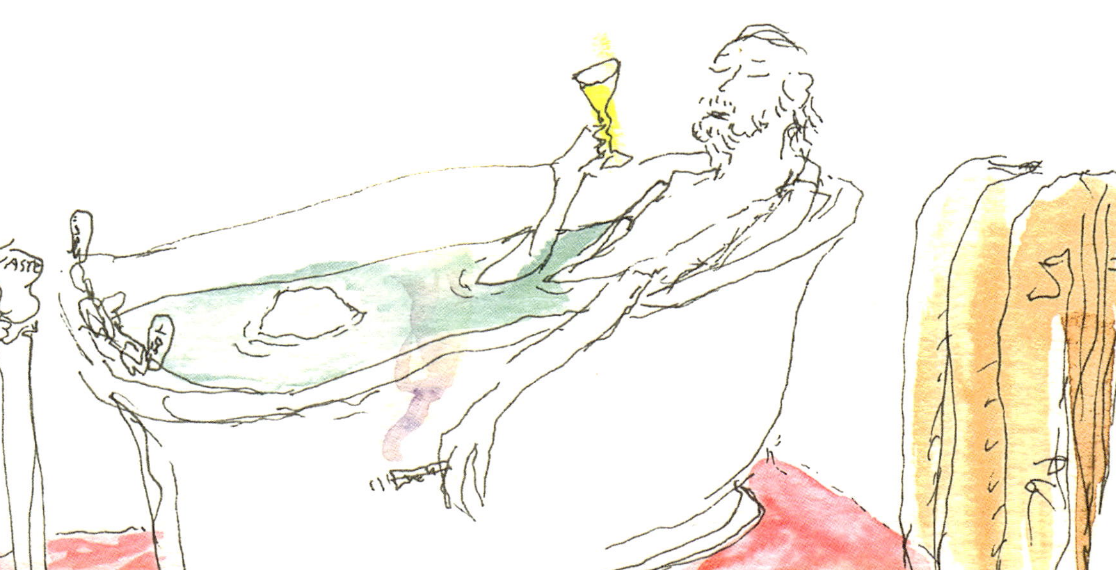

Drawing by Ragnar Kjartansson, 2007

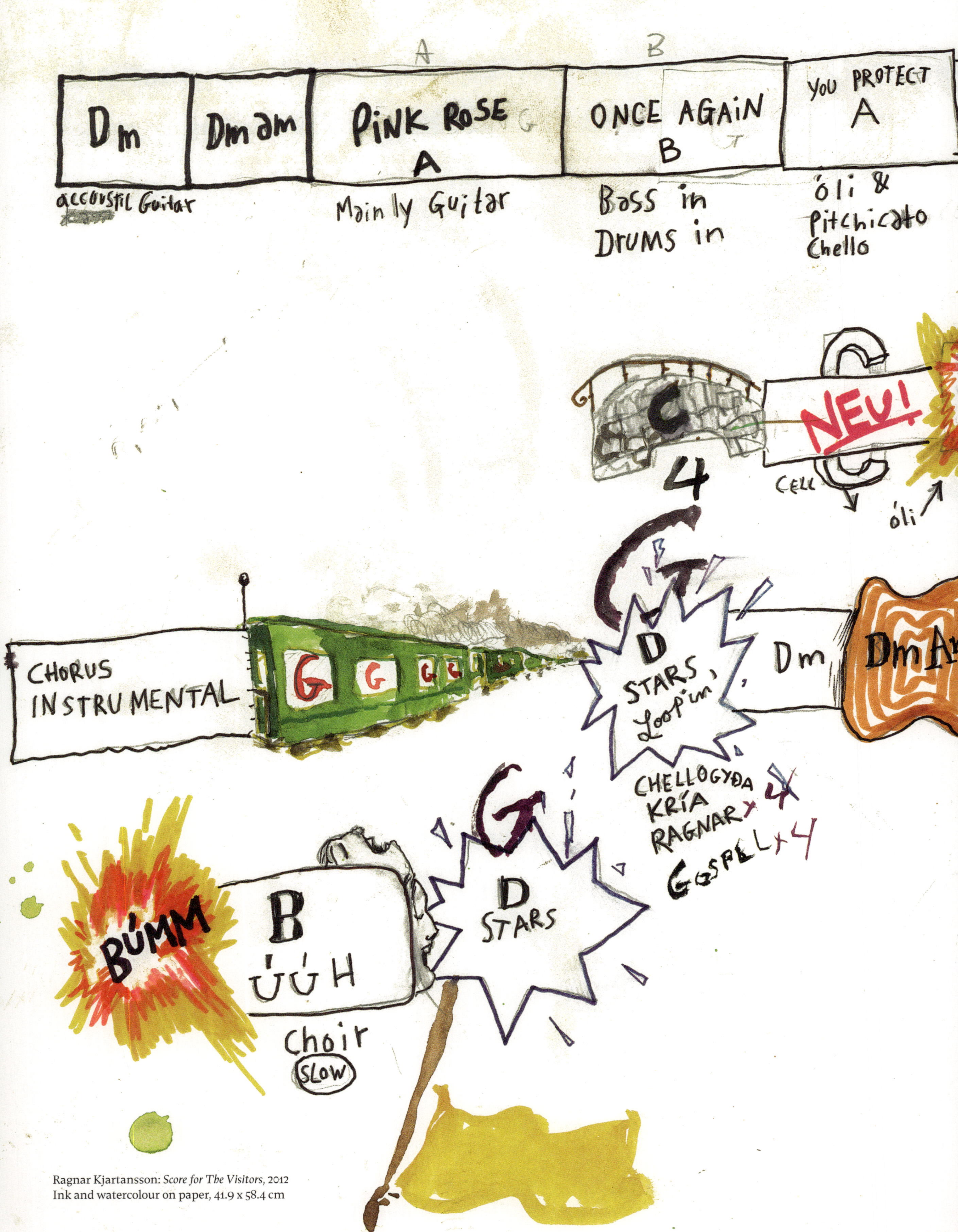

Ragnar Kjartansson: *Score for The Visitors*, 2012
Ink and watercolour on paper, 41.9 x 58.4 cm

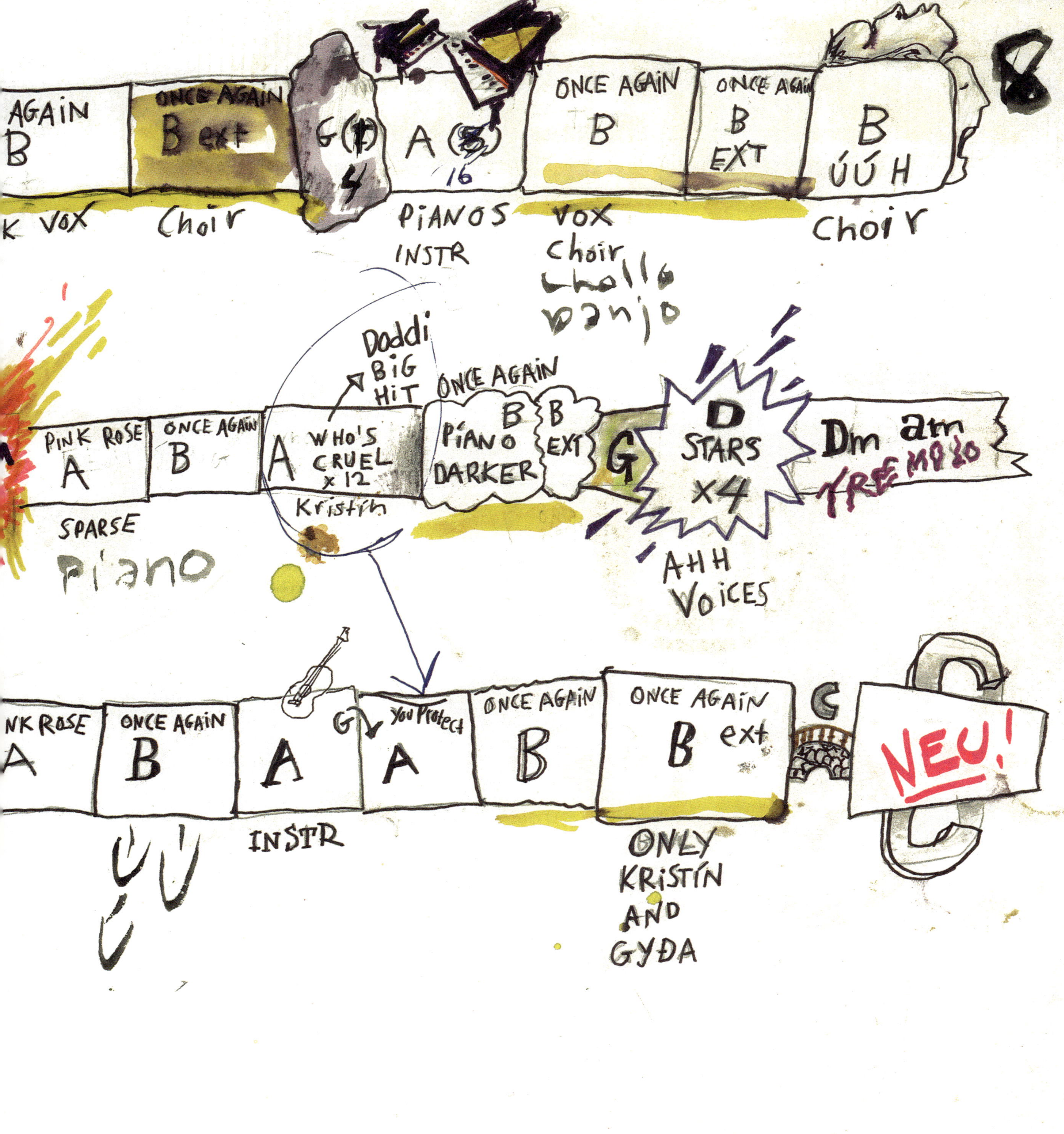

AGAIN B
K VOX
ONCE AGAIN B ext
Choir
G(F) 4
A 16
PIANOS INSTR
ONCE AGAIN B
VOX choir
ONCE AGAIN B EXT
B ÚÚH
Choir
PINK ROSE A
SPARSE piano
ONCE AGAIN B
A WHO'S CRUEL x 12
Kristín
Doddi BIG HIT
ONCE AGAIN B PIANO DARKER
B EXT
G
D STARS x4
AHH VOICES
Dm am
TREMOLO
NK ROSE A
ONCE AGAIN B
A
INSTR
G A You Protect
ONCE AGAIN B
ONCE AGAIN B ext
ONLY KRISTÍN AND GYDA
C
NEU!

A pink rose
In the glittery frost
A diamond heart
And the orange red fire

Once again I fall into
My feminine ways

You protect the world from me
As if I'm the only one who's cruel
You've taken me
To the bitter end

Once again I fall into
My feminine ways

There are stars exploding
And there is nothing you can do

Lyrics by Ásdís Sif Gunnarsdóttir

Opposite page: From the recordings of *The Visitors*, 2012
The following spread: Installation view, Louisiana Museum of Modern Art, 2023

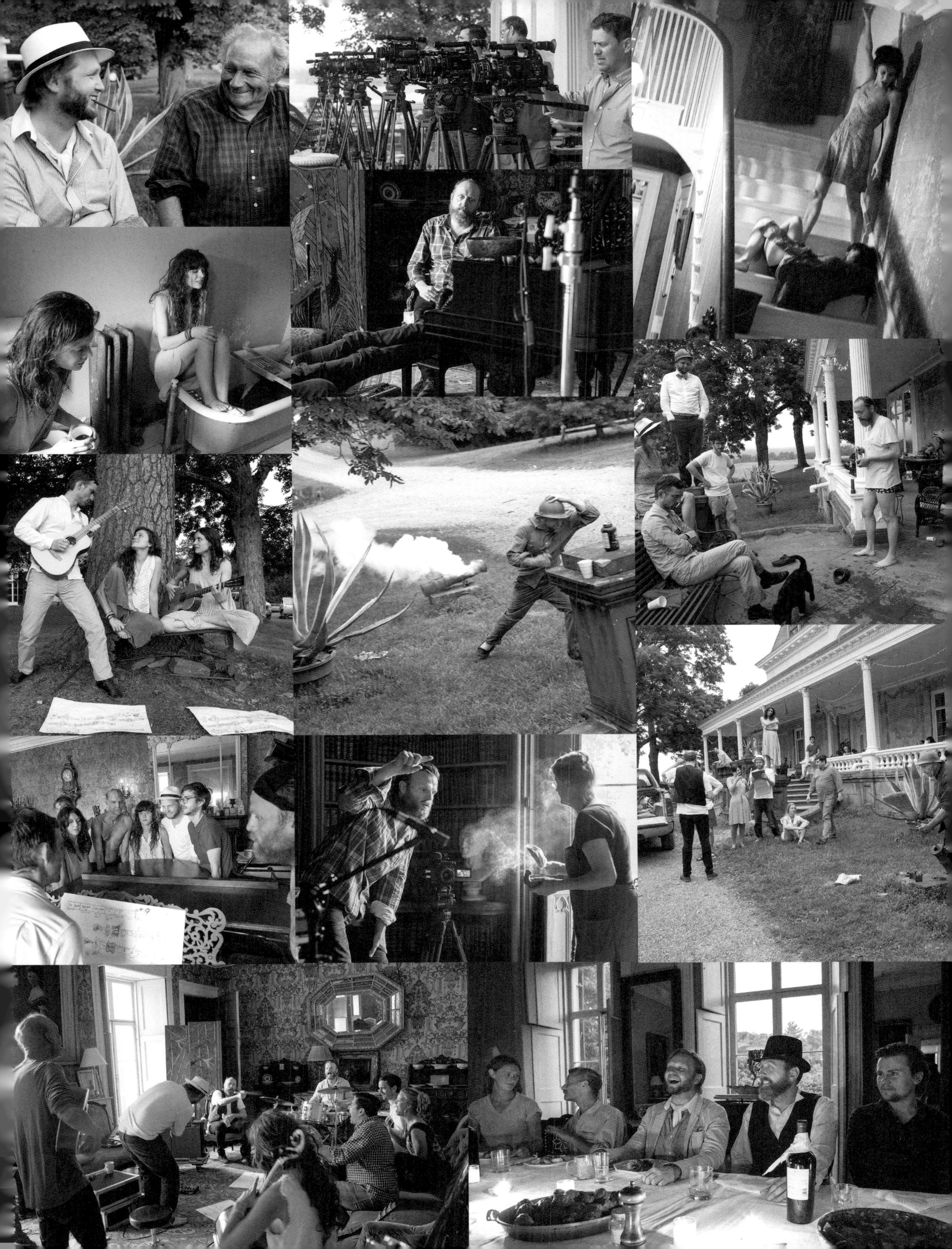

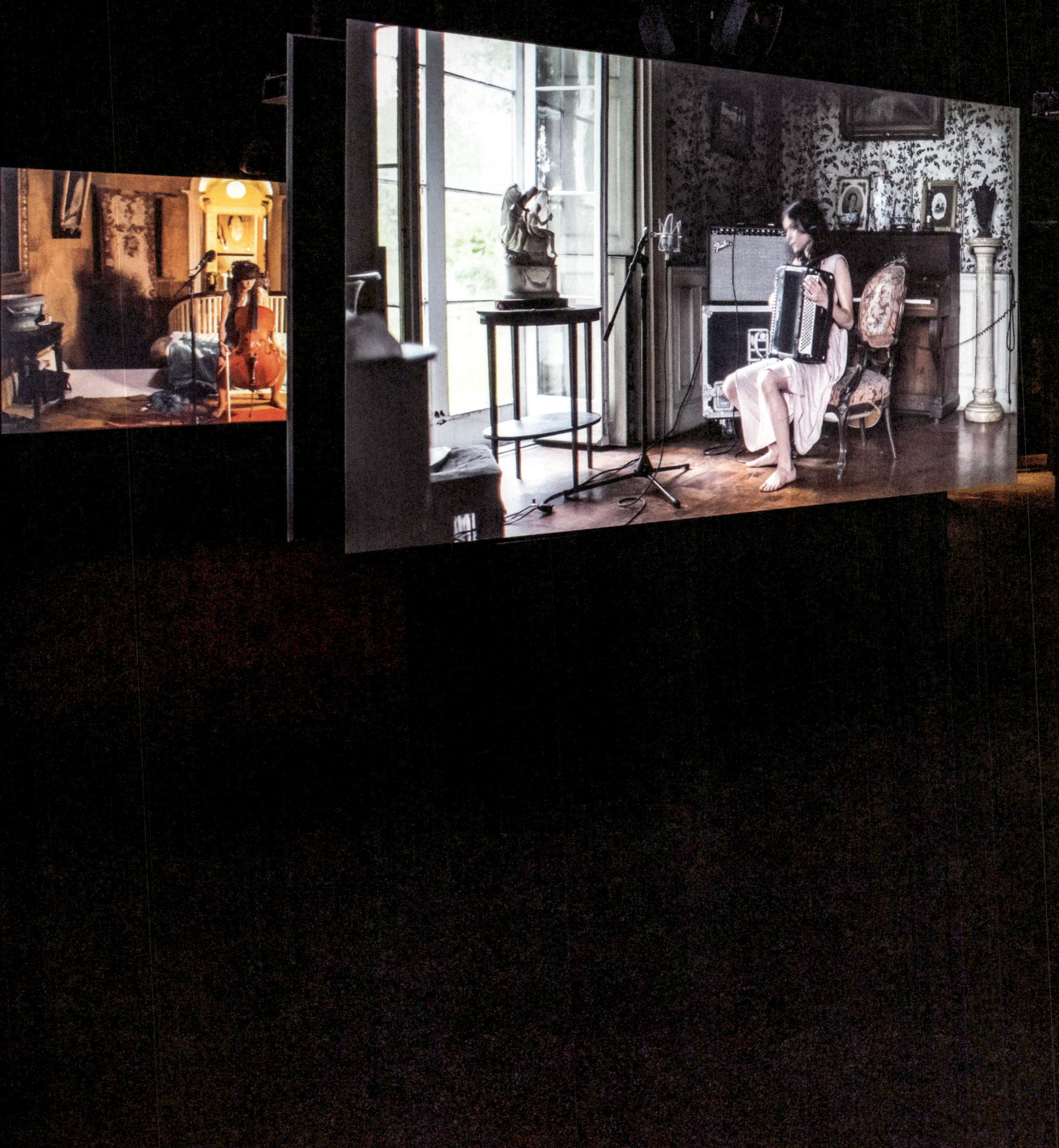

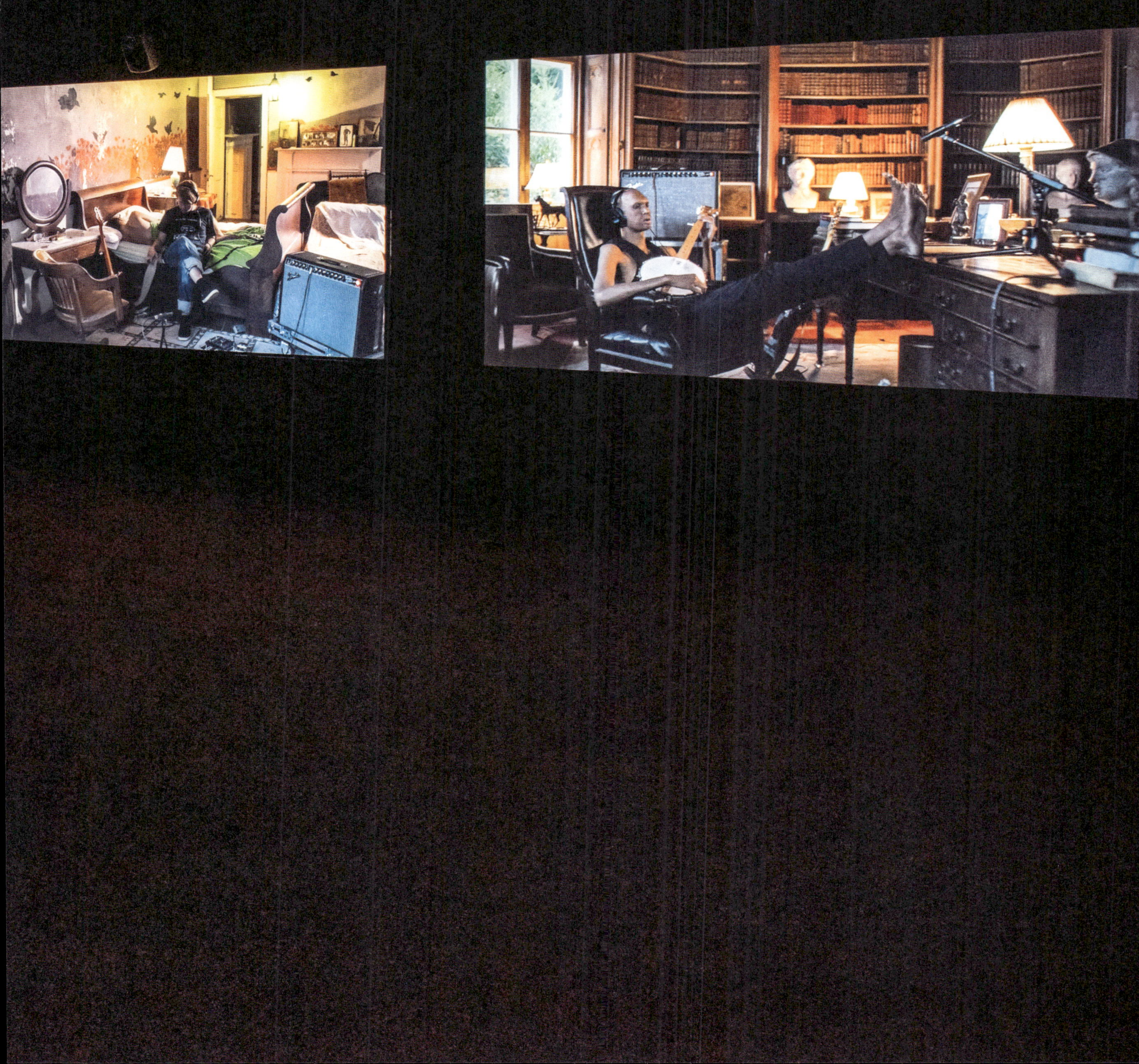

BANGEMAND — 2023

Scaredman
Performance
Courtesy of the artist, Luhring Augustine, New York, and i8 Gallery, Reykjavik

By Tine Colstrup

A man in a tuxedo finds himself on a ledge with his back against the wall. The motif is a familiar Hollywood cliche. Is he fleeing? Will he fall? As always with Kjartansson, *Bangemand* (Scaredman) is as much a self-portrait as it is a proposition for a destilled image of the ongoing debates around masculinity, power and privilege.

The performance was created for the exhibition at Louisiana and will run throughout the exhibition period.

TINE COLSTRUP is curator at Louisiana Museum of Modern Art and curated *Epic Waste of Love and Understanding*.

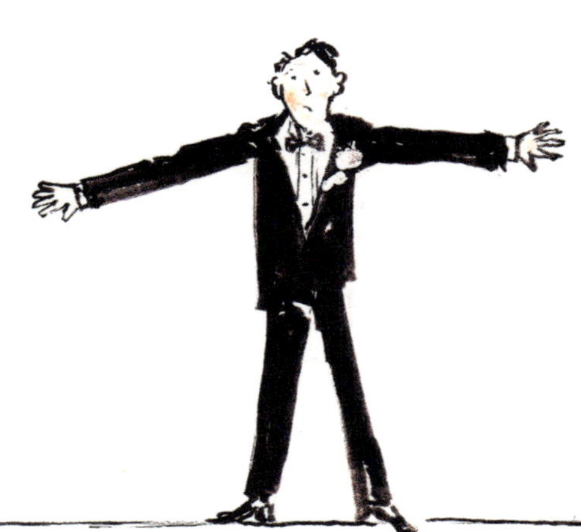

Drawing by Ragnar Kjartansson, 2023
Opposite page and the following spread: Installation views, Louisiana Museum of Modern Art, 2023

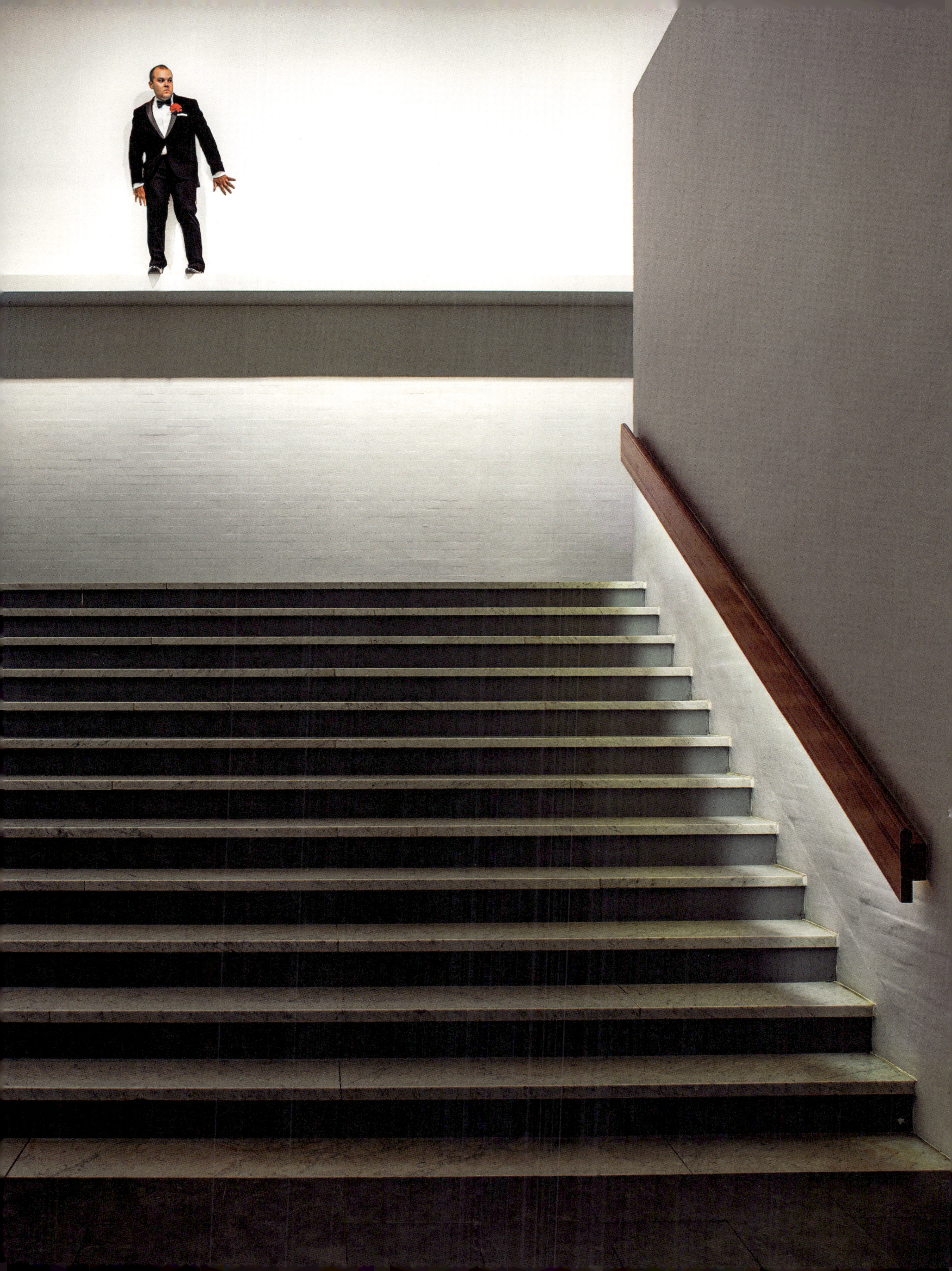

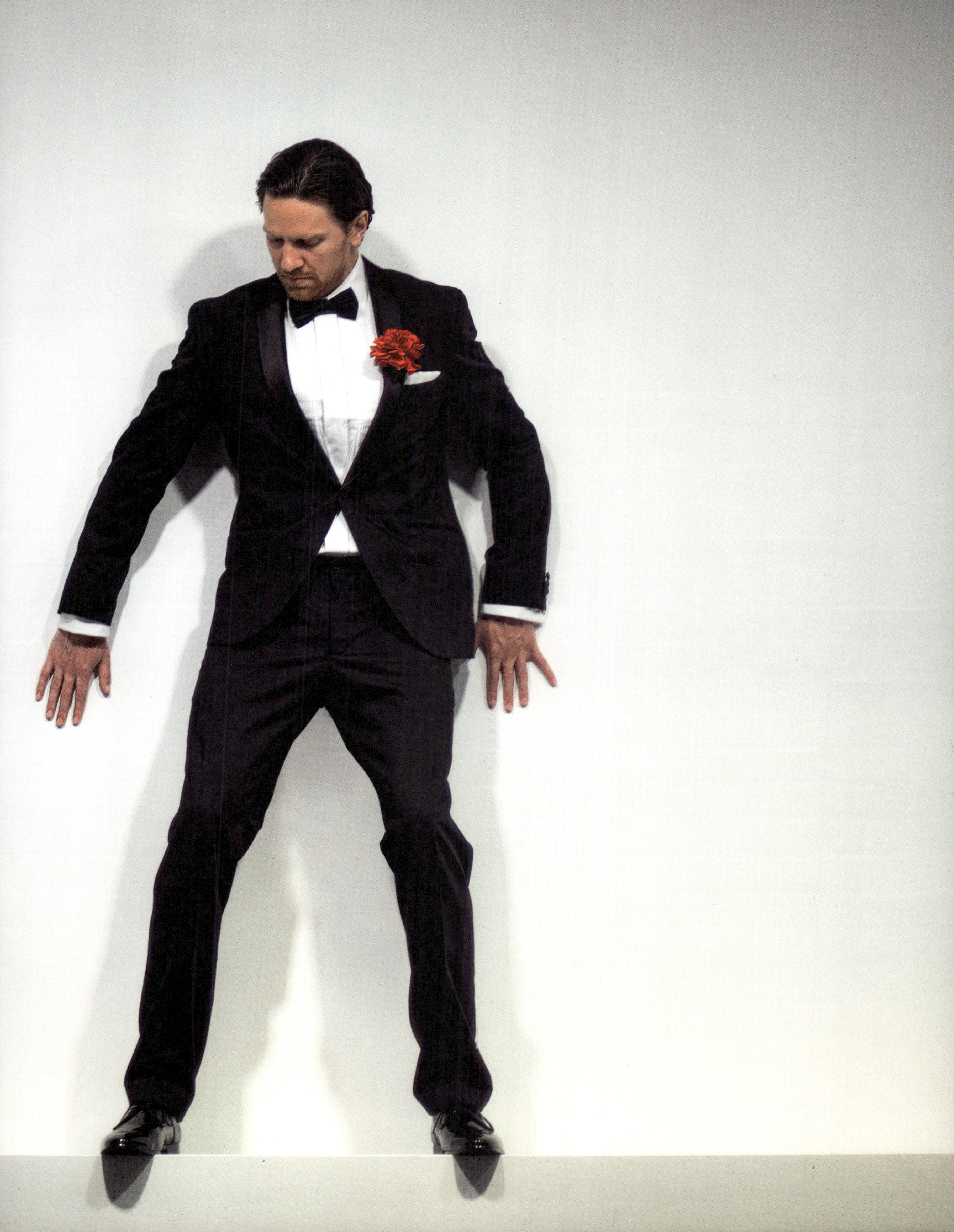

GREY SUITS — 2008

Drawings on paper
102 × 81 × 4.5 cm
Private collections, Reykjavik

By Dóri DNA

Hello, my dear.

I just wanted to let you know that your mother has left. She is gone and she will never return. If a woman who looks like your mother tries to contact you, it's not her but an actress trying to deceive you for a new reality show. Pure evil.

I know that the two of you had a deep connection, but lately, it has felt like you were just pretending. Like you were just loving each other to make me look like a fool. I think one evening, you and I should go through the household accounts, and then you can at least see your mother's disappearance in financial terms. If you're going to cry, then I ask you to do it outside, by the shed, where the weeds are growing. But I wouldn't cry for your mother, I mean, she wasn't even strong enough anymore to hold you in the air. Now it will just be you and me. It will be grand.

Regards, Dad.

DÓRI DNA (Halldór Laxness Halldórsson) is an Icelandic actor, author, comedian, rapper and television personality.

Opposite page: *Grey Suits (09)*
The following spread: *Grey Suits (05)* and *Grey Suits (12)*

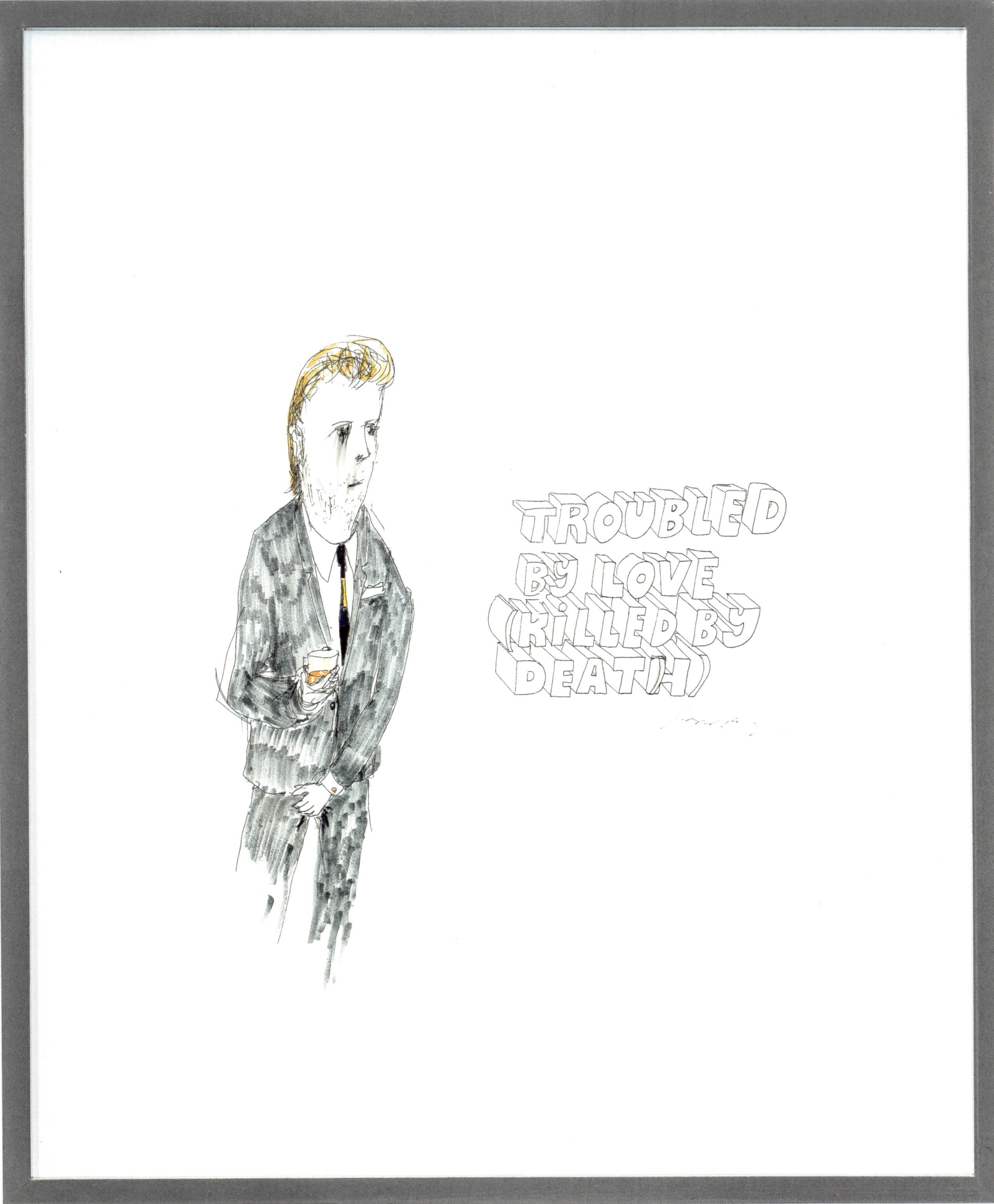
TROUBLED
BY LOVE
(KILLED BY
DEATH)

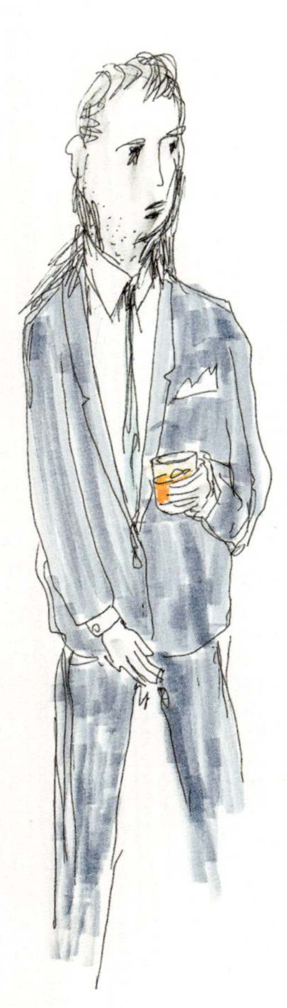
Troubled
by love
(killed by
death)

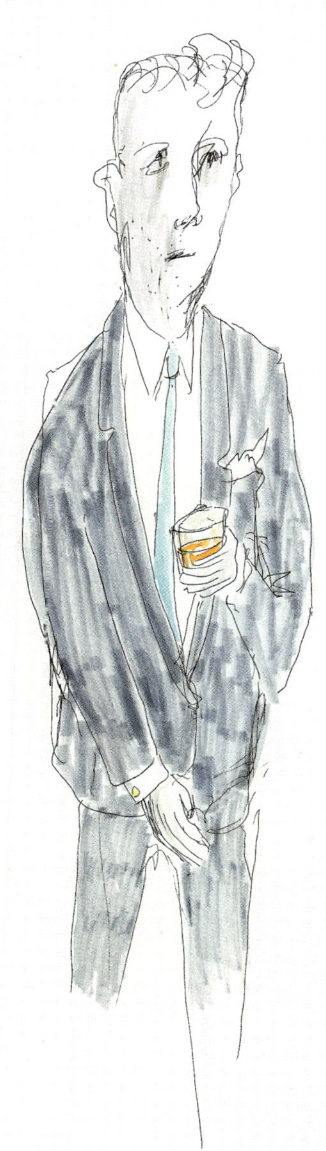
Troubled
by love
(killed by
death)

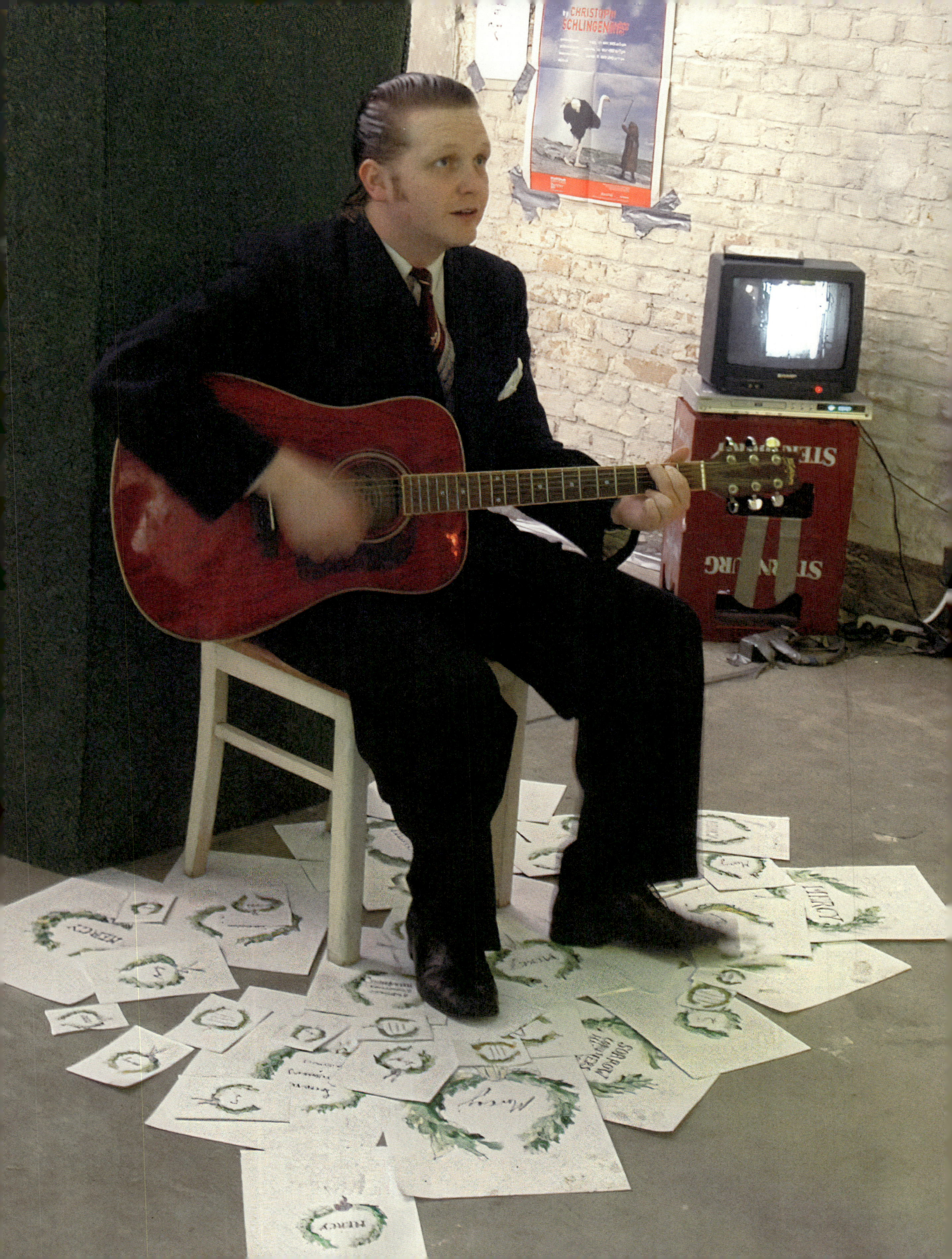
CHRISTOPH
MERCY

DRAWINGS OF MERCY — 2005

Watercolour and pencil on paper
Dimensions variable
Private collections, Copenhagen
Private collection, Reykjavik

By Tine Colstrup

All media are intrinsically interconnected in Kjartansson's practice. Every performance starts as a drawing in the sketchbook – and drawings and paintings are often created in the context of a performance.

The *Mercy* series of drawings were made for a performance in Berlin in 2005. They were lying on the floor beneath the artist who was sitting on a chair with his guitar, dressed as a 1950s-style crooner. The crooner figure was one of the masculine stereotypes that Kjartansson explored over and over again at the time, for instance also in the filmed performance *Mercy* from the previous year, 2004 (see pp. 30-35).

In the drawings, we find a self-contradictory statement: a laurel wreath encircles the word "Mercy". The history of the laurel wreath is almost as long as history itself, and at least since antiquity, the wreath has been associated with victory, glory and honour. While the laurel wreath is a mark of distinction that you *receive*, mercy is something you *ask for* when, for one reason or another, you need forgiveness or compassion. This ambiguous clash set the stage for the well-dressed crooner with slicked-back hair, who repeated the phrase "Sorrow conquers happiness" over and over again in the performance, which lasted some hours. Stuck in the same melancholic groove, the crooner surrounded by the drawings could be grappling with a contradictory mess of success, privilege, sadness and shame? Or perhaps something else entirely. The drawings have traces of dirt and shoes that have walked all over them. That their excess of pathos has been trampled on adds another melodramatic layer to the works.

Repetition is Kjartansson's most consistent method across all media, and in numerous series of drawings and watercolours he repeats the same motif in a kind of homemade graphic mass production.

The performance took place in connection with the art fair Berliner Liste in 2005, where Kjartansson participated with the artist-run exhibition platform Kling & Bang in Reykjavik. In the snapshot from the event, there is a poster behind Kjartansson – perfectly installed with gaffer tape – from an exhibition at Kling & Bang with German artist Christoph Schlingensief (1960-2010). When the *Mercy* performance was over, Schlingensief asked permission to buy one of the walked-on drawings, which Kjartansson has described as an ultimate honour and a decisive encouragement from one of his artistic heroes.

TINE COLSTRUP is curator at Louisiana Museum of Modern Art and curated *Epic Waste of Love and Understanding*.

Opposite page: Photograph from the *Mercy* performance in Berlin, 2005
The following spread: Installation view, Louisiana Museum of Modern Art, 2023

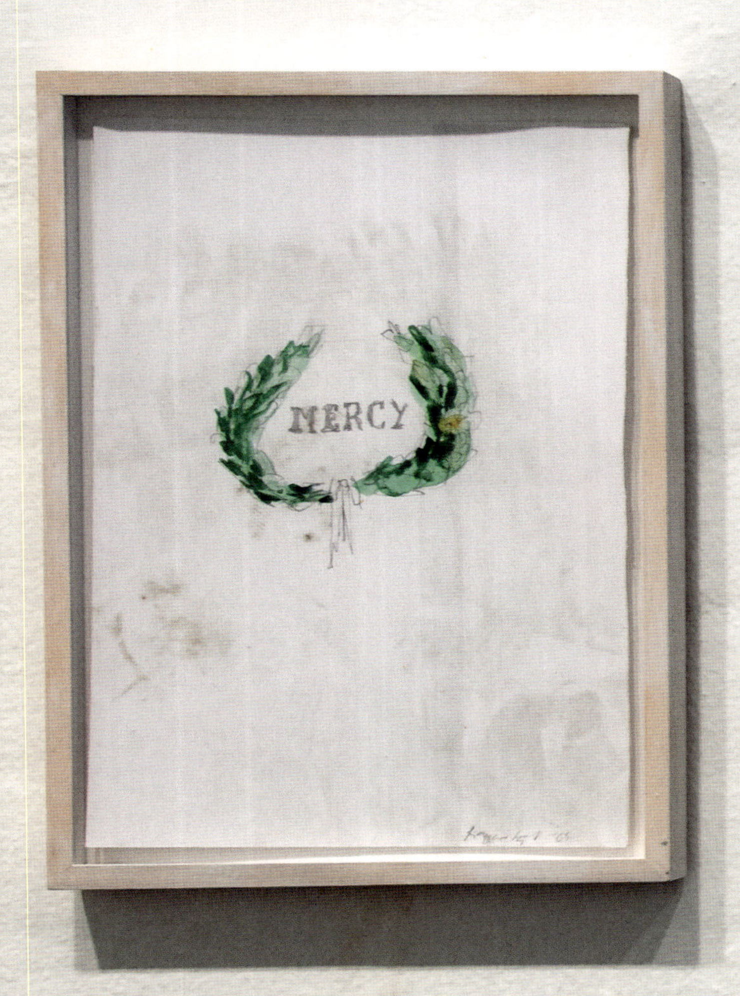
MERCY

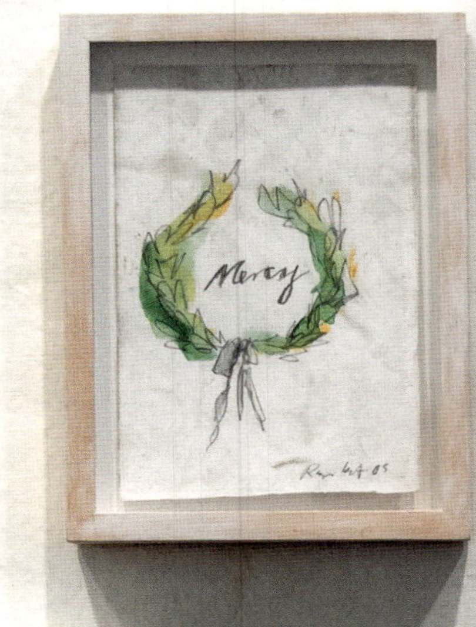
Mercy

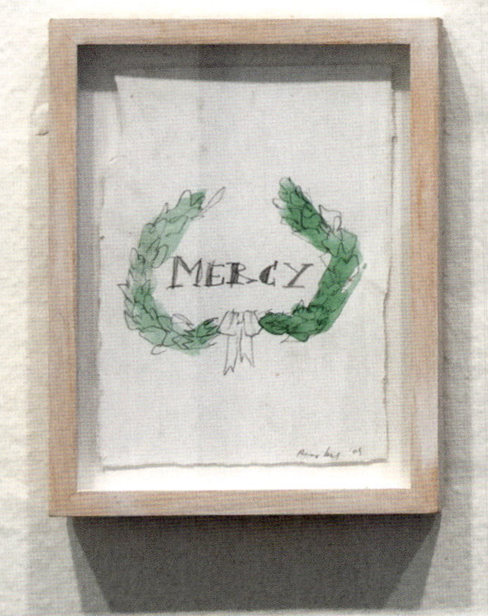
MERCY

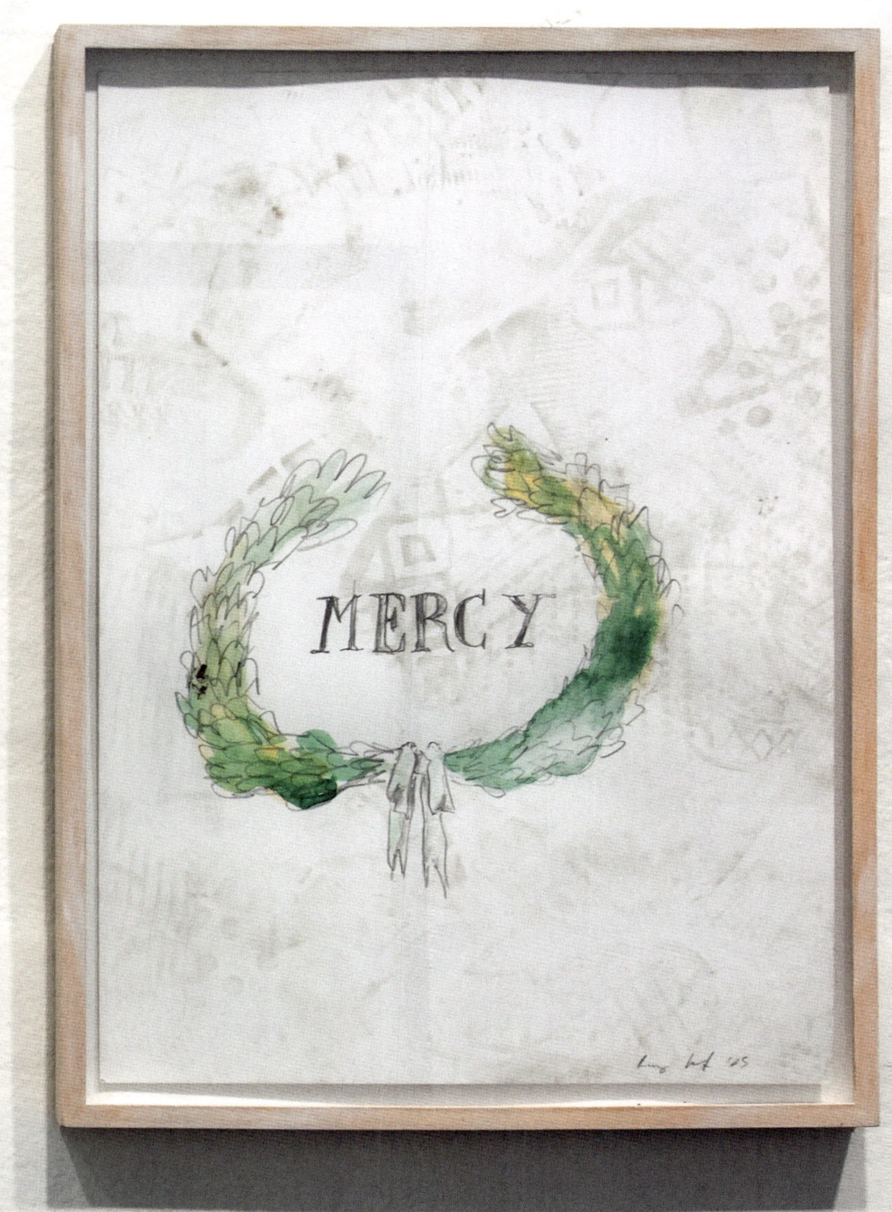
MERCY

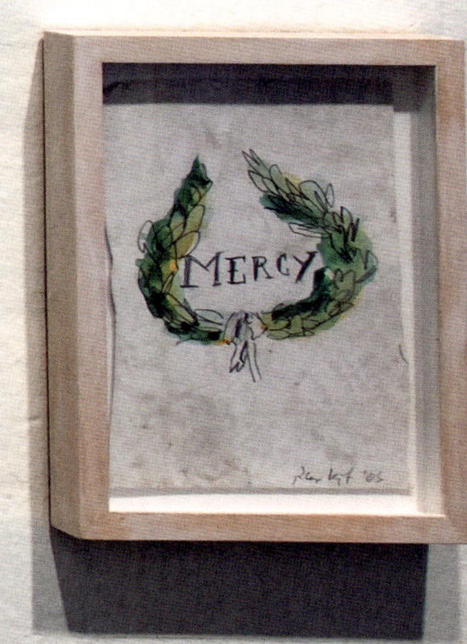
MERCY

RAGNAR KJARTANSSON, MARGRÉT BJARNADÓTTIR & BRYCE DESSNER

NO TOMORROW — 2022

Six-channel video installation
Duration: 29:18 min.
Commissioned by Sigurður Gísli Pálmason, based on a commission by the Iceland Dance Company

By Maria Schnyder

Back in 2021, during one of the virtual studio visits we held in preparation for his solo exhibition at De Pont (in Tilburg, Netherlands, ed.), Ragnar Kjartansson told us about a live performance he had developed in collaboration with choreographer Margrét Bjarnadóttir (born 1981), musician Bryce Dessner (born 1976) and eight dancers from the Icelandic Dance Company. *No Tomorrow* was first shown at the SACRIFICE Festival in Reykjavik in 2017 and was a piece, Kjartansson said, in which "the dance is the music, and the music is the dance". For the exhibition, he wanted to translate the performance into a monumental audiovisual sculpture: in effect "carving it into marble", as he jokingly put it. He envisioned a sonic experiment in which the original stage set would be replaced by six screens and thirty audio channels encircling the viewer. We were all game, of course, so off he went, sending us sketches and images along the way until the actual recording session took place just shy of one month before we began installing the exhibition.

I vividly remember my first glimpses of *No Tomorrow* while we were installing the piece, the encounter with the eight dancers, appearing life-size in front of a muted teal-and-white striped curtain backdrop. The dancers, all women in blue jeans with white T-shirts and white socks, were moving gracefully across the stage, from one screen to the next, disappearing and reemerging as they strummed their guitars, which they had learned to play especially for the occasion. The sounds each dancer produced travelled seamlessly with her image, eventually culminating in ethereal, melancholy vocals. The lyrics were a kind of collage that Kjartansson and his wife, artist Ingibjörg Sigurjónsdóttir (born 1985), had assembled from texts by the ancient Greek poet Sappho (c. 610-570 BC) and French artist and author Dominique Vivant Denon (1747-1825), whose 18th-century novella *No Tomorrow* supplied the title for the piece. It was nothing short of spellbinding.

I returned to the installation many more times over the course of the exhibition, trying to pinpoint where the magic was coming from. The work is unmistakably Kjartansson's, but also quite different from what I was used to seeing from him up to this point. Although it indisputably nods to Rococo, specifically through Vivant Denon and more generally in its staging of idyllic beauty, it lacks any overt theatricality; and while it shares with many of Kjartansson's other works a deep sense of longing that Goethe (1749-1832) would be proud of, here, that longing appears in a more distilled form. There is no challenging durational aspect to the performance and the dancers' movements have a purposeful simplicity to them. Their guitar playing is somewhat unpolished and at times a bit rough, their vocals not entirely flawless. The viewer might even be tempted

Opposite page: Still from *No Tomorrow*, 2022

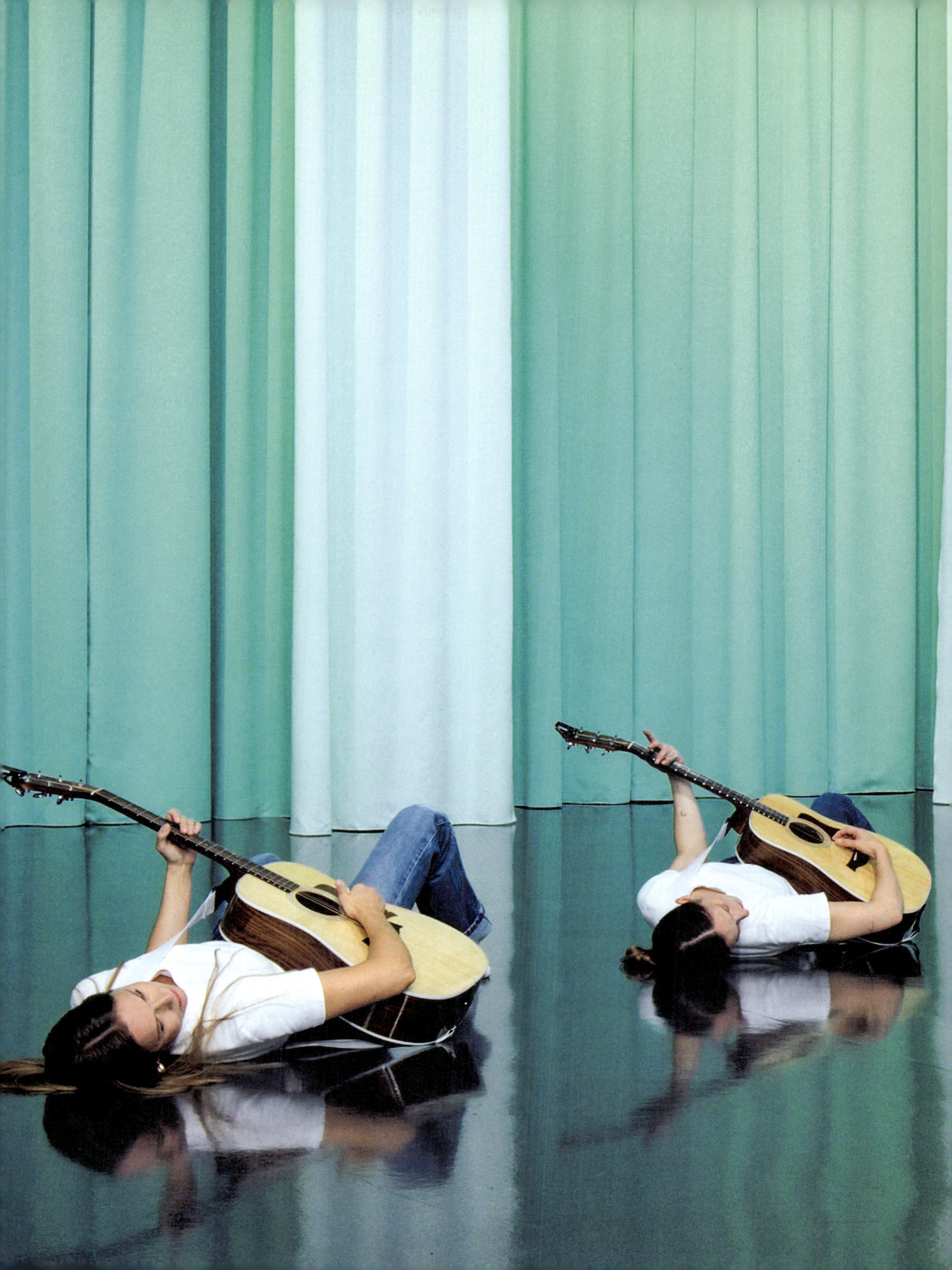

to think that with the right amount of training, they themselves might eventually be able to join in. It depicts a world of beauty and harmony to which one is irresistibly drawn, yet at the same time, it conveys a sense that this world is not entirely out of reach.

Perhaps this is because it is less concerned with a demonstration of skills than with human qualities. The beauty of the piece stems from the fragile balance between its elements – a balance that can exist only by virtue of sensitivity, empathy and responsiveness. The dancers' bodies seem to be propelled by one another; they move as one in carefully shifting formations, playing their guitars while the guitars, in turn, lead their movements. The dance is, indeed, the music, and the music the dance. Each dancer is subtly aware of her responsibility to the others and to the whole, mindful of the ripple effect caused by her faintest gesture. As a viewer, standing in the middle of it all, you catch the glances the dancers exchange and their subtle interactions; you sense the underlying complicity. Their space bleeds into yours, you adapt to their rhythm. Due to the size and positioning of the screens, viewing the dancers' performance means moving with them as well as in concert with the other viewers in attendance, sometimes losing sight of the dancers but maintaining an awareness of their presence.

Yet the piece is as hopeless as it is beautiful. "Looked hard for the moral / Of this whole adventure / And found none / Stand to face me beloved / And open out the grace of your eyes / Oh babe, no tomorrow," the dancers sing. When Kjartansson, Bjarnadóttir and Dessner began preparing the live performance, Donald Trump (born 1946) had just been elected president in the US. By the time they were filming the video installation, Russia had invaded Ukraine and the war was in full swing. Facing these troublesome political times, they drew inspiration from the 1940s dance movies, made while the world was going to hell. They were committed to creating a piece that was all image and sound – yet ultimately, about nothing. "I am a nihilist", Kjartansson once said. "But being such a nihilist, I have to be a romantic, just to have more fun in the abyss."

If *No Tomorrow* is a reflection of this attitude, it is also a *pars pro toto* for Kjartansson's collaborative approach to making art. Having initially wanted to be a musician, collaborations offer the artist a way to recapture the feeling of being in a band. *No Tomorrow*, a "total soup of collaboration" as he called it, is likely his most ambitious one to date, in which music, dance and visual art come together to be gently but irrevocably changed by one another. The qualities that make *No Tomorrow* so irresistible as a work of art are the same ones that made it possible in the first place: it is built on the human capacity for tuning into one another. Maybe the melancholy in Kjartansson's work is so enticing because he has turned the romantic's longing-in-solitude into a nihilist's longing-in-togetherness. And that, most certainly, is more fun than Werther ever had.

MARIA SCHNYDER is a Swiss deputy director and curator at De Pont museum, Tilburg, Netherlands, who, with Martijn van Nieuwenhuyzen, curated the museum's Ragnar Kjartansson exhibition *Time Changes Everything* (2022-2023).

The following spreads: Installation views, Louisiana Museum of Modern Art, 2023, and stills from *No Tomorrow*, 2022

Thought myself to be
The best loved lover
And therefore the happiest of men
I never thought to touch the sky
With two arms

Oh babe, no tomorrow

Looked hard for the moral
Of this whole adventure
And found none
Stand to face me beloved
And open out the grace of your eyes

Oh babe, no tomorrow

Lyrics collaged by Ragnar Kjartansson and Ingibjörg Sigurjónsdóttir
from texts by Sappho (poems translated by Anne Carson) and
Vivant Denon (the short novel *Point de lendemain* (1777), translated by Lydia Davis)

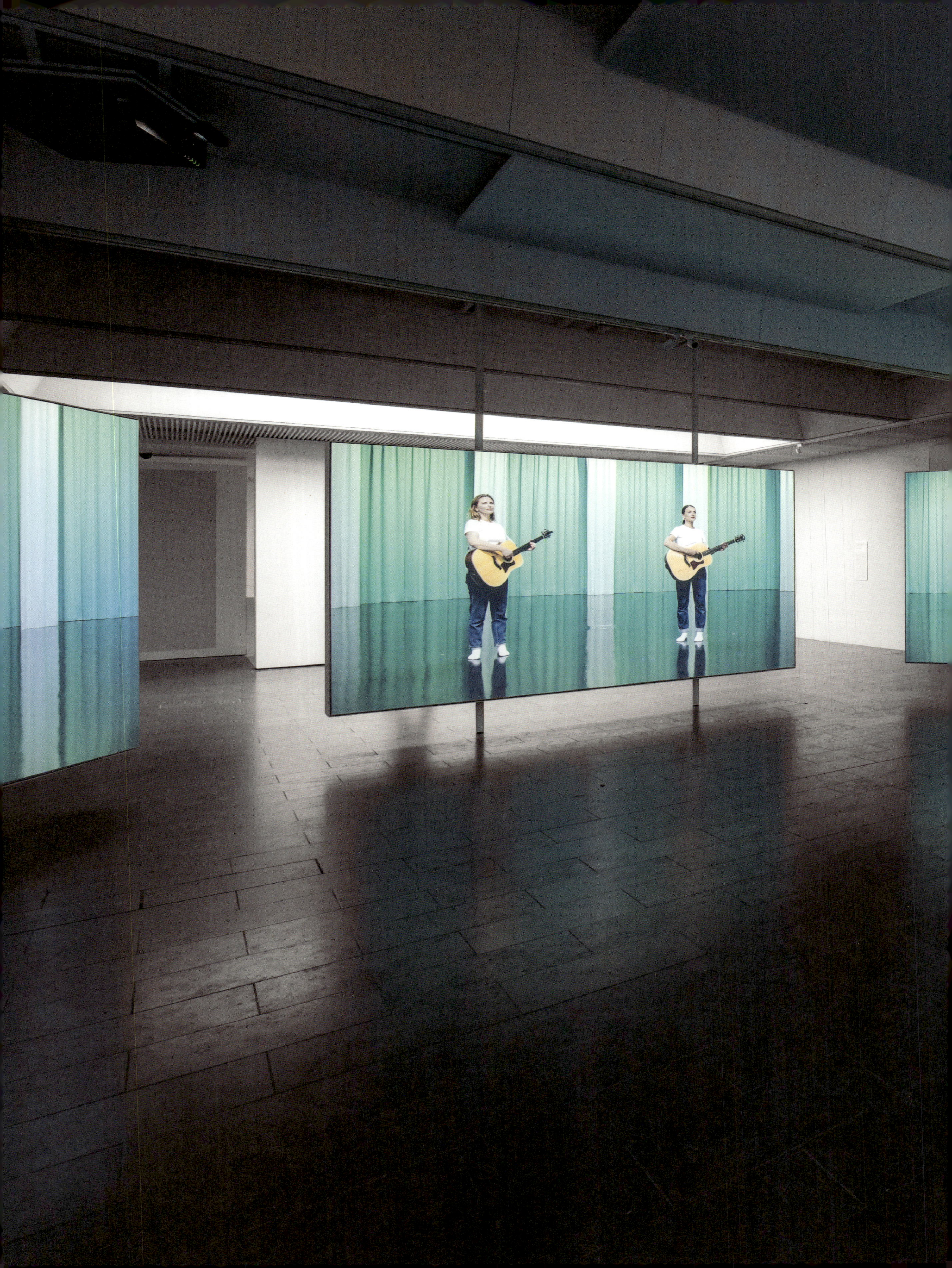

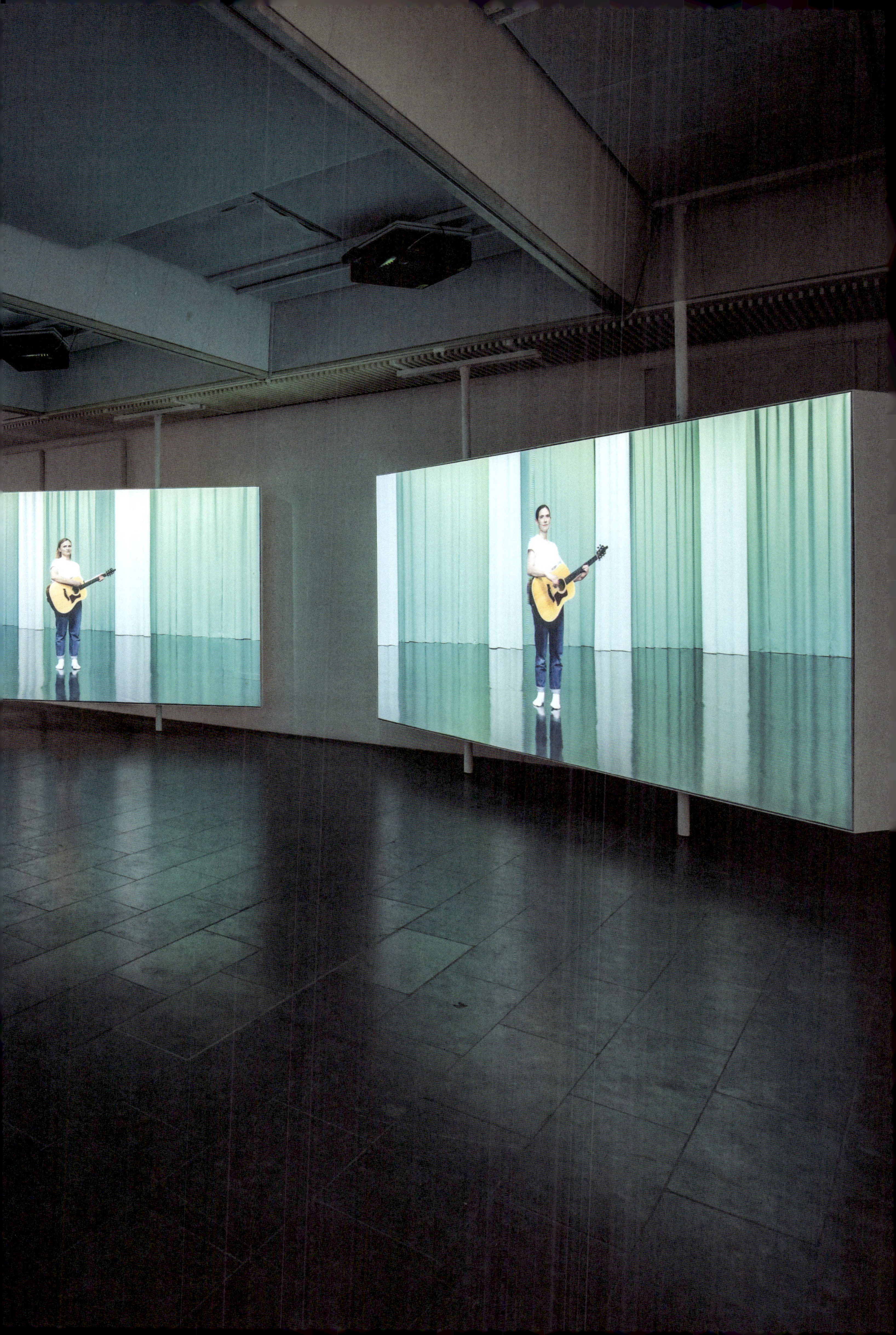

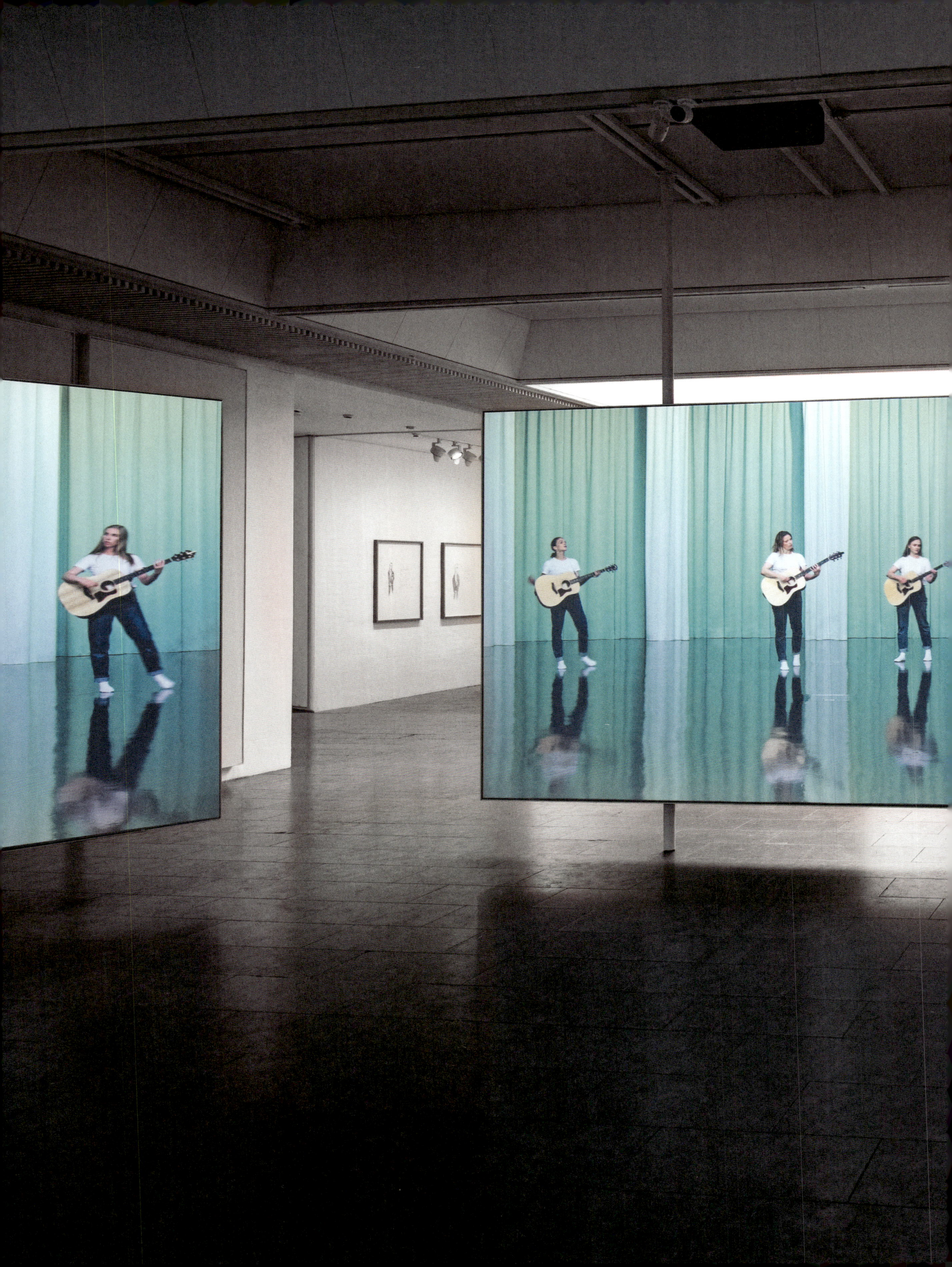

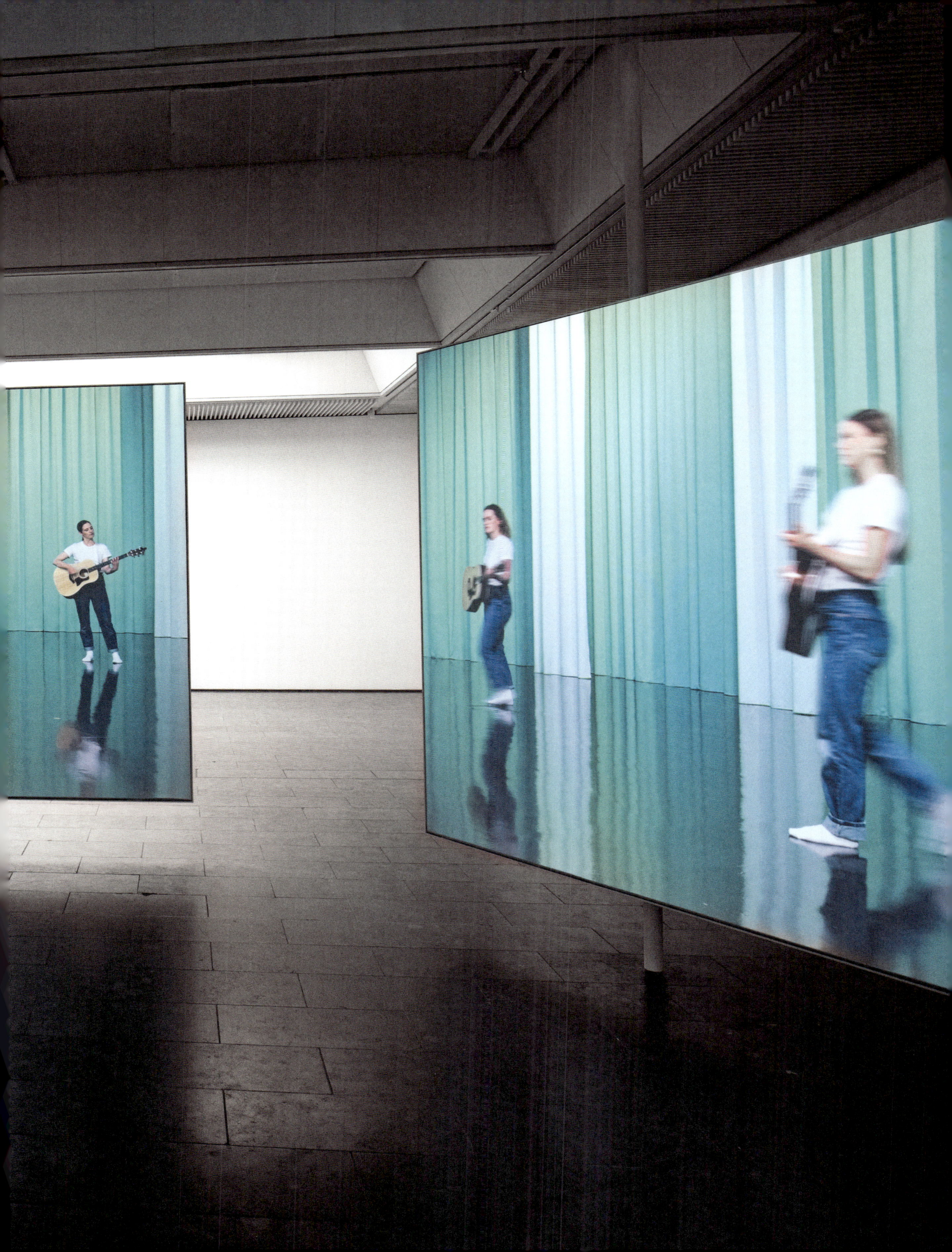

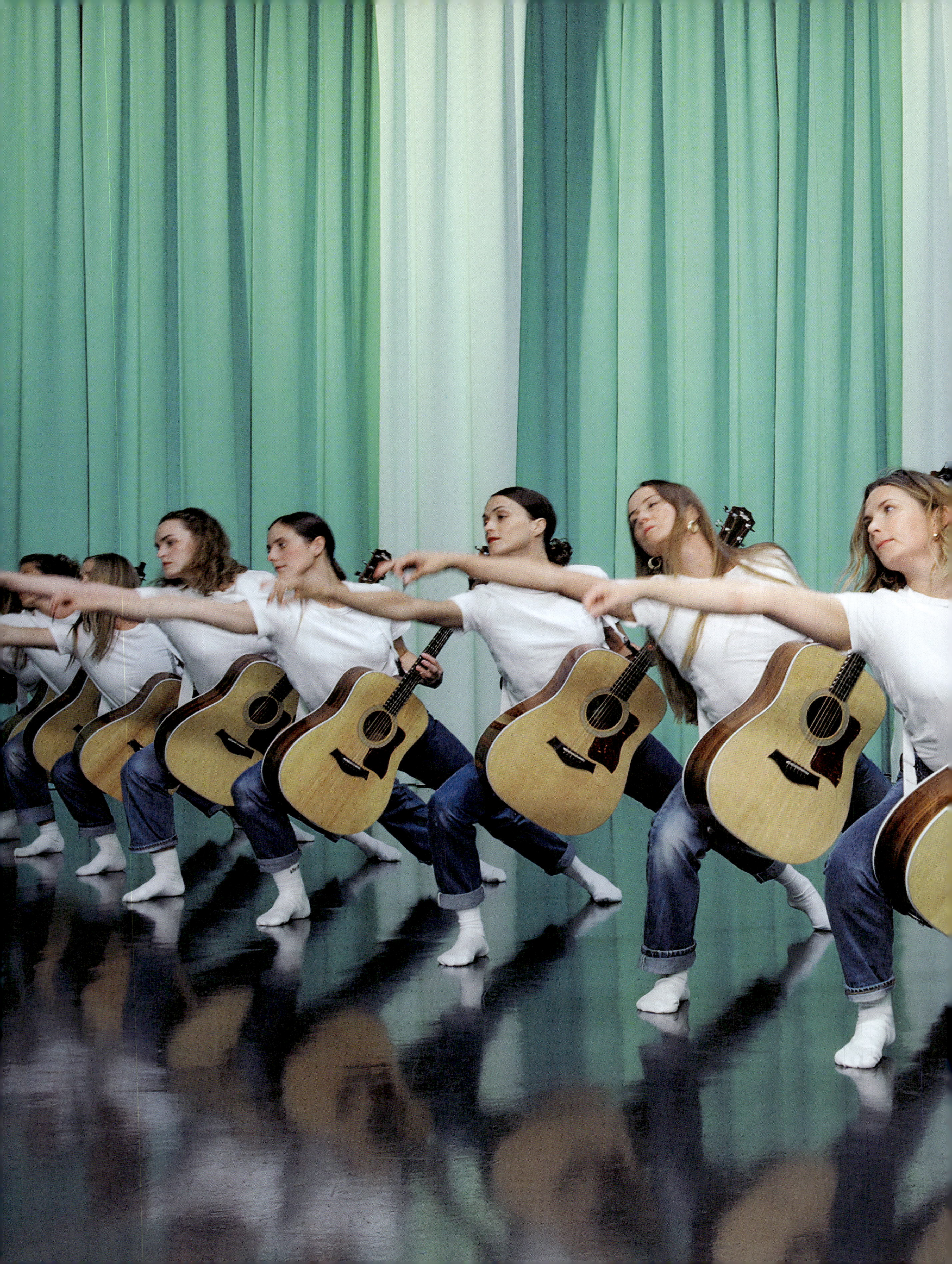

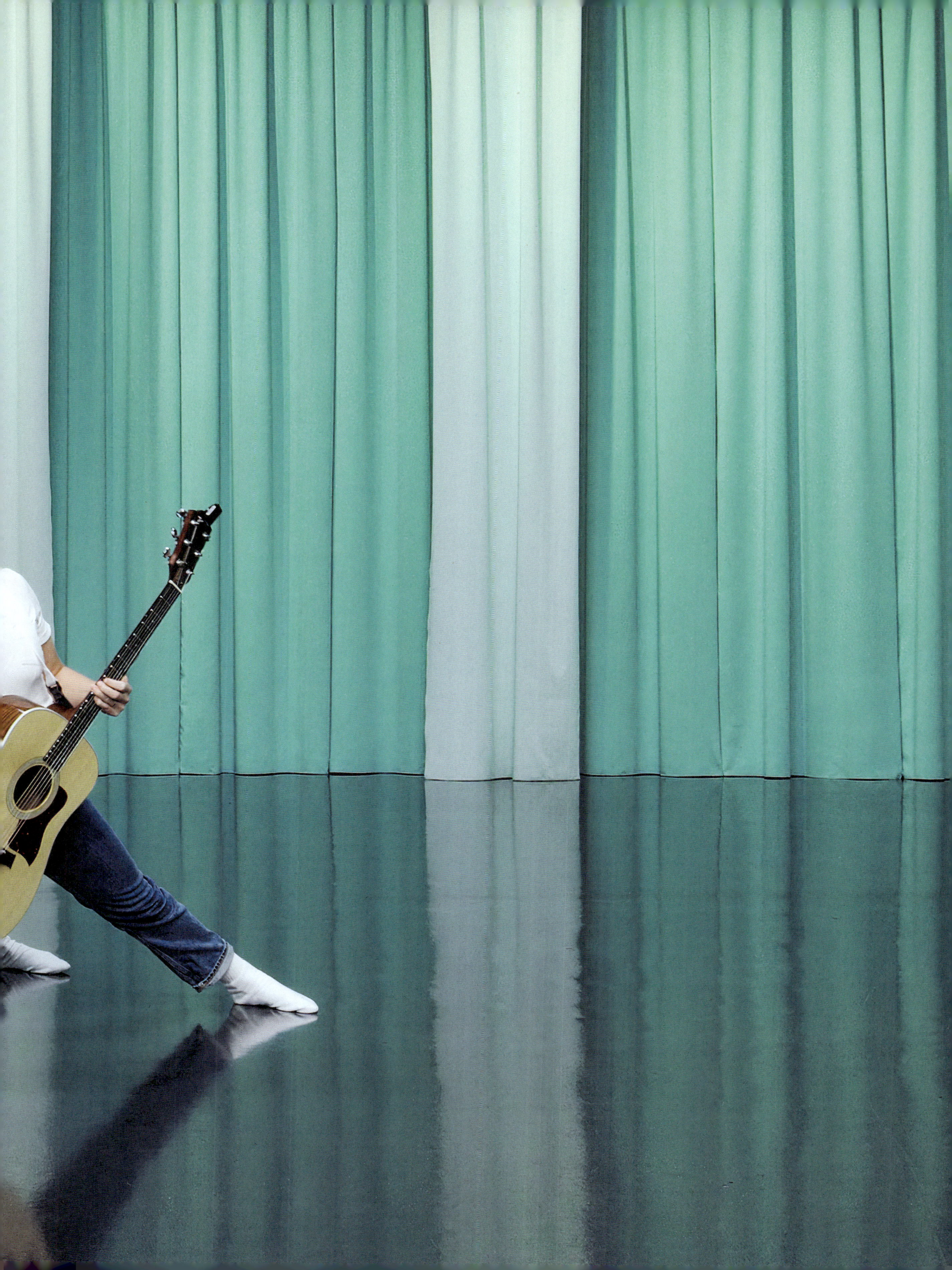

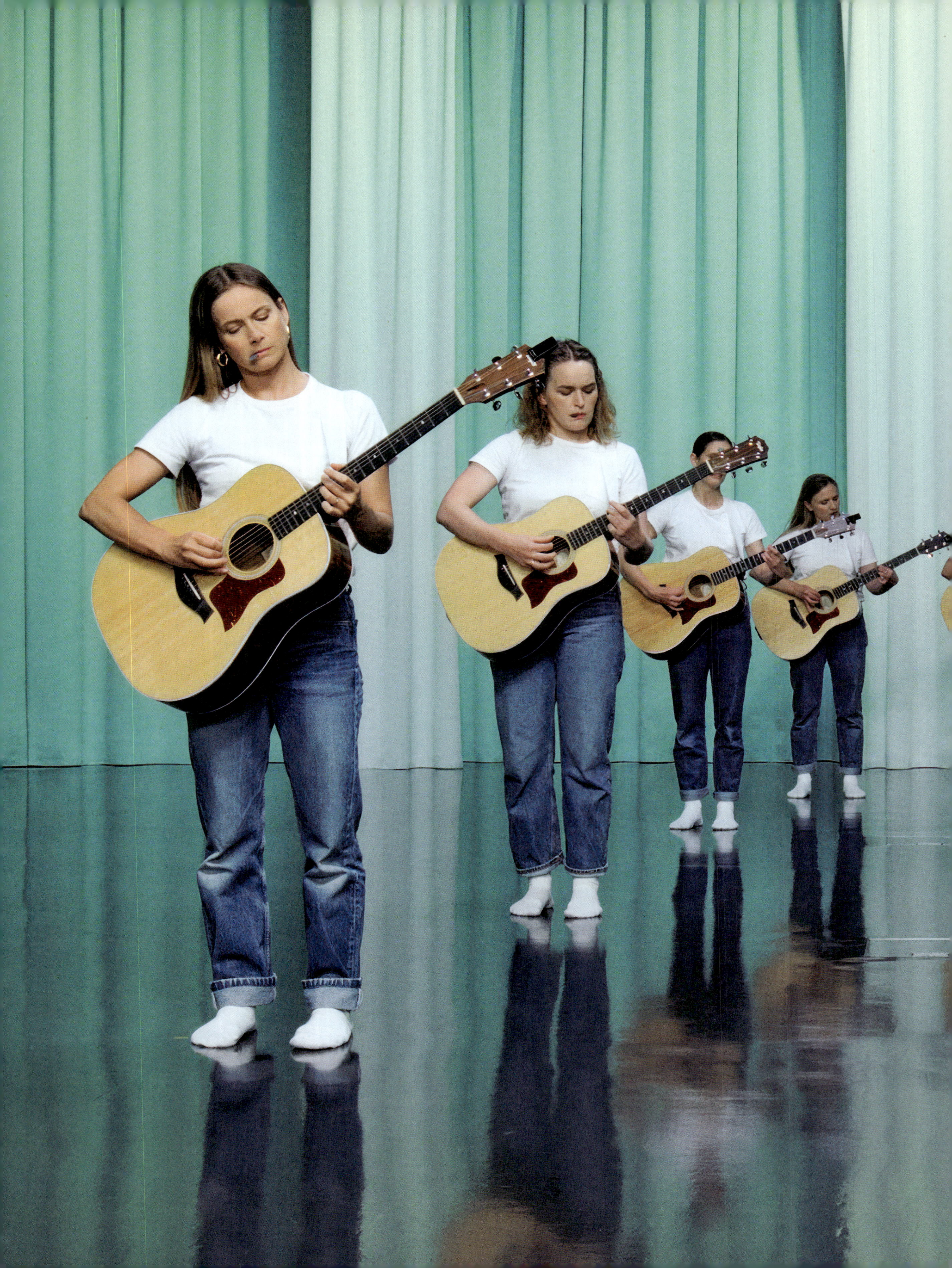

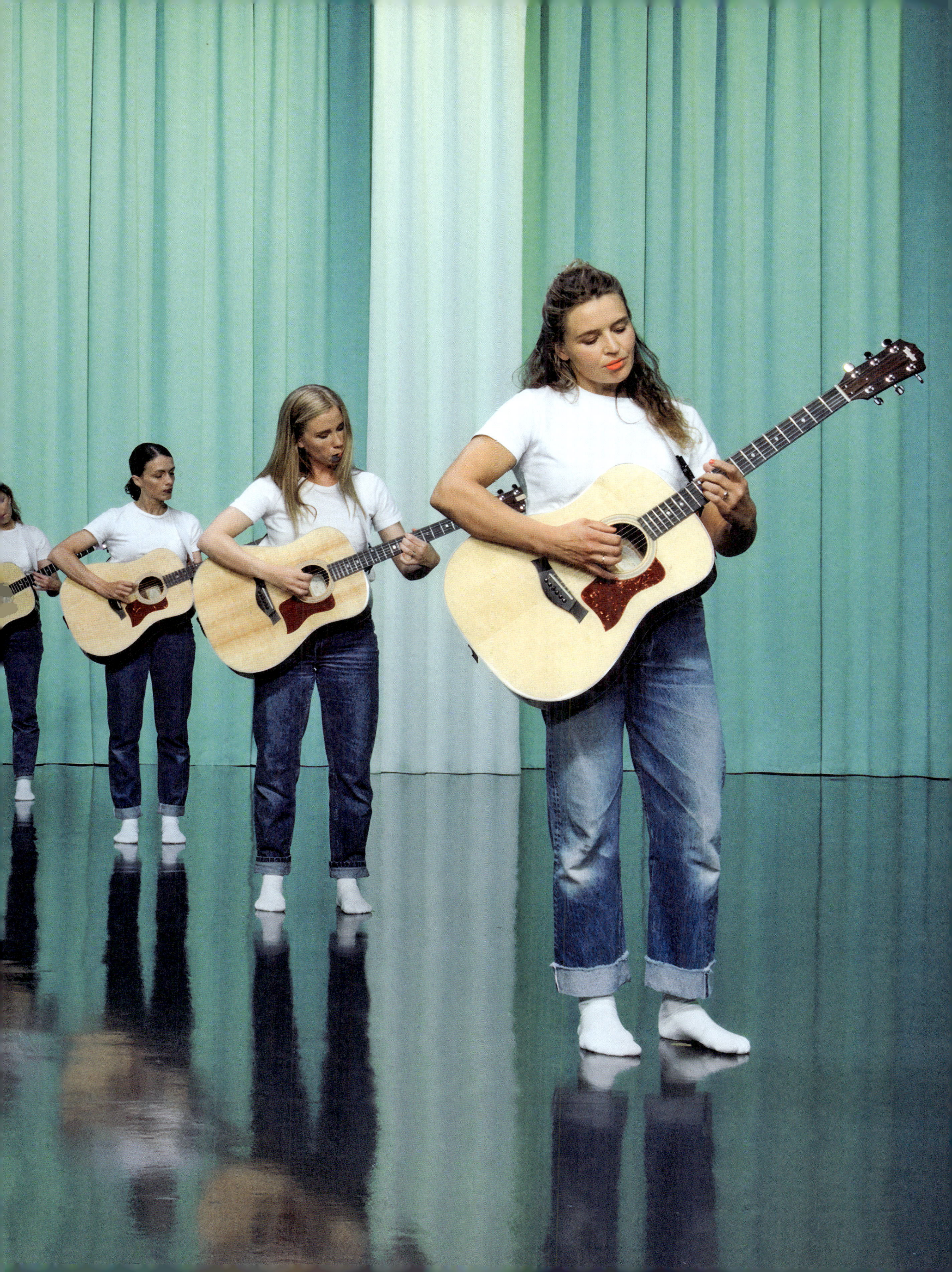

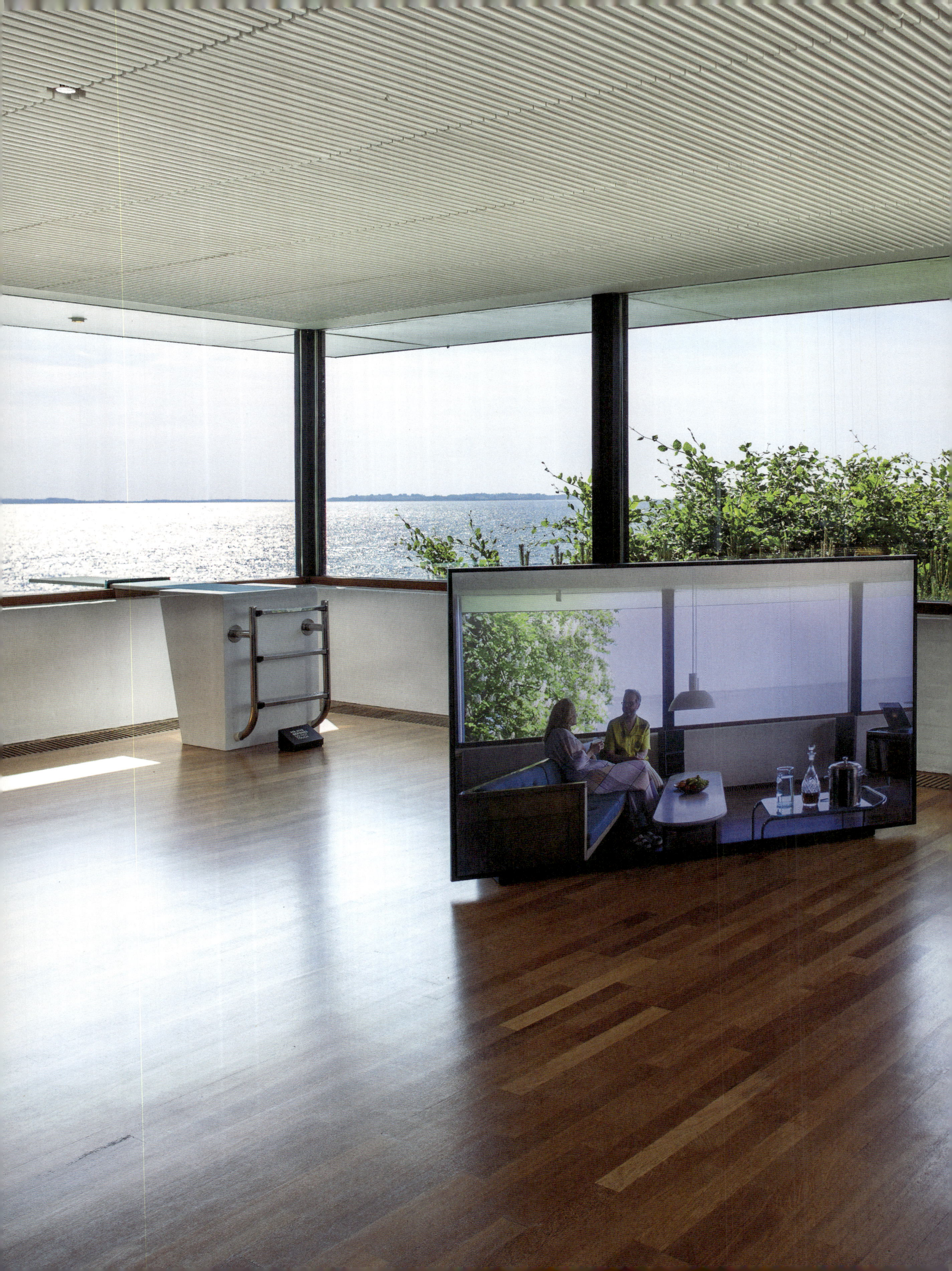

HVAD HAR VI DOG GJORT FOR AT HA' DET SÅ GODT — 2023

What Have We Done to Deserve This
Single-channel video
Duration: 11:05 hr.
Commissioned by Louisiana Museum of Modern Art, Humlebæk

By Tine Colstrup

The work is a filmed performance, 11 hours long, that took place at Louisiana Museum of Modern Art on 30 May 2023 in a panorama room with a view to Sweden across the Øresund strait. Icelandic actress Saga Garðarsdóttir (born 1987) and Ragnar Kjartansson play a Danish couple in a beautiful living room. All day long, they repeat a Danish happy-ironic phrase, which is also familiar in Iceland: "What have we done to deserve this?" In a field of tension between nihilism and *hygge*, we're left to ponder the answer ourselves, but typically for Kjartansson the work is an ambiguous cocktail of pathos and politics.

The scene is both a symbol of the best of Scandinavian welfare society and a tragicomic hint of its decadence. The couple's repeated affirmation becomes forced and slightly, to say the least, desperate, while the turntable plays a melodious yet minor-key Danish religious song, "Hver dag er en sjælden gave" ("Every day is a rare gift", 1939). It is sung by Icelandic-Danish singer Elsa Sigfúss (1908-1979) and is like the phrase "What have we done ...", one of many Danish imprints that still inhabits Icelandic culture.

TINE COLSTRUP is curator at Louisiana Museum of Modern Art and curated *Epic Waste of Love and Understanding*.

Opposite page: Installation view, Louisiana Museum of Modern Art, 2023. In the panorama room where the performance was filmed, and where it is displayed during the exhibition, the springboard sculpture is a permanent installation by Elmgreen & Dragset: *Powerless Structures, Fig. 11* (1997)
Following spreads: Stills from *Hvad har vi dog gjort for at ha' det så godt*, 2023

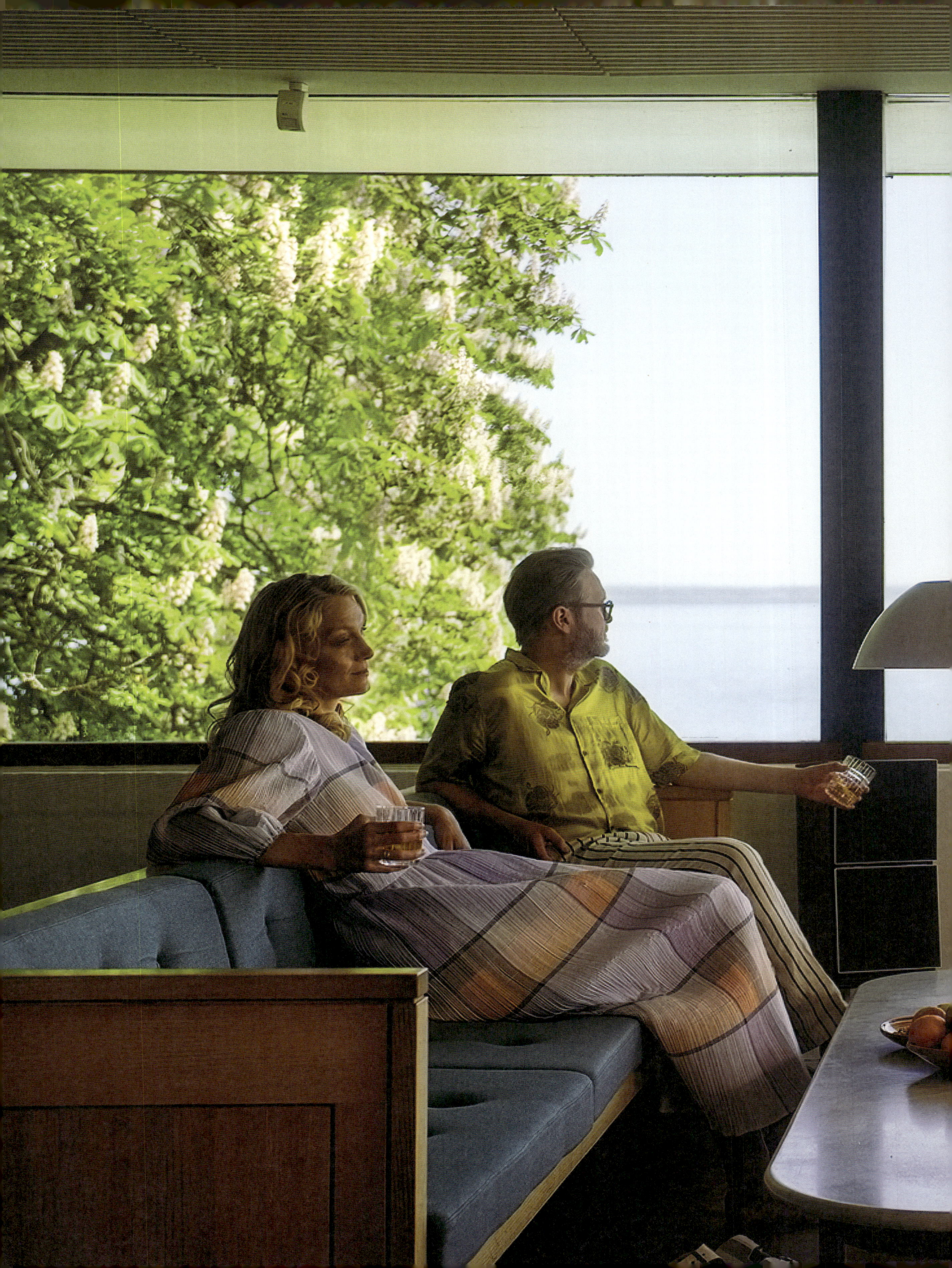

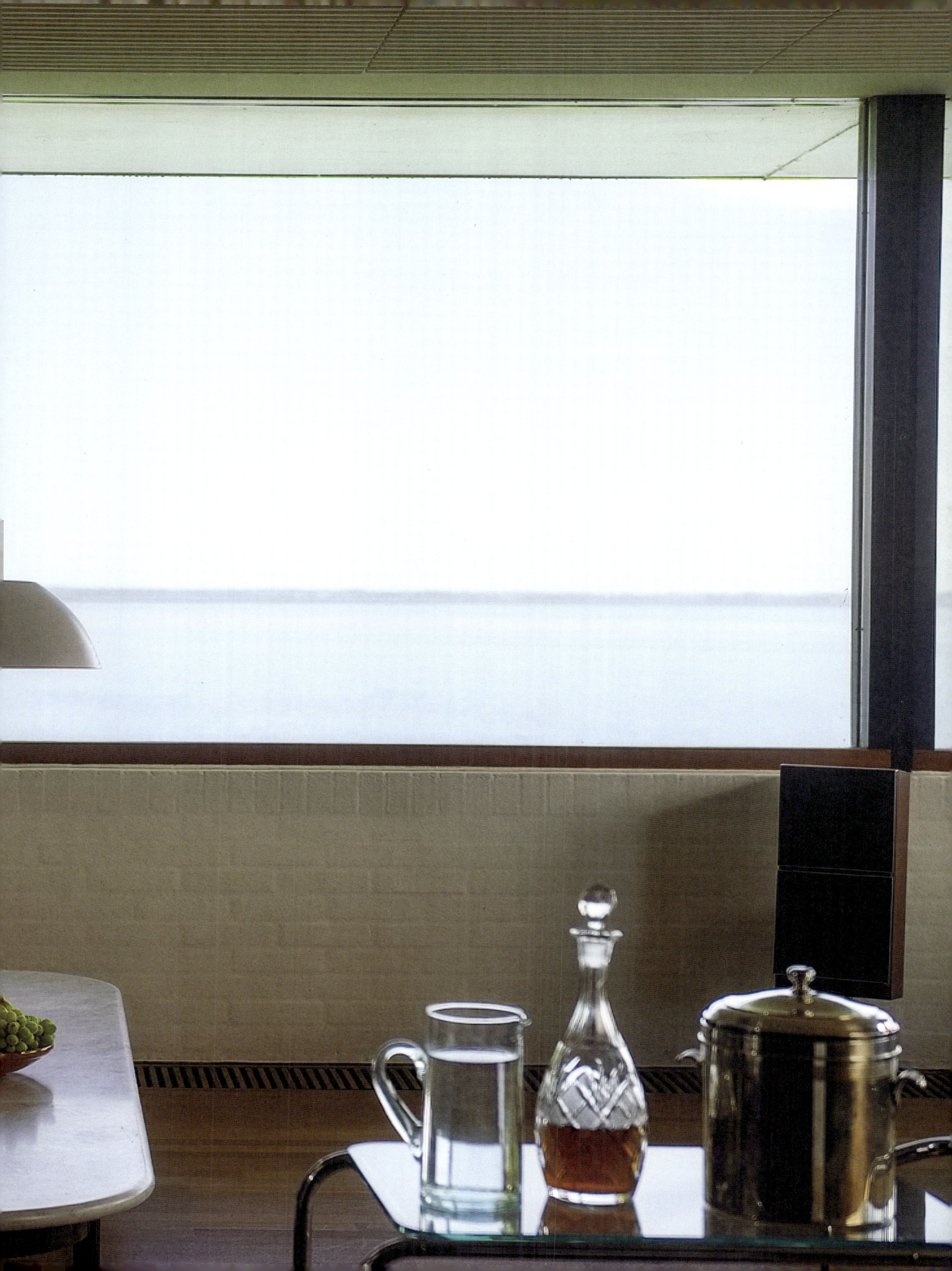

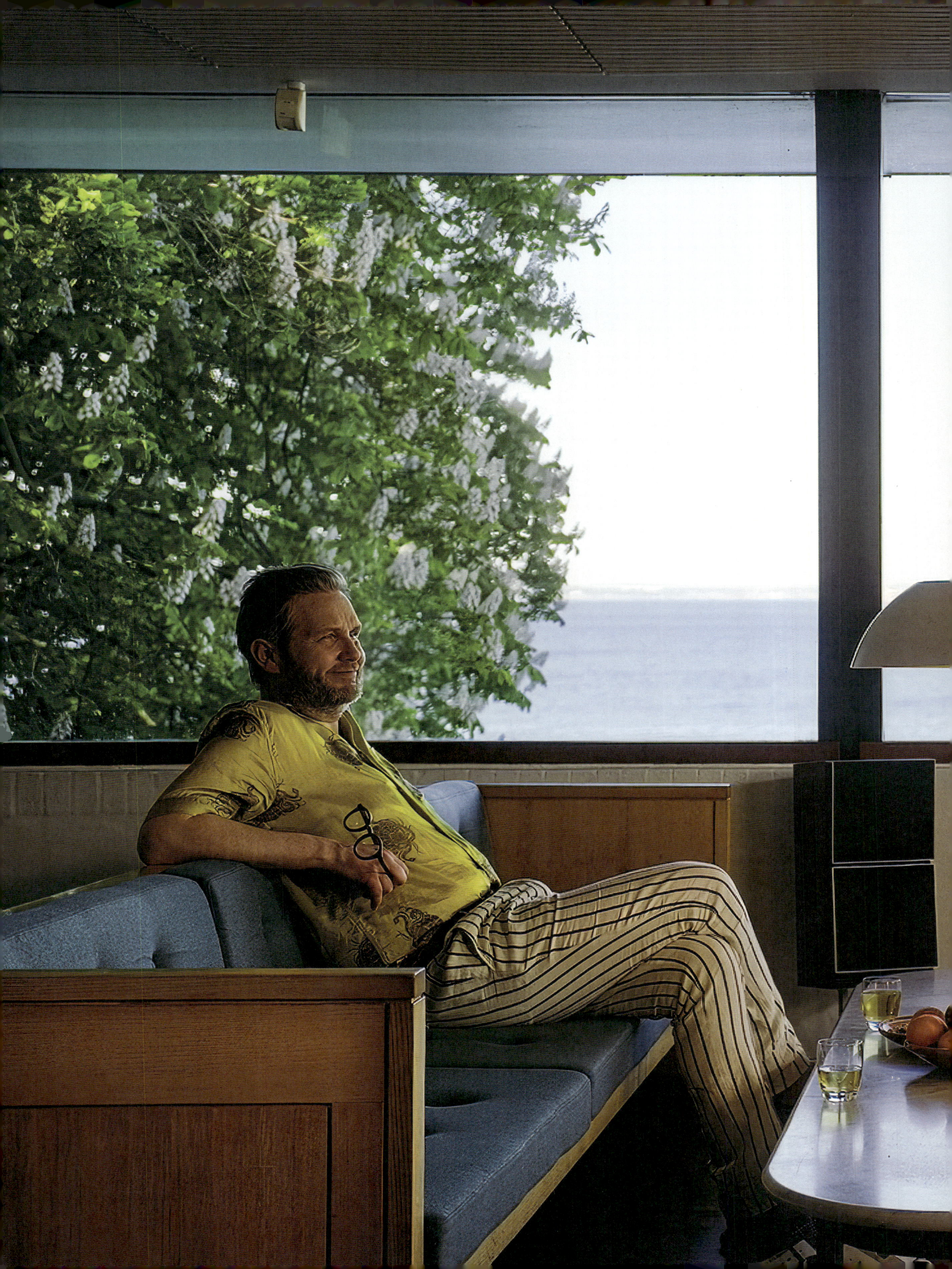

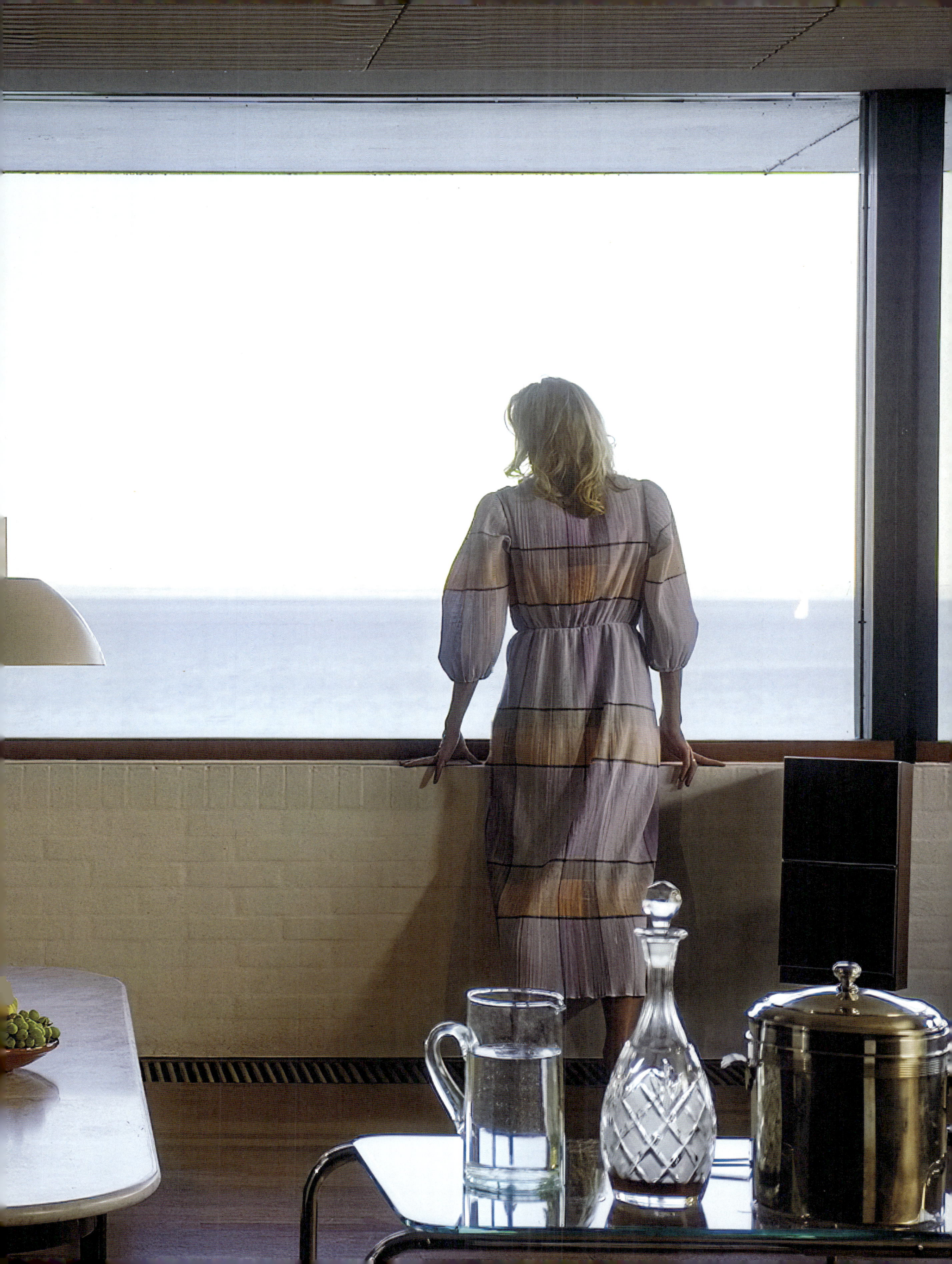

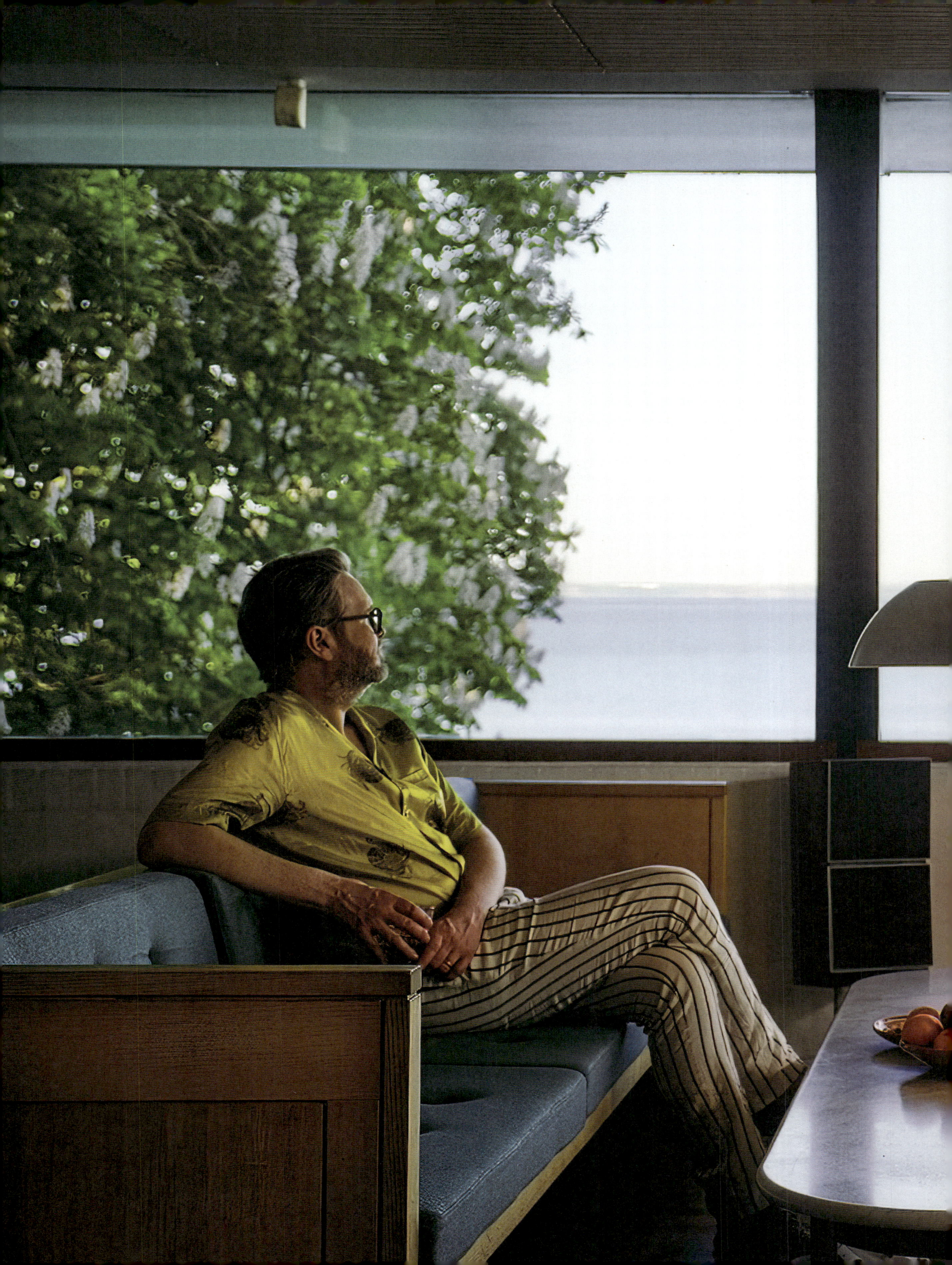

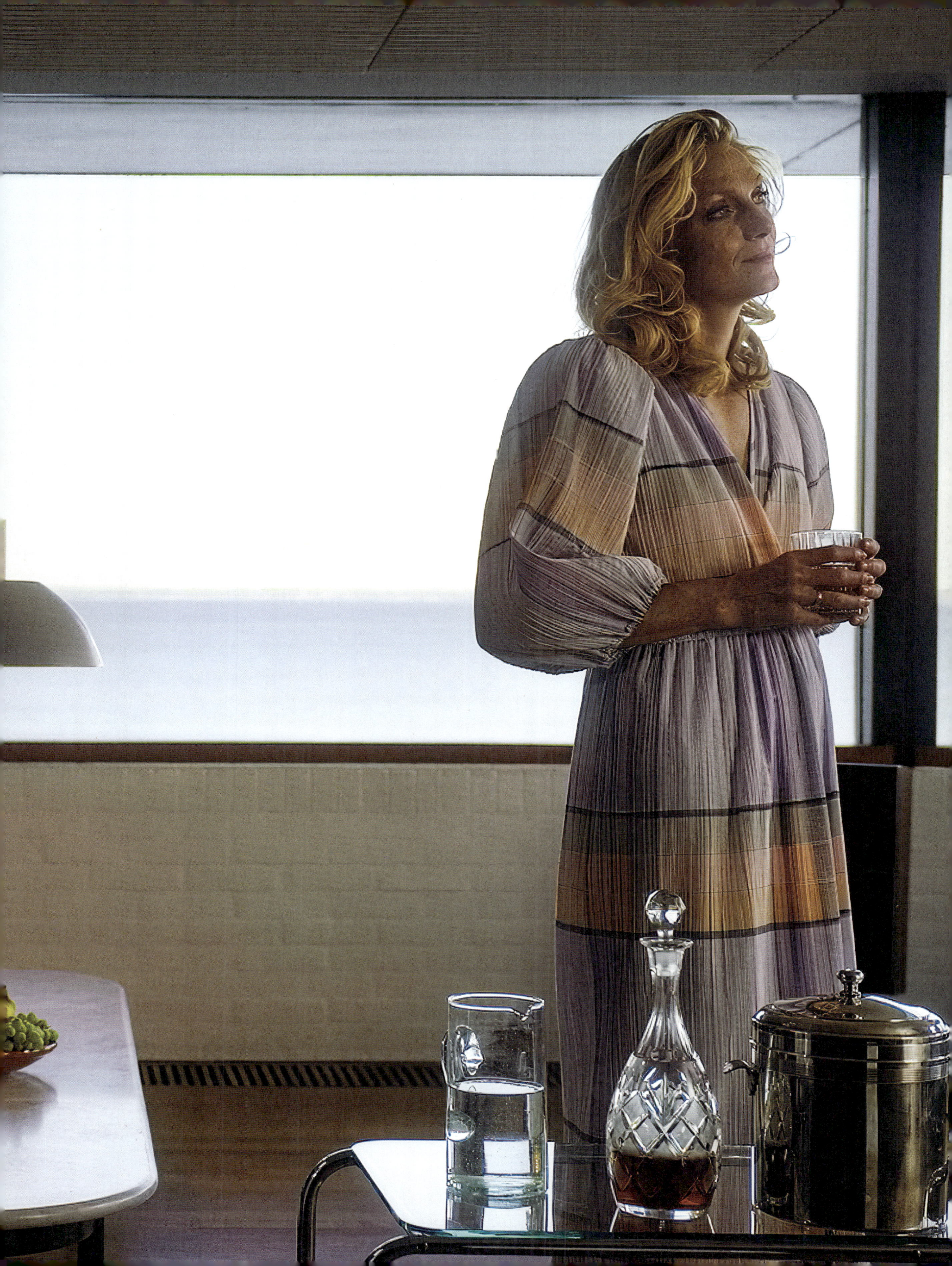

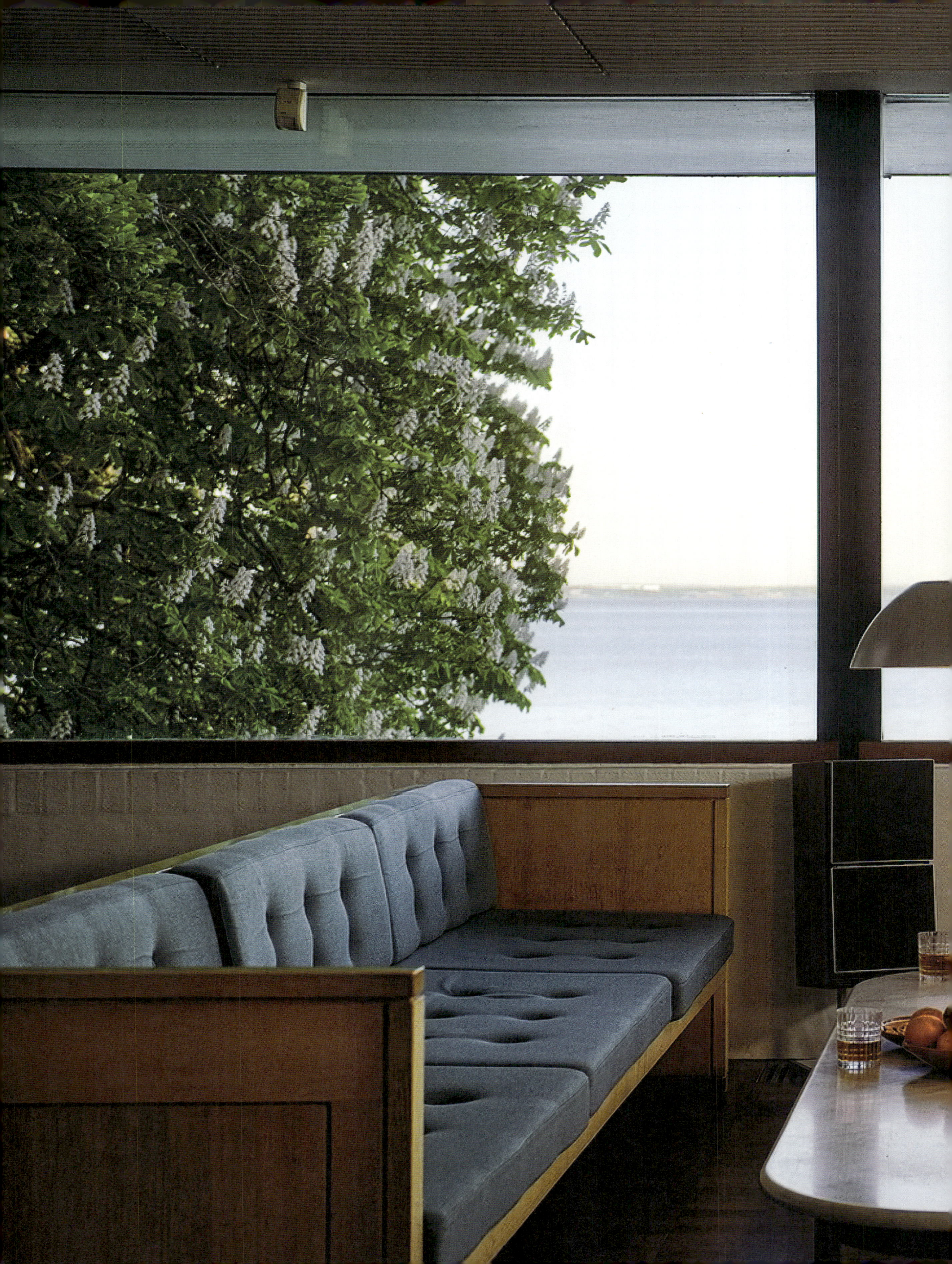

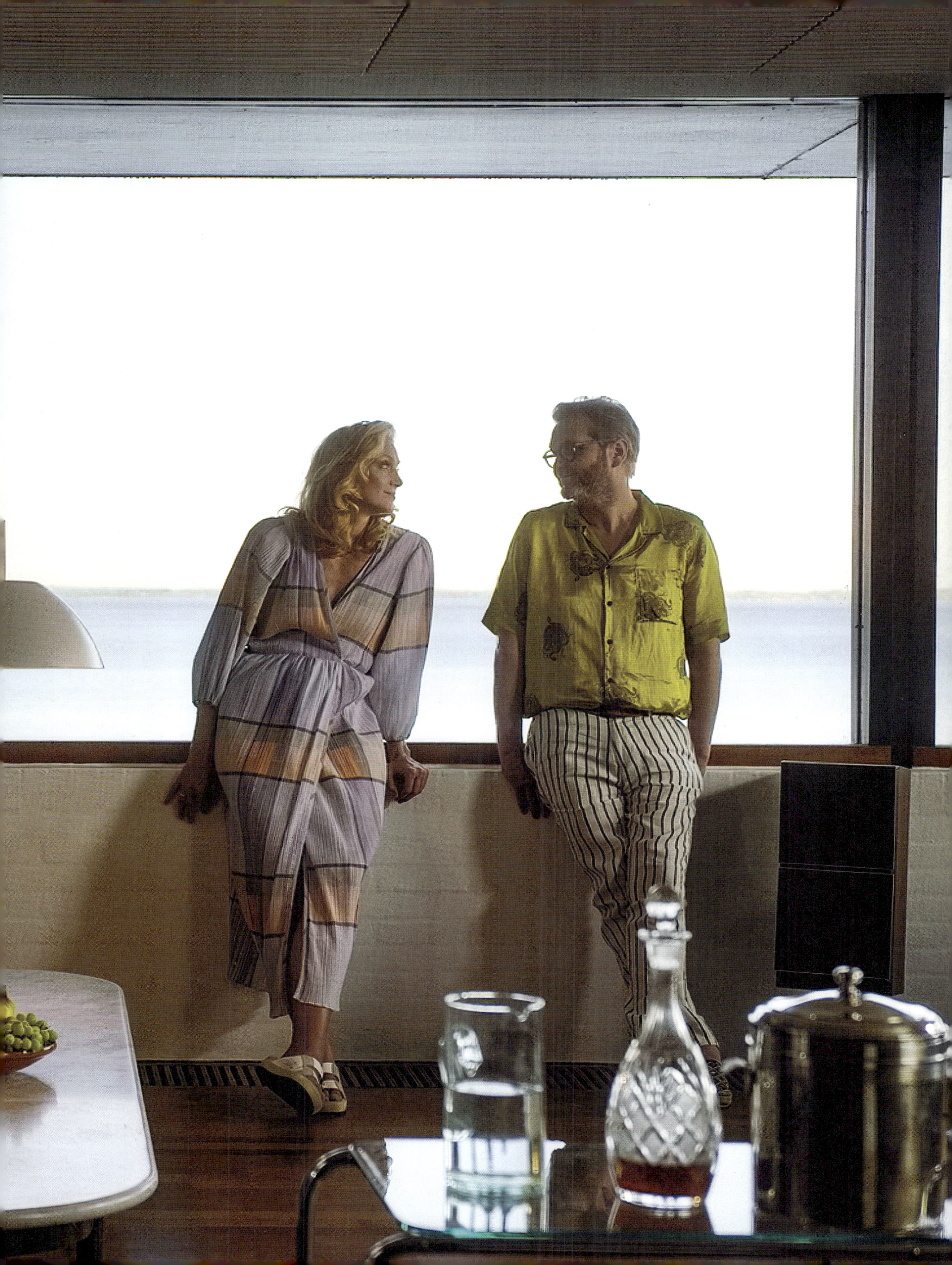

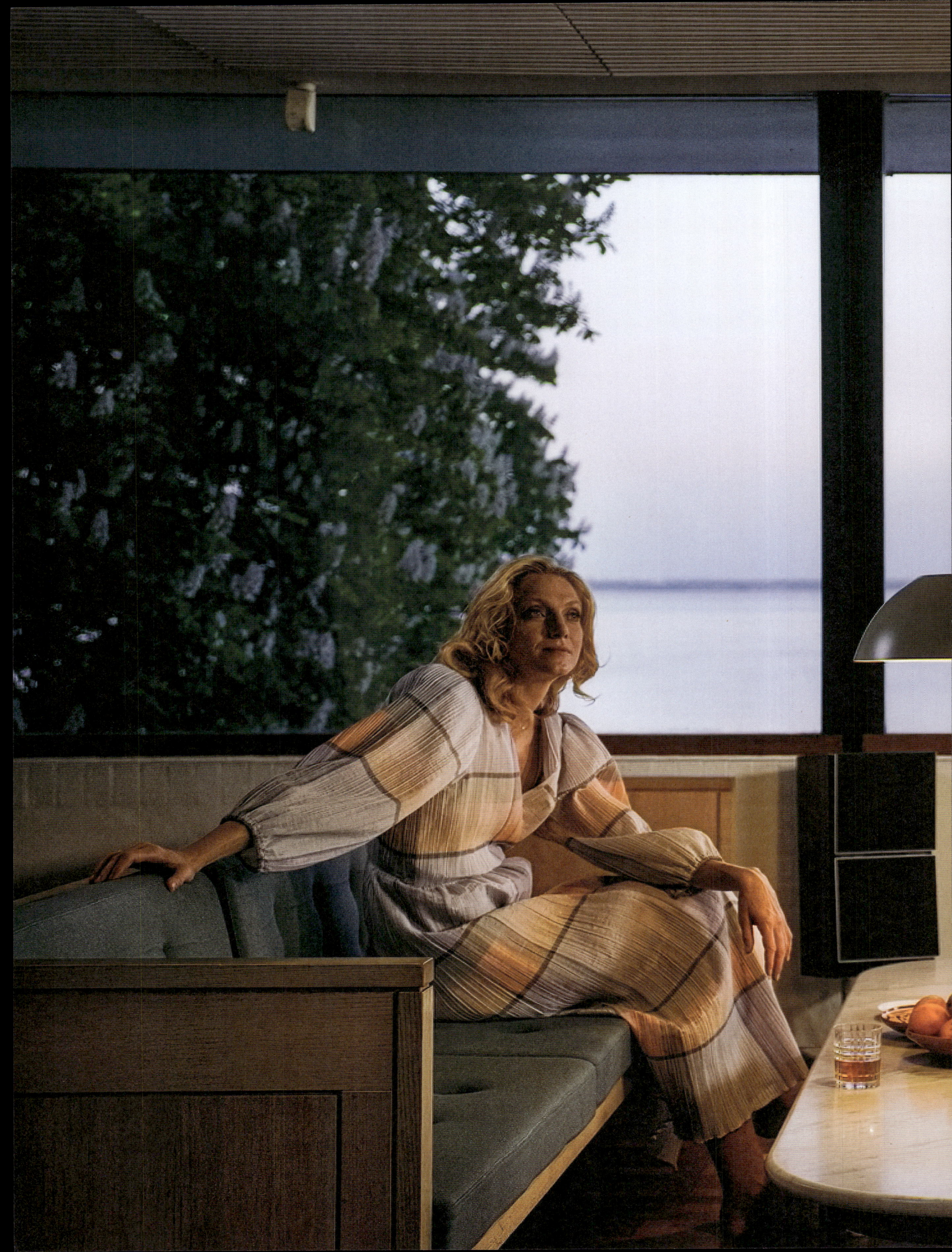

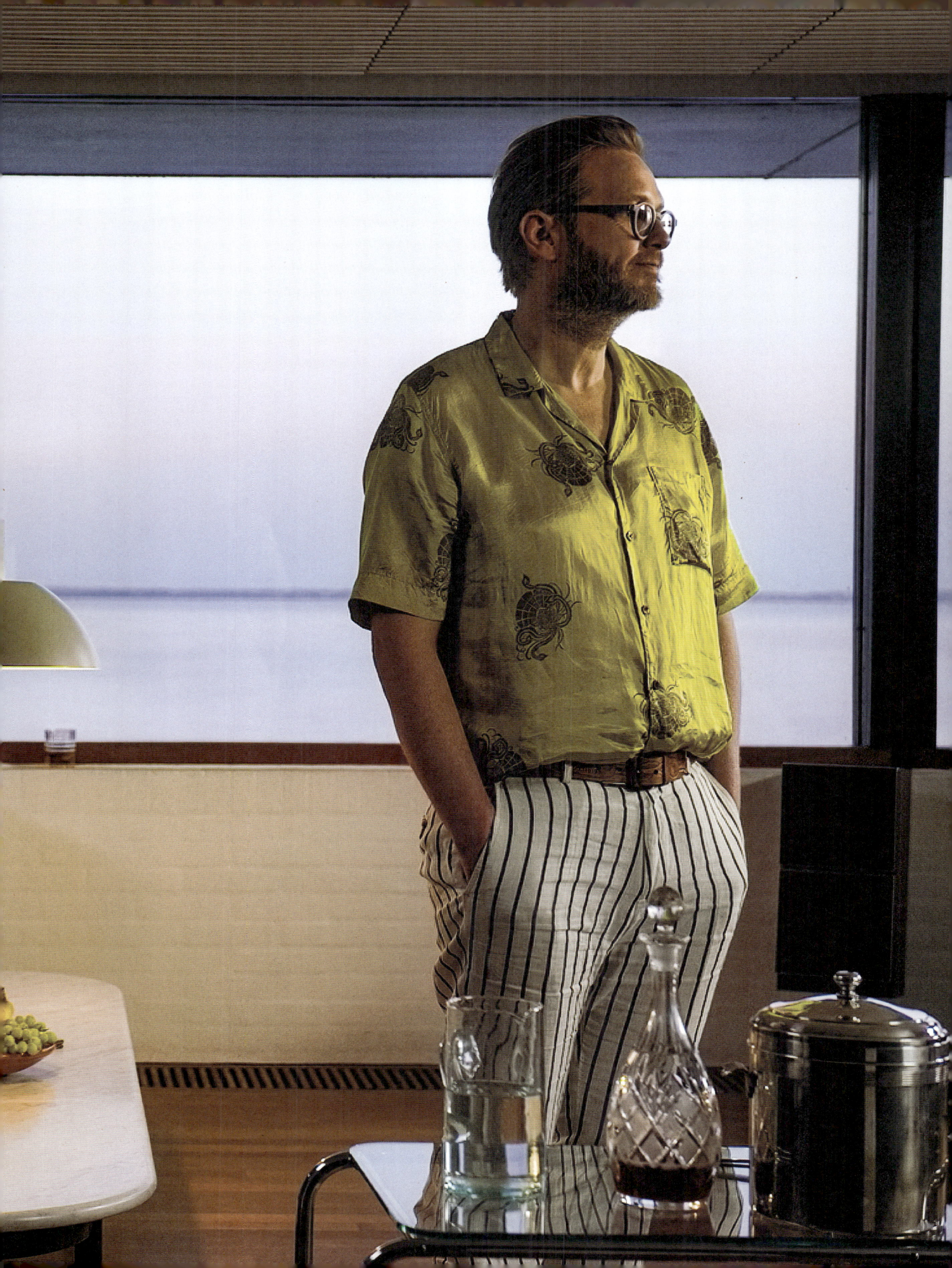

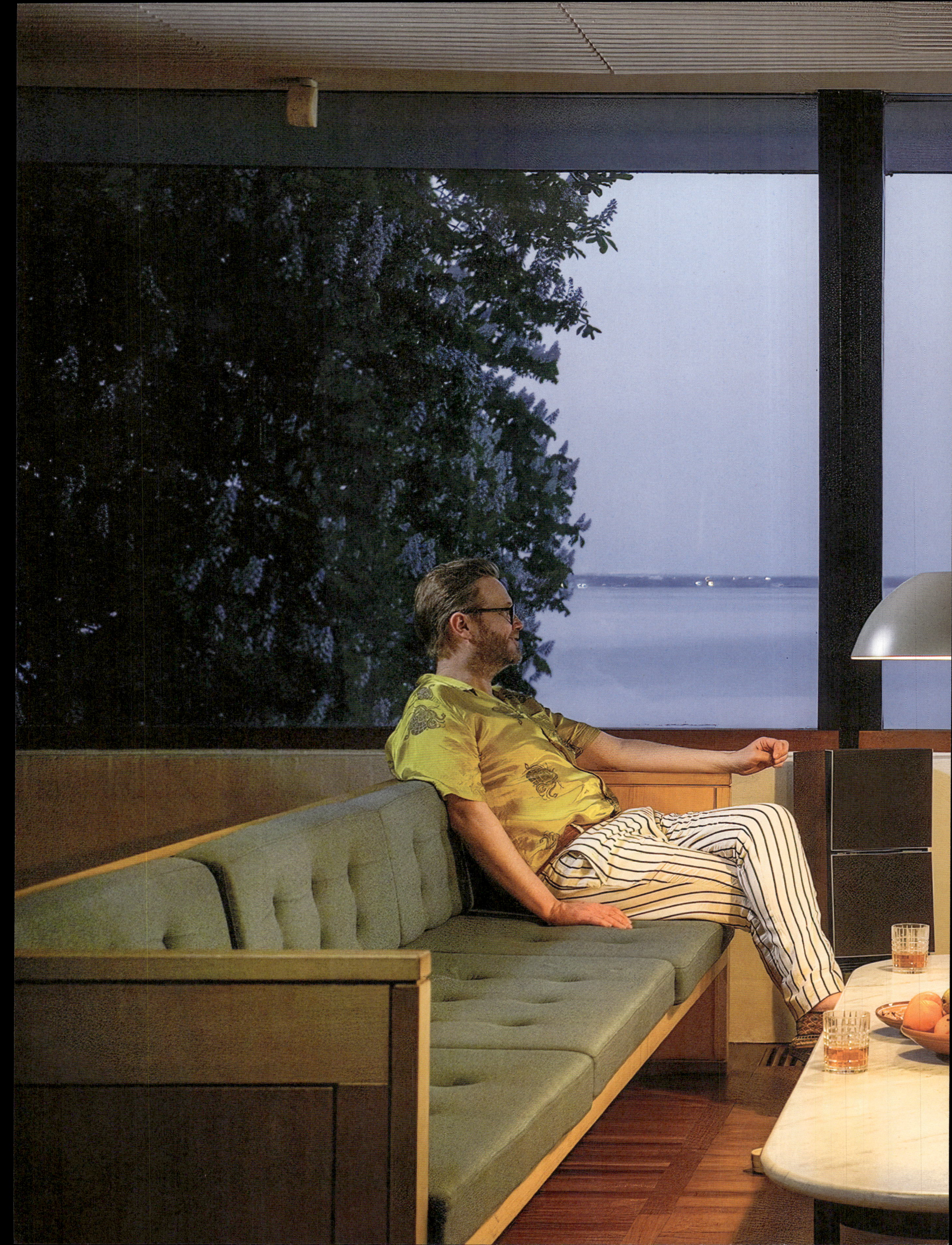

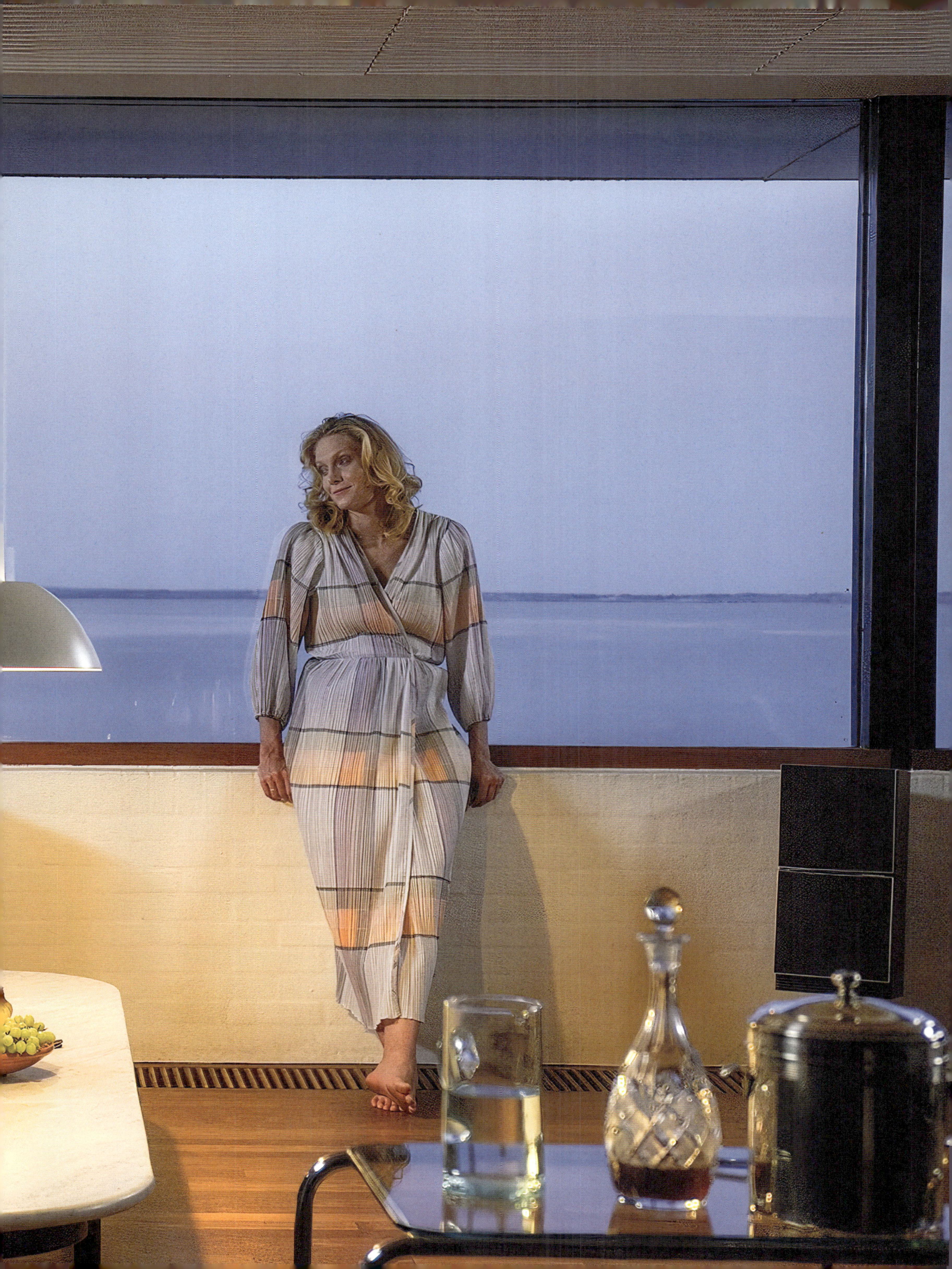

BLISS — 2020

Single-channel video
Duration: 11:59 hr.
Recorded at REDCAT as part of Los Angeles Philharmonic's Fluxus Festival curated by Christopher Roundtree 25 May 2019, originally a commission for Performa 11
AMA Collection, Venezia

By Tine Colstrup

When entering the exhibition at Louisiana you hear the repeated lines "Oh, why do I keep on hurting you", from the work *Mercy* (2004). You leave the exhibition with a symbol of a Sisyphean state of wrongdoing and forgiveness in the work *Bliss*. Here, a short excerpt from the final scene in Wolfgang Amadeus Mozart's opera *The Marriage of Figaro* from 1786 is repeated non-stop for 12 hours.

The famous scene is a distillation of dramatic emotions: guilt, shame, desire, humiliation, anger, forgiveness and reconciliation. The count begs his wife for forgiveness for his lust for other women. Being more docile than him, as she remarks, the countess forgives him. The chorus rushes to smooth things over, singing that now all is forgiven, happiness may last forever! The mood, however, is tense.

Kjartansson himself is part of the ensemble, playing the part of the drunken gardener Antonio (with the dead hare). He has described the scene as a portrait of the patriarchy, with the man being forgiven again and again – in this piece *ad absurdum*.

TINE COLSTRUP is curator at Louisiana Museum of Modern Art and curated *Epic Waste of Love and Understanding*.

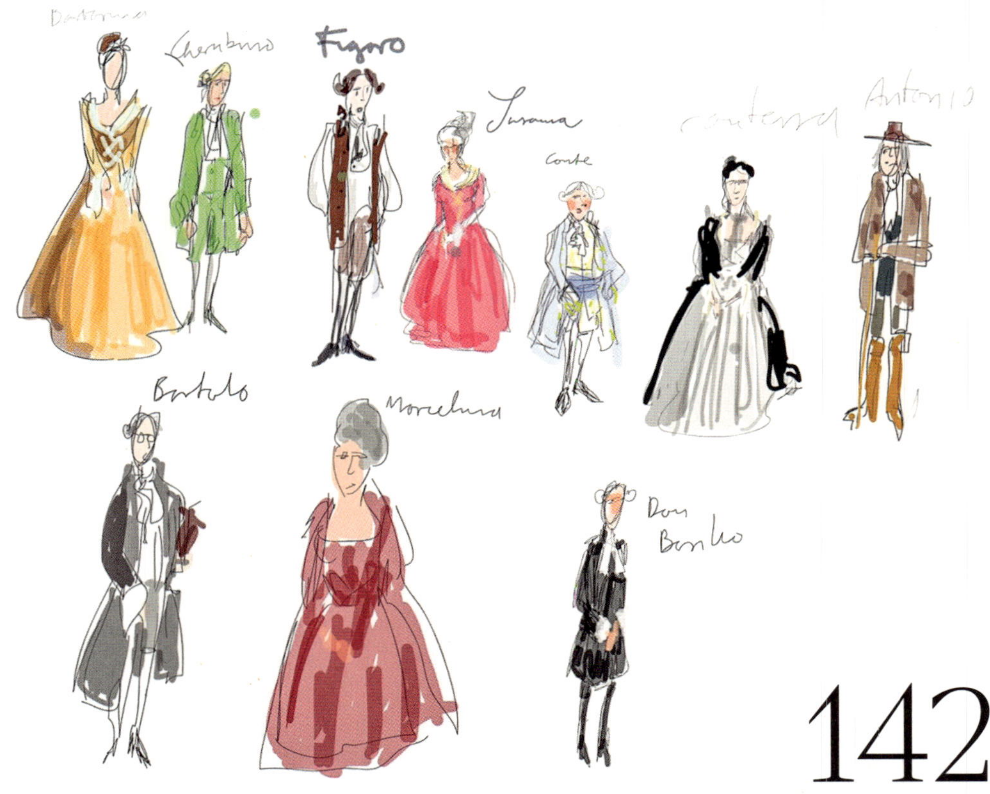

Drawing by Ragnar Kjartansson, 2011
Opposite page: Stills from *Bliss*, 2020

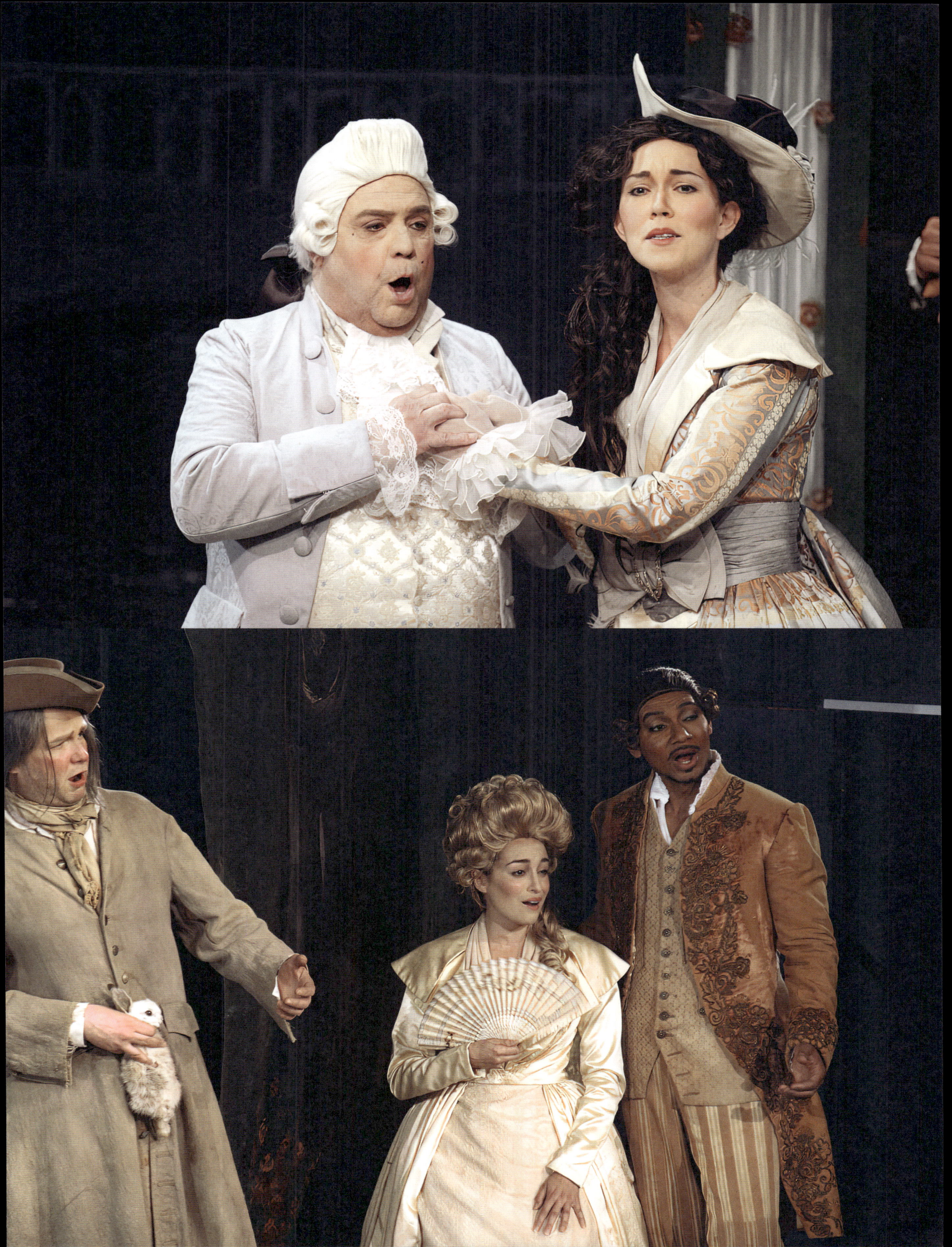

CONTE [*inginocchiandosi*]
Contessa perdono! Perdono, perdono!

CONTESSA
Più docile sono,
e dico di sì.

TUTTI
Ah! Tutti contenti
saremo così.

COUNT [*kneeling*]
Countess, your pardon! Pardon!

COUNTESS
I am more docile,
and answer, yes.

ALL
Ah! All happy
we will be like this.

Le nozze di Figaro (The Marriage of Figaro):
Libretto, Act Four, No. 28: Finale (excerpt)

Music by Wolfgang Amadeus Mozart, libretto by Lorenzo Da Ponte, 1786

Opposite page: Stills from *Bliss*, 2020
The following spread: Installation view, Louisiana Museum of Modern Art, 2023

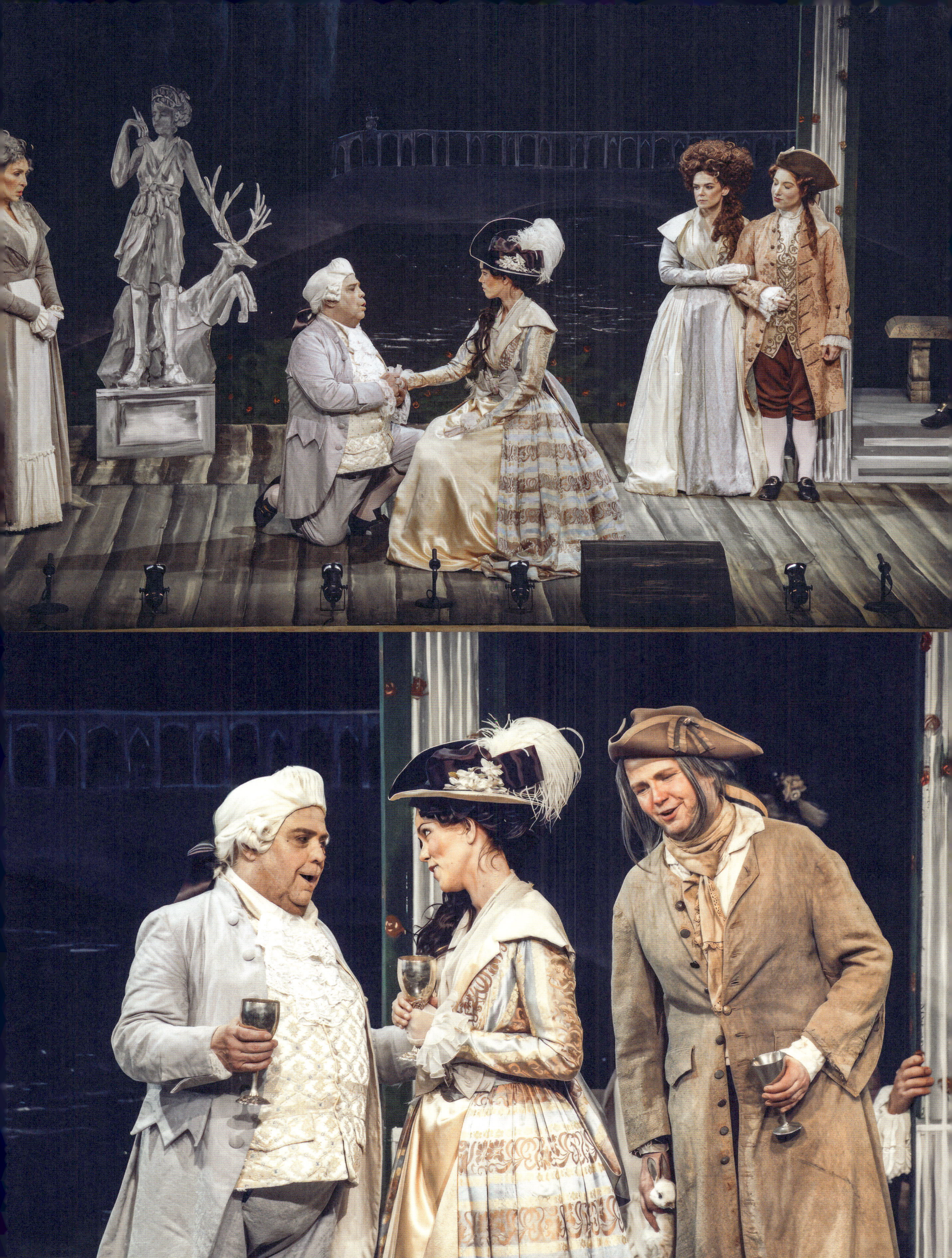

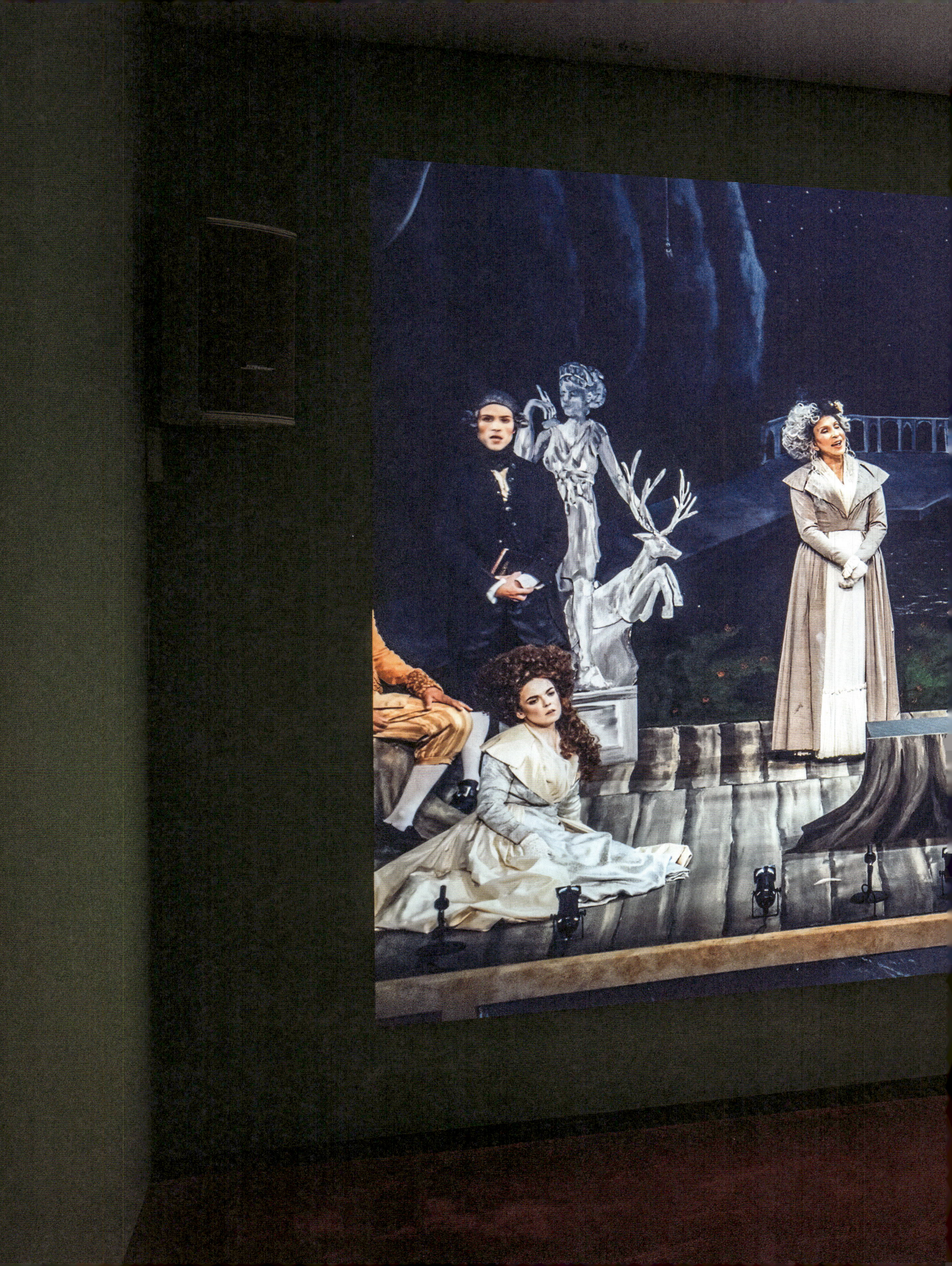

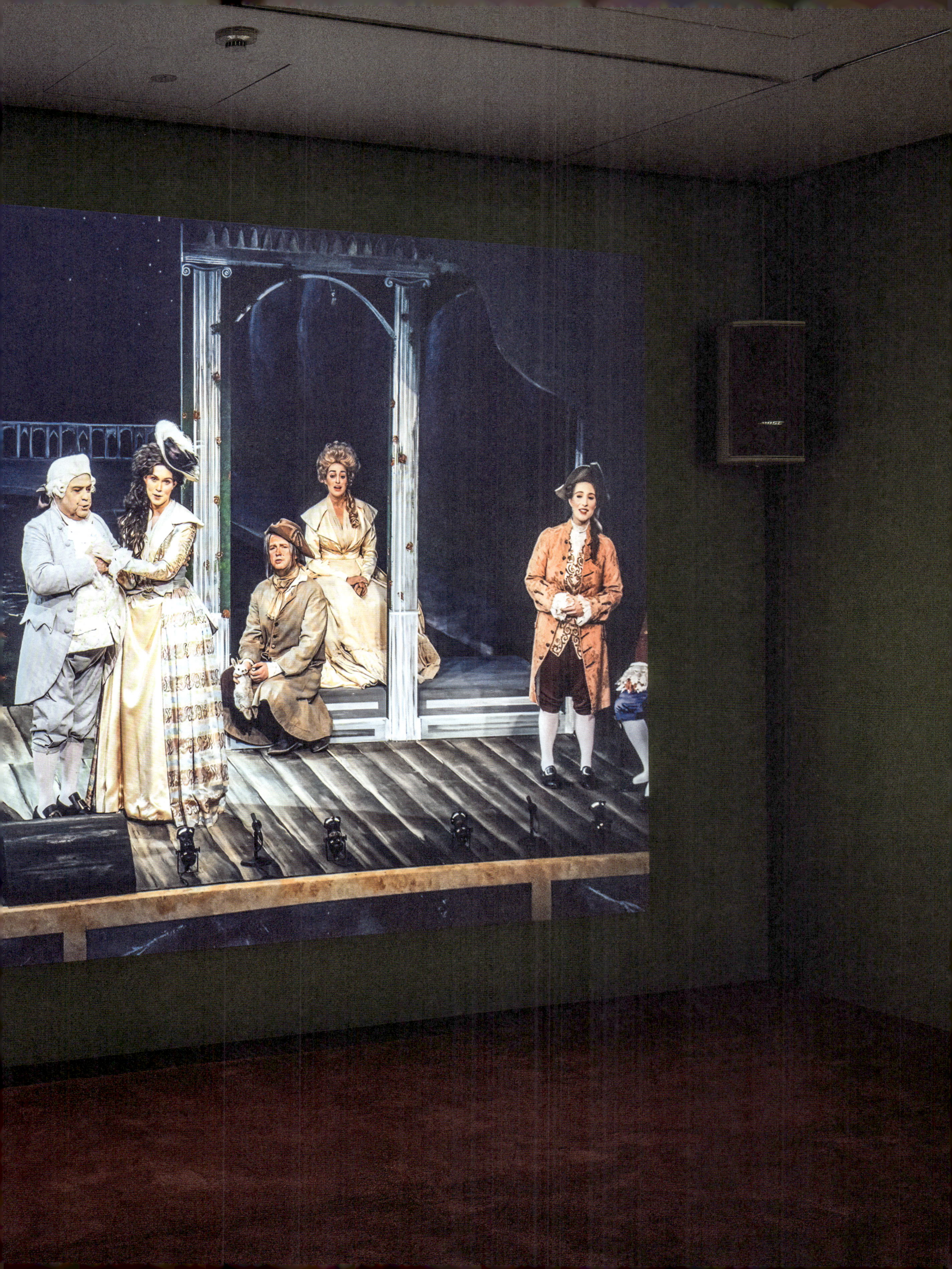

SCANDINAVIAN PAIN — 2006-2012

Neon, aluminium
57.6 × 1,219 × 20 cm
National Gallery of Iceland, Reykjavik

By Jonatan Habib Engqvist

"Success is only preparation for the next failure."
– August Strindberg (1849-1912)

Constantly trying to save nature from man, and adapting reality to the system instead of the other way around; a cliche culture of melancholia, suicide, silence, intoxication and a breeding season ... Perhaps the Nordic pathology has new meaning in contemporary society? Maybe this culture can transfigure several pathological states of mind that characterise a neoliberal society currently experiencing something like a dark Nordic December without snow. Don't those shadowy page-turners, laconic works by Halldór Laxness (1902-1998), films by Aki Kaurismäki (born 1957) or Ingmar Bergman (1918-2007), or Norwegian black metal, *The Girl with the Dragoon Tattoo* (2005) and Danish thrillers that have reached international acclaim, portray something of relevance for our time?

Indeed, the self-chosen attitude of Scandinavian melancholia, where we only live two months a year, calmly seems to declare that work which receives economic compensation, but no other vital justification, is sucking up life in Western society. It asks why we are working and for whom do we suffer. From a post-welfare state condition where the visions of a better society in the future might be behind us, this soft Northern whisper suggests that life-projects are impossible under the regime of unbearable employment markets, where not even large corporations expect sustainable long-term profit. The significance of the politically depressed emerges: if you're not 'living the dream', you virtually need a religious conviction, a belief in the afterlife, a new age vision, or consider other occult dimensions of reality for life to have any meaning.

Furthermore, the sentiment of this geographic and cultural seclusion can be described as a form of tunnel vision, providing yet another prospect on our predicament. While technological development encourages individualism and simultaneously cultivates segregated communities into which we can escape through a personalised internet, the cookies and matching metadata algorithms create filter-bubbles and you-loops, which collect and deploy data in a manner that determines not only what we find online, but also what we look for. Laxness writes, "a man finds what he seeks, and he who believes in a ghost finds a ghost".

It is only in this darkness we can find the fairy-tale-like glow that affirms the pious, self-righteous clarity and silent feast – and ecstatic states of exception created by apartment-isolated winter life. A mysterious radiance, albeit of hopelessness, that shows other forces, another vitality, which might save us from zombie-life or suffocating from despair.

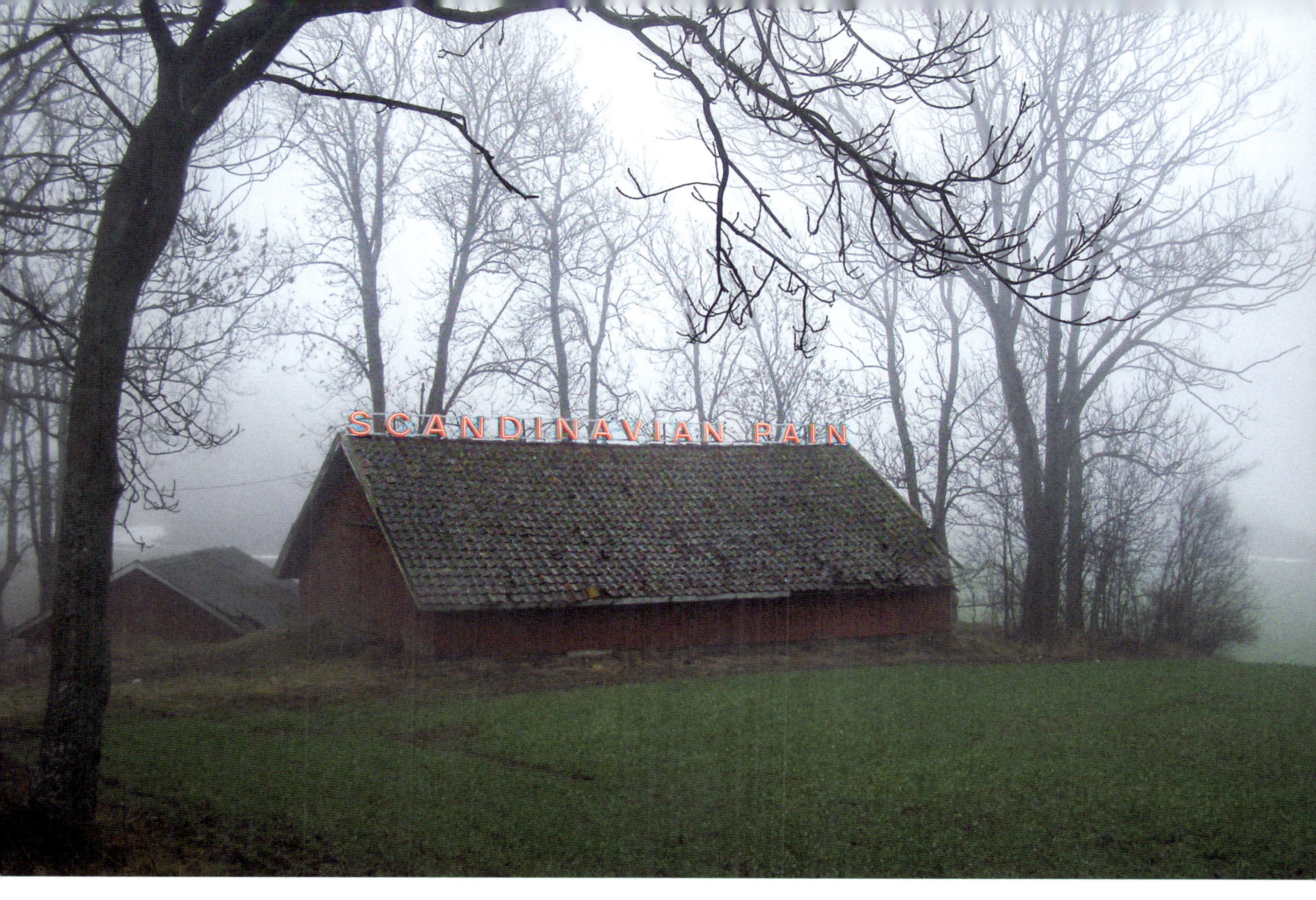

In many of Ragnar Kjartansson's repetitious works (he once told me that artists only make the same work over, and over, and over again) there is a kind of tainted magical realism, with its own variations and language of culturally historic laden terms like melancholia, the fantastic, realism, loneliness, and the pre-individual collectiveness of Dionysus. And by cannibalising the Nordic myth, *Scandinavian Pain* speaks of hopelessness, yet also reveals its transfiguration into 'magic', absurdity, and humour: a strategy with the potential to create a cultural machine that can turn the hopelessness of contemporary reality into a form of intelligence.

JONATAN HABIB ENGQVIST is a Swedish author and curator. He is also an editor as well as an occasional teacher.

Installation view, Momentum, 2006
The following spread: Installation view, Louisiana Museum of Modern Art, 2023

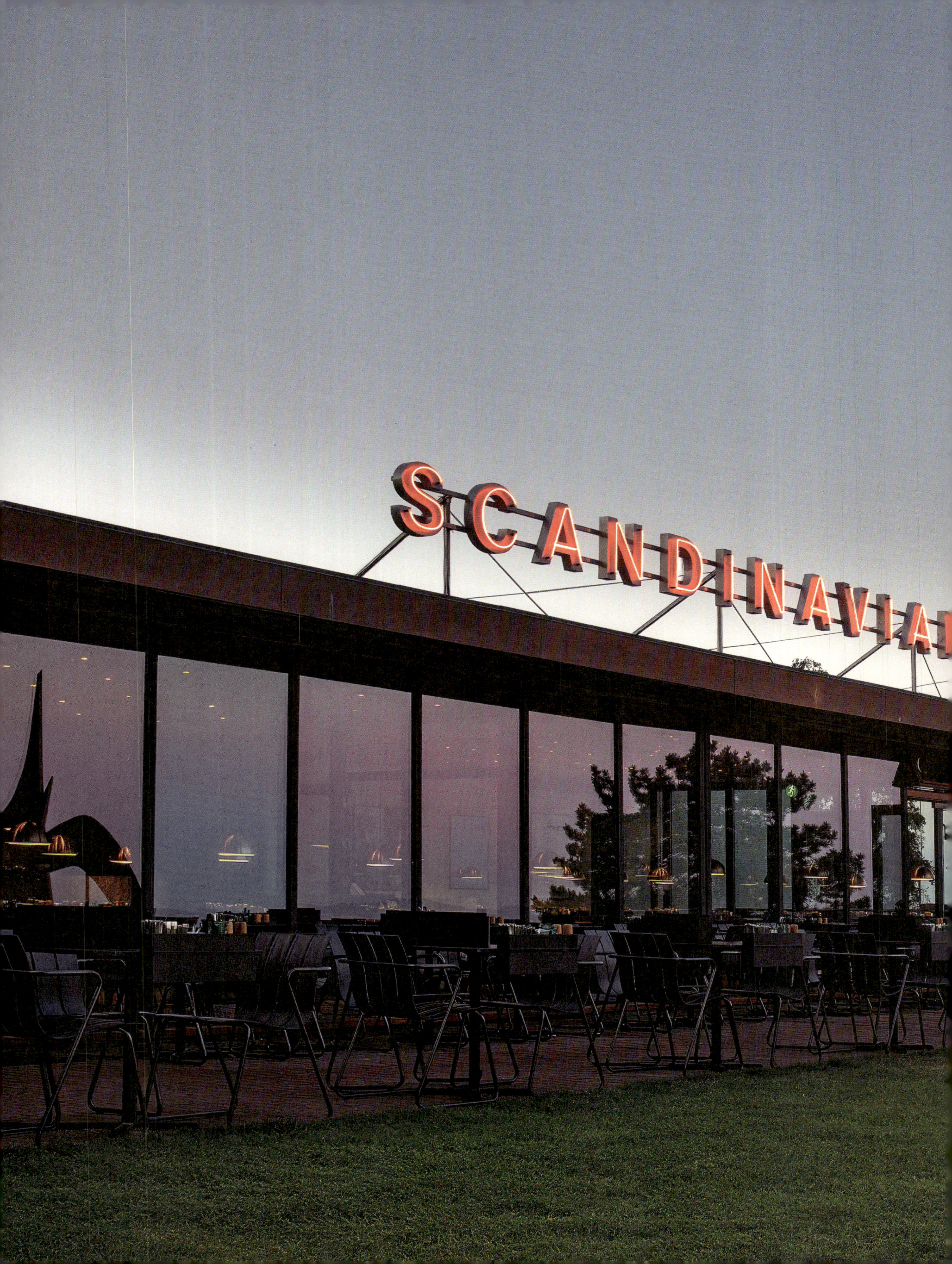
SCANDINAVIA

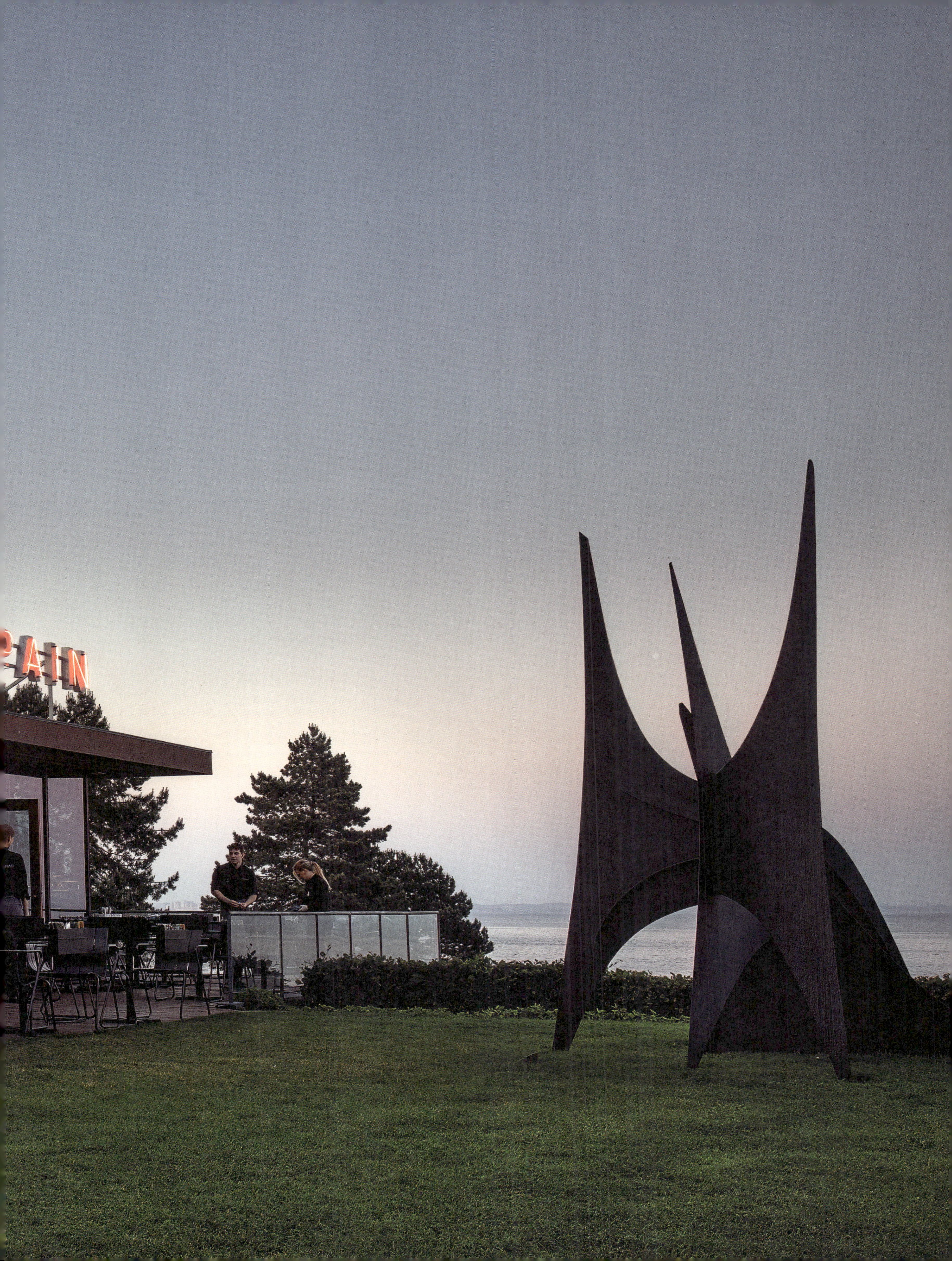
PAIN

"I CAN'T SEE 'EM COMIN' DOWN MY EYES, SO I GOTTA MAKE THE SONG CRY"

By Ragnar Kjartansson

The power of a song is a suspended idea of something deeply human. A room becomes alight when the record spins or digits explode. In the 21st century, every space is song. Song is seeping through every moment of our lives like water. Imagine when song was just performed, just confined to the space and time of a performance. My godmother was an artist in that time. Recording techniques were new and vulgar to her. The idea of "hyggemusik" from a speaker in a restaurant – an insult to Apollo.

I learned the power of song from my Danish godmother, Engel Lund (1900-1996). She was born in Reykjavik, on Bastille Day in the year 1900. She was daughter of the pharmacist couple in Reykjavik, Michael Lars Lund and Emilie Marie Magdalene Hansen. Reykjavík Apotek was situated on Reykjavik's main square, with a view to Bertel Thorvaldsen's (1770-1844) statue and the newly built parliament crowned with Christian IX's (1818-1906) crown.

Her youth was one of bliss in this makeshift Danish town on the edge of the world. Her father would entertain the family with playing Zeus, lying on a cupboard with a duvet under him and a silver fork as his stick of reign. Her parents would attend costume balls at the governor-general's or *landshöfding* mansion. A 17th century cello belonging to the French baron Charles Gauldrée-Boilleau (1863-1901) was stored at the home. The baron was a mystery man who held the first classical concert to 200 awestruck souls in Reykjavik where he played his Cappa di Saluzzo cello. But the baron was destined for doomed business ventures in Iceland and shot himself, penniless on a train in outside London in 1901. But the cello was always there in the corner of the home. A swan in hibernation. Engel often talked about that cello and the mystery of what became of it. Engel came to study music and became a singer of *Lieder* and folksongs and had a long and eventful career in Europe in between the wars and until 1960. Always dressed in black, she lived sparsely in hotel rooms and sang the songs of the world, mostly Icelandic and Jewish folk songs with her collaborator, the pianist Ferdinand Rauter (1902-1987).

Just take a listen to her singing *Guð gaf mér eyra*. An ancient Icelandic children's psalm of how God gave us our eyes, ears and tongue to communicate to the beauty of the world.

Engel reluctantly released one record of Icelandic folk songs at the end of her career, which is heavenly. There a song is a song. Stripped of everything, character, emotion, beauty. Of course, those elements are there, but her artistic attitude was about freeing the song from the personal. Engel had a truly modernist approach to song. She was a friend of Olivier Messiaen (1908-1992) and Oskar Kokoschka

(1886-1980), and held a salon concert at Sigmund Freud's (1856-1939) home. The 20th century pulsated in her veins. She left Germany in the 1930's when Adolf Hitler (1889-1945) asked her give a private concert. Proudly she told me she sent a telegram to the Führer, with just one word, "Nein". I often think of that telegram in relation to Yoko Ono's (born 1933) "yes".

The absence of the self was such an important fact for her. There was nothing but the song. I often remember her saying "Nobody cares what you, the performer, feels – the song is the only thing there is." Never let your persona get in the way of a song. That's why she always wore a black dress with white pearl neckless. In her old age, she was the teacher of Björk Guðmundsdóttir (born 1965). Her legacy lives on in Björk's massive clarity. Björk uses the method of outrageous costume to distil the song away from the celebrity.

Engel never listened to music on recordings. She was of a generation of performance. It was just concerts and then memories of concerts. I remember her telling me about going to the premiere of Charlie Chaplin's (1889-1977) *The Great Dictator* (1940) in London during air raids and Duke Ellington (1899-1974) played before the movie. She loved Duke Ellington, never listened to him again though. Music was a moment in time.

I did not follow her example. Like most people nowadays, music is constantly playing on the stereo, in the car, the headphones. I am soaked in dead people's emotional clarity.

George Jones (1931-2013) sang, "Take me, take me to your darkest room / Close every window and bolt every door". Oppression and suffering in between lines of beauty. "Take Me" was recorded in Nashville in 1966. One of endless tracks laid down by musicians making hits for a living on Music Row. George Jones was the greatest voice of them all. Constantly drunk, violent, angry and literally flushed his money down the toilet. This song creates a space, a space so narrow, dark and loaded with sorrow. It is a black hole deep in the heart in the form of a song. I can't get enough of it ... those twangy guitars and those opening lines. It continues into lines asking his lover to take him to her most barren desert and to Siberia in the coldest weather of the wintertime.

Relationships are not always great. The demanding patriarchal ownership comes to life in the earnest delivery of the lines, "Darlin', if you would just show a sign / Of love, I could bear any loss". Seems sweet, but it's the essence of untrue love. The one that demands the lover to deliver. George Jones could not live or talk about emotions except through song. He only lived when he sang. The rest was pure suffering, for him and especially those around him. Talk about just being the song.

I love that just before his death the songwriter, Californian vegetarian and pioneer hippie Eden Ahbez (1908-1995) said that he wanted to change the end of his glorious song "Nature Boy" that Nat King Cole (1919-1965) first released and immortalised in 1948. The profound wisdom of the young boy who travelled "very far, very far" is in the lines:

The greatest thing you'll ever learn
Is just to love
And be loved
In return

After walking barefoot through life, camping with his family under the first "L" in the Hollywood sign, losing his wife and young son. Sun in the old man's face for decades. The myth has it Eden wanted the lines to be changed to:

The greatest thing you'll ever learn
Is just to love
love
And love

I give Joni Mitchell (born 1943) a Tchaikovskyan cannon-at-the-sky salute for writing the greatest starting lines of a song. It gorgeously disses male romantic melodrama found in song in abundance. As painting a picture, it is in a class with Herman Melville's (1819-1891) opening lines of *Moby-Dick* (1851):

Call me Ishmael. Some years ago – never mind how long precisely – having little or no money in my purse, and nothing particular to interest me on shore, I thought I would sail about a little and see the watery part of the world.

Here is Joni's opener that creates an Elysian field or sea:

Just before our love got lost you said
"I am as constant as a northern star"
And I said, "Constantly in the darkness
Where's that at?
If you want me I'll be in the bar".

How she riffs that dobro is constant lit stars shining through bourbon in a smoky hippie room. They all left. They are most of them gone now. The rooms have become a building with people in clothes of exquisite quality drinking fresh smoothies. "I'll rather be thin than famous", Jack Kerouac (1922-1969) wrote and died vomiting blood.

Art is about transformation of space. People making ideas and objects that transform space. There is one song that addresses this essence of art, and it was written in a brothel in Genoa in 1959. Gino Paoli (born 1934) got the idea for Italy's most loved love song lying beside a sex worker whose identity is a mystery. Gino was so intoxicated with love for the human being lying beside him in that moment that the walls stopped existing, they became endless woods and the purple ceiling in the 1950's Genoa brothel did not exist, he only saw the heavens. The two of them were in the sky in a room. The song is a James Turrell (born 1943) „eat your heart out," played on the radio in the café and in the butcher's shop.

Nina Simone (1933-2003) wrote songs by singing them, they became so totally her. I recommend seeing her in a state of shock singing the Brazilian pop song "Feelings" at Montreux Jazz Festival. "Who gets into such an emotional space to write such a song?" she asks appalled and in awe. Then she becomes the song with such intensity it is heart-wrenching. Yes and did you know Gino Paoli shot himself in the heart and survived, a few years after writing "Il Cielo in Una Stanza"? But Nina was the song and she was constantly shooting herself in the heart. Imagine, she was by Martin Luther King's (1929-1968) side. She cried for two weeks.

It's hard to pin down one song when it comes to her. Maybe it's "Wild is the Wind". Her version of "Wild is the Wind" is maybe a pinnacle of collaboration in culture. A Russian emigre composer wrote this song for a movie with the same title. Some Hollywood hired hand wrote the lyrics, for the opening credits where a plane flies through the sky. Nina then 20 years later took the song, burrowed deep into its roots in Rachmaninovian bliss and when we play it we soak up, longing like an English Christmas cake. David Bowie's (1947-2016) version is OK. But I know he would agree with me it's just a tribute.

I use art to say it all. Other people's art and my own. This world and myself in it are just so mind-blowingly beautiful and terrible that it's beyond words. Jay-Z (born 1969) put it so well in "Song Cry".

Again we come to life lived in song, lived in art. He can't show it, say it, do it in life. All the regret, guilt and fear. But he can in song. We can allow ourselves to reach for the holy in song:

I can't see 'em comin' down my eyes
So I gotta make the song cry

This is exactly what Engel meant. We are not interested in Jay-Z's tears, we are interested in his song.

Opposite page: From the recordings of *No Tomorrow*, 2022

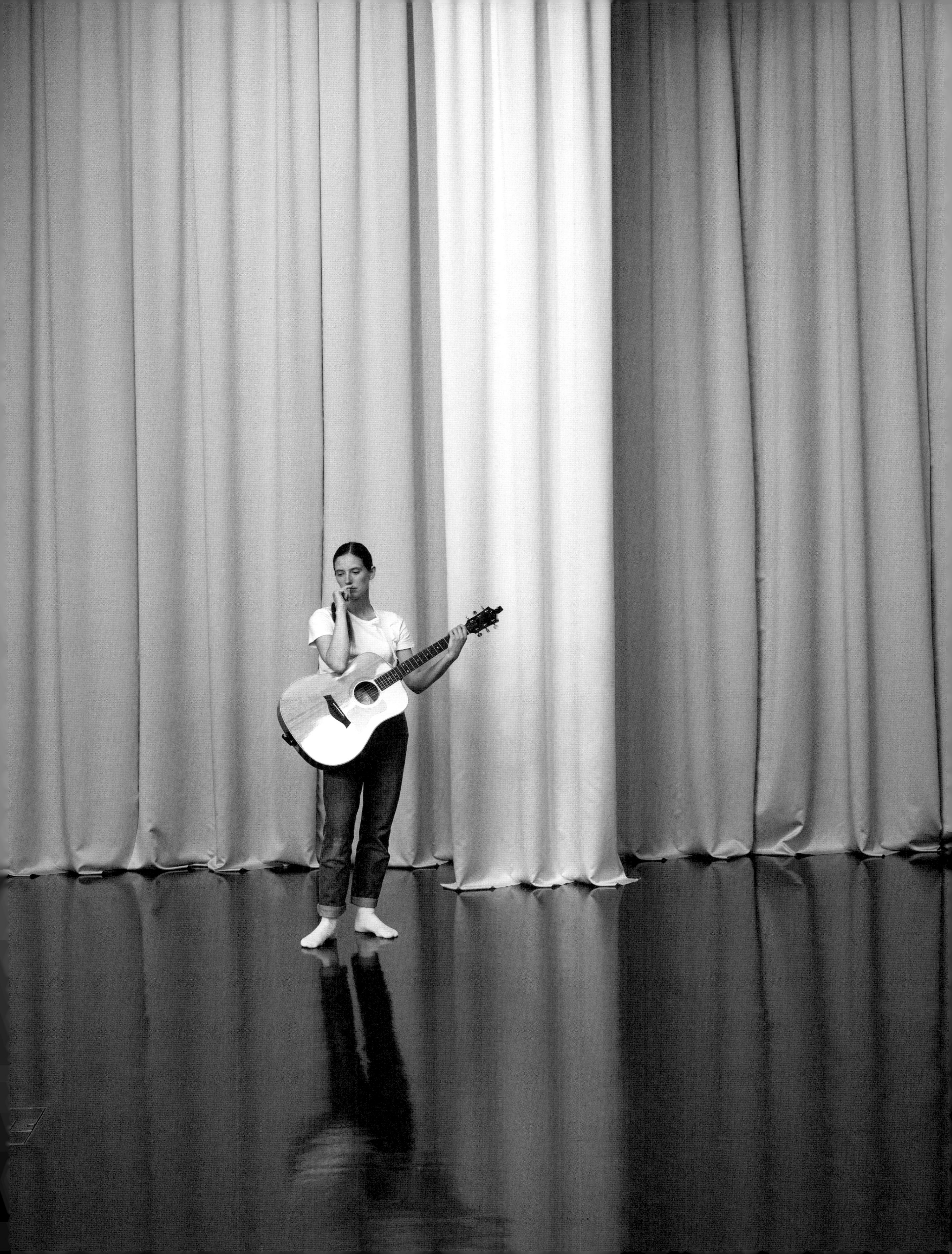

Quando sei qui con me,
questa stanza non ha più pareti
ma alberi,
alberi infiniti ...
Quando sei qui vicino a me,
questo soffitto viola
no, non esiste più:
io vedo il cielo sopra noi
che restiamo qui, abbandonati
come se non ci fosse più
niente, più niente al mondo ...
Suona un'armonica,
mi sembra un organo
che vibra per te e per me
su nell'immensità del cielo.
Suona un'armonica,
mi sembra un organo
che vibra per te e per me
su nell'immensità del cielo,
Per te, e per me
nel cielo ...

When you are here with me
this room no longer has walls
but trees,
infinite trees ...
When you are here next to me,
this purple ceiling
no, it no longer exists:
I see the sky above us
and we stay here, abandoned
as if there were no more,
nothing, nothing more in the world ...
I hear a harmonica
it seems like an organ to me
it plays for you and for me
up in the immense sky.
I hear a harmonica
it seems like an organ to me
it plays for you and for me
up in the immense sky
for you, and for me
in the sky ...

157

Il cielo in una stanza (The Sky in a Room)

Lyrics and music by Gino Paoli, 1959

LIST OF WORKS IN CHRONOLOGICAL ORDER

Me and My Mother, 2000
Single-channel video
Duration: 7:07 min.
Hirshhorn Museum and Sculpture Garden,
Smithsonian Institution, Washington, D.C.,
Joseph H. Hirshhorn Purchase Fund, 2018

Colonization, 2003
Single-channel video
Duration: 12:08 min.
National Gallery of Iceland, Reykjavik

Mercy, 2004
Single-channel video
Duration: 62:30 min.
National Gallery of Iceland, Reykjavik

Me and My Mother, 2005
Single-channel video
Duration: 3:40 min.
Hirshhorn Museum and Sculpture Garden,
Smithsonian Institution, Washington, D.C.,
Joseph H. Hirshhorn Purchase Fund, 2018

Drawings of Mercy, 2005
Watercolour and pencil on paper
18.2 × 13.8 cm
Private collection, Copenhagen

Drawings of Mercy, 2005
Watercolour and pencil on paper
44.5 × 33 cm
Private collection, Copenhagen

Drawings of Mercy, 2005
Watercolour and pencil on paper
18.2 × 13.8 cm
Private collection, Copenhagen

Drawings of Mercy, 2005
Watercolour and pencil on paper
18.2 × 13.8 cm
Private collection, Copenhagen

Drawings of Mercy, 2005
Watercolour and pencil on paper
33 × 24 cm
Private collection, Reykjavik

Hitler's Loge, 2006
Remains of a theatre loge, inscribed marble slab
Dimensions variable
National Gallery of Iceland, Reykjavik

Scandinavian Pain, 2006-2012
Neon, aluminium
57.6 × 1,219 × 20 cm
National Gallery of Iceland, Reykjavik

Guilt Trip, 2007
Single-channel video
Duration 10:24 min.
Courtesy of the artist, Luhring Augustine, New York,
and i8 Gallery, Reykjavik

Grey Suits (5), 2008
Drawing on paper
102 × 81 × 4.5 cm
Private collection, Reykjavik

Grey Suits (9), 2008
Drawing on paper
102 × 81 × 4.5 cm
Private collection, Reykjavik

Grey Suits (12), 2008
Drawing on paper
102 × 81 × 4.5 cm
Private collection, Reykjavik

The End – Venezia, 2009
Oil on canvas
144 paintings
Dimensions variable
Performed at the Icelandic Pavilion during the 53rd Venice Biennale,
14 June-22 November, daily for six hours
Commissioned by the Center for Icelandic Art, Reykjavik
Fondazione Sandretto Re Rebaudengo, Torino

Me and My Mother, 2010
Single-channel video
Duration: 20:00 min.
Hirshhorn Museum and Sculpture Garden, Smithsonian Institution,
Washington, D.C., Joseph H. Hirshhorn Purchase Fund, 2018

The Visitors, 2012
Nine-channel video installation
Duration: 64:00 min.
Commissioned Migros Museum für Gegenwartskunst, Zürich
Sammlung Migros Museum für Gegenwartskunst, Zürich

Ragnar Kjartansson & The National
A Lot of Sorrow, 2013-2014
Single-channel video
Duration: 6:09 hr.
The performance took place at MoMA PS1, New York,
as part of Sunday Sessions
The Art Institute of Chicago, purchased with funds provided by
Stephanie Skestos Gabriele

Me and My Mother, 2015
Single-channel video
Duration: 20:25 min.
Louisiana Museum of Modern Art, Humlebæk
Acquired with funding from Museumsfonden af 7. december 1966

Bliss, 2020
Single-channel video
Duration: 11:59 hr.
Recorded at REDCAT as part of Los Angeles Philharmonic's Fluxus
Festival curated by Christopher Roundtree 25 May 2019,
originally a commission for Performa 11
AMA Collection, Venezia

Me and My Mother, 2020
Single-channel video
Duration: 10:38 min.
Hirshhorn Museum and Sculpture Garden, Smithsonian
Institution, Washington, D.C., Joseph H. Hirshhorn Purchase
Fund, 2018

Magnús Stephensen, governor-general in full regalia, 2021
Oil on canvas
120.5 × 80 × 2.5 cm
Private collection, Reykjavik

Terrible, Terrible 2021
Two-channel video
Duration: 3:30 min.
Commissioned by the V-A-C Foundation, Moscow
Courtesy of the artist, Luhring Augustine, New York,
and i8 Gallery, Reykjavik

Guilt and Fear, 2022
Porcelain salt and pepper shakers
Dimensions variable
Courtesy of the artist, Luhring Augustine, New York,
and i8 Gallery, Reykjavik

Die Nacht der Hochzeit, 2022
Watercolour on paper
Dimensions variable
Courtesy of the artist, Luhring Augustine, New York
and i8 Gallery, Reykjavik
Private collection, New York
collection De Pont museum, Tilburg

Ragnar Kjartansson, Margrét Bjarnadóttir & Bryce Dessner
No Tomorrow, 2022
Six-channel video
Duration: 29:18 min.
Commissioned by Sigurður Gísli Pálmason,
based on a commission by the Iceland Dance Company

Bangemand, 2023
Scaredman
Performance
Courtesy of the artist, Luhring Augustine, New York,
and i8 Gallery, Reykjavik

Die Nacht der Hochzeit, 2023
Watercolour on paper
Dimensions variable
Courtesy of the artist, Luhring Augustine, New York,
and i8 Gallery, Reykjavik

Epic Waste of Love and Understanding, 2023
Plywood and paint
230 × 600 × 230 cm
Courtesy of the artist, Luhring Augustine, New York,
and i8 Gallery, Reykjavik

Hvad har vi dog gjort for at ha' det så godt, 2023
What Have We Done to Deserve This
Single-channel video
Duration: 11:05 hr.
Commissioned by Louisiana Museum of Modern Art, Humlebæk

Ragnar Kjartansson
Epic Waste of Love and Understanding

Edited by Malou Wedel Bruun and Tine Colstrup
Graphic design: Marie Lübecker
Special consultants: Lilja Gunnarsdóttir, Ingibjörg Sigurjónsdóttir and Ragnar Kjartansson
Editorial assistance: Pernille Gøtze Johansson
Photo editor: Grethe Røndal Christensen
Translations: Adam King (Preface + all texts by Tine Colstrup), Brian FitzGibbon (Auður Ava Ólafsdóttir) and Glen Garner (*Colonization* transcript)
Proofreading: Henry Broome

Cover: Ragnar Kjartansson: *Epic Waste of Love and Understanding*, 2023 (detail)

Litho/Print: Narayana Press
ISBN: 978-87-93659-68-1
Printed in Denmark 2023
First edition, second print-run
www.louisiana.dk

The text by Roni Horn was written and commissioned for and previously published in Massimiliano Gioni and Margot Norton (ed.): *Ragnar Kjartansson: Me, My Mother, My Father, and I*, New Museum, New York, 2014

The text by Anne Carson was previously published in Ragnar Kjartansson & The All Star Band: *The Visitors*, Bel-Air Glamour Records, The Vinyl Factory, 2016

The transcription of *Colonization* was made by Pernille Gøtze Johansson

The conversation between Theaster Gates and Ragnar Kjartansson was adapted for print by Malou Wedel Bruun

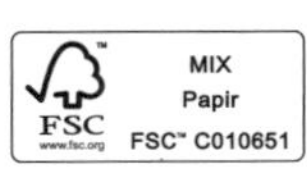

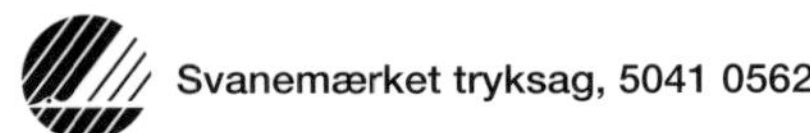

The exhibition at Louisiana Museum of Modern Art is supported by:

C.L. DAVIDS FOND OG SAMLING

Myndlistarsjóður
Icelandic Visual
Arts Fund

Drawing by Ragnar Kjartansson, 2022
The line reads: "Just throw up, love"

The catalogue is published on the occasion of the exhibition

Ragnar Kjartansson
Epic Waste of Love and Understanding
Louisiana Museum of Modern Art, Humlebæk, Denmark
9 June-22 October 2023

Curator: Tine Colstrup
Curatorial coordinator/Registrar: Arne Schmidt-Petersen
Conservator/Exhibition producer: Ulrik Staal Strange Dinesen
Curatorial assistant: Louis Nitze
Exhibition architects: Brian Lottenburger and Jens Kamp
Architect student: Lovisa My Lorén
Graphic design: Maria Hviid Bengtson and Marie Lübecker

Performers in *Bangemand* (Scaredman), Louisiana Museum of Modern Art, 9 June-22 October 2023:
Daniel Peder Askeland
Simon Boysen
Johan Buch
Timothy Gray
Lukas Gregory
Jakob Juul Heide
Jacob Østergaard Johansson
Malthe Møhr Johnsen
Johan Michelsen Kjeldahl
Sven Buster Krauch
Ivan Nylander
Ayaz Shah
Robert Morsing Thyssen

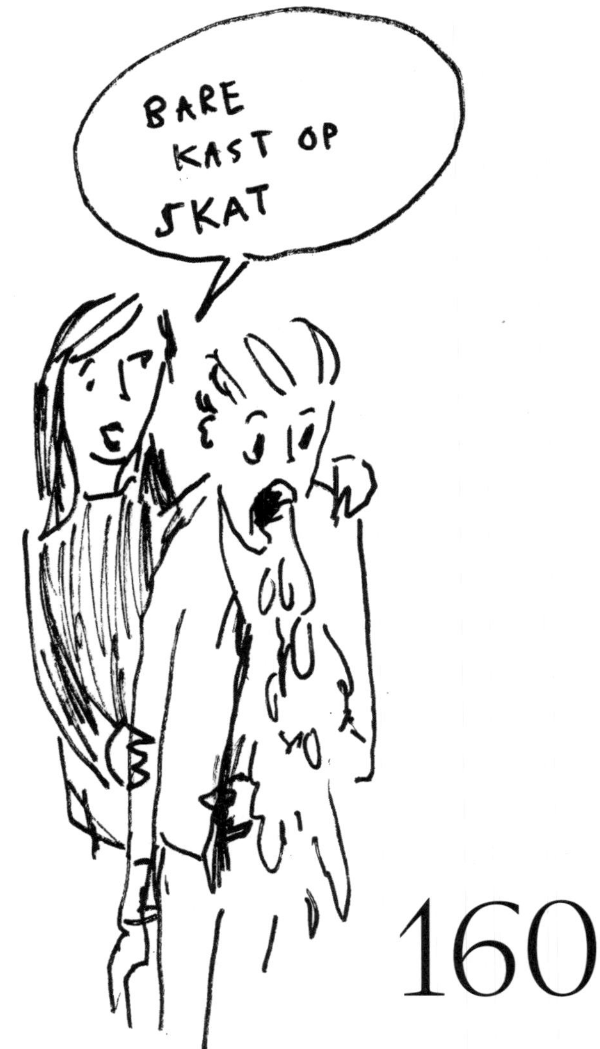